Criminal Justice in Action
THE CORE
SECOND EDITION

Larry K. Gaines

California State University—San Bernardino

Roger LeRoy Miller

Institute for University Studies
Arlington, Texas

THOMSON

WADSWORTH

Australia • Canada • Mexico • Singapore • Spain
United Kingdom • United States

THOMSON

WADSWORTH

Editor in Chief: Eve Howard
Acquisitions Editor: Jay Whitney
Development Editor: Julie Sakaue
Assistant Editor: Dawn Mesa
Editorial Assistant: Paul Massicotte
Technology Project Manager: Susan DeVanna
Marketing Manager: Dory Schaeffer
Marketing Assistant: Neena Chandra
Advertising Project Manager: Stacey Purviance
Project Manager, Editorial Production: Ann Borman

Print/Media Buyer: Karen Hunt
Permissions Editor: Sarah Harkrader
Text Designers: Bill Stryker, Ann Borman
Photo Researcher: Anne Sheroff
Copy Editor: Suzie DeFazio
Cover Designer: Bill Stryker
Cover Image: David McGlynn, Getty Images, 2003
Cover and Text Printer: Transcontinental/Interglobe
Compositor: Parkwood Composition
Index: Bob Marsh

Printed in Canada

2   3   4   5   6   7   07   06   05   04   03

For more information about our products, contact us at:
Thomson Learning Academic Resource Center
1-800-423-0563

For permission to use material from this text, contact us by:
Phone: 1-800-730-2214 • **Fax:** 1-800-730-2215
Web: htto://www.thomsonrights.com

Library of Congress Control Number: 2003100794
ISBN 0-534-61623-2

Student Edition with InfoTrac College Edition: ISBN 0-534-61623-2
Instructor's Edition: ISBN 0-534-61639-9

Wadsworth/Thomson Learning
10 Davis Drive
Belmont, CA 94002-3098
USA

Asia
Thomson Learning
5 Shenton Way #01-01
UIC Building
Singapore 068808

Australia
Nelson Thomson Learning
102 Dodds Street
South Melbourne, Victoria 3205
Australia

Canada
Nelson Thomson Learning
1120 Birchmount Road
Toronto, Ontario M1K 5G4
Canada

Europe/Middle East/Africa
Thomson Learning
High Holborn House
50/51 Bedford Row
London WC1R 4LR
United Kingdom

Latin America
Thomson Learning
Seneca, 53
Colonia Polanco
11560 Mexico D.F.
Mexico

Spain
Paraninfo Thomson Learning
Calle/Magallanes, 25
28015 Madrid, Spain

Chapter Opening Photos are credited on the last page of the Index.

DEDICATION

This book is dedicated to my
good friend and colleague,
Lawrence Walsh, of the Lexington,
Kentucky Police Department.
When I was a rookie, he taught me
about policing. When I became a
researcher, he taught me about the
practical applications of knowledge.
He is truly an inspiring professional
in our field.

L.K.G.

To my sister, Lorraine,

Whose generosity, love,
and care for our family
knows no bounds.

R.L.M.

Contents in Brief

CONTENTS

ALL CHAPTERS INCLUDE: **Key Terms • Chapter Summary • Questions for Critical Analysis • Selected Print and Electronic Resources • Logging On • Using the Internet for Criminal Justice Analysis • Notes**

Chapter 6
POLICE AND THE RULE OF LAW 142

Chapter 7
CHALLENGES TO EFFECTIVE POLICING 169

Chapter 8
COURTS AND THE QUEST FOR JUSTICE 195

Chapter 9
PRETRIAL PROCEDURES AND THE CRIMINAL TRIAL 219

Chapter 10

PUNISHMENT AND SENTENCING 250

Chapter 11

PROBATION AND COMMUNITY CORRECTIONS 279

CAREERS IN
CRIMINAL JUSTICE:
Scott T. Ballock 286

CRIMINAL JUSTICE
& TECHNOLOGY:
Satellite Tracking: The Next Step
in Electronic Monitoring 293

Chapter 12

PRISONS AND JAILS 301

CJ IN FOCUS:
Myth versus Reality:
Does Placing Criminals in Prison
Reduce Crime? 307

CRIMINAL JUSTICE
& TECHNOLOGY:
The Electronic Head Count 312

CAREERS IN
CRIMINAL JUSTICE:
Penny Lucero 314

Chapter 13

BEHIND BARS: THE LIFE OF AN INMATE 325

CRIMINAL JUSTICE
& THE MEDIA:
Prison Chic 329

Chapter 14
THE JUVENILE JUSTICE SYSTEM   354

PREFACE

Why are more students than ever enrolling in criminal justice programs throughout the country? No doubt, the sincere desire to serve the public and help others has motivated many students to major in criminal justice. The heroism demonstrated by the members of the New York Police Department in the wake of the terrorist attacks of September 11, 2001, has also certainly inspired a large number of young Americans to consider criminal justice professions. Other students are hoping to find lucrative and secure jobs at a time when the career possibilities and challenges in this field are greater than ever before.

In this text, we have attempted to impart to the reader an idea of the grand scope of the criminal justice system in the United States. The problems of American society are the problems that American police officers, prison administrators, judges, and other criminal justice professionals must contemplate on a daily basis. Consider the following:

- Perhaps the most important battles of the "war" on terrorism are being fought on the home front by law enforcement officers and other criminal justice professionals. Federal, state, and local police departments have greatly expanded their counterterrorism efforts, placing more demands on already overburdened police officers.

- New technologies have influenced nearly every aspect of the criminal justice process. DNA techniques have allowed police to solve more crimes, sometimes years after they occurred, and have resulted in the release of a number of prisoners who were falsely accused. Satellites and other technological devices can be configured to keep an "electronic eye" on those convicted of committing crimes, whether they are incarcerated or under supervision in the community.

- Prison overcrowding continues to be a problem. Today, more than two million individuals are being held in federal and state prisons as well as in county and local jails. Indeed, more Americans are under the control of the criminal justice system than at any other point in our nation's history.

These are the kinds of issues that students going into the field of criminal justice will need to be prepared to confront, and this text will help them get there. It not only focuses on the many topics and issues all students must know and understand, but addresses these topics in a variety of interesting ways.

A COMPLETE LEARNING EXPERIENCE

While the text of *Criminal Justice in Action: The Core,* Second Edition, is filled with numerous eye-catching, instructive, and penetrating features, we have not stopped there. You will notice that the first page of every chapter starts with the chapter outline and learning objectives. The following page has an Introduction in the form of a case study and an appropriate photo. The pedagogy continues all the way through to the end of each chapter, with the pedagogical devices listed below:

- **Criminal Justice in Action:** Every chapter ends with this important feature. It wraps up the topics and issues discussed in the chapter using a current news item or controversy to demonstrate how the concepts apply to the "real world."

- **Criminal Justice & Technology:** Because the criminal justice field is changing so rapidly as a result of new technology, we made sure that students cannot miss learning about important new technologies and the related issues confronting practitioners in the field today by including at least one of these features in each chapter.

- **Careers in Criminal Justice:** Most students reading this book are planning a career in criminal justice. To support their professional interests, we have provided them with insight into a number of careers by offering first-person accounts of what it is like to work in a variety of criminal justice professions. Using an in-margin icon, we have also indicated when the enclosed *Careers in Criminal Justice Interactive CD-ROM*, Release 2.0 covers a position that is relevant to the text at hand.

- **CJ in Focus:** This feature covers important topics such as excerpts from significant United States Supreme Court cases and the age-old struggle between the need to protect society and the rights of individuals. Because the issues addressed are so important to future practitioners, we've included this feature in every chapter. Moreover, students will find a variety of information and activities associated with the Supreme Court cases covered in this feature on our companion Web site.

- **You Be the Judge:** Students are put into the position of a judge in a hypothetical criminal case (based, though, on an actual court case). The facts of the case are presented with alternative possible outcomes. The student is asked to make a decision as if he or she were the judge. What the courts actually ruled in each case can be found by the student in Appendix A at the end of the text.

- **Cross-National CJ Comparison:** Because it is sometimes easier to teach by comparison, in this feature we present students with information about how our criminal justice system compares with those of other countries.

- **Criminal Justice & the Media:** Many aspects of the criminal justice system have invaded the media. We felt this feature was important to reveal these "invasions" while at the same time commenting on their accuracy.

- **The Diversity Challenge:** Diversity issues in the criminal justice system continue to create friction both within and without the system. This feature examines the role of women and minorities in the criminal justice system today.

- **Mastering Concepts:** This feature helps students to master essential concepts of criminal justice. Because it is often important to compare and contrast two similar concepts to help the student understand them, many of the concept summaries are based on comparisons.

- **In-Margin Online Features:** Our teaching/learning package offers numerous opportunities for using online technology in the classroom. Two new margin items have been added for this edition. *Stories from the Street* features audio clips of co-author Larry Gaines sharing some of his experiences as a participant and observer of the criminal justice system in action. The **Great Debates** feature, found on our companion Web site, presents controversial topics, provides the relevant arguments and Web links that students can use to gather more information, and poses questions that students can answer with the opportunity to express their opinions with supporting statements. Also in the margins, you will find *InfoTrac®* citations that lead students to very important research articles in this powerful, private, password-protected, online database. In addition, there are relevant Web citations in the margins of every chapter. Finally, when appropriate, there is a CD-ROM logo displayed to show that a career feature is available in the text's companion careers CD-ROM.

CYBER CRIMES ON THE RISE

Because cyber crimes are on the rise, we have devoted an entire chapter, Chapter 15, to this increasingly important problem that faces Americans and the rest of the world alike. Because the world of computer technology and online communication is expanding so rapidly, criminal justice personnel often have a difficult time keeping up with those who use such technology to perpetrate crimes. And obviously, as the threat of terrorist activities continues to grow, this crucial field will expand in importance.

ALL NEW—THE *CRIMINAL JUSTICE IN ACTION* Board of Mentors

By going online, you and your students can find our new Board of Mentors. The board is grouped according to each expert's field of specialization. We believe that career information is critical to those students entering the field of criminal justice today. Therefore, to round out the information we provide both in the text and on the enclosed *Careers in Criminal Justice Interactive CD-ROM, Release 2.0*, we've included the Board of Mentors. After all, what better way to advise students than to get answers from those who know? To get these answers, students need only go to **http://cj.wadsworth.com/gainescore2e/**, click Board of Mentors on the left navigation bar, and select a board member in the student's area of interest.

THE SUPPLEMENTS

Our entire team—the two authors plus numerous individuals at Wadsworth— have put together a complete teaching package. In this package you will find the following resources.

For the Instructor

Instructor's Resource Manual This revised and updated *Instructor's Resource Manual* includes the following for every text chapter: learning objectives, detailed chapter outlines, chapter summaries, key terms, student activities, Internet connections, and a test bank. The completely new test bank features the following for each text chapter: 45 multiple-choice, 25 true/false, 20 fill-in-the-blank, and five essay questions.

ExamView® Create, deliver, and customize printed and online tests and study guides in minutes with this easy-to-use assessment and tutorial system. *ExamView* includes a Quick Test Wizard and an Online Test Wizard to guide instructors step by step through the process of creating tests. The test appears on screen exactly as it will print or display online. Using *ExamView's* complete word processing capabilities, instructors can enter an unlimited number of new questions or edit questions included with *ExamView. ExamView* offers flexible delivery and the ability to test and grade online.

Criminal Justice Faculty Development: Teaching Professors to Teach,
Second Edition   Written by Laura B. Myers, Sam Houston State University,
this newly revised guide includes valuable teaching tips, lecture outlines for the
introduction to criminal justice course, and so much more!

Classroom Presentation Tools for the Instructor

Multimedia Manager for Criminal Justice 2004: A Microsoft®
PowerPoint® Link Tool   With this one-stop digital library and presentation
tool, instructors can assemble, edit, and present custom lectures with ease. The
MultiMedia Manager contains a selection of digital media from this book and
other Wadsworth criminal justice textbooks, including figures and tables. Also
included are CNN video clips and pre-assembled Microsoft PowerPoint lecture
slides. Instructors can use the material as is or add their own material for a truly
customized lecture presentation in the classroom or online for student reference
and distance learning.

Introduction to Criminal Justice 2003: Transparency Acetates   Fifty
full-color transparencies will enhance your discussion of concepts and research
findings.

Introduction to Criminal Justice 2003: A Microsoft® PowerPoint®
Presentation Tool   More than 500 engaging PowerPoint® slides that correspond with each chapter's subject matter are available.

CJ in Action: The Core CNN® DVD   With this DVD, you get not only the
up-to-the-minute programming power of CNN that comes with every volume of
our *CNN® Today: Introduction to Criminal Justice Video Series* but also the programming power of CNN *tailored to CJ in Action: The Core,* Second Edition. We
selected video clips based on the text's table of contents. Next, we included an
instructor's manual with instructions on how to run the DVD, background stories
on the clips, creative teaching tips on how to incorporate the DVD into your lectures, and discussion questions and answers that tie the DVD to the related chapter topics and encourage student participation in class discussions. In no time at
all, you'll be seamlessly incorporating the latest technology into your class and
delivering lectures with even greater impact!

CNN® Today: Video Series, Introduction to Criminal Justice (for-
merly CJ in the News), Vols. I–VI   Now you can integrate the up-to-the-
minute programming power of CNN and its affiliate networks right into your
course. These videos feature short, high-interest clips perfect for launching
your lectures. A current new volume is available to adopters each year. Ask your
Thomson/Wadsworth representative about our video policy by adoption size.

America's New War: CNN® Looks at Terrorism   This great discussion
starter includes 16 two- to five-minute segments featuring CNN news footage,
commentator remarks, and speeches dealing with terrorist attacks on U.S targets
throughout the world. Topics include anthrax and biological warfare, new security measures, Osama bin Laden, Al Qaeda, asset freezing, homeland defense,
renewed patriotism, new weapons of terrorism, the bombing of U.S. embassies in
Kenya and Tanzania, the American psyche, and the Arab-American response to
recent events that have occurred. Ask your Thomson/ Wadsworth representative
about our video policy by adoption size.

The Wadsworth Criminal Justice Video Library   So many exciting, new
videos, so many great ways to enrich your lectures and spark discussion of the
material in this text! Your Thomson/Wadsworth representative will be happy to

provide details on our video policy by adoption size. The library includes these selections and many others:

- Court TV Videos—one-hour videos presenting seminal and high-profile court cases
- Plus videos from the *A & E American Justice Series, Films for the Humanities,* and the *National Institute of Justice Crime File Videos*

Customized Criminal Justice Videos   Produced by Wadsworth and *Films for the Humanities*, these videos include short 5- to 10-minute segments that encourage classroom discussion. Topics include white-collar crime, domestic violence, forensics, suicide and the police officer, the court process, the history of corrections, prison society, and juvenile justice. Now available: Volume I and Volume II.

For the Student

Study Guide   This helpful guide contains learning objectives, chapter outlines, key points/chapter summaries, key terms and concepts, and a variety of test questions, including 25 multiple-choice, 20 true/false, 20 fill-in-the-blank, and five essay questions for each chapter in the text.

InfoTrac® College Edition   With every new copy of this text, adopters and their students automatically receive four months of FREE access to **InfoTrac College Edition**, a world-class, online university library that offers complete articles (not just abstracts) from thousands of scholarly and popular publications. Updated daily and going back as far as 22 years, **InfoTrac College Edition** is a great way to expand your course beyond the pages of this text.

InfoTrac College Edition Student Guide for Criminal Justice   This booklet provides detailed user guidelines for students, illustrating how to use the InfoTrac® College Edition database. Special features include log-in help, a complete search tips worksheet, and a topic list of suggested keyword search terms for criminal justice.

Careers in Criminal Justice 2.0 Interactive CD-ROM   FREE with every new copy of this book, and updated with many new career profile videos, this CD-ROM is designed to help students focus on the criminal justice career choices right for them. This engaging self-exploration provides an interactive discovery of careers in criminal justice with such exciting features as FREE online access to the Holland Personalized Self-Assessment Test, video profiles of practicing professionals, and information and references to assist students in learning more not only about various jobs but also about effective job search strategies and practices.

***Seeking Employment in Criminal Justice and Related Fields,* Fourth Edition**   Written by J. Scott Harr and Karen M. Hess, this completely updated book provides students with extensive information on the wide range of criminal justice professions. It also helps students develop a job search strategy and provides information on résumés and interviewing techniques.

***Wadsworth's Guide to Careers in Criminal Justice,* Second Edition**   Fully updated, this comprehensive guide includes information on careers in law enforcement, courts, and corrections. It includes job descriptions and requirements, training and salary/benefits information, and contact details for many of the top employers and associations in criminal justice.

Handbook of Selected Court Cases   This handbook features 35 relevant, seminal Supreme Court cases. Co-author Roger LeRoy Miller has organized the presentation of each case into five parts: the case citation, introduction, WESTLAW summary, case excerpts, and decision. Miller's excellent, explanatory preface introduces and summarizes relevant general information about court cases to help readers better understand the specific cases discussed.

Crime Scenes: An Interactive Criminal Justice CD-ROM Awarded the gold medal in higher education and silver medal for video interface by *New Media* magazine's *Invision Awards,* this interactive CD-ROM features six vignettes that allow students to adopt various roles as they explore all aspects of the criminal justice system, such as policing/investigation, courts, and sentencing and corrections.

Mind of a Killer CD-ROM Voted one of the top 100 CD-ROMs by an annual *PC* magazine survey, *Mind of a Killer* gives students a chilling glimpse into the realm of serial killers with over 80 minutes of video, 3-D simulations, an extensive mapping system, a library, and much more.

Internet Activities for Criminal Justice, **Second Edition** This completely updated booklet shows how to best utilize the Internet for research through fun and informative exercises, searches, and activities.

Internet Guide for Criminal Justice, **Second Edition** Intended for the less-experienced Internet user, the first part of this completely revised booklet explains the background and vocabulary necessary for navigating the Internet while the second part focuses on Internet applications in criminal justice, doing criminal justice research online, and criminal justice career information on the Web.

The Criminal Justice Internet Investigator, **Third Edition** This colorful tri-fold brochure lists some of the most popular Internet addresses for criminal justice–related Web sites.

Terrorism: An Interdisciplinary Perspective, **Second Edition** This 80-page booklet (with companion Web site) discusses terrorism in general and the issues surrounding the events of September 11, 2001. This information-packed booklet examines the origins of terrorism in the Middle East, focusing on Osama bin Laden in particular, as well as issues involving bioterrorism; the specific role played by religion in Middle Eastern terrorism; globalization as it relates to terrorism; and the reactions to and repercussions of terrorist attacks.

Internet-Based Supplements

The Criminal Justice Resource Center's Companion Web site for *Criminal Justice in Action: The Core, 2nd Edition*
www.cj.wadsworth.com/gainescore2e/
At the ***Criminal Justice in Action: The Core*** page, students will find many useful learning resources for their course. Some of those resources include audio clips of co-author Larry Gaines, Tutorial Quizzing, Flashcards, Chapter Outlines and Summaries, *Great Debates* activities with a discussion forum, and many other valuable resources! In addition to all that's available to students, instructors can access the *Instructor's Manual, NewsEdge,* and a MultiMedia Manager demonstration on the password-protected Instructor Resources site.

The Criminal Justice Resource Center
www.cj.wadsworth.com
This Web site provides instructors and students alike with a wealth of FREE information and resources, such as:

- *Terrorism: An Interdisciplinary Perspective* Web page
- The NEW Criminal Justice lecture series
- The NEW Crime and Technology interactive resource/activity module
- *What Americans Think* Web polls
- The NEW Timeline, highlighting significant events and developments from before 601 C.E. to the present

And so much more!

WebTutor® on WebCT and Blackboard This Web-based software takes a course beyond the classroom to an anywhere, anytime environment. Students gain access to a full array of study tools, including chapter outlines and chapter-specific quizzing material. Instructors can provide virtual office hours, post syllabi, track student progress with the quizzing material, and even customize the content to suit their needs, doing such things as uploading images and other resources, adding Web links, and creating customized practice materials. Instructors can also use the communication tools to do such things as set up threaded discussions and conduct "real time" chats. "Out of the box" or customized, WebTutor provides powerful tools for instructors and students alike.

ACKNOWLEDGMENTS

Throughout the creation of the first and second editions of this text, we have been aided by literally hundreds of experts in various criminal justice fields, by professors throughout the country, and by numerous students who have used the text. We list below the reviewers and class-test participants for the first edition as well as the survey respondents for the first edition. Next, we present the reviewers for the second edition.

Reviewers of the First Edition

We are especially grateful for the participation of the following reviewers, who read and reviewed portions of our manuscript throughout its development:

Angela Ambers-Henderson
Montgomery County Community College

Judge James Bachman
Bowling Green State University

Tom Barclay
University of South Alabama

Julia Beeman
University of North Carolina at Charlotte

Anita Blowers
University of North Carolina at Charlotte

John Bower
Bethel College

Steven Brandl
University of Wisconsin—Milwaukee

Charles Brawner III
Heartland Community College

Susan Brinkley
University of Tampa

Paula Broussard
University of Southwestern Louisiana

Michael Brown
Ball State College

Joseph Bunce
Montgomery College—Rockville

Paul Campbell
Wayne State College

Dae Chang
Wichita State University

Steven Chermak
Indiana University

Charlie Chukwudolue
Northern Kentucky University

Monte Clampett
Asheville-Buncombe Community College

John Cochran
University of South Florida

Mark Correia
University of Nevada—Reno

John Del Nero
Lane Community College

John Dempsey
Suffolk County Community College

Joyce Dozier
Wilmington College

M. G. Eichenberg
Wayne State College

Frederick Galt
Dutchess Community College

James Gilbert
University of Nebraska—Kearney

Dean Golding
West Chester University of Pennsylvania

Debbie Goodman
Miami-Dade Community College

Donald Grubb
Northern Virginia Community College

Sharon Halford
Community College of Aurora

Michael Hallett
Middle Tennessee State University

Mark Hansel
Moorhead State University

Michelle Heward
Weber State University

Dennis Hoffman
University of Nebraska—Omaha

Richard Holden
Central Missouri State University

Ronald Holmes
University of Louisville

Marilyn Horace-Moore
Eastern Michigan University

Matrice Hurrah
Shelby State Community College

Nicholas Irons
County College of Morris

Michael Israel
Kean University

J. D. Jamieson
Southwest Texas State University

James Jengeleski
Shippensburg University

Paul Johnson
Weber State University

Matthew Kanjirathinkal
Texas A & M University—Commerce

Bill Kelly
University of Texas—Austin

John H. Kramer
Pennsylvania State University

Kristen Kuehnle
Salem State University

Karl Kunkel
Southwest Missouri State

Barry Latzer
John Jay College of Criminal Justice

Deborah Laufersweiler-Dwyer
University of Arkansas—Little Rock

Paul Lawson
Montana State University

Nella Lee
Portland State University

Walter Lewis
St. Louis Community College—Meramec

Faith Lutze
Washington State University

Richard Martin
Elgin Community College

Bill Matthias
University of South Carolina—Columbia

Janet McClellan
Southwestern Oregon Community College

Pat Murphy
State University of New York—Geneseo

Rebecca Nathanson
Housatonic Community-Technical College

Michael Palmiotto
Wichita State University

Gary Prawel
Monroe Community College

Mark Robarge
Mansfield University

Matt Robinson
Appalachian State University

Debra Ross
Buffalo State College

William Ruefle
University of South Carolina

Gregory Russell
Washington State University

John Scheb II
University of Tennessee—Knoxville

Ed Selby
Southwestern College

Ronald Sopenoff
Brookdale Community College

Gregory Talley
Broome Community College

Kimberly Vogt
University of Wisconsin—La Crosse

Robert Wadman
Weber State University

Ron Walker
Trinity Valley Community College

John Wyant
Illinois Central College

Class-Test Participants

We also want to acknowledge the participation of the professors and their students who agreed to class-test portions of the text. Our thanks go to:

Tom Arnold
College of Lake County

Paula M. Broussard
University of Southwestern Louisiana

Mike Higginson
Suffolk Community College

Andrew Karmen
John Jay College of Criminal Justice

Fred Kramer
John Jay College of Criminal Justice

Anthony P. LaRose
Western Oregon University

Anne Lawrence
Kean University

Jerry E. Loar
Walters State Community College

Phil Reichel
University of Northern Colorado

Albert Sproule
Allentown College

Gregory B. Talley
Broome Community College

Karen Terry
John Jay College of Criminal Justice

Angelo Tritini
Passaic County Community College

Gary Uhrin
Westmoreland County Community College

Robert Vodde
Fairleigh Dickinson University

Survey Respondents

Edward Abair, Madonna University

Samuel Ackah, Delaware State University

Charles Adams, Savannah State College

Leanne Alarid, University of Missouri

R. B. Allen, Anson Community College

James Amos, Alvernia College

Allen Anderson, Indiana University—Kokomo

William Arnold, University of Kansas

Kelly Asmussen, Peru State College

Thomas Austin, Shippensburg University

James Bachman, Bowling Green State University

Thomas Baker, University of Scranton

Gregg Barak, Eastern Michigan University

Tom Barclay, University of South Alabama

Allan Barnes, University of Alaska, Anchorage

Peter Barone, St. Thomas University

Thomas Barry, University of Texas at San Antonio

Elaine Bartgis, Fairmont State College

Lincoln Barton, Anna Maria College

Larry Bassi, State University of New York College at Brockport

Mary Ellen Batiuk, Wilmington College

Chris Beard, California State University—Sacramento

Frank Beck, College of the Sequoias

Joe Becraft, Portland Community College

Julia Beeman, University of North Carolina at Charlotte

Richard Bennett, American University

Charles Biggs, Oakland City University

Donna Bishop, University of Central Florida

John Bower, Bethel College

Gary Boyer, University of Great Falls

Chuck Brawner, Heartland Community College

Susan Brinkley, University of Tampa

Ronald Brooks, Clinton Community College

Paula Broussard, University of Southwestern Louisiana

Carolyn Brown, Fayetteville Technical Community College

Michael Brown, Ball State University

Joseph Bunce, Montgomery College

John Burchill, Kansas Wesleyan University

Tod Burke, Radford University

Michael Burnette, Southwestern Community College

Deborah Burris-Kitchen, University of LaVerne

Orman Buswell, Fairmont State College

Timothy Buzzell, Baker University

David Calihan, Longwood College

Paul Campbell, Wayne State College

Leon Cantin, Mount Marty College

Timothy Carboreau, University of Cincinnati

Joseph Carlson, University of Nebraska at Kearny

David Cary, Mary Baldwin College

William Castleberry, University of Tennessee at Martin

Darl Champion, Methodist College

Dae Chang, Wichita State University

Charles Chastain, University of Arkansas at Little Rock

Russ Cheothem, Cumberland University

Steven Chermak, Indiana University

Art Chete, Central Florida Community College

Steven Christiansen, Green River Community College

Charlie Chukwudolue, Northern Kentucky University

Monte Clampett, Asheville-Buncombe Technical Community College

Ray Clarkson, Kings River Community College

Kenneth Clontz, Western Illinois University

Jean Clouatre, New Hampshire Technical Institute

John Cochran, University of South Florida

Keith Coleman, Fayetteville State University

Kim Cook, University of Southern Maine

Richard Cook, Evergreen Valley College

Tom Cook, Wayne State College

William Cook, Jr., Westfield State College

Walt Copley, Metropolitan State College of Denver

Gary Copus, University of Alaska at Fairbanks

David Corbett, Pensacola Christian College

Mark Correia, University of Nevada at Reno

Stephen Cox, Central Connecticut State University

Beverly Curl, Long Beach City College

Dean Dabney, Georgia State University

John Daly, Cazenovia College

Carol Davis, Indiana University Northwest

Rita Davis, New Mexico State University

Peggy De Stefano, Bakersfield College

Tim Dees, Floyd College

Darrel Degraw, Delta State University

John Del Nero, Lane Community College

Tom Dempsey, Christopher Newport University

Holly Dershem-Bruce, Dawson Community College

John Doherty, Marist College

Rita Dorsey, Shelby State Community College

Marion Doss, Jr., James Madison University

Yvonne Downes, Hilbert College

Daniel Doyle, University of Montana

Joyce Dozier, Wilmington College

J. C. Drake, Roanoke-Chowan Community College

David Duffee, State University of New York at Albany

Gary Dull, Mesa Community College

William Dunford, Erie Community College

Steve Dunker, Casper College

Tim Durham, Thomas College

Mary Ann Eastep, University of Central Florida

Peter Eckert, Broward Community College

David Emmons, Richard Stockton College of New Jersey

Don Ernst, Joliet Junior College

Dave Evans, University of North Carolina

Larry Field, Western New England College

Tom Fields, Cape Fear Community College

Charles Fieramusca, Medaille College

Frank Fischer, Kankakee Community College

Terry Fisk, Grand Valley State University

Michael Foley, Western Connecticut State University

Walt Francis, Central Wyoming College

Carl Franklin, Cloud County Community College

Crystal Garcia, Indiana University

Barry Garigen, Genesee Community College

Godfrey Garner, Hinds Community College

Carole Garrison, University of Akron

Andrew Giacomazzi, University of Texas at San Antonio

John Gillespie, Pennsicola Christian College

J. Ginger, St. Mary's University

Mary Glazier, Millersville University

Dean Golding, West Chester University of Pennsylvania

Michael Goodman, Illinois State University

Dirk Grafton, Mt. Aloysius College

Charles Graham, Solano Community College

James Green, St. Thomas Aquinas College

Peter Grimes, Nassau Community College

Edmund Grosskopf, Indiana State University

Donald Grubb, Northern Virginia Community College

George Guay, Salem State College

Stephen Haas, California State University at Bakersfield

Jan Hagemann, San Jose State University

Sharon Halford, Community College of Aurora

Doris Hall, California State University at Bakersfield

Cynthia Hamilton, West Virginia State College

Hil Harper, Valdosta State University

Judith Harris, University of South Carolina—Spartanburg

Lou Harris, Faulkner University

Robert Harvie, St. Martin's College

Curtis Hayes, Western New Mexico University

Kay Henriksen, MacMurray College

Gary Hill, Cisco Junior College

Vincent Hoffman, Michigan State University

Joe Hogan, Central Texas College

Ronald Holmes, University of Louisville

John Homa, Murray State University

David Hough, University of Findlay

John Hudgens, Weatherford College

James Hudson, Bob Jones University

Wendelin Hume, University of North Dakota

G. Hunt, Wharton County Junior College

William Hyatt, Western Carolina University

Timothy Ireland, Niagara University

Michael Israel, Kean University

Mary Jackson, East Carolina University

Theron Jackson, Los Angeles Southwest College

Caron Jacobson, Wayne State University

J. D. Jamieson, Southwest Texas State University

Shirley Jarreo, Texas A & M University at Commerce

Denise Jenne, Montclair State University

H. Johnson, University of Iowa

Kathrine Johnson, Kentucky State University

Paul Johnson, Weber State University

W. Johnson, Sam Houston State University

Fred Jones, Simpson College

Ken Jones, Coastal Carolina Community College

Casey Jordan, Western Connecticut State University

Lamar Jordan, Southern Utah University

Judy Kaci, California State University—Long Beach

George Kain, Western Connecticut State University

Michael Kane, Coastal Bend College

Richard Kania, Guilford College

Mathew Kanjirathinkal, Texas A & M University at Commerce

Kimberly Kempf-Leonard, University of Missouri—St. Louis

Patrick Kinkade, Texas Christian University

Douglas Kirk, University of South Carolina—Aiken

Paul Kish, Elmira College

Dan Klotz, Los Angeles Valley College

F. Knowles, Jr., Central Methodist College

Junius Koonce, Edgecombe Community College

John Kozlowicz, University of Wisconsin—Whitewater

Fred Kramer, John Jay College of Criminal Justice

Pete Kraska, Eastern Kentucky University

Bob Kristic, College of the Redwoods

A. Kuennen, Briar Cliff College

Karl Kunkel, Southwest Missouri State University

Lon Lacey, The Victoria College

Jerry Lane, Central Virginia Community College

Peter Lango, Gateway Technical College

Anthony LaRose, Western Oregon University

Michael Lauderdale, University of Texas at Austin

Deborah Laufersweiler-Dwyer, University of Arkansas at Little Rock

Alan Lavallee, Delaware Technical College

George Lawless, South Plains College

Richard Lawrence, St. Cloud State University

Nella Lee, Portland State University

Tazinski Lee, Mississippi Valley State University

Thomas Lenahan, Herkimer Community College

B. H. Levin, Blue Ridge Community College

Elizabeth Lewis, Waycross College

Walter Lewis, St. Louis Community College

Lee Libby, Shoreline Community College

Charles Linder, John Jay College of Criminal Justice

Bobby Little, University of North Alabama

Jay Livingston, Montclair State University

Robert Lockwood, Portland State University

Thomas Long, Vance-Granville Community College

Beth Lord, Louisiana State University

Albert Lugo, El Camino College

Dennis Lund, University of Nebraska at Kearney

Faith Lutze, Washington State University

Richard Mangan, Florida Atlantic University

Larry Marshall, Methodist College

Brad Martin, University of Findlay

William Mathias, University of South Carolina

Nancy Matthews, Northeastern Illinois University

Rick Matthews, Ohio University

Richard Mays, Cameron University

Stephen McAndrew, Hessen College

Thomas McAninch, Scott Community College

William McCamey, Western Illinois University

James McCarten, Mt. Senario College

Maureen McCleod, Russell Sage College

Kenneth McCreedy, Ferrum College

Susan McGuire, San Jacinto College North

Barry McKee, Bristol Community College

Michael McMorris, Ferris State University

M. McShane, Northern Arizona University

Jim Meko, Gannon University

D. Miller, Alvin Community College

Robin Miller, Sterling College

Al Miranne, Gonzaga University

John Mockry, Clinton Community College

Dale Mooso, San Antonio College

Karen Mullin, Southwest State University

William Muraskin, Queens College

Pat Murphy, State University of New York at Geneseo

Stephen Muzzatti, Clark College

Johnnie Myers, Morris Brown College

Alisa Nagler, Edgecombe Community College

Brian Nanavaty, Indiana University—Purdue University

Rebecca Nathanson, Housatonic Community College

Marc Neithercutt, California State University at Hayward

Steve Nelson, University of Great Falls

Robert Neville, College of the Siskiyous

Deborah Newman, Middle Tennessee State University

Frederica Nix, Missouri Western State University

Robert Nordvall, Gettysburg College

Paul North, Spoon River College

Patrick O'Guinn, Howard Community College

John O'Kane, Adirondack Community College

John O'Sullivan, Mt. San Antonio College

Robert Oatis, Indiana Wesleyan University

Willard Oliver, Glenville State College

Ihekwoaba Onwudiwe, University of Maryland—Eastern Shore

Kenneth Orr, College of the Albemarie

Alejandrina Ortiz, Catholic University of Puerto Rico

Gregory Osowski, Henry Ford Community College

Ted Paddack, Midwestern State University

Don Palmer, Union County College

Michael Palmiotto, Wichita State University

Peter Parilla, University of St. Thomas

Dan Partrich, Mid-America Nazarene University

Jill Payne, American International College

Michael Penrod, Ellsworth Community College

Francine Perretta, Mater Dei College

Morgan Peterson, Palomar College

Vincent Petrarca, Salve Regina University

Peter Phillips, University of Texas at Tyler

William Pitt, Del Mar College

Joy Pollock, Southwest Texas State University

Darrell Pope, Pensacola Christian College

Edward Porter, Halifax Community College

Harry Porter, Mississippi College

Wayne Posner, Los Angeles City College

Ronald Powell, Taylor University

Gary Prawel, Monroe Community College

Chester Quarles, University of Mississippi

Norman Raasch, Lakeland Community College

Alfred Reed, Jr., Los Angeles Southwest College

Jack Reinwand, Ricks College

George Rengert, Temple University

Marylee Reynolds, Caldwell College

Jayne Rich, Atlantic Community College

Mark Robarge, Mansfield University

Matt Robinson, Appalachian State University

Herman Roe, The Victoria College

Darrell Ross, East Carolina University

Debra Ross, Buffalo State College

William Ruefle, University of South Carolina

Walter Ruger, Nassau Community College

Jeffrey Rush, Jacksonville State University

Gregory Russell, Washington State University

Carl Russell, Scottsdale Community College

Ronald Ryan, Bladen Community College

Julie Salazano, Pace University

Beth Sanders, Kent State University
Wayne Schaffter, Anderson University
Barry Schelzer, St. Ambrose University
Harry Schloetter, Napa Valley College
Patrick Schuster, El Centro College
Edward Selby, Southwestern College
Allen Settles, Mid-Plains Community College
Tim Sexton, University of Northern Iowa
Martin Seyler, San Antonio College
Stan Shernock, Norwich University
Daniel Simpson, Delaware Technical and Community College—Terry Campus
Barbara Sims, Pennsylvania State University
John Sloan, University of Alabama at Birmingham
Neal Slone, Bloomsburg University
Martha Smithey, University of Texas at El Paso
Beverly Smith, Illinois State University
Brian Smith, Northern Arizona University
Lynne Snowden, University of North Carolina—Wilmington
Diann Sollie, Meridian Community College
Ronald Sopenoff, Brookdale Community College
John Spiva, Walla Walla Community College
Phoebe Stambaugh, Northern Arizona University
Debra Stanley, Central Connecticut State University
Katherine Steinbeck, Lakeland Community College
Rick Steinmann, Lindenwood University
G. Stevens, Carteret Community College
Jeffrey Stewart, Howard University
Sandra Stone, State University of West Georgia
Thomas Stoney, Lees-McRae College
Danny Stover, Kaskaskia College
Gene Straughan, Lewis-Clark State College
David Struckhoff, Loyola University

Leslie Sue, Tacoma Community College
Thomas Sullenberger, Southeastern Louisiana University
Kathryn Sullivan, Hudson Valley Community College
Margaret Sylvia, St. Mary's University
Susette Talarico, University of Georgia
Michael Tatum, Ricks College
Carol Thompson, Texas Christian University
Shurunda Thrower, University of Arkansas at Pine Bluff
George Tielsch, College of the Desert
Amy Tobol, Empire State College
James Todd, Tiffin University
C. Toler, Coastal Georgia Community College
Bonnie Toothaker, Mt. Wachusett Community College
Lawrence Travis, University of Cincinnati
Cecilia Tubbs, Jefferson State Community College
Jarrod Tudor, Kent State University—Stark Campus
Steve Turner, East Central University
Gary Uhrin, Westmoreland County Community College
Prabha Unnithan, Colorado State University
Dean Van Bibber, Fairmont State College
Ellen Van Valkenburgh, Jamestown Community College
Eddyth Vaughan, Hillsborough Community College
B. Vericker, Honolulu Community College
Kimberly Vogt, University of Wisconsin—La Crosse
Ron Walker, Trinity Valley Community College
Anthony Walsh, Boise State University
Thomas Ward, New Mexico Highlands University
Glenn Ware, North Harris College
Gene Waters, Georgia Southern University

John Watkins, Jr., University of Alabama
Ralph Weisheit, Illinois State University
Karen Weston, Gannon University
Christine Westphal, Mt. Ida College
Giselle White, South Carolina State University
Martin White, Garland County Community College
Paul White, Quincy College
Stephanie Whitus, Sam Houston State University
Terri Wies-Haithcuck, Lima Technical College
Robert Wiggins, Cedarville College
Frank Williams, California State University—San Bernadino
Kathryn Williams, Southern Nazarene University
Deborah Wilson, University of Louisville
Deborah Wilson, Ohio State University
Michael Witkowski, University of Detroit—Mercy
Grace Witte, Briar Cliff College
Kevin Woods, Becker College
Alissa Worden, State University of New York at Albany
Robert Worden, State University of New York at Albany
John Wyant, Illinois Central College
Bert Wyatt, University of Arkansas at Pine Bluff
Lisa Wyatt-Diaz, Nassau Community College
Coary Young, Sr., Jefferson College
Dawn Young, Bossier Parish Community College
Rosalie Young, State University of New York at Oswego
Steve Zabetakis, Hagerstown Junior College
Edward Zamarin, Catonsville Community College
Otho Zimmer, Jr., Essex Community College
Glenn Zuern, State University of New York at Albany

Reviewers of The Core, Second Edition

David A. Armstrong,
McNeese State University

Roland C. Dart, III,
California State University, Sacramento

Donald E. Ernst,
Joliet Junior College

Daniel Kearney,
Henry Ford Community College

Dale T. Mooso,
San Antonio College

John J. Sloan, III,
University of Alabama at Birmingham

James Walker,
Grand Valley State University

We sincerely thank the reviewers listed above for their participation in the revision of *Criminal Justice in Action: The Core.* We believe that the second edition responds even more to the needs of today's criminal justice instructors and students alike because we have taken into account the constructive comments and criticisms of our reviewers.

Others helped us bring this second edition to fruition. We again used the research efforts of Shawn G. Miller, perhaps more than he had anticipated. William Eric Hollowell added additional legal assistance. Our developmental editor, Julie Sakaue, provided guidance and analysis of the numerous reviews that she obtained. Our editors, Jay Whitney and Eve Howard, came up with dozens of new ideas, trends, and changes made for this revision. We'd also like to acknowledge Dawn Mesa, the assistant editor, who coordinated production of all of the many print supplements for this book and Susan DeVanna, the technology project editor, who oversaw the creation of the Web site and the Careers CD-ROM. At the production end, as always, we feel fortunate to have had the services of Bill Stryker and Ann Borman. This design/production team continues to produce the most eye-catching and accessible text in the field. To all of those just mentioned, we extend our sincere appreciation for efforts beyond the call of duty.

Any criminal justice text has to be considered a work in progress. We know that there are improvements that we can make. Therefore, write us with any suggestions that you may have.

L.K.G.
R.L.M.

WHAT IS CRIME?

Many Americans wondered why John Walker Lindh had not been charged with treason, a crime that reflects serious betrayal of one's own country and carries the death penalty. The easy answer is that his situation failed to meet the legal conditions that make treason a crime. Article III of the U.S. Constitution defines treason as "levying war" against the United States, "adhering" to the country's enemies, or providing these enemies with "aid and comfort." The text goes on to state that "no person shall be convicted of treason unless on the testimony of two witnesses to the same overt act, or on confession in open court."

Lindh would certainly never admit to committing a crime for which he could be executed, and prosecutors were unable to find two witnesses who actually saw Lindh give aid to Al Qaeda or fire on American troops.[5] While Lindh may have behaved in a treasonous manner, his actions did not meet the legal definition of treason.

A *crime* can be defined as a wrong against society proclaimed by law and, if committed under certain circumstances, punishable by society.[6] The problem with this definition, however, is that it obscures the complex nature of societies. A society is not static—it evolves and changes, and its concept of criminality evolves and changes as well. Different societies can have vastly different ideas of what constitutes "a wrong." In Singapore, for example, the sale of chewing gum is illegal; this is a prohibition that many Americans may find incomprehensible.

To more fully understand the concept of crime, it will help to examine the two most common models of how society "decides" which acts are criminal: the consensus model and the conflict model.

The Consensus Model

The **consensus model** assumes that as people gather together to form a society, its members will naturally come to a basic agreement with regard to shared norms and values. Those individuals whose actions deviate from the established norms and values are considered to pose a threat to the well-being of society as a whole and must be sanctioned (punished). The society passes laws to control and prevent deviant behavior, thereby setting the boundaries for acceptable

Stories from the Street

Go to the Stories from the Street feature at http://www.cj.wadsworth.com/gainescore2e to hear Larry Gaines tell insightful stories related to this chapter and his experiences in the field.

CONSENSUS MODEL
A criminal justice model in which the majority of citizens in a society share the same values and beliefs. Criminal acts are those acts that conflict with these values and beliefs and are deemed harmful to society.

At the Cannabis Buyers' Cooperative in Oakland, California, "bartender" Pamela Powers picks out a marijuana muffin for quadriplegic Ken Estes. In the mid-1990s, voters in California approved Proposition 215, which allows those with a physician's approval to purchase marijuana for medical purposes. The U.S. Department of Justice declared Proposition 215 illegal, as it countered federal drug laws that prohibit the production and sale of marijuana. U.S. District Judge Charles Breyer agreed, ordering the closing of the Oakland Cannabis Cooperative. In response, the city kept the Cooperative open, with an official telling the federal government to "butt out." How does the debate over medical marijuana reflect the consensus model in action? (AP Photo/Ben Margot)

British au pair Louise Woodward was found guilty of second degree murder for her role in the death of eight-month-old Matthew Eappen, who had been in her care. Woodward apparently caused Eappen's death by treating him roughly in a fit of annoyance when the infant would not stop crying. Massachusetts Superior Court Judge Hiller Zobel, who presided over the case, disagreed with the jury and reduced the murder conviction to involuntary manslaughter, setting Woodward free in the process. How does this case show the flexibility in the punishment of homicide in the American legal system? (AP Photo/ Jim Bourg)

CONFLICT MODEL
A criminal justice model in which the content of criminal law is determined by the groups that hold economic, political, and social power in a community.

VIOLENT CRIME
Crimes committed against persons, including murder, rape, assault and battery, and robbery.

behavior within the group.[7] Use of the term *consensus* implies that a majority of the citizens agree on what activities should be outlawed and punished as crimes.

The consensus model, to a certain extent, assumes that a diverse group of people can have similar *morals.* That is, they share an ideal of what is "right" and "wrong." Consequently, as public attitudes toward morality change, so do laws. In colonial times, those found guilty of adultery were subjected to corporal punishment; a century ago, one could walk into a pharmacy and purchase heroin. Today, social attitudes have shifted to consider adultery a personal issue, beyond the purview of the state, and the sale of heroin a criminal act. When a consensus does not exist as to whether a certain act falls within the parameters of acceptable behavior, a period of uncertainty ensues as society struggles to formalize its attitudes as law. (For an example of the consensus model at work, see *Cross-National CJ Comparison—Doctor-Assisted Death and the Dutch.*)

The Conflict Model

Those who reject the consensus model do so on the ground that moral attitudes are not absolute. In large, democratic societies such as the United States, different segments of society will inevitably have different value systems and shared norms. According to the **conflict model,** these different segments—separated by social class, income, age, and race—are engaged in a constant struggle with each other for control of society. The victorious groups exercise their power by codifying their value systems into criminal laws.[8]

Consequently, criminal activity is determined by whichever group happens to be holding power at any given time. Because certain groups do not have access to political power, their interests are not served by the criminal justice system. To give one example, the penalty (five years in prison) for possession of 5 grams of crack cocaine is the same as for possession of 500 grams of powder cocaine. This 1:100 ratio has had widespread implications for inner-city African Americans, who are statistically more likely to get caught using crack cocaine than are white suburbanites, who appear to favor the illicit drug in its powdered form.

An Integrated Definition of Crime

Considering both the consensus and conflict models, we can construct a definition of crime that will be useful throughout the textbook. For our purposes, crime is an action or activity that is:

1 Punishable under criminal law, as determined by the majority of a society or, in some cases, a powerful minority.

2 Considered an *offense against society as a whole* and prosecuted by public officials, not by victims.

3 Punishable by statutorily determined sanctions that bring about the loss of personal freedom or life.

Types of Crime

The manner in which crimes are classified depends on their seriousness. Federal, state, and local legislation has provided for the classification and punishment of hundreds of thousands of different criminal acts, ranging from jaywalking to first degree murder. For general purposes, we can group criminal behavior into six groups: violent crime, property crime, public order crime, white-collar crime, organized crime, and high-tech crime.

Violent Crime.   Crimes against persons, or **violent crimes,** have come to dominate our perspectives on crime. There are four major categories of violent crime:

Cross-National CJ COMPARISON

Doctor-Assisted Death and the Dutch

In 2001, the Netherlands became the first nation to legalize physician-assisted suicide and euthanasia ("mercy killing"). The new law simply formalized practices that had been taking place since 1973, when this European nation's courts decided that doctors can help terminate a patient's life if certain conditions are met: the patient must explicitly request such an action, the request must be voluntary, and the patient's suffering must be unbearable and without any hope of improvement. The law requires youths aged twelve to sixteen to obtain parental consent before requesting assisted suicide. From the age of sixteen, all patients have the right to discuss the matter with their doctors without obtaining their parents' approval.

In explaining why the Netherlands accepts actions that many other countries would consider objectionable, observers point to several characteristics of Dutch society. First, doctors hold exalted positions, and their actions are rarely questioned. Not only are doctors authorized to terminate "meaningless" lives, but they are also expected to do so. Second, the country lacks a strong religious influence, which might place the question of assisted suicide in a different moral perspective. As it is, hopelessly ill patients who fail to request euthanasia are seen as adhering to outdated ethical values. Third, and most important, is the Dutch emphasis on personal autonomy; the choice to die is considered the responsibility of the individual, not of the state.

In 1998, an elderly Oregon woman whose breast cancer left her unable to breathe easily became the first American

On April 10, 2000, thousands of protesters gather outside the Upper House of Parliament in The Hague, Netherlands, as Dutch government officials debate the legalization of euthanasia. (AP Photo/ Serge Ligtenberg)

to legally commit suicide with the aid of a doctor. Oregon's Death with Dignity Act—which is modeled in many respects after the Dutch system—was upheld by a federal court ruling in 2002 that reconfirmed each state's authority to legalize assisted suicide. To date, about seventy people have ended their lives with a physician's help in Oregon, the only state that allows such a practice.

FOR CRITICAL ANALYSIS
What social attitudes make it unlikely that physician-assisted suicide and euthanasia will become widely accepted in this country?

- *Murder,* or the unlawful killing of a human being.
- *Sexual assault,* or *rape,* which refers to coerced actions of a sexual nature against an unwilling participant.
- *Assault and battery,* two separate acts that cover situations in which one person intentionally leads another to believe that he or she will be assaulted (assault) or physically attacks another (battery).
- *Robbery,* or the taking of money, personal property, or any other article of value from a person by means of force or fear.

As we shall see in Chapter 3, these violent crimes are further classified by *degree,* depending on the circumstances surrounding the criminal act. These circumstances include the intent of the person committing the crime, whether a weapon was used, and (in cases other than murder) the level of pain and suffering experienced by the victim.

Property Crime. The most common form of criminal activity is **property crime,** or those crimes in which the goal of the offender is some form of economic gain or the damaging of property. Pocket-picking, shoplifting, and the

> "**Murder is unique in that it abolishes the party it injures, so that society has to take the place of the victim and on his behalf demand atonement or grant forgiveness; it is the one crime in which society has a direct impact.**"
>
> —W. H. Auden, *Anglo-American poet* (1949)

PROPERTY CRIME
Crimes committed against property, including larceny/theft, burglary, and arson.

PUBLIC ORDER CRIME
Behavior that has been labeled criminal because it is contrary to shared social values, customs, and norms.

WHITE-COLLAR CRIME
Nonviolent crimes committed by corporations and individuals to gain a personal or business advantage.

stealing of any property that is not accomplished by force are covered by laws against *larceny/theft*. *Burglary* refers to the unlawful entry of a structure with the intention of committing a felony such as theft. *Motor vehicle theft* describes the theft or attempted theft of a motor vehicle, including all cases in which automobiles are taken by persons not having lawful access to them. The willful and malicious burning of a home, automobile, commercial building, or any other structure, known as *arson*, is also a property crime.

Public Order Crime. The concept of **public order crimes** is linked to the consensus model discussed earlier. Historically, societies have always outlawed activities that are considered contrary to public values and morals. Homosexual acts, for example, have been designated criminal for most of this nation's history[9] and are still banned (though rarely prosecuted) in nearly half the states. Today, the most common public order crimes include public drunkenness, prostitution, gambling, and illicit drug use. These crimes are sometimes referred to as *victimless crimes* because they usually harm only the offender. As we shall see throughout this textbook, however, that term is rather misleading. Public order crimes often create an environment that gives rise to property and violent crimes.

White-Collar Crime. Crimes occur in the business world too. Business-related crimes are popularly referred to as **white-collar crimes.** The term *white-collar crime* is broadly used to describe an illegal act or series of acts committed by an individual or business entity using some nonviolent means to obtain a personal or business advantage. Figure 1.1 lists various types of white-collar crime;

FIGURE 1.1
White-Collar Crime

Embezzlement	A form of employee fraud in which an individual uses his or her position within a corporation to *embezzle,* or steal, the corporation's money, property, or other assets.
Pilferage	A less serious form of employee fraud in which the individual steals items from the workplace.
Credit-Card and Check Fraud	The unauthorized use of credit cards costs billions of dollars annually. This form of white-collar crime involves obtaining credit-card numbers through a variety of schemes (such as stealing them from the Internet) and using the numbers for personal gain. Check fraud includes writing checks that are not covered by bank funds, forging checks, and stealing traveler's checks.
Insurance Fraud	Insurance fraud involves making false claims in order to collect insurance payments under false pretenses. Faking an injury in order to receive payments from a workers' compensation program, for example, is a form of insurance fraud.
Securities Fraud	This area covers illegal activity in the stock market. It includes stockbrokers who steal money from their clients and *insider trading,* which is the illegal trading in a stock by someone (or on behalf of someone) who has inside knowledge of the company in question.
Bribery	Also known as *influence peddling,* bribery occurs in the business world when somebody within a company sells influence, power, or information to a person outside the company who can benefit. A county official, for example, could give a construction company a lucrative county contract to build a new jail. In return, the construction company would give a sum of money, also known as a *kickback,* to the official.
Consumer Fraud	This term covers a wide variety of activities designed to defraud consumers, from selling counterfeit art to offering "free" items, such as electronic devices or vacations, that include a number of hidden charges.
Tax Evasion	The practice by which taxpayers either underreport (or do not report) their taxable income or otherwise purposely attempt to evade a tax liability.

CJ in F⊙CUS

A Question of Ethics: The Boom in White-Collar Crime

"The business pages of American newspapers should not read like a scandal sheet," lectured President George W. Bush to a group of Wall Street professionals. "At this moment America's greatest economic need is higher ethical standards." During the summer of 2002, it did seem as if the world of commerce was suffering from an ethical crisis. Corporate fraud involving billions of dollars had been uncovered at giant companies such as Enron, Xerox, Adelphia, and WorldCom. One in five American workers said they knew of colleagues who had lied on expense reports, stolen items from supply cabinets, accepted personal gifts from clients, or skimmed money off of cash sales. The country appeared to be suffering from an epidemic of white-collar crime, causing many to believe that we were somehow less ethical as a people than we used to be.

Such generalizations rarely tell the whole story. As we will see in the next chapter and throughout this textbook, an important aspect of understanding crime is understanding the conditions that contribute to criminal behavior. White-collar criminals, for example, are generally older and better educated than those who commit "street" crimes. Thus, as society ages and its educational level rises—two factors that presently exist in the United States—corporate crimes should increase. Furthermore, the Internet offers opportunities for perpetrating financial crimes that were not possible even a decade ago. When compared with the risks that one runs in committing a petty crime such as purse snatching, stealing a credit-card number online seems a safer alternative, not to mention that, if caught, the punishment generally is less. (We will examine crime on the Internet in Chapter 15.)

On February 12, 2002, Kenneth Lay is sworn in before a U.S. Senate committee. Lay had been the head of the Enron Corporation, a giant energy company, when it went bankrupt in December 2001, causing thousands of shareholders in the company to lose their investments. Enron's downfall was blamed on a series of illegal and unethical business practices that provided executives like Lay with healthy profits. The Enron scandal, along with evidence of other misdeeds in American boardrooms, created intense pressure for stricter laws punishing white-collar crime. (AP Photo/Ron Edmonds)

FOR CRITICAL ANALYSIS

In general, the rise in the white-collar crime rate has coincided with a decline in violent and property crimes, such as assault and theft, since the late 1970s. How might the higher average age and greater educational levels in America during this time period contribute to these trends?

note that certain property crimes fall into this category when committed in a corporate context.

White-collar crime costs corporate America about $600 billion annually.[10] Some observers see the relatively light penalties given to wealthy white-collar criminals—in contrast to harsher penalties for poorer "blue-collar" (or street) criminals convicted of burglary, larceny, and the sale of illegal drugs—as supporting the conflict model of criminality. Following a series of high-profile corporate fraud cases in 2002, President George W. Bush tried to change the perception of law enforcement's "slap on the wrist" mentality toward white-collar crime by signing a bill that greatly increased the criminal penalties for a variety of types of business-related wrongdoing.[11] (See the feature *CJ in Focus—A Question of Ethics: The Boom in White-Collar Crime.*)

Organized Crime. White-collar crime involves the use of legal business facilities and employees to commit illegal acts. For example, a bank teller can't

In April 1999, John A. "Junior" Gotti pled guilty to racketeering, bribery, extortion, and several other charges related to the illegal takeover of a topless club in Manhattan, New York. The son of legendary Mafia boss John "The Dapper Don" Gotti, "Junior" was sentenced to a seven-year prison term. (AP Photo/Mitch Jacobson)

INFOTRAC®
COLLEGE EDITION

Keywords: organized crime, computer crime

ORGANIZED CRIME
A conspiratorial relationship between any number of persons engaged in the market for illegal goods or services, such as pornography, illicit drugs, or firearms.

embezzle unless she is hired first as a legal employee of the bank. In contrast, **organized crime** describes illegal acts by illegal organizations, usually geared toward satisfying the public's demand for unlawful goods and services. Organized crime broadly implies a conspiratorial and illegal relationship between any number of persons engaged in unlawful acts. More specifically, groups engaged in organized crime employ criminal tactics such as violence, corruption, and intimidation for economic gain. The hierarchical structure of organized crime operations often mirrors that of legitimate businesses, and, like any corporation, these groups attempt to capture a sufficient percentage of any given market to make a profit. For organized crime, the traditional preferred markets are gambling, prostitution, illegal narcotics, and loan sharking (lending money at higher than legal rates), along with more recent ventures into counterfeiting and credit-card scams.[12]

High-Tech Crime. The newest type of crime is directly related to the increased use of computers in everyday life. The Internet, with approximately 700 million users worldwide, is the site of numerous *cybercrimes,* such as selling pornographic materials, soliciting minors, and defrauding consumers with bogus financial investments. The dependence of businesses on computer operations has left corporations vulnerable to sabotage, fraud, embezzlement, and theft of proprietary data. (See Figure 1.2 for several types of cybercrimes.)

According to the annual Computer Crime and Security Survey, 85 percent of the businesses and large governmental organizations polled reported that the security of their computer systems had been breached within the past year, with nearly two-thirds suffering financial losses as a result.[13] Corporations worldwide spend nearly $20 billion a year to ward off these Internet-based attacks,[14] and law enforcement agencies are increasing efforts to combat cybercrimes. In 2001, for example, the Federal Bureau of Investigation charged sixty-two people with cheating 56,000 American consumers out of $117 million through various Internet scam operations. We will explore the various types of cybercrimes and their impact on society in more detail in Chapter 15.

THE CRIMINAL JUSTICE SYSTEM

Defining which actions are to be labeled "crimes" is only the first step in safeguarding society from criminal behavior. Institutions must be created to apprehend alleged wrongdoers, determine whether these persons have indeed committed crimes, and punish those who are found guilty according to society's wishes. These institutions combine to form the *criminal justice system.* As we begin our examination of the American criminal justice system in this introductory chapter, it is important to have an idea of its purpose.

The Purpose of the Criminal Justice System

In 1967, the President's Commission on Law Enforcement and Administration of Justice stated that the criminal justice system is obliged to enforce accepted standards of conduct so as to "protect individuals and the community."[15] Given this general mandate, we can further separate the purpose of the modern criminal justice system into three general goals:

1 To control crime
2 To prevent crime
3 To provide and maintain justice

Though many observers differ on the precise methods of reaching them, the first two goals are fairly straightforward. By arresting, prosecuting, and punishing wrongdoers, the criminal justice system attempts to *control* crime. In the process,

FIGURE 1.2 Types of Cybercrime

Cybercrime against Persons

- *Obscene material and pornography:* The selling, posting, and distributing of obscene material such as pornography, indecent exposure, and child pornography.
- *Cyber stalking:* The act of using a computer and the Internet to continually attempt to contact and/or intimidate another person.
- *Cyber harassment:* The harassment of a person through electronic mail, on chat sites, or by printing information about the person on Web sites.

Cybercrime against Property

- *Hacking:* The act of using programming abilities with malicious intent.
- *Cracking:* The act of using programming abilities in an attempt to gain unauthorized access to a computer or network.
- *Piracy:* Copying and distributing software or other items belonging to someone else over the Internet.
- *Viruses:* The creation and distribution of harmful computer programs.

Cybercrime against the Government

- *Cyber terrorism:* The use of a computer and/or the Internet to further political goals of terrorism against a country and its citizens.

Source: Susan Brenner and Rebecca Cochran, University of Dayton School of Law at **http://www.cybercrimes.net**

On the Web

You can find a wealth of information on cybercrimes at the CyberSpace Law Center's Web site. For a link to this Web site, go to the Hypercontents page for this chapter at **http://www.cj.wadsworth.com/gainescore2e.**

the system also hopes to *prevent* new crimes from taking place. The prevention goal is often used to justify harsh punishments for wrongdoers, which some see as deterring others from committing similar criminal acts. The third goal—of providing and maintaining justice—is more complicated, largely because *justice* is a difficult concept to define. Broadly stated, justice means that all citizens are equal before the law and that they are free from arbitrary arrest or seizure as defined by the law.[16] In other words, the idea of justice is linked with the idea of fairness. Above all, we want our laws and the means by which they are carried out to be fair.

Justice and fairness are subjective terms; different people may have different concepts of what is just and fair. If a woman who has been beaten by her husband retaliates by killing him, what is her just punishment? Reasonable persons could disagree, with some thinking that the homicide was justified and she should be treated leniently, and others insisting that she should not have taken the law into her own hands. Police officers, judges, prosecutors, prison administrators, and other employees of the criminal justice system must decide what is "fair." Sometimes, their course of action is obvious; often, as we shall see, it is not.

Society places the burden of controlling crime, preventing crime, and determining fairness on those citizens who work in the three main institutions of the criminal justice system: law enforcement, courts, and corrections. In the next section, we take an introductory look at these institutions and their role in the criminal justice system as a whole.

"The American people have been very clear; . . . keep the streets and the neighborhoods of America safe. The first responsibility of Government is law and order. Without it, people can never really pursue the American dream. And without it, we're not really free."

—President Bill Clinton (1994)

The Structure of the Criminal Justice System

To understand the structure of the criminal justice system, one must understand the concept of **federalism,** which means that government powers are shared by the national (federal) government and the states. The framers of the U.S. Constitution, fearful of tyranny and a too-powerful central government, chose the system of federalism as a compromise. The appeal of federalism was that it allowed for state powers and local traditions while establishing a strong national government capable of handling large-scale problems.

The Constitution gave the national government certain express powers, such as the power to coin money, raise an army, and regulate interstate commerce. All

FEDERALISM

A form of government in which a written constitution provides for a division of powers between a central government and several regional governments. In the United States, the division of powers between the federal government and the fifty states is established by the Constitution.

FIGURE 1.3 **Local, State, and Federal Employees in Our Criminal Justice System**

	Law Enforcement	Judicial and Legal	Corrections	Total
	104,096	56,099	30,974	191,169
	99,686			
	814,140	250,420	228,846	1,293,406
		148,463	456,753	704,902

Federal   State   Local

Source: Bureau of Justice Statistics, *Justice Expenditure and Employment Extracts, 1999* (Washington, D.C.: U.S. Department of Justice, 2002), Table 5.

other powers were left to the states, including police power, which allows the states to enact whatever laws are necessary to protect the health, morals, safety, and welfare of their citizens. As the American criminal justice system has evolved, the ideals of federalism have ebbed somewhat; in particular, federal involvement has expanded significantly. Crime is still, however, for the most part a local concern, and the majority of all employees in the criminal justice system work for local government (see Figure 1.3).

Law Enforcement. The ideals of federalism can be clearly seen in the local, state, and federal levels of law enforcement. Though agencies from the different levels will cooperate if the need arises, they have their own organizational structures and tend to operate independently of one another. In addition to this brief introduction, each level of law enforcement will be covered in more detail in Chapters 4, 5, 6, and 7.

Local Law Enforcement. On the local level, the duties of law enforcement agencies are split between counties and municipalities. The chief law enforcement officer of most counties is the county sheriff. The sheriff is usually an elected official, with a two- or four-year term. In some areas, where city and county governments have merged, there is a county police force, headed by a chief of police. The bulk of local police officers—nearly 500,000—are employed by municipalities. The majority of these forces consist of fewer than ten officers, though a large city such as New York can have a police force of more than 35,000.

Local police are responsible for the "nuts and bolts" of law enforcement work. They investigate most crimes and attempt to deter crime through patrol activities. They apprehend criminals and participate in trial proceedings, if necessary. Local police are also charged with "keeping the peace," a broad set of duties that includes crowd and traffic control and the resolution of minor conflicts between citizens. In many areas, local police have the added obligation of providing social services, such as dealing with domestic violence and child abuse. Furthermore, since September 11, 2001, local law enforcement officers are taking on many jobs that in the past have been the responsibility of federal agencies. New York City detectives, for example, are accepting assignments in foreign countries such as Canada and Israel as part of the city's counterterrorism efforts.[17]

State Law Enforcement. Hawaii is the only state that does not have a state law enforcement agency. Generally, there are two types of state law enforcement agencies, those designated simply as "state police" and those designated as

Criminal Justice & TECHNOLOGY

Weathering the Storm in Alaska

Few states face the law enforcement challenges found in Alaska. Covering more than 586,000 square miles, the state is filled with mountains, glaciers, millions of lakes, and thousands of rivers. Alaska State Troopers, pictured below, and other law enforcement personnel must cope with blizzards, avalanches, and winter temperatures that average twenty degrees below zero. "Snow is a big problem," says one officer. "When everything is white, it's impossible to get your

↑ Few states face the law enforcement challenges that are found in Alaska. One-fifth the size of the continental United States, Alaska is filled with mountains, glaciers, thousands of lakes and rivers, and has a coastline of more than 6,600 miles. The Alaska State Troopers, pictured here, must cope with blizzards, avalanches, subzero temperatures, and limited roads. Many isolated communities can be reached only by airplane or dog sled. Obviously, environment plays a large role in law enforcement on a state and local level. (Photo courtesy of the Alaska State Troopers)

bearings." Shutter releases on cameras often stop working in the cold, which can severely hamper efforts to photograph crime scenes. Police vehicles must be kept running to prevent oil and transmission fluid from freezing, often leaving the cruisers susceptible to theft. To make things worse, nearly 30 percent of Alaska's population lives in communities inaccessible by road or ferry, making it arduous not only to reach many locations, but also to transport suspects back to police stations.

To deal with these challenges, Alaska has the fewest law enforcement personnel of any state in the Union—around 1,200 sworn officers. As a result, many of the crime-fighting technologies that will be discussed in this textbook are crucial to police work in Alaska. Portable crime-processing kits are necessary to gather clues at remote crime scenes. Geographic information systems (GISs) allow officials to "map crime" and place resources where they are most needed. Satellite tracking and electronic monitoring permit correctional officials to supervise nonviolent criminals in their own communities, saving the cost and trouble of transporting them to, and housing them in, jails. Finally, using thermal imaging devices that measure heat, officers can "see" in the dark and through snowstorms. "If it's 38 below and a moose walks through town," notes the police chief of Wasilla, Alaska, "we can find the heat signature in the snow two hours later."

IN THE FUTURE

One of the greatest difficulties in policing large areas such as Alaska is communication. If various agencies are not able to transfer information to one another, the quality of law enforcement will inevitably suffer. Alaska is in the process of creating an Integrated Criminal Justice Information System that will connect police departments, courts, district attorneys' offices, probation departments, and social services agencies, allowing them to exchange data no matter how geographically isolated they may be.

 For more information on the technology described in this box, go to the Crime and Technology feature at http://www.cj.wadsworth.com

"highway patrols." State highway patrols concern themselves mainly with infractions on public highways and freeways. Other state law enforcers include fire marshals, who investigate suspicious fires and educate the public on fire prevention, and fish, game, and watercraft wardens, who police a state's natural resources and often oversee its firearms laws. Some states also have alcoholic beverage control officers plus agents who investigate welfare and food stamp fraud. (To see how one state deals with the challenge of law enforcement, see the feature *Criminal Justice & Technology—Weathering the Storm in Alaska*.)

Federal Law Enforcement. The creation of new national gun, drug, and violent crime laws over the past thirty years has led to an expansion in the size and scope of the federal government's participation in the criminal justice system. Federal agencies with police powers include the Federal Bureau of Investigation

(FBI), the Drug Enforcement Administration (DEA), the U.S. Secret Service, and the Bureau of Alcohol, Tobacco, and Firearms (ATF). In fact, almost every federal agency, including the postal and forest services, has some kind of police power. On November 25, 2002, President George W. Bush created a Department of Homeland Security, which combined the police powers of twenty-two federal agencies in order to protect the United States from terrorist attacks.

The Courts. The United States has a *dual court system;* that is, we have two independent judicial systems, one on the federal level and one on the state level. In practice, this translates into fifty-one different court systems: one national court system and fifty different state court systems. The federal system consists of district courts, circuit courts of appeals, and the United States Supreme Court. The state systems include trial courts at the local and state levels, intermediate courts of appeals, and state supreme courts.

The *criminal court* and its work group—the judge, prosecutors, and defense attorneys—are charged with the weighty responsibility of determining the innocence or guilt of criminal suspects. We will cover these important participants, their role in the criminal trial, and the court system as a whole in Chapters 8, 9, and 10.

Corrections. Once the court system convicts and sentences an offender, she or he is delegated to the corrections system. Depending on the seriousness of the crime and their individual needs, offenders are placed on probation, incarcerated, or transferred to community-based corrections facilities.

- *Probation,* the most common correctional treatment, allows the offender to return to the community and remain under the supervision of an agent of the court known as a probation officer. While on probation, the offender must follow certain rules of conduct. If probationers fail to follow these rules, they may be incarcerated.

- If the offender's sentence includes a period of incarceration, he or she will be remanded to a corrections facility for a certain amount of time. *Jails* hold those convicted of minor crimes with relatively short sentences, as well as those awaiting trial or involved in certain court proceedings. *Prisons* house those convicted of more serious crimes with longer sentences. Generally speaking, counties and municipalities administer jails, while prisons are the domain of federal and state governments.

- *Community-based corrections* have increased in popularity, as jails and prisons have been plagued with problems of overcrowding. Community-based correctional facilities include halfway houses, residential centers, and work-release centers; they operate on the assumption that all convicts do not need, and are not benefited by, incarceration in jail or prison.

The majority of those inmates released from incarceration are not finished with the correctional system. The most frequent type of release from a jail or prison is *parole,* in which an inmate, after serving part of his or her sentence in a correctional facility, is allowed to serve the rest of the term in the community. Like someone on probation, a parolee must conform to certain conditions of freedom, with the same consequences if these conditions are not followed. Issues of probation, incarceration, community-based corrections, and parole will be covered in Chapters 11, 12, and 13.

The Criminal Justice Process

In its 1967 report, the President's Commission on Law Enforcement and Administration of Justice asserted that the criminal justice system:

> "What is legal is not necessarily—not even usually—about what is right, just, or ethical. It is about order. Similarly, 'justice' is a process that makes things work, not necessarily a result that is good or moral or ethical."
>
> —Charles R. Gregg, *President, Houston Bar Association* (1995)

PACKAGE CONTAINS 6/2052

SCANTRON
A HARLAND COMPANY

Counted on most.

is not a hodgepodge of random actions. It is rather a continuum—an orderly progression of events—some of which, like arrest and trial, are highly visible and some of which, though of great importance, occur out of public view.[18]

The commission's assertion that the criminal justice system is a "continuum" is one that many observers would challenge.[19] Some liken the criminal justice system to a sports team, which is the sum of an indeterminable number of decisions, relationships, conflicts, and adjustments.[20] Such a volatile mix is not what we generally associate with a "system." For most, the word *system* indicates a certain degree of order and discipline. That we refer to our law enforcement agencies, courts, and correctional facilities as part of a "system" may reflect our hopes rather than reality.

Just as there is an idealized image of the criminal justice system as a smooth continuum, there also exists an idealized version of the *criminal justice process,* or the procedures through which the criminal justice system meets the expectations of society. Professor Herbert Packer, for example, compared the idealized criminal justice process to an assembly line,

> down which moves an endless stream of cases, never stopping, carrying the cases to workers who stand at fixed stations and who perform on each case as it comes by the same small but essential operation that brings it one stop closer to being a finished product, or, to exchange the metaphor for the reality, a closed file.[21]

As Packer himself was wont to point out, the daily operations of criminal justice are not nearly so perfect. In this textbook, the criminal justice process will be examined as the end product of literally thousands of decisions made by the police, courtroom workers, and correctional administrators. It should become clear that, in fact, the criminal justice process functions as a continuous balancing act between its formal and informal nature, both of which are discussed below.

The Formal Criminal Justice Process.   In Packer's image of assembly-line justice, each step of the process "involves a series of routinized operations whose success is gauged primarily by their tendency to pass the case along to a successful conclusion."[22] These "routinized" steps are detailed in the fold-out Figure 1.4 in this chapter.

The Informal Criminal Justice Process.   Each step described in Figure 1.4 is the result of a series of decisions that must be made by those who work in the criminal justice system. This **discretion**—which can be defined as the authority to choose between and among alternative courses of action—leads to the development of the informal criminal justice process, discussed below.

Discretionary Basics.   One New York City public defender called his job "a pressure cooker." That term could apply to the entire spectrum of the criminal justice process. Law enforcement agencies do not have the staff or money to investigate *every* crime; they must decide where to direct their restricted resources. Increasing caseloads and a limited amount of time with which to dispose of them constrict many of our nation's courts. Overcrowding in prisons and jails affects both law enforcement agencies and the courts—there is simply not enough room for all convicts.

The criminal justice system uses discretion to alleviate these pressures. Police decide whether to arrest a suspect; prosecutors decide whether to prosecute; magistrates decide whether there is sufficient probable cause for a case to go to a jury; judges decide on sentencing; and so on. Collectively, these decisions are said to

DISCRETION
The ability of individuals in the criminal justice system to make operational decisions based on personal judgment instead of formal rules or official information.

Although discretion is absolutely necessary in the criminal justice system, it can be abused. Several years ago, Damien "Pookie" Burris, above with his young son, spent more than five months in a Los Angeles jail for a murder he did not commit. Witnesses to the killing said the assailant was nicknamed "Pookie," and, after several identified Burris from mug shots, he was arrested by the police. Burris claimed he was in church at the time of the murder, an alibi detectives chose not to validate. In fact, it took the discretionary intervention of a patrol officer to prove that Burris had in fact been in church and the police had arrested the wrong "Pookie." How can criminal justice procedure be seen as a system of "checks and balances" in which discretionary errors are eventually corrected? (Patrick Downs, *Los Angeles Times*)

"WEDDING CAKE" MODEL
A wedding cake–shaped model that explains why different cases receive different treatment in the criminal justice system. The cases at the "top" of the cake receive the most attention and have the greatest effect on public perception of criminal justice, while those cases at the "bottom" are disposed of quickly and virtually ignored by the media.

FELONY
A serious crime punishable by death or by imprisonment in a federal or state corrections facility for more than a year.

produce an *informal criminal justice system* because discretion is informally exercised by the individual and is not enclosed by the rigid confines of the law. Even if prosecutors believe that a suspect is guilty, they may decide not to prosecute if the case is weak or if they know that the police erred in the investigative process. In most cases, prosecutors will not squander the scarce resource of court time on a case they might not win. Some argue that the informal process has made our criminal justice system more just. Given the immense pressure of limited resources, the argument goes, only rarely will an innocent person end up before a judge and jury.[23]

Of course, not all discretionary decisions are based on scarce resources. Sometimes, discretion is based on political considerations, such as when a police administrator orders a crackdown on public order crimes because of citizen complaints. Furthermore, employees of the criminal justice system may make decisions based on their personal values or morality, which, depending on what those personal and moral values are, may make the system less just in the eyes of some observers. For that reason, discretion is closely connected to questions of *ethics* in criminal justice and will be discussed in that context throughout this textbook.

The "Wedding Cake Model" of Criminal Justice. Some believe that the prevailing informal approach to criminal justice creates a situation in which all cases are not treated equally. They point to the highly publicized O. J. Simpson trial of 1994, during which the defendant was treated differently than most double-murder suspects. To describe this effect, criminal justice researchers Lawrence M. Friedman and Robert V. Percival came up with a **"wedding cake" model** of criminal justice.[24] This model posits that discretion comes to bear depending on the relative importance of a particular case to the decision makers.

Like any wedding cake, Friedman and Percival's model has the smallest layer at the top and the largest at the bottom (see Figure 1.5).

❶ The "top" layer consists of a handful of "celebrity" cases that attract the most attention and publicity. Recent examples of top-level cases include the trials of Kennedy cousin Michael Skakel and terrorism suspect Zacarias Moussaoui.

❷ The second layer consists of "high-profile" felonies. A **felony** is a serious crime such as murder, rape, or burglary that in most states is punishable either by death or by incarceration for a period longer than one year. This layer includes crimes committed by persons with criminal records, crimes in which the victim was seriously injured, and crimes in which a weapon was used, as well as crimes in which the offender and victim were strangers. These types of felonies are considered "high profile" because they usually draw a certain amount of public attention, which places pressure on the prosecutors to bring the case to trial instead of accepting a guilty plea for a lesser sentence.

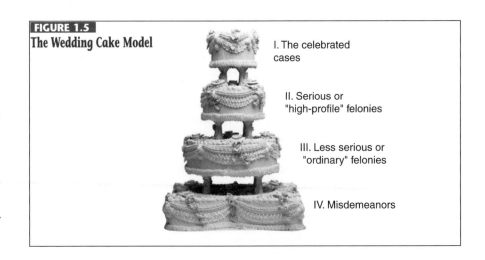

FIGURE 1.5
The Wedding Cake Model

I. The celebrated cases

II. Serious or "high-profile" felonies

III. Less serious or "ordinary" felonies

IV. Misdemeanors

❸ The third layer consists of "ordinary" felonies, which include less violent crimes such as burglaries and thefts or even robberies in which no weapon was used. Because of the low profile of the accused—usually a first-time offender who has had a prior relationship with his or her victim—these "ordinary" felonies often do not receive the full formal process of a trial.

❹ Finally, the fourth layer consists of **misdemeanors,** or crimes less serious than felonies. Misdemeanors include petty offenses such as shoplifting, disturbing the peace, and violations of local ordinances; they are usually punishable by fines, probation, or short jail times. More than three-quarters of all arrests made by police are for misdemeanors.

The irony of the wedding cake model is that the cases on the top level come closest to meeting our standards of ideal criminal justice. In these celebrity trials, we get to see committed (and expensive) attorneys argue minute technicalities of the law, sometimes for days on end. The further one moves down the layers of the cake, the more informal the process becomes. Though many of the cases in the second layer are brought to trial, only rarely does this occur for the less serious felonies in the third level of the wedding cake. By the fourth level, cases are dealt with almost completely informally, and the end goal appears to be speed rather than what can be called "justice."

Public fascination with celebrity cases obscures a truth of the informal criminal justice process: trial by jury is relatively rare (only about 3 percent of those arrested for felonies go to trial), and most cases are disposed of with an eye more toward convenience than ideals of justice or fairness. Consequently, the summary of the criminal justice system provided by the wedding cake model is much more realistic than the impression many Americans have obtained from the media.

VALUES OF THE CRIMINAL JUSTICE SYSTEM

If the general conclusion of the wedding cake model—that some defendants are treated differently than others—bothers you, then you probably question the values of the system. Just as individuals have values—a belief structure governing individual conduct—our criminal justice system can be said to have values, too. These values form the foundation for Herbert Packer's two models of the criminal justice system.

Crime Control and Due Process: To Punish or Protect?

In his landmark book, *The Limits of the Criminal Sanction,* Packer introduced two models for the American criminal justice system: the crime control model and the due process model.[25] The underlying value of the crime control model is that the most important function of the criminal justice process is to punish and repress criminal conduct. Though not in direct conflict with crime control, the underlying values of the due process model focus more on protecting the rights of the accused through legal constraints on police, courts, and corrections.

The Crime Control Model. Under the **crime control model,** law enforcement must be counted on to control criminal activity. "Controlling" criminal activity is at best difficult, and probably impossible. For the crime control model to operate successfully, Packer writes, it

> must produce a high rate of apprehension and conviction, and must do so in a context where the magnitudes being dealt with are very large and the resources for dealing with them are very limited.[26]

MISDEMEANOR
Any crime that is not a felony; punishable by a fine or by confinement for up to a year.

CRIME CONTROL MODEL
A criminal justice model that places primary emphasis on the right of society to be protected from crime and violent criminals. Crime control values emphasize speed and efficiency in the criminal justice process; the benefits of lower crime rates outweigh any possible costs to individual rights.

DUE PROCESS MODEL
A criminal justice model that places primacy on the right of the individual to be protected from the power of the government. Due process values hold that the state must prove a person's guilt within the confines of a process designed to safeguard personal liberties as enumerated in the Bill of Rights.

In other words, the system must be quick and efficient. In the ideal crime control model, any suspect who most likely did not commit a crime is quickly jettisoned from the system, while those who are transferred to the trial process are convicted as quickly as possible. It was in this context that Packer referred to the criminal justice process as an assembly line.

The crime control model also assumes that the police are in a better position than the courts to determine the guilt of arrested suspects. Therefore, not only should judges operate on a "presumption of guilt" (that is, any suspect brought before the court is more likely guilty than not), but as few restrictions as possible should be placed on police investigative and fact-gathering activities. The crime control model relies on the informality in the criminal justice system, as discussed earlier.

The Due Process Model. Packer likened the **due process model** to an obstacle course rather than an assembly line. Rather than expediting cases through the system, as is preferable in the crime control model, the due process model strives to make it more difficult to prove guilt. It rests on the belief that it is more desirable for society that ninety-nine guilty suspects go free than that a single innocent person be condemned.[27]

The due process model is based on the assumption that the absolute efficiency that is the goal of the crime control model can be realized only if the power of the state is absolute. Because fairness, and not efficiency, is the ultimate goal of the due process model, it rejects the idea of a criminal justice system with unlimited powers. As a practical matter, the model also argues that human error in any process is inevitable; therefore, the criminal justice system should recognize its own fallibility and take all measures necessary to ensure that this fallibility does not impinge on the rights of citizens.

Finally, whereas the crime control model relies heavily on the police, the due process model relies just as heavily on the courts and their role in upholding the legal procedures of establishing guilt. The due process model is willing to accept that a person who is factually guilty will go free if the criminal justice system does not follow legally prescribed procedures in proving her or his culpability.[28] Therefore, the due process model relies on formality in the criminal justice system. The *Mastering Concepts* feature compares and contrasts the two models.

Which Model Prevails Today?

Though both the crime control and the due process models have always been present to a certain degree, during different time periods one has taken precedence over the other. The twentieth century saw an ebb and flow between them. The influx of immigrants and problems of urbanization in the early 1900s caused somewhat of a panic among the American upper class. Considering that most, if not all, politicians and legal theorists were members of this class, it not surprising that crime control principles prevailed during the first half of the century.

As the nation became more secure and prosperous in the 1950s and 1960s, a "due process revolution" took place. Under the leadership of Chief Justice Earl Warren, the United States Supreme Court significantly expanded the rights of the accused. Following a series of landmark cases that will be referred to throughout this textbook, suspected offenders were guaranteed, among other things, that an attorney would be provided to them by the state if they could not afford one,[29] and that they would be notified of their right to remain silent and retain counsel on being arrested.[30] The 1960s also saw severe limits placed on the power of the police, as the Court required law enforcement officers to follow strictly specific guidelines on gathering evidence or risk having that evidence invalidated.[31]

MASTERING CONCEPTS	Crime Control Model versus Due Process Model	
	Crime Control Model	**Due Process Model**
Goals of the Criminal Justice System	• Deter crime. • Protect citizens from crime. • Incapacitate criminals. • Provide quick and efficient justice.	• Protect the individual against the immense power of the state. • Rehabilitate those convicted of crimes.
Goals Can Best Be Met by	• Promoting discretion and limiting bureaucratic red tape in criminal justice institutions. • Making it easier for police to arrest criminals. • Reducing legal restrictions on proving guilt in a criminal trial.	• Limiting state power by assuring the constitutional rights of the accused. • Providing even guilty offenders with full protection of the law, and allowing those offenders to go free if due process procedures are not followed. • Assuring that all accused criminals receive the same treatment from the law, regardless of class, race, gender, or sexual orientation. • Protecting the civil rights of prisoners.
Favored Policies	• More police. • More jails and prisons. • Harsher penalties (including increased use of the death penalty) and longer sentences.	• Open the criminal justice process to scrutiny by the media and public. • Abolish the death penalty. • Limit police powers to arbitrarily search, interrogate, and seize criminal suspects. • Limit discretion and formalize criminal justice procedures so that all suspects and convicted offenders receive the same treatment. • Increase funding for rehabilitation and education programs in jails and prisons.
View of Criminality	• Wrongdoers are responsible for their own actions. • Wrongdoers have violated the social contract and can therefore be deprived of many of the rights afforded to law-abiding citizens.	• Criminal behavior can be attributed to social and biological factors. • Criminals can be rehabilitated and returned to the community.
Case in Point	• *Ohio v. Robinette* (519 U.S. 33 [1996]), which allows police greater freedom to search the automobile of a driver stopped for speeding.	• *Mapp v. Ohio* (367 U.S. 643 [1961]), which invalidates evidence improperly gathered by the police, even if the evidence proves the suspect's guilt.

Rising crime rates in the late 1970s and early 1980s led to increased pressure on politicians and judges to get "tough on crime." This certainly slowed down the due process revolution and perhaps returned the principles of the crime control model to our criminal justice system. This trend has become even more obvious as the criminal justice system tries to adjust to the threat of domestic terrorism, a process we will examine in the chapter-ending *Criminal Justice in Action—Terrorism and the Law* on the next page.

Criminal Justice in Action
Terrorism and the Law

The law evolves. Generally, this process is slow and deliberate, influenced by numerous different factors and circumstances. In 2001, however, the outlook concerning our antiterrorism laws changed in an instant—to be precise, at 8:45 A.M. on the morning of September 11, when hijackers flew American Airlines Flight 11 into the north tower of the World Trade Center in New York City. Could the tragedy of September 11 have been prevented, many Americans wondered, if we had been better prepared; that is, if we had had better laws in place to prevent acts of terrorism? In this *Criminal Justice in Action* feature, we will see that changing laws is never a straightforward process, even when the need for such change seems evident.

CONGRESS ACTS

On September 16, 2001, U.S. Attorney General John Ashcroft met with congressional leaders, asking that law enforcement agencies be given more authority to follow and apprehend those suspected of terrorist activities. "We need to make sure that we provide maximum capacity against terrorists in the United States," Ashcroft said after the meeting.[32]

Few members of Congress would dispute Ashcroft's statement. Just five days earlier, the United States had experienced one of the most traumatic events in its history. On September 11, nineteen terrorists had hijacked four commercial jetliners for use as "flying bombs." Two of the planes were deliberately crashed into the World Trade Center in New York City, destroying those cultural and financial landmarks. A third plane demolished a section of the Pentagon in Washington, D.C., while the fourth—apparently due to the heroic efforts of its passengers—went down in an uninhabited woodland area near Pittsburgh, Pennsylvania. The final death toll, which included hundreds of firefighters and police officers who perished when the World Trade Center collapsed, was over three thousand.

In response to Ashcroft's request, Congress produced legislation giving the government new powers to monitor electronic communications among terrorism suspects and wiretap any phone that might be used by such suspects.[33] In particular, legislators expanded the FBI's ability to use Carnivore, the agency's Internet wiretap system. Once it is installed in an Internet service provider, Carnivore (discussed further in Chapter 15) "samples" all e-mails that pass through that system in its search for terrorist activity.

The bill also allows law enforcement agents to detain terrorism suspects for up to seven days without filing charges against them, and makes it a crime to "harbor" terrorists.[34]

THE QUESTION OF CIVIL LIBERTIES

The FBI had been requesting similar changes for a number of years.[35] Many members of the law enforcement agency community feel that these measures, and others like them, are necessary to face the particular challenges presented by the crime of terrorism. Suicide terrorism, for example, is particularly suited to frustrate law enforcement efforts: the perpetrators do not need to plan an escape route; they do not need to be "rescued" by comrades; and there is no risk of being captured and questioned by law enforcement agents or government officials.[36] Furthermore, notes Professor Ronald Steel of the University of Southern California, lawmakers may have been influenced by a sense that the old methods were not working.[37] Following the bombing of the World Trade Center by terrorists in 1993, those responsible were captured, tried, and sentenced under the rules of the criminal justice system that form the basis of this textbook. Given the strong evidence that the same network of fundamentalist Islamic terrorists was connected to both the 1993 bombing and the 2001 attacks, it seemed that a new approach was needed.

Support for the stronger measures is not, however, universal. Many observers fear that one of the casualties of the "war against terrorism" will be long-cherished civil liberties.[38] *Civil liberties* can be loosely defined as those rights guaranteed to American citizens by the Bill of Rights, and they include freedom of speech, freedom of religion, freedom of assembly, and freedom to a certain amount of privacy. The day following the attacks in New York City and Washington, D.C., Republican Senator Trent Lott of Mississippi said, "When you are at war, civil liberties are treated differently."[39]

SECURITY VERSUS FREEDOM

The question is, then, how differently are Americans willing to see their civil liberties treated? Or, in other words, how much freedom are we willing to trade for security? As far as privacy is concerned, most Americans seem relatively untroubled by the prospect of more thorough screening processes and a higher law enforcement presence in airports and on airplanes (a situation we will discuss in Chapter 4). But what about increased surveillance capabilities, such as more power for law enforcement agents to listen in on phone conversations and greater access to information on personal computer systems? Should Americans be given smart cards that will allow the government to follow their movements via satellite?

Other incidents in the week following the September 11 tragedy raised questions of civil liberties, particularly freedom of speech and freedom of religion. In Union City, New Jersey, five men with Middle Eastern appearances were detained by the Immigration and Naturalization Service after they had been reported as "celebrating" the attacks.[40] A day later, Sher J. B. Singh, an Indian American Sikh, was handcuffed by police on a train from Boston to Washington, D.C. Apparently, Singh was detained because he was carrying a ceremonial knife less than four inches long, known as a Kirpan, that Sikhs are required to carry as a symbol of their religious beliefs.[41]

"REASONABLE SUSPICION" AND TERRORIST SUSPECTS

Singh's detention was particularly disturbing to some observers because his appearance seemed to play a large role in the police officers' actions. (Singh, as is customary for Sikhs, wears a turban and has a long beard, making him look similar to many of the images of known terrorists seen in the media.) As you will learn in Chapter 6, a police officer has the authority to stop a civilian if that officer has a "reasonable suspicion" of wrongdoing. While the officer may take many factors into consideration in making a "reasonable" decision to stop someone, he or she cannot legally rely on race or ethnicity alone. Indeed, the U.S. Constitution protects us from being treated differently simply because of our race or ethnicity.[42]

In reality, the protection of the Constitution has not been as strong for certain minority groups in times of crisis in this country. During World War II, 120,000 Japanese Americans were held in internment camps because of suspicions concerning their loyalty, an action that was upheld by the Supreme Court.[43] In the present struggle against terrorism, the primary focus of antiterrorism efforts has been fundamentalist Islamic extremists, particularly Saudi Arabian Osama bin Laden and his Al Qaeda terrorist organization. Bin Laden is believed to be primarily responsible for the bombing of the World Trade Center in 1993, the bombing of American embassies in Kenya and Tanzania in 1998—in which 224 people were killed and thousands injured—and the attack on the U.S.S. *Cole* in Yemen in 2000, which left 17 Americans dead and 19 wounded. He is also the primary suspect in the September 11 tragedy. Each of the nineteen hijackers believed by the FBI to have been responsible for those attacks was of Middle Eastern descent.

Following the 1993 World Trade Center bombing and the 1995 destruction of the Alfred P. Murrah Federal Building in Oklahoma City, Oklahoma, by American citizen Terry McVeigh, President Clinton signed the Anti-Terrorism and Effective Death Penalty Act of 1996 into law.[44] Among other things, this law allows the government to hold foreign nationals (that is, non–American citizens) indefinitely if they are suspected of terrorist activity. The law established special "removal courts" to oversee such proceedings, and such courts may hear evidence against the suspected terrorist without making the evidence available to that person.[45] Since the passage of the act in 1996, nearly all of the "secret evidence cases" brought under its authority have involved Arab or Muslim immigrants, leading Georgetown University law professor David Cole to remark that "if the [government] used this tactic against a group that was less subject to terrorist stereotype, there would be a much broader outcry."[46]

THE DETAINEES

Indeed, in the year following the September 11 attacks, the federal government detained more than 1,200 people, almost all of whom were Arab or Muslim males, on suspicion of terrorist connections. The majority of those detained were picked up because they had violated immigration laws

Continued on next page

Jose Padilla, who was arrested on May 8, 2002, under suspicion of conspiring with Al Qaeda terrorists to detonate a "dirty" bomb in the United States. Labeled an "enemy combatant," Padilla was denied many rights normally provided to criminal suspects. (AP Photo/Broward County Sheriff's Office)

CJ in Action: Terrorism and the Law *continued*

(by overstaying the amount of time they were permitted to reside in the United States, for example) and, as of July 2002, not one had been charged with any crime in relation to terrorist activities.[47]

The federal government insisted that the detentions were necessary for security reasons. But the practice has been criticized on three grounds. First, the names of many of the detainees were kept secret, and their initial appearances before immigration judges were closed to the public. Second, several were held as "material witnesses"; that is, though not suspected of criminal activities themselves, they were believed to have information on terrorist organizations. Third, two detained Americans—Jose Padilla and Yaser Hamdi—were labeled "enemy combatants" and denied rights fundamental to U.S. citizens, such as the right to be represented by a lawyer and the right to trial before a judge or jury.[48]

Throughout this textbook, we will be addressing how the criminal justice system attempts to balance the need to control crime with the need to protect individual rights. You will see that the tactics of the New York City Police Department over the past decade have been both lauded for their contribution to lowering crime rates nationwide and criticized for a perceived disregard for civil rights, especially those of minorities. In the context of the fight against terrorism, the "balancing act" is essential to an understanding of how the law enforcement community will respond to this threat.

MAKING SENSE OF TERRORISM AND THE LAW

1 Do you think the measures passed by Congress mentioned in this feature will help prevent terrorist attacks? How might they do so? What civil liberties, if any, might other citizens be giving up in allowing law enforcement agencies such powers?

2 Consider the incident mentioned in which five Middle Eastern men were detained because they had "celebrated" the terrorist attacks on New York City and Washington, D.C. Do you think it was "reasonable" of the police officers to detain these men? What about the First Amendment, which protects freedom of speech? Would it change your answer to learn that the night before the terrorist attacks, three Middle Eastern men whom authorities believed to be connected to the attacks were heard loudly predicting coming bloodshed in America at a sports bar in Daytona Beach, Florida?

3 Do you think racial profiling on commercial airplanes of people who appear to be Middle Eastern is "reasonable"? In other words, are law enforcement agents justified in stopping those who appear to be Middle Eastern more frequently than members of other racial or ethnic groups? Explain your argument.

INFOTRAC®
COLLEGE EDITION

Keywords: terrorism;
World Trade Center bombing:
Oklahoma City bombing

KEY TERMS

conflict model 4

consensus model 3

crime control model 15

discretion 13

due process model 16

federalism 9

felony 14

misdemeanor 15

organized crime 8

property crime 5

public order crime 6

violent crime 4

"wedding cake" model 14

white-collar crime 6

CHAPTER SUMMARY

1 Describe the two most common models of how society determines which acts are criminal. The consensus model argues that the majority of citizens will agree on which activities should be outlawed and punished as crimes; it rests on the assumption that a diverse group of people can have similar morals. In contrast, the conflict model argues that in a diverse society, the dominant groups exercise power by codifying their value systems into criminal laws.

2 Define crime and the different types of crime. Crime is any action punishable under criminal statutes and is considered an offense against society. Therefore, alleged criminals are prosecuted by the state rather than by victims. Crimes are punishable by sanctions that bring about a loss of personal freedom, fines, or, in extreme cases, death. There are six groups of crimes: (a) violent crimes—murder, rape, assault, battery, and robbery; (b) property crimes—pickpocketing, shoplifting, larceny/theft, burglary, and arson; (c) public order crimes—public drunkenness, prostitution, gambling, and illicit drug use; (d) white-collar crime—fraud and embezzlement; (e) organized crime—crime undertaken by a number of persons who operate their activities much as legal businesses do; and (f) high-tech crime—sabotage, fraud, embezzlement, and theft of proprietary data from computer systems as well as cybercrimes, such as selling pornographic materials to minors on the Internet.

3 Outline the three levels of law enforcement. Because we have a federal system of government, law enforcement occurs at both the federal and the state levels and within the states at local levels. Because crime is primarily a local concern, most employees in the criminal justice system work for local governments. Agencies at the federal level include the FBI, the DEA, and the U.S. Secret Service, among others.

4 List the essential elements of the corrections system. Criminal offenders are placed on probation, incarcerated in a jail or prison, transferred to community-based correction facilities, or released on parole.

5 Explain the difference between the formal and informal criminal justice processes. The formal criminal justice process involves procedures such as booking, setting bail, and the like. For every step in the formal process, though, someone has discretion, and such discretion leads to an informal process. Even when prosecutors believe that a suspect is guilty, they have the discretion not to prosecute, for example.

6 Describe the layers of the "wedding cake" model. The top layer consists of celebrity cases, which are most highly publicized; the second layer involves high-profile felonies, such as rape and murder; the third layer consists of property crimes such as larcenies and burglaries; the fourth layer consists of misdemeanors.

7 Contrast the crime control and due process models. The crime control model assumes that the criminal justice system is designed to protect the public from criminals; thus, its most important function is to punish and repress criminal conduct. The due process model presumes that the accused are innocent and provides them with the most complete safeguards, usually within the court system.

QUESTIONS FOR CRITICAL ANALYSIS

1 How is it possible to have a consensus about what should or should not be illegal in a country with several hundred million adults from all races, religions, and walks of life?

2 Why are criminals prosecuted by the state, through its public officials, rather than by the victims themselves?

3 Why are public order crimes sometimes referred to as victimless crimes?

4 At what political level is most law enforcement carried out? Relate your answer to the concept of federalism.

5 Assume that all of the officials involved in the criminal justice process were deprived of most of the discretion they now have. What might be some of the results?

SELECTED PRINT AND ELECTRONIC RESOURCES

SUGGESTED READINGS

Henry, Stuart, and William G. Hinkle, eds., *Careers in Criminal Justice: The Inside Story,* 2d ed., Salem, WI: Sheffield Publishing Company, 2000. This is a direct and concise explanation of careers in the criminal justice system. You will obtain a real feel for the career that you may enter.

Penzler, Otto, and Thomas H. Cook, eds., *Best American Crime Reporting 2002,* New York: Vintage Books USA, 2002. With seventeen selections, this analogy offers a variety of angles on criminal behavior while covering some of the most important crime stories of 2001. The collection focuses not only on criminals, but also on victims and their families, and, in some cases, the wider sociological implications of the criminal act. Included are pieces on widespread corruption within the Los Angeles Police Department, executing mentally deficient convicts in Texas, and the September 11 terrorist attack.

Price-Lee, Mary, et al., *100 Best Careers in Crime Fighting: Law Enforcement, Criminal Justice, Private Security, and Cyberspace Crime Detection,* New York: Macmillan General Reference, 1998. This is a relatively short (224 pages) guide to job opportunities in crime fighting from local to state to federal law enforcement positions as well as private security careers. Also presented are opportunities for women and minorities.

MEDIA RESOURCES

The Siege **(1998)** A series of deadly bomb attacks have paralyzed New York City, providing FBI terrorist task force leader Anthony "Hub" Hubbard (played by Denzel Washington) with the challenge of his career. With the help of CIA agent Elise Kraft (Annette Bening) and FBI agent Frank Haddad (Tony Shalhoub), Hub is able to link the attacks to an Arab terrorist group with cells in the city.

When he proves unable to stop them, however, the president of the United States declares martial law and orders Gen. William Devereaux (Bruce Willis) to lead the Army into Brooklyn. Soldiers cordon off the borough and subject Arab Americans living there to highly intrusive (and unconstitutional) treatment in order to locate the terrorists.

Critically analyze this film:

1. Many viewers have been struck by the similarities between the plot of *The Siege* and the events of September 11, 2001. In what ways did the film "predict" the terrorist attacks on New York and Washington, D.C.?

2. Do you find the quick declaration of martial law by the president to be realistic? In light of the September 11, 2001, terrorist attacks, do you think Americans would accept such a harsh restriction of civil liberties by the military, including the placement of Arab Americans in detention camps? Would you support a reduction of civil liberties if terrorist activity in the United States intensifies in the next several years?

3. In the film, Gen. Devereaux justifies torturing a suspect by saying that the "time has come for one man to suffer in order to save hundreds of lives." Do you agree that torture can be justified in this manner? Should our government consider it as a "tool" to fight terrorism? Why or why not?

4. Following September 11, 2001, many observers criticized government law enforcement agencies for failing to cooperate in the fight against terrorism. How does the relationship between Hub and Elise in the film anticipate this criticism?

Bonnie and Clyde and Me: True Tales of Crime and Punishment by Floyd Hamilton, et al., Greattapes audiocassettes, 1995. These four audio tapes are enjoyable listening for anyone who wants to hear a "true" account of what it was like to go on a "job" with Bonnie and Clyde.

LOGGING ON

Go to <u>http://cj.wadsworth.com/gainescore2e</u>, **and click Hypercontents.** There, you will find URLs for the organizations in the following list:

- An organization called **360degrees** offers a helpful overview of the American criminal justice system on its Web site.

- The **Urban Institute** also provides a wealth of information on crime in the United States through its Web site.

- Not surprisingly, a large number of Web sites deal with the issue of terrorism. The Web site for the **Terrorism Research Center** is one of the most informative.

USING THE INTERNET FOR CRIMINAL JUSTICE ANALYSIS

1. Log on to your InfoTrac College Edition at **http://www.infotrac-college.com/wadsworth/**. Then type in the words **"Terrorism threats at home: Two years after Oklahoma City."** Read the entire article and answer the following questions:

   a. What groups did federal and local law enforcement agencies target after the bombing of the Oklahoma City federal building?

   b. What are the fastest growing hard-core violence-prone groups?

   c. Describe the radical right group called the Odinists.

2. See Internet Activities 1.1 and 1.2 on the companion Web site for *CJ in Action: The Core.* To get to the activities, go to **http://www.cj.wadsworth.com/gainescore2e**, select the appropriate chapter from the drop down list, then click Internet Activities on the left navigation bar.

NOTES

1. David Johnston, "Walker Will Face Terrorism Counts in a Civilian Court," *New York Times* (January 16, 2002), A1.
2. Neil A. Lewis, "American Who Joined Taliban Pleads Guilty to Felony Charges," *New York Times* (July 16, 2002), A1.
3. William Glaberson, "Whether Walker Knew of Counsel Is Issue," *New York Times* (January 17, 2002), A15.
4. Edwin Dobb, "Should John Walker Lindh Go Free?" *Harper's Magazine* (May 2002), 3141.
5. Linda R. Monk, "The Act of Treason Is in the Eye of the Beholder," *Chicago Tribune* (February 25, 2002), 15.
6. Kenneth W. Clarkson, Roger LeRoy Miller, Gaylord A. Jentz, and Frank B. Cross, *West's Business Law: Texts; Cases; Legal, Ethical, Regulatory, and International Environment*, 9th ed. (Minneapolis/St. Paul, MN: West Publishing Co., 2004), 165.
7. Herman Bianchi, *Justice as Sanctuary: Toward a New System of Crime Control* (Bloomington: Indiana University Press, 1994), 72.
8. George B. Vold, *Theoretical Criminology* (New York: Oxford Press, 1994), 72.
9. In 1962, the Supreme Court ruled that a person could not be criminally prosecuted because of his or her status as a homosexual. *Robinson v. California*, 376 U.S. 660 (1962). Many United States Supreme Court decisions will be cited in this book, and it is important to understand these citations. In this citation, *Robinson v. California* refers to the parties in the case that the Court is reviewing. "U.S." is the abbreviation for *United States Reports*, the official publication of United States Supreme Court decisions. "376" refers to the volume of the *United States Reports* where the case appears, and "660" refers to the page number. The citation ends with the year the case was decided in parentheses. Most, though not all, case citations in this book will follow this formula. For general information on how to read case citations and find court decisions, see the appendix at the end of the chapter.
10. *2002 Report to the Nation: Occupational Fraud and Abuse* (Austin, TX: The Association of Certified Fraud Examiners, 2002), 5.

11. Sarbanes-Oxley Act of 2002.
12. Chicago Crime Commission, *The New Faces of Organized Crime* (Chicago, IL: Chicago Crime Commission, 1997).
13. *Computer Crime and Security Survey* (San Francisco: Computer Security Institute, 2001).
14. Charles E. Ramirez, "Cybercrimes Cost Businesses Billions," *Detroit News* (May 29, 2001), 1.
15. President's Commission on Law Enforcement and Administration of Justice, *The Challenge of Crime in a Free Society* (Washington, D.C.: U.S. Government Printing Office, 1967), 7.
16. John Rawls, *A Theory of Justice* (Cambridge, MA: Belknap Press of Harvard University Press, 1971), 60–1.
17. William K. Rashbaum, "Counterterrorism Becomes a Local Beat in New York," *New York Times* (July 15, 2002), A15.
18. President's Commission on Law Enforcement and Administration of Justice, 7.
19. John Heinz and Peter Manikas, "Networks among Elites in a Local Criminal Justice System," *Law and Society Review* 26 (1992), 831–61.
20. James Q. Wilson, "What to Do about Crime: Blaming Crime on Root Causes," *Vital Speeches* (April 1, 1995), 373.
21. Herbert Packer, *The Limits of the Criminal Sanction* (Stanford, CA: Stanford University Press, 1968), 154–73.
22. *Ibid.*
23. Daniel Givelber, "Meaningless Acquittals, Meaningful Convictions: Do We Reliably Acquit the Innocent?" *Rutgers Law Review* 49 (Summer 1997), 1317.
24. Lawrence M. Friedman and Robert V. Percival, *The Roots of Justice* (Chapel Hill, NC: University of North Carolina Press, 1981).
25. Packer, 154–73.
26. *Ibid.*
27. Givelber, 1317.
28. Guy-Uriel E. Charles, "Fourth Amendment Accommodations: (Un) Compelling Public Needs, Balancing Acts, and the Fiction of Consent," *Michigan Journal of Race and Law* (Spring 1997), 461.
29. *Gideon v. Wainwright*, 372 U.S. 335 (1963).

30. *Miranda v. Arizona*, 384 U.S. 436 (1966).
31. *Mapp v. Ohio*, 367 U.S. 643 (1961).
32. Bob Kemper and Jill Zuckman, "More Powers Sought to Combat Terrorism," *Chicago Tribune* (September 17, 2001), A1.
33. Public Law No. 107-56, USA Patriot Act of 2001.
34. *Ibid.*
35. Kemper and Zuckman.
36. Ehud Sprinzak, quoted in Jodi Wilgoren, "A Terrorist Profile Emerges That Confounds the Experts," *New York Times* (September 15, 2001), A2.
37. Ronald Steel, "The Weak at War with the Strong," *New York Times* (September 14, 2001), A27.
38. Linda Greenhouse, "The Clamor of a Free People," *New York Times* (September 16, 2001), Sec. 4, p. 1.
39. Robin Toner, "Some Foresee a Sea Change in Attitude on Freedoms," *New York Times* (September 15, 2001), A16.
40. James Risen and Don Van Natta, Jr., "Authorities Have Learned the Identities of 18 Hijackers, Attorney General Says," *New York Times* (September 14, 2001), A4.
41. Erica Noonan, "Sikh Protests Police Detention, Behavior," *Boston Globe* (September 16, 2001), 1.
42. *Holland v. Illinois,* 493 U.S. 479 (1990).
43. *Korematsu v. United States,* 323 U.S. 214 (1944).
44. Public Law No. 104-132, 110 Stat. 1214 (1996).
45. Roberta Smith, "America Tries to Come to Terms with Terrorism," *Cardozo Journal of International Law and Comparative Law* 5 (Spring 1997), 249.
46. Quoted in Christopher Marquis, "U.S. Frees Palestinian Held 3 Years on Secret Evidence," *New York Times* (December 16, 2000), A8.
47. Tamaia Audi, "U.S. Detained 600 for Secret Hearings," *Chicago Tribune* (July 19, 2002), 13.
48. Adam Liptak, Neil A. Lewis, and Benjamin Weiser, "After Sept. 11, a Legal Battle on the Limits of Civil Liberty," *New York Times* (August 4, 2002), 1.

HOW TO READ CASE CITATIONS AND FIND COURT DECISIONS

Many important court cases are discussed throughout this book. Every time a court case is referred to, you will be able to check its citation using the endnotes on the final pages of the chapter. Court decisions are recorded and published. When a court case is mentioned, the notation that is used to refer to, or to cite, the case denotes where the published decision can be found.

State courts of appeals decisions are usually published in two places, the state reports of that particular state and the more widely used *National Reporter System* published by West Group. Some states no longer publish their own reports. The *National Reporter System* divides the states into the following geographic areas: Atlantic (A. or A.2d), South Western (S.W., S.W.2d, or S.W.3d), North Eastern (N.E. or N.E.2d), North Western (N.W. or N.W.2d), Southern (So. or So.2d), and Pacific (P., P.2d, or P.3d). The *2d* and *3d* in these abbreviations refer to the *Second Series* and *Third Series,* respectively.

Federal trial court decisions are published unofficially in West's *Federal Supplement* (F.Supp. or F.Supp.2d), and opinions from the circuit courts of appeals are reported unofficially in West's *Federal Reporter* (F., F.2d, or F.3d). Opinions from the United States Supreme Court are reported in the *United States Reports* (U.S.), the *Lawyers' Edition of the Supreme Court Reports* (L.Ed.), West's *Supreme Court Reporter* (S.Ct.), and other publications. The *United States Reports* is the official publication of United States Supreme Court

decisions. It is published by the federal government. Many early decisions are missing from these volumes. The citations of the early volumes of the *United States Reports* include the names of the actual reporters, such as Dallas, Cranch, or Wheaton. *McCulloch v. Maryland,* for example, is cited as 17 U.S. (4 Wheat.) 316. Only after 1874 did the present citation system, in which cases are cited based solely on their volume and page numbers in the *United States Reports,* come into being. The *Lawyers' Edition of the Supreme Court Reports* is an unofficial and more complete edition of Supreme Court decisions. West's *Supreme Court Reporter* is an unofficial edition of decisions dating from October 1882. These volumes contain headnotes and numerous brief editorial statements of the law involved in the case.

State courts of appeals decisions are cited by giving the name of the case; the volume, name, and page number of the state's official report (if the state publishes its own reports); and the volume, unit, and page number of the *National Reporter.* Federal court citations are also listed by giving the name of the case and the volume, name, and page number of the reports. In addition to the citation, this textbook lists the year of the decision in parentheses. Consider, for example, the case *Miranda v. Arizona,* 384 U.S. 436 (1966). The Supreme Court's decision in this case may be found in volume 384 of the *United States Reports* on page 436. The case was decided in 1966.

CHAPTER 2
MEASURING AND EXPLAINING CRIME

CHAPTER OUTLINE

- **The Uniform Crime Report**

- **Alternative Measuring Methods**

- **Crime Trends and Patterns**

- **Exploring the Causes of Crime**

- **Criminal Justice in Action—The Link between Guns and Crime**

Chapter Objectives

After reading this chapter, you should be able to:

1. Identify the publication in which the FBI reports crime data and list the three ways it does so.

2. Distinguish between Part I and Part II offenses as defined in the UCR.

3. Explain how the National Incident-Based Reporting System differs from the UCR.

4. Distinguish between the National Crime Victimization Survey and self-reported surveys.

5. Explain the underlying assumption on which choice theories of crime are based.

6. Identify two social process theories of crime.

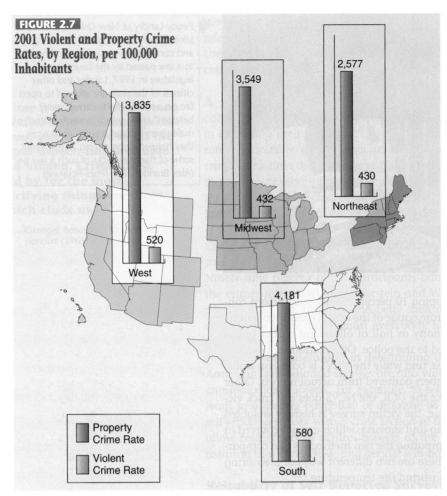

FIGURE 2.7

2001 Violent and Property Crime Rates, by Region, per 100,000 Inhabitants

3,835
520
West

3,549
432
Midwest

2,577
430
Northeast

4,181
580
South

■ Property Crime Rate

□ Violent Crime Rate

Source: Federal Bureau of Investigation, *Crime in the United States, 2001* (Washington, D.C.: U.S. Department of Justice, 2002), Figure 2.4, page 17.

patterns of crime, police departments are increasingly able to divert resources to the areas that need them the most. We will further discuss the use of this technology in police operations in Chapter 5.

Class and Crime

The general assumption that the poorest citizens are those most likely to commit serious crimes is borne out by official crime statistics. The highest crime rates in the United States are consistently recorded in low-income, urban neighborhoods. A rise of one percentage point in male unemployment appears to increase the violent crime rate by 9 percent, and a one percentage point rise in the poverty rate increases property crime by nearly 3 percent.[31]

It may seem logical that those who believe they lack a legal opportunity to gain the consumer goods and services that dominate American culture would turn to illegal methods to do so. But, logic aside, many criminologists are skeptical of such an obvious class-crime relationship. After all, poverty does not *cause* crime; the majority of residents in low-income neighborhoods are law abiding. Furthermore, higher-income citizens are also involved in all sorts of criminal activities and are more likely to commit white-collar crimes, which are not measured by the UCR or NCVS.

Furthermore, self-reported data have been used extensively in studying the crime-class relationship. The results have shown that as far as less serious crimes are concerned, criminal behavior differs very little among the lower, middle, and upper classes.[32] These findings tend to support the theory that high crime rates in low-income communities are at least partly the result of a greater willingness of police to arrest poor citizens, and of the court system to convict them.

> "**The common argument that crime is caused by poverty is a kind of slander on the poor.**"
>
> —H. L. Mencken, *American journalist* (1956)

Race and Crime

The class-crime relationship and the class-race relationship are invariably linked. Official crime data seem to indicate a strong correlation between minority status and crime: according to the UCR, African Americans—who make up 12.9 percent of the population—constitute 38 percent of those arrested for violent crimes and 31 percent of those arrested for property crimes.[33] Furthermore, according to the NCVS, African Americans are victims of violent crime at a rate of 31.2 per 1,000, compared to 24.5 per 1,000 for whites.[34]

The racial differences in the crime rate are one of the most controversial areas of the criminal justice system (see *CJ in Focus—Myth versus Reality: Race Stereotyping and Crime*). At first glance, crime statistics seem to support the idea that the subculture of African Americans in the United States is disposed toward criminal behavior. Not all of the data, however, support that assertion. A num-

INFOTRAC®
COLLEGE EDITION

Keywords: race and crime

CJ in F⊙CUS

Myth versus Reality: Race Stereotyping and Crime

In an effort to study the effect of race on perception, Birt Duncan gathered 104 white undergraduate students at the University of California and had them observe an argument between two people in which one person shoved the other. The undergraduates were randomly assigned to view one of four different conditions: (1) white shover/African American victim, (2) white shover/white victim, (3) African American shover/white victim, and (4) African American shover/African American victim. The students were then asked to rate the behavior of the person who did the shoving.

Duncan found that when the shover was African American and the victim was white, 75 percent of the students considered the shove to be "violent behavior" and 6 percent saw it as "playing around." In contrast, when the shover was white and the victim black, only 17 percent characterized the shove as violent, while 42 percent saw it as playful.

The Myth

The results of Duncan's study are not, in the end, surprising. Racial stereotyping is not an aberration in our society. Negative stereotypes of minorities, especially African Americans, label them as prone to violence and more likely to be criminals or members of gangs than others.

The Reality

According to the University of Maryland's Katheryn K. Russell, the best-kept secret in criminology is that the United States has a "white crime" problem. Whites, Russell points out, are the subject of about two-thirds of the arrests in this country each year and account for a majority of those Americans in prison and jail. Russell's point is that public and academic obsession with "black crime" has severely limited discussion of "white crime." This fascination can be explained, at least from a criminological standpoint, by the different *proportional* involvement of racial minorities in crime. As Figure 2.8 shows, although white involvement in crime is high, it is "relatively" low given the percentage of the American population that is of European descent. In contrast, minorities have a disproportionate involvement in crime based on their population statistics.

FIGURE 2.8
Crime and Race in the United States

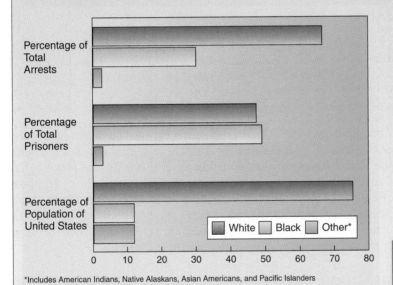

*Includes American Indians, Native Alaskans, Asian Americans, and Pacific Islanders

NOTE: For purposes of crime statistics, government agencies distinguish between race and ethnicity. Hispanic Americans are seen as a separate ethnicity, not a separate race. Therefore, most crime statistics will make a distinction between "white non-Hispanic" and "black non-Hispanic" if they aim to draw conclusions about ethnicity in the criminal justice system.

Source: U.S. Census, U.S. Department of Justice, Federal Bureau of Investigation.

FOR CRITICAL ANALYSIS
According to Figure 2.8, although African Americans are arrested at less than half the rate of whites, they comprise about 3 percent more of the prison population. How might this statistical anomaly be explained?

ber of crime-measuring surveys show consistent levels of crime and drug abuse across racial lines.[35] Why, then, are proportionally more minorities arrested and incarcerated than whites? This discrepancy has been attributed to inherent racism in the criminal justice system, though criminologists are by no means of one mind regarding this possibility. (See *The Diversity Challenge—Disparity or Discrimination?*) A number of other factors, including poor economic and social conditions in the low-income neighborhoods where many minorities reside, have been offered to explain the complex problem of race and crime. We will address this issue throughout this textbook.

Another point to remember when reviewing statistical studies of minority offenders and victims is that they tend to focus on *race,* which distinguishes groups based on physical characteristics such as skin color, rather then *ethnicity,* which denotes national or cultural background. Thus, the bulk of criminological

Disparity or Discrimination?

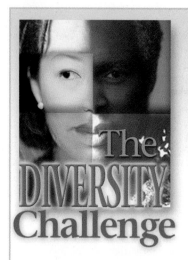

The statistics seem clear—and outrageous. African Americans make up 12.9 percent of the country's population, but they account for 27.9 percent of its arrests. In Massachusetts, blacks and Hispanics are imprisoned for drug offenses at rates that are, respectively 39 and 81 times higher than for whites. The question for many criminal justice experts is whether these figures represent discrimination or disparity. *Discrimination* reflects illegitimate influences (such as race) that affect the decision-making process of judges, prosecutors, police officers, and other authority figures in the criminal justice system. *Disparity,* in contrast, refers to inconsistencies that result from legitimate factors in this decision making.

A great deal of research has been done on the treatment of minorities by the criminal justice system, but no simple answers to the question of discrimination versus dis-

parity have emerged. While there are certainly many crime experts who make strong arguments that the system if biased (and we shall hear from them throughout this textbook), a number of observers believe that evidence of racial discrimination often in fact reveals a pattern of disparity. For example, social indicators other than overt racism may explain higher arrest rates of minorities. When compared with whites, minorities have higher instances of living conditions that can be correlated with crimes. Research done in Massachusetts shows that a person of *any* race living in a neighborhood designated as an "extreme poverty" area is nineteen times more likely to be arrested for a drug offense than someone who lives in a nonpoverty area. Racism and other forms of discrimination may very well have created the living conditions that place minorities at a greater risk of being arrested. But many observers believe that the criminal justice system if merely reacting to these conditions and is not responsible for them.

FOR CRITICAL ANALYSIS

Place yourself in the position of a police officer. Why might you find it easier to make arrests in a poor neighborhood than in a middle- or upper-class one?

research in this area has focused on the differences between European Americans and African Americans, both because the latter have been the largest minority group in the United States for most of its history and because the racial differences between the two groups are easily identifiable. Americans of Hispanic descent have either been excluded from many crime studies or been linked with whites or blacks based on racial characteristics.[36] Other minority groups, such as Asian Americans, Native Americans, and immigrants from the South Pacific or Eastern Europe, have been similarly underreported in crime studies.

Age and Crime

The strongest statistical determinant of criminal behavior appears to be age. Each of the three sources of crime data supports the hypothesis that criminal activity has been, and continues to be, most pronounced among younger citizens.[37] According to the latest UCR, 41.1 percent of arrests for violent crimes involve Americans aged 24 and younger, with the highest crime rate occurring between the ages of 16 and 19. By the same token, those aged 50 years and older are responsible for only 5.6 percent of the violent crime arrests in this country.[38] The young are also in more danger of being crime victims than any other age group. Those aged 12 to 19 are about twice as likely as those aged 25 to 34 and almost three times as likely as those aged 35 to 49 to be victims of violent crimes.[39] We will take a comprehensive look at juvenile delinquency and crime in Chapter 14.

Guns and Crime

Since at least the 1930s, young people have committed more violent crimes than have their elders. Since the mid-1980s, however, such rates have increased *significantly.* Between 1985 and 1992, homicide rates went up by 50 percent for white males aged fourteen to seventeen and tripled for African Americans of the

INFOTRAC®
COLLEGE EDITION

Keywords: crime and age; guns and crime; drugs and alcohol and crime; gender and crime

same age.[40] This sharp increase has been linked to the role guns play in juvenile criminal behavior. The rise in gun ownership among gang members in high-crime urban areas has been well documented,[41] but these high rates of violence also reflect a growing pattern of gun ownership among suburban youths as well.[42]

According to the UCR, 63.4 percent of all homicides in 2001 were committed with a firearm. In addition, 42 percent of all robberies and 18.3 percent of all aggravated assaults were carried out by someone brandishing a gun.[43] Victims' rights groups and gun control advocates argue that America's high rates of violence reflect the ease with which firearms are available to its citizens; hence, they push for legislation to restrict the ability to sell and purchase such weapons. William Wells of Southern Illinois University—Carbondale and Julie Horney of the University of Nebraska at Omaha point to two facts that link guns and violent crime. First, according to the "weapon effect," a violent situation (such as an argument or a fight) in which a firearm is involved is more likely to result in assault or murder than if no firearm were involved. Second, guns increase the probability of an attack because they give the attacker a feeling of confidence that would not exist if she or he were unarmed.[44] (For a discussion of gun policies and their possible impact on violent crimes, see the feature *Criminal Justice in Action—The Link between Guns and Crime* at the end of this chapter.)

Drugs and Alcohol and Crime

Because of methodology, neither the UCR nor the NCVS is well suited to measure the effect of drugs and alcohol on criminal behavior. The National Incident-Based Reporting System may improve official crime data in this area. Other institutions, however, have studied the role that drugs and alcohol play in crime trends. A recent report published by the National Center on Addiction and Substance Abuse at Columbia University concluded that eight out of every ten prisoners in the United States were involved with alcohol or other drugs at the time of their crimes. That is to say, 80 percent were either under the direct influence of alcohol or other drugs while committing the crime, had a history of drug abuse, committed the crime to support a drug habit, or were arrested for violating drug or alcohol laws.[45] Furthermore, a number of studies, the latest published in 2002 by Graham C. Ousey of the University of Kentucky and Matthew R. Lee of Mississippi State University, have concluded that as drug use in a particular area increases, so does the violent crime rate.[46]

Gender and Crime

As with age patterns, UCR, self-reported, and victimization data consistently show similar patterns with regard to gender and crime; that is, males commit significantly more crime than females. For example, men commit murder at almost ten times the rate of females. The male-female crime ratio does not change when other factors—such as age, race, or class—are considered. This lower female involvement in crime has been attributed to a number of factors including the influence of gender roles, different social expectations for women and men, biology, and physical ability to commit crime; we will examine this issue in Chapter 10.

Career Criminals

A final pattern that crime data have uncovered is that of the career criminal, or **chronic offender.** The idea of the chronic offender was established by the pioneering research of Marvin Wolfgang, Robert Figlio, and Thorsten Sellin. The trio used official records to follow a **cohort** of 9,945 males born in Philadelphia in 1945 until they turned eighteen years of age in 1963. Released in 1972, the resulting study showed that 6 percent of the cohort had committed five or more offenses. Furthermore, this "chronic 6 percent" were responsible for 71 percent of

Police officers gather outside Stamps High School in Stamps, Arkansas, following the early morning shooting of two students, seventeen-year-old Grover Henderson and fifteen-year-old LeTisia Finley. Henderson and Finley, who eventually recovered from their wounds, were the target of fourteen-year-old Joseph Todd, who told police that the shootings were revenge for being "picked on" by his fellow students. Do you think measures such as police officers and metal detectors in schools could alleviate this problem? What negative consequences might result from such dramatic steps? (AP Photo/Danny Johnston)

On the Web

The issue of guns and crime is widely debated on the Web. For the pro–gun control view, visit the Coalition to Stop Gun Violence's Web site. For the anti–gun control view, go to the National Rifle Association's Web site. For links to both sites, go to the Hypercontents page for this chapter at http://www.cj.wadsworth.com/gainescore2e.

CHRONIC OFFENDER
A delinquent or criminal who commits multiple offenses and is considered part of a small group of wrongdoers who are responsible for a majority of the antisocial activity in any given community.

COHORT
A group of persons gathered for study because they share a certain characteristic, such as age, income, or criminal background.

"Once I've armed myself and I go in and do the robbery, my mind and my heart are racing a thousand miles an hour—yeah, I got a hell of an adrenaline rush. For me, before a crime, it's getting myself pumped up for that rush, and while committing the crime it's like being scared and excited at the same time, and it's from gaining that power over another human being. That rush gets going and doesn't stop until I succeed in whatever I am doing."

—Inmate, *interviewed by criminologist Peter B. Wood* (1997)

Keywords: career criminals

CHOICE THEORY
A school of criminology that holds that wrongdoers act as if they weigh the possible benefits of criminal or delinquent activity against the costs of being apprehended. When the benefits are greater than the costs, the offender will make a rational choice to commit a crime or delinquent act.

the murders attributed to the cohort, 82 percent of the robberies, 69 percent of the aggravated assaults, and 73 percent of the rapes.[47] The existence of chronic offenders has been corroborated by further research, such as that done by Lawrence Sherman in Kansas City. Sherman found that although only 2.7 percent of the city's roughly 500,000 inhabitants were arrested twice or more in 1990, these offenders accounted for over 60 percent of all arrests that year.[48]

Chronic offender patterns have had a significant impact on the criminal justice system. Law enforcement agencies and district attorneys' offices have devised specific strategies to apprehend and prosecute repeat offenders. As we shall see in Chapter 10, the federal government and most states have instituted sentencing policies designed to incapacitate career criminals for long periods of time.

EXPLORING THE CAUSES OF CRIME

Why do chronic offenders persist in their criminal behavior? Criminologists have advanced a number of theories to explain this pattern, including learning disabilities or poor school performance, an unsettled home life, familial history of criminality, and hyperactivity. Some observers feel that criminal behavior is linked to certain biological or genetic traits, while others think that some people are driven to commit crimes because they like it. Serial killer John Wayne Gacy claims to have "realized that death was the ultimate thrill" after murdering the first of his more than thirty victims.[49]

Research shows at least a *correlation* between each of the above theories and the phenomenon of the chronic offender. The research community has not, however, been able to reach a consensus on the cause of career criminality. The question that is the underpinning of a career in criminology—what causes crime?—is yet to be fully answered. Many variables must be accounted for. But criminologists have uncovered a wealth of information concerning a different, and more practically applicable, inquiry: Given a certain set of circumstances, why do individuals commit certain crimes?

Various schools of criminology have developed numerous theories of crime causation. In the following sections, we will examine the most widely recognized ones: choice theories, trait theories, sociological theories, social process theories, and social conflict theories.

Choice Theories

For those who subscribe to **choice theory**, the answer to why a person commits a crime is rather straightforward: because that person chooses to do so. Social scientist James Q. Wilson sums up choice theory as follows:

> At any given moment, a person can choose between committing a crime and not committing it. The consequences of committing a crime consist of rewards . . . and punishments; the consequences of not committing the crime also entail gains and losses. The larger the ratio of net rewards of [committing a crime], the greater the tendency to commit a crime.[50]

In other words, before a person commits a crime, he or she weighs the benefits (which may be money in the case of a robbery) against the costs (the possibility of being caught and going to prison or jail). If the perceived benefits are greater, the person is more likely to commit the crime.

Sociologist Jack Katz has noted that the "rewards" of crime may be sensual as well as financial. The inherent danger of criminal activity, according to Katz, increases the "rush" a criminal experiences on successfully committing a crime. Katz labels this rush the *seduction of crime*.[51] He believes that seemingly "senseless" crimes—where no obvious reward is involved—can be explained by choice theory only if the seduction of crime is considered.

Criminal Justice & TECHNOLOGY

Mapping Crime in the Brain

During the trial of John Hinckley, Jr., who attempted to assassinate President Ronald Reagan in 1981, the defense offered the jury a black-and-white photo of Hinckley's brain. This picture, the defense claimed, showed that Hinckley was schizophrenic and not responsible for his actions. In a controversial decision, the defendant was found not guilty by reason of insanity.

Twenty years later, "brain mapping" techniques make the black-and-white photo of Hinckley's brain look like the drawing of a child.

By placing electrodes on a subject's scalp, scientists can use computerized electroencephalography (CEEG) to measure the brain's spontaneous electrical activity, or its electrical response to visual and auditory stimuli. Using CEEG, scientists can present a color-coded display of brain activity. Other neuroimaging measures include positron emission computer tomography (PET scanning), which produces a computerized image of molecular variations in brain metabolism, and magnetic resonance imaging (MRI), which depicts the brain's form and structure by bombarding it with magnetic fields and radio waves.

Scans that measure brain activity can be particularly helpful in identifying *attention deficit/hyperactivity disorder (ADHD)*, a condition most commonly found in children of

elementary school age. The symptoms of ADHD include an inability to concentrate and a tendency to be impulsive and hyperactive. The condition—which is believed to affect between 3 and 5 percent of the

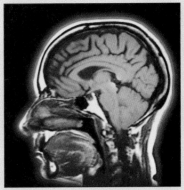
An MRI scan showing the human brain.

children in the United States—is associated with substance abuse, learning disabilities, and delinquency. Observers believe that because those who suffer from ADHD perform poorly in school, they are at much greater risk to develop antisocial and delinquent behavioral patterns. Brain scans can identify ADHD in "problem" children and lead to treatment that lessens the risk of future criminality.

IN THE FUTURE

The use of brain scanning to show a proclivity toward criminal behavior or as a defense strategy in criminal trials is dismissed as "junk science" by many criminologists. A number of studies, though, have established that certain brain patterns are associated with criminal behavior. As scientific methods improve, brain mapping may allow physicians to "predict" crime—with all the controversial implications that ability would bring.

The theory that wrongdoers choose to commit crimes is a cornerstone of the American criminal justice system. Because crime is seen as the end result of a series of rational choices, policymakers have reasoned that severe punishment can deter criminal activity by adding another variable to the decision-making process. Supporters of the death penalty—now used by thirty-eight states and the federal government—emphasize its deterrent effects, and legislators are increasingly using harsh mandatory sentences to control illegal drug use and trafficking.

Trait Theories

The Italian physician Cesare Lombroso (1835–1909), who is known as the "father of criminology," believed that criminals were throwbacks to the savagery of early humankind and could therefore be identified by certain physical characteristics such as sharp teeth and large jaws. Such far-fetched notions have long been rejected as ludicrous. But many criminologists do believe that *trait theories* are valid. They believe that the secret to crime is locked in the human body and the human brain. (See the feature *Criminal Justice & Technology—Mapping Crime in the Brain.*)

One trait theory is that biochemical conditions can influence criminal behavior. Criminal activity in males, for example, has been linked to hormones—specifically *testosterone,* which controls secondary sexual characteristics (such as the growth of facial and pubic hair) and has been linked to traits of aggression.

GREAT DEBATES

Perhaps the most controversial trait theory holds that some persons are more genetically disposed to committing crimes than others. For information on scientific research in the area of the "crime gene," as well as a discussion of the many political and ethical issues raised by these studies, go to the Great Debates feature on the text's companion Web site at http://www.cj.wadsworth.com/gainescore2e.

On June 20, 2001, Andrea P. Yates methodically drowned her five children, aged six months to seven years, in the family bathtub. A state psychiatrist found that Yates, shown here in a Houston courtroom, suffered from severe depression with "psychotic features." After her arrest, Yates told doctors that she saw Satan in the walls of her jail cell. What if Yates's psychological problems could be successfully treated? Do you believe that she should still be severely punished for her crimes? (AP Photo/Steve Ueckert, Pool)

SOCIAL DISORGANIZATION THEORY

The theory that deviant behavior is more likely in communities where social institutions such as the family, schools, and criminal justice system fail to exert control over the population.

Assistant Fire Chief Scott Roberts provides a helping hand to neighborhood children during Kids Night Out Against Crime, held in Petal, Mississippi, on June 14, 2002. Under social disorganization theory, how can the involvement of firefighters or police officers in these types of community activities help prevent crime? (AP Photo/Hattiesburg American, Joe Lovett)

Testing of inmate populations has shown that those incarcerated for violent crimes have higher testosterone levels than other prisoners.[52]

The study of psychology has also been incorporated in trait theories. During the middle of the twentieth century, the concept of the criminal as *psychopath* gained a great deal of popularity. The psychopath was seen as a person who had somehow lost her or his "humanity": the ability to control criminal impulses or to understand the consequences of her or his decisions.[53] More recently, psychological studies of crime have focused on more measurable areas such as intelligence. A study of six hundred grade school students by researchers from the University of Wisconsin, for example, found that low IQs were prevalent in those students who later became delinquents.[54] Many criminologists mistrust such data, however, as there is no way to prove that low intelligence leads to crime.

Trait theorists believe that criminal behavior should be identified and treated and do not necessarily agree with choice theorists that punishment is the most effective way to lessen crime. Though this focus on treatment has diminished somewhat in the past three decades, it is still common in the criminal justice system.

Sociological Theories

The problem with trait theory, many observers maintain, is that it falters when confronted with certain crime patterns. Why is the crime rate in Detroit, Michigan, twenty-five times that of Sioux Falls, South Dakota? Do high levels of air pollution cause lower intelligence or high levels of testosterone? As no evidence has been found to suggest such conclusions, many reject the idea that crime is something a person is "born to do." Instead, they say, crime is the result of the social conditions in a person's environment. Juvenile researchers Clifford Shaw and Henry McKay popularized this idea with their **social disorganization theory,** developed in the early 1900s. Shaw and McKay studied various high-crime neighborhoods in Chicago and found that these "zones" were characterized by "disorganization," or a breakdown of the traditional institutions of social control such as family, school systems, and local businesses.[55] (See Figure 2.9 to better understand social disorganization theory.) These types of sociological theories contend that those who are disadvantaged because of poverty or other factors such as racial discrimination are more likely to commit crimes because other avenues to "success" have been closed off. High-crime areas will develop their own cultures that are in constant conflict with the dominant culture and create a cycle of crime that claims the youth who grow up in the area and go on to be career criminals.

FIGURE 2.9
The Stages of Social Disorganization Theory

Social disorganization theory holds that crime is related to the environmental pressures that exist in certain communities or neighborhoods. These areas are marked by the desire of many of their inhabitants to "get out" at the first possible opportunity. Consequently, residents tend to ignore the important institutions in the community, such as business and education, causing further erosion and an increase in the conditions that lead to crime.

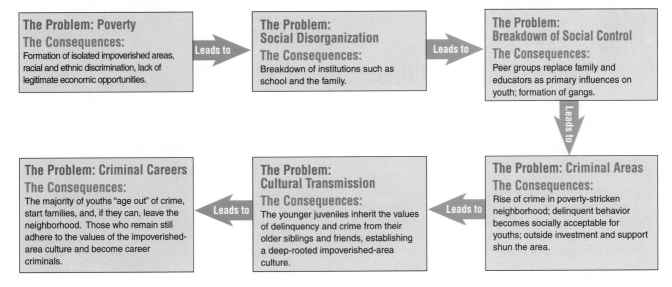

Source: Adapted from Larry J. Siegel, *Criminology*, 8th ed. (Belmont, CA: Thomson/Wadsworth, 2003), 183.

If criminal behavior can be explained by the conditions in which certain groups of people live, then it stands to reason that changing those conditions can prevent crime. Indeed, government programs to decrease unemployment, reduce poverty, and improve educational facilities in low-income neighborhoods have been partly justified as part of large-scale attempts at crime prevention.

Social Process Theories

Some criminologists reject the above arguments as being too narrow. As numerous self-report surveys have shown, the criminal instinct is pervasive in "good" neighborhoods as well as in "bad" ones. Anybody, these criminologists argue, has the potential to act out criminal behavior, regardless of his or her surroundings. **Social process theories** hold that the major influence on any individual is not society in general, but the interactions that dominate everyday life. (One "interaction" that can be said to "dominate" daily life is the media. To see how the media have been blamed for a certain type of crime, see *Criminal Justice & the Media—Turning Kids into Killers?* on the next page.)

Therefore, individuals are drawn to crime not by general factors such as "society" or "community," but by family, friends, and peer groups. **Learning theory,** popularized by Edwin Sutherland in the 1940s, saw crime as learned behavior.[56] The "teacher" is usually a family member or friend, who exposes the "student" to criminal behavior. Therefore, those who form positive social relations instead of destructive ones have a better chance of avoiding criminal activity. Another social process theory known as **labeling theory** contends that if someone is labeled "delinquent" or "criminal" by authority figures, there is a better chance that the person will consider himself or herself as such and continue the criminal behavior.[57]

Because adult criminals are seen as too "hardened" to unlearn their criminal behavior, crime prevention policies associated with social process theory focus on

INFOTRAC®
COLLEGE EDITION

<u>Keywords: social disorganization theory, social control theory; labeling theory</u>

SOCIAL PROCESS THEORIES
A school of criminology that considers criminal behavior to be the predictable result of a person's interaction with his or her environment. According to these theories, everybody has the potential for wrongdoing. Those who act on this potential are conditioned to do so by family or peer groups, or institutions such as the media.

LEARNING THEORY
The hypothesis that delinquents and criminals must be taught both the practical and emotional skills necessary to partake in illegal activity.

LABELING THEORY
The hypothesis that society creates crime and criminals by labeling certain behavior and certain people as deviant. The stigma that results from this social process excludes a person from the community, thereby increasing the chances that she or he will adopt the label as her or his identity and engage in a pattern of criminal behavior.

Criminal Justice & THE MEDIA

Turning Kids into Killers?

In the weeks following the shooting deaths of fourteen students and one teacher at Columbine High School in Littleton, Colorado, a great deal of attention was focused on the video game Doom. A favorite of the killers, Eric Harris and Dylan Klebold, Doom is a "shooter" game that allows players to choose from an array of weaponry to take out their targets. CBS's *60 Minutes* broadcast a segment entitled, "Are Video Games Turning Kids into Killers?" Several bills attempting to ban the sale of violent video games to minors were introduced on the floor of Congress. One psychologist called the video game a "mass-murder simulator" and blamed Doom for providing the stepping-stone between being "a normal kid" and "massacring kids."

Professor John Murray, a child psychologist at Kansas State University who has been studying the effects of television violence on children for three decades, does not write off such concerns as media hype. In his studies of the brain, Murray has found what he believes to be a link among memory, learning, and violent images. Repeated viewing of violent films such as *Natural Born Killers* (another favorite of Harris and Klebold), violent television programs, and violent video games may cause images of violence to be stored in memory, to be recalled as a "hair-trigger" response to frustration or anger. Murray holds that repeated exposure to violence changes the values of the children, making them more likely to "act out aggressively."

Such theories are not universally accepted. Many observers point out that millions of children play violent video games and watch violent films without becoming violent themselves. Harris and Klebold did what they did not because they watched *Natural Born Killers*, or played Doom, or were "outsiders" who wore black trenchcoats, these observers maintain, but because they were psychotic. For his part, pop star Marilyn Manson, who did not escape criticism for his violent videos and song lyrics in the wake of Columbine, focused on another aspect of the mass media. Noting that television news channels had saturated the airwaves with coverage of every detail of the Columbine tragedy, Manson warned, "Don't be surprised if every kid who gets pushed around has two new idols."

Jay Wilbur poses with Doom, the video game he helped create. (AP Photo/Tim Sharp)

juvenile offenders. Many youths, for example, are diverted from the formal juvenile justice process to keep them from being labeled "delinquent." Furthermore, many schools have implemented programs that attempt to steer children away from crime by encouraging them to "just say no" to drugs and stay in school.

Social Conflict Theories

The most recent movement in criminology focuses not on psychology, biology, or sociology, but on *power*. Those who identify power—seen as the ability of one person or group of persons to control the economic and social positions of other people or groups—as the key component in explaining crime entered the mainstream of American criminology during the 1960s. These theorists saw social ills such as poverty, racism, sexism, and destruction of the environment as the "true crimes," perpetrated by the powerful, or ruling, classes. Burglary, robbery, and even violent crimes were considered reactions by the powerless against laws that were meant to repress, not protect, them.

Social conflict theories are often associated with a critique of our capitalist economic system. Capitalism is seen as leading to high levels of violence and crime because of the disparity of income it encourages. The poor commit prop-

SOCIAL CONFLICT THEORIES
A school of criminology that views criminal behavior as the result of class conflict. Certain behavior is labeled illegal not because it is inherently criminal, but because the ruling class has an economic or social interest in restricting such behavior in order to protect the *status quo*.

erty crimes for reasons of need and because, as members of a capitalist society, they desire the same financial rewards as everybody else. They commit violent crimes because of the frustration and rage they feel when these rewards seem unattainable. Laws, instead of reflecting the value of society as a whole, reflect only the values of the segment of society that has achieved power and is willing to use the criminal justice system as a tool to keep that power.[58] Thus, the harsh penalties for "lower-class" crimes such as burglary can be seen as a means of protecting the privileges of the "haves" from the aspirations of the "have-nots."

Given its radical nature, social conflict theory has had a limited impact on public policy. Even in the aftermath of situations where class conflict has had serious and obvious repercussions, such as the Los Angeles riots of 1991, few observers feel that enough has been accomplished to improve the conditions that led to the violence. (For an overview of the different theories discussed in this chapter, see *Mastering Concepts*.)

Jacqueline Castillo, 13, left, Jasmin Amaya, 13, top, and Jacquelyn Rodriguez, 20, right, are members of Aspira, a national organization devoted to developing leadership skills and strengthening community ties among Latino youth. In 2002, Florida's Department of Juvenile Justice awarded Aspira and several other groups $7.5 million in grants to help prevent delinquency. According to learning theory, how might organizations comprised of young people like Jacqueline, Jasmin, and Jacquelyn be able to affect levels of juvenile delinquency in areas with high concentrations of young offenders? (AP Photo/Angela Gaul)

MASTERING CONCEPTS   The Causes of Crime

Choice Theories

Crime is the result of rational choices made by those who want to engage in criminal activity for the rewards it offers. The rewards may be financial or they may be psychological—criminals enjoy the "rush" that comes with committing a crime. According to choice theorists, the proper response to crime is harsh penalties, which force potential criminals to weigh the benefits of wrongdoing against the costs of punishment if they are apprehended.

Trait Theories

Criminal behavior is explained by biological and psychological attributes of the individual. Those who support biological theories of crime believe that the secret to crime is locked in the human body: in genes, brain disorders, reaction to improper diet or allergies, and so on. Psychological attempts to explain crime are based on the study of personality and intelligence and the development of a person's behavioral patterns during infancy.

Sociological Theories

Crime is not something a person is "born to do." Instead, it is the result of the social conditions in a person's environment. Those who are socially disadvantaged—because of poverty or other factors such as racial discrimination—are more likely to commit crimes because other avenues to "success" have been closed off. High-crime areas will develop their own cultures that are in constant conflict with the dominant culture and create a cycle of crime that claims the youth who grow up in the area and go on to be career criminals.

Social Process Theories

The major influence on any individual is not society in general, but the interactions that dominate everyday life. Therefore, individuals are drawn to crime not by general factors such as "society" or "community," but by family, friends, and peer groups. Crime is "learned behavior"; the "teacher" is usually a family member or friend. Everybody has the potential to become a criminal. Those who form positive social relationships instead of destructive ones have a better chance of avoiding criminal activity. Furthermore, if a person is labeled "juvenile" or "criminal" by the authority figures or organizations in his or her life, there is a better chance he or she will create a personality and actions to fit that label.

Social Conflict Theories

Criminal laws are a form of social control. Through these laws, the dominant members of society control the minority members, using institutions such as the police, courts, and prisons as tools of oppression. Crime is caused by the conflict between the "haves" and "have-nots" of society. The poor commit crimes because of the anger and frustration they feel at being denied the benefits of society.

Criminal Justice in Action

The Link between Guns and Crime

Approximately 40,000 Americans are killed each year by guns in incidents ranging from suicide to homicide. According to the most recent FBI statistics, firearms are used in 63.4 percent of murders and 42 percent of robberies in the United States.[59] Roughly speaking, there is one gun per person in this country, and half of our households own at least one firearm.[60] The link between guns and violent behavior seems obvious, but in this chapter we noted that drawing conclusions from statistics is often problematic. As we will see in this *Criminal Justice in Action* feature, there is considerable debate as to whether there is in fact any causal relationship between the prevalence of firearms in our society and their use in criminal activity and, if so, whether gun control laws can affect this relationship.

DO GUNS MEAN MORE CRIME?

Supporters of the theory that gun ownership promotes crime have a wealth of information at their fingertips, some of it reaching back more than one hundred years. Criminologist Gregory Weaver of Auburn University has suggested that a dramatic increase in homicides by gunfire in the final decades of the 1800s is directly related to a rise in the availability of guns following the Civil War (1861–1865).[61] The national supply of guns grew sharply after the end of the war, as the Union army sold its stockpile of weapons back to private manufacturers, which in turn sold the firearms to the public. Furthermore, soldiers on both sides were often allowed to keep their guns as they returned home.

Weaver also cites a significant increase in the size of gun sections in the Sears, Roebuck and Montgomery Ward mail-order catalogues between 1880 and 1900 to show that Americans were becoming more interested in gun ownership during that time period.[62] Mark Duggan of the University of Chicago has used a similar technique in one of the latest studies to connect gun ownership with violent crime.[63] One of the problems of research on this subject is that it is very difficult to know exactly how many people own guns and how many guns they own. To tackle this problem, Duggan obtained information concerning state- and county-level sales of gun magazines, reasoning that readers of such publications were likely to be gun owners. Using data covering 1990 to 1998, Duggan found that a 10 percent average increase in a state's gun ownership (as measured by sales of the magazines) was associated with a 2 percent rise in its homicide rate.

DO GUNS MEAN MORE CRIME? PART II

Figures that show violent crime rates increasing with gun ownership are often interpreted one of two ways: either crime rises when people have more guns, or people buy more guns to defend themselves when crime rises. Economist John Lott of Yale Law School supports a third, and controversial, point of view. Lott believes that gun ownership deters crime. By comparing UCR data in communities before and after they passed "right-to-carry" gun laws (which allow an adult applicant to be granted a concealed-weapon permit unless he or she is a felon or has a history of mental illness), Lott has estimated that such laws reduced homicide by 8 percent, sexual assault by 5 percent, aggravated assault by 7 percent, and robbery by 3 percent. In the thirty-one states that currently have right-to-carry laws on the books, violent crime is 13 percent lower than in those states that do not have such laws.[64] Though even Lott is not willing to say that right-to-carry laws directly cause a drop in violent crime—other contributing factors could include population density and sentencing lengths—he does believe that these reductions are partly attributable to the deterrent effect that weapons have on criminal behavior by reducing the number of "helpless victims" who are often targets of criminals.[65]

THE BRADY BILL

For government and law enforcement agencies, the important question is not "Do guns cause crime?" but rather, "How can we keep people from using guns to commit crimes?" Statistically, most guns will never be used to inflict harm on another human being; only 1.1 percent of all handguns and 0.1 percent of "long guns" (shotguns, rifles, and so on) in the United States are involved in criminal activity each year.[66] The challenge, therefore, is first to determine who might use a gun to commit a crime and then to keep the gun out of that person's hands.

In general, a criminal obtains a firearm in one of three ways: by stealing it, by purchasing it from a gun dealer, or by purchasing it from a private citizen.[67] As it is almost impossible to control the private gun market among law-abiding citizens, and law enforcement agencies already expend a great deal of energy trying to control traffic in stolen guns, most recent gun control laws focus on gun dealers.

To that end, Congress passed the Brady Handgun Violence Prevention Act in 1993.[68] Commonly known as

Maryland State Police Col. David Mitchell explains how law enforcement agents use the Integrated Ballistics Identification System to "fingerprint" firearms. The computer monitor in the photo displays the markings of a bullet that has been successfully matched to a stolen gun. (AP Photo/Gail Burton)

"Saturday night specials," cheap handguns that are often used in crimes.

FINGERPRINTING FIREARMS

Perhaps the most important development in this area is the ability of the federal government to "fingerprint" guns. Today, almost every gun is manufactured with a serial number, and firearm companies provide the Bureau of Alcohol, Tobacco and Firearms (ATF) with detailed information concerning the marks made on shell casings by every weapon they produce. With this information, the ATF can "trace" a gun used in a crime to its original owner and the store where it was purchased. Data from this system show that 1.2 percent of the nation's 83,000 licensed dealers sell almost 60 percent of the guns used in crime.[72] Targeting these "rogue" dealers can have a substantial effect on violent crime. In Boston, for example, only one juvenile was killed by a handgun in the two years after local agents used the "fingerprinting" system to sanction gun dealers who had not been doing proper background checks.[73]

the Brady Bill, this measure requires local law enforcement agencies to conduct background checks of potential handgun purchasers. In the first twenty-eight months after the effective date of the Brady Bill, 130,200 convicted or indicted felons were prevented from buying a gun because of the new background checks.[69] From 1993 to 1998, the Justice Department found that crimes committed with handguns fell 52 percent, or twice the rate that crimes fell overall.[70]

The Brady Bill has been criticized for not going far enough. The law requires background checks only for those who purchase guns from federally licensed firearms dealers. It does not cover purchases made at gun shows or from private dealers, which represent between 30 and 40 percent of the market.[71] Indeed, a number of states have enacted much more restrictive gun control laws than are required under the Brady Bill. In a reaction to the fatal shootings at Columbine High School, in 2001 Colorado became the twentieth state to require background checks for all public gun sales, including sales at gun shows. In Massachusetts, gun dealers may not sell a firearm unless it has a safety device that enables a user to know whether the gun is loaded and a "trigger lock" designed to prevent accidental shootings. That state also banned all sales of

MAKING SENSE OF THE LINK BETWEEN GUNS AND CRIME

1 After reviewing the various theories concerning ownership of guns and crime in this feature, which one do you think is most likely to be correct? Why?

2 In a single year, guns are used to murder about 15 people in Japan, 30 people in Great Britain, 100 people in Canada, and close to 10,000 in the United States. Are these figures relevant for the gun control debate in our country? Explain your answer.

3 With the "fingerprinting" system described above, law enforcement agents can now trace guns back to their dealers. Should a gun dealer be charged with a crime if he or she improperly sells a handgun that is later used to commit a homicide? Why or why not?

INFOTRAC®
COLLEGE EDITION

Keywords:
crime and age;
guns and crime;
Brady Handgun Violence
Prevention Act

KEY TERMS

choice theory   40

chronic offender   39

cohort   39

criminology   27

dark figure of crime   32

index crimes   27

labeling theory   43

learning theory   43

Part II offenses   28

self-reported surveys   33

social conflict theories   44

social disorganization theory   42

social process theories   43

Uniform Crime Report (UCR)   27

victim surveys   32

CHAPTER SUMMARY

1 Identify the publication in which the FBI reports crime data and list the three ways it does so. Every year the FBI releases the Uniform Crime Report (UCR), in which it presents different crimes as (a) a rate per 100,000 people; (b) a percentage change from the previous year; and (c) an absolute, or aggregate, number.

2 Distinguish between Part I and Part II offenses as defined in the UCR. Part I offenses are always felonies and include the most violent crimes. They are called index crimes and yield the index crime rate. Part II offenses can be either misdemeanors or felonies and constitute the majority of crimes committed.

3 Explain how the National Incident-Based Reporting System differs from the UCR. The NIBRS, yet to be widely adopted, involves collection of data on each single crime occurrence with twenty-two offense categories made up of forty-six different crimes; the data are recorded on computer systems financed in part by the federal government.

4 Distinguish between the National Crime Victimization Survey and self-reported surveys. The NCVS involves an annual survey of about 50,000 households conducted by the Bureau of the Census along with the Bureau of Justice Statistics. The survey queries citizens on crimes that have been committed against them. As such, the NCVS includes crimes not necessarily reported to police. Self-reported surveys, in contrast, involve asking individuals about criminal activity to which they may have been a party.

5 Explain the underlying assumption on which choice theories of crime are based. According to choice theory, people commit crimes because they choose to do so after weighing the possible benefits of the criminal act against the possible costs of getting caught.

6 Identify two social process theories of crime. Learning theory holds that crime is learned behavior, taught by a family member or friend. Labeling theory contends that once a person is designated "delinquent" or "criminal" by authority figures, that person is more likely to act in a delinquent or criminal manner.

QUESTIONS FOR CRITICAL ANALYSIS

1 What is the distinction between the crime rate and crime in America?

2 Although Part II offenses constitute the bulk of crimes, Part I offenses get the most publicity. Is this necessarily irrational? Why or why not?

3 Why might you consider the UCR a biased source of crime statistics?

4 What is one possible reason for higher crime rates in lower-income communities?

5 If you believe that fear of punishment can have a deterrent effect on criminal activity, to what view of human behavior are you subscribing?

6 If you believe that criminals learn how to be criminals, to what theory are you subscribing?

SELECTED PRINT AND ELECTRONIC RESOURCES

SUGGESTED READINGS

Cote, Suzette, ed., *Criminological Theories: Bridging the Past to the Future,* Thousand Oaks, CA: Sage Publications, 2002. This anthology covers all the major criminological theories, including articles on social, biological, and cultural causes of crime. It also offers a criminological perspective on white-collar crime and investigates feminist criminal theory. Though most of the thirty-six articles were originally published in scholarly journals, they have been edited in this edition to make them accessible to students interested in delving deeper into the various explanations of criminal behavior.

Lott, John R., *More Guns, Less Crime: Understanding Crime and Gun-Control Laws,* Chicago: University of Chicago Press, 2000. This controversial book contains the statistical results of an economist's research. He purports to show that those states that allow concealed weapons have less crime than other states. In other words, Lott argues that when citizens can legally carry guns, crime rates fall.

Rhodes, Richard, *Why They Kill: The Discoveries of a Maverick Criminologist,* New York: Alfred A. Knopf, 1999. This biography details the life and theories of criminologist Lonnie Adams, who rejects the idea that violence can be traced to factors such as race or poverty. Instead, Adams believes that most criminals are "trained" to be violent, and that most violent acts are the result of rational planning rather than spontaneous surges of emotion.

MEDIA RESOURCES

***Minority Report* (2002)** The year is 2054. No murder has been committed in Washington, D.C., in a half decade, thanks to the city's Pre-Crime law enforcement unit. Pre-Crime relies on the powers of the Pre-Cognitives, three beings that can predict when a killing is going to take place and the identity of the killer. The Pre-Cogs pass this information on to law enforcement officers, who are almost always able to stop the crime before it is committed. Pre-Crime Chief John Anderton (Tom Cruise) is dedicated to the system, which is in the process of going nationwide, until the Pre-Cogs finger him as a future murderer. Convinced of his future innocence, Anderton kidnaps one of the Pre-Cogs (Samantha Morton) and leads his old colleagues at Pre-Crime on a classic Hollywood chase.

Critically analyze this film:

1. Which one of the five different theories (choice, trait, sociological, social process, and social conflict) discussed in this chapter is most similar to the process used by the Pre-Cogs? Why?

2. What are the ethical questions the film raises about being able to predict who will commit a crime in the future? How might the same concerns be raised with regard to trait theories?

3. Why is premeditated murder almost nonexistent in the Washington, D.C., of the film, meaning that most of the murders handled by Pre-Crime are of the "crime of passion" variety? Is the reasoning offered by the film in keeping with choice theory?

LOGGING ON

Go to http://cj.wadsworth.com/gainescore2e, **and click Hypercontents.** There, you will find URLs for the organizations in the following list:

- Your basic source for crime statistics is the **U.S. Department of Justice, Bureau of Justice Statistics.** There you can look at files on crime and arrest data and criminal justice data.

- The **Criminology-Mega–Site** provides a helpful introduction to this particular branch of study.

- On the **National Archive of Criminal Justice Data** Web site, you can obtain time-series data for criminal justice information.

USING THE INTERNET FOR CRIMINAL JUSTICE ANALYSIS

1. Go to your InfoTrac College Edition at
http://www.infotraccollege.com/wadsworth/.
After you log on, type in the words:
National Crime Control Policies
This article offers a social theory of the causes of crime.
Read it and answer the following questions:

a. What is control theory, and where did it have its beginnings?

b. Why does the author make a distinction between crimes and criminals and between events and people?

c. According to the author, what characteristic of the offender is most relevant to crime control?

d. Why does the author believe that in criminology an increase in the seriousness of sanctions does not influence the crime rate?

e. Why does control theory prefer local over central responsibility for crime prevention?

f. Briefly summarize the eight rules or recommendations for crime control to which control theory leads.

g. Which is the most important rule in your opinion, and why?

2. See Internet Activities 2.1 and 2.2 on the companion Web site for *CJ in Action: The Core.* To get to the activities, go to http://www.cj.wadsworth.com/gainescore2e, select the appropriate chapter from the drop down list, then click Internet Activities on the left navigation bar.

NOTES

1. Kim Murphy, "Serial Killer Yates Offers Apologies But No Explanations," *Idaho Statesman* (October 27, 2000), 1.

2. William A. Niskanen, "Washington's Misdirected Efforts at Curbing Crime," *USA Today Magazine* (July 1995), 22–5.

3. *Ibid.*

4. Federal Bureau of Investigation, *Crime in the United States, 2001* (Washington, D.C.: U.S. Government Printing Office, 2002), 2. Uniform Crime Report, or UCR, statistics cited in this chapter will reflect the latest data available.

5. *Ibid.*

6. *Ibid.*, 10.

7. Jeffrey Reiman, *The Rich Get Richer and the Poor Get Prison*, 4th ed. (Boston: Allyn & Bacon, 1995), 59–60.

8. *Crime in the United States, 2001*, 25.

9. *Ibid.*, Figure 2.3, page 16.

10. *Ibid.*, Table 29, page 233.

11. Marcus Felson, *Crime in Everyday Life* (Thousand Oaks, CA: Pine Forge Press, 1994), 3.

12. Donald J. Black, "Production of Crime Rates," *American Sociological Review* 35 (1970), 733–48.

13. Bureau of Justice Statistics, *Crime Victimization 2001* (Washington, D.C.: U.S. Department of Justice, 2002), 1.

14. Victoria W. Schneider and Brian Wiersema, "Limits and Use," in Doris Layton MacKenzie, Phyllis Jo Baunach, and Roy R. Robergs, eds., *Measuring Crime: Large Scale, Long Range Efforts* (Albany, NY: State University of New York Press, 1990), 21–7.

15. Alabama Code Sections 13A-6-60(8), 13A-6-61(a)(1) (1994).

16. W. Chambliss, *Exporting Criminology* (New York: Macmillan, 1988), 30.

17. Samuel Walker, *The Police in America*, 2d ed. (New York: McGraw-Hill, 1992), 295–6.

18. *Crime in the United States, 2000*, 3.

19. Domingo Ramirez, Jr., and Betsy Blaney, "FBI Revises Crime Log Categories," *Ft. Worth Star-Telegram* (December 1, 1996), 1.

20. Romana R. Rantala, *The Effect of NIBRS on Crime Statistics* (Washington, D.C.: Bureau of Justice Statistics, 2000), 3.

21. Victor E. Kappeler, Mark Blumberg, and Gary W. Potter, *The Mythology of Crime and Criminal Justice*, 2d ed. (Prospect Heights, IL: Waveland Press, 1993), 31.

22. Alfred D. Biderman and James P. Lynch, *Understanding Crime Statistics: Why the UCR Diverges from the NCVS* (New York: Springer-Verlag, 1991).

23. L. Edward Vells and Joseph Rankin, "Juvenile Victimization: Convergent Validation of Alternative Measurements," *Journal of Research and Crime in Delinquency* 32 (1995), 287–307.

24. James S. Wallerstein and Clement J. Wyle, "Our Law-Abiding Law Breakers," *Probation* 35 (April 1947), 107–18.

25. Michael Hindelang, "Causes of Delinquency: A Partial Replication and Extension," *Social Problems* 20 (1973), 471–87.

26. Thomas Gray and Eric Walsh, *Maryland Youth at Risk: A Study of Drug Use in Juvenile Detainees* (College Park, MD: Center for Substance Abuse Research, 1993).

27. John Braithwaite, *Inequality, Crime, and Public Policy* (London: Routledge & Kegan Paul, 1979), 21.

28. Dan Eggen, "Survey Shows Continuing Drop in Violent Crime," *Washington Post* (June 14, 2001), A1.

29. *Crime in the United States, 2001*, Figure 2.4, page 17.

30. *Ibid.*

31. Niskanen.

32. Charles Tittle and Robert Meier, "Specifying the SES/Delinquency Relationship," *Criminology* 28 (1990), 270–301.

33. *Crime in the United States, 2001*, Table 43, page 252.

34. Bureau of Justice Statistics, *Criminal Victimization, 2001* (Washington, D.C.: U.S. Department of Justice, 2002), Table 2, page 4.

35. Arthur H. Garrison, "Disproportionate Minority Arrests: A Note on What Has Been Said and How It Fits Together," *New England Journal on Criminal and Civil Confinement* 23 (Winter 1997), 29.

36. Margaret Farnworth, Raymond H. C. Teske, Jr., and Gina Thurman, "Ethnic, Racial, and Minority Disparity in Felony Court Processing," in *Race and Criminal Justice*, ed. Michael J. Lynch and E. Britt Patterson (New York: Harrow & Heston, 1991), 55–7.

37. Darrell Steffensmeier and Cathy Steifel, "Age, Gender, and Crime across Three Historical Periods," *Social Change* 69 (1991), 869–94.

38. *Crime in the United States, 2001*, Table 38, pages 245–6.

39. *Criminal Victimization 2001*, 6.

40. James Q. Wilson, "What to Do about Crime," *Commentary* 86 (September 1994), 25–35.

41. Beth Bjerregaard and Alan J. Lizotte, "Gun Ownership and Gang Membership," *Journal*

of Criminal Law and Criminology (Fall 1995), 37–58.

42. Joseph F. Sheley and Victoria E. Brewer, *Public Health Reports* (January–February 1995), 18–27.

43. *Crime in the United States, 2001,* page 23 and pages 35, 38.

44. William Wells and Julie Horney, "Weapon Effects and Individual Intent to Do Harm," *Criminology* (May 1, 2002), 265.

45. The National Center on Addiction and Substance Abuse at Columbia University, *Behind Bars: Substance Abuse and America's Prison Population* (New York: The National Center on Addiction and Substance Abuse at Columbia University, 1998), 6.

46. Graham C. Ousey and Matthew R. Lee, "Examining the Conditional Nature of the Illicit Drug Market–Homicide Relationship," *Criminology* (February 1, 2002), 73.

47. Marvin Wolfgang, Robert Figlio, and Thorsten Sellin, *Delinquency in a Birth Cohort* (Chicago: University of Chicago Press, 1972).

48. Lawrence W. Sherman, "Attacking Crime: Police and Crime Control," in *Modern Policing,* Michael Tonry and Norval Morris eds. (Chicago: University of Chicago Press, 1992), 159.

49. Tim Cahill, *Buried Dreams: Inside the Mind of a Serial Killer* (New York: Bantam Books, 1986), 349.

50. James Q. Wilson and Richard J. Hernstein, *Crime and Human Nature: The Definitive Study of the Causes of Crime* (New York: Simon & Schuster, 1985), 515.

51. Jack Katz, *Seductions of Crime: Moral and Sensual Attractions of Doing Evil* (New York: Basic Books, 1988).

52. L. E. Kreuz and R. M. Rose, "Assessment of Aggressive Behavior and Plasma Testosterone in a Young Criminal Population," *Psychosomatic Medicine* 34 (1972), 321–32.

53. Hervey M. Cleckley, *The Mask of Sanity,* 4th ed. (St. Louis: Mosby, 1964.)

54. "Delinquents as Dummies," *Psychology Today* (January–February 1994), 16.

55. Clifford R. Shaw, Henry D. McKay, and Leonard S. Cottrell, *Delinquency Areas* (Chicago: University of Chicago Press, 1929).

56. Edwin H. Sutherland, *Criminology,* 4th ed. (Philadelphia: Lippincott, 1947).

57. Howard S. Becker, *Outsiders: Studies in the Sociology of Deviance* (New York: Free Press, 1963).

58. Robert Meier, "The New Criminology: Continuity in Criminology Theory," *Journal of Criminal Law and Criminology* 67 (1977), 461–9.

59. *Crime in the United States, 2001,* pages 23 and 35.

60. Gary Kleck, *Targeting Guns* (New York: Aldine de Gruyter, 1997), 8.

61. William Claiborne, "Decades of Murders Restored to Life," *Washington Post* (March 6, 2001), A3.

62. *Ibid.*

63. Mark Duggan, *More Guns, More Crime* (Cambridge, MA: National Bureau of Economic Research, October 2000).

64. John R. Lott, Jr., "Does Allowing Law-Abiding Citizens to Carry Concealed Handguns Save Lives?" *Valparaiso University Law Review* 31 (Spring 1997), 355.

65. John R. Lott, Jr., and David Muster, "Crime, Deterrence, and Right to Carry Concealed Handguns," *Journal of Legal Studies* 26 (1997), 1.

66. Kleck, 8.

67. Jerry J. Phillips, "The Relation of Constitutional and Tort Law to Gun Injuries and Deaths in the United States," *Connecticut Law Review* (Summer 2000), 1342.

68. Pub. L. No. 103-159, 107 Stat. 1536 (1993); codified as amended at 18 U.S.C. Sections 922(s)-(t) (1995).

69. Bureau of Justice Statistics, *Presale Firearm Checks* (Washington, D.C.: U.S. Department of Justice, February 1997), 1.

70. Fox Butterfield, "Study Disputes Success of the Brady Law," *New York Times* (August 2, 2000), A12.

71. Jens Ludwig and Philip J. Cook, "Homicide and Suicide Rates Associated with Implementation of the Brady Handgun Violence Prevention Act," *Journal of the American Medical Association* 284 (August 2, 2000), 585–91.

72. Fox Butterfield, "Guns: The Law as Selling Tool," *New York Times* (August 13, 2000), 4.

73. *Ibid.*

CHAPTER 3
CRIMINAL LAW

Chapter Objectives

After reading this chapter, you should be able to:

1. List the four written sources of American criminal law.

2. Explain the two basic functions of criminal law.

3. List and explain the six basic elements of any crime.

4. Delineate the elements required to establish *mens rea* (a guilty mental state).

5. Explain how the doctrine of strict liability applies to criminal law.

6. List and briefly define the most important excuse defenses for crimes.

7. Describe the four most important justification criminal defenses.

8. Distinguish between substantive and procedural criminal law.

9. Determine where Americans find most of their criminal procedural safeguards.

INTRODUCTION
Murder or a Dog Attack?

The death of Diane Whipple sent shock waves through San Francisco, California, a city that prides itself on being one of the most animal-friendly metropolitan areas in the country. On January 26, 2001, as she was trying to enter her apartment, Whipple was attacked and killed by Bane and Hera, two Canary Island mastiffs owned by Whipple's neighbors, Marjorie Knoller and Robert Noel. Bane was put to death that night, and city authorities took Hera into custody. But the dogs were not the only ones to be punished for Whipple's death. Noel was found guilty of involuntary manslaughter, while Knoller became the first person in the nation's history to be convicted of second degree murder for a death by dog attack.[1]

That a person could spend fifteen years to life in prison (the penalty Knoller was facing) for an act clearly committed by one of her pets struck some observers as overly harsh. Under California law, however, an unintentional killing caused by "implied malice" is considered second degree murder.[2] In other words, if Knoller knew that her dogs possessed violent natures and posed a threat to others, and did nothing to lessen this threat, she had done the legal equivalent of "setting a lethal mantrap."[3] Prosecutors felt they had ample evidence that Knoller did, in fact, have such knowledge. The dogs had been trained to fight and

attack by a previous owner, and police collected numerous statements from neighbors who said the animals had lunged at and bitten them.

As it turned out, Judge James Warren of the Superior Court in San Francisco overturned Knoller's conviction, on the ground that the evidence did not support the jury's finding that she had any way of knowing that her dog was a deadly threat to a neighbor. Instead, he found her guilty of involuntary manslaughter, which carried only a four-year prison term. The many critics of the decision claimed the city had been robbed of its "sense of justice," but Judge Warren felt that the law did not sustain Knoller's conviction of the very serious crime of murder.[4]

In previous chapters, we discussed crime in relation to society. In this chapter, we will focus on the substance and procedure of criminal law, which defines those actions that are labeled crimes and sets the guidelines by which the criminal justice system determines and punishes criminal guilt. As the Knoller case suggests, criminal law must be flexible enough to encompass activities that are not obvious crimes, yet still pose a threat to society. That flexibility, as this case also shows, can often lead to results that disappoint society's sense of what is "just" or "right"—an issue to which we shall return throughout this textbook.

Robert Noel and his wife, Marjorie Knoller, appear in a San Francisco courtroom in conjunction with their dog Hera's fatal mauling of Diane Whipple in 2001. (AP Photo/Paul Sakuma)

INFOTRAC®
COLLEGE EDITION

Keywords: Diane Whipple

Go to the Stories from the Street feature at http://www.cj. wadsworth.com/gainescore2e to hear Larry Gaines tell insightful stories related to this chapter and his experiences in the field.

"Justice?—You get justice in the next world, in this world you have the law."

—William Gaddis, *American novelist* (1994)

CONSTITUTIONAL LAW
Law based on the U.S. Constitution and the constitutions of the various states.

STATUTORY LAW
The body of law enacted by legislative bodies.

▌FIGURE 3.1▐
Sources of American Law

WRITTEN SOURCES OF AMERICAN CRIMINAL LAW

One of the most important aspects of American criminal law is that it is *codified;* that is, it is written down and accessible to all. This allows citizens to know which acts are illegal and understand the procedures that must be followed by the government to establish innocence or guilt. U.S. history has seen the development of several written sources of criminal law, also known as "substantive" criminal law. These sources include:

① The U.S. Constitution and the constitutions of the various states.

② Statutes, or laws, passed by Congress and by state legislatures, plus local ordinances.

③ Regulations, created by regulatory agencies, such as the federal Food and Drug Administration.

④ Case law (court decisions).

We describe each of these important written sources of law in the following pages (see Figure 3.1).

Constitutional Law

The federal government and the states have separate written constitutions that set forth the general organization and powers of, and the limits on, their respective governments. **Constitutional law** is the law as expressed in these constitutions.

The U.S. Constitution is the supreme law of the land. As such, it is the basis of all law in the United States. Any law that violates the Constitution, as ultimately determined by the United States Supreme Court, will be declared unconstitutional and will not be enforced. The Tenth Amendment, which defines the powers and limitations of the federal government, reserves to the states all powers not granted to the federal government. Under our system of federalism (see Chapter 1), each state also has its own constitution. Unless they conflict with the U.S. Constitution or a federal law, state constitutions are supreme within their respective borders. (You will learn more about how constitutional law applies to our criminal justice system in later chapters.)

Statutory Law

Statutes enacted by legislative bodies at any level of government make up another source of law, which is generally referred to as **statutory law.** *Federal statutes* are

❶ Constitutional law—The law as expressed in the U.S. Constitution and the various state constitutions. The U.S. Constitution is the supreme law of the land. State constitutions are supreme within state borders to the extent that they do not violate the U.S. Constitution or a federal law.

❷ Statutory law—Laws or ordinances created by federal, state, and local legislatures and governing bodies. None of these laws can violate the U.S. Constitution or the relevant state constitution. Uniform laws, when adopted by a state legislature, become statutory law in that state.

❸ Administrative law—The rules, orders, and decisions of federal or state government administrative agencies. Federal administrative agencies are created by enabling legislation enacted by the U.S. Congress. Agency functions include rulemaking, investigation and enforcement, and adjudication.

❹ Case law and common law doctrines—Judge-made law, including interpretations of constitutional provisions, of statutes enacted by legislatures, and of regulations created by administrative agencies. The common law—the doctrines and principles embodied in case law—governs all areas not covered by statutory law (or agency regulations issued to implement various statutes).

laws that are enacted by the U.S. Congress. *State statutes* are laws enacted by state legislatures, and statutory law also includes the ordinances passed by cities and counties. A federal statute, of course, applies to all states. A state statute, in contrast, applies only within that state's borders. City or county ordinances (statutes) apply only to those jurisdictions where they are enacted. As mentioned, statutory law found by the Supreme Court to violate the U.S. Constitution will be overturned. In the late 1980s, for example, the Court ruled that any state laws banning the burning of the American flag were unconstitutional because they impinged on the individual's right to freedom of expression.

Until the mid–twentieth century, state statutes were disorganized, inconsistent, and generally inadequate for modern society. In 1952, the American Law Institute began to draft a uniform penal code in hopes of solving this problem. The first Model Penal Code was released ten years later and has had a broad effect on state statutes.[5] Though not a law itself, the code defines the general principles of criminal responsibility and codifies specific offenses; it is the source for many of the definitions of crime in this textbook. The majority of the states have adopted parts of the Model Penal Code into their statutes, and some states, such as New York, have adopted a large portion of the Code.[6]

It is important to keep in mind that there are essentially fifty-one different criminal codes in this country—one for each state and the federal government. Even if a state has adopted a large portion of the Model Penal Code, there may be certain discrepancies. Indeed, a state's criminal code often reflects certain values of its citizens, which may not be in keeping with those of the majority of other states. New Mexico, Oklahoma, and Louisiana, for example, are the only states where cockfighting is still legal.

George Washington, standing at right, presided over the Constitutional Convention of 1787. The convention resulted in the U.S. Constitution, the source of a number of laws that continue to form the basis of our criminal justice system today. (The Granger Collection)

Administrative Law

A third source of American criminal law consists of **administrative law**—the rules, orders, and decisions of regulatory agencies. A regulatory agency is a federal, state, or local government agency established to perform a specific function. The Occupational Safety and Health Administration (OSHA), for example, oversees the safety and health of American workers; the Environmental Protection Agency (EPA) is concerned with protecting the natural environment; and the Food and Drug Administration (FDA) regulates food and drugs produced in the United States. Disregarding certain laws created by regulatory agencies can be a criminal violation. Many modern federal statutes, such as the Clean Air Act, designate authority to a specific regulatory agency, such as the EPA, to promulgate regulations to which criminal sanctions are attached. The number of criminal investigators employed by the EPA has grown from six in 1982 to more than 150 at present. These investigators help the U.S. Department of Justice deliver nearly two hundred environmental crime indictments each year.[7] (As you will learn in Chapter 9, an indictment is a written accusation, issued by a grand jury, that a suspect has committed a crime.)

On the Web

You can learn about some of the constitutional questions raised by various criminal laws and procedures by going to the Web site of the American Civil Liberties Union. For a link to this Web site, go to the Hypercontents page for this chapter at **http://www.cj.wadsworth.com/gainescore2e.**

Case Law

As is evident from the earlier discussion of the common law tradition, another basic source of American law consists of the rules of law announced in court decisions. These rules of law include interpretations of constitutional provisions, of statutes enacted by legislatures, and of regulations created by administrative agencies. Today, this body of law is referred to variously as the common law, judge-made law, or **case law.**

Case law relies to a certain extent on how courts interpret a particular statute. If you wanted to learn about the coverage and applicability of a particular statute, for example, you would need to locate the statute and study it. You would

ADMINISTRATIVE LAW
The body of law created by administrative agencies (in the form of rules, regulations, orders, and decisions) in order to carry out their duties and responsibilities.

CASE LAW
The rules of law announced in court decisions. Case law includes the aggregate of reported cases that interpret judicial precedents, statutes, regulations, and constitutional provisions.

Surfing the Law

At no time in the nation's history have the sources of American law been as accessible as they are today. One recent study estimates that the World Wide Web has more than nine million "sites," hundreds of thousands of which are dedicated to the law. (A search using "United States Constitution" results in more than 160,000 "hits.") Consequently, the Internet has become an essential legal research tool. Documents such as state and federal legislation, agency regulations, and court opinions are generally made available online. The Web also offers a wealth of factual information and links to interest groups, and can even be used to learn about the laws of other countries. In fact, there is almost too much information on the Internet—trying to find one partic-

ular regulation or case is often like trying to find the proverbial needle in the haystack. For that reason, research sites such as Westlaw.com are crucial tools for the legal researcher, as are various search engines such as Findlaw, Catalaw, the Internet Law Library, and the Cornell University Legal Information Institute. Links to these sites are provided on the Hypercontents page for this chapter at http://www.cj.wadsworth.com/gainescore2e.

IN THE FUTURE

As far as most Internet users are concerned, faster is better. While most of the 62 million American households with Internet access get online through dial-up services, nearly 20 percent have "high-speed" access through digital subscriber lines (DSL) or a cable television hookup. Many observers are concerned about the "digital divide" caused by high-speed connections, which can be more than twice as costly as dial-up service, and thus are not affordable for many low-income Americans. Industry experts expect, however, that competition between DSL and cable companies will drive down prices, allowing high-speed legal research to become available to the majority of Americans.

also need to see how the courts in your jurisdiction have interpreted the statute—in other words, what precedents have been established in regard to that statute. The use of precedent means that judge-made law varies from jurisdiction to jurisdiction. (To learn how sources of law have become more accessible through the Internet, see the feature *Criminal Justice & Technology—Surfing the Law.*)

THE PURPOSES OF CRIMINAL LAW

Why do societies need laws? Many criminologists believe that criminal law has two basic functions: one relates to the legal requirements of a society, and the other pertains to its need to maintain and promote social values.[8]

Protect and Punish: The Legal Function of the Law

The primary legal function of the law is to maintain social order by protecting citizens from "criminal harm." This term refers to a variety of harms that can be generalized to fit into two categories:

1 Harms to individual citizens' physical safety and property, such as the harm caused by murder, theft, or arson.

2 Harms to society's interests collectively, such as the harm caused by unsafe foods or consumer products, a polluted environment, or poorly constructed buildings.[9]

The first category is self-evident, although even murder has different degrees, or grades, of offense to which different punishments are assigned. The second, however, has proved more problematic, for it is difficult to measure society's "collective" interests. Often, laws passed to reduce such harms seem overly intrusive and marginally necessary. An extreme example would seem to be the Flammable Fabrics Act, which makes it a crime for a retailer to willfully remove a precautionary instruction label from a mattress that is protected with a chemical fire retardant.[10]

Yet even in this example, a criminal harm is conceivable. Suppose a retailer removes the tags before selling a large number of mattresses to a hotel chain. Employees of the chain then unknowingly wash the mattresses with an agent that lessens their flame-resistant qualities. After the mattresses have been placed in rooms, a guest falls asleep while smoking a cigarette, starting a fire that burns down the entire hotel and causes several deaths.[11]

Maintain and Teach: The Social Function of the Law

If criminal laws against acts that cause harm or injury to others are almost universally accepted, the same cannot be said for laws that criminalize "morally" wrongful activities that may do no obvious, physical harm outside the families of those involved. Why criminalize gambling or prostitution if the participants are consenting?

Expressing Public Morality.   The answer lies in the social function of criminal law. Many observers believe that the main purpose of criminal law is to reflect the values and norms of society, or at least of those segments of society that hold power. Legal scholar Henry Hart has stated that the only justification for criminal law and punishment is "the judgment of community condemnation."[12]

Take, for example, the misdemeanor of bigamy, which occurs when someone knowingly marries a second person without terminating her or his marriage to an original husband or wife. Apart from moral considerations, there would appear to be no victims in a bigamous relationship, and indeed many societies have allowed and continue to allow bigamy to exist. In the American social tradition, however, as John L. Diamond of the University of California's Hastings College of the Law points out:

> Marriage is an institution encouraged and supported by society. The structural importance of the integrity of the family and a monogamous marriage requires unflinching enforcement of the criminal laws against bigamy. The immorality is not in choosing to do wrong, but in transgressing, even innocently, a fundamental social boundary that lies at the core of social order.[13]

When discussing the social function of criminal law, it is important to remember that a society's views of morality change over time. Puritan New England society not only had strict laws against adultery, but also considered lying and idleness to be criminal acts.[14] Today, such acts may carry social stigmas, but only in certain extreme circumstances do they elicit legal sanctions.

Teaching Societal Boundaries.   Some scholars believe that criminal laws not only express the expectations of society, but "teach" them as well. Professor Lawrence M. Friedman of Stanford University believes that just as parents teach children behavioral norms through punishment, criminal justice "'teaches a lesson' to the people it punishes, and to society at large." Making burglary a crime, arresting burglars, placing them in jail—each step in the criminal justice process reinforces the idea that burglary is unacceptable and is deserving of punishment.[15]

This teaching function can also be seen in traffic laws. There is nothing "natural" about most traffic laws; Americans drive on the right side of the street, the British on the left side, with no obvious difference in the results. These laws, such as stopping at intersections, using headlights at night, and following speed limits, do lead to a more orderly flow of traffic and fewer accidents—certainly socially desirable goals. Various forms of punishment for breaking traffic laws teach drivers the "social" order of the road.

> "If he who breaks the law is not punished, he who obeys it is cheated. This, and this alone, is why lawbreakers ought to be punished; to authenticate as good, and to encourage as useful, law-abiding behavior. The aim of criminal law cannot be correction or deterrence, it can only be the maintenance of the legal order."
>
> —Thomas Szasz, *American psychiatrist* (1973)

On the Web

Many state criminal codes are now online. To find your state's code, go to the Hypercontents page for this chapter at **http://www.cj.wadsworth.com/ gainescore2e, click the Findlaw.com link, then select 'State Codes.'"**

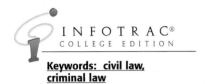

CLASSIFICATION OF CRIMES

The huge body of the law may be broken down according to various classifications. Three of the most important distinctions can be made between (1) civil law and criminal law, (2) felonies and misdemeanors, and (3) crimes *mala in se* and *mala prohibita.*

Civil Law and Criminal Law

All law can be divided into two categories: civil law and criminal law. As U.S. criminal law has evolved, it has diverged from U.S. civil law. The two categories of law are distinguished by their primary goals. The criminal justice system is concerned with protecting society from harm by preventing and prosecuting crimes. A crime is an act so reprehensible that it is considered a wrong against society as a whole, as well as against the individual victim.[16] Therefore, the state prosecutes a person who commits a criminal act. If the state is able to prove that a person is guilty of a crime, the government will punish her or him with imprisonment or fines, or both.

Civil law, which includes all types of law other than criminal law, is concerned with disputes between private individuals and between entities. Proceedings in civil lawsuits are normally initiated by an individual or a corporation (in contrast to criminal proceedings, which are initiated by public prosecutors). Such disputes may involve, for example, the terms of a contract, the ownership of property, or an automobile accident. Under civil law, the government provides a forum for the resolution of torts, or private wrongs, in which the injured party, called the *plaintiff,* tries to prove that a wrong has been committed by the accused party, or the *defendant.* (Note that the accused party in both criminal and civil cases is known as the defendant.) Most civil cases involve a request for monetary damages in recognition that a wrong has been committed. If, for example, a driver runs a red light and hits a pedestrian, the pedestrian could file a civil suit asking for monetary compensation for the "pain and suffering" caused by his or her injuries. (See *Mastering Concepts* for a comparison of civil and criminal law.)

Although criminal law proceedings are completely separate from civil law proceedings in the modern legal system, the two systems do have some similarities. Both attempt to control behavior by imposing sanctions on those who violate the law. Furthermore, criminal and civil law often supplement each other. In certain instances, a victim may file a civil suit against an individual who is also the target of a criminal prosecution by the government.

Because the burden of proof is much greater in criminal trials than civil ones, it is usually easier to win monetary damages than a criminal conviction.[17] After shooting sixteen-year-old exchange student Yoshihiro Hattori of Japan, for

CIVIL LAW
The branch of law dealing with the definition and enforcement of all private or public rights, as opposed to criminal matters.

MASTERING CONCEPTS	Civil Law versus Criminal Law	
ISSUE	**CIVIL LAW**	**CRIMINAL LAW**
Area of concern	Rights and duties between individuals	Offenses against society as a whole
Wrongful act	Harm to a person	Violation of a statute that prohibits some type of activity
Party who brings suit	Person who suffered harm (plaintiff)	The state
Party who responds	Person who supposedly caused harm (defendant)	Person who allegedly committed crime (defendant)
Standard of proof	Preponderance of the evidence	Beyond a reasonable doubt
Remedy	Damages to compensate for the harm	Punishment (fine, imprisonment, or death)

example, Rodney Pearis was acquitted of manslaughter charges by a Louisiana jury. Pearis claimed he thought Hattori—who mistook the defendant's home for the site of a Halloween party—was an intruder. After the criminal trial, however, Hattori's family brought a civil suit against Pearis and was awarded more than $650,000 in damages.[18] While the government had been unable to prove *beyond a reasonable doubt* (the burden of proof in criminal cases) that Pearis had intended to kill Hattori, the civil trial established that a *preponderance of the evidence* (the burden of proof in civil cases) showed this to be the case.

Felonies and Misdemeanors

Depending on their degree of seriousness, crimes are classified as felonies or misdemeanors. Felonies are serious crimes punishable by death or by imprisonment in a federal or state penitentiary for one year or longer (though some states, such as North Carolina, consider felonies to be punishable by at least two years' incarceration). The Model Penal Code provides for four degrees of felony:

❶ Capital offenses, for which the maximum penalty is death.

❷ First degree felonies, punishable by a maximum penalty of life imprisonment.

❸ Second degree felonies, punishable by a maximum of ten years' imprisonment.

❹ Third degree felonies, punishable by a maximum of five years' imprisonment.[19]

Degrees of Murder. Though specifics vary from state to state, some general rules apply when grading crimes. For example, most jurisdictions punish a burglary that involves a nighttime forced entry into a home more seriously than one that takes place during the day and involves a nonresidential building or structure. Murder in the first degree occurs under two circumstances:

❶ When the crime is *premeditated,* or considered beforehand by the offender, instead of being a spontaneous act of violence.

❷ When the crime is *deliberate,* meaning that it was planned and decided on after a process of decision making. Deliberation does not require a lengthy planning process; a person can be found guilty of first degree murder even if she or he made the decision to murder only seconds before committing the crime.

Second degree murder occurs when no premeditation or deliberation was present, but the offender did have *malice aforethought* toward the victim. In other words, the offender acted with wanton disregard of the consequences of his or her actions. The difference between first and second degree murder is clearly illustrated in a case involving a California man who beat a neighbor to death with a partially full brandy bottle. The crime took place after Ricky McDonald, the victim, complained to Kazi Cooksey, the offender, about the noise coming from a late-night barbecue Cooksey and his friends were holding. The jury could not find sufficient evidence that Cooksey's actions were premeditated, but he certainly acted with wanton disregard of his victim's safety. Therefore, the jury convicted Cooksey of second degree murder rather than first degree murder.

A homicide committed without malice toward the victim is known as *manslaughter* and is usually punishable by up to fifteen years in prison. *Voluntary manslaughter* occurs when the intent to kill may be present, but malice was lacking. Voluntary manslaughter covers crimes of passion, in which the emotion of an argument between two friends may lead to a homicide. Voluntary manslaughter can also occur when the victim provoked the offender to act violently. *Involuntary manslaughter* covers incidents in which the offender's acts were negligent, even

Fred Goldman, center, celebrates the verdict in the wrongful death suit against O. J. Simpson in 1997. The civil jury found that Simpson was liable for the deaths of Fred's son Ron Goldman and Simpson's ex-wife Nicole Brown, and awarded $8.5 million in compensatory damages to the Goldman and Brown families. Two years earlier, a criminal court had found Simpson not guilty of the murders of Goldman and Brown. Do you believe that defendants found innocent in criminal trials should be subject to civil trials for the same incident? (AP Photo/Nick Ut)

though there was no intent to kill. In 2002, for example, Thomas Junta was convicted of involuntary manslaughter in the beating death of Michael Costin following an argument over their sons' rough play during a youth hockey practice in Reading, Massachusetts. Junta had apparently struck Costin repeatedly while the latter lay on the ground, severing an artery near his brain. Though Junta undoubtedly intended to injure Costin, there was no evidence that he intended to kill him.[20]

Degrees of Misdemeanor.   Under federal law and in most states, any crime that is not a felony is considered a misdemeanor. Misdemeanors are crimes punishable by a fine or by confinement for up to a year. If imprisoned, the guilty party goes to a local jail instead of a penitentiary. Disorderly conduct and trespassing are common misdemeanors. Like felonies, misdemeanors are graded by level of seriousness. In Illinois, for example, misdemeanors are either Class A (confinement for up to a year), Class B (not more than six months), or Class C (not more than thirty days).

Most states similarly distinguish between *gross misdemeanors,* which are offenses punishable by thirty days to a year in jail, and *petty misdemeanors,* or offenses punishable by fewer than thirty days in jail. The least serious form of crime is a *violation* (such as a traffic offense), which is punishable only by a small fine and does not appear on the wrongdoer's criminal record. Whether a crime is a felony or a misdemeanor can also determine whether the case is tried in a magistrate's court (for example, by a justice of the peace) or in a general trial court (for example, superior court).

Probation and community service are often imposed on those who commit misdemeanors, especially juveniles.[21] Also, most states have decriminalized all but the most serious traffic offenses. These infractions are treated as civil proceedings, and civil fines are imposed. In many states, the violator has "points" assessed against her or his driving record.

Mala in Se and Mala Prohibita

Criminologists often express the social function of criminal law in terms of *mala in se* or *mala prohibita* crimes. A criminal act is referred to as **mala in se** if it would be considered wrong even if there were no law prohibiting it. *Mala in se* crimes are said to go against "natural laws"; that is, against the "natural, moral, and public" principles of a society.[22] Murder, rape, and theft are examples of *mala in se* crimes. These crimes are generally the same from country to country or culture to culture. In contrast, the term **mala prohibita** refers to acts that are considered crimes only because they have been codified as such through statute—"human-made" laws. A *mala prohibita* crime is considered wrong only because it has been prohibited; it is not inherently a wrong, though it may reflect the moral standards of a society at a given time.[23] Thus, the definition of a *mala prohibita* crime can vary from country to country or even from state to state. Bigamy, as discussed earlier, could be considered a *mala prohibita* crime.

Some observers believe that the distinction between *mala in se* and *mala prohibita* is problematic. First, it is difficult to define a "pure" *mala in se* crime; that is, it is difficult to separate a crime from the culture that has deemed it a crime.[24] Even murder, in certain cultural circumstances, is not considered a criminal act. In a number of poor, traditional areas of the Middle East and Asia, for example, the law excuses "honor killings" in which men kill female family members suspected of sexual indiscretion. Our own legal system excuses homicide in extreme situations, such as self-defense or when a law enforcement agent kills in the course of upholding the law. Therefore, all "natural" laws can be seen as culturally specific. Second, similar difficulties occur in trying to define a "pure" *mala prohibita* crime.[25] As already noted, an argument could be made that a law prohibiting the removal of instruction tags from a mattress could prevent the loss of human life.

MALA IN SE
A descriptive term for acts that are inherently wrong, regardless of whether they are prohibited by law.

MALA PROHIBITA
A descriptive term for acts that are made illegal by criminal statute and are not necessarily wrong in and of themselves.

CORPUS DELICTI
The body of circumstances that must exist for a criminal act to have occurred.

ACTUS REUS
(pronounced *ak*-tus *ray*-uhs). A guilty (prohibited) act. The commission of a prohibited act is one of the two essential elements required for criminal liability, the other element being the intent to commit a crime.

THE ELEMENTS OF A CRIME

In fictional accounts of police work, the admission of guilt is often portrayed as *the* crucial element of a criminal investigation. Although an admission is certainly useful to police and prosecutors, it alone cannot establish the innocence or guilt of a suspect. Criminal law normally requires that the **corpus delicti,** a Latin phrase for "the body of the crime," be proved before a person can be convicted of wrongdoing.[26] *Corpus delicti* can be defined as "proof that a specific crime has actually been committed by someone."[27] It consists of the basic elements of any crime, which include (1) *actus reus,* or a guilty act; (2) *mens rea,* or a guilty intent; (3) concurrence, or the coming together of the criminal act and the guilty mind; (4) a link between the act and the legal definition of the crime; (5) any attendant circumstances; and (6) the harm done, or result of the criminal act. (See *Mastering Concepts* for an example showing some of the various elements of a crime.)

In a Cambridge, Massachusetts, courtroom, Thomas Junta demonstrates "what happened" during his fight with Michael Costin during a youth hockey practice in which their sons were participating. In 2002, Junta was found guilty of involuntary manslaughter and sentenced to six to ten years imprisonment. Junta, a large man, had beaten Costin, a smaller man, severely and severed an artery in Costin's head during the fight, but the judge in the matter was unwilling to infer that Junta had intended to kill his opponent. What purpose is served by punishing people for what they *intended* to occur rather than for what *actually* occurred? (AP Photo/Steven Senne, Pool)

Criminal Act: *Actus Reus*

Suppose Mr. Smith walks into a police department and announces that he just killed his wife. In and of itself, the confession is insufficient for conviction unless the police find Mrs. Smith's corpse with a bullet in her brain and establish through evidence that Mr. Smith fired the gun. (This does not mean that an actual dead body has to be found in every homicide case. Rather, it is the fact of the death that must be established in such cases.)

Most crimes require an act of *commission;* that is, a person must *do* something in order to be accused of a crime. The prohibited act is referred to as the **actus reus,** or guilty act. Furthermore, the act of commission must be voluntary. For

---

MASTERING CONCEPTS   **The Elements of a Crime**

Carl Robert Winchell walked into the SunTrust Bank in Volusia County, Florida, and placed a bag containing a box on a counter. He announced that the box held a bomb, and demanded to be given an unspecified amount of money. After being provided with several thousand dollars in cash, Winchell fled, leaving the box behind. A Volusia County Sheriff's Office bomb squad subsequently determined that the box did not in fact contain any explosive device. Winchell was eventually arrested and charged with robbery.

Winchell's actions were criminal because they satisfy the three elements of a crime:

1. ***Actus reus***—The physical act of a crime took place. In this case, Winchell committed bank robbery.
2. ***Mens rea***—The offender must intentionally, knowingly, or willingly commit the criminal act. In this case,

Winchell obviously planned to rob the SunTrust Bank using the false threat of a bomb.

3. A **concurrence** of *actus reus* and *mens rea*—The criminal act must be the result of the offender's intention to commit that particular criminal act. In this case, the robbery was the direct result of Winchell's intent to take property using the threat of the fake bomb. If, in addition, a bank customer had died of a heart attack during the robbery attempt, Winchell could not be charged with first degree murder, because he did not intend to harm anyone.

Note that the fact that there was no bomb in the box has no direct bearing on the three elements of the crime. It could, however, lead to Winchell receiving a lighter punishment than if he had used a real bomb.

YOU be the JUDGE
A Voluntary Act?

THE FACTS

On a bright, sunny afternoon, Emil was driving on Delaware Avenue in Buffalo, New York. As he was making a turn, Emil suffered an epileptic seizure and lost control of his automobile. The car careened onto the sidewalk and struck a group of six schoolgirls, killing four of them. Emil knew that he was subject to epileptic attacks that rendered him likely to lose consciousness.

THE LAW

An "act" committed while one is unconscious is in reality not an act at all. It is merely a physical event or occurrence over which the defendant has no control; that is, such an act is involuntary. If the defendant, however, voluntarily causes the loss of consciousness by, for example, using drugs or alcohol, then he or she will usually be held criminally responsible for any consequences.

YOUR DECISION

Emil was charged in the deaths of the four girls. He asked the court to dismiss the charges, as he was unconscious at the time of the accident and therefore had not committed a voluntary act. In your opinion, is there an *actus reus* in this situation, or should the charges against Emil be dismissed?

[To see how an appellate court in New York ruled in this case, go to Example 3.1 in Appendix A.]

On the Web

For an overview of criminal law and links to an extensive number of documents relating to criminal justice, go to the Web site of Cornell University's Legal Information Institute. For a link to this Web site, go to the Hypercontents page for this chapter at http://www.cj.wadsworth.com/gainescore2e.

example, if Mr. Smith had an epileptic seizure while holding a hunting rifle and accidentally shot his wife, he would normally not be held criminally liable for her death. (See the feature *You Be the Judge—A Voluntary Act?*)

In some cases, an act of *omission* can be a crime, but only when a person has a legal duty to perform the omitted act. One such legal duty is assumed to exist based on a "special relationship" between two parties, such as a parent and child, adult children and their aged parents, and spouses.[28] For example, a Milwaukee woman was arrested for allowing her teenage daughter to be sexually assaulted and then sending her back to the scene of the assault to purchase crack cocaine.[29] Those persons involved in contractual relationships with others, such as physicians and lifeguards, must also perform legal duties to avoid criminal penalty. Some states, including Rhode Island and Vermont, have passed statutes requiring their citizens to report criminal conduct and to aid victims of such conduct if possible.[30] Another example of a criminal act of omission is failure to file a federal income tax return when required by law to do so.

The *guilty act* requirement is based on one of the premises of criminal law—that a person is punished for harm done to society. Planning to kill someone or to steal a car may be wrong, but the thoughts do no harm and are therefore not criminal until they are translated into action. Of course, a person can be punished for attempting murder or robbery, but normally only if he or she took substantial steps toward the criminal objective. Furthermore, the punishment for an *attempt* normally is less severe than if the act had succeeded.

Mental State: *Mens Rea*

A wrongful mental state—**mens rea**—is as necessary as a wrongful act in establishing guilt. The mental state, or requisite *intent,* required to establish guilt of a crime is indicated in the applicable statute or law. For theft, the wrongful act is the taking of another person's property, and the required mental state involves both the awareness that the property belongs to another and the desire to deprive the owner of it.

The Categories of *Mens Rea*.   A guilty mental state includes elements of purpose, knowledge, negligence, and recklessness.[31] A defendant is said to have *purposefully* committed a criminal act when he or she desires to engage in certain criminal conduct or to cause a certain criminal result. For a defendant to have *knowingly* committed an illegal act, he or she must be aware of the illegality, must

MENS REA
(pronounced *mehns* ray-uh). Mental state, or intent. A wrongful mental state is as necessary as a wrongful act to establish criminal liability.

believe that the illegality exists, or must correctly suspect that the illegality exists but fail to do anything to dispel (or confirm) his or her belief. Criminal **negligence** involves the mental state in which the defendant grossly deviates from the standard of care that a reasonable person would use under the same circumstances. The defendant is accused of taking an unjustified, substantial, and foreseeable risk that resulted in harm. In Texas, for example, a parent or handgun owner commits a felony if she or he fails to secure a loaded firearm or leaves it in such a manner that it could easily be accessed by a child.

A defendant who commits an act *recklessly* is more blameworthy than one who is criminally negligent. The Model Penal Code defines criminal recklessness as "consciously disregard[ing] a substantial and unjustifiable risk."[32] Some courts, particularly in those jurisdictions adhering to the Model Penal Code, will not find criminal recklessness on the part of a defendant who was subjectively unaware of the risk when she or he acted.

Criminal Liability.   Intent plays an important part in allowing the law to differentiate among varying degrees of criminal liability for similar, though not identical, guilty acts. The role of intent is clearly seen in the different classifications of homicide, defined generally as the willful killing of one human being by another. It is important to emphasize the word *willful*, as it precludes deaths caused by accident or negligence and those deemed justifiable. A death that results from negligence or accident normally is considered a private wrong and a matter for civil law, although some statutes allow for culpable negligence, which permits certain negligent homicides to be criminalized. As we saw earlier, when the act of killing is willful, deliberate, and premeditated (planned beforehand), it is considered first degree murder. When premeditation does not exist but intent does, the act is considered second degree murder. (See Figure 3.2 for an example of the different homicide statutes in Florida.)

Different degrees of criminal liability for various categories of homicide lead to different penalties. The distinction between murder and manslaughter was evident in the punishment given to Terry Nichols, the co-conspirator in the 1995 Oklahoma City bombing. Nichols was spared the death penalty when the prosecution at his trial could not prove that the defendant had planned for the deaths of those who perished in the Alfred P. Murrah Federal Building. Nichols was acquitted of first degree murder and instead was convicted of involuntary manslaughter. In a lesser known but equally demonstrative example, a judge convicted Theodore

NEGLIGENCE
A failure to exercise the standard of care that a reasonable person would exercise in similar circumstances.

FIGURE 3.2
Florida Homicide Statutes (Excerpts)

782.02 Justifiable use of deadly force.—The use of deadly force is justifiable when a person is resisting any attempt to murder such person or to commit any felony upon him or her or upon or in any dwelling house in which such person shall be.

782.03 Excusable homicide.—Homicide is excusable when committed by accident and misfortune in doing any lawful act by lawful means with usual ordinary caution, and without any unlawful intent, or by accident and misfortune in the heat of passion, upon any sudden and sufficient provocation, or upon a sudden combat, without any dangerous weapon being used and not done in a cruel or unusual manner.

782.04 Murder.—

(1)(a) The unlawful killing of a human being:

1. When perpetrated from a premeditated design to effect the death of the person killed or any human being;

2. When committed by a person engaged in the perpetration of, or in the attempt to perpetrate, any: [such acts as arson, robbery, burglary, etc.]; . . .

is murder in the first degree and constitutes a capital felony, ...

(2) The unlawful killing of a human being, when perpetrated by any act imminently dangerous to another and evincing a depraved mind regardless of human life, although without any premeditated design to effect the death of any particular individual, is murder in the second degree and constitutes a felony of the first degree, punishable by imprisonment for a term of years not exceeding life . . . .

782.07 Manslaughter; aggravated manslaughter of an elderly person or disabled adult; aggravated manslaughter of a child.—

(1) The killing of a human being by the act, procurement, or culpable negligence of another, without lawful justification according to the provisions of chapter 776 and in cases in which such killing shall not be excusable homicide or murder, according to the provisions of this chapter, is manslaughter, a felony of the second degree, ...

Stevens of involuntary manslaughter instead of first degree murder in the killing of Eno Bailey, his common law wife. Stevens had become convinced that Bailey was casting "evil spells" on him before he shot her in the chest, and the judge believed that this fear eliminated the intent necessary for first degree murder.[33]

Strict Liability. For certain crimes, criminal law holds the defendant to be guilty even if intent to commit the offense is lacking. These acts are known as **strict liability** crimes and generally involve endangering the public welfare in some way.[34] Drug control statutes, health and safety regulations, and traffic laws are all strict liability laws. To a certain extent, the concept of strict liability is inconsistent with the traditional principles of criminal law, which hold that *mens rea* is required for an act to be criminal. The goal of strict liability laws is to protect the public by eliminating the possibility that wrongdoers could claim ignorance or mistake to absolve themselves of criminal responsibility.[35] Thus, a person caught dumping waste in a protected pond or driving 70 miles per hour in a 55-miles-per-hour zone cannot plead a lack of intent in his or her defense.

One of the most controversial strict liability crimes is statutory rape, in which an adult engages in a sexual relationship with a minor. In most states, even if the minor consents to the sexual act, the crime still exists because, being underage, he or she is considered incapable of making a rational decision on the matter.[36] Therefore, statutory rape has been committed even if the adult was unaware of the minor's age or had been misled to believe that the minor was older.

Accomplice Liability. Under certain circumstances, a person can be charged with and convicted of a crime that he or she did not actually commit. This occurs when the suspect has acted as an *accomplice to* a crime; that is, he or she has helped another person commit the crime. Generally, to be found guilty as an accomplice a person must have the "dual intent" (1) to aid the person who committed the crime and (2) that such aid would lead to the commission of the crime.[37] As for the *actus reus,* the accomplice must have helped the primary actor in either a physical sense (providing the getaway car) or a psychological sense (encouraging her or him to commit the crime).[38]

In some states, a person can be convicted as an accomplice even without intent if the crime was a "natural and probable consequence" of his or her actions.[39] Suppose that Jim and Mary enter Frank's home with the goal of burglary. Frank walks in on them while they are carrying out his television, and Jim shoots and kills Frank with a shotgun. Mary could be charged as an accomplice to murder because it is reasonably foreseeable that if one illegally enters another's home with a dangerous weapon, a homicide could occur.

On the Web

You can gain some insights into criminal law and procedures, including some of the defenses that can be raised to avoid criminal liability, by looking at some of the famous criminal law cases included on Court TV's Web site. For a link to this Web site, go to the Hypercontents page for this chapter at **http://www.cj.wadsworth.com/ gainescore2e.**

Concurrence

According to criminal law, there must be *concurrence* between the guilty act and the guilty intent. In other words, the guilty act and the guilty intent must occur together.[40] Suppose, for example, that a woman intends to murder her husband with poison in order to collect his life insurance. Every evening, this woman drives her husband home from work. On the night she plans to poison him, however, she swerves to avoid a cat crossing the road and runs into a tree. She survives the accident, but her husband is killed. Even though her intent was realized, the incident would be considered an accidental death because she had not planned to kill him by driving the car into a tree.

Causation

Criminal law also requires that the criminal act cause the harm suffered. In Michigan, for example, two defendants were convicted of murder even though their victim died in an unrelated basketball game several years after the initial crime.[41] In the course of a robbery, the defendants had shot the victim in the heart and abdomen and abandoned him in a sewer. Though the victim survived, his heart remained very weak. Four years later, the victim collapsed during a basketball game and died. Medical examination established that his heart failed as a direct result of the earlier injury, and the Michigan Supreme Court ruled that, despite the passage of time, the defendants' criminal act had been the cause of the man's death.[42] (It is interesting to contrast this decision with the common law rule that a victim's death must occur within a year and a day from the date of the defendant's crime.)

Attendant Circumstances

In certain crimes, attendant circumstances—also known as accompanying circumstances—are relevant to the *corpus delicti*. Most states, for example, differentiate between simple assault and the more serious offense of aggravated assault depending on whether the defendant used a weapon such as a gun or a knife while committing the crime. Criminal law also classifies degrees of property crimes based on the amount stolen. According to federal statutes, robbing a bank of less than $100 is a misdemeanor, while taking any amount over $100 results in a felony.[43]

Some states have used attendant circumstances to impose harsher penalties on hate crimes. Under Missouri's Ethnic Intimidation Law, for example, if someone commits any of a number of crimes "by reason of any motive relating to the race, color, religion, or national origin of another individual or group of individuals," she or he is guilty of the crime of "ethnic intimidation." The statute increases the penalty for certain crimes if such motives can be proved. Consequently, property damage, normally punished as a misdemeanor, is elevated to a felony when ethnic intimidation is involved.[44] Although the United States Supreme Court has upheld these types of laws,[45] a number of legal scholars believe that in many cases a court of law is ill-equipped to prove racist intent.[46] (See *Criminal Justice in Action—Punishing Hate* at the end of the chapter.)

Harm

For most crimes to occur, some harm must have been done to a person or to property. A certain number of crimes are actually categorized depending on the harm done to the victim, regardless of the intent behind the criminal act. Take two offenses, both of which involve one person hitting another in the back of the head with a tire iron. In the first instance, the victim dies, and the offender is charged with murder. In the second, the victim is only knocked unconscious, and the offender is charged with battery. Because the harm in the second instance was less severe, so was the crime with which the offender was charged, even though the act was exactly the same. Furthermore, most states have different degrees of battery depending on the extent of the injuries suffered by the victim.

Many acts are deemed criminal if they could do harm that the laws try to prevent. Such acts are called **inchoate offenses.** They exist when only an attempt at a criminal act was made. If Jenkins solicits Peterson to murder Jenkins's business partner, this is an inchoate offense on the part of Jenkins, even though Peterson fails to carry out the act. Conspiracies are also a general category of inchoate offenses.

THE LEGAL DEFINITION OF CRIME

The elements of a crime are integral to **substantive criminal law,** which is a general term that refers to the body of legislative action that defines the acts that

The concept of "harm" in criminal law does not apply only to property and violent crimes. Prostitution, for example, is illegal in almost all U.S. jurisdictions because of the perceived harm the practice causes society. This harm includes the spread of sexually transmitted diseases such as AIDS, the linkage of prostitution to illicit drug use (as many prostitutes sell their services to obtain the cash to buy drugs), and the violence done to prostitutes by customers and pimps. Under certain circumstances, however, the state of Nevada has legalized prostitution. How might legalized prostitution reduce some of the social harms attributed to the practice? (AP Photo/Timothy Jacobsen)

INCHOATE OFFENSES
Conduct deemed criminal without actual harm being done, provided that the harm that would have occurred is one the law tries to prevent.

SUBSTANTIVE CRIMINAL LAW
Law that defines the rights and duties of individuals with respect to each other.

the government will punish. In essence, substantive criminal law, in the form of penal codes, defines precisely what is illegal. The key points of most criminal laws are the *actus reus, mens rea,* attendant circumstances, and harm done to society.

Penal codes provide the framework for defining criminal acts, but they are not unchanging. Police, prosecutors, judges, and other employees of the criminal justice system must interpret the codes, and social pressures and the changing legal environment often influence these interpretations. For example, Nushawn Williams was the first person in New York to face a felony charge of reckless endangerment on the ground that he had unprotected sex with a teenage girl months after he learned he was infected with HIV, the virus that can lead to AIDS. According to New York law:

> A person is guilty of reckless endangerment in the first degree when, under circumstances evincing a depraved indifference to human life, he recklessly engages in conduct that creates a grave risk of death to another person.[47]

The elements of reckless endangerment in New York, therefore, include engaging in conduct that creates a grave risk of death to another person (the *actus reus*) while evincing a depraved indifference to human life (the *mens rea*). The attendant circumstances are the concurrence between the guilty act and the guilty mind to create a criminal act.

The difficulty for New York prosecutors was proving that Williams was indifferent to the possibility that he was infecting his sexual partner with a deadly disease.[48] Prosecutors in other states have encountered similar problems when pressing criminal charges against HIV–infected individuals who fail to warn sexual partners that they have contracted the virus. In Maryland, officials initially succeeded in convicting Dwight Ralph Smallwood—who knew he had HIV when he raped three women—of attempted first degree murder. Maryland state law, however, holds as follows:

> All murder which shall be perpetrated by means of poison, or lying in wait, or by any kind of willful, deliberate and premeditated killing shall be murder in the first degree.[49]

Referring to this definition, a higher court overturned Smallwood's conviction. In explaining the reversal, the state judge noted that there was no medical proof that a single sexual exposure to Smallwood would necessarily result in the victim's contracting HIV. Therefore, the defendant could not have had the proper state of mind ("willful, deliberate, and premeditated") to satisfy the *mens rea* requirement for attempted murder.[50]

CRIMINAL RESPONSIBILITY AND THE LAW

In overturning Dwight Ralph Smallwood's conviction for attempted murder, the Maryland court was following a precedent set by the United States Supreme Court, which has held that a defendant's intent must be proved beyond a reasonable doubt.[51] The Maryland court, in essence, ruled that Smallwood could not be held responsible for a crime that he did not intend to commit. The idea of responsibility plays a significant role in criminal law. In certain circumstances, the law recognizes that a person is not responsible for wrongdoing because he or she does not meet certain mental conditions. In many jurisdictions, for example, children under a specific age are believed incapable of committing crimes because they are too young to understand the ramifications of their actions. Thus, *infancy* is an "excuse" defense, or a defense that argues that the accused's wrongdoing should be excused because he or she lacked the capacity to be held liable for the crime. Other important excuse defenses include insanity, intoxication, and mistake.

Insanity

In 2002, Andrea Pia Yates unsuccessfully pled not guilty to drowning her five children by reason of insanity. If Yates's defense team had succeeded in convincing a Houston jury that Yates was suffering from a form of psychosis that made her delusional and caused her to lose touch with reality, the defendant could have been sentenced to a mental hospital rather than a jail.[52] Thus, **insanity** may be a defense to a criminal charge when the defendant's state of mind is such that she or he cannot claim legal responsibility for her or his actions.

Measuring Sanity. Although criminal law has accepted the idea that an insane person cannot be held responsible for criminal acts, society has long debated what standards should be used to measure sanity for the purposes of a criminal trial. One of the oldest tests for insanity resulted from a case in 1843 in which Daniel M'Naughten shot and killed Edward Drummond in the belief that Drummond was Sir Robert Peel, the British prime minister. At trial, M'Naughten claimed that he was suffering from delusions at the time of the murder, and he was found not guilty by reason of insanity. In response to public outcry over the decision, the British court established the **M'Naughten rule.** Also known as the right-wrong test, the *M'Naughten* rule states that a person is legally insane and therefore not criminally responsible if, at the time of the offense, he or she was *not* able to distinguish between right and wrong.[53] (Andrea Pia Yates, mentioned above, was found guilty of murder because the Texas jury felt that, even though she may have been mentally ill, she knew drowning her children was wrong at the time of the act.)

As Figure 3.3 shows, sixteen states still use a version of the *M'Naughten* rule. Several other jurisdictions, reacting to criticism of the *M'Naughten* rule as too narrow, have supplemented it with the less restrictive **irresistible impulse test.** Under this combined approach, a person may be found insane even if he or she was aware that a criminal act was "wrong," provided that some "irresistible impulse" resulting from a mental deficiency drove him or her to commit the crime.[54]

INSANITY
A defense for criminal liability that asserts a lack of criminal responsibility. According to the law, a person cannot have the requisite state of mind to commit a crime if she or he did not know at the time of the act that it was wrong, or did not know the nature and quality of the act.

M'NAUGHTEN RULE
A common law test of criminal responsibility derived from *M'Naughten's Case* in 1843 that relies on the defendant's inability to distinguish right from wrong.

IRRESISTIBLE IMPULSE TEST
A test for the insanity defense under which a defendant who knew his or her action was wrong may still be found insane if he or she was nonetheless unable, as a result of a mental deficiency, to control the urge to complete it.

FIGURE 3.3
Insanity Defenses

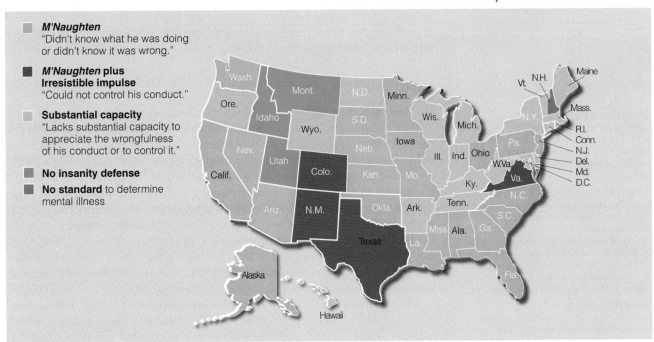

Source: Bureau of Justice Statistics, *State Court Organization 1998* (Washington, D.C.: U.S. Department of Justice, 2000), 257–59.

On March 12, 2002, Andrea Yates is led from a Houston courtroom after being found guilty of murdering her five children. Yates had pleaded innocent by reason of insanity, a defense that the jury—who had heard thirty-eight witnesses during the three week trial—ultimately rejected. For what reasons do mentally ill convicts receive more lenient penalties? (AP Photo/KHOU-TV, Pool)

DURHAM RULE
A test of criminal responsibility adopted in a 1954 case: "an accused is not criminally responsible if his unlawful act was the product of mental disease or mental defect."

SUBSTANTIAL CAPACITY TEST
From the Model Penal Code, a test that states that a person is not responsible for criminal behavior if when committing the act "as a result of mental disease or defect he lacks substantial capacity either to appreciate the wrongfulness of his conduct or to conform his conduct to the requirements of the law."

INTOXICATION
A defense for criminal liability in which the defendant claims that the taking of intoxicants rendered him or her unable to form the requisite intent to commit a criminal act.

Another method of determining criminal sanity—the **Durham rule**—rejects the *M'Naughten* test by focusing on the many personality factors that lead to mental instability. Under the *Durham* test, mental illness may be viewed as a permanent defect in the defendant or as a disease that can be treated. Created in New Hampshire in the nineteenth century, the *Durham* rule was adopted by the Court of Appeals for the District of Columbia in the 1954 case *Durham v. United States.* [55] Judge David Bazelon, who presided over the case, placed the burden on prosecutors to prove beyond a reasonable doubt that the defendant was not insane. The jury is then expected to determine whether the criminal act was the product of a mental defect or disease; for this reason the rule is referred to as the *products test.* Eventually, this rule was rejected as being too vague.

Today, all federal courts and nearly half the states use the **substantial capacity test** to determine sanity. Characterized as a modern improvement on the *M'Naughten* test, substantial capacity guidelines state that:

> A person is not responsible for criminal conduct if at the time of such conduct as a result of mental disease or defect he lacks substantial capacity either to appreciate the wrongfulness of his conduct or to conform his conduct to the requirements of the law.[56]

The key element of this rule is that it requires only a lack of "substantial capacity" to release a defendant from criminal responsibility. This standard is considerably easier to meet than the "right-wrong" requirements of the *M'Naughten* rule or the irresistible impulse test.

Guilty but Mentally Ill. Partly as a response to public backlash against the insanity defense, some state legislatures have passed "guilty but mentally ill" statutes. Under these laws, a defendant is guilty but mentally ill if

> at the time of the commission of the act constituting the offense, he had the capacity to distinguish right from wrong . . . but because of mental disease or defect he lacked sufficient capacity to conform his conduct to the requirements of the law.[57]

In other words, the laws allow a jury to determine that a defendant is "mentally ill," though not insane, and therefore criminally responsible for his or her actions. Defendants found guilty but mentally ill generally spend the early years of their sentences in a psychiatric hospital and the rest of the time in prison, or they receive treatment while in prison.

Intoxication

The law recognizes two types of **intoxication**, whether from drugs or from alcohol: *voluntary* and *involuntary*. Involuntary intoxication occurs when a person is physically forced to ingest or is injected with an intoxicating substance, or is unaware that a substance contains drugs or alcohol. Involuntary intoxication is a viable defense to a crime if the substance leaves the person unable to form the mental state necessary to understand that the act committed while under the influence was wrong.[58] In Colorado, for example, the murder conviction of a man who shot a neighbor was overturned on the basis that the jury in the initial trial was not informed of the possibility of involuntary intoxication. At the time of the crime, the man had been taking a prescription decongestant that contained phenylpropanolamine, which has been known to cause psychotic episodes.[59]

Voluntary drug or alcohol intoxication is also used to excuse a defendant's actions, though it is not a defense in itself. Rather, it is used when the defense attorney wants to show that the defendant was so intoxicated that *mens rea* was negated. In other words, the defendant could not possibly have had the state of mind that a crime requires. Many courts are reluctant to allow voluntary intoxication arguments to be presented to juries, however. After all, the defendant, by definition, voluntarily chose to enter an intoxicated state.

Twelve states have eliminated voluntary intoxication as a possible defense, a step that has been criticized by many legal scholars but was upheld by the United States Supreme Court in *Montana v. Egelhoff* (1996).[60] The case concerned a double murder committed by James Allen Egelhoff, who was extremely drunk at the time of the crime. Egelhoff was convicted on two counts of deliberate homicide, which is defined by Montana law as "knowingly" or "purposefully" causing the death of another human being.[61] Egelhoff appealed his conviction, arguing that the state statute prohibiting evidence of voluntary intoxication kept his attorneys from showing the jury that he was too inebriated to "knowingly" or "purposefully" commit the murders.[62] The Court allowed Egelhoff's conviction, ruling that states were constitutionally within their rights to abolish the voluntary intoxication defense.

Mistake

Everyone has heard the saying, "Ignorance of the law is no excuse." Ordinarily, ignorance of the law or a *mistaken idea* about what the law requires is not a valid defense.[63] A few years ago, for example, Gilbert A. Robinson appealed his conviction for possession of sexually explicit photographs of teen-age boys, claiming he did not know that such an act had become illegal. Chief Judge Juan R. Torruella del Valle upheld Robinson's conviction, stating that child pornography is "inherently deleterious" and that the "probability of regulation is so great that anyone who is aware that he is in possession of [it] . . . must be presumed to be aware of the regulation."[64]

In some states, however, that rule has been modified. People who claim that they honestly did not know that they were breaking a law may have a valid defense if (1) the law was not published or reasonably known to the public or (2) the person relied on an official statement of the law that was erroneous.[65]

A *mistake of fact,* as opposed to a *mistake of law,* operates as a defense if it negates the mental state necessary to commit a crime. If, for example, Oliver mistakenly walks off with Julie's briefcase because he thinks it is his, there is no theft. Theft requires knowledge that the property belongs to another. The mistake-of-fact defense has proved very controversial in rape and sexual assault cases, where the accused claims that the sex was consensual while the alleged victim claims it was coerced.

JUSTIFICATION CRIMINAL DEFENSES AND THE LAW

In certain instances, a defendant will accept responsibility for committing an illegal act, but contend that—given the circumstances—the act was justified. In other words, even though the guilty act and the guilty intent are present, the particulars of the case relieve the defendant of criminal liability. In 2001, for example, there were 585 "justified" killings of felons who were in the process of committing a felony: 370 were killed by law enforcement officers, and 215 by private citizens.[66] Four of the most important justification defenses are duress, self-defense, necessity, and entrapment.

Duress

Duress exists when the *wrongful* threat of one person induces another person to perform an act that she or he would otherwise not perform. In such a situation, duress is said to negate the *mens rea* necessary to commit a crime. For duress to qualify as a defense, the following requirements must be met:

1 The threat must be of serious bodily harm or death.

> "You know how it is, Dr. Ellsworth. You go to a party, have a few drinks, somebody gets killed."
>
> —Letter from a death row inmate to Phoebe Ellsworth, *Professor at the University of Michigan* (1999)

DURESS
Unlawful pressure brought to bear on a person, causing the person to perform an act that he or she would not otherwise perform.

2 The harm threatened must be greater than the harm caused by the crime.

3 The threat must be immediate and inescapable.

4 The defendant must have been involved in the situation through no fault of his or her own.[67]

When ruling on the duress defense, courts often examine whether the defendant had the opportunity to avoid the threat in question. Two narcotics cases illustrate this point. In the first, the defendant claimed that an associate threatened to kill him and his wife unless he participated in a marijuana deal. Although this contention was proved true during the course of the trial, the court rejected the duress defense because the defendant made no apparent effort to escape, nor did he report his dilemma to the police. In sum, the drug deal was avoidable—the defendant could have made an effort to extricate himself, but he did not, thereby surrendering the protection of the duress defense.[68]

In the second case, a taxi driver in Bogotá, Colombia, was ordered by a passenger to swallow cocaine-filled balloons and take them to the United States. The taxi driver was warned that if he refused, his wife and three-year-old daughter would be killed. After a series of similar threats, the taxi driver agreed to transport the drugs. On arriving at customs at the Los Angeles airport, the defendant consented to have his stomach X-rayed, which led to discovery of the contraband and his arrest. During trial, the defendant told the court that he was afraid to notify the police in Colombia because he believed them to be corrupt. The court accepted his duress defense, on the grounds that it met the four requirements listed above and the defendant had notified American authorities when given the opportunity to do so.[69]

Justifiable Use of Force—Self-Defense

A person who believes he or she is in danger of being harmed by another is justified in defending himself or herself with the use of force, and any criminal act committed in such circumstances can be justified as **self-defense.** Other situations that also justify the use of force include the defense of one's dwelling, the defense of other property, and the prevention of a crime. In all these situations, it is important to distinguish between deadly and nondeadly force. Deadly force is likely to result in death or serious bodily harm.

Generally speaking, people can use the amount of nondeadly force that seems necessary to protect themselves, their dwellings, or other property or to prevent the commission of a crime. Deadly force can be used in self-defense if there is a *reasonable belief* that imminent death or bodily harm will otherwise result, if the attacker is using unlawful force (an example of lawful force is that exerted by a police officer), if the defender has not initiated or provoked the attack, and if there is no other possible response or alternative way out of the life-threatening situation.[70] In the past several years, for example, a number of states have enacted so-called battered women self-defense statutes. These laws allow defendants charged with murder or manslaughter to present evidence that they had been the victims of repeated acts of violence by the deceased. This evidence may then be used to establish that any violent action taken by the woman against her abuser was done in self-defense.[71] (See *The Diversity Challenge—The Battered Woman Defense.*) In contrast, deadly force normally can be used to defend a dwelling only if the unlawful entry is violent and the person believes deadly force is necessary to prevent imminent death or great bodily harm or—in some jurisdictions—if the person believes deadly force is necessary to prevent the commission of a felony (such as arson) in the dwelling.

Necessity

According to the Model Penal Code, the **necessity** defense is justifiable if "the harm or evil sought to be avoided by such conduct is greater than that sought to

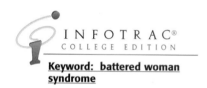

INFOTRAC®
COLLEGE EDITION

Keyword: battered woman syndrome

SELF-DEFENSE
The legally recognized privilege to protect one's self or property from injury by another. The privilege of self-defense protects only acts that are reasonably necessary to protect one's self or property.

NECESSITY
A defense against criminal liability in which the defendant asserts that circumstances required her or him to commit an illegal act.

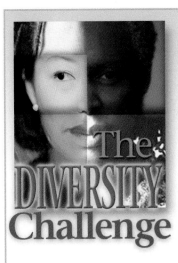

The Battered Woman Defense

When Albert Hampton beat his companion Evelyn Humphrey, he tried to hit her in the back of the head, where, he told her, "it won't leave bruises." Driving back from a camping trip to their home in Fresno, California, Albert told Evelyn that the mountains would be a good place to kill her because nobody would find the body. The next day, he started hitting her again and went to grab his gun. Evelyn got the gun first, said "you're not going to hit me anymore," and shot him. Evelyn then waited outside their home for the police. She was charged with murder.

During her trial, Dr. Lee Bowker testified that Evelyn suffering from "battered woman's syndrome (BWS)," a term that has come to describe the psychological state a person descends into following a lengthy period of being beaten. Experts say that those suffering from BWS lost self-esteem and feel helpless, trapped in a relationship because of a lack of money, socially isolated, and fearful of reprisals. Evelyn's lawyers tried to use BWS as a defense on two levels. First, they used the "partial responsibility" defense, claiming that although Evelyn's actions were wrong, she was not in a mental state to comprehend what she was doing. Second, they presented the justification defense, admitting that Evelyn killed Albert, buy saying that the act was justified as self-defense.

These defenses were difficult to prove, given that, although Albert had acted violently in the past, he had never attempted to actually kill Evelyn, and she had never felt obliged to protect herself by such drastic means. In other words, why was this time different? Furthermore, the trial judge ordered that the jury not consider the BWS testimony when deciding whether Evelyn's actions were reasonably justified. Evelyn was found guilty of voluntary manslaughter and sentenced to eight years in prison. On appeal, however, the California Supreme Court ruled that the trial judge erred in his jury instructions and that BWS should be considered when trying to determine a battered woman's belief that her life is in danger. The court's ruling set an important precedent by allowing a jury to consider whether a "reasonable battered woman" would feel her life to be threatened under any given set of circumstances. If jurors do find this, they can decide that homicide was justifiable and, as happened with Evelyn Humphrey on retrial, set the defendant free.

FOR CRITICAL ANALYSIS

In another case, a woman was found not guilty after she shot her batterer-husband while he was sleeping. Under what circumstances do you believe that such an act would be considered justifiable? What might be some unexpected implications of allowing BWS to be used as a defense to homicide?

---

be prevented by the law defining the offense charged."[72] For example, in one case a convicted felon was threatened by an acquaintance with a gun. The felon grabbed the gun and fled the scene, but subsequently he was arrested under a statute that prohibits convicted felons from possessing firearms. In this situation, the necessity defense was viable because the defendant's crime avoided a "greater evil."[73] The one crime for which the necessity defense is not viable is murder.[74] (For a classic case in which the necessity defense was offered for homicide, see *CJ in Focus—Landmark Cases: Regina v. Dudley and Stephens* on the next page.)

Entrapment

Entrapment is a justification defense that criminal law allows when a police officer or government agent deceives a defendant into wrongdoing. Although law enforcement agents can legitimately use various forms of subterfuge—such as informants or undercover agents—to gain information or apprehend a suspect in a criminal act, the law places limits on these strategies. Police cannot persuade an innocent person to commit a crime, nor can they coerce a suspect into doing so, even if they are certain she or he is in fact a criminal.

PROCEDURAL SAFEGUARDS

To this point, we have focused on the substantive aspects of criminal law. We will now turn our attention to **procedural criminal law.** The section that follows

ENTRAPMENT
A defense in which the defendant claims that he or she was induced by a public official—usually an undercover agent or police officer—to commit a crime that he or she would otherwise not have committed.

PROCEDURAL CRIMINAL LAW
Rules that define the manner in which the rights and duties of individuals may be enforced.

CJ in F⊙CUS

Landmark Cases: *Regina v. Dudley and Stephens*

Three sailors and a cabin boy were forced into a lifeboat after their ship sank. After nearly three weeks on the open seas, they ran out of food and water, and the cabin boy was seriously ill and near death. Two of the men, Dudley and Stephens, killed the cabin boy and ate his flesh in order to survive. Four days later, the three survivors were rescued. Dudley and Stephens were prosecuted for murdering the cabin boy and raised a necessity defense. A British court found that even though the cabin boy would likely have died of natural causes, the killing was not justified.

Regina v. Dudley and Stephens
Queen's Bench Division
14 Q.B.D. 173 (1884)

IN THE WORDS OF THE COURT . . .

LORD COLERIDGE, C.J. [chief justice]

* * * *

There remains to be considered the real question in the case whether killing under the circumstances set forth in the verdict be or be not murder. The contention that it could be anything else was, to the minds of us all, both new and strange, and we stopped the Attorney General in his negative argument in order that we might hear what could be said in Support of a proposition which appeared to us to be at once dangerous, immoral, and [opposed] to all legal principle and analogy. * * *

* * * *

Note: Triple asterisks (* * *) indicate that a few words or sentences have been deleted, and quadruple asterisks (* * * *) indicate that an entire paragraph (or more) has been omitted from the opinion.

Is there, then, any authority for the proposition which has been presented to us? Decided cases there are none. * * * The American case, * * * in which it was decided, correctly indeed, that sailors had no right to throw passengers overboard to save themselves, but on the somewhat strange ground that the proper mode of determining who was to be sacrificed was to vote upon the subject by ballot, can hardly * * * be an authority satisfactory to a court in this country. * * *

* * * *

Now it is admitted that the deliberate killing of this unoffending, and unresisting boy was clearly murder, unless the killing can be justified by some well-recognised, excuse admitted by the law. It is further admitted that there was in this case no such excuse, unless the killing was justified by what has been called "necessity." But the temptation to the act which existed here was not what the law has ever called necessity. Nor is this to be regretted. Though law and morality are not the same, and many things may be immoral which are not necessarily illegal, yet the absolute divorce of law from morality would be of fatal consequence; and such divorce would follow if the temptation to murder in this case were to be held by law an absolute defence of it. It is not so. To preserve one's life is generally speaking a duty, but it may be the plainest and the highest duty, to sacrifice it.

DECISION

The court sentenced the two prisoners to death. The Crown later commuted the sentence to six months' imprisonment.

FOR CRITICAL ANALYSIS
Are there ever any circumstances under which sacrificing one person for the good of others is justified?

 For more information and activities related to this case, go to the Landmark Cases feature at http://cj.wadsworth.com/ gainescore2e

will provide only a short overview of criminal procedure. In later chapters, many other constitutional issues will be examined in more detail. Criminal law brings the force of the state, with all its resources, to bear against the individual. Criminal procedures, drawn from the ideals stated in the Bill of Rights, are designed to protect the constitutional rights of individuals and to prevent the arbitrary use of power by the government (see Figure 3.4).

The Bill of Rights

For various reasons, proposals related to the rights of individuals were rejected during the framing of the U.S. Constitution in 1787. Yet the importance of a written declaration of rights of individuals eventually caused the first Congress to draft ten amendments to the Constitution and submit them for approval by the states. These amendments, commonly known as the **Bill of Rights,** were adopted in 1791. Since then, seventeen more amendments have been added.

The Bill of Rights, as interpreted by the United States Supreme Court, has served as the basis for procedural safeguards of the accused in this country. These safeguards include the following:

1 The Fourth Amendment protection from unreasonable searches and seizures.

2 The Fourth Amendment requirement that no warrants for a search or an arrest can be issued without probable cause.

3 The Fifth Amendment requirement that no one can be deprived of life, liberty, or property without the "due process" of law.

4 The Fifth Amendment prohibition against *double jeopardy* (trying someone twice for the same criminal offense).

5 The Fifth Amendment guarantee that no person can be required to be a witness against (incriminate) himself or herself.

6 The Sixth Amendment guarantees of a speedy trial, a trial by jury, a public trial, the right to confront witnesses, and the right to a lawyer at various stages of criminal proceedings.

7 The Eighth Amendment prohibitions against excessive bails and fines and cruel and unusual punishments.

The Bill of Rights offered citizens protection only against the federal government. Over the years, the procedural safeguards of most of the provisions of the Bill of Rights have been incorporated into the protections afforded by the Fourteenth Amendment (and the states are free to grant even more protection than is required by the federal Constitution). As these protections are crucial to criminal justice procedures in the United States, they will be afforded much more attention in Chapter 6, with regard to police action, and in Chapter 9, with regard to the criminal trial.

Due Process

Both the Fifth and the Fourteenth Amendments provide that no person should be deprived of "life, liberty, or property without the due process of law." This clause, the **due process clause,** basically requires that any government decisions taken in the course of prosecuting a person be made fairly. For example, fair procedures must be used in determining whether a person will be subjected to punishment or have some burden imposed on her or him. Fair procedure has been interpreted as requiring that the person have at least an opportunity to object to a proposed action before a fair, neutral decision maker (which need not be a judge).

The Supreme Court's Role in Due Process. The due process clause has played a defining role in the restrictions that the Supreme Court has placed on the criminal justice system over the past century. In 1936, for example, the Court ruled that a criminal confession gained through brutality was not admissible under the Fourteenth Amendment.[75] Nearly thirty years later in 1963, in *Gideon v. Wainwright,*[76] the Court held that due process requires the government to provide defendants who cannot afford to hire a defense lawyer with counsel in all felony trials, later extended to all trials resulting in a sentence of incarceration. (See Figure 3.5 for a list of important Supreme Court due process cases.)

Changes in Due Process. Some observers feel that recent due process decisions have eroded the rights of the accused. For example, two rulings involving the search and seizure of suspicious vehicles are seen as evidence of the Supreme Court's weakening of Fourth Amendment protections. In *Whren v. United States*

FIGURE 3.4

Provisions in the Unamended U.S. Constitution Pertaining to Criminal Procedure

Article I, Section 9, clause 2

The privilege of the Writ of Habeas Corpus shall not be suspended, . . .

Article I, Section 9, clause 3

No Bill of Attainder or ex post facto Law shall be passed.

Article III Section 2, clause 3

The Trial of all Crimes, . . . , shall be by Jury; and such crimes shall be held in the State where the said Crimes shall have been committed; . . .

BILL OF RIGHTS
The first ten amendments to the U.S. Constitution.

DUE PROCESS CLAUSE
The provisions of the Fifth and Fourteenth Amendments to the Constitution that guarantee that no person shall be deprived of life, liberty, or property without due process of law. Similar clauses are found in most state constitutions.

FIGURE 3.5

Important United States Supreme Court Due Process Decisions

YEAR	ISSUE	AMENDMENT INVOLVED	COURT CASE
1948	Right to a public trial	VI	*In re Oliver*, 333 U.S. 257
1949	No unreasonable searches and seizures	IV	*Wolf v. Colorado*, 338 U.S. 25
1961	Exclusionary rule	IV	*Mapp v. Ohio*, 367 U.S. 643
1963	Right to a lawyer in all criminal felony cases	VI	*Gideon v. Wainwright*, 372 U.S. 335
1964	No compulsory self-incrimination	V	*Malloy v. Hogan*, 378 U.S. 1
1964	Right to have counsel when taken into police custody and subjected to questioning	VI	*Escobedo v. Illinois*, 378 U.S. 478
1965	Right to confront and cross-examine witnesses	VI	*Pointer v. Texas*, 379 U.S. 911
1966	Right to an impartial jury	VI	*Parker v. Gladden*, 385 U.S. 363
1966	Confessions of suspects not notified of due process rights ruled invalid	V	*Miranda v. Arizona*, 384 U.S. 436
1967	Right to a speedy trial	VI	*Klopfer v. North Carolina*, 386 U.S. 21
1967	Juveniles have due process rights, too	V	*In re Gault*, 387 U.S. 1
1968	Right to a jury trial ruled a fundamental right	VI	*Duncan v. Louisiana*, 391 U.S. 145
1969	No double jeopardy	V	*Benton v. Maryland*, 395 U.S. 784

(1996),[77] the Court held that a police officer could stop an automobile for a traffic violation even if the officer's ultimate intent was to search the car for drugs. A year later, in *Maryland v. Wilson* (1997),[78] the Court ruled that an officer could order passengers, as well as the driver, out of the car during traffic stops without requiring either probable cause or reasonable suspicion. Critics of these decisions believe that the Court has severely damaged due process by giving the police too much power to stop automobiles and search their contents.[79]

As part of heightened airport security following the September 11, 2001, terrorist attacks, a police officer leads a bomb-sniffing dog through Boston's Logan Airport. Other new measures included increased scrutiny of luggage, a ban on customer parking within three hundred feet of a terminal, and not allowing any visitor without a ticket allowed past airline checkpoints. Do any of these steps appear to infringe on the due process clause of the U.S. Constitution? Would they if they were applied only, or mostly, to passengers of Middle Eastern descent? (AP Photo/ Bizuayehu Tesfaye)

Criminal Justice in Action

Punishing Hate

In this chapter, we have seen that a crime, as traditionally understood, has two basic elements: an *actus reus* and a *mens rea*. Criminal law, however, is not set in stone; it changes with the values of the society it is meant to protect. Under certain circumstances, many state penal codes have expanded to include a third element: motive. In most cases, a person's motive for committing a crime is irrelevant—a court will not try to read the accused's mind. But, as we will discuss in this *Criminal Justice in Action* feature, when the motive involves hate or bias, many jurisdictions have decided that the harm done by the crime is more serious, and therefore the punishment should be as well.

TWO BRUTAL CRIMES

Shortly after midnight on June 7, 1998, an African American named James Byrd was walking to his home in Jasper, Texas. Three white men in a pickup pulled over and offered Byrd a ride, which he accepted. The driver and his companions proceeded to take Byrd into the nearby woods and beat him unconscious. Then they chained him to the back of their truck and dragged him until he was dead.

Four months later, the body of twenty-one-year-old University of Wyoming freshman Matthew Shepard was found tied to a deer fence off Snowy Mountain View Road, one mile east of Laramie. Shepard's head and face had been brutally beaten, his arms were scorched with burn marks, and he had been left unconscious and bleeding on the fence for nearly eighteen hours. Five days later, he died in a local hospital. Investigators quickly learned that Shepard's two assailants had been aware that he was homosexual and had lured him to their truck by feigning romantic interest.

Byrd and Shepard were two of the approximately 9,700 Americans who are victims of violent crimes motivated by hate or bias each year.[80] At the time of these murders, Wyoming and Texas were two of only nine states that did not have a **hate crime law**—a fact mentioned numerous times in the wake of both deaths by those who felt that the lack of such a law created a climate in which verbal and physical attacks against minorities were subtly tolerated. (Texas has since passed such a law.) In general, hate crime laws provide for greater sanctions against those who commit crimes motivated by animosity against a person or group because of race, ethnicity, religion, gender, sexual orientation, disability, or age. (See Figure 3.6.)

PENALTY ENHANCEMENT STATUTES

Due to the lack of a federal hate crime statute, the full weight of prosecuting these crimes has fallen on those states that have passed relevant laws. In general, these laws are based on a model created by the Anti-Defamation League (ADL) in 1981. The ADL model was centered around the concept of "penalty enhancement": just as someone who robs a convenience store using a gun will face a greater penalty than if he or she had been unarmed, so will someone who commits a crime because of prejudice against her or his victim or victims.[81]

FIGURE 3.6

Offenses Motivated by Bias

In 2001, the Federal Bureau of Investigation reported 9,726 bias-motivated offenses. This chart shows the percentage distribution of the motivating factors.

Source: Adapted from Federal Bureau of Investigation, *Crime in the United States, 2001* (Washington, D.C.: U.S. Department of Justice, 2002), Figure 2.19 at page 61.

HATE CRIME LAW
A statute that provides for greater sanctions against those who commit crimes motivated by animosity against an individual or a group based on race, ethnicity, religion, gender, sexual orientation, disability, or age.

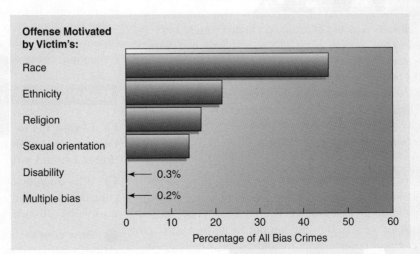

Offense Motivated by Victim's:

- Race
- Ethnicity
- Religion
- Sexual orientation
- Disability ← 0.3%
- Multiple bias ← 0.2%

Percentage of All Bias Crimes
0   10   20   30   40   50   60

Continued on next page

CJ in Action: Punishing Hate *continued*

The specifics of hate crime legislation vary from jurisdiction to jurisdiction. Not all states follow the penalty enhancement model, preferring instead to create new categories of crimes committed "because of" or "by reason of" the victim's characteristics. Some states do not specify which groups are protected by the legislation, while others list some aspects, such as race, but not others, such as mental or physical disability. Furthermore, some states establish training in dealing with hate crimes for law enforcement personnel. A number of police departments have created specialized bias units to prevent hate crimes and collect data on them.

SUPREME COURT RULINGS

The legal basis for hate crime legislation was established by two cases heard by the Supreme Court in the early 1990s. In *R.A.V. v. St. Paul* (1992),[82] the Court reviewed a case involving a group of white teenagers who burned a cross on the lawn of an African American family in St. Paul, Minnesota. One of the youths, who had been arrested and convicted under the city's Bias-Motivated Crime Ordinance, claimed that the law violated his right to free speech. The Minnesota Supreme Court upheld the conviction, ruling that the law was constitutional because it applied only to "fighting words," or speech that is likely to evoke a violent response. The United States Supreme Court, however, reversed the state court's decision, holding that the statute was too broad and therefore could be used to outlaw forms of expression that are protected under the First Amendment, as well as "fighting words."

The following year, however, the Supreme Court upheld Wisconsin's penalty enhancement statute in *State of Wisconsin v. Todd Mitchell* (1993).[83] The case involved Todd Mitchell, a nineteen-year-old African American who incited his friends to attack a white teenager after viewing the film *Mississippi Burning*. The victim was left in a coma for two days, and Mitchell was convicted of felony aggravated battery and sentenced to two years in prison, plus an additional two years under the state's hate crime law. The Court upheld the statute, reasoning that the results of hate crime, such as community fear, justify harsher punishments. Furthermore, it ruled that speech could be used as evidence of motive, and because motive is an integral part of sentencing, hate speech could be used to augment sentences.

QUESTIONING HATE LAWS

Many of those who question the validity of hate crime legislation do so on First Amendment grounds. Punish Todd Mitchell for his acts, they say, but not for his beliefs, which he has a constitutional right to hold. Some of these opponents also question laws that seem to indicate that some victims are worthy of more protection than others. They

Participants in the "Hike for Hope"—a seventy-mile trek to raise awareness of hate crimes—pause at the site where Matthew Shepard was beaten to death. (AP Photo/Ed Andrieski)

find it disturbing that Mitchell would have received a lesser sentence if he and his friends had beaten an African American youth instead of a white youth.[84]

In addition, James B. Jacobs, a professor of law at New York University, points out that it is difficult enough to establish the *mens rea* of someone who has committed a criminal act without trying to establish his or her motivation.[85] Jacobs envisions court cases becoming bogged down as prosecutors try to establish the defendant's levels of prejudice and bias, a difficult task considering the deep psychological and sociological roots of such feelings. Law enforcement officials are also wary of the demands of hate crime legislation. "I'm very fearful of the concept of thought police," said a commander in the Kenosha (Wisconsin) police department. "It makes me nervous."[86]

MAKING SENSE OF HATE CRIME LAWS

❶ Review the last two paragraphs of this feature. Do you agree with any of the arguments presented there? Explain your answer.

❷ Why do you suppose that motive is usually not considered in criminal law? Why might determining motive be difficult?

❸ How does society suffer a greater "harm" from crimes motivated by bias than from those driven by greed, jealousy, or some other emotion?

KEY TERMS

CHAPTER SUMMARY

1 **List the four written sources of American criminal law.** (a) The U.S. Constitution and state constitutions; (b) statutes passed by Congress and state legislatures (plus local ordinances); (c) administrative agency regulations; and (d) case law.

2 **Explain the two basic functions of criminal law.** The primary function is to protect citizens from harms to their safety and property and from harms to society's interest collectively. The second function is to maintain and teach social values as well as social boundaries; for example, laws against bigamy and speed limits.

3 **List and explain the six basic elements of any crime.** (a) The *actus reus,* or the guilty act; (b) the *mens rea,* or the proof of guilty intent by the alleged criminal; (c) a concurrence of act and intent; (d) a link between the act and the crime; (e) any attendant circumstances; and (f) the existence of harm done, or the result of a criminal act.

4 **Delineate the elements required to establish *mens rea* (a guilty mental state).** (a) Purpose, (b) knowledge, (c) negligence, or (d) recklessness.

5 **Explain how the doctrine of strict liability applies to criminal law.** Strict liability crimes are ones that do not allow the alleged wrongdoer to claim ignorance or mistake to avoid criminal responsibility; for example, exceeding the speed limit and statutory rape.

6 **List and briefly define the most important excuse defenses for crimes. Insanity**—different tests of insanity can be used including (a) the *M'Naughten* rule (right-wrong test); (b) the irresistible impulse test; (c) the *Durham* rule, also called the products test—where the criminal act was the product of a mental defect or disease; and (d) the substantial capacity test. **Intoxication**—voluntary and involuntary, the latter being a possible criminal defense.

Mistake—sometimes valid if the law was not published or reasonably known or if the alleged offender relied on an official statement of the law that was erroneous. Also, a mistake of fact may negate the mental state necessary to commit a crime.

7 **Describe the four most important justification criminal defenses. Duress**—requires that (a) the threat is of serious bodily harm or death; (b) the harm is greater than that caused by the crime; (c) the threat is immediate and inescapable; and (d) the defendant became involved in the situation through no fault of his or her own. **Justifiable use of force**—the defense of one's person, dwelling, or property, or the prevention of a crime. **Necessity**—justifiable if the harm sought to be avoided is greater than that sought to be prevented by the law defining the offense charged. **Entrapment**—if the criminal action was induced by certain governmental persuasion or trickery.

8 **Distinguish between substantive and procedural criminal law.** The former concerns questions about what acts are actually criminal. The latter concerns procedures designed to protect the constitutional rights of individuals and to prevent the arbitrary use of power by the government.

9 **Determine where Americans find most of their criminal procedural safeguards.** Basic safeguards for the accused are found in the Bill of Rights; for example, Fourth Amendment protections from unreasonable searches and seizures, as well as the requirements that no warrants for a search or an arrest can be issued without probable cause, and the Fifth Amendment's due process requirement, prohibition against double jeopardy, and rule against self-incrimination.

QUESTIONS FOR CRITICAL ANALYSIS

1 Give an example of how the criminal justice system teaches societal boundaries.

2 Give an example of how the same person could be involved in a civil lawsuit and a criminal lawsuit for the same action.

3 What is the difficulty in defining which criminal acts are *mala in se?*

4 Many people are careless. At what point can such carelessness be deemed criminal negligence?

5 Assume you are planning to pay someone to set fire to an old barn (arson) for the insurance money. Before you get a chance to carry out your plan, you accidentally drop a tool on another metal object, creating a spark that ignites some dry hay and burns the barn down. What essential element of a crime is missing in your actions?

6 Why are accompanying, or attendant, circumstances sometimes important to alleged perpetrators of certain acts?

7 What is the most often used test for insanity, and how does it differ from the other tests?

8 Under what circumstances is the use of deadly force a justified criminal defense?

SELECTED PRINT AND ELECTRONIC RESOURCES

SUGGESTED READINGS

Duhl, Robert Alan, *How Democratic Is the American Constitution?* New Haven, CT: Yale University Press, 2002. In this thin volume, Yale University professor Duhl challenges the democratic credentials of the U.S. Constitution. From its inception, Duhl notes, the Constitution was stained by several "undemocratic elements," including the acceptance of slavery and limitation of voting rights to white males. While these elements have been removed, Duhl points out that some of the most sacred aspects of our modern political system—federalism, the bicameral legislature, judicial review, and the electoral college—often contradict "the will of the people." Most disturbing, Duhl suggests that the framers "rigged" the Constitution to discourage democratic reform.

Robinson, O. S., *The Criminal Law of Ancient Rome,* Baltimore: Johns Hopkins University Press, 1996. Would you like to find out how the ancient Romans dealt with muggings on the street, theft at the public bath, and assassination plots? Then read this excellent overview of criminal law in ancient Rome. The author also shows how Rome dealt with violent crimes and offenses against the public order.

Schopp, Robert F., *Justification Defenses and Just Convictions,* Cambridge, England: Cambridge University Press, 1998. The author interprets the different criminal justification defenses in such a way that he concludes that they are an integral part of the structure of criminal law. He examines both the legal and the philosophical ramifications of justification defenses.

MEDIA RESOURCES

***Primal Fear* (1996)** In this film, Richard Gere plays Martin "Marty" Vail, a high-powered, arrogant defense attorney who takes on the case of Aaron Stampler (Edward Norton). Altar boy Aaron is almost certainly responsible for the grisly murder of a local archbishop, but Marty believes that his client is innocent. It eventually becomes apparent, however, that the quiet, stuttering Aaron has a second personality: that of Roy, a crude man who certainly seems capable of doing great violence. Marty decides to rely on the insanity defense, arguing that Aaron is not responsible for the archbishop's death because Roy actually committed the crime. To do so, however, Marty must get Roy to "show" himself at the trial—a dangerous proposition indeed.

Critically analyze this film:

1. Throughout Aaron's trial, the prosecution spends a great deal of time trying to establish his motive for killing the archbishop. Why is it so important to establish motive? Is "motive" part of the *corpus delicti* of a crime? What motive is eventually established in the film?

2. Suppose that Aaron does indeed suffer from multiple personality disorder, and that he committed the murder when acting as Roy. Would this mean that Aaron is not responsible for the crime? What role does "intent" play in answering this question?

3. Check Figure 3.3. What standard for determining insanity is used in Illinois? Given this standard, what would Marty have to prove to succeed in offering the insanity defense for Aaron?

4. During the trial, prosecutor Janet Venable (Laura Linney) asks expert witness Dr. Molly Arrington (Frances McDormand) if Aaron "knows the difference between right and wrong." Janet also asks Molly if Aaron knew that he had broken the law. Given Illinois's standard for determining sanity, are these questions relevant?

5. From what you have read in this chapter, is it likely that Aaron would be back on the streets "in a month"—as Janet says—if he is found not guilty by reason of insanity?

Without Due Process by J. A. Jance, is an audiocassette, produced by Books in Motion, that presents views on due process.

LOGGING ON

Go to http://cj.wadsworth.com/gainescore2e, **and click Hypercontents.** There, you will find URLs for the organizations in the following list:

- You can find a very concise summary of criminal law at the **West Group's West Legal Directory**

Web site, as well as an exhaustive summary of the constitutional due process issue.

- You can also access a checklist of the subjects that are important in criminal law by accessing the Web site **'Lectric Law Library.**

USING THE INTERNET FOR CRIMINAL JUSTICE ANALYSIS

INFOTRAC®
COLLEGE EDITION

1. Go to InfoTrac College Edition at http://www.infotrac-college.com/wadsworth/.
   After you log on, type in **dangerous games and the criminal law**
   This essay concerns dangerous games such as drag racing and Russian roulette. After reading the essay, answer the following questions:

   a. What movie does the author discuss when he talks about drag racing? Why?

   b. Why does the author argue that such dangerous activities should be criminalized?

   c. Why does he think that those who engage in dangerous games should be penalized more severely than they are today?

   d. What is the maximum fine in California for drivers who exceed 100 miles an hour?

2. See Internet Activities 3.1 and 3.2 on the companion Web site for *CJ in Action: The Core.* To get to the activities, go to http://www.cj.wadsworth.com/gainescore2e, select the appropriate chapter from the drop down list, then click Internet Activities on the left navigation bar.

NOTES

1. Evelyn Nieves, "Couple Convicted of All Charges in Dog Mauling Fatal to Neighbor," *New York Times* (March 22, 2002), A1.
2. California Penal Code Sections 188–189.
3. *Berry v. Superior Court,* 256 Cal.Rptr. 348 (1989).
4. Evelyn Nieves, "Woman Gets 4-Year Term in Fatal Dog Attack," *New York Times* (July 16, 2002), A8.
5. Joshua Dressler, *Understanding Criminal Law,* 2d ed. (New York: Richard D. Irwin, 1995), 22–3.
6. *Ibid.,* 23.
7. Thomas R. Bartman, "High Criminal Intent Standard Needed for Complex Environmental Laws," *Legal Backgrounder* (September 15, 1995), 4.
8. *State v. Saunders,* 75 N.J. 200, 381 A.2d 333 (1977).
9. Joel Feinberg, *The Moral Limits of the Criminal Law: Harm to Others* (New York: Oxford University Press, 1984), 221–32.
10. Flammable Fabrics Act, 15 U.S.C. Section 1196 (1994).
11. Stuart P. Green, "Why It's a Crime to Tear the Tag Off a Mattress," *Emory Law Journal* 46 (Fall 1997), 1533–1614.
12. Henry M. Hart, Jr., "The Aims of the Criminal Law," *Law & Contemporary Problems* 23 (1958), 405–6.

13. John L. Diamond, "The Myth of Morality and Fault in Criminal Law Doctrine," *American Criminal Law Review* 34 (Fall 1996), 111.
14. Lawrence M. Friedman, *Crime and Punishments in American History* (New York: Basic Books, 1993), 34.
15. *Ibid.,* 10.
16. Robert W. Drane and David J. Neal, "On Moral Justifications for the Tort/Crime Distinction," *California Law Review* 68 (1980), 398.
17. Gail Heriot, "An Essay on the Civil-Criminal Distinction with Special Reference to Punitive Damages," *Journal of Contemporary Legal Issues* 7 (1996), 43.
18. Joan Treadway, "Judgment Against Son's Killer Applauded," *New Orleans Times-Picayune* (January 17, 1996), A1.
19. Model Penal Code 1.04 (2).
20. David Flick, "Hockey Dad Guilty of Manslaughter," *Dallas Morning News* (January 12, 2002), 1A.
21. Advisory Task Force on the Juvenile Justice System, *Final Report* (Minneapolis, MN: Minnesota Supreme Court, 1994), 5–11.
22. *Black's Law Dictionary,* 6th ed. (St. Paul, MN: West Publishing Co., 1990), 959.
23. *Ibid.,* 960.
24. Johannes Andenaes, "The Moral or Educative Influence of Criminal Law," *Journal of Social Issues* 27 (Spring 1971), 17, 26.

25. Green, 1533–1614.
26. Thomas A. Mullen, "Rule without Reason: Requiring Independent Proof of the *Corpus Delicti* as a Condition of Admitting Extrajudicial Confession," *University of San Francisco Law Review* 27 (1993), 385.
27. *Hawkins v. State,* 219 Ind. 116, 129, 37 N.E.2d 79 (1941).
28. David C. Biggs, "'The Good Samaritan Is Packing': An Overview of the Broadened Duty to Aid Your Fellowman, with the Modern Desire to Possess Concealed Weapons," *University of Dayton Law Review* 22 (Winter 1997), 225.
29. Jessica McBride, "Mom Accused of Not Trying to Stop Assault on Daughter," *Milwaukee Journal Sentinel* (July 31, 1997), 3.
30. Daniel B. Yeager, "A Radical Community of Aid: A Rejoinder to Opponents of Affirmative Duties to Help Strangers," *Washington University Law Quarterly* 71 (1993), 1.
31. Model Penal Code Section 2.02.
32. Model Penal Code Section 2.02 (c).
33. Marisol Bello, "Man Who Says He Feared Wife's Voodoo Acquitted of Murder," *Orange County Register* (November 27, 1997), A18.
34. *Black's Law Dictionary,* 1423.
35. *United States v. Dotterweich,* 320 U.S. 277 (1943).

36. *State v. Stiffler,* 763 P.2d 308, 311 (Idaho Ct. App. 1988).

37. *State v. Harrison,* 425 A.2d 111 (1979).

38. Richard G. Singer and John Q. LaFond, *Criminal Law: Examples and Explanations* (New York: Aspen Law & Business, 1997), 322.

39. *State v. Linscott,* 520 A.2d 1067 (1987).

40. *Morissette v. United States,* 342 U.S. 246, 251–2 (1952).

41. Stacey M. Studnicki, "Annual Survey of Michigan Law, June 1, 1993–May 31, 1994," *Wayne Law Review* 41 (Winter 1995), 589.

42. *People v. Harding,* 443 Mich. at 699–703, 506 N.W.2d at 486–7 (1994).

43. Federal Bank Robbery Act, 18 U.S.C.A. Section 2113.

44. Missouri State Statutes 574.090 and 574.093, RSMo Supp. 1993.

45. *Wisconsin v. Mitchell,* 508 U.S. 476 (1993).

46. Sandra D. Scott and Timothy S. Wynes, "Should Missouri Retain Its 'Ethnic Intimidation' Law?" *Journal of the Missouri Bar* 49 (November/December 1993), 445.

47. New York Penal Section 120.25.

48. "Bronx D.A. Charges Nushawn Williams with Reckless Endangerment, Assault," *New York Law Journal* (August 20, 1998), 1.

49. Maryland Code 1957, Art. 27, Code 1957, Section 407.

50. *Smallwood v. State,* 680 A.2d 512 (Md. 1996).

51. *In re Winship,* 397 U.S. 358, 364 (1970).

52. Jim Yardley, "Trial in Case of Drowned Children Opens," *New York Times* (February 19, 2002), 3.

53. *M'Naughten's Case,* 10 Cl. & F. 200, Eng. Rep. 718 (1843). Note that the name of the rule is also spelled M'Naghten and McNaughten.

54. Joshua Dressler, *Cases and Materials on Criminal Law,* 2d ed. (St. Paul, MN: West Group, 1999), 599.

55. 214 F.2d 862 (D.C. Cir., 1954).

56. Model Penal Code 401 (1952).

57. South Carolina Code Ann. Section 17-24-20(A) (Law. Co-op. Supp. 1997).

58. Lawrence P. Tiffany and Mary Tiffany, "Nosologic Objections to the Criminal Defense of Pathological Intoxication: What Do the Doubters Doubt?" *International Journal of Law and Psychiatry* 13 (1990), 49.

59. John Sanko, "Murder Conviction Overturned," (Denver, Colorado) *Rocky Mountain News* (April 11, 1997), 25A.

60. 518 U.S. 37 (1996).

61. Mont. Code Ann. Section 45-5-102 (1997).

62. Mont. Code Ann. Section 45-2-203 (1997).

63. Kenneth W. Simons, "Mistake and Impossibility, Law and Fact, and Culpability: A Speculative Essay," *Journal of Criminal Law and Criminology* 81 (1990), 447.

64. *United States v. Robinson,* 119 F.3rd 1205 (5th Cir. 1997).

65. *Lambert v. California,* 335 U.S. 225 (1957).

66. Federal Bureau of Investigation, *Crime in the United States, 2001* (Washington, D.C.: U.S. Government Printing Office, 2002), 28.

67. Craig L. Carr, "Duress and Criminal Responsibility," *Law and Philosophy* 10 (1990), 161.

68. *United States v. May,* 727 F.2d 764 (1984).

69. *United States v. Contento-Pachon,* 723 F.2d 691 (1984).

70. *People v. Murillo,* 587 N.E.2d 1199, 1204 (Ill. App. Ct. 1992).

71. Michael K. Molitor, "The 'Battered Child Syndrome' As Self-Defense," *Wayne Law Review* 40 (Fall 1993), 237.

72. Model Penal Code Section 3.02.

73. *United States v. Paolello,* 951 F.2d 537 (3rd Cir. 1991).

74. *People v. Petro,* 56 P.2d 984 (Cal. Ct. App. 1936); and *Regina v. Dudley and Stephens,* 14 Q.B.D. 173 (1884).

75. *Brown v. Mississippi,* 279 U.S. 278 (1936).

76. 372 U.S. 335 (1963).

77. 116 U.S. 1769 (1996).

78. 117 U.S. 882 (1997).

79. "Traffic Stops," *Harvard Law Review* 111 (November 1997), 299.

80. *Crime in the United States, 2001,* 60.

81. Steve M. Freeman, "Hate Crime Laws: Punishment which Fits the Crime," *Annual Survey of American Law* 4 (1992/93), 581–5.

82. 505 U.S. 377 (1992).

83. 508 U.S. 476 (1993).

84. Nat Hentoff, "Letting Loose the Hate Crimes Police," *The Village Voice* (July 13, 1993).

85. James B. Jacobs, "Should Hate Be a Crime?" *The Public Interest* (Fall 1993), 3–14.

86. Quoted in Hentoff.

CHAPTER 4
POLICE: AGENTS OF LAW AND ORDER

Chapter Objectives

After reading this chapter, you should be able to:

1. Tell how the patronage system affected policing.

2. Indicate the results of the Wickersham Commission.

3. List five main types of law enforcement agencies.

4. List some of the most important federal law enforcement agencies.

5. Identify the five investigative priorities of the FBI.

6. Analyze the importance of private security today.

7. List the four basic responsibilities of the police.

8. Explain how some states have reacted to perceived leniency to perpetrators of domestic violence.

INTRODUCTION
Operation Reunion and Elian Gonzalez

Early on the morning of April 22, 2000, 131 federal law enforcement agents, some of them wearing body armor and carrying automatic weapons, executed "Operation Reunion" in the Little Havana section of Miami, Florida. The purpose of the operation was to forcibly remove six-year-old Cuban citizen Elian Gonzalez from the house of his relatives, whom the U.S. government felt were illegally holding the boy in defiance of the law. Three minutes after an eight-member "high-risk" team broke down the front door and entered the home, Gonzalez was in a van, speeding toward the airport and a flight to Washington, D.C., to meet with his father.

By objective standards, "Operation Reunion" was a success. Media images of the raid, however, sparked a nationwide debate on the strategy used by the federal law enforcement agents. Many observers, such as Geoffrey Alpert, a criminologist at the University of South Carolina, maintained that the use of force was necessary to subdue any possible resistance. "Someone breaks the door down and you see these commandos come in. No one in his right mind is going to pick a fight," said Alpert.[1] In contrast, critics such as ex–Federal Bureau of Investigation agent Robert Ressler argued, "This was not the type of thing that warranted killing anyone, yet they went in with lethal force."[2]

In addition, the government's strategy outraged many local Cuban Americans. "They were animals," one resident said of the agents. "They gassed women and children to take a defenseless child out of there."[3] News that a Miami assistant police chief had been riding in the vehicle that took the boy to the airport led to further confrontations, as protesters pelted local police officers with chairs, stones, and garbage cans.[4]

The turmoil surrounding these events points to the complex position of the law enforcement agent in modern society. Police are the most visible representatives of our criminal justice system; indeed, they symbolize the system for the many Americans who may never see the inside of a courtroom or a prison cell. The police are entrusted with immense power to serve and protect the public good: the power to use weapons and the power to arrest. But that same power alarms many citizens, who fear that it may be turned arbitrarily against them.[5] The role of the police is constantly debated as well. Is their primary mission to fight crime, or should they also be concerned with the social conditions that presumably lead to crime?

This chapter will lay the foundation for our study of the police and the work that they do. A short history of policing will be followed by an examination of the many different agencies that make up American law enforcement. We will also look at the various responsibilities of police officers.

A family friend holds six-year-old Cuban citizen Elian Gonzalez as a federal agent armed with an MP-5 submachine gun attempts to grab the boy. (AP Photo/Alan Diaz)

A HISTORY OF THE AMERICAN POLICE

Although modern society relies on law enforcement officers to control and prevent crime, in the early days of this country police services had little to do with crime control. The policing efforts in the first American cities were directed toward controlling certain groups of people (mostly slaves and Native Americans), delivering goods, regulating activities such as buying and selling in the town market, maintaining health and sanitation, controlling gambling and vice, and managing livestock and other animals.[6] Furthermore, these police services were for the most part performed by volunteers, as a police force was an expensive proposition. Most communities simply could not afford to pay a group of law enforcement officers.[7]

Eventually, of course, as the populations of American cities grew, so did the need for public order and the willingness to devote resources to the establishment of formal police forces. Policing in the United States and in England evolved along similar lines, and many of our policing institutions have their roots in English tradition. Consequently, we will begin our discussion of the history of American police with a look back at its English beginnings.

English Roots

Before William the Conqueror invaded the island in 1066, the dominant system of law enforcement in England was the **tithing system.** Every male was enrolled in a group of ten families, which was called a *tithing.* If one person in the tithing committed a crime, then every person in the group was responsible for paying the fine. The theory was that this obligation would be an incentive for the tithing to engage in collective community policing. Later, ten tithings were joined together to form a *hundred,* whose top law official was the *reeve.* Finally, the hundreds were consolidated into *shires* (the equivalent of modern counties), and the law enforcement official became known as the **shire-reeve.** As the phonetics suggest, this official is the earliest example of what is now the county sheriff.

In 1326, the office of the **justice of the peace** was established to replace the shire-reeve. Over the next centuries, in most English cities the justice of the peace, with the help of a constable, came to oversee various law enforcement activities, including organizing the night watch, investigating crimes, and securing criminals for trial. In the countryside, the hundred was replaced by the parish, which corresponded to the territory served by a particular church and included its members. Under the *parish constable system,* the parish hired a person to oversee criminal justice for its parishioners.

The London Experiments.   By the mid-1700s, London, England—one of the largest cities in the Western world—still did not have an organized system of law enforcement. Crime was endemic to city life, and the government's only recourse was to *read the riot act* (call in the military when the lawbreaking became unbearable). Such actions were widely unpopular, as the townspeople did not appreciate being disciplined (and fired on) by soldiers whose salaries they were paying. Furthermore, the soldiers proved unreliable peacemakers, as they were hesitant to use force against their fellow London citizens. Despite rampant crime in the city, most Londoners were not in favor of a police force under the control of the city government. English history is rife with instances in which the king or some other government official abused military power by turning it against the citizens. Therefore, the citizenry were wary of any formal, armed organization that could restrict their individual liberties.

This mistrust began to ebb in 1829, when British Home Secretary Sir Robert "Bobbie" Peel pushed the Metropolitan Police Act through Parliament. This legislation has had lasting impact, as many of its operating goals were similar to

Go to the Stories from the Street feature at http://www.cj. wadsworth.com/gainescore2e to hear Larry Gaines tell insightful stories related to this chapter and his experiences in the field.

"Every society gets the kind of criminal it deserves. What is equally true is that every community gets the kind of law enforcement it insists on."

—Robert Kennedy, *U.S. attorney general* (1964)

TITHING SYSTEM
In Anglo-Saxon England, a system of law enforcement in which groups of ten families, known as tithings, were collectively responsible for law and order within their groups.

SHIRE-REEVE
The chief law enforcement officer in an early English shire, or county. The forerunner of the modern sheriff.

JUSTICE OF THE PEACE
Established in fourteenth-century England, a government official who oversaw various aspects of local law enforcement. The post eventually became strictly identified with judicial matters.

A satirical English cartoon depicts Sir Robert Peel fighting a group of night watchmen. The cartoon refers to the organization of the London Metropolitan Police in 1829, through which Peel tried to bring a measure of control and organization to law enforcement in the city. In doing so, Peel made obsolete the night watchmen, who were generally ineffective in preventing crime and, in many cases, were themselves of questionable character. The cartoonist appears to take a slightly sarcastic view of Peel as a "savior." What attitudes in early nineteenth-century London might cause citizens to be suspicious of an organized police force? (Corbis/Hulton-Deutsch Collection)

those of modern police forces (see Figure 4.1 for a summary of the act). Under the terms of this act, the London Metropolitan Police was formed. One thousand members strong at first, the members of this police force were easily recognizable in their uniforms that included blue coats and top hats. Under Peel's direction, the "bobbies," as the police were called in honor of their founder, had four specific operating philosophies:

1 To reduce tension and conflict between law enforcement officers and the public.

2 To use nonviolent means (they did not carry firearms) in keeping the peace, with violence to be used only as a last resort. This point was crucial, because, as mentioned earlier, the English were suspicious of armed government military organizations. Being unarmed, the bobbies could hardly be confused with soldiers.

3 To relieve the military from certain duties, such as controlling urban violence. (Peel specifically hoped that his police would be less inclined to use excessive force than the military had been.)

4 To be judged on the absence of crime rather than through high-visibility police action.[8]

London's police operation was so successful that it was soon imitated in smaller towns throughout England and, eventually, in the United States.

The Early American Police Experience

In colonial America and immediately following the American Revolution, law enforcement virtually mirrored the English system. Constables and night watchmen were taken from the ranks of ordinary citizens. The governor of each colony hired a sheriff in each county to oversee the formal aspects of law enforcement, such as selecting juries and managing jails and prisons.[9] These colonial appointees were not always of the highest moral character. In 1730, the Pennsylvania colony felt the need to pass laws specifically prohibiting sheriffs from extorting money from prisoners or selling "strong liquors" to "any person under arrest."[10]

The First Police Department. In 1801, Boston became the first American city to acquire a formal night watch; the watchmen were paid 50 cents a night. For the next three decades, most major cities went no further than the watch sys-

FIGURE 4.1

Fundamental Principles of the Metropolitan Police Act of 1829

The first modern police force was established in London by the Metropolitan Police Act of 1829. Sir Robert Peel, the politician who pushed through the legislation, wanted a police force that would provide citizens with "the full and complete protection of the law" and "check the increase of crime." To fulfill these objectives, Peel's early police were guided by the basic principles listed here.

1 The police force must be organized along military lines.

2 Police administrators and officers must be under government control.

3 Emphasis must be placed on hiring qualified persons and training them properly.

4 New police officers must complete a probationary period; if they fail to meet standards during this time, they will not be hired as permanent officers.

5 Police personnel should be assigned to specific areas of the city for a specific time period.

6 Police headquarters must be centrally located in the city.

7 Police officers must maintain proper appearances at all times in order to gain and keep the respect of citizens.

8 Individual police officers should be able to control their tempers and refrain from violence whenever possible.

9 Police records must be kept in order to measure police effectiveness.

tem. Finally, facing the same pressures as London, major American metropolitan areas began to form "reactive patrol units" geared toward enforcing the law and preventing crime.[11] In 1833, Philadelphia became the first city to employ both day and night watchmen. Five years later, working from Sir Robert Peel's model, Boston formed the first organized police department, consisting of six full-time officers. In 1844, New York City set the foundation for the modern police department by combining its day and night watches under the control of a single police chief. By the onset of the Civil War in 1861, a number of American cities, including Boston, Baltimore, New Orleans, Philadelphia, Cincinnati, and Chicago, had similarly consolidated police departments, modeled on the Metropolitan Police of London.

Like their modern counterparts, many early police officers were hard working, honest, and devoted to serving and protecting the public. On the whole, however, in the words of historian Samuel Walker, "The quality of American police service in the nineteenth century could hardly have been worse."[12] This poor quality can be attributed to the fact that the recruitment and promotion of police officers were intricately tied into the politics of the day. Police officers received their jobs as a result of political connections, not because of any particular skills or knowledge. Whichever political party was in power in a given city would hire its own cronies to run the police department; consequently, the police were often more concerned with serving the interests of the political powers than with protecting the citizens.[13]

The Spoils System. Corruption was rampant during this *political era* of policing, which lasted roughly from 1840 to 1930. (See Figure 4.2 for an overview of the three eras of policing, which are discussed in this chapter and referred to

A horse-drawn police wagon used by the New York City Police Department, circa 1886. In the 1880s a number of American cities introduced patrol wagon services, which included transporting prisoners and drunks as well as performing ambulance duties. Along with signal service, or "call boxes," the police wagon represented a "revolution" in police methods. If a patrol officer made an arrest far from headquarters, he could now call the station and request a police wagon to pick up and deliver the arrested person (instead of having to deliver the arrestee himself). (Corbis/Bettmann)

FIGURE 4.2

The Three Eras of American Policing

George L. Kelling and Mark H. Moore have separated the history of policing in the United States into three distinct periods. Here is a brief summarization of these three eras.

| 1840 1850 1860 1870 1880 1890 1900 1910 1920 1930 1940 1950 1960 1970 1980 1990 2000 |

The Political Era

Time Period—1840 to 1930
Primary Function of Police—Provide range of social services to citizenry.
Organization—Decentralized
Police/Community Relationship—Intimate
Tactics—Patrolling neighborhoods on foot
Strategic Goal—Satisfy the needs of citizens and political bosses
Strategic Weakness—Widespread police corruption and brutality

The Reform Era

Time Period—1930 to 1980
Primary Function of Police—Crime control
Organization—Centralized
Police/Community Relationship—Professional and distant
Tactics—Patrolling neighborhoods in cars, rapid response to emergency calls for service (911 calls)
Strategic Goal—Crime control
Strategic Weakness—Lack of communication with citizens fostered mistrust and community violence (riots)

The Community Era

Time Period—1980 to present
Primary Function of Police—Continue to control crime while providing a broader range of social services
Organization—Decentralized, with specialized units and task forces
Police/Community Relationship—Return to intimate
Tactics—Foot patrol, problem solving, and public relations
Strategic Goal—Improve the quality of life of citizens
Strategic Weakness—An over-reliance on police officers to solve all of society's problems

Source: Adapted from George L. Kelling and Mark H. Moore, "From Political to Reform to Community: The Evolving Strategy of Police," in *Community Policing: Rhetoric or Reality,* ed. Jack R. Green and Stephen D. Mastrofski (New York: Praeger Publishers, 1991), 14–15, 22–23; plus authors' updates. Reproduced with permission of Greenwood Publishing Group, Inc., Westport, CT.

throughout the book.) Police salaries were relatively low; thus, many police officers saw their positions as opportunities to make extra income through any number of illegal activities. Bribery was common, as police would use their close proximity to the people to request "favors," which went into the police officers' own pockets or into the coffers of the local political party as "contributions."[14] This was known as the **patronage system,** or the "spoils system," because to the political victors went the spoils.

The political era also saw police officers take an active role in providing social services for their bosses' constituents. In many instances, this role even took precedence over law enforcement duties. Politicians realized that they could attract more votes by offering social services to citizens than by arresting them, and they required the police departments under their control to act accordingly.

The Modernization of the American Police

The abuses of the political era of policing did not go unnoticed. But it was not until 1929 that President Herbert Hoover appointed the national Commission on Law Observance and Enforcement to assess the American criminal justice system. The Wickersham Commission, named after its chairman, George Wickersham, focused on two areas of American policing that were in need of reform: (1) police brutality and (2) "the corrupting influence of politics." According to the commission, this reform should come about through higher personnel standards, centralized police administrations, and the increased use of technology.[15] Reformers of the time took the commission's findings as a call for the professionalization of American police and initiated the progressive (or *reform*) era in American policing.

Professionalism.   In truth, the Wickersham Commission was not ground breaking. Many of its recommendations echoed the opinions of one of its contributors—August Vollmer, the police chief of Berkeley, California, from 1905 until 1932. Known as "the father of modern police administration," Vollmer pioneered the training of potential police officers in institutions of higher learning. The first program to grant a degree in law enforcement, at San Jose State College (now a university), was developed under Vollmer.

Along with increased training, Vollmer also championed the use of technology in police work. His Berkeley police department became the first in the nation to use automobiles to patrol city streets and to hire a scientist to assist in solving crimes.[16] Furthermore, Vollmer believed that police could prevent crime by involving themselves in the lives of *potential* criminals, which led to his establishing the first juvenile crime unit in the nation.

Vollmer's devotion to modernism was also apparent in the career of his most successful protégé, police reformer O. W. Wilson, who promoted a style of policing known as the **professional model.** In an attempt to remove politics from police work, Wilson stressed the need for efficiency through bureaucracy and technology.

Administrative Reforms.   Under the professional model police chiefs, who had been little more than figureheads during the political era, took more control over their departments. A key to these efforts was the reorganization of police departments in many major cities. To improve their control over operations, police chiefs began to add midlevel positions to the force. These new officers, known as majors or assistant chiefs, could develop and implement crime-fighting strategies and more closely supervise individual officers. Police chiefs also tried to consolidate their power by bringing large areas of a city under their control so that no local ward, neighborhood, or politician could easily influence a single police department.

Finally, police chiefs set up special units such as criminal investigation, vice, and traffic squads with jurisdiction-wide power. Previously, all police powers

PATRONAGE SYSTEM
A form of corruption in which the political party in power hires and promotes police officers, receiving job-related "favors" in return.

PROFESSIONAL MODEL
A style of policing advocated by August Vollmer and O. W. Wilson that emphasizes centralized police organizations, increased use of technology, and a limitation of police discretion through regulations and guidelines.

Criminal Justice & TECHNOLOGY

Going Wireless

Despite the many technological advances that have transformed police work since August Vollmer sent out the first patrol cars in the early 1900s, law enforcement agents have always faced one important limitation. Any information taken down on paper by a police officer in the field—such as speeding tickets or arrest warrants—would have to be refiled when he or she returned to the station. Time that could be better spent on providing services to citizens was taken up with paperwork that, essentially, had already been done.

Thanks to a new technology known as wireless-fidelity, or Wi–Fi, police departments can set up wide-area networks (WANs) that connect computer systems via directional antennas. Each one of these antennas has a radius of fifteen to thirty miles, and they can be chained together to create large areas of coverage. Any police officer with a laptop or dashboard computer that has the proper network card (and an antenna on the roof of the patrol car) can use this wireless technology to link up not only with local police headquarters, but also with other law enforcement agencies, courtrooms, and government departments. The potential for Wi–Fi as an information transmitter goes well beyond saving police officers from having to fill out an arrest report twice. Jail authorities could, for example, use Wi–Fi to send a mug shot of an escaped convict to all law enforcement agencies in the immediate vicinity.

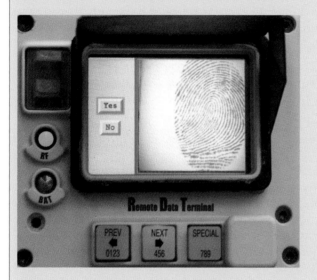

The "ISBS" is a wireless device that can record a fingerprint at the scene of an investigation and then send the image to be checked against a database. (AP Photo/Nick Ut)

IN THE FUTURE

Today, Wi–Fi systems are often limited by the range of the antennae or "access points." Thus, if a patrol car moves out of range of an access point, the police officer will enter a "dead zone" with no wireless access. Some systems have developed a back-up plan in which the connection is immediately reestablished through a cellular WAN (using the same technology as a cellular phone), but many experts worry that any information transferred in this manner can easily be intercepted by someone with the proper tools. The scope of this problem may be reduced, however, as more WANs use satellite links, which both increases their range and protects against information theft. Furthermore, until 2002 the Federal Communications Commission required all WANs to be licensed. Now that the networks are unregulated, it will be much easier for law enforcement agencies to create and use them.

within a precinct were controlled by the politicians in that precinct. By creating specialized units that worked across all precincts, the police chiefs increased their own power at the expense of the political bosses.

Technological innovations on all fronts—including patrol cars, radio communications, public records systems, fingerprinting, toxicology (the study of poisons), and forensics (the application of chemistry to the examination of physical evidence)—allowed police operations to move even more quickly toward O. W. Wilson's professional model. By the 1950s, America prided itself on having the most modern and professional police force in the world. (The pace of technological innovation continues to this day, as you can see in the feature *Criminal Justice & Technology—Going Wireless*.) As efficiency became the goal of the reform era police chief, however, relations with the community suffered. Instead of being members of the community, police officers were now seen almost as intruders, patrolling the streets in the anonymity of their automobiles. The drawbacks of this perception—and the professional model in general—would soon become evident.

"He may be a very nice man. But I haven't got the time to figure that out. All I know is, he's got a uniform and a gun and I have to relate to him that way."

—James Baldwin, *American author* (1971)

Turmoil in the 1960s.   The 1960s was one of the most turbulent decades in American history. The civil rights movement, though not inherently violent, intensified feelings of helplessness and impoverishment in African American communities. These frustrations resulted in civil unrest, and many major American cities experienced race riots in the middle years of the decade.

Even though police brutality often provided the spark for riots—and there is little question that police departments often overreacted to antiwar demonstrations during the Vietnam era (1963–1975)—it would be simplistic to blame the strife of the 1960s on the police. The rioters were reacting to social circumstances that they found unacceptable. Their clashes with the police were the result rather than the cause of these problems. Many observers, however, believed that the police *contributed* to the disorder. The National Advisory Commission on Civil Disorders stated bluntly that poor relations between the police and African American communities were partly to blame for the violence that plagued many of those communities.[17] In striving for professionalism, the police appeared to have lost touch with the citizens they were supposed to be serving. To repair their damaged relations with a large segment of the population, police would have to rediscover their community roots.

Returning to the Community

The beginning of the third era in American policing, the *community era,* may have started with several government initiatives that took place in 1968. Of primary importance was the Omnibus Crime Control and Safe Streets Act, which was passed that year.[18] Under this act, the federal government provided state and local police departments with funds to create a wide variety of police-community programs. Most large-city police departments established entire units devoted to community relations, implementing programs that ranged from summer recreation activities for inner-city youths to "officer-friendly" referral operations that encouraged citizens to come to the police with their crime concerns.

In the 1970s, as this vital rethinking of the role of the police was taking place, the country was hit by a crime wave. Thus, police administrators were forced to combine efforts to improve community relations with aggressive and innovative crime-fighting strategies. At first, these strategies were *reactive;* that is, they focused on reducing the amount of time the police took to react to crime—how quickly they were able to reach the scene of a crime, for example. Eventually, police departments began to focus on *proactive* strategies—that is, strategies aimed at stopping crimes before they are committed. A dedication to proactive strategies led to widespread acceptance of community policing in the 1980s. Community policing is based on the notion that meaningful interaction between officers and citizens will lead to a partnership in preventing and fighting crime.[19] Though the idea of involving members of the community in this manner is hardly new—a similar principle was set forth by Sir Robert Peel—innovative tactics in community policing, many of which will be discussed in Chapter 5, have had a significant impact on modern police work.

LAW ENFORCEMENT AGENCIES

Another aspect of modern police work is the fragmentation of law enforcement. For example, when seven inmates escaped from prison in Kennedy, Texas, on December 13, 2000, prison officials relied on a wide network of local, state, and federal law enforcement agencies to recapture the fugitives. The inspector general's office of the Texas Department of Criminal Justice, acting as the lead agency, coordinated the search efforts of dozens of local police departments and the Texas Rangers, as well as the Immigration and Naturalization Service, the

U.S. Marshals Service, the Federal Bureau of Investigation, the Drug Enforcement Administration, the Bureau of Alcohol, Tobacco and Firearms, and the Border Patrol.[20]

The manhunt illustrates how many agencies can become involved in a single incident. There are over 13,500 law enforcement agencies in the United States, employing over 940,000 people. The various agencies include:

- 3,088 sheriffs' departments.
- 1,332 special police agencies, limited to policing parks, schools, airports, and so on.
- 49 state police departments, with Hawaii being the one exception.
- 50 federal law enforcement agencies.[21]

Each level has its own set of responsibilities, which we shall discuss starting with local police departments.

Irving (Texas) Police Department Public Information Officer David Tull posts artists' renditions of the seven inmates who escaped a South Texas prison in late 2000. After committing several robberies and killing a Dallas police officer, the fugitives were finally apprehended in Colorado thanks to a tip prompted by the television show *America's Most Wanted*. Why would local law enforcement agencies seek the aid of state and federal law enforcement agencies in a situation such as this one? (AP Photo/Jerry W. Hoefer)

Municipal Law Enforcement Agencies

According to the Federal Bureau of Investigation, there are 2.5 state and local police officers for every 1,000 citizens in the United States.[22] This average somewhat masks the discrepancies between the police forces in urban and rural America. As noted in Chapter 1, the vast majority of all police officers work in small and medium-sized police departments (see Figure 4.3). While the New York City Police Department has more than 38,000 employees, almost 800 small towns have only one police officer. Most of the nearly 2,000 "nontraditional" law enforcement agencies—those that police transit systems, schools and colleges, airports, parks, and other special jurisdictions—in the United States also operate on a local level.

Of the three levels of law enforcement, municipal agencies have the broadest authority to apprehend criminal suspects, maintain order, and provide services to the community. Whether the local officer is part of a large force or the only law enforcement officer in the community, he or she is usually responsible for a wide spectrum of duties, from responding to noise complaints to investigating homicides. (To learn about a new duty that is being given to some local police officers, see the feature *CJ in Focus—The Balancing Act: A Question of Immigrants* on the next page.) Much of the criticism of local police departments is based on the belief that local police are too underpaid or poorly trained to handle these various responsibilities. Reformers have suggested that residents of smaller American towns would benefit from greater statewide coordination of local police departments, though little progress has been made in this area.[23]

Sheriffs and County Law Enforcement

A vestige of the English shire-reeve discussed earlier in the chapter, the **sheriff** is still an important figure in American law enforcement. Almost every one of the more than three thousand counties in the United States (except those in Alaska) has a sheriff. In every state except Rhode Island and Hawaii, sheriffs are elected

FIGURE 4.3

Full-Time Police Personnel, by Size of Population Served

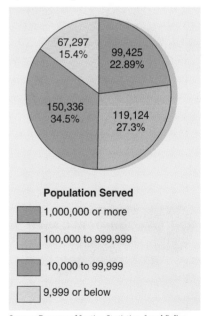

67,297
15.4%

99,425
22.89%

150,336
34.5%

119,124
27.3%

Population Served

- 1,000,000 or more
- 100,000 to 999,999
- 10,000 to 99,999
- 9,999 or below

Source: Bureau of Justice Statistics, *Local Police Departments—1999* (Washington, D.C.: U.S. Department of Justice, May 2000), Table 3, p. 3.

SHERIFF
The primary law enforcement officer in a county, usually elected to the post by a popular vote.

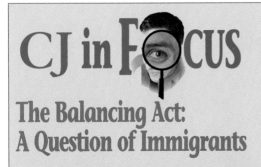

CJ in FOCUS

The Balancing Act: A Question of Immigrants

Each one of the nineteen hijackers involved in the September 11, 2001, terrorist attacks had been living in the United States on a temporary visa, a document that sets out the terms under which noncitizens can stay in this country. At least two of the nineteen were in violation of their visas, meaning they were in America illegally. Following the strikes, the Immigration and Naturalization Service (INS) came under a great deal of criticism for failing to regulate the actions of the hijackers. But, as defenders of the INS pointed out, the federal agency concentrates its law enforcement efforts mostly on our borders with Canada and Mexico, and has fewer than two thousand agents to police the rest of the country.

In 2002, Florida became the first state to supplement INS efforts by authorizing thirty-five local and state law enforcement officers to make arrests of immigrants who have overstayed their visas or entered the country illegally. While many applauded the move as a first step in shoring up our ramparts against terrorism, it also raised a number of concerns. As you will see in Chapter 6, local and state police officers generally have to meet certain standards before they can arrest someone. Specifically, they must either convince a judge that there is sufficient evidence to make the arrest, or have probable cause that the suspect has committed a crime. Furthermore, law enforcement officers are not permitted to make arrests based on a person's skin color or ethnicity.

In contrast, INS agents can arrest foreigners for violating immigration law without having either a warrant or probable cause. And, almost by definition, they can single out persons on the basis of race. Consequently, the Florida officers, as deputized immigration agents, would have much greater powers to arrest a foreign national who was believed to be a member of a terrorist group or was even simply "acting suspiciously." Because of a belief that local police should not have such authority, states with large immigrant populations such as New York, Illinois, New Jersey, and Michigan have said that they will not follow Florida's lead in allowing local and state agents to enforce federal immigration laws.

FOR CRITICAL ANALYSIS

In general, the INS can forcibly remove an immigrant who is in the United States without permission from this country at any time. How might Florida's plan discourage illegal aliens who are victims of a crime from reporting the criminal activity to local law enforcement officers?

---

by members of the community for two- or four-year terms and are paid a salary set by the state legislature or county board. As elected officials who do not necessarily need a background in law enforcement, modern sheriffs resemble their counterparts from the political era of policing in many ways. Simply stated, the sheriff is also a politician. When a new sheriff is elected, she or he will sometimes repay political debts by appointing new deputies or promoting those who have given her or him support. This high degree of instability and personnel turnover in many states is seen as one of the weaknesses of county law enforcement.[24]

Video Profile of Charlotte East, Senior Deputy Sheriff

Size and Responsibility of Sheriffs' Departments.   Like municipal police forces, sheriffs' departments vary in size. The largest is the Los Angeles County Sheriffs' Department, with more than 8,000 full-time employees. Of the 3,088 sheriffs' departments in the country, 17 employ more than 1,000 officers, while 35 have only one.[25]

The image of the sheriff as a powerful figure patrolling vast expanses is not entirely misleading. Most sheriffs' departments are assigned their duties by state law. Almost 90 percent of all sheriffs' departments have the primary responsibility for investigating violent crimes in their jurisdictions. Other common responsibilities of a sheriff's department include:

- Protecting the public.
- Administering the county jail.
- Carrying out civil and criminal processes within county lines, such as serving eviction notices and court summonses.
- Keeping order in the county courthouse.
- Collecting taxes.

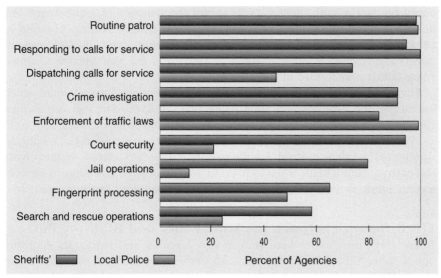

Source: Bureau of Justice Statistics, *Sheriffs' Departments—1997* (Washington, D.C.: U.S. Department of Justice, February 2000), 14.

FIGURE 4.4
The Functions of Sheriffs' and Local Police Departments

Sheriffs' and local police departments perform many of the same functions. As you see here, however, they often emphasize the functions differently. Sheriffs' departments are much more involved in operating local jails, while police departments are more likely to deal with traffic control.

- Enforcing orders of the court, such as overseeing the sequestration of a jury during a trial.[26]

It is easy to confuse sheriffs' departments and local police departments, for good reason. As Figure 4.4 shows, both law enforcement agencies are responsible for many of the same tasks, including crime investigation and routine patrol. There are differences, however, also evident in Figure 4.4: sheriffs' departments are more likely to be involved in county court and jail operations and to perform certain services such as search and rescue. Local police departments, for their part, are more likely to perform traffic-related functions than are sheriffs' departments.

The County Coroner.   Another elected official on the county level is the **coroner,** or medical examiner. Duties vary from county to county, but the coroner has a general mandate to investigate "all sudden, unexplained, unnatural, or suspicious deaths" reported to the office. The coroner is ultimately responsible for determining the cause of death in these cases. Coroners also perform autopsies and assist other law enforcement agencies in homicide investigations.[27] In certain rare circumstances, such as when the sheriff is arrested or otherwise forced to leave his or her post, the coroner becomes the leading law enforcement officer of the county.

State Police and Highway Patrols

The most visible state law enforcement agency is the state police or highway patrol agency. Historically, state police agencies were created for four reasons:

1. To assist local police agencies, which often did not have adequate resources or training to handle their law enforcement tasks.
2. To investigate criminal activities that crossed jurisdictional boundaries (such as when bank robbers committed a crime in one county and then fled to another part of the state).
3. To provide law enforcement in rural and other areas that did not have local or county police agencies.
4. To break strikes and control labor movements.

The first statewide police organization was the Texas Rangers. When this organization was initially created in 1835, the Rangers' primary purpose was to

CORONER
The medical examiner of a county, usually elected by popular vote.

patrol the border with Mexico as scouts for the Republic of Texas Army. The Rangers evolved into a more general-purpose law enforcement agency, and in 1874 they were commissioned as police officers and given law enforcement duties. The Arizona Rangers (created in 1901) and the New Mexico Mounted Police (1905) were formed in a similar manner.

The first state to operate a modern state police force was Pennsylvania, which established the Pennsylvania State Police (PSP) in 1905. The PSP was formed specifically as a response to the Great Anthracite Coal Strike of 1902.

Within twenty years, state police forces were common, though their jurisdiction was limited by public mistrust. For the most part, the state police were the private tool of the governor to use when local police were unable, or unwilling, to perform a certain task, such as violently breaking labor strikes (as in Pennsylvania).

The Difference between the State Police and Highway Patrols. Today, there are twenty-three state police agencies and twenty-six highway patrols in the United States. State police agencies have statewide jurisdiction and are authorized to perform a wide variety of law enforcement tasks. Thus, they provide the same services as city or county police departments and are limited only by the boundaries of the state. Such full-service state police agencies exist in Virginia, Michigan, Texas, New Mexico, Louisiana, Oregon, New York, Kentucky, Pennsylvania, and Rhode Island.

In contrast, highway patrols have limited authority. They are limited either by their jurisdiction or by the specific types of offenses they have the authority to control. As their name suggests, most highway patrols concentrate primarily on regulating traffic; specifically, they enforce traffic laws and investigate traffic accidents. Furthermore, they usually limit their activity to patrolling state and federal highways. States such as Florida, Georgia, Ohio, Nevada, and North Carolina have highway patrols.

Limited-Purpose Law Enforcement Agencies. Even with the agencies just discussed, a number of states have found that certain law enforcement areas need more specific attention. As a result, a wide variety of limited-purpose law enforcement agencies have sprung up in the fifty states. For example, most states have an alcoholic beverage control commission (ABC), or a similarly named organization, which monitors the sale and distribution of alcoholic beverages. The ABC monitors alcohol distributors to assure that all taxes are paid on the beverages and is responsible for revoking or suspending the liquor licenses of establishments that have broken relevant laws.

Many states have fish and game warden organizations that enforce all laws relating to hunting and fishing. Motor vehicle compliance (MVC) agencies monitor interstate carriers or trucks to make sure that they are in compliance with state and federal laws. MVC officers generally operate the weigh stations that are commonly found on interstate highways. Other limited-purpose law enforcement agencies deal with white-collar and computer crime, regulate nursing homes, and provide training to local police departments.

Federal Law Enforcement Agencies

Statistically, employees of federal agencies do not make up a large part of the nation's law enforcement force. In fact, the New York City Police Department has nearly half as many employees as all of the federal law enforcement agencies combined.[28] The influence of these federal agencies, however, is substantial. Unlike local police departments, which must deal with all forms of crime, federal agencies have been authorized, usually by Congress, to enforce specific laws or attend to specific situations. The U.S. Coast Guard, for example, patrols the nation's waterways, while U.S. Postal Inspectors investigate and prosecute crimes

Video Profile of Keith Ray, National Park Services Ranger

perpetrated through the use of the U.S. mails. In response to the terrorist attacks of September 11, 2001, the Federal Aviation Administration has resurrected a program that places law enforcement agents on passenger aircraft.

The federal government maintains about fifty agencies that play a role in law enforcement. (See Figure 4.5 for a list of federal law enforcement agencies.) We will address the most important ones here, grouping them according to the federal department or bureau to which they report.

The Department of Justice.   The U.S. Department of Justice, created in 1870, is the primary federal law enforcement agency in the country. With the responsibility of enforcing criminal law and supervising the federal prisons, the Justice Department plays a leading role in the American criminal justice system. To carry out its responsibilities to prevent and control crime, the department has a number of law enforcement agencies, including the Federal Bureau of Investigation, the federal Drug Enforcement Administration, the U.S. Marshals Service, and the Immigration and Naturalization Service.

The Federal Bureau of Investigation (FBI).   Initially created in 1908 as the Bureau of Investigation, this agency was renamed the **Federal Bureau of Investigation (FBI)** in 1935. One of the primary investigative agencies of the federal government, the FBI has jurisdiction over nearly two hundred federal crimes, including sabotage, espionage (spying), kidnapping, extortion, interstate transportation of stolen property, bank robbery, interstate gambling, and civil rights violations. Note that the FBI is not considered a "national" police force. In general, law enforcement is seen as the responsibility of state and local governments. There is no doubt, however, that the agency plays a crucial role in today's law enforcement landscape. With its network of agents across the country and the globe, the FBI is uniquely positioned to combat worldwide criminal activity such as terrorism and drug trafficking. Furthermore, in times of national emergency the FBI is the primary arm of federal law enforcement. Within hours after suicide airline hijackers caused more than 3,000 deaths in New York, Washington, D.C., and Pennsylvania on September 11, 2001, more than 7,000 FBI employees in 57 different countries had begun an intense search for those responsible.

Today, the FBI has more than 25,000 employees and an annual budget of over $3 billion. The agency has five investigative priorities: (1) terrorism, (2) organized crime, (3) foreign intelligence operations in the United States, (4) federal drug offenses, and (5) white-collar crime.[29] The agency also offers valuable assistance

FEDERAL BUREAU OF INVESTIGATION (FBI)
The branch of the Department of Justice responsible for investigating violations of federal law. The bureau also collects national crime statistics and provides training and other forms of aid to local law enforcement agencies.

INFOTRAC®
COLLEGE EDITION
Keyword: FBI

FIGURE 4.5
Federal Law Enforcement Agencies

A number of federal agencies employ law enforcement officers who are authorized to carry firearms and make arrests. The most prominent ones are under the control of either the U.S. Department of Justice or the U.S. Department of the Treasury.

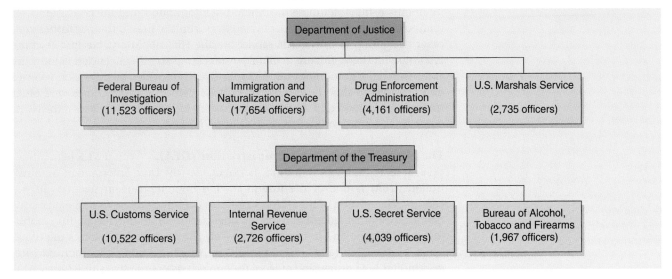

Source: Bureau of Justice Statistics, *Federal Law Enforcement Officers—2000* (Washington, D.C.: U.S. Department of Justice, July 2001), Table 1, page 2.

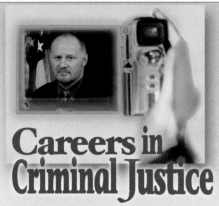

Careers in Criminal Justice

Growing up in a small town in rural West Virginia, I always knew that I wanted to be an FBI agent. There were probably a lot of other kids in America who shared this dream, but the murder of a woman who at one time was my baby-sitter convinced me to do everything that I could to make my dream of becoming a law enforcement officer come true.

I received a B.S. in biology from John Marshall University in West Virginia and subsequently earned a master's degree in biochemistry from there as well. During college, I worked at several part-time jobs, loading trucks and bagging groceries, and also served in the Coast Guard as a reservist.

Following college, I went to work for the West Virginia State Police (WVSP) as a forensic toxicologist, a job that prepared me well for my current position with the FBI. These four years were well spent, because it was an interesting and challenging job and

Jim Rice

Federal Bureau of Investigation (FBI) Supervisory Special Agent

also because the FBI seeks to attract candidates who are competitive and who bring a specialty or work experience to the job.

I joined the FBI as a Special Agent in 1988 and spent the first sixteen weeks of my Bureau career at the FBI Academy in Quantico, Virginia, as do all new agents. The FBI Academy is similar to a small college campus, with classrooms, dormitories, a cafeteria, and a gymnasium, with hundreds of students in residence at any given time, including new agents, experienced agents who are back for a week or two of specialized training, and police officers from all over the country and the world.

Following graduation from the FBI Academy, agents are subject to transfer to one of the fifty-six field offices in the United States for their first assignment. I was sent to the Indianapolis (Indiana) office, where I was assigned to a "reactive squad," which handled violent criminal violations, such as bank robberies, fugitives, kidnappings, and extortions.

A rotational transfer brought me to the Washington, D.C., field office in 1992, where I joined the SWAT team

and worked on a "Safe Streets Gang Task Force" and then on a Cold Case Homicide Squad. Soon thereafter, a Joint Terrorism Task Force was formed to address domestic terrorism matters in the nation's capital, an area filled with symbolic targets for would-be terroristic activities.

I volunteered to be part of this task force in late 1992 and was promoted to the position of Supervisory Special Agent of the squad in 1998. My duties include the operational and emergency response to incidents of domestic terrorism; bombings and bomb threats; chemical, biological, and nuclear incidents; and the security for special events, such as presidential inaugurations and the fiftieth anniversary celebration of NATO, which brought dozens of heads of state to Washington in 1999, without incident.

Go to the *Careers in Criminal Justice Interactive CD* **for more profiles in the field of criminal justice.**

to local and state law enforcement agencies. The FBI's Identification Division maintains a huge database of fingerprint information and offers assistance in finding missing persons and identifying the victims of fires, airplane crashes, and other disfiguring disasters. The services of the FBI Laboratory, the largest crime laboratory in the world, are available at no charge to other agencies. Finally, the FBI's National Crime Information Center (NCIC) provides lists of stolen vehicles and firearms, missing license plates, vehicles used to commit crimes, and other information to local and state law enforcement officers who may access the NCIC database. (See the feature *Careers in Criminal Justice.*)

The Drug Enforcement Administration (DEA).　With a $1.5 billion budget and more than four thousand special agents, the Drug Enforcement Administration (DEA) is one of the fastest-growing law enforcement agencies in the country. The mission of the DEA is to enforce domestic drug laws and regulations and to assist other federal and foreign agencies in combating illegal drug manufacture and trade on an international level. The agency also enforces the provisions of the Controlled Substances Act, which controls the manufacture, distribution, and dispensing of legal drugs, such as prescription drugs.

The federal government has had a role in policing the manufacture and sale of illicit drugs since 1914. The first federal drug agency, the Federal Bureau of Narcotics (FBN), was established in 1930 under President Herbert Hoover. The FBN's main priorities were cocaine and opiates such as heroin. As the level of illegal drug use expanded over the decades, and international trafficking became an increasingly pressing problem, several more agencies were formed to deal with drug enforcement. Then, in 1970 Congress passed the comprehensive Drug Abuse Prevention and Control Act,[30] which gave Congress the authority to regulate interstate commerce of legal drugs. With the Bureau of Narcotics and Dangerous Drugs (a successor to the FBN), the U.S. Customs Service, the FBI, and hundreds of state and local law enforcement agencies all working to enforce drug laws—as well as the government's new responsibility with regard to legal drugs—it was evident that a new "superagency" was needed. In 1973, by order of President Richard Nixon, the DEA was formed.

The U.S. Marshals Service.   The oldest federal law enforcement agency is the U.S. Marshals Service. In 1789, President George Washington assigned thirteen U.S. Marshals to protect his attorney general. That same year, Congress created the office of the U.S. Marshals and Deputy Marshals. Originally, the U.S. Marshals acted as the main law enforcement officers in the western territories. Following the Civil War, when most of these territories had become states, these agents were assigned to work for the U.S. district courts, where federal crimes are tried. The relationship between the U.S. Marshals Service and the federal courts continues today and forms the basis for the officers' main duties, which include:

1. Providing security at federal courts for judges, jurors, and other courtroom participants.
2. Controlling property that has been ordered seized by federal courts.
3. Protecting government witnesses who place themselves in danger by testifying against the targets of federal criminal investigations. This protection is sometimes accomplished by relocating the witnesses and providing them with different identities.
4. Transporting federal prisoners to detention institutions.
5. Investigating violations of federal fugitive laws.[31]

The Immigration and Naturalization Service (INS).   The Immigration and Naturalization Service (INS) monitors and polices the flow of immigrants into the United States. Agents of the INS patrol the borders of the continental United States and American territories to ensure that immigrants do not enter the country illegally. They also apprehend and deport aliens who have not complied with U.S. naturalization laws that would allow them to live within American borders.

The INS's role in national security was questioned with regard to the terrorist attack of September 11, 2001, when it became clear that several of the hijackers had entered the country illegally via the United States' border with Canada. This border is often referred to as "soft" because it does not receive the attention or the funding provided to policing our southern border with Mexico. In recent years, the large number of illegal immigrants and huge amounts of illicit drugs entering the United States across its borders with Mexico and with Canada have become a pressing concern. As a result, the U.S. Border Patrol has seen its budget rise to over $4.2 billion, a nearly 200 percent increase since 1993. Furthermore, the number of border patrol agents doubled to 7,000 during the same time period, with plans to add an additional 1,000 agents each year until 2008. The results have been dramatic—agents arrested a record 1.6 million illegal aliens in 2000. Though the number of United States–Mexico border arrests dropped by nearly a quarter in the first half of 2001, few observers believe this signifies a

INFOTRAC®
COLLEGE EDITION
Keyword: DEA

Video Profile of Tom Riley, Special Agent in Charge, U.S. Fish & Wildlife Service

Video Profile of Joycelyn Barnes, Special Agent Recruiter

Video Profile of Irene Holth, Deportation Officer, INS

On the Web

The Del Rio Sector of the United States Border Patrol is responsible for controlling 205 miles of the Rio Grande, the natural border between the United States and Mexico. For a link to this Web site, go to the Hypercontents page for this chapter at http://www.cj.wadsworth.com/ gainescore2e.

Border patrol agents frisk illegal aliens captured in Nogales, Arizona. Starting in 1994, Operation Gatekeeper increased the number of border patrol agents in the southwestern United States from 800 to 2,300, resulting in a dramatic increase in the number of illegal aliens captured and returned to Mexico. The increase in agents also appears to have led to an increase in violent confrontations between agents and aliens. In four separate incidents in October 1998, border agents opened fire on rock-throwing illegal aliens. Two Mexicans were killed in the exchanges, and several agents were badly injured. Do you believe society benefits from efforts to keep illegal aliens out of the country? Is the use of force to carry out these efforts justifiable? (Paul Conklin/ PhotoEdit)

trend.[32] According to estimates, at least 800,000 immigrants enter the United States illegally each year in the Tucson (Arizona) area alone.[33]

The Department of the Treasury.

The Department of the Treasury, formed in 1789, is mainly responsible for all financial matters of the federal government. It pays all the federal government's bills, borrows money, collects taxes, mints coins, and prints paper currency. The department also has several law enforcement agencies, including the Bureau of Alcohol, Tobacco and Firearms, the U.S. Secret Service, the Internal Revenue Service, and the Customs Service.

The Bureau of Alcohol, Tobacco and Firearms (ATF).

As its name suggests, the Bureau of Alcohol, Tobacco and Firearms (ATF) is primarily concerned with the illegal sale, possession, and use of firearms and the control of untaxed tobacco and liquor products. The Firearms Division of the agency has the responsibility of enforcing the Gun Control Act of 1968, which sets the circumstances under which firearms may be sold and used in this country. The bureau also regulates all gun trade between the United States and foreign countries and collects taxes on all firearm importers, manufacturers, and dealers. In keeping with these duties, the ATF is also responsible for policing the illegal use and possession of explosives. Furthermore, the ATF is charged with enforcing federal wagering laws.

Because it has jurisdiction over such a wide variety of crimes, especially those involving firearms and explosives, the ATF is a constant presence in federal criminal investigations. Since 1982, for example, the agency has been working in conjunction with the FBI to prevent the bombing of abortion clinics. Recently, the agency, along with the FBI, has begun to place undercover informants inside antiabortion groups to gain information about proposed bombings. Furthermore, the ATF has been active in forming multijurisdictional drug task forces with other federal and local law enforcement agencies to investigate drug crimes involving firearms.

The U.S. Secret Service.

When initially created in 1865, the Secret Service was primarily responsible for combating currency counterfeiters. In 1901, the agency was given the added responsibility of protecting the president of the United States, the president's family, the vice president, the president-elect, and ex-presidents. These duties have remained the cornerstone of the agency, with several expansions. After a number of threats against presidential candidates in the 1960s and early 1970s, including the shootings of Robert Kennedy and Governor George Wallace of Alabama, in 1976 Secret Service agents became responsible for protecting those political figures as well.

In addition to its special plainclothes agents, the agency also directs two uniformed groups of law enforcement officers. The Secret Service Uniformed Division protects the grounds of the White House and its inhabitants, and the Treasury Police Force polices the Treasury Building in Washington, D.C. This responsibility includes investigating threats against presidents and those running for presidential office.

To aid its battle against counterfeiters and forgers of government bonds, the agency has the use of a laboratory at the Bureau of Engraving and Printing in the nation's capital.

The Internal Revenue Service (IRS). The largest bureau of the Treasury Department, the Internal Revenue Service (IRS), is concerned with violations of tax laws and regulations. The bureau has three divisions, only one of which is involved in criminal investigations. The examination branch of the IRS audits the tax returns of corporations and individuals. The collection division attempts to collect taxes from corporations or citizens who have failed to pay the taxes they owe. Finally, the criminal investigation division investigates cases of tax evasion and tax fraud. Criminal investigation agents can make arrests. The IRS has long played a role in policing criminal activities such as gambling and selling drugs for one simple reason: those who engage in such activities almost never report any illegally gained income on their tax returns. Therefore, the IRS is able to apprehend them for tax evasion. The most famous instance of this took place in the 1920s, when the IRS finally arrested crime boss Al Capone—responsible for numerous violent crimes—for not paying his taxes.

President George W. Bush promotes the Department of Homeland Security, a large federal agency designed to protect the United States against terrorist attacks that was formed in November 2002. Considering that the United States already has a federal crime-fighting agency—the FBI—why might a Department of Homeland Security be necessary? (AP Photo/Ron Edmonds)

The U.S. Customs Service. The U.S. Customs Service stations agents at ports of entry and exit to the United States to police the flow of people and goods into and out of the country. A primary goal of the bureau is to prevent the smuggling of contraband (anything that is unlawful to produce or possess). Customs agents have widespread authority to investigate and search all international passengers, including those arriving on airplanes, ships, or other forms of transportation. Furthermore, the Customs Service is responsible for ensuring that proper tariffs and taxes have been paid on all goods imported into the United States. As efforts to stop the international flow of illicit drugs have become a higher priority, customs agents are increasingly working in tandem with the federal Drug Enforcement Administration.

Department of Homeland Security. In the wake of the terrorist attacks of September 11, 2001, the federal law enforcement community came under scrutiny for failing to foresee the strikes. The FBI in particular was singled out for severe disapproval. Critics said that the agency failed to properly analyze the large

The day after the September 11, 2001, terrorist attacks, extra private security guards patrol the front entrance to the Three Mile Island nuclear power plant near Middletown, Pennsylvania. In the wake of the attacks, American corporations rushed to hire extra security, placing a strain on the industry. "We're swamped with people who have concerns," said an executive at Global Options, a Washington, D.C.–based security firm. "[Businesspeople] are frightened, perplexed." What are the positive consequences of a sharp increase in private security in the United States? Are there any possible negative consequences? (AP Photo/Paul Vathis)

amount of information it received on possible terrorist activity in the United States. Even when FBI agents did come across "clues," superiors often ignored their reports. On July 10, for example, barely two months before the attacks, an FBI field agent in Phoenix, Arizona, sent a memo to headquarters warning that certain groups could be sending terrorists to flight schools to train them as pilots.[34] The memo was shelved. "The FBI is the greatest in the world in investigating a crime after it happened," said one former agency official, "but is not equipped to prevent crimes."[35]

In an effort to prevent the crime of terrorism, during the fall of 2002 President George W. Bush signed a bill creating a new federal crime-fighting agency, called the Department of Homeland Security. The department will combine twenty-two existing federal agencies, including the Customs Service, the Secret Service, the INS, and the Coast Guard, and will have an annual budget of almost $40 billion.[36] The FBI will not be part of this new department, but may be required to turn over any information on domestic terrorist activities to one of its bureaus.

Private Security

Even with the increasing numbers of local, state, and federal law enforcement officers, the police do not have the ability to prevent every crime. Recognizing this, many businesses and citizens have decided to hire private security. The results of such a decision can be striking. In the mid–1990s, residents in a six-block section of Georgetown, an upper-class neighborhood in Washington, D.C., were concerned over rising rates of auto theft. They hired a security guard from the Wells Fargo Company to patrol the area at a cost of 44 cents per household per day. After a year, burglaries had decreased by 55 percent and robberies by 50 percent. The security guard even thwarted a kidnapping attempt. Soon after, 90 percent of the entire Georgetown neighborhood was being policed by security guards.[37] This anecdote hints at the massive increase in the use of **private security** in the United States over the past three decades.

A Growing Industry. Allan Pinkerton, a Scottish immigrant, started the first private security company in the United States in 1860. Today, Pinkerton, Inc., is part of the Swedish firm Securitas. It is just one of nearly 60,000 private security firms in the country.[38] In 1970, the ratio of private security officers to police officers paid by the government was 1.4 to 1. As Figure 4.6 shows, the discrepancy has continued to grow since then. From 1964 to 1991, employment by private security firms increased by nearly 750 percent, and the number of firms offering such services grew by 543 percent.[39] Today, there are three times as many private police as public, and Americans are spending $90 billion a year on private security, compared to $40 billion in taxes for public police.[40] In California, even though the crime rate is at its lowest level in more than thirty years, the number of private security guards grew 22 percent from 1996 to 2000.[41]

This increase in private security can be traced to several social and economic trends. The Hallcrest Report II, a far-reaching overview of private security trends funded by the National Institute of Justice, identifies four main factors in the growth of the industry:

1 An increase in fear on the part of the public triggered by the growing rate of crime, either real or perceived.

PRIVATE SECURITY
The practice of private corporations or individuals offering services traditionally performed by police officers.

2 The problem of crime in the workplace.

3 Budget cuts in states and municipalities that have forced reductions in the number of public police, which raises the demand for private ones.

4 A rising awareness of private security products (such as home burglar alarms) and services as cost-effective protective measures.[42]

William Cunningham, the author of the report, does not believe that the growth of private security is a "put-down" of the police. Instead, he says, "people are taking a greater stake in protecting themselves" rather than relying on public services.

Authority of Private Police. Partly because of the speed at which the industry has grown, consensus has yet to be reached on the restrictions that should be placed on private security employees. Some courts have ruled that these personnel are not held to the same rules of action that govern public police in the use of force, interrogation, and other issues of law. Other courts have found that private police are bound by the same laws as their public counterparts because people perceive them as having the same legal authority.[43] The situation is further complicated by the fact that many members of local and state police forces **moonlight** as private security guards; that is, they work private security details during "off hours" to earn extra income.

THE RESPONSIBILITIES OF THE POLICE

Some observers, including police executives, believe that giving an increased role to private security employees—allowing them to respond to burglar alarms, for example, or handle misdemeanor reports—would free up police officers to deal with "more important" duties.[44] For the most part, the incidents that make up a police officer's daily routine would not make it onto television dramas such as *Law and Order.* Besides catching criminals, police spend a great deal of time on such mundane tasks as responding to noise complaints, confiscating firecrackers, and poring over paperwork. Thirty years ago, sociologist Egon Bittner warned against the tendency to see the police primarily as agents of law enforcement and crime control. A more inclusive accounting of "what the police do," Bittner believed, would recognize that they provide "situationally justified force in society."[45] In other words, the function of the police is to solve any problem that may *possibly,* though not *necessarily,* require the use of force. (For a discussion of one social and criminal problem that confronts law enforcement agents, see the chapter–ending feature *Criminal Justice in Action—The Police and Domestic Violence.*)

Within Bittner's rather broad definition of "what the police do," we can pinpoint four basic responsibilities of the police:

1 To enforce laws.

2 To provide services.

3 To prevent crime.

4 To preserve the peace.

As will become evident over the next three chapters, there is a great deal of debate among legal and other scholars and law enforcement officers over which responsibilities deserve the most police attention and what methods should be employed by the police in meeting those responsibilities.

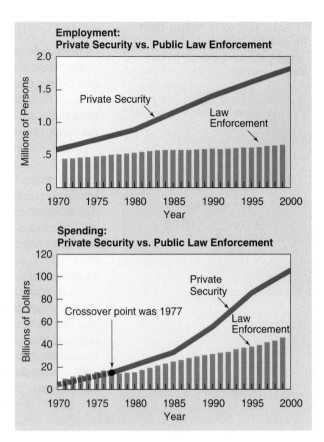

FIGURE 4.6
The Rise of Private Security in the United States

Source: Adapted from William C. Cunningham, John J. Strauchs, and Clifford W. Van Meter, *Private Security Trends, 1970–2000: The Hallcrest Report II* (Boston: Butterworth-Heinemann, 1990), 237–239; plus authors' update.

MOONLIGHTING
The pract ice of a police officer holding a second job in the private security field.

"That's the only thing that made me feel safe last night when I came home from work."

—Penny Baily, *resident of Indianapolis,* commenting on the police car patrolling her neighborhood (1996)

Enforcing Laws

In the public mind, the primary role of the police is to enforce society's laws—hence, the term *law enforcement officer.* In their role as "crime fighters," police officers have a clear mandate to seek out and apprehend those who have violated the law. The crime-fighting responsibility is so dominant that all police activity—from the purchase of new automobiles to a plan to hire more minority officers—must often be justified in terms of its law enforcement value.[46]

Police officers also primarily see themselves as crime fighters, or "crook catchers," a perception that often leads people into what they believe will be an exciting career in law enforcement. Although the job certainly offers challenges unlike any other, police officers do not normally spend the majority of their time in law enforcement duties. Several studies from the 1970s suggested that police officers spent a very small percentage of their workday on law enforcement matters. Both Thomas Bercal, who examined police calls in St. Louis and Detroit, and John A. Webster, who made a similar study on a wider basis, estimated that only 16 percent of those calls were related to law enforcement.[47]

More recently, police experts have come to the conclusion that these early studies of police activities were flawed in several ways, not the least of which was that they tended to focus only on general patrol officers while discounting criminal investigation units or special response units, which have heavier law enforcement duties. In 1991, Jack Greene and Carl Klockars revisited questions of police workload in Wilmington, Delaware, with the goal of improving on the earlier research.[48] Using a more methodical set of data, they found that police officers spend about half of their time enforcing the law or dealing with crimes.

Providing Services

If Greene and Klockars are correct, what are police officers doing the other half of working hours? The emphasis on crime fighting and law enforcement tends to overshadow the fact that a great deal of a police officer's time is spent providing services for the community. The motto "To Serve and Protect" has been adopted by thousands of local police departments, and the *Law Enforcement Code of Ethics* recognizes the duty "to serve the community" in its first sentence.[49] The services that police provide are numerous—a partial list would include directing traffic, performing emergency medical procedures, counseling those involved in domestic disputes, providing directions to tourists, and finding lost children. Along with firefighters, police officers are among the first public servants to arrive at disaster scenes to conduct search and rescue operations. This particular duty adds considerably to the dangers faced by law enforcement agents (discussed in more detail in Chapter 7). When the World Trade Center collapsed in September 2001 following the terrorist attack, for example, more than sixty New York City police officers lost their lives. As mentioned earlier, many police departments have adopted the strategy of community policing, and as a consequence, many officers find themselves providing assistance in areas that have not until recently been their domain.[50] For example, police are required to deal with the problems of the homeless and the mentally ill to a greater extent than in past decades.

Preventing Crime

Perhaps the most controversial responsibility of the police is to prevent crime. According to Jerome Skolnick of the University of California at Berkeley, there are two predictable public responses when crime rates begin to rise in a community. The first is to punish convicted criminals with stricter laws and more severe penalties. The second is to demand that the police "do something" to prevent crimes from occurring in the first place. Is it, in fact, possible for the police to

Pasadena, California police officers honor their New York City Police Department counterparts who lost their lives in the September 11 terrorist attacks. More than sixty NYPD officers were killed in their attempts to save World Trade Center tenants.
(AP Photo/Damian Dovarganes)

"prevent" crimes? The strongest response that Professor Skolnick is willing to give to this question is "maybe."[51]

On a limited basis, police can certainly prevent some crimes. If a rapist is dissuaded from attacking a solitary woman because a patrol car is cruising the area, then that police officer behind the wheel has prevented a crime. In general, however, the deterrent effects of police presence are unclear. Carl Klockars has written that the "war on crime" is a war that the police cannot win because they cannot control the factors—such as unemployment, poverty, immorality, inequality, political change, and lack of educational opportunities—that lead to criminal behavior in the first place.[52] As we shall see in the next chapter, many police stations have adopted the idea of community policing in an attempt to better prevent crime.

Preserving the Peace

To a certain extent, the fourth responsibility of the police, that of preserving the peace, is related to preventing crime. Police have the legal authority to use the power of arrest, or even force, in situations in which no crime has yet occurred, but might occur in the immediate future.

In the words of James Q. Wilson, the police's peacekeeping role (which Wilson believes is the most important role of law enforcement officers) often takes on a pattern of simply "handling the situation."[53] For example, when police officers arrive on the scene of a loud late-night house party, they may feel the need to disperse the party and even arrest some of the party goers for disorderly conduct. By their actions, the officers have lessened the chances of serious and violent crimes taking place later in the evening. The same principle is often used when dealing with domestic disputes, which, if escalated, can lead to homicide. Such situations are in need of, to use Wilson's terminology again, "fixing up," and police can use the power of arrest, or threat, or coercion, or sympathy, to do just that.

The basis of Wilson and George Kelling's "broken windows" theory is similar: street disorder—such as public drunkenness, urination, and loitering—signals to both law-abiding citizens and criminals that the law is not being enforced and therefore leads to more violent crime. Hence, if police preserve the peace and "crack down" on the minor crimes that make up street disorder, they will in fact be preventing serious crimes that would otherwise occur in the future.[54]

Criminal Justice in ACTION
The Police and Domestic Violence

When police officers use their judgment in deciding which offenses to punish and which to ignore, they are said to be using *discretion*. One factor that often influences police discretion is the relationship between the person committing the criminal act and the victim. The closer this relationship, the less likely many police officers are to respond to the victim's complaints and arrest the wrongdoer.[55] This tendency is often evident in police action (or lack thereof) concerning *domestic violence*. The statistics surrounding this crime speak volumes regarding the extent of the problem in the United States. An estimated three to four million American women are battered—subjected to physical, emotional, or sexual force—by their partners every year.[56] According to research cited by Congress, domestic violence is the leading cause of injury for women between the ages of fifteen and forty-four in the United States.[57] Nearly one-third of all female murder victims in the United States are killed by current or former husbands or boyfriends.[58] For most of this nation's history, the police role in domestic violence was limited to "calming" the situation, a short-term response that did little to prevent future violence. Today, as we shall see in this feature, more is expected.

THE PROBLEM: LACK OF POLICE INVOLVEMENT IN "FAMILY MATTERS"

As we will discuss in more detail in Chapter 6, police have a great deal of discretion in deciding whether to make an arrest. Basically, if a police officer has good reason (known as "probable cause") to believe that a person has committed a crime or is about to commit a crime, that officer can arrest the suspect.

Historically, police officers have been hesitant to make arrests when the dispute involves a "family matter," even when faced with strong evidence that domestic violence has taken place. This hesitancy has been obvious in studies such as the one conducted by James J. Fyfe of Temple University, David Klinger of the University of Houston, and Jeanne Flavin of Fordham University with regard to the Chester (Pennsylvania) Police Department.[59] The researchers found that Chester police were less likely to arrest male felony assailants who had attacked former or present female partners than other males who had committed similarly violent acts against strangers. Among the cases that did not lead to arrests were 4 attacks on domestic partners with guns, 38 attacks involving cutting instruments (including one with an ax), and 27 attacks with blunt instruments such as baseball bats or hammers. In one incident that did not result in arrest, a woman was held by her feet over a second-floor landing and dropped on her head.

A number of factors have been considered to explain this leniency. Many police officers see domestic violence cases as the responsibility of social service providers, not law enforcement officers. Furthermore, officers are often uncomfortable with the intensely private nature of domestic disputes.[60] Finally, even when a police officer does arrest the abuser, the victim often chooses to drop the charges.

THE RESPONSE: MANDATORY ARREST LAWS

Whatever the reasons for this reluctance to arrest domestic abusers, many jurisdictions have responded by severely limiting police discretion in domestic violence cases.[61] Today, twenty-three states and the District of Columbia have

Women in Charlotte, North Carolina, take part in a silent march to mark the start of Domestic Violence Awareness Week. Pressure from activist citizens played a large role in the passage of state mandatory arrest laws for those who commit domestic violence. (AP Photo/*The Charlotte Observer,* Patrick Schneider)

passed *mandatory arrest laws.*[62] Under these laws, a police officer *must* arrest a person who has battered a spouse or domestic partner. No discretion is involved.

Several early studies encouraged the passage of these laws. In the landmark Minneapolis Domestic Violence Experiment of 1983, the Minneapolis Police Department and Professors Lawrence Sherman and Richard Berk attempted to determine the consequences of police inaction in domestic violence cases. The researchers found that the most effective deterrent to repeat incidents of battering was the arrest of the batterer.[63] A similar project in Duluth, Minnesota, had similar results, with rates of rearrest of domestic abusers dropping to levels as low as 16 percent seven to twelve months after the initial arrest.[64]

The theory behind mandatory arrest laws is relatively straightforward: they act as a deterrent to criminal behavior. Costs are imposed on a person who is arrested. He or she must go to court and face the possibility of time in jail. Arrest may also lead to humiliation, loss of job, and separation from family and friends. To avoid these unpleasant consequences, the argument goes, potential abusers will not act in a manner that increases the risk that they will be arrested.

QUESTIONING MANDATORY ARRESTS

Despite the popularity of mandatory arrest statutes, not all of the evidence supports limiting police discretion in this manner. The National Institute of Justice commissioned studies in six other cities to verify the findings of the Minneapolis experiment. In only one of the sites—Miami, Florida—were researchers able to match the Minneapolis results.[65]

More troubling are recent findings by Professor Sherman that led him to conclude that "mandatory arrests in domestic violence cases may cause more violence against women in the long run."[66] After completing a research project in Milwaukee, Wisconsin, Sherman found that while arrest deterred employed men from committing domestic violence, being arrested increased repeat violence by 44 percent in unemployed men.[67] Thus, it seems that only those who have "more to lose" by being arrested (such as their jobs, standing in the community, and so on) are likely to be deterred by arrest. As Sherman noted, "Mandatory arrest puts us in the moral dilemma of reducing violence against women who are relatively well off [living with or married to an employed assailant], at the price of increasing violence against women whose abusers are unemployed."[68]

A RETURN TO DISCRETION?

Mandatory arrest statutes raise other questions. For the most part, the police rely on the victim to report incidents of domestic abuse. Under certain circumstances, the risk that the abuser will be arrested may actually keep the victim from calling the police. A victim in a low-income family might not want to lose the wages that the abuser provides. Similarly, immigrant victims might not want to run the risk that they or their abusers will be deported.[69]

Furthermore, what should the police consider evidence of abuse? In 2000, professional hockey player Patrick Roy was taken into custody under Colorado's mandatory arrest law even though he did not physically harm his wife. Instead, during an argument, he had torn a door off its hinges, and under state law destruction of property is considered a form of domestic violence.[70]

Finally, what if a victim uses force to protect himself or herself against an abuser? Statistics show that in jurisdictions with mandatory arrest laws, arrests of women under domestic abuse charges have increased dramatically. These women may be less willing to report domestic violence in the future, fearing that they themselves will be arrested again for "abusing" their attackers in self-defense.[71]

To reduce some of the harsher effects of mandatory arrest laws and resolve some of these inconsistencies, Professors Sherman and Berk favor a policy of "presumption of arrest." That is, after finding evidence of domestic violence, police should make an arrest unless there are "good, clear reasons why an arrest would be counterproductive."[72] Of course, it would be up to the police officers to determine whether these "good, clear reasons" exist, in effect returning to them the ability and the responsibility of using discretion to make the final decision.

MAKING SENSE OF POLICE DISCRETION AND DOMESTIC VIOLENCE

1 What reasons can be given to support widespread police discretion in general? What reasons can be given to limit police discretion in general?

2 Why might police officers welcome mandatory arrest laws or any other limitation on their discretionary abilities?

3 Can you think of any other reasons why a victim might *not* call the police if she or he was sure that it would result in the arrest of the abuser?

INFOTRAC®
COLLEGE EDITION

Keywords: police and
domestic violence

KEY TERMS

coroner 91

Federal Bureau of Investigation
  (FBI) 93

justice of the peace 83

moonlighting 99

patronage system 86

private security 98

professional model 86

sheriff 89

shire-reeve 83

tithing system 83

CHAPTER SUMMARY

① Tell how the patronage system affected policing. During the political era of policing (1840–1930), bribes paid by citizens and business owners often went into the coffers of the local political party. This became known as the patronage system.

② Indicate the results of the Wickersham Commission. The Wickersham Commission of 1929 called for reform to eliminate police brutality and the corrupting influence of politics. The result was the professionalization of American police, sometimes called the progressive era in American policing. Potential police officers began to be trained in institutes of higher learning. Another result was the increased use of technology in police work.

③ List five main types of law enforcement agencies. (a) Municipal police departments (the largest and most active); (b) sheriffs' departments; (c) special police agencies, such as those limited to school protection or airport security; (d) state police departments (in all states except Hawaii); and (e) federal law enforcement agencies.

④ List some of the most important federal law enforcement agencies. (a) Department of Justice—FBI, Drug Enforcement Administration, U.S. Marshals Service, and Immigration and Naturalization Service; (b) Department of Treasury—Bureau of Alcohol, Tobacco and Firearms, U.S. Secret Service, Internal Revenue Service, and U.S. Customs Service; and (c) Department of Homeland Security.

⑤ Identify the five investigative priorities of the FBI. (a) Terrorism, (b) organized crime, (c) foreign intelligence operations in the United States, (d) federal drug offenses, and (e) white-collar crime.

⑥ Analyze the importance of private security today. Private security officers outnumber public police officers by a ratio of 3 to 1. Heightened fear of crime and increased crime in the workplace have led to the growth in spending on private security.

⑦ List the four basic responsibilities of the police. (a) To enforce laws, (b) to provide services, (c) to prevent crime, and (d) to preserve the peace.

⑧ Explain how some states have reacted to perceived leniency to perpetrators of domestic violence. Some states have passed mandatory arrest laws, requiring a police officer to arrest a person who has battered a spouse or domestic partner. Such laws eliminate police officers' discretion.

QUESTIONS FOR CRITICAL ANALYSIS

① Increased professionalism in police forces has been made possible by two-way radios, telephones, and automobiles. In what way has society not benefited from this increased professionalism? Explain your answer.

② The latest era in policing has been called the community era and dates from the 1980s. How does this "new" era differ from the era of professionalism?

③ To what extent are state police complementary to, rather than substitutes for, local law enforcement agencies?

④ Besides the FBI's five principal investigative priorities, how does that agency benefit local policing units?

⑤ In many neighborhoods, residents have banded together to pay for and hire private security services. What problems arise under this system?

⑥ Which of the four basic responsibilities of the police do you think is most important? Why?

SELECTED PRINT AND ELECTRONIC RESOURCES

SUGGESTED READINGS

Douglas, John E., *Guide to Careers in the FBI,* Princeton: Kaplan, 1998. The author argues that the FBI is more selective than Harvard University. He provides tips on how to overcome the odds if you would like to become an FBI agent. He outlines the skills, volunteer experiences, and personal attributes, as well as the academic fields, that are most highly valued by FBI recruiters. He takes you through the step-by-step application process.

Hutton, Donald B., and Anna Mydiarz, *Guide to Law Enforcement Careers,* Huappuage, NY: Barrons Educational Publishing, 2001. This useful guide lists hundreds of different jobs at the local, state, and federal levels, as well as in the military and special law enforcement agencies. Numerous helpful Web sites are also listed.

MacDonald, Peter, *From the Cop Shop,* North York, Ontario: Stoddart Publishing, 1997. This relatively light reading gives you some insights into what law enforcement personnel do around the world. Police officers from Australia, Canada, England, France, India, and the United States talk about their craziest experiences.

MEDIA RESOURCES

Die Hard **(1988)** This highly popular action movie starring Bruce Willis as John McClane spawned a series of films. McClane is a New York City policeman on his way back to Los Angeles to reconcile with his wife, Holly, played by Bonnie Bedelia. When he goes to visit her, the building in which she works is taken over by a group of apparent terrorists led by a character played by Alan Rickman. When viewing this movie, focus on the interaction among the various law enforcement agencies.

Critically analyze this film:

1. List the different law enforcement agencies represented by the various characters in this movie.
2. What are the problems faced by the "beat" policeman in this movie, played by Reginald VelJohnson?
3. How is the chief of police portrayed in this movie, and does his portrayal seem realistic?
4. What type of tension is exhibited between the FBI and the local Los Angeles Police Department?
5. How do the screenwriter and director portray the FBI agents?
6. What type of negotiating skills do these agents have?

LOGGING ON

Go to http://cj.wadsworth.com/gainescore2e, **and click Hypercontents.** There, you will find URLs for the organizations in the following list:

- The Web site of the **Federal Bureau of Investigation (FBI)** offers a mountain of information about this very visible crime-fighting agency, including information about careers in federal law enforcement.

- Go to the **Drug Enforcement Administration** Web site for career information.

- The **U.S. Marshals Service,** the oldest law enforcement agency in the United States, operates a Web site as well.

USING THE INTERNET FOR CRIMINAL JUSTICE ANALYSIS

INFOTRAC®
COLLEGE EDITION

1. Access your InfoTrac account at:
http://www.infoTrac.college.com/wadsworth/
Once you are at the InfoTrac College Edition, type in the words **"police forces."** Read the article out of the *Readers' Companion to American History*. Now answer the following questions:

a. List the three ways American police have always been different from the police of other Western nations.

b. When were African Americans first employed as police in America?

c. How did Allan Pinkerton become well known?

2. See Internet Activities 4.1 and 4.2 on the companion Web site for *CJ in Action: The Core*. To get to the activities, go to **http://www.cj.wadsworth.com/gainescore2e**, select the appropriate chapter from the drop down list, then click Internet Activities on the left navigation bar.

NOTES

1. Amy Worden and Hans Chen, "Seizing Elian: Lawmen Call It Good, Bad, Ugly," *APBNews.Com* (April 24, 2000).

2. *Ibid.*

3. "Disturbances in Miami after Elian Handed Over to Father," *Inter Press Service* (April 22, 2000).

4. *Ibid.*

5. Jerome H. Skolnick and James J. Fyfe, *Above the Law: Police and the Excessive Use of Force* (New York: Free Press, 1993), 69.

6. M. K. Nalla and G. R. Newman, "Is White Collar Crime Policing, Policing?" *Policing and Society* 3 (1994), 304.

7. Richard Maxwell Brown, "Vigilante Policing," in *Thinking about Police*, Carl Klockars and Stephen Mastrofski, eds. (New York: McGraw-Hill, 1990), 66.

8. Peter K. Manning, *Police Work* (Cambridge, MA: MIT Press, 1977), 82.

9. Carol S. Steiker, "Second Thoughts about First Principles," *Harvard Law Review* 107 (1994), 820.

10. Lawrence M. Friedman, *Crime and Punishment in American History* (New York: Basic Books, 1993), 29.

11. Mark H. Moore and George L. Kelling, "'To Serve and Protect': Learning from Police History," *Public Interest* 70 (1983), 53.

12. Samuel Walker, *The Police in America: An Introduction* (New York: McGraw-Hill, 1983), 7.

13. Moore and Kelling, 54.

14. Mark H. Haller, "Chicago Cops, 1890–1925," in *Thinking about Police*, Carl Klockars and Stephen Mastrofski, eds. (New York: McGraw-Hill, 1990), 90.

15. William J. Bopp and Donald O. Shultz, *A Short History of American Law Enforcement* (Springfield, IL: Charles C Thomas, 1977), 109–10.

16. Roger G. Dunham and Geoffrey P. Alpert, *Critical Issues in Policing: Contemporary Issues* (Prospect Heights, IL: Waveland Press, 1989).

17. National Advisory Commission on Civil Disorders, *Report* (Washington, D.C.: U.S. Government Printing Office, 1968), 157–60.

18. 18 U.S.C.A. Sections 2510–2521.

19. Jayne Seagrave, "Defining Community Policing," *American Journal of Police* 1 (1996), 1–22.

20. John Moritz, "Many Agencies Cooperate in Manhunt for Escapees," *Fort Worth Star-Telegram* (December 27, 2000), 7.

21. Federal Bureau of Investigation, *Crime in the United States, 2001* (Washington, D.C.: Government Printing Office, 2002), 316.

22. *Ibid.*

23. G. Robert Blakey, "Federal Criminal Law," *Hastings Law Journal* 46 (April 1995), 1175.

24. Vern L. Folley, *American Law Enforcement* (Boston: Allyn & Bacon, 1980), 228.

25. Bureau of Justice Statistics, *Sheriffs' Departments 1997* (Washington, D.C.: U.S. Department of Justice, 2000), 2.

26. *Ibid.*, 10–11.

27. *Black's Law Dictionary*, 982.

28. Bureau of Justice Statistics, *Federal Law Enforcement Officers, 2000* (Washington, D.C.: U.S. Department of Justice, January 2001), 1.

29. "Feds Have a Plan if Terrorists Strike," *UPI Online* (February 19, 1998).

30. Pub. L. No. 91-513, 84 Stat. 1242 (1970), codified as amended at 21 U.S.C. Section 801 (1994).

31. http://www.usdoj.gov/marshals/factsheets/general.htm.

32. Ken Ellingwood, "Arrests of Illegal Migrants Plunge," *Los Angeles Times* (April 4, 2001), A3.

33. "One Agent's Night," *Economist* (September 12, 1998), 33.

34. David Johnston and Don Van Natta, Jr., "Wary of Risk, Slow to Adapt, F.B.I. Stumbles in Terror War," *New York Times* (June 2, 2002), 24.

35. *Ibid.*, 25.

36. Stephen Dinan, "House Approves Last Security Changes," *Washington Times* (November 23, 2002), A2.

37. Tucker Carlson, "Safety Inc.," *Policy Review* (Summer 1995), 72–73.

38. *Ibid.*, 67.

39. Bruce L. Benson, *Privatization in Criminal Justice* (Oakland, CA: Independent Institute, 1996), 1.

40. "Welcome to the New World of Private Security," *Economist* (April 19, 1997).

41. Teri Sforza, "Firm's Private Canine Patrols," *Orange County Register* (April 3, 2000), B1.

42. William C. Cunningham, John J. Strauchs, and Clifford W. Van Meter, *The Hallcrest Report II: Private Security Trends, 1970 to the Year 2000* (Boston: Butterworth-Heinemann, 1990), 236.

43. *People v. Zelinski*, 594 P.2d 1000 (1979).

44. Norman R. Bottom, Jr., "Privatization: Lessons of the Hallcrest Report," *Law Enforcement News* (June 23, 1986), 13.

45. Egon Bittner, *The Functions of the Police in a Modern Society*, Public Health Service Publication No. 2059 (Chevy Chase, MD: National Institute of Mental Health, 1970), 38–44.

46. Carl Klockars, "The Rhetoric of Community Policing," in *Community Policing: Rhetoric and Reality*, ed. Jack Greene and Stephen Mastrofski (New York: Praeger Publishers, 1991), 244.

47. Thomas Bercal, "Calls for Police Assistance," *American Behavioral Scientist* 13 (1970), 681–91; John A. Webster, "Police Task and Time Study," *Journal of Criminal Law, Criminology, and Police Science* 61 (1970), 94–100.

48. Jack R. Greene and Carl B. Klockars, "What Do Police Do?" in *Thinking about Police*, 2d ed., Carl B. Klockars and Stephen B. Mastrofski, eds. (New York: MacGraw-Hill, 1991), 273–84.

49. Reprinted in *Police Chief* (January 1990), 18.

50. Eric J. Scott, *Calls for Service: Citizen Demand and Initial Police Response* (Washington, D.C.:

U.S. Government Printing Office, 1981), 28–30.

51. Jerome H. Skolnick, "Police: The New Professionals," *New Society* (September 5, 1986), 9–11.

52. Klockars, 250.

53. James Q. Wilson, *Varieties of Police Behavior: The Management of Law and Order in Eight Communities* (Cambridge, MA: Harvard University Press, 1968).

54. James Q. Wilson and George L. Kelling, "Broken Windows," *Atlantic Monthly* (March 1982), 29.

55. Stephen D. Mastrofski, Jeffrey B. Snipes, Roger B. Parks, and Christopher D. Maxwell, "The Helping Hand of the Law: Police Control of Citizens on Request," *Criminology* 38 (May 2000), 307.

56. Georgia Pabst, "Slayings Underscore Domestic Violence's Toll," *Milwaukee Journal-Sentinel* (March 4, 1998), 4.

57. Violent Crime Control and Law Enforcement Act of 1994, H.R. Conf. Rep. No. 103-711, p. 391 (1994).

58. Ronet Bachman and Linda E. Saltzman, "Violence against Women: Estimates from the Redesigned Survey," in *Bureau of Justice Statistics Special Report: National Crime Victimization Survey* (Washington, D.C.: Office of Justice Programs, 1995), 4.

59. James J. Fyfe, David A. Klinger, and Jeanne M. Flavin, "Differential Police Treatment of Male-on-Female Spousal Violence," *Criminology* 35 (August 1997), 455–73.

60. L. Craig Parker, Robert D. Meier, and Lynn Hunt Monahan, *Interpersonal Psychology for Criminal Justice* (St. Paul, MN: West Publishing Co., 1989), 113.

61. Douglas R. Marvin, "The Dynamics of Domestic Abuse," *FBI Law Enforcement Bulletin* (July 1997), 13–19.

62. Machaela M. Hoctor, "Domestic Violence as a Crime against the State: The Need for Mandatory Arrest in California," *California Law Review* 85 (May 1997), 643.

63. Lawrence W. Sherman and Ellen G. Cohn, "The Impact of Research on Legal Policy: The Minneapolis Domestic Violence Experiment," *Law and Society Review* 23 (1989), 261.

64. Ellen Pence, "The Duluth Domestic Abuse Intervention Project," *Hamline Law Review* 6 (1983), 258.

65. J. David Hirschel and Ira W. Hutchison, "Realities and Implications of the Charlotte Spousal Abuse Experiment," in *Do Arrests and Restraining Orders Work?* ed. Eve S. Buzawa and Carl G. Buzawa (Thousand Oaks, CA: Sage Publications, 1996), 54–55.

66. Franklyn W. Dunford et al., "The Role of Arrest in Domestic Assault: The Omaha Police Experiment," *Criminology* 28 (1990), 167.

67. *Ibid.*

68. Quoted in Roger Worthington, "Value of Mandatory Arrest for Women Beaters Questioned," *Chicago Tribune* (November 19, 1991), C5.

69. Donna Coker, "Shifting Power for Battered Women: Law, Material Resources, and Poor Women of Color," *University of California at Davis Law Review* (Summer 2000), 1042.

70. John Ingold, "Law May Hinge on Roy Motion," *Denver Post* (December 23, 2000), B1.

71. Cecelia M. Expenoza, "No Relief for the Weary: VAWA Relief Denied for Battered Immigrants," *Marquette Law Review* 83 (1999), 163.

72. Lawrence W. Sherman and Richard A. Berk, "The Specific Deterrence Effects of Arrest for Domestic Assault," *American Society Review* 49 (1984), 270.

CHAPTER 5
POLICING: ORGANIZATION AND STRATEGIES

Chapter Objectives

After reading this chapter, you should be able to:

❶ Explain the difference between arrest rates and clearance rates.

❷ List the three primary purposes of police patrol.

❸ Identify the different types of patrol.

❹ Describe the steps that an investigator must take after a crime occurs.

❺ Indicate some investigation strategies that are considered aggressive.

❻ Explain community policing and its strategies.

❼ Indicate the five principles of problem-solving policing.

INTRODUCTION
Calling for Help at Columbine

Just before noon on April 20, 1999, Patti Nielson, a teacher at Columbine High School in Littleton, Colorado, made a frantic call to Jefferson County 911. She was trapped in the school library and had been wounded by glass shards after a student named Eric Harris had shattered a door with a shotgun blast. "He's outside this hall!" Nielson told the dispatcher, speaking of Harris. "He's outside the door!" she added, before being interrupted by the sound of gunfire. "Oh my God," Nielson continued, "that was really close!"[1]

Nielson was one of hundreds of Littleton residents, both inside and outside the school, who used 911 to report the destruction being wrought by Harris and fellow student Dylan Klebold. Almost seventy dispatchers worked the local 911 lines for more than twenty-four hours following the first reports of shooting.[2] One dispatcher began asking all callers, "Jefferson County 911, are you reporting the incident at Columbine High School?"[3] That an entire community reacted in such a similar manner is not necessarily surprising. The reflex to call 911 in emergencies is so deeply ingrained in our national consciousness that Americans have been socialized to "call the cops" at the first sign of trouble.[4]

Rapid response to 911 calls was indeed a benchmark of police reform in the period from the 1960s to the 1980s.[5] The system is far from infallible, however. Miscommunication between personnel who answer 911 calls and law enforcement officers can occur. At Columbine, for example, where twelve students and one teacher were killed, the heavy volume of calls caused a great deal of confusion, and contributed to the failure of law enforcement agents to enter the school until more than an hour after the first gunshots. Furthermore, 911 systems are being clogged by crank calls and summonses from citizens who do not understand that the service is for emergencies only. Some cities, such as Baltimore, Maryland, are implementing 311 systems to divert noncritical calls.[6] Others, such as Dayton, Ohio, are making misuse of 911 a misdemeanor, subject to a $100 fine and, after multiple infractions, jail time.[7]

Many observers are critical of the reliance on 911 for theoretical, as well as practical, reasons. Focusing on calls for service reflects a reactive rather than proactive philosophy of policing. In this chapter, we will examine a range of police strategies and discuss how the latest generation of police reformers is trying to temper professionalism with some values from the nation's law enforcement past. The chapter opens with an overview of how police departments are organized to best implement their strategies for enforcing the law and preventing crime.

Charles Haneca answers 911 calls in Minneapolis, Minnesota. (AP Photo/Damian Dovarganes)

Go to the Stories from the Street feature at http://www.cj. wadsworth.com/gainescore2e to hear Larry Gaines tell insightful stories related to this chapter and his experiences in the field.

POLICE ORGANIZATION

Each police department is organized according to its environment: the size of its jurisdiction, the type of crimes it must deal with, and the demographics of the population it must police. A police department in a racially diverse city often faces different challenges than a department in a homogeneous one. Geographic location also influences police organization. The make-up of the police department in Miami, Florida, for example, is partially determined by the fact that the city is a gateway for illegal drugs from Central and South America. The department directs a high percentage of its resources to special drug-fighting units and has formed cooperative partnerships with federal agencies such as the Federal Bureau of Investigation and the U.S. Customs Service in an effort to stop the flow of narcotics and weapons into the South Florida area.

The ultimate goal for any police department is to reach its maximum efficiency—to provide the best service to the community with limited resources such as staff and budget. Although some police departments are experimenting with alternative structures based on a partnership between management and the officers in the field,[8] most continue to rely on the hierarchical structure described below.

The Structure of the Police Department

FIGURE 5.1

The Command Chain of the Lombard (Illinois) Police Department

The Lombard (Illinois) Police Department is made up of seventy-three sworn law enforcement officers and thirty-three civilians. As you can see, the chain of command runs from the chief of police down to crossing guards and part-time secretaries.

One of the goals of the police reformers, especially beginning in the 1950s, was to lessen the corrupting influence of politicians. The result was a move toward a militaristic organization of police.[9] As you can see in Figure 5.1, a typical police department is based on a chain of command that leads from the police chief down through the various levels of the department. In this formalized structure, all persons are aware of their place in the chain and of their duties and responsibilities within the organization.

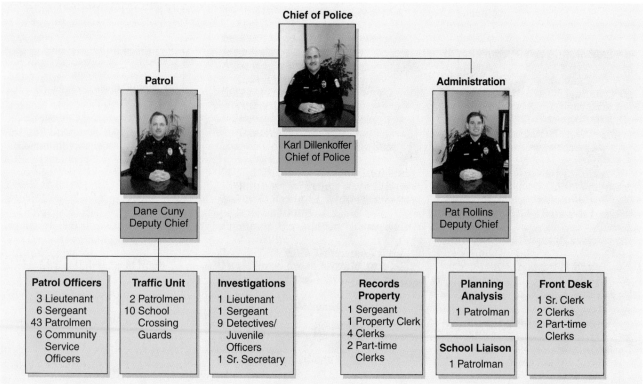

Source: Lombard Police Department.

"HOT" CALLS FOR SERVICE—IMMEDIATE RESPONSE

Complaint to 911 Officer	Rationale
"I just got home from work, and I can see someone in my bedroom through the window."	Possibility that the intruder is committing a crime.
"My husband has a baseball bat, and he says he's going to kill me."	Crime in progress.
"A woman in a green jacket just grabbed my purse and ran away."	Chances of catching the suspect are increased with immediate action.

"COLD" CALLS FOR SERVICE—ALTERNATIVE RESPONSE

Complaint to 911 Officer	Rationale
"I got to my office about two hours ago, but I just noticed that the fax machine was stolen at some point during the night."	The crime occurred at least two hours earlier.
"The guy in the apartment above me has been selling pot to his hippy friends for years, and I'm sick and tired of it."	Not an emergency situation.
"My husband came home late two nights ago with a black eye, and I finally got him to admit that he didn't run into a doorknob. Larry Smith smacked him."	Past crime with a known suspect who is unlikely to flee.

Source: Adapted from John S. Dempsey, *An Introduction to Policing*, 2d ed. (Belmont, CA: West/Wadsworth Company, 1999), Table 8.1, page 175.

FIGURE 5.3

Putting the Theory of Differential Response into Action

Differential response strategies are based on a simple concept: treat emergencies like emergencies and nonemergencies like nonemergencies. As you see, calls for service that involve "hot crimes" will be dealt with immediately, while those that report "cold crimes" will be dealt with at some point in the future.

Again, practice does not necessarily follow theory. As we saw in Chapter 2, the amount of crime is not a function of arrest rates; self-reported surveys show that many, if not most, criminal acts do not lead to arrests. To make a generalization, police will never be able to make an arrest for *every* crime that is committed. Observers have offered other, more specific reasons for a possible disconnect between arrest rates and crime rates. One explanation is that, given the amount of paperwork each arrest forces on a police officer, more arrests mean less time for crime prevention.[13] Perhaps arrest rates and crime rates would prove more consistent if all arrests were made for serious crimes. But, as we have discussed, this is not the case. Most arrests are for misdemeanors, not felonies. Furthermore, arrests are poor predictors of incarceration: one study found that nearly sixty times more Americans are arrested than are sent to prison each year.[14]

Perhaps a more meaningful indicator of the job a police force is doing is the *clearance rate,* or the percentage of crimes solved over any given time. This measurement allows statisticians to differentiate among types of crime. The clearance rates for violent crimes, in which the victims tend to know their assailants, are generally much higher (around 45 percent) than those for burglaries (around 17 percent), which generally are committed by strangers.[15] Low clearance rates for a certain type of crime, as compared to national averages or past performance, can indicate that police response to that crime is lacking.

Citizen Satisfaction. An additional measure of police effectiveness, which has only recently been recognized, is *citizen satisfaction.* As we saw in Chapter 1, fear of crime continues to exist even though violent crime rates have dropped over the past decade. Part of the reason for

Fairfax County, Virginia, police officers search a manhole near the site of the ninth sniper attack in a series of murders that terrorized the Washington, D.C., area in the fall of 2002. Law enforcement officers enlisted the aid of the U.S. Army's RC-7 Airborne Reconnaissance Low as part of their efforts to protect the community. This high-tech surveillance plane was expected to cut police response time to ninety seconds in sniper shootings, down from three and a half minutes. Why would it be so important for police to reach a crime scene quickly? (AP Photo/Alan Diaz)

this may be found in public attitudes toward the police. A poll found that one out of every two Americans had little or no confidence that the police would protect them from violent crime.[16] Many police administrators believe that this trend can be reversed if departments begin to treat citizens as "customers" who pay for the services provided by law enforcement agencies.[17]

As all businesspersons know, the customers are the most important people in any service industry (which includes police work), and the greater the effort to listen to customers' concerns, the greater their levels of satisfaction will be. In analyzing the results of a foot patrol experiment in Flint, Michigan, in which the police department made a concerted effort to forge bonds with citizens, Robert Trojanowicz of Michigan State University found a significant increase in citizen satisfaction.[18] A number of observers believe that the strategy of increasing police presence in the community, which we will discuss later in the chapter under the heading "Community Policing," is a crucial step toward improving citizen satisfaction with police performance.

In sum, it is difficult to measure the effectiveness of the police. Even crime rates are at least partially determined by elements beyond police control, such as the sociological, biological, and psychological factors discussed in Chapter 2. Hence, crime rates cannot be relied on as definitive indicators of the job a police department is doing.

POLICE ON PATROL: THE BACKBONE OF THE DEPARTMENT

One of the great ironies of the police organization is that the people lowest on the hierarchical "stepladder"—the patrol officers—are considered the most valuable members of the force. (Many patrol officers, considering their pay and work hours, would call the situation unjust, not ironic.) As many as two-thirds of the *sworn officers,* or those officers authorized to make arrests and use force, in some large police departments are patrol officers, and every department has a patrol unit.

"Life on the street" is not easy. Patrol officers must be able to handle any number of difficult situations, and experience is often the best, and, despite training programs, the only, teacher. As one patrol officer commented:

> You never stop learning. You never get your street degree. The person who says . . . they've learned it all is the person that's going to wind up dead or in a very compromising position. They've closed their minds.[19]

It may take a patrol officer years to learn when a gang is "false flagging" (trying to trick rival gang members into the open) or what to look for in a suspect's eyes to sense if he or she is concealing a weapon. This learning process is the backdrop to a number of different general functions that a patrol officer must perform on a daily basis.

The Purpose of Patrol

As was noted in Chapter 4, patrol officers do not spend a great deal of time chasing, catching, and handcuffing suspected criminals. The vast majority of patrol shifts are completed without a single arrest.[20] An influential study of Kansas City patrol operations—which will be discussed in detail later in this chapter—found that 60 percent of a patrol officer's time was uncommitted;[21] that is, officers spend a great deal of time meeting with other officers, taking breaks, and patrolling with the goal of preventing crime in general rather than any specific crime or criminal activity. This does not mean that the image of the patrol officer as a crime fighter is altogether incorrect. Instead, the study suggests that the activities of the patrol officer are more varied than most would expect.

On the Web

The Los Angeles Police Department, Dallas Police Department, and New York Police Department broadcast radio reports from patrol officers live on the Web. For a link to a site at which you can listen to these reports, go to the Hypercontents page for this chapter at http://www.cj.wadsworth.com/ gainescore2e.

As Samuel Walker noted, the basic purposes of the police patrol have changed very little since 1829, when Sir Robert Peel founded the modern police department. These purposes include:

1 The deterrence of crime by maintaining a visible police presence.

2 The maintenance of public order and a sense of security in the community.

3 The twenty-four-hour provision of services that are not crime related.[22]

The first two goals—deterring crime and keeping order—are generally accepted as legitimate police functions. The third, however, has been more controversial.

We saw in the last chapter that the provision of services unrelated to crime was a hallmark of police activity in the political era of policing and was discouraged in the professional era. The community era has seen a resurgence of the patrol officer as a provider of community services, many of which have little to do with crime. The extent to which noncrime incidents dominate patrol officers' time is evident in the Police Services Study, a survey of 26,000 calls to police in sixty different neighborhoods. The study found that only one out of every five calls involved the report of criminal activity.[23] (See Figure 5.4.)

There is some debate over whether community services should be allowed to dominate patrol officers' duties. The question, however, remains: If the police do not handle these problems, who will? Few cities have the financial resources to hire public servants to deal specifically with, for example, finding shelter for homeless persons. Furthermore, the police are the only public servants on call twenty-four hours a day, seven days a week, making them uniquely accessible to citizen needs.

Police officers spend a great deal of time performing community services such as visiting classrooms and interacting with students. Do you think that the time police officers dedicate to community services is time well spent, or should they concentrate on fighting and preventing crime? (Paul Conklin/PhotoEdit)

Patrol Activities

To recap, the purposes of police patrols are to prevent and deter crime and also to provide social services. How can the police best accomplish these goals? Of course, each department has its own methods and strategies, but William Gay, Theodore Schell, and Stephen Schack are able to divide routine patrol activity into four general categories:

| **NONSERIOUS CRIME CALLS** | |
Description of Violation	Percentage of Total Calls for Service
Assistance (missing persons, traffic accident, damaged property, etc.)	9.8
Public disorder (drunk, disorderly, begging, prostitution, etc.)	11.1
Nonviolent disputes	41.7
Minor violations (shoplifting, trespassing, traffic/parking offense, refusal to pay, etc.)	4.5

| **SERIOUS CRIME CALLS** | |
Description of Violation	Percentage of Total Calls for Service
Assaults (using violence against a person, kidnapping, child abuse, injured person, etc.)	26
Serious theft (motor vehicle theft, burglary, purse snatching, etc.)	5.1
General disorder (illicit drugs, fleeing police, leaving the scene of an accident, etc.)	1.8

Source: Stephen D. Mastrofski, Jeffrey B. Snipes, Roger B. Parks, and Christopher D. Maxwell, "The Helping Hand of the Law: Police Control of Citizens on Request," *Criminology* 38 (May 2000), Table 5, page 328.

FIGURE 5.4
Calls for Service

Over a period of two years, the Project on Policing Neighborhoods gathered information on calls for service in Indianapolis, Indiana, and St. Petersburg, Florida. As you can see, the largest portion of these calls involved disputes where no violence or threat of violence existed.

1 *Preventive patrol.* By maintaining a presence in a community, either in a car or on foot, patrol officers attempt to prevent crime from occurring. This strategy, which O. W. Wilson called "omnipresence," was a cornerstone of policing philosophy and still takes up roughly 40 percent of patrol time.

2 *Calls for service.* Patrol officers spend nearly a quarter of their time responding to 911 calls for emergency service or other citizen problems and complaints.

3 *Administrative duties.* Paperwork takes up nearly 20 percent of patrol time.

4 *Officer-initiated activities.* Incidents in which the patrol officer initiates contact with citizens, such as stopping motorists and pedestrians and questioning them, account for 15 percent of patrol time.[24]

The estimates made by Gay, Schell, and Schack are not universally accepted. Professor of law enforcement Gary W. Cordner argues that administrative duties account for the largest percentage of patrol officers' time and that when these officers are not consumed with paperwork and meetings, they are either answering calls for service (which takes up 67 percent of the officers' time on the street) or initiating activities themselves (the remaining 33 percent).[25]

Indeed, there are dozens of academic studies that purport to answer the question of how patrol officers spend their days and nights. Perhaps it is only fair, then, to give a police officer the chance to describe the duties patrol officers perform. In the words of Anthony Bouza, a former police chief:

> [Patrol officers] hurry from call to call, bound to their crackling radios, which offer no relief—especially on summer weekend nights. . . . The cops jump from crisis to crisis, rarely having time to do more than tamp one down sufficiently and leave for the next. Gaps of boredom and inactivity fill the interims, although there aren't many of these in the hot months. Periods of boredom get increasingly longer as the nights wear on and the weather gets colder.[26]

Bouza paints a picture of a routine beat as filled with "noise, booze, violence, drugs, illness, blaring TVs, and human misery." This may describe the situation in high-crime neighborhoods, but it certainly does not represent the reality for the majority of patrol officers in the United States. Duties that all patrol officers have in common, whether they work in Bouza's rather nightmarish city streets or in the quieter environment of rural America, include controlling traffic, conducting preliminary investigations, making arrests, and patrolling public events.

Controlling Traffic.   Enforcing traffic laws is a critical function of patrol officers. More than three times as many people lose their lives to traffic accidents than to criminal activity each year, and many more are injured in such accidents than as a result of criminal assaults.[27] Police can lessen the danger to drivers and pedestrians by facilitating an orderly flow of traffic. Patrol officers are also called on to manage and investigate the circumstances of accidents, as well as to educate citizens on automobile and bicycle safety.

Preliminary Investigations.   Because patrol officers are on duty and available for quick response, they are usually the first law enforcement officers to respond to a call for service and to reach the scene of a crime. In this capacity, their initial responsibility is to provide first aid for the victims of the crime, if there are any. Then, the crime scene must be made safe by eliminating hazards and arresting any suspects who are still in the area. After taking these steps, the officers will normally secure the crime scene by blocking it off and then will interview witnesses and victims. In smaller departments, the patrol officer may continue the investigation, but in larger ones, that task, along with the fruits of the patrol officer's initial investigations, is turned over to a detective.

Making Arrests. Making an arrest is the most dangerous duty of the patrol officer. Luckily, for most officers, an arrest is a relatively rare occurrence. According to Egon Bittner, patrol officers average about one arrest per month.[28] Furthermore, the majority of arrests do not involve violent crimes such as murder, rape, robbery, and aggravated assault. More than 15 million arrests for criminal violations (excluding traffic violations) take place in the United States each year. Eleven million of those arrests concern quality-of-life and public order crimes such as:

- Driving while intoxicated (DWI) or driving under the influence (DUI).
- Drug abuse violations.
- Liquor law violations, public drunkenness, and disorderly conduct.
- Misdemeanor assaults.
- Vagrancy and loitering.[29]

These arrests, though not as "flashy" as those for more violent crimes, are an important part of the patrol officer's duty as a civil servant. The power to make an arrest is a patrol officer's primary mode of law enforcement and crime control. Patrol officers are not, however, given a free rein to place citizens under the control of the state. The law heavily regulates patrol officers' actions before, during, and after arrests. At the same time, officers have a great deal of discretion in whether to make arrests and how to conduct themselves during the process. The legal aspects of arrests will be discussed in Chapter 6 and police discretion in Chapter 7.

Patrolling Public Events. Uniformed police officers are a deterrent to disruptive behavior. Thus, patrol officers are often called to be present at sporting events, concerts, political rallies, and parades.

Methods of Patrol

Police administrators often give officers specific assignments such as patrolling high-crime areas or writing traffic citations at an intersection where a large number of accidents occur. These activities are considered forms of **directed patrol.** Such patrols are specifically designed to deal with crimes that commonly occur in certain locations and under circumstances that provide police with opportunity for preparation. In Chicago, for example, police noted a pattern of taxi holdups that took place in a single neighborhood. Officers began disguising themselves as taxi drivers in the area and were soon able to apprehend the robber. Because of their proactive nature, these police actions are also sometimes known as *aggressive patrols.*

Most police work, in contrast, is done on **general patrol,** during which officers make the rounds of a specific area with the purpose of carrying out the various patrol functions. In a sense, general patrol is random because the officers spend a substantial amount of their shift hoping to notice any crimes that may be occurring. General patrol takes place when officers are not responding to calls for service. Some observers have compared a patrol officer to a scarecrow because it is hoped that the officer's presence alone will deter any would-be criminals from attempting a crime.[30]

Patrols can be conducted by a number of different methods. For example, the Los Angeles Police Department uses sixteen patrol helicopters with 30 million candlepower searchlights to detect crimes that no land-bound patrol vehicle could hope to uncover.[31] The most common methods of patrol, however, include foot, automobile, motorcycle, mounted (on horseback), bicycle, boat, and K-9 (with the aid of a dog).

DIRECTED PATROL
Patrol strategies that are designed to respond to a specific criminal activity at a specific time.

GENERAL PATROL
Patrol strategies that rely on police officers monitoring a certain area with the goal of detecting crimes in progress or preventing crime due to their presence. Also known as random or preventive patrol.

Foot Patrol.   Thanks in large measure to the theories of police reformer O. W. Wilson (discussed in Chapter 4), American police departments in big cities generally abandoned foot patrol in favor of automobiles during the middle of the twentieth century. In recent years, however, the oldest form of patrolling has made a comeback. Officers on foot are now seen as more responsive to community needs and less physically separated from citizens.[32] A study done by police scholar George L. Kelling showed that increased foot patrols in Newark, New Jersey, while having no impact on crime rates, did succeed in lowering citizens' fear of crime by heightening the perception of safety in the areas patrolled.[33]

Automobile Patrols.   Automobile patrols are the most common of all patrol methods. In most cases, they offer the greatest speed and flexibility. They are also the least expensive. One automobile can cover the same area as five to ten foot patrol officers. With onboard computers providing a direct link between patrol officers and criminal information databases and traffic centers, automobiles are becoming even more effective.[34] This form of patrol does have some distinct disadvantages, however; most obviously, automobiles cannot pursue suspects into certain locations such as narrow alleys or buildings. Furthermore, officers in cars are less likely than those on foot patrol to notice certain "tip-off" details, such as a broken window or an open door. Finally, as noted earlier, automobiles tend to separate the police from the public they serve.

Motorcycle Patrol.   The main advantage of a motorcycle over an automobile is maneuverability: a motorcycle can weave in and out of traffic and through alleys to a much greater degree than even a compact car. On the negative side, officers on motorcycles are more exposed than those riding in automobiles and are more likely to be injured in an accident. Furthermore, motorcycles cannot be used effectively in inclement weather such as heavy rain or snow.

Mounted Patrol.   There are approximately two hundred mounted patrol units in the United States. Many departments have found that mounted police are useful in crowd-control situations, as the horses retain their mobility even in the midst of a riot. The elevation of an officer on horseback seems to convey the presence of authority. The officers can better scan an unruly crowd from their high perch. Furthermore, mounted patrols are useful for public relations: they can help convey a "softer" image of police to citizens, especially children.[35] Despite these advantages, mounted patrol use is on the decline in the United States, mostly due to the cost of keeping the horses.

Bicycle Patrol.   Historically one of the least popular methods of patrol, at least for police officers, bicycle patrols have been gaining in popularity in recent years. As a unit, bicycle officers are the most physically fit members of any department, and they are often preferred in tourist communities that do not appreciate the severe image of police cars. Because of their mobility, bicycles are useful in areas such as beaches and

Mounted patrol offers a number of benefits. In crowd control, people faced with the impressive stature of a horse are less likely to challenge the authority of the police officer sitting on top of it. Also, because of the positive feelings many citizens have toward horses, mounted patrols present a softer, if not "lovable," image of the patrol officer. What are some of the potential drawbacks—both strategic and economic—of mounted patrols? (Spencer Grant/Photo Edit)

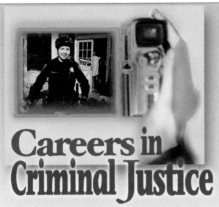

Careers in Criminal Justice

Lois Perillo,
Bicycle Community Policing Officer

I did not always want to be a police officer. I wanted to be an astronaut. So I graduated with a B.S. in aeronautics and promptly went to work as an accountant for the city of New York. Loving the Broadway theater and my Italian/Ukrainian family, yet knowing there was something more, I emptied my bank account of its $700, bought a bike rack, packed my '76 Datsun B-210 hatchback, and drove across the country to join my college roommate in San Francisco. Seventeen years later, I still live in the Bay Area, working as a police officer for fourteen of those years.

A career in law enforcement first entered my mind when I saw a recruitment poster hanging in a very bohemian San Francisco restaurant. It depicted a United Nations of women in uniform and encouraged that I join them. I did. However, the hiring process, inclusive of background checks and written, oral, physical, and polygraph testing, took two years. Concerned with my ability to scale the

six-foot wall, I talked my way into a specialized physical prep class designed for female firefighter candidates. To stay motivated, I enrolled in a pre-academy study class and I hunkered down for the wait.

In late June 1994, I received a letter from the San Francisco Police Department: my academy class was to begin in four weeks. By July, my hair was significantly shorter, and I was starching a gray rookie uniform weekly and polishing my brass and shoes daily. Those of us who could write easily were forced to do pushups, and those whose pushup style was one hand behind the back were compelled to write. After three months, my star was pinned to my navy blue wool uniform by the chief of police, and I was off to four years of midnights before falling into the daylight and community policing.

I began my career as the S.F.P.D.'s first bicycle officer by going undercover on my beat, riding a bicycle. At first we rode our personal bicycles with rubber bands around pant legs to protect ourselves from chain snags. After ten years of bicycles on the beat, we are now fully funded with departmental supplies, equipment, and uniforms.

As a bicycle community officer, I don't just lock 'em up and go to court

to testify. I am charged to be a problem solver and to stem repeat calls to dispatch. For example, after catching graffiti vandals in the act, I contracted with the teens and their parents that they remove their markings in lieu of facing arrest. I managed a crime alert system that the merchants use to share information and hopefully avert criminal activity. I helped organize the community to encourage a judge to compel a once ever-present, panhandling heroin addict to choose drug treatment over jail time. And when Headquarters called me into action, I've switched into cop-and-robber mode to chase and catch bike thieves, shoplifters, burglars, and drug dealers on my bike.

I think of myself as an old-fashioned beat officer (with the plus of my bicycle) who was fortunate enough to fall into my life's work. And while off duty, I still keep a watchful eye on the space program and the stars.

Go to the
***Careers in Criminal Justice Interactive CD* for more profiles in the field of criminal justice.**

---

parks that are inaccessible to automobiles but too vast for officers to patrol on foot. Bicycle patrols also have the advantage of being able to approach crimes in progress without making much noise. Finally, due to the speed of the bicycle, officers can more easily catch suspects who attempt to flee on foot.[36] For the most part, bicycle patrols are rendered useless in inclement weather. For that reason they are more common in warm-weather jurisdictions. (See the feature *Careers in Criminal Justice.*)

Boat Patrol.   Many departments in cities on or near large bodies of water operate boat patrols. This method of patrol is used to enforce narcotics and firearms smuggling laws and, in some areas, to combat illegal immigration. Due to the expense of maintaining the type of boats required, many coastal cities have surrendered at least part of this responsibility to the U.S. Coast Guard.

K-9 Patrol.   Dog units, or K-9 patrols, perform very specific tasks: detecting illegal narcotics, finding hidden bombs, assisting in searches for missing persons, and searching buildings and other areas for burglars and other suspects. With their powerful sense of smell, dogs are responsible for the seizure of millions of dollars' worth of narcotics and drug-contaminated currency a year. (One legendary golden retriever sniffed out $63 million worth of drugs and was responsible for the conviction of twenty drug dealers in Miami over a two-year period.[37])

Dogs can often search buildings and track down fleeing suspects more quickly and effectively than human police officers. Well-trained dogs are incredibly loyal and commonly go to great lengths to protect their handlers. When accompanying officers on foot patrol, a dog can have the double impact of giving the officers a sense of protection and intimidating any potential wrongdoers in the immediate area. As with horses, the primary drawback with K-9 patrols is cost. (To learn more about a career in canine enforcement, go to the *Careers in Criminal Justice Interactive CD* and click on the Career Rolodex.)

Preventive Patrol and the Kansas City Experiment

In theory, as has been noted, police patrol—whether it takes place on foot, in a car, on a bicycle, or with a dog—is a *preventive* measure; that is, the presence of officers on general patrol is believed to have the effect of preventing crimes before they occur. O. W. Wilson was particularly optimistic about the preventive power of automobile patrols, believing that cruising police cars would give the impression that officers could be anywhere at any time. This impression, in turn, would keep would-be criminals from committing crimes, would-be jaywalkers from jaywalking, and would-be speeders from speeding.[38]

A number of police administrators have questioned Wilson's strong belief in preventive patrolling. On a practical level, cities simply could not afford to pay the large numbers of uniformed patrol officers who would be needed to blanket a city.[39] With existing levels of police presence, criminals still could figure that the chances of a patrol officer "catching them in the act" were slight. Furthermore, preventive patrol would have little effect on crimes committed indoors or crimes of passion committed without any thought as to whether a police officer was nearby.

The Kansas City Preventive Patrol Experiment.   The suspicions of those who questioned the efficacy of preventive patrols were somewhat justified by the results of the Kansas City Preventive Patrol Experiment, conducted in 1972 and 1973. With the cooperation of the local police department, researchers chose three areas, comprised of five beats each, with similar crime statistics.[40] Over the course of one year, the police applied different patrol strategies to each designated area:

- On the *control* beats, normal preventive measures were taken, meaning that a single automobile drove the streets when not answering a call for service.

- On the *proactive* beats, the level of preventive measures was increased, with automobile patrols being doubled and tripled.

- On the *reactive* beats, preventive patrol was eliminated entirely, and patrol cars only answered calls for service.

Before, during, and after the experiments, the researchers also interviewed residents of the three designated areas to determine their opinion of police service and fear of crime.

The results of the Kansas City experiment were somewhat shocking. Researchers found that increasing or decreasing preventive police patrol had little or no impact on:

- Crime rates.
- Fear of crime.
- Public opinion on the effectiveness of police.
- Police response time.
- Traffic accidents.
- Reports of crime to the police.

Criminologists were, and continue to be, somewhat divided on how to interpret these results. For some, the Kansas City experiment and other similar data proved that patrol officers, after a certain threshold, were not effective in preventing crime, and therefore scarce law enforcement resources should be diverted to other areas. "It makes about as much sense to have police patrol routinely in cars to fight crime as it does to have firemen patrol routinely in fire trucks to fight fire," noted University of Delaware professor Carl Klockars.[41]

Others saw the experiment as proving only one conclusion in a very specific set of circumstances and were unwilling to accept the results as universal. Professor James Q. Wilson, for example, said that the study showed only that random patrols in marked automobiles were of questionable value and that it proved nothing about other types of police presence such as foot patrols or patrols in unmarked automobiles.[42]

The Lasting Effects of the Kansas City Study. Indeed, despite the Kansas City Preventive Patrol Experiment, most modern police departments continue to assign officers to random, preventive patrols. Such patrols bring local governments revenue through traffic tickets and also are believed to reassure citizens. The lasting benefit of the Kansas City study, according to researchers Robert Sheehan and Gary Cordner, seems to be that it has freed police departments from their reliance on the random patrol.[43] In light of the study, police departments realized that they could divert patrol officers from their traditional patrol duties without setting off an increase in crime. Therefore, administrators felt free to experiment with alternative strategies and tactics.

We will examine some of these more aggressive approaches—such as undercover operations and the use of informants—in the following section on police investigations.

POLICE INVESTIGATIONS: THE CRIME SCENE AND BEYOND

Investigation is the second main function of police, along with patrol. Whereas patrol is primarily preventive, investigation is reactive. After a crime has been committed and the patrol officer has gathered the preliminary information from the crime scene, the responsibility of finding "who dunnit" is delegated to the investigator, most commonly known as the **detective.** Today detectives make up about 15 percent of the personnel in the average midsized and large-city police department.[44] Detectives have not been the focus of nearly as much reform attention as their patrol counterparts, mainly because the scope of the detective's job is limited to law enforcement, with less emphasis given to social services or maintaining order.

INFOTRAC®
COLLEGE EDITION

Keywords: police and investigations

DETECTIVE
The primary police investigator of crimes.

The detective—and the work a detective does—has been romanticized to a certain degree. From Sherlock Holmes to Dirty Harry to Andy Sipowicz, the detective has been portrayed in popular culture as an antiestablishment maverick with a success rate in solving crimes close to—if not at—100 percent. There is some truth to the "maverick" characterization. Detectives, on the whole, have more room for innovation in their operations than patrol officers; their work hours are more flexible; they are not required to wear uniforms; and they are not as closely supervised.

The job is not a glamorous one, however. Detectives spend much of their time investigating common crimes such as burglaries and are more likely to be tracking down stolen property than a murderer. They must also prepare cases for trial, which involves a great deal of time-consuming paperwork. The other media-driven perception of the detective—that she or he always finds the suspect—is also somewhat exaggerated.

Even with advances in technology such as DNA identification methods, the clearance rate of murder cases has decreased dramatically over the past three decades. In 1968, police solved 86 percent of all murders.[45] By 1998, that number had dropped to 64 percent. Experts link this decline to the fact that strangers, rather than easier-to-find spouses and friends, commit proportionally more murders today than they did in the past.[46] Furthermore, a landmark Rand Corporation study estimated that more than 97 percent of cases that are "solved" can be attributed to a patrol officer making an arrest at the scene, witnesses or victims identifying the perpetrator, or detectives undertaking routine investigative procedures that could easily be performed by clerical personnel.[47] "There is no Sherlock Holmes," said one investigator. "The good detective on the street is the one who knows all the weasels and one of the weasels will tell him who did it."[48]

The Detection Function

A detective division in large police departments usually has a number of sections. These sections often include crimes against persons, such as homicide or sexual assault, and crimes against property, such as burglary and robbery. Many departments have separate detective divisions that deal exclusively with *vice,* a broad term that covers a number of public order crimes such as prostitution, gambling, and pornography. In the past, vice officers have also been primarily responsible for narcotics violations, but many departments now devote entire units to that growing social and legal problem.

The ideal case for any detective, of course, is one in which the criminal stays on the scene of the crime, has the weapon in his or her hands when apprehended, and, driven by an overriding sense of guilt, confesses immediately. Such cases are, needless to say, rare. University of Cincinnati criminal justice professor John E. Eck, in attempting to improve the understanding of the investigative process, concluded that investigators face three categories of cases:

- *Unsolvable cases,* or weak cases that cannot be solved regardless of investigative effort.
- *Solvable cases,* or cases with moderate evidence that can be solved with considerable investigative effort.
- *Already solved cases,* or cases with strong evidence that can be solved with minimum investigative effort.[49]

Eck found that the "unsolvable cases," once identified as such, should not be investigated because the effort would be wasted, and that the "already solved cases" require little additional effort or time on the part of detectives. Therefore, Eck concluded, the investigation resources of a law enforcement agency should primarily be aimed at "solvable cases." Further research by Steven G. Brandl and James Frank found that detectives had relatively high success rates in investigating burglary and robbery cases for which a moderate level of evidence was available.[50] Thus, the Rand study cited above may be somewhat misleading, in that investigators can routinely produce positive results as long as they concentrate on those cases that potentially can be solved.

The Preliminary Investigation

When police are notified of a crime, the investigation process begins. Though each investigation has its own idiosyncrasies, the steps that are taken are fairly uniform. First comes the **preliminary investigation,** which consists of the duties of the first law enforcement officer to arrive on the scene (usually a patrol officer). The initial responsibility is to attend to the well-being of the victim of the crime, if there is one. Next, the investigator must secure the crime scene.

Securing the Crime Scene. The **crime scene** is the physical area that may hold evidence that will aid in the investigation of a crime. Crime scenes contain fingerprints, bloodstains, footprints, weapons, strands of hair, and other pieces of evidence that are crucial to the investigation. The first officers to arrive at the crime scene are to protect it from being disturbed, or **contaminated,** so that these clues can be effectively collected and used to solve the case.

Gathering Information. After the scene has been secured, the investigator's next task is to gather information that may be useful as the investigation continues or in a subsequent court case. The information may also aid the investigator's memory, should it falter further along in the process. Information can be gathered in a number of ways, including taking notes and photographs. Regardless of the investigator's artistic skills, a rough sketch can also provide a useful overall picture of the crime scene. (See Figure 5.5 for a sample sketch of a crime scene.) Officers must also identify all possible witnesses. Given that a witness could at some point become a suspect, this step is crucial. Then, one by one, the victims and witnesses should be given an **interview,** or detailed questioning to determine what information each can provide concerning the case.[51]

Gathering Evidence Using Forensic Techniques. Aside from information, the crime scene is also the primary source of physical evidence. An investigator must be able to locate, store, and transport the evidence without contamination. Fingerprints—the result of sweat and grease from the pores of the skin—bloodstains, footprints, tire impressions, fiber from clothing, hair and skin samples, and weapons are the primary forms of physical evidence.

Recently, technology has greatly improved law enforcement officers' ability not only to gather physical evidence, but also to use that evidence to solve crimes. The use of scientific technology in criminal investigations is known alternatively as *forensic science* or *criminalistics.* The two terms are often used interchangeably, but they are not synonymous.

PRELIMINARY INVESTIGATION
The procedure, usually conducted by a patrol officer, that must be followed immediately on initial arrival at a crime scene. Includes securing the crime scene, interviewing witnesses and suspects, and searching the scene for evidence.

CRIME SCENE
The physical area that contains or is believed to contain evidence of a crime.

CONTAMINATED
When evidence of a crime is rendered useless because of exposure to a foreign agent or improper removal from a crime scene.

INTERVIEW
The process of questioning a suspect or witness during the preliminary and follow-up investigations.

Washington, D.C., police stand guard in Rock Creek Park where the remains of former congressional intern Chandra Levy were found on May 22, 2002. The yellow police tape is designed to keep everyone except police officers away from the crime scene to avoid contamination. What are some of the ways that the presence of civilians can ruin a crime scene for investigators? (AP Photo/Ron Edmonds)

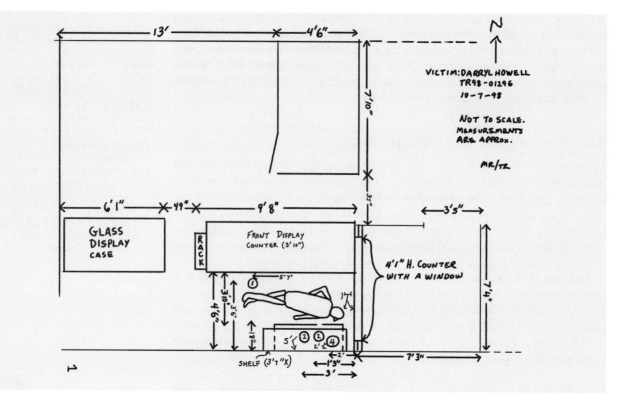

FIGURE 5.5

Sketching a Crime Scene

On October 7, 1998, four law enforcement officers entered Darryl Howell's gun shop in the small town of Taft, California. Their goal: to arrest Howell for weapons violations. The attempt ended in disaster, as Howell died with four bullet wounds; one was self-inflicted and three came from the gun of Taft Police Sergeant Ed Whiting. Whiting was eventually cleared of any wrongdoing, and Howell's death was ruled a suicide. Here, you see a police sketch of the scene of the incident.

On the Web

You can find a detailed "handbook" on the ins and outs of a crime scene investigation on the Web. For a link to the Crime Scene Investigator site, go to the Hypercontents page for this chapter at http://www.cj.wadsworth.com/gainescore2e.

FORENSICS
The application of scientific methods to finding and utilizing criminal evidence.

Source: *The Bakersfield Californian.* Photo courtesy of Kern County, CA, Sheriff's Dept.

Forensic science refers specifically to the use of science to examine, evaluate, and explain physical evidence in a court of law. Criminalistics is a branch of forensic science that deals with the collection and study of physical evidence such as fingerprints, blood, semen, hairs, clothing fibers, and firearms. To simplify matters, we will use the term *forensics* to refer to both forensic science and criminalistics.

The goal of **forensics** is to take physical evidence from the crime scene and to use that evidence either to prove that a particular person committed the crime or to clear the name of someone who did not commit the crime. (See *Criminal Justice & Technology—Putting the Finger on Unsolved Crimes.*) If, for example, forensic technicians are able to match fibers of a jacket found at the crime scene with fibers from a jacket worn by a suspect at the time of her or his arrest, then detectives have been provided with a valuable clue to use in solving the case. Most large police departments operate their own laboratories to which physical evidence can be delivered directly from the crime scene. Smaller police departments, lacking the budget to run such a facility, are usually able to use county, state, or FBI crime labs (for a price). Today, there are more than three hundred crime labs in the United States, about 80 percent of which are operated by police departments.[52] (To learn more about a career as a forensic science examiner, go to the *Careers in Criminal Justice Interactive CD* and click on the Career Rolodex.)

Many observers believe that the area of forensics with the greatest potential to change the criminal justice landscape involves DNA technology. As we will see in the *Criminal Justice in Action* feature at the end of this chapter, this technology, while inspiring hope in many, is also the focus of a great deal of controversy and consternation.

The Follow-Up Investigation

If a case is not solved—that is, if a suspect is not arrested—during the preliminary investigation, police must decide whether to pursue the matter with a **follow-up**

Criminal Justice &TECHN LOGY

Putting the Finger on Unsolved Crimes

On February 17, 1982, Janet Nickel was raped and severely beaten in Room 121 of the Classic Inn Motel in Giddings, Texas. Her assailant managed to escape, leaving behind a pair of smudgy fingerprints, one on a light bulb and another on a doorknob. The local police unsuccessfully tried to match the prints with samples from numerous suspects, and the Nickel case became one of the thousands of violent crimes that go unsolved in the United States in the average year. Thanks to a new fingerprinting technology, however, it would not go unsolved indefinitely.

The Automated Fingerprint Identification System

Thirteen years later, Joe Goodson, the Lee County sheriff who worked on the Nickel case, learned about an addition to the state's technological arsenal, known as the Automated Fingerprint Identification System (AFIS). With AFIS, fingerprints are converted to algorithms—sets of mathematical equations used in problem solving. The computer compares the algorithms with other fingerprints found at crime scenes, as well with other samples recorded and stored by other law enforcement agencies. Using this program, law enforcement agencies can search and compare millions of samples in minutes. When combined with other new technology such as Live Scan—which electronically scans fingerprints instead of using black printer's ink to make a record of the print—AFIS greatly increases the chances that fingerprints will lead to a suspect. "Fifteen years ago, I only dreamed of something like this," said one fingerprint specialist.

In the Nickel case, the old fingerprints were matched through AFIS, and the attacker, who was not considered a suspect at the time of the crime, was tried and convicted for attempted capital murder and sentenced to ninety-nine years in prison. Other states have seen similar successes:

during the first two years after installing AFIS, the Oklahoma state police resolved more than two thousand sexual assault and property crimes.

The technology received an additional boost in 2001 when the FBI launched its new Integrated Automated Fingerprint Identification System. Besides aiding the agency's own law enforcement efforts, the FBI's system dramatically increases the speed at which state and local police departments receive fingerprint identification. (To learn more about a career as a fingerprint specialist, go to the *Careers in Criminal Justice Interactive CD* and click on the Career Rolodex.)

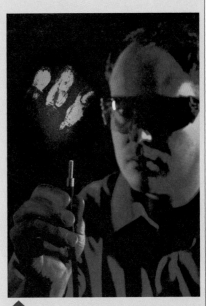

A special light designed to illuminate fingerprints is tested at Sandia National Laboratories in Livermore, California. (AP Photo/Sandia National Laboratories)

IN THE FUTURE

In several jurisdictions, law enforcement agencies are equipping patrol cars with portable devices that permit troopers to conduct on-the-spot fingerprint checks of people they have pulled over. These devices allow the officer to find out in less than thirty seconds whether the subject is listed in an FBI database as a fugitive or a missing person. Law enforcement experts predict that use of such devices will be commonplace by the end of the decade. Do note, however, that even as this technology advances, some courts are questioning its reliability, a development we cover in Chapter 9.

investigation. In most instances, the police will make a pragmatic decision about whether to continue the investigation based on a number of **solvability factors.** In violent crimes, these factors include the presence of a witness, useful physical evidence such as fingerprints, a possible suspect, and the amount of time between the criminal act and its discovery.[53] In burglary and robbery cases, the value of the stolen property often dictates whether an investigation will continue.[54] If the department decides to conduct a follow-up investigation, detectives will search for new physical evidence and reinterview witnesses.

There are three general types of follow-up investigations: (1) walk-throughs, (2) where-are-theys, and (3) whodunits.[55] Walk-throughs, comparable to Eck's "already solved cases" mentioned earlier, occur when the suspect is identified and

FOLLOW-UP INVESTIGATION
The steps taken by investigative personnel once it has been determined, based on the results of the preliminary investigation, that the crime is solvable.

SOLVABILITY FACTORS
Those factors that affect the probability that a case will be solved.

Anthony Porter celebrates his release in Chicago after spending sixteen years on death row. Porter was released when a follow-up investigation—spurred by information unearthed by a professor and five journalism students at Northwestern University—led to the taped confession of another man to the murder for which Porter was convicted. (AP Photo/Mike Fisher)

apprehended during preliminary procedures. In where-are-theys, the suspect has been identified but remains at large. Finally, the whodunits are cases for which the preliminary investigation did not produce the identification of the person responsible for the crime.

If the suspect has already been arrested, a detective's primary duty in the follow-up investigation is to provide the prosecutor with all relevant material and evidence that will be needed to show the suspect's guilt in court. In some cases, the detective will gather more evidence to give the prosecutor a stronger case.

If the identity of the suspect is not known, the follow-up investigation can take several paths. Sometimes an investigator will retrace the steps already taken by patrol officers to make sure no evidence was overlooked. He or she may attempt to locate additional witnesses by contacting everybody in the area where the crime was committed. Informants can be interviewed to determine whether they have information about the crime, and attempts can be made to trace any property—such as an automobile—that was involved in the crime. Another useful tool for detectives is the *modus operandi* file, which contains descriptions of how known criminals commit specific crimes. The detective can check to see if the circumstances surrounding the crime in question match those of any crimes described in the *modus operandi* file.

Aggressive Investigation Strategies

Detective bureaus also have the option of implementing more aggressive strategies during a follow-up investigation. For example, if detectives suspect that a person was involved in the robbery of a Mercedes-Benz parts warehouse, one of them might pose as a "fence"—or purchaser of stolen goods. In what is known as a "sting" operation, the suspect is deceived into thinking that the detective (fence) wants to buy stolen car parts; after the transaction takes place, the suspect can be arrested.

Perhaps the most dangerous and controversial operation a detective can undertake is to go *undercover,* or to assume a different identity in order to obtain information concerning illegal activities. Though each department has its own guidelines on when undercover operations are necessary, all that is generally required is the suspicion that illegal activity is taking place.[56] (As you may recall from the discussion of entrapment in Chapter 3, police officers are limited in what they can do to convince the target of an undercover operation to participate in the illegal activity.) Today, undercover officers are most commonly used to infiltrate large-scale narcotics operations or those run by organized crime.

New York detective Mary Glatzke, wearing a gray wig and the nonthreatening clothes of a civilian, sits on a park bench. By posing as a "Muggable Mary," Detective Glatzke is using herself as bait to lure would-be robbers. This sort of undercover strategy hopes to deter crime as well as catch criminals in the act. What might be some of the deterrent effects of Detective Glatzke's assignment? (Corbis/Bettmann)

A Question of Ethics: The Informant Problem

The use of informants poses a variety of ethical problems for law enforcement agents. In general, for an informant to be useful, she or he must continue her or his illegal activities. Police officers often agree to turn a blind eye to such activities as long as the informant continues to provide quality information. Furthermore, this arrangement may give the informant the impression that the police have given her or him permission to commit criminal acts.

The dangers of using informants were highlighted by the extraordinary case of Stephen Flemmi and James Bulger, two Boston-area organized crime figures who provided information to the Federal Bureau of Investigation (FBI) for more than thirty years. In return, FBI agents went to great lengths to "protect" the pair, including warning Flemmi that he was being indicted on state murder charges, allowing him to skip town and thereby avoid arrest. In another incident, agents told Flemmi and Bulger that a third FBI informant named Brian Halloran had implicated them in a murder; within a year, Halloran was killed under suspicious circumstances. The Massachusetts State Police Department went to great lengths to exclude the FBI from its investigation into organized crime in Boston, for fear that the agency would tip off Flemmi and Bulger. Indeed, at one dinner attended by Flemmi, Bulger, and several FBI agents, the two informants were told that "you can do anything you want as long as you don't 'clip' anyone."

In 2000, responding to these revelations, the U.S. Justice Department released a new set of guidelines for managing informants. Among other provisions, the guidelines stated that federal law enforcement agents do not have the authority to promise informants that they will not be prosecuted for illegal activity. Only the federal prosecuting office with jurisdiction over the criminal investigation may do so. Furthermore, agents may not withhold the identities of informants from other federal law enforcement agencies.

FOR CRITICAL ANALYSIS
For all the alleged crimes they committed while acting as informants for the FBI, Flemmi and Bulger did provide the agency with a wealth of information, leading to dozens of arrests. In light of this service, is it ethical for law enforcement agencies to tolerate some criminal activity in order to prevent other criminal activity? What restrictions would you place on the use of informants, if any?

In some cases, a detective bureau may not want to take the risk of exposing an officer to undercover work or may believe that an outsider cannot infiltrate an organized crime network. When the police need access and information, sometimes they turn to a **confidential informant (CI).** A CI is a person who is involved in criminal activity and gives information about the activity and those who engage in it to the police. The United States Supreme Court, in *Rovario v. United States* (1957),[57] held that the state has a confidential informant privilege, which means that it is not required to disclose the identity of an informant unless a court finds that such information is needed to determine the guilt or innocence of a suspect. (To learn more about some of the difficulties of this kind of investigative device, see the feature *CJ in Focus—A Question of Ethics: The Informant Problem.*)

THE GLOBALIZATION OF LAW ENFORCEMENT

Criminal investigations are not, of course, limited to American soil. As modes of international transportation and communication have improved, so has the "global" scope of crime. Take the example of Ludwig Feinberg, an American citizen living in Moscow, Russia, who arranged to sell a diesel submarine to Colombian drug runners so they could deliver illegal narcotics from Panama to the West Coast of the United States.[58] In such a scenario, law enforcement officers must obviously expand their investigative efforts beyond the nation's borders.

Jurisdiction outside the United States

As you may recall from our discussion in Chapter 3, a law enforcement agency must have jurisdiction in a certain area in order to uphold the law (make arrests,

CONFIDENTIAL INFORMANT (CI)
A human source for police who provides information concerning illegal activity in which he or she is involved.

Women in Multan, Pakistan, protest FBI activity in their country. The Pakistani government has allowed the agency to conduct raids of terrorist cells and detain suspects within its borders. Even without permission, under what theory of jurisdiction would the FBI have the right to conduct these sorts of anti-terrorism operations? (AP Photo/Khaled Tanveer)

and so on) in that area. How, then, might an American detective have jurisdiction to travel to Moscow and apprehend Ludwig Feinberg? In general, the detective would have no legal authority in Russia, just as a Russian detective would have no authority in Los Angeles. U.S. courts, however, recognize several bases for extraterritorial jurisdiction, including:

- *Territorial jurisdiction.* The idea that a nation has jurisdiction within its own borders is the fundamental basis for criminal law. U.S. courts have, in addition, held that acts done outside a jurisdiction but *intended* to produce detrimental effects within that jurisdiction are to be treated as if they were committed within national boundaries.[59] Thus, for example, the U.S. Coast Guard had jurisdiction to board a shrimping vessel carrying a load of marijuana near the Yucatan Peninsula of Mexico because the captain had maps of Alabama and Florida, and the boat was headed toward the United States.[60]

- *Nationality principle of jurisdiction.* This holds that a nation can require its citizens to follow its laws outside of its boundaries. So, when a U.S. citizen commits murder on an island in the Caribbean, he can be charged with homicide under American law.[61]

- *Universal jurisdiction.* International law recognizes that some crimes are so heinous that any country may have jurisdiction if one of its citizens is the target or the perpetrator of such a crime, or she or he has committed the crime and is afterward found within that country's boundaries.[62] In general, the United States recognizes that war crimes, crimes against humanity (such as genocide), torture, and hijacking fall under universal jurisdiction.[63]

Cooperation and Extradition

Besides these legal and theoretical bases for international jurisdiction, governments can enter into agreements providing law enforcement agents with powers outside their own borders. In 2000, for example, the FBI opened an office in Budapest, Hungary, to combat the Russian Mafia. In the aftermath of the September 11, 2001, terrorist attacks, hundreds of FBI agents were allowed to search for terrorist suspects in Pakistan and Afghanistan.

The past few years have also witnessed an increased cooperation between the U.S. and Mexican governments with regard to law enforcement. In fact, a Mexican prosecutor is working in the U.S. Justice Department, and an American prosecutor has been stationed in the Mexican attorney general's office. These cooperative efforts seem to be paying off. In 2001 alone, more than one hundred fugitives wanted in the United States were arrested in Mexico (three times the number arrested in 2000).[64] Because the two countries have an extradition treaty, many of these fugitives are sent from Mexico to the United States. **Extradition** refers to the surrender by one jurisdiction to another of a person charged with a crime. Usually, the person has been charged with a crime in the jurisdiction requesting extradition, and that jurisdiction demands his or her return to face charges.

REFOCUSING ON THE COMMUNITY

One of the centerpieces of the Violent Crime Control and Law Enforcement Act of 1994 (the Crime Bill) was a provision to place 100,000 new police officers on the streets of America by the end of the decade. The statute also established the Office of Community Oriented Policing Services (COPS) to distribute nearly $9 billion in federal grant money. On a practical level, the Crime Bill failed to live up to its promise, falling 40,000 officers short by its target date. But in the opinions of a number of law enforcement experts, the law was philosophically flawed as well. Although it did provide funding for the modern policing approaches discussed in this section, to a certain extent the Crime Bill was a throwback to an earlier era, reflecting the theory that more patrol officers and investigators will result in quicker response times and higher arrest rates, and thereby lower crime rates.

Many observers, however, question such conclusions. University of Arizona professors Michael Gottfredson and Travis Hirschi have found that the assumption that increasing the number of police will have a negative effect on crime rates is contrary to empirical research.[65] These researchers, along with many of their peers, believe that although incident-oriented policing—a reactive strategy—certainly has its place in law enforcement, more emphasis should be placed on proactive strategies that prevent rather than simply react to crime.[66] In other words, the number of police is often not as important as what those police are doing.

Over the past two decades, notions about what the police should be doing have experienced, in the words of George Kelling, a "quiet revolution."[67] This revolution has been fueled by the emergence of two theories of police strategy, now combined under the umbrella term of *community policing:* community-oriented policing and problem-oriented policing. Though conceptually different, both theories are based on the philosophy that to prevent and control crime effectively, police need to form partnerships with members of the community.

Community Policing

For all its negative associations, the political era of policing did have characteristics that many observers have come to see as advantageous. During the nineteenth century, police were much more involved in the community than they were after the reforms. Police officers performed many duties that today are associated with social services, such as operating soup kitchens and providing lodging for homeless people. They also played a more direct role in keeping public order by "running in" drunks and intervening in minor disturbances.[68]

Return to the Community.   To a certain extent, **community policing** advocates a return to this understanding of the police mission. In general, community policing can be defined as an approach that promotes community-police

"**The poorest man may in his cottage bid defiance to all the forces of the Crown. It may be frail; its roof may shake; the wind may blow through it; the storm may enter; the rain may enter; but the King of England cannot enter—all his force dares not cross the threshold of the ruined tenement!**"

—William Pitt, *English statesman* (1777)

INFOTRAC®
COLLEGE EDITION

Keywords: community policing

EXTRADITION
The surrender of a fugitive offender by one jurisdiction to another in which the offender has been convicted or is liable for punishment.

COMMUNITY POLICING
A policing philosophy that emphasizes community support for and cooperation with the police in preventing crime. Community policing stresses a police role that is less centralized and more proactive than reform era policing strategies.

The Professional Model of Policing and Community Policing

The past sixty years have seen two dominant trends in the style of American policing. The first was the professional model, designed to reduce corruption and improve performance by emphasizing efficiency. The second, community policing, was a reaction against the professional model, which many thought went too far in relying on statistics and technology. The main characteristics of these two trends are summarized below.

Professional Model of Policing

- The separation of policing from politics.
- Reduced emphasis on the social service function of police, with resources and strategies directed toward crime control.
- Limits placed on police discretion; emphasis placed on following guidelines and respecting the authority of the law.
- Centralized, bureaucratic police departments.
- The promotion of a certain distance between police officers and citizens, also the result of increased use of automobile patrols as opposed to foot patrols.
- Main strategies:
  1. Rapid response to calls for service, made possible by technological innovations such as the two-way radio.
  2. Preventive patrol, which attempts to use police presence to deter criminal activity.

Community Policing

- Although professionalism is still valued, it is tempered by recognition that police serve the community and its citizens, as well as the ideal of the law.
- Decentralized, less bureaucratic police departments, allowing more authority and discretion to rest in the hands of police officers.
- Recognition that crime control is only one function of law enforcement, to be included with crime prevention and the provision of social services.
- A more intimate relationship between police and citizens, which comes from an understanding that police officers can do only so much to fight crime; ultimately, they need the cooperation of the community to be successful.
- Main strategies:
  1. Return to foot patrol to "reconnect" with the community.
  2. Problem solving, which treats crimes not just as isolated incidents but as "problems" that can be "solved" with innovative, long-term approaches.

INFOTRAC®
COLLEGE EDITION

Keywords: problem-solving policing

partnerships, proactive problem solving, and community engagement to address issues such as fear of crime and the causes of crime in a particular area.[69] In the reform era, the police were, in a sense, detached from the community. They did their jobs to the best of their ability, but were more concerned with making arrests or speedily answering calls for service than learning about the problems or concerns of the citizenry. In their efforts to eliminate police corruption, administrators put more emphasis on segregating the police from the public than on cooperatively working with citizens to resolve community problems. Under community policing, patrol officers have much more freedom to improvise. They are expected to develop personal relationships with residents and to encourage those residents to become involved in making the community a safer place. (See *Mastering Concepts—The Professional Model of Policing and Community Policing.*)

Thinking Locally. Local initiatives have played a significant role in the community era of policing. When the Bridgeport (Connecticut) Police Department decided to target a high-crime neighborhood known as the "Beirut of Bridgeport," it adopted community policing methodology. The department opened a Strategic Interventions for High-Risk Youth office in the neighborhood and invited citizens to attend meetings there to discuss their crime problems. A Neighborhood Watch Council was founded, and both police and citizens worked to improve the appearance of the area. Within four years, overall crime rates in the neighborhood dropped 75 percent.[70]

The Columbia (South Carolina) Police Department has taken the idea of community involvement to the extreme with its adoption of the Japanese *koban* system. A *koban* is a mini–police station where police officers live as well as work. The initial *koban* in Columbia was set up on Lady Street, which runs through one of the city's high-crime neighborhoods. Two volunteer police officers stay rent-free in the upper floor of the building, while the lower floor is a police station/community center. Residents are encouraged to come to the *koban* to report crimes, and it also serves as a work station for social and educational services. According to Charles Austin, Columbia's police chief, the *koban* is a sign to residents that the police have "a vested stake in the community."[71]

These programs and others across the country typify the essence of community policing. First, they show how the police can engage in problem solving as opposed to only responding to calls for service. Second, they are examples of how the police are attempting to forge partnerships with neighborhoods or community groups. Finally, the programs illustrate how the police can engage the community by encouraging citizens' active involvement in crime and disorder problems.

PROBLEM-SOLVING POLICING
A policing philosophy that requires police to identify potential criminal activity and develop strategies to prevent or respond to that activity.

Problem-Solving Policing

Problem solving is a key component of community policing. Problem solving has its roots in **problem-solving policing**, which was introduced by Herman Goldstein of the Police Executive Research Forum in the late 1970s. Goldstein's basic premise was that police departments were devoting too many of their resources to reacting to calls for service and too few to "acting on their own initiative to prevent or reduce community problems."[72] To rectify this situation, problem-solving policing moves beyond simply responding to incidents and attempts instead to control or even solve the root causes of criminal behavior.

Goldstein's theory was in direct contrast to the reform era theories of policing, discussed in this chapter and the previous one.[73] Goldstein was suggesting that patrol officers must become intimately involved with citizens. For example, instead of responding to a call concerning illegal drug use by simply arresting the offender—a short-term response—the patrol officers should also look at the long-term implications of the situation. They should analyze the pattern of similar arrests in the area and interview the arrestee to determine the reasons, if any, that the site had been selected for drug activity.[74] Then additional police actions should be taken to prevent further drug sales at the identified location. (See Figure 5.6 for the environmental aspects of a neighborhood that can contribute to drug activity.)

"We have a hard enough time dealing with real crime, let alone somebody's fantasy of it."

—Los Angeles patrol officer, *complaining about the difficulty in implementing community policing programs (1998)*

1. Heavy traffic volume at certain hours of the night.
2. Poor street lighting, which may be the result of poor public maintenance (burned-out bulbs) or broken lights.
3. Abandoned automobiles.
4. Public property (street signs, light poles, telephone poles, statues) with graffiti.
5. Private property (homes, apartment buildings, businesses) with graffiti.
6. Large numbers of people "hanging out," that is, not working or engaging in some other obvious pursuit (such as playing street hockey or basketball).
7. An excessive amount of litter.
8. An excessive number of vacant lots in obvious disuse.
9. An excessive number of abandoned or vacant buildings.

Source: "Appendix B: Example of a Block Environmental Problem" in *Bureau of Justice Assistance, A Police Guide to Surveying Citizens in Their Environment* (Washington, D.C.: U.S. Department of Justice, October, 1993), 69–79.

FIGURE 5.6
A Police Guide to Surveying Citizens in Their Environment

One of the basic truths of problem-solving policing is that crimes are not always isolated incidents, but may be part of a pattern of life in a certain neighborhood or community. Therefore, changing the environment of a high-crime area is an essential part of solving that area's crime problems. John Meeks of the Philadelphia Police Department has identified physical characteristics that may be indicative of drug activity in an area and should be "fixed" to lessen such activity.

HOT SPOTS
Concentrated areas of high criminal activity that draw a directed police response.

INFOTRAC®
COLLEGE EDITION

Keywords:
crime and hot spots;
crime mapping;
broken windows theory

On the Web

MapInfo and Vertical Mapping are computer programs law enforcement agencies use to determine "hot spots." To see how this technology works, find a link to MapInfo on the Hypercontents page for this chapter at http://www.cj.wadsworth.com/gainescore2e.

Police and "Problems."   During the reform era, police officers were trained to respond to "incidents," or violations of the law. Once an incident had taken place, officers were judged by the speed at which they arrived at the scene and how quickly they were able to arrest those responsible for the incident. The introduction of problem solving represents a distinct change in strategy. Although a criminal act certainly qualifies as a "problem," the term also covers circumstances that may lead to criminal activity. To assist departments with the transformation from incident-driven policing to problem solving, the Department of Justice identified five principles of problem-solving policing:

1 A problem is something that concerns the community and its citizens, not just police officers. Issues that may be important only to police are worthy of attention, but they are not necessarily community concerns.

2 A problem is a group or pattern of incidents and therefore demands a different set of responses than does a single incident.

3 A problem must be understood in terms of the competing interests at stake. Police must be aware of these interests and respect them in dealing with the problem.

4 Responding to a problem involves more than a "quick fix," such as an arrest. Problem solving is a long-term strategy.

5 Problem solving requires a heightened level of creativity and initiative on the part of the patrol officer.[75]

Hot Spots.   According to the tenets of reform era policing, patrol officers should be spread evenly throughout a precinct, giving each citizen the same level of service. Many observers find this shortsighted, at best. Professor Lawrence Sherman compares it to giving every citizen an equal dose of penicillin—whether that person is sick or not.[76]

Some say a more practical response is for police to concentrate on **hot spots**, or areas of high criminal activity. Minneapolis police discovered, for example, that 100 percent of the robberies in a certain year occurred in only 2 percent of the city's zip codes.[77] Similarly, law enforcement officials in Jersey City, New Jersey, found that fifty-six hot spots of drug activity (occupying 4.4 percent of the city's street sections) accounted for 45 percent of the city's narcotics sales arrests and 46 percent of emergency calls for service.[78]

In both cases, the city's police department took part in experiments in which extra patrol coverage—in brief bursts of activity—was directed to a select number of the hot spots. In Minneapolis, robbery rates in the targeted hot spots fell by more than 20 percent, and in both cities, calls for service reporting public disorder also decreased. Neither police department, however, concluded that the hot spots experiment had decreased overall crime. Criminals had simply moved to other areas, or "scattered like cockroaches in the light," as one observer put it.[79]

Crime Mapping.   Many police departments are using *crime mapping* technology to locate and identify hot spots. A new generation of geographic information systems (GISs) provides departments with colored maps that allow them to easily spot patterns of crime and determine where increased coverage is needed.[80] (See Figure 5.7.) With the press of a button, GIS software can find and predict crime patterns by matching variables such as time of day, type of crime, and type of weapon used. When Fontana, California, recently experienced a spate of burglaries, for example, the police department's GIS was able to direct officers to virtually the exact spot where the next attempt would take place. Deputies were able to follow the burglars into a target house, where they were arrested and confessed to more than thirty other similar crimes.[81] Crime mapping is critical to establishing police targets for directed patrols, as described earlier in the chapter.

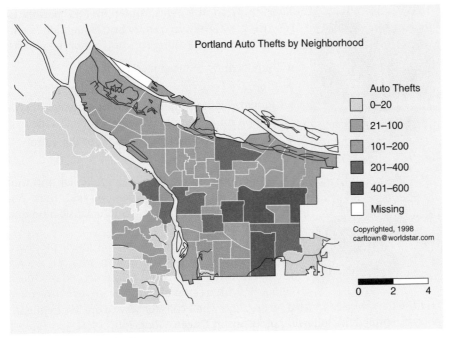

Portland Auto Thefts by Neighborhood

Auto Thefts
- 0–20
- 21–100
- 101–200
- 201–400
- 401–600
- Missing

Copyrighted, 1998
carltown@worldstar.com

0   2   4

Source: City of Portland Police Bureau.

FIGURE 5.7

Geographic Information Systems and Auto Theft in Portland, Oregon

A geographic information system (GIS) uses digital maps to highlight areas in which crime occurs. As you can see, the Portland (Oregon) Police Department has taken advantage of GIS technology to pinpoint the incidence of auto theft in the city.

Broken Windows: Popularizing Community Policing

If Herman Goldstein introduced the idea of problem-solving policing, James Q. Wilson and George L. Kelling brought it widespread attention. Many observers believe that Wilson and Kelling set the modern wave of community policing in motion with their 1982 article in *Atlantic Monthly* entitled "Broken Windows."[82]

The Broken Windows Theory. In "Broken Windows," Wilson and Kelling argued that reform era police strategies focused on violent crime to the detriment of the vital police role of promoting the quality of life in neighborhoods. As a result, many American communities, particularly in large cities, had fallen into a state of disorder and disrepute, with two very important consequences. First, these neighborhoods—with their broken windows, dilapidated buildings, and lawless behavior by citizens—send out "signals" that criminal activity is tolerated. Second, this disorder promotes fear among law-abiding citizens, dissuading them from leaving their homes or attempting to improve their surroundings.

The **broken windows theory,** therefore, is based on "order maintenance" of neighborhoods by cracking down on "quality-of-life" crimes such as panhandling, public drinking and urinating, loitering, and graffiti painting. Only by encouraging police diligence with regard to these quality-of-life crimes, the two professors argued, could American cities be rescued from rising crime rates.

Community policing played a prominent role in Wilson and Kelling's article. To reduce fear and crime, they insisted, police had to rely on the cooperation of the citizens. Many cities have found that a crucial step in "reconnecting" with the community has been the reintroduction of foot patrols in high-crime neighborhoods. Studies have shown that foot patrol officers pay more attention to "order maintenance crimes" such as drunkenness, vagrancy, and panhandling than do patrol officers in police cars. Although these crimes are not serious, they do increase fear of crime in a community.

Foot patrol officers are also in a better position to interact with citizens, forming relationships that allow them to deal with threatening or inappropriate behavior—such as a domestic dispute—that could eventually lead to violence.[83]

BROKEN WINDOWS THEORY
Wilson and Kelling's theory that a neighborhood in disrepair signals that criminal activity is tolerated in the area. Thus, by cracking down on quality-of-life crimes, police can reclaim the neighborhood and encourage law-abiding citizens to live and work there.

Redlands (California) police officer Stephen Crane takes part in a one-legged jumping race with neighborhood children. The race was sponsored by Redlands's Risked Focus Policing Program, which works to reduce juvenile delinquency in the community. How can establishing friendly relations with citizens help law enforcement agencies reduce crime? (AP Photo/Damian Dovarganes)

> "A stable neighborhood of families who care for their homes, mind each other's children, and confidently frown on unwanted intruders can change, in a few years or even a few months, to an inhospitable and frightening jungle. A piece of property is abandoned, weeds grow up, a window is smashed. . . . Such an area is vulnerable to criminal invasion."
>
> —James Q. Wilson and George L. Kelling, *American crime researchers* (1982)

After studying the reinstitution of foot patrols in Newark, New Jersey, in a study briefly mentioned earlier in the chapter, Kelling concluded that the patrols:

- Significantly reduced levels of fear.
- Improved citizen satisfaction with the police.
- Provided foot patrol officers with a greater appreciation for the values of neighborhood residents.
- Provided greater job satisfaction for the patrol officers.[84]

It is important to note that Kelling *did not* find that foot patrols affected crime rates. Instead, their primary benefits were to increase citizen satisfaction and reduce citizen fear.

Philadelphia police officers used problem-solving concepts to put the broken windows theory into effect in the high-crime neighborhood of Queen Village.[85] With a series of "Sunday Surveys" (so-called because they were conducted on Sundays when calls for service are less frequent), police identified the following problems in Queen Village:

- Twenty dilapidated buildings.
- Twenty abandoned cars.
- Seven blocks with serious litter problems.
- Eleven blocks with serious graffiti problems.
- Five littered vacant lots.
- Six blocks with poor overhead lighting.

In cooperation with other city agencies, the Philadelphia police aggressively worked to alleviate these shortcomings. Although the city did not conduct a formal survey of crime rates in the neighborhood after this strategy shift, the police department noted that residents felt a great deal safer than they had before.

Crackdowns.   In many American cities, the implementation of the broken windows theory has been accompanied by aggressive patrol tactics known as "crackdowns." When police intensely focus their energies on a particular crime or set of crimes in a given area, they are said to be conducting a "crackdown." Crackdowns, which are related to the "hot spot" tactics discussed earlier, are one of the most widely used forms of directed patrol and are typically used to solve a significant crime or disorder problem in an area. New York City, which experienced a dramatic drop in violent crime in the 1990s, is often held up as the ultimate example of what can be accomplished when the broken windows theory and aggressive police actions are combined.

In light of the broad acceptance of the broken windows theory, it must be noted that police abuse of their power to make "order maintenance" arrests was one of the reasons for police reform in the first place. In the 1950s and 1960s, for example, such laws were used to provide a legal shield for police harassment of civil rights and anti–Vietnam War demonstrators. During that period, courts restricted the police's freedom to make "vagrancy" arrests because such arrests were politically motivated.[86] Some scholars believe that a resurgence of police power in this area may result in similar problems in the future.[87]

Criminal Justice in Action

The DNA Revolution

As mentioned earlier in this chapter, forensics, or the application of science to criminal investigations, plays a key role in police work. Forensic scientists can now flood a crime scene with ultraviolet light to pick up hidden fingerprints or footprints, or identify a criminal's "signature" by the type of weapon he or she uses, among other advanced techniques. But could forensics help solve a multiple murder that occurred eight years earlier, for which the only evidence is the remains of a half-eaten chicken? Until recently, the case would have been closed, as dead chickens tell no tales. Today, however, police officers in Chicago relied on the eight-year-old meal to lead to the person or persons who killed seven diners at Brown's Chicken and Pasta restaurant on January 8, 1993. They are using a relatively new technology—the subject of this *Criminal Justice in Action* feature—that is revolutionizing the criminal justice system.

The DNA "Miracle at Work"

In 1979, Diane Gregory was stabbed to death in her apartment in Mount Vernon, New York. A good deal of physical evidence was found at the site of the crime, including a pillowcase, a jagged piece of glass, and a sheet, all covered with blood. At the time, police officers were certain that some of the blood belonged to Walter Gill, the main suspect. But, as there was no proof, investigators lacked evidence to charge Gill with the crime.[88]

Twenty-one years later, local police finally obtained the evidence they needed. A new state law allowed them to take a deoxyribonucleic acid (DNA) sample from Gill, who was serving a prison term for robbery. Investigators retrieved the pillowcase, glass shard, and sheet from a storage bin and were able to analyze the DNA in the decades-old blood. The samples matched those taken from Gill, placing him at the scene of the crime. In March 2001, a jury convicted him of first degree manslaughter in the death of Diane Gregory. It was, said the prosecuting district attorney, "like the finger of God pointing 21 years later, saying, 'You can't get away with it.'"[89]

DNA, which is the same in each cell of a person's body, provides a "genetic blueprint" or "code" for every living organism. DNA "profiling" is useful in criminal investigations because no two people, save for identical twins, have the same genetic code. Therefore, lab technicians, using

the process described in Figure 5.8 on the following page, can compare the DNA sample of a suspect such as Gill to the evidence found at the crime scene. If the match is negative, it is certain that the two samples did not come from the same source. If the match is positive, the lab will determine the odds that the DNA sample could have come from somebody other than the subject. These odds are so high—sometimes reaching 30 billion to one—that juries often see the match as conclusive.[90]

Storing Genetic Information

The initial use of DNA to establish criminal guilt took place in Britain in 1986; the Federal Bureau of Investigation (FBI) used it for the first time in the United States two years later. The process begins when forensic technicians gather blood, semen, skin, saliva, or hair from the scene of the crime. Blood cells and sperm are rich in DNA, making the practice particularly useful in murder and rape cases. Once a suspect is identified, her or his DNA can be tested to determine whether she or he can be placed at the crime scene. In cases of murder or when the victim is unable to provide a suspect, police rely on DNA databases.

Today, every state allows law enforcement agencies to collect DNA samples from certain types of criminals for inclusion in state databases. At the least, these state laws require DNA samples to be taken from convicted sex offenders. Six states allow such samples to be taken from anybody convicted of any felony, and Wisconsin goes so far as to require samples from everyone who is incarcerated, on probation, paroled, or found not guilty by reason of mental disease.[91] In addition to these state databases, there is also a national information retrieval service. Operated by the FBI since 1998, the Combined DNA Index System (CODIS) gives local and state law enforcement agencies access to the DNA profiles of a wide variety of felons who have been convicted of homicide and sexual assault.

Cold Hits and Second Chances

These databases can lead to what police call a *cold hit,* or the solving of a case where there are no suspects. For example, the first cold hit using CODIS occurred when Leon Dundas was found dead after being shot in the back in Jacksonville, Florida. An investigator with the local sheriff's office took a blood sample from Dundas, who had a history of drug arrests, and ran it through CODIS. The sample matched DNA evidence at the scene of eleven different unsolved rape cases, three in Jacksonville and eight in Washington, D.C.[92] In its first fifteen months of operation,

Continued on next page

CJ in Action: The DNA Revolution *continued*

CODIS aided twenty-four states in over 1,100 criminal investigations.[93]

In addition to helping police find criminals, DNA profiling also offers hope for those who are unjustly convicted of crimes. Since the technology was introduced in this country, nearly ninety wrongfully convicted people have been exonerated after DNA testing was applied to their cases. Ten of those won release from death row.[94]

PRIVACY CONCERNS

There is not much doubt that in little more than a decade, DNA testing has transformed many aspects of crime investigation. One government official has gone so far as to call the process a "scientific miracle for human justice" that "shines the light of irrefutable truth into our courtrooms for our juries."[95] But many observers are wary of DNA's ability to give government agencies information about citizens that goes beyond the scope of their criminal liability.

The main issue of contention concerns personal privacy, which the United States Supreme Court has identified as a "fundamental right" guaranteed by our Constitution.[96]

Having been found guilty of a crime by a jury, convicted felons are said to have relinquished their right to privacy. But what of those who have only been arrested and have not been convicted? Do they have a right to keep certain information that DNA testing can reveal—such as a genetic predisposition to disease—private? Observers such as Barry Steinhardt, associate director of the American Civil Liberties Union, are troubled by laws such as the one recently passed in California that allow DNA searches before conviction for those arrested for violent crimes such as murder, sexual assault of a child, and kidnapping.[97] Steinhardt points out that about half of those charged with such violent crimes ultimately have their cases dismissed, and therefore California's law imposes a heavy burden on possibly innocent people. Further, he is worried that the law will encourage police officers to make "pretextual" arrests solely for the purpose of collecting DNA from suspects whom the officers do not have enough evidence to arrest.[98]

The issue of privacy was at the heart of a lawsuit brought by a convicted sex offender against the state of Connecticut.[99] The convict argued that the state did not

---

FIGURE 5.8

Unlocking Evidence in DNA

Deoxyribonucleic acid, or DNA, is the genetic material that carries the code for all living cells. DNA is useful to crime solvers thanks to the discovery that the DNA of one person is different from the DNA of all other persons (except identical twins). Through DNA profiling, a process explained here, forensic scientists test DNA samples to see if they match with the DNA profile of a known criminal or other test subject.

1. Collection of Samples. DNA samples can be taken from a number of sources, including saliva, blood, hair, or skin. These samples are labeled and shipped to a forensic lab.

2. Extraction and Purification. At the lab, the sample is mixed with chemicals that break open the cells and let the DNA seep out. The broken cell fragments are removed from the mixture, and the remains are placed in a test tube. This tube is then spun very quickly, which makes the pure DNA sink to the bottom.

3. Separation and Binding The double helix is then separated into two single strands. Lab technicians add "probes" to the single strands. These probes are short pieces of single-stranded DNA: A pairs with T and C pairs with G. Because the probes are tagged with radioactivity, technicians follow them as they form connections, and figure out the strand of the original DNA sample. (For example, whenever a T probe connects, it connects with an A strand, etc.)

4. Replication. DNA samples are very small and difficult to see. Consequently, scientists have invented a way to "photocopy" them using a process called polymerase chain reaction (PCR). In PCR, when a probe attaches itself to a rung in the original DNA, it very quickly creates a large number of copies of the new pair. (Imagine that the probe acts like a finger pressing the "copy" button on a photocopying machine, producing repeated patterns such as ATGCTAGCAT, and so on.)

5. Identification. Next, technicians place a drop containing millions of DNA fragments at one end of a sheet of gel. An electric current is then run through the sheet, a process that pulls the DNA fragments across the gel. The larger a fragment is, the slower it will move. In order to measure these movements, the DNA fragments are tagged with dye, and they show up as colored bands when exposed to ultraviolet light.

6. Matching. Normally, a crime lab will analyze thirteen places on a person's DNA in the profiling process. These thirteen markers will be compared to a suspect's DNA profiles that are already on file. If a match is found for each of the thirteen markers, there is almost no chance that the two DNA samples did not come from the same person.

have reasonable cause to store his DNA in its database because it could not be sure that he would commit another crime. Therefore, he argued, the DNA collection was an illegal search.[100] The U.S. Court of Appeals for the Second Circuit rejected this argument, holding that Connecticut's interest in protecting its citizens from possible sex offenders was greater than an individual convict's interest in keeping his or her blood from being tested.[101]

THE PORTABLE DNA LAB

A number of other courts have agreed with the Second Circuit ruling, making it likely that government agencies will have a relatively free hand in collecting DNA information from both suspects and convicts.[102] As the technology continues to improve, then, so will the effect of DNA on crime-fighting efforts. For example, today many police officers should have access to portable DNA labs. These labs allow an officer to place saliva onto a DNA analysis chip. The chip is then read by a laser, creating a DNA "fingerprint" that can be tested against information in a central database. Within twelve minutes of the initial contact, the officer knows whether the subject is wanted for any outstanding crimes.[103]

MAKING SENSE OF DNA PROFILING

1 Do you agree that the positive impact of DNA profiling on crime-fighting efforts outweighs an individual's interest in privacy? Why or why not?

2 How far should the government be allowed to go in collecting DNA samples from citizens? Should such methods be limited to felons convicted of violent crimes? To anybody convicted of any felony? To those who have only been arrested?

3 Considering how successful DNA is in identifying criminals, should those accused or convicted of crimes automatically be given access to DNA material in preparing their defense? What might be the pros and cons of such a policy? In making your answer, note that only three states—New York, Illinois, and Minnesota—have laws that require courts to honor such a request. In most other states, judges can deny such a request under most circumstances.

INFOTRAC®
COLLEGE EDITION

Keywords:
crime and DNA;
CODIS

KEY TERMS

broken windows theory 133

bureaucracy 111

community policing 129

confidential informant (CI) 127

contaminated 123

crime scene 123

delegation of authority 111

detective 121

differential response 112

directed patrol 117

extradition 129

follow-up investigation 125

forensics 124

general patrol 117

hot spots 132

incident-driven policing 111

interview 123

preliminary investigation 123

problem-solving policing 131

response time 111

solvability factors 125

CHAPTER SUMMARY

1 **Explain the difference between arrest rates and clearance rates.** Arrest rates simply indicate the number of individuals arrested by a police department. In contrast, clearance rates show the percentage of crimes a police department has solved over any given time.

2 **List the three primary purposes of police patrol.** (a) The deterrence of crime, (b) the maintenance of public order, and (c) the provision of services that are not related to crime.

3 **Identify the different types of patrol.** Most patrols are general patrols as opposed to directed. The most common methods of general patrol include (a) foot, (b) automobile, (c) motorcycle, (d) mounted on horseback, (e) bicycle, (f) boat, and (g) K-9 (with a dog).

4 **Describe the steps that an investigator must take after a crime occurs.** The first responsibility during the preliminary investigation is to attend to the well-being of the victim. Next, the crime scene must be secured so that it does not become contaminated. Then comes the information-gathering stage, which involves taking notes, sketching, taking photographs, and identifying and interviewing victims and witnesses. Then physical evidence, such as footprints and bloodstains, is collected.

5 **Indicate some investigation strategies that are considered aggressive.** Using undercover officers is considered an aggressive (and often dangerous) investigative technique. The use of informants is also aggressive, but involves danger for those who inform.

6 **Explain community policing and its strategies.** Community policing involves proactive problem solving and a community-police partnership in which the community engages itself along with the police to address crime and the fear of crime in a particular geographic area. Strategies include sending police officers to schools, opening community intervention offices for high-risk youths, and encouraging police officers to live in high-crime neighborhoods.

7 **Indicate the five principles of problem-solving policing.** (a) Problems are concerns of the community, not just police officers. (b) Problems demand different sets of responses than do single incidents. (c) Competing interests are at stake in all problems. (d) Problem solving is a long-term strategy. (e) The patrol officer must become more creative and use more initiative to solve problems.

QUESTIONS FOR CRITICAL ANALYSIS

1 What type of police organization resulted from the desire to eliminate politicians' influence on the police?

2 What two criteria are most often used to measure police efficiency, and what are the weaknesses of such statistical indicators?

3 How can a differential response strategy help a police department become more effective?

4 "The number of police is often not as important as what those police are doing." Analyze this statement.

5 The Kansas City Preventive Patrol Experiment involved control beats, proactive beats, and reactive beats. Did the results of that experiment show any benefits to increasing preventive police patrol? If yes, how? If not, why not?

6 Contrast the community policing model with the professional policing model.

7 Relate the concept of "broken windows" to high-crime neighborhoods and potential ways to combat crime in such neighborhoods.

8 How effective are detectives in solving crimes? If they are not that effective, who or what is responsible for solving most crimes?

9 How has the DNA revolution changed forensics?

SELECTED PRINT AND ELECTRONIC RESOURCES

SUGGESTED READINGS

DeLong, Candice, and Elisa Petrini, *Special Agent: My Life on the Front Lines as a Woman in the FBI,* New York: Hyperion Press, 2001. DeLong explains her twenty-year career in the FBI, especially the grueling training process at the Quantico training academy. She tells the stories of numerous dangerous arrests that she made. She also refers to the initial hostility to female agents in the 1980s.

Dwyer, Jim, Peter Neufeld, and Barry Scheck, *Actual Innocence: Five Days to Execution and Other Dispatches from the Wrongly Convicted,* New York: Doubleday, 2000. Neufeld and Scheck run the Innocence Project, a program that works to reopen old convictions using DNA evidence. This book explores the case histories of men imprisoned for rape and murder who are eventually able to prove their innocence because of DNA technology.

Peak, Kenneth J., and Ronald W. Glensor, *Community Policing and Problem Solving: Strategies and Practices,* 2d ed., Englewood Cliffs, NJ: Prentice Hall, 1998. This book looks into the processes of community policing and problem-solving policing. The authors explore the efforts of police agencies across the United States. The book shows how police are moving away from traditional methods of responding to crime.

MEDIA RESOURCES

***Rush* (1991)** This is the story of two undercover narcotics agents who find themselves hooked on the drugs that they are buying and illegally using. The experienced undercover agent, Raynor (played by Jason Patric), is helping break in the recruit, Kristen (played by Jennifer Jason Leigh). Raynor believes he is the master of the drug world. He shoots up drugs himself in the presence of big-time dealers so that they cannot possibly believe he is a cop. This movie was inspired by Kim Wozencraft's book about a true story. While viewing this film, think about the different types of law enforcement agents who are involved.

Critically analyze this film:

1. In addition to narcotics agents, what other types of "workers" in this film are at least somewhat connected to law enforcement?

2. Why does an undercover agent have to pretend to be the very thing that he or she has pledged to defeat?

3. Is the story believable?

4. What is the moral game that undercover agents have to play in order to bring in the dealers?

5. At any point in this film do you believe that the law enforcement officers could be accused of entrapment? Explain your answer.

6. What might induce a police officer to become an undercover narcotics agent?

LOGGING ON

Go to http://cj.wadsworth.com/gainescore2e, and click Hypercontents. There, you will find URLs for the organizations in the following list:

- A web site entitled **Forensic Science Resources** contains a wealth of information on this subject, including a run-through of a criminal fact investigation, a bibliography, and a reference guide to the field of forensic science.

- You may also want to get information on a criminal investigation developed for a course at **Lake Superior State University.**

- The **Community Policing Consortium** offers an electronic library and information-access, links to other community policing Web site, and links to Popnet, the Problem-Oriented Policing Network.

USING THE INTERNET FOR CRIMINAL JUSTICE ANALYSIS

INFOTRAC®
COLLEGE EDITION

1. Access your InfoTrac account at:
http://www.infoTrac.college.com/wadsworth/
Type in **"Community policing: the process of transitional change."** This article from the *FBI Law Enforcement Bulletin* covers a study undertaken to evaluate the extent of law enforcement agencies' involvement with community policing in terms of strategies, philosophy, and officers' skills.

   a. What percentage of agencies surveyed had implemented community policing?

   b. Why do the authors of this article mention the Violent Crime Control and Law Enforcement Act of 1994?

   c. Which of the ten principles that encompass the community-oriented policing philosophy were incorporated by the agencies surveyed in the Minneapolis–St. Paul metropolitan area?

   d. What were the two most popular community policing strategies implemented by the agencies surveyed?

   e. What were the three guidelines that led to successful implementation of community-oriented policing policies?

2. See Internet Activities 5.1 and 5.2 on the companion Web site for *CJ in Action: The Core*. To get to the activities, go to **http://www.cj.wadsworth.com/gainescore2e**, select the appropriate chapter from the drop down list, then click Internet Activities on the left navigation bar.

NOTES

1. Howard Pankratz, "Columbine 911 Calls Released to Kin," *Denver Post* (May 12, 2000), B1.

2. Berny Morson, "911 Workers Honored for Effort during Columbine," *Denver Rocky Mountain News* (April 10, 2000), 21A.

3. Pankratz, B1.

4. Samuel Walker, *The Police in America: An Introduction*, 2d ed. (New York: McGraw-Hill, 1992), 16.

5. George L. Kelling and Mark H. Moore, "From Political to Reform to Community: The Evolving Strategy of Police," in *Community Policing: Rhetoric or Reality,* Jack Greene and Stephen Mastrofski, eds. (New York: Praeger Publishers, 1988), 13.

6. Leef Smith, "Manassas Wants to Ease 911 Load," *Washington Post* (January 28, 1998), V3.

7. Laura A. Bischoff, "Abusers of 911 May Face Jail," *Dayton Daily News* (February 18, 1998), 3B.

8. H. Nees, "Policing 2001," *Law and Order* (January 1990), 257–64.

9. Walker, 14.

10. Kelling and Moore, 11–12.

11. Henry M. Wrobleski and Karen M. Hess, *Introduction to Law Enforcement and Criminal Justice*, 5th ed. (Minneapolis/St. Paul, MN: West Publishing Company, 1997), 326.

12. Lori Stahl and Stephen Power, "Response Slows on 911 Calls," *Dallas Morning News* (September 28, 1997), 1A.

13. Lawrence W. Sherman, "Attacking Crime: Police and Crime Patrol," in *Modern Policing*, ed. Michael H. Tonry and Norval Morris, vol. 16 of *Crime and Justice: A Review of Research* (Chicago: University of Chicago Press, 1992), 335.

14. Ibid., 338.

15. Federal Bureau of Investigation, *Crime in the United States,* 2001 (Washington, D.C.: U.S. Government Printing Office, 2002), 220.

16. Survey by the Gallup organization for *CNN/USA Today*, September 22–24, 1995.

17. David C. Couper and Sabine Lobitz, "The Customer Is Always Right," *The Police Chief* (May 1991), 17–23.

18. Robert Trojanowicz, *An Evaluation of the Neighborhood Foot Patrol Program in Flint, Michigan* (East Lansing, MI: Michigan State University, 1982), 85–87.

19. Connie Fletcher, "What Cops Know," *OnPatrol* (Summer 1996), 44–45.

20. David H. Bayley, *Police for the Future* (New York: Oxford University Press, 1994), 20.

21. George L. Kelling, Tony Pate, Duane Dieckman, and Charles Brown, *The Kansas City Preventive Patrol Experiment: A Summary Report* (Washington, D.C.: The Police Foundation, 1974), 3–4.

22. Walker, *Police in America,* 2d ed., 103.

23. Eric J. Scott, *Calls for Service: Citizens Demand and Initial Police Response* (Washington, D.C.: National Institute of Justice, 1981), 28–30.

24. William G. Gay, Theodore H. Schell, and Stephen Schack, *Routine Patrol: Improving Patrol Productivity*, vol. 1 (Washington, D.C.: National Institute of Justice, 1977), 3–6.

25. Gary W. Cordner, "The Police on Patrol," in *Police and Policing: Contemporary Issues*, ed. Dennis Jay Kenney (New York: Praeger Publishers, 1989), 60–71.

26. Anthony V. Bouza, *The Police Mystique: An Insider's Look at Cops, Crime, and the Criminal Justice System* (New York: Plenum Press, 1990), 27.

27. Noel C. Bufe, "Traffic Services" in *The Encyclopedia of Police Sciences,* 2d ed., William G. Bailey, ed. (New York: Garland, 1995), 776–82.

28. Egon Bittner, *The Functions of Police in a Modern Society*, Public Health Service Publication No. 2059 (Chevy Chase, MD: National Institute of Mental Health, 1970), 127.

29. Kathleen Maguire and Ann L. Pastore, eds., *Sourcebook of Criminal Justice Statistics, 1996* (Washington, D.C.: U.S. Department of Justice, Bureau of Justice Statistics, 1997), 368.

30. Dale O. Cloninger, "Enforcement Risks and Deterrence: A Reexamination," *Journal of Socio-Economics* 23 (1994), 273.

31. Todd S. Purdum, "Vigilant Eyes Fill Skies over Los Angeles," *New York Times* (March 18, 1998), A1, A14.

32. James Q. Wilson and George L. Kelling, "Making Neighborhoods Safe," *Atlantic Monthly* (February 1989), 36–38.

33. Police Foundation, *The Newark Foot Patrol Experiment* (1981), 122–24.

34. Tom Yates, "Magic Patrol Cars: Police Travel 'Information Superhighway,'" *Law and Order* (April 1995), 77–81.

35. Kimberly Rinker, "There's No Horsing Around in These Units," *Police* (July 1997), 26–31.

36. Bonnie Bobit, "Bicycle Patrols," *Police* (February 1998), 32–35.

37. Samuel G. Chapman, *Police Dogs in North America* (Springfield, IL: Charles C Thomas Pub., 1990), 71.

38. Jerome H. Skolnick and James J. Fyfe, *Above the Law: Police and the Excessive Use of Force* (New York: Free Press, 1993), 251–52.

39. Andrew Halper and Richard Ku, *An Exemplary Project: New York City Police Department Street Crimes Unit* (Washington, D.C.: U.S. Government Printing Office, 1975), 1.

40. Kelling, Pate, Dieckman, and Brown.

41. Carl B. Klockars and Stephen D. Mastrofski, "The Police and Serious Crime," in *Thinking about Police*, Carl Klockars and Stephen Mastrofski, eds. (New York: McGraw-Hill, 1990), 130.

42. James Q. Wilson, *Thinking about Crime* (New York: Basic Books, 1983), 65–66.

43. Robert Sheehan and Gary W. Cordner, *Introduction to Police Administration*, 2d ed. (Cincinnati, OH: Anderson, 1989), 367–68.

44. Federal Bureau of Investigation data cited in Tim McLaughlin, "Fewer Detectives Working on More Cases, Study Shows," *Capital Times* (Madison, Wisconsin) (September 5, 1997), 1A.

45. Laura Parker and Gary Fields, "Unsolved Killings on the Rise," *USA Today* (February 23, 2000), 1A.

46. *Ibid.*

47. Peter W. Greenwood and Joan Petersilia, *The Criminal Investigation Process: Summary and Policy Implications* (Santa Monica, CA: Rand Corporation, 1975).

48. Fletcher, 46.

49. John E. Eck, *Solving Crimes: The Investigation of Burglary and Robbery* (Washington, D.C.: Police Executive Research Forum, 1983).

50. Steven G. Brandl and James Frank, "The Relationship between Evidence, Detective Effort, and the Disposition of Burglary and Robbery Investigations," *American Journal of Police* 1 (1994), 149–68.

51. Gerald W. Garner, "Investigating Death," *Police* (May 1997), 26–33.

52. Joseph L. Peterson, *Use of Forensic Evidence by the Police and Courts* (Washington, D.C.: National Institute of Justice, 1987), 5.

53. Joel Samaha, *Criminal Justice*, 3d ed. (St. Paul, MN: West Publishing Co., 1994), 198.

54. Steven Brandl, "The Impact of Case Characteristics on Detectives' Decision Making," *Justice Quarterly* 10 (1993), 141.

55. J. Kuykendall, "The Municipal Police Detective: An Historical Analysis," *Criminology*, 24 (1) (1986), 175–201.

56. *Hoffa v. United States*, 385 U.S. 293, 298 (1966).

57. 353 U.S. 53 (1957).

58. Robert I. Friedman, "Land of the Stupid," *New Yorker* (April 10, 2000), 47–48.

59. *Strassheim v. Daily*, 221 U.S. 280 (1911), 285.

60. *United States v. DeWeese*, 632 F.2d 1267 (Fifth Cir. 1980), 1271–2.

61. *Jones v. United States*, 137 U.S. 202 (1890), 224.

62. 49 U.S.C. Section 46502(b) (2001).

63. Frank Turkheimer, "Globalization of U.S. Law Enforcement: Does the Constitution Come Along?" *Houston Law Review* (Summer 2002), 324.

64. Bruce Zagaris, "Extradition: Mexico Arrests and Hands over U.S. Citizens Wanted for Oregon Murders," *International Enforcement Law Reporter* (March 2002), 102.

65. Michael R. Gottfredson and Travis Hirschi, *A General Theory of Crime* (Stanford, CA: Stanford University Press, 1990), 270.

66. Lawrence W. Sherman, "Attacking Crime: Police and Crime Patrol," in *Modern Policing*, Michael H. Tonry and Norval Morris, eds., vol. 16 of *Crime and Justice: A Review of Research* (Chicago: University of Chicago Press, 1992), 327.

67. George Kelling, "Police and Community: The Quiet Revolution," in *Perspectives on Policing* (Washington, D.C.: National Institute of Justice, 1988).

68. Mark H. Moore and George L. Kelling, "'To Serve and Protect': Learning from Police History," *Public Interest* (Winter 1983), 54–57.

69. A. Steven Dietz, "Evaluating Community Policing: Quality Police Service and Fear of Crime," *Policing: An International Journal of Police Strategies and Management* 20 (1997), 83–100.

70. Bureau of Justice Assistance, *Crime Prevention and Community Policing: A Vital Partnership* (Washington, D.C.: Office of Justice Programs, September 1997), 7–8.

71. "Fighting Crime, Japanese Style," *Economist* (August 7, 1999), 24.

72. Herman Goldstein, "Improving Policing: A Problem-Oriented Approach," *Crime and Delinquency* 25 (1979), 236–58.

73. Kelling and Moore, 12.

74. Bureau of Justice Assistance, *Problem-Oriented Drug Enforcement: A Community-Based Approach for Effective Policing* (Washington, D.C.: Office of Justice Programs, 1993), 5.

75. *Ibid.*, 5–6.

76. Sherman, 331–32.

77. Lawrence W. Sherman, Patrick R. Gartin, and Michael E. Buerger, "Hot Spots of Predatory Crime: Routine Activities and the Criminology of Place," *Criminology* 27 (1989), 27–55.

78. *National Institute of Justice Research Preview: Policing Drug Hot Spots* (Washington, D.C.: Office of Justice Programs, January 1996).

79. Brian J. Taylor, "The Screening of America," *Reason* (May 1, 1997), 44.

80. William M. Bulkeley, "Information Age: Police Turn to Database to Link Crimes," *Wall Street Journal* (March 8, 1993), B5.

81. Elizabeth Douglass, "Crime Mapping Software Helps Officers Put Pieces Together," *Los Angeles Times* (February 16, 1998), D3.

82. James Q. Wilson and George L. Kelling, "Broken Windows," *Atlantic Monthly* (March 1982), 29–38.

83. *Ibid.*

84. George L. Kelling, *Foot Patrol* (Washington, D.C.: National Institute of Justice, 1987).

85. *Problem-Oriented Drug Enforcement: A Community-Based Approach for Effective Policing*, 53–54.

86. *Coates v. City of Cincinnati*, 402 U.S. 611 (1971); *Cox v. Louisiana*, 379 U.S. 536 (1965); *Papachristou v. City of Jacksonville*, 405 U.S. 156 (1972).

87. Debra Livingston, "Police Discretion and the Quality of Life in Public Places: Courts, Communities, and the New Policing," *Columbia Law Review* (April 1997), 551.

88. C. J. Chivers, "Larger DNA Database Links an Inmate to a 1979 Murder, Officials Say," *New York Times* (March 13, 2000), A21.

89. *Ibid.*

90. Judith E. Lewter, "The Use of Forensic DNA in Criminal Cases in Kentucky as Compared with Other Selected States," *Kentucky Law Journal* 86 (1997–1998), 223.

91. Deborah F. Barfield, "DNA Fingerprinting—Justifying the Special Need for the Fourth Amendment's Intrusion into the Zone of Privacy," *Richmond Journal of Law and Technology* (Spring 2000), 4.

92. Gerald Mizejewski, "DNA Bank Helps Solve 8 Rape Cases," *Washington Times* (July 22, 1999), C4.

93. Dwight E. Adams, Deputy Assistant Director, Forensic Analysis Branch, Federal Bureau of Investigation, "Statement for the Record before the Subcommittee on Crime of the House Judiciary Committee," Washington, D.C., March 23, 2000.

94. Kim Curtis, "Inmates Slow to Seek DNA Testing under New Law," *Associated Press Newswire* (May 17, 2001).

95. George Pataki, quoted in DeWayne Wickham, "Don't Use DNA Test to Excuse Bad Idea," *USA Today* (February 29, 2000), 15A.

96. *Katz v. United States*, 389 U.S. 347 (1967).

97. Barry Steinhardt, "Law Opens Door to Abuse," *USA Today* (January 2, 2001), 10A.

98. *Ibid.*

99. *Roe v. Marcotte*, 193 F.3d 76 (2d Cir. 1999).

100. *Ibid.*

101. *Ibid.*, at 82.

102. Barfield, 16.

103. Kevin Flynn, "Police Gadgets Aim to Fight Crime with 007-Style Ingenuity," *New York Times* (March 7, 2000), A21.

CHAPTER 6
POLICE AND THE RULE OF LAW

Chapter Objectives

After reading this chapter, you should be able to:

1. Outline the four major sources that may provide probable cause.

2. Explain the exclusionary rule.

3. Distinguish between a stop and a frisk, and indicate the importance of the case *Terry v. Ohio*.

4. List the four elements that must be present for an arrest to take place.

5. Explain under what circumstances officers need not announce themselves before entering a dwelling and under what circumstances arrest warrants are not required.

6. List the four categories of items that can be seized by use of a search warrant.

7. Explain when searches can be made without a warrant.

8. Recite the *Miranda* warning.

9. Indicate situations in which a *Miranda* warning is unnecessary.

10. List the three basic types of police identification.

INTRODUCTION
The Seat Belt Case

When Gail Atwater was pulled over by a police officer on a local street in Lago Vista, Texas, she did not appear to be engaged in any serious wrong-doing. She was driving her two children home from soccer practice at 15 miles per hour. There was no contraband in her pickup truck—rather, it was filled with two tricycles, a bag of charcoal, a cooler, toys, food, and two pairs of children's shoes.[1] In fact, Atwater had been stopped because neither she nor her children were wearing a seat belt. Under Texas law, this offense is a misdemeanor, punishable by a maximum fine of $50.

While the police officer's stop was unremarkable, his actions following the stop led Atwater and the city of Lago Vista to the United States Supreme Court. Instead of writing a ticket, he ordered Atwater out of her car, placed her in handcuffs, and informed her that she would be taken to jail. He threatened to take Atwater's children into custody as well, but a neighbor happened onto the scene of the incident and took them home.

Atwater's lawyers argued that the police officer had overstepped his discretion, and asked the United States Supreme Court to rule that it is unreasonable for an officer to arrest someone for a minor traffic offense that carries only a fine. The Court refused this request.[2] Justice David Souter, while agreeing that Atwater had been subjected to "gratuitous humiliations," said that the Court was not willing to limit an officer's ability to make an arrest as long as he or she believes that a law—any law—has been broken.[3]

Note that this was not an easy case for the Supreme Court. Four of the nine justices agreed with Atwater that the police officer had acted unreasonably. In effect, each member of the Court was forced to weigh Atwater's personal freedoms against the ability of the local police department to do its job. This balance between the need for effective law enforcement and the rights of American citizens under the U.S. Constitution has been, and remains, a controversial issue. Many observers feel that courts go too far in protecting the rights of the accused, but others think that police have been given a dangerous amount of leeway in using their powers. In this chapter we will examine the extent to which police behavior is controlled by the law, starting with a discussion of the constitutional principles on which such control is grounded.

Gail Atwater, left, with her children Anya and Mac at their home in Lago Vista, Texas. (AP Photo/Pat Sullivan.)

Go to the Stories from the Street feature at http://www.cj. wadsworth.com/gainescore2e to hear Larry Gaines tell insightful stories related to this chapter and his experiences in the field.

Keyword: Fourth Amendment

SEARCHES AND SEIZURES
The legal term, as found in the Fourth Amendment of the U.S. Constitution, that generally refers to the searching for and the confiscating of evidence by law enforcement agents.

PROBABLE CAUSE
Reasonable grounds to believe the existence of facts warranting certain actions, such as the search or arrest of a person.

FIGURE 6.1
The Meaning of Unreasonable Searches and Seizures and Probable Cause

THE FOURTH AMENDMENT

As pointed out in the introduction to this chapter, in the *Atwater v. City of Lago Vista* case, the United States Supreme Court did not address the defendant's illegal activity. (In fact, Atwater pleaded no contest to the seat belt charge.) Rather, it ruled that the police officer had not overstepped the boundaries of his authority in making the arrest. To understand these boundaries, law enforcement officers must understand the Fourth Amendment,[4] which reads as follows:

> The right of the people to be secure in their persons, houses, papers, and effects, against unreasonable searches and seizures, shall not be violated, and no Warrants shall issue, but upon probable cause, supported by Oath or affirmation, and particularly describing the place to be searched, and the persons or things to be seized.

This amendment contains two critical legal concepts: a prohibition against *unreasonable* **searches and seizures** and the requirement of *probable cause* to issue a warrant (see Figure 6.1).

Reasonableness

Law enforcement personnel use searches and seizures to look for and collect the evidence they need to convict individuals suspected of crimes. As you have just read, when conducting a search or seizure, they must be *reasonable*. Though courts have spent innumerable hours scrutinizing the word, no specific meaning for "reasonable" exists. A thesaurus can provide useful synonyms—logical, practical, sensible, intelligent, plausible—but as each case is different, those terms are relative.

In the *Atwater* case, the Court rejected the argument that the arrest had been so unreasonable as to violate the Fourth Amendment's prohibition against unreasonable searches and seizures. That does not mean that the officer's actions would have been unreasonable under any circumstances. What if Atwater could have proved that there was no way the officer could have known whether she was wearing a seat belt and that he had pulled her over in retaliation for contesting a speeding ticket that he had written her two months earlier? The officer's conduct would almost certainly have been considered unreasonable.

Probable Cause

The concept of reasonableness is linked to **probable cause.** The Supreme Court has ruled, for example, that any arrest or seizure is unreasonable unless it is supported by probable cause.[5] The burden of probable cause requires more than

UNREASONABLE SEARCH AND SEIZURE
The Fourth Amendment provides that individuals have the right to be "secure in their persons" against "unreasonable searches and seizures" conducted by government agents. In practice, this means that law enforcement officers must normally obtain a search warrant prior to a search and seizure. Basically, the search warrant is the acknowledgment by a judge that probable cause exists for law enforcement officers to search for or take a person or property. In other words, the search and seizure must be "reasonable."

PROBABLE CAUSE
Before a search can take place or an individual can be arrested, the requirement of probable cause must be met. Probable cause exists if there is a substantial likelihood that (1) a crime was committed and (2) the individual committed the crime. Note that probable cause involves a *likelihood*—not just a possibility—that the suspect committed the crime. Probable cause must exist before police can get an arrest warrant or a search warrant from a judge.

mere suspicion on a police officer's part; that officer must know of facts and circumstances that would reasonably lead to "the belief that an offense has been or is being committed."[6]

If no probable cause existed when a police officer took a certain action, it cannot be retroactively applied. If, for example, a police officer stops a person for jaywalking and then finds several ounces of marijuana in that person's pocket, the arrest for marijuana possession would probably be disallowed. Remember, suspicion does not equal probable cause. If, however, an informant had tipped off the officer that the person was a drug dealer, probable cause might exist and the arrest could be valid. Informants are one of several sources that may provide probable cause. Others include:

For a link to Findlaw's summary of the many laws regarding police procedure that can be traced to the Fourth Amendment, go to the Hypercontents page for this chapter at http://www.cj.wadsworth.com/ gainescore2e.

1. *Personal observation.* Police officers may use their personal training, experience, and expertise to infer probable cause from situations that may not be obviously criminal. If, for example, a police officer observes several people in a car slowly circling a certain building in a high-crime area, that officer may infer that the people are "casing" the building in preparation for a robbery. Probable cause could be established for detaining the suspects.

2. *Information.* Law enforcement officers receive information from victims, eyewitnesses, informants, and official sources such as police bulletins or broadcasts. Such information, as long as it is believed to be reliable, is a basis for probable cause.

3. *Evidence.* In certain circumstances, which will be examined later in this chapter, police have probable cause for a search or seizure based on evidence—such as a shotgun—in plain view.

4. *Association.* In some circumstances, if the police see a person with a known criminal background in a place where criminal activity is openly taking place, they have probable cause to stop that person. Generally, however, association is not adequate to establish probable cause.[7]

In a sense, the concept of probable cause allows police officers to do their job effectively. Most arrests are made without a warrant because most arrests are the result of quick police reaction to the commission of a crime. Indeed, it would not be practical to expect a police officer to obtain a warrant before making an arrest on the street. Thus, probable cause provides a framework that limits the situations in which police officers can make arrests, but also gives officers the freedom to act within that framework. Once an arrest is made, however, the arresting officer must prove to a judge that probable cause existed. In *County of Riverside v.*

EXCLUSIONARY RULE
A rule under which any evidence that is obtained in violation of the accused's rights under the Fourth, Fifth, and Sixth Amendments, as well as any evidence derived from illegally obtained evidence, will not be admissible in criminal court.

FRUIT OF THE POISONED TREE
Evidence that is acquired through the use of illegally obtained evidence and is therefore inadmissible in court.

INFOTRAC®
COLLEGE EDITION
Keyword: Exclusionary Rule

McLaughlin (1991),[8] the Supreme Court ruled that this judicial determination of probable cause must be made within forty-eight hours after the arrest, even if this two-day period includes a weekend or holiday.

The Exclusionary Rule

Historically, the courts have looked to the Fourth Amendment for guidance in regulating the activity of law enforcement officers, as the language of the Constitution does not expressly do so. The courts' most potent legal tool in this endeavor is the **exclusionary rule,** which prohibits the use of illegally seized evidence. According to this rule, any evidence obtained by an unreasonable search or seizure is inadmissible (may not be used) against a defendant in a criminal trial.[9] Even highly incriminating evidence, such as a knife stained with the victim's blood, usually cannot be introduced at a trial if illegally obtained. Furthermore, any physical or verbal evidence police are able to acquire by using illegally obtained evidence is known as the **fruit of the poisoned tree** and is also inadmissible. For example, if the police use the existence of the blood-stained knife to get a confession out of a suspect, that confession will be excluded as well.

One of the implications of the exclusionary rule is that it forces police to gather evidence properly. If they follow appropriate procedures, they are more likely to be rewarded with a conviction. If they are careless or abuse the rights of the suspect, they are unlikely to obtain a conviction. Critics of the exclusionary rule, however, argue that its strict application may permit guilty people to go free because of police carelessness or innocent errors.

STOPS AND FRISKS

Several years ago, an off-duty Miami–Dade County police officer named Aaron Campbell was driving on the Florida turnpike when he was pulled over by two Orange County deputies, allegedly for changing lanes without properly signaling. A fistfight ensued. At the resulting trial, Campbell claimed that he was stopped because he fit a drug courier profile in use by the deputies; he was an African American and had South Florida license plates. A circuit judge agreed, ruling that Campbell had been stopped illegally.[10]

The problem was not that the deputies had stopped Campbell. Law enforcement officers are expected to stop and question people if there is a suspicion of illegal behavior. The problem was that the Orange County deputies did not have a "reasonable" suspicion that Campbell was breaking the law. Instead, they had only a "mere" suspicion based on the drug courier profile—without any other specific facts. (See the feature *Criminal Justice in Action—Racial Profiling and the Constitution* at the end of the chapter.) When reasonable suspicion exists, police officers are well within their rights to *stop and frisk* a suspect (described in more detail later). In a stop and frisk, law enforcement officers (1) briefly detain a person they reasonably believe to be suspicious, and (2) if they believe the person to be armed, proceed to pat down, or "frisk," that person's outer clothing.[11]

Terry v. Ohio

The precedent for the ever-elusive definition of a "reasonable" suspicion in stop-and-frisk situations was established in *Terry v. Ohio* (1968).[12] In that case, a detective named McFadden observed two men (one of whom was Terry) acting strangely in downtown Cleveland. The men would walk past a certain store, peer into the window, and then stop at a street corner and confer. While they were talking, another man joined the conversation and then left quickly. Several minutes later the three men met again at another corner a few blocks away. Detective McFadden believed the trio was planning to break into the store. He approached

GREAT DEBATES
Does the exclusionary rule allow the guilty to go free on technicalities? Is it unfair to police? In contrast, is it necessary to protect citizens against unethical actions by the police? To better understand the many issues that surround the exclusionary rule, go to the Great Debates feature on the text's companion Web site at **http://www.cj.wadsworth. com/gainescore2e.**

Cross-National CJ COMPARISON

French Identity Checks

As the Christmas holiday approached, the people of France were understandably nervous. Christmas Eve would mark the second anniversary of the hijacking of a French airplane by terrorists who accused France of supporting a repressive regime in Algeria. On December 4, 1995, four people had been killed and dozens injured when a bomb exploded on a commuter train in Paris. French law enforcement responded to the unease with a massive security operation—on December 18 alone, the police stopped and questioned six thousand people. Few, if any, of those stops would have been ruled constitutional in the United States.

French "identity checks," in which police require people to show identification, and American "stop and frisks" have similar goals. Both are tools that police officers use to detect and prevent crime. French police have much greater free-dom in carrying out identity checks than do their American counterparts, though. First, French law does not require that police have a reasonable suspicion that criminal activity is about to take place. Second, a French police officer does not need to establish imminent danger to do a weapons frisk.

These conditions are the direct result of terrorist activity. For a short time before 1986, the French Procedural Code required that all identity checks be based on individualized suspicion or the threat of immediate danger. After an Iranian-backed Lebanese group carried out a bombing campaign that year, the law was changed to its present form in an attempt to better protect French citizens from terrorist acts.

FOR CRITICAL ANALYSIS
What role does "reasonable suspicion" play in police stops in the United States? In the wake of the September 11, 2001, terrorist attacks on New York and Washington, D.C., do you think American police should be able to carry out French-style "identity checks" of suspicious persons? Do you think the U.S. public would accept such measures?

them, told them who he was, and asked for identification. After receiving a mumbled response, the detective frisked the three men and found handguns on two of them, who were tried and convicted of carrying concealed weapons.

The United States Supreme Court upheld the conviction, ruling that Detective McFadden had reasonable cause to believe that the men were armed and dangerous and that swift action was necessary to protect himself and other citizens in the area.[13] The Court accepted McFadden's interpretation of the unfolding scene as based on objective facts and practical conclusions. It therefore concluded that his suspicion was reasonable. In the Florida case described above, the deputies' reasons for stopping Campbell—his race and place of car registration—were not seen as reasonable. (For information on the role "reasonableness" plays in France's equivalent to the stop and frisk, see the feature *Cross-National CJ Comparison—French Identity Checks*.)

For the most part, the judicial system has refrained from placing restrictions on police officers' ability to make stops. In *Terry*, the Supreme Court did say that the officer must have "specific and articulable facts" before making a stop, but added that the facts may be "taken together with rational inferences."[14] The Court has consistently ruled that because of their "street" experience, police officers are in a unique position to make such inferences and should be given a great deal of freedom in doing so. In *United States v. Cortez* (1981),[15] the Court augmented a police officer's discretion to stop citizens by holding that reasonable suspicion should be based on the "totality of the circumstances," which may include inferences and deductions made by a trained officer. So, for example, if a person flees at the mere sight of a police car in an area known for heavy narcotics trafficking, the "totality of circumstances" test may sometimes, though not always, provide the officer with sufficient justification to conduct a stop-and-frisk search.[16]

INFOTRAC®
COLLEGE EDITION
Keyword: Terry v. Ohio

A Stop

The terms *stop* and *frisk* are often used in concert, but they describe two separate acts. A **stop** takes place when a law enforcement officer has reasonable suspicion

STOP
A brief detention of a person by law enforcement agents for questioning. The agents must have a reasonable suspicion that a crime has been committed, or will be committed, involving the person before making a stop.

FRISK
A pat-down or minimal search by police to discover weapons; conducted for the express purpose of protecting the officer or other citizens, and not to find evidence of illegal substances for use in a trial.

ARREST
To take into custody a person suspected of criminal activity. Police may use only reasonable levels of force in making an arrest.

> "A highly sophisticated set of rules, qualified by all sorts of ifs, ands, and buts and requiring the drawing of subtle nuances and hairline distinctions, may be the sort of heady stuff upon which the facile minds of lawyers and judges eagerly feed, but they may be literally impossible of application by the officer in the field."
>
> —Wayne R. LaFave, *American law professor* (1974)

A police officer frisks a suspect in Lockhart, Texas. What is the main purpose behind a frisk? When are police justified in frisking someone who has been detained? (Photo Edit/John Boykin)

that a criminal activity is taking place or is about to take place. In 2002, the United States Supreme Court ruled that police can use their practical experience to determine whether a situation is reasonably suspicious. Consequently, certain otherwise innocent behavior—such as a driver abruptly slowing down when seeing a patrol car—can be grounds for a stop if, as in one case, it takes place on a dirt road that is commonly used by drug smugglers.[17] Because an investigatory stop is not an arrest, there are limits to the extent police can detain someone who has been stopped. For example, in one situation an airline traveler and his luggage were detained for ninety minutes while the police waited for a drug-sniffing dog to arrive. The Court ruled that the initial stop of the passenger was constitutional, but that the ninety-minute wait was excessive.[18]

A Frisk

The Supreme Court has stated that a **frisk** should be a protective measure. Police officers cannot conduct a frisk as a "fishing expedition" simply to try to find items besides weapons, such as illegal narcotics, on a suspect.[19] A frisk does not necessarily follow a stop and in fact may occur only when the officer is justified in thinking that the safety of police officers or other citizens may be endangered.

Again, the question of reasonable suspicion is at the heart of determining the legality of frisks. In the *Terry* case, the Court accepted that Detective McFadden reasonably believed that the three suspects posed a threat. The suspects' refusal to answer McFadden's questions, though within their rights because they had not been arrested, provided him with sufficient motive for the frisk.

ARRESTS

As in the *Terry* case, a stop and frisk may lead to an **arrest.** An arrest is the taking into custody of a citizen for the purpose of detaining him or her on a criminal charge.[20] It is important to understand the difference between a stop and an arrest. In the eyes of the law, a stop is a relatively brief intrusion on a citizen's rights, whereas an arrest—which involves a deprivation of liberty—is deserving of a full range of constitutional protections, which we shall discuss throughout the chapter (see *Mastering Concepts—The Difference between a Stop and an Arrest*). Consequently, while a stop can be made based on a reasonable suspicion, a law enforcement officer needs a probable cause, as defined earlier, to make an arrest.[21]

Elements of an Arrest

When is somebody under arrest? The easy—and false—answer would be whenever the police officer says so. In fact, the state of being under arrest is dependent not only on the actions of the law enforcement officers but also on the perception of the suspect. Suppose Mr. Jones is stopped by plainclothes detectives, driven to the police station, and detained for three hours for questioning. During this time, the police never tell Mr. Jones he is under arrest, and in fact, he is free to leave at any time. But if Mr. Jones or any other reasonable person *believes* he is not free to leave, then, according to the United States Supreme Court, that person is in fact under arrest and should be afforded the necessary constitutional protections.[22]

Criminal justice professor Rolando V. del Carmen of Sam Houston State University has identified four elements that must be present for an arrest to take place:

1 The *intent* to arrest. In a stop, though it may entail slight inconvenience and a short detention period, there is no intent on the part of the law enforcement officer to take the person into custody. Therefore, there is no arrest. As intent is a subjective term, it is sometimes difficult to determine

MASTERING CONCEPTS | The Difference between a Stop and an Arrest

Both stops and arrests are considered seizures because both police actions involve the restriction of an individual's freedom to "walk away." Both must be justified by a showing of reasonableness as well. You should be aware, however, of the important differences between a stop and an arrest:

	STOP	ARREST
Justification:	Reasonable suspicion	Probable cause
Warrant:	None	Required in some, though not all, situations
Intent of Officer:	The investigation of suspicious activity	To make a formal charge against the suspect
Search:	May frisk, or "pat down," for weapons	Full search for weapons and evidence
Scope of Search:	Outer clothing only	Area within the suspect's immediate control, or "reach"

The stop is an important part of police activity. Police officers therefore have the right to stop and frisk a person if they suspect that a crime is about to be committed. Police may stop those who are acting strangely, do not "fit" the time or place, are knwn to associate with criminals, or are loitering. They may also stop a person who reasonably fits a description of a person who is wanted in conjunction with a crime. During a stop, police can interrogate the person and make a limited search of his or her outer clothing. If anything occurs during the stop, such as the discovery of an illegal weapon, then officers may arrest the person. If an arrest is made, the suspect is now in police custody and is protected by the U.S. Constitution in a number of ways that will be discussed later in the chapter.

Source: Adapted from J. Scott Harr and Karen M. Hess, *Criminal Procedure* (St. Paul, MN: West Publishing Company, 1990), 140

whether the police officer intended to arrest. In situations in which the intent is unclear, courts often rely—as in our hypothetical case of Mr. Jones—on the perception of the arrestee.[23]

2 The *authority* to arrest. State laws give police officers the authority to place citizens under custodial arrest, or take them into custody. Like other state laws, the authorization to arrest varies among the fifty states. Some states, for example, allow off-duty police officers to make arrests, while others do not.

3 *Seizure or detention.* A necessary part of an arrest is the detention of the subject. Detention is considered to have occurred as soon as the arrested individual submits to the control of the officer, whether peacefully or under the threat or use of force.

4 The *understanding* of the person that she or he has been arrested. Through either words—such as "you are now under arrest"—or actions, the person taken into custody must understand that an arrest has taken place. If a subject has been forcibly subdued by the police, handcuffed, and placed in a patrol car, that subject is believed to understand that an arrest has been made. This understanding may be lacking if the person is intoxicated, insane, or unconscious.[24]

INFOTRAC®
COLLEGE EDITION

Keywords: arrest and warrants

Arrests with a Warrant

When law enforcement officers have established a probable cause to arrest an individual who is not in police custody, they obtain an **arrest warrant** for that person. An arrest warrant contains information such as the name of the person suspected and the crime he or she is suspected of having committed. (See Figure 6.2 on the next page for an example of an arrest warrant.) Judges or magistrates issue arrest warrants after first determining that the law enforcement officers have indeed established probable cause.

ARREST WARRANT
A written order, based on probable cause and issued by a judge or magistrate, commanding that the person named on the warrant be arrested by the police.

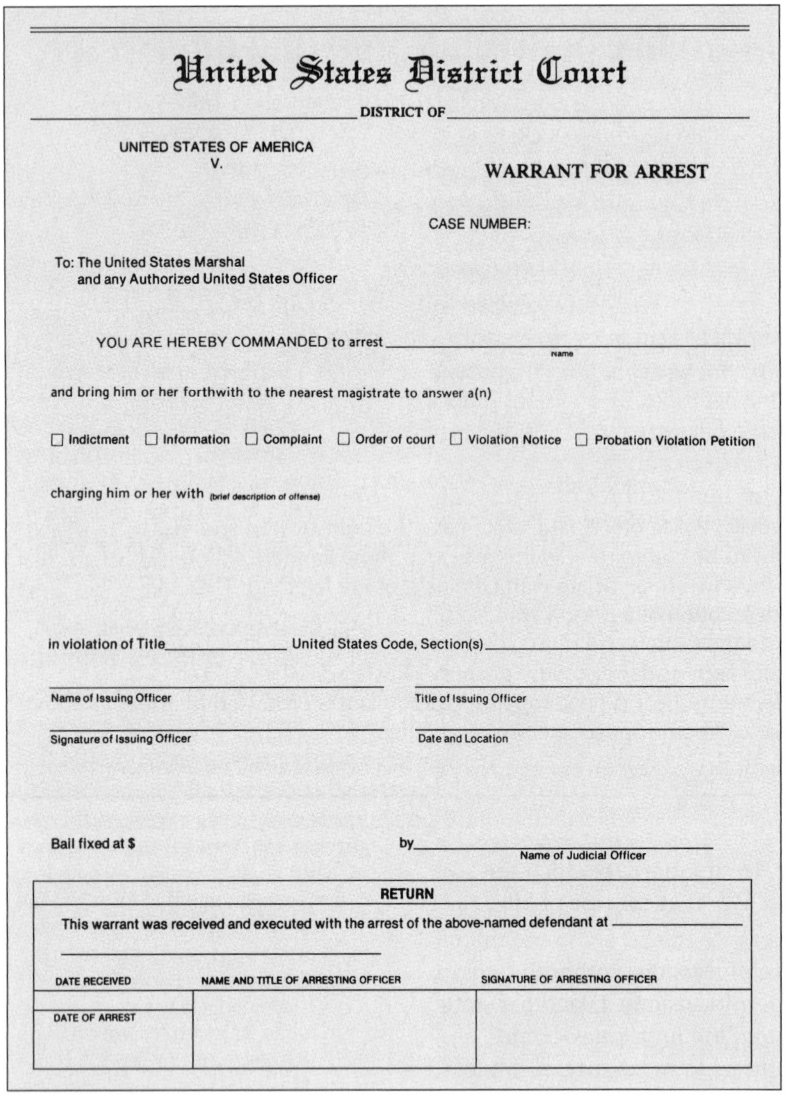

United States District Court

_____ DISTRICT OF _____

UNITED STATES OF AMERICA
V.

WARRANT FOR ARREST

CASE NUMBER:

To: The United States Marshal
and any Authorized United States Officer

YOU ARE HEREBY COMMANDED to arrest _____
_____ Name

and bring him or her forthwith to the nearest magistrate to answer a(n)

☐ Indictment ☐ Information ☐ Complaint ☐ Order of court ☐ Violation Notice ☐ Probation Violation Petition

charging him or her with (brief description of offense)

in violation of Title _____ United States Code, Section(s) _____

Name of Issuing Officer | Title of Issuing Officer

Signature of Issuing Officer | Date and Location

Bail fixed at $ _____ by _____
_____ Name of Judicial Officer

RETURN

This warrant was received and executed with the arrest of the above-named defendant at _____

DATE RECEIVED | NAME AND TITLE OF ARRESTING OFFICER | SIGNATURE OF ARRESTING OFFICER

DATE OF ARREST

FIGURE 6.2
Example of an Arrest Warrant

EXIGENT CIRCUMSTANCES
Situations that require extralegal or exceptional actions by the police. In these circumstances, police officers are justified in not following procedural rules, such as those pertaining to search and arrest warrants.

WARRANTLESS ARREST
An arrest made without first seeking a warrant for the action; permitted under certain circumstances, such as when the arresting officer has witnessed the crime or has a reasonable belief that the suspect has committed a felony.

There is a perception that an arrest warrant gives law enforcement officers the authority to enter a dwelling without first announcing themselves. This is not accurate. In *Wilson v. Arkansas* (1995),[25] the United States Supreme Court reiterated the common law requirement that police officers must knock and announce their identity and purpose before entering a dwelling. Under certain conditions, known as **exigent circumstances**, law enforcement officers need not announce themselves. These circumstances include situations in which the officers have a reasonable belief of any of the following:

● The suspect is armed and poses a strong threat of violence to the officers or others inside the dwelling.

● Persons inside the dwelling are in the process of destroying evidence or escaping because of the presence of the police.

● A felony is being committed at the time the officers enter.[26]

For example, in *Minnesota v. Olson* (1990),[27] the Court ruled that officers acted legally when they forcibly entered the home of an armed robber who had been fleeing arrest.

Arrests without a Warrant

Arrest warrants are not required, and in fact, most arrests are made on the scene without a warrant.[28] A law enforcement officer may make a **warrantless arrest** if:

1 The offense is committed in the presence of the officer; or

2 The officer has knowledge that a crime has been committed and a probable cause to believe the crime was committed by a particular suspect.[29]

The type of crime also comes to bear in questions of arrests without a warrant. As a general rule, officers can make a warrantless arrest for a crime they did not see if they have probable cause to believe that a felony has been committed. For misdemeanors, the crime must have been committed in the presence of the officer for a warrantless arrest to be valid.

In certain situations, warrantless arrests are unlawful even though a police officer can establish probable cause. In *Payton v. New York* (1980),[30] for example, the Supreme Court held that when exigent circumstances do not exist and the suspect does not give consent to enter a dwelling, law enforcement officers cannot force themselves in for the purpose of making a warrantless arrest. The *Payton* ruling was expanded to cover the homes of third parties when, in *Steagald v. United States* (1981),[31] the Court ruled that if the police wish to arrest a criminal suspect in another person's home, they cannot enter that home to arrest the suspect without first obtaining a search warrant, a process we will discuss in the following section.

Criminal Justice & TECHN LOGY

Biometrics

Americans have become accustomed to being watched. Surveillance cameras are commonplace in banks, malls, lobbies of office buildings, and other private and public places. But these cameras are only recorders; they do not "recognize" us, or send information about us to a third party. The technology does exist, however, that would let these cameras do just this, and much more.

Broadly known as "biometrics," this technology allows a camera to identify anyone who comes into view by scanning her or his physical characteristics, and matching the results of the scan with information in a database. Airports in Iceland and Great Britain, for example, utilize face recognition biometrics to protect against terrorism. A computer linked to surveillance cameras in these airports profiles individuals based on as many as eighty different facial structural features, such as cheekbone formation, the width of the nose bridge, and the space between the eyes. These facial "signatures," once noted, are compared to facial features of known criminals or terrorists.

In the United States, privacy concerns have limited the use of biometrics. Facial recognition cameras, after all, would circumvent the anonymity that is important to many Americans. But as security concerns have become paramount after the terrorist attacks of September 11, 2001, resistance to biometrics seems to have weakened. One company that markets facial recognition technology received nearly a hundred inquiries a day in the weeks following the tragedy. The possibilities of biometrics in fighting terrorism are intriguing. A video taken at a terrorist training camp, for example, could be fed into a computer, which would log the features of the faces. This information would then be distributed to airports, embassies, and other locations for use in their own systems.

IN THE FUTURE
The International Air Transport Association favors a slightly more advanced form of biometrics that scans a person's eyes by measuring the distinct colors in the iris or the patterns of blood vessels in the retina. This technology is less invasive than face recognition. A veiled Muslim woman, for example, could be identified without having to drop her veil.

 For more information on the technology described in this box, go to the Crime and Technology feature at http://www.cj.wadsworth.com/gainescore2e

LAWFUL SEARCHES AND SEIZURES

How far can law enforcement agents go in searching and seizing private property? Consider the steps taken by Jenny Stracner, an investigator with the Laguna Beach (California) Police Department. After receiving information that a suspect, Greenwood, was engaged in drug trafficking, Stracner enlisted the aid of the local trash collector in procuring evidence. Instead of taking Greenwood's trash bags to be incinerated, the collector agreed to give them to Stracner. The officer found enough drug paraphernalia in the garbage to obtain a warrant to search Greenwood's home. Subsequently, he was arrested and convicted on narcotics charges.[32]

Remember, the Fourth Amendment is quite specific in forbidding unreasonable searches and seizures. Were Stracner's search of Greenwood's garbage and her seizure of its contents "reasonable"? The United States Supreme Court thought so, holding that Greenwood's garbage was not protected by the Fourth Amendment.[33]

The Role of Privacy in Searches

A crucial concept in understanding search and seizure law is *privacy.* By definition, a **search** is a governmental intrusion on a citizen's reasonable expectation of privacy. The recognized standard for a "reasonable expectation of privacy" was established in *Katz v. United States* (1967).[34] The case dealt with the question of whether the defendant was justified in his expectation of privacy in the calls he made from a public phone booth. The Supreme Court held that "the Fourth Amendment protects people, not places." Katz prevailed.

In his concurring opinion, Justice John Harlan, Jr., set a two-pronged test for a person's expectation of privacy:

SEARCH
The process by which police examine a person or property to find evidence that will be used to prove guilt in a criminal trial.

SEARCH WARRANT
A written order, based on probable cause and issued by a judge or magistrate, commanding that police officers or criminal investigators search a specific person, place, or property to obtain evidence.

AFFIDAVIT
A written statement of facts, confirmed by the oath or affirmation of the party making it and made before a person having the authority to administer the oath or affirmation.

INFOTRAC®
COLLEGE EDITION

Keywords: search and seizure

FIGURE 6.3
Example of a Search Warrant

United States District Court

DISTRICT OF_____

In the Matter of the Search of
(Name, address or brief description of person or property to be searched)

SEARCH WARRANT

CASE NUMBER:

TO:_____ and any Authorized Officer of the United States

Affidavit(s) having been made before me by_____ who has reason to
                            Affiant
believe that ☐ on the person of or ☐ on the premises known as (name, description and/or location)

in the_____District of_____there is now
concealed a certain person or property, namely (describe the person or property)

I am satisfied that the affidavit(s) and any recorded testimony establish probable cause to believe that the person or property so described is now concealed on the person or premises above-described and establish grounds for the issuance of this warrant.

YOU ARE HEREBY COMMANDED to search on or before_____
                                              Date
(not to exceed 10 days) the person or place named above for the person or property specified, serving this warrant and making the search (in the daytime — 6:00 A.M. to 10:00 P.M.) (at any time in the day or night as I find reasonable cause has been established) and if the person or property be found there to seize same, leaving a copy of this warrant and receipt for the person or property taken, and prepare a written inventory of the person or property seized and promptly return this warrant to_____
as required by law.   U.S. Judge or Magistrate

_____ at _____
Date and Time Issued   City and State

_____   _____
Name and Title of Judicial Officer   Signature of Judicial Officer

---

❶ The individual must prove that she or he expected privacy, and

❷ Society must recognize that expectation as reasonable.[35]

Accordingly, the Court agreed with Katz's claim that he had a reasonable right to privacy in a public phone booth. (Remember, however, that the *Terry* case allows for conditions under which a person's privacy rights are submerged by a reasonable suspicion on the part of a law enforcement officer that a threat to public safety is present.)

In contrast, in *California v. Greenwood* (1988)[36] described above, the Court did not believe that the suspect had a reasonable expectation of privacy when it came to his garbage bags. The Court noted that when we place our trash on a curb, we expose it to any number of intrusions by "animals, children, scavengers, snoops, and other members of the public."[37] In other words, if Greenwood had truly intended for the contents of his garbage bags to remain private, he would not have left them on the side of the road. "Reasonable" expectations of privacy can, and do, change. (For a discussion of one possible change following the September 11, 2001, terrorist attacks on New York and Washington, D.C., see the feature *Criminal Justice & Technology—Biometrics* on the previous page.)

Search and Seizure Warrants

To protect against charges that they have unreasonably infringed on privacy rights during a search, law enforcement officers can obtain a **search warrant.** (See Figure 6.3 for an example of a search warrant.) Similar to an arrest warrant, a search warrant is a court order that authorizes police to search a certain area. Before a judge or magistrate will issue a search warrant, law enforcement officers must generally provide:

- Information showing probable cause that a crime has been or will be committed.
- Specific information on the premises to be searched, the suspects to be found and the illegal activities taking place at those premises, and the items to be seized.

The purpose of a search warrant is to establish, before the search takes place, that a *probable cause to search* justifies infringing on the suspect's reasonable expectation of privacy.

The members of the First Congress specifically did not want law enforcement officers to have the freedom to make "general, exploratory" searches through a person's belongings.[38] Consequently, the Fourth Amendment requires that a warrant describe with "particularity" the place to be searched and the things—either people or objects—to be seized.

This "particularity" requirement places a heavy burden on law enforcement officers. Before going to a judge to ask for a search warrant, they must prepare an **affidavit** in which they provide specific, written information on the property that they wish to search and seize. They must know the specific address of any place they wish to search; general addresses of apartment buildings or office complexes are not sufficient. Furthermore, courts generally frown on vague descriptions of goods to be seized. "Stolen goods" would most likely be consid-

YOU be the JUDGE
A Valid Search?

THE FACTS

Baltimore police officers obtained a valid warrant to search Larry's apartment for marijuana. Larry's address, as described on the warrant, was "the premises known as 2036 Park Avenue third floor apartment." When the officers conducted the search, they reasonably believed that there was only one apartment on the third floor of the building. In fact, the third floor was divided into two apartments, the second one rented by Harold. Before the officers became aware that they were actually searching Harold's apartment, for which they had no warrant, they discovered illegal drugs there. Harold was eventually charged with possession of heroin with intent to distribute.

THE LAW

To prevent general searches, the Fourth Amendment requires warrants to describe with particularity "the place to be searched." Police officers are required to make a "reasonable effort" to make sure that the place they are searching is the place specified in the warrant.

YOUR DECISION

Harold claims that the evidence against him is invalid, because "the officers, not having a warrant for [his] apartment, had no right to go into that apartment." Do you agree?

[To see how the United States Supreme Court ruled in this case, go to Example 6.1 in Appendix A.]

ered unacceptably imprecise, while "1 Optra S 1650 Lexmark Laser Printer" would be preferred.

A **seizure** is the act of taking possession of property by the government because of a (suspected) violation of the law. In general, four categories of items can be seized by use of a search warrant:

1 Items that resulted from the crime, such as stolen goods.

2 Items that are inherently illegal for anybody to possess (with certain exceptions), such as narcotics and counterfeit currency.

3 Items that can be called "evidence" of the crime, such as a blood-stained sneaker.

4 Items used in committing the crime, such as an ice pick or a printing press used to make counterfeit bills.[39]

No matter how "particular" a warrant is, it cannot provide for all the conditions that are bound to come up during its service. Consequently, the law gives law enforcement officers the ability to act "reasonably" during a search and seizure in the event of unforeseeable circumstances. For example, if a police officer is searching an apartment for a stolen Optra S 1650 Lexmark laser printer and notices a vial of crack cocaine sitting on the suspect's bed, that contraband is considered to be in "plain view" and can be seized. (See *You Be the Judge—A Valid Search?*)

Searches and Seizures without a Warrant

Although the United States Supreme Court has established the principle that searches conducted without warrants are *per se* (by definition) unreasonable, it has set "specifically established" exceptions to the rule.[40] In fact, most searches, like most arrests, take place in the absence of a judicial order. Warrantless searches and seizures can be lawful when police are in "hot pursuit" of a subject or when they search bags of trash left at the curb for regular collection. Because of the magnitude of smuggling activities in "border areas" such as airports, seaports, and international boundaries, a warrant is normally not needed to search property in those places. The two most important circumstances in which a warrant is not needed, however, are (1) searches incidental to an arrest and (2) consensual searches.

SEIZURE
The forcible taking of a person or property in response to a violation of the law.

On the Web

CourtTV hosts a useful Web site on search and seizure law. The site offers FAQs and links to other sites that deal with this issue. For access to CourtTV's Web site, go to the Hypercontents page for this chapter at http://www.cj.wadsworth.com/gainescore2e.

**SEARCHES INCIDENTAL
TO ARRESTS**
Searches for weapons and evidence of
persons who have just been arrested. The
fruit of such searches is admissible if any
items found are within the immediate
vicinity or control of the suspect.

CONSENT SEARCHES
Searches by police that are made after the
subject of the search has agreed to the
action. In these situations, consent, if given
of free will, validates a warrantless search.

In 1999, New York City implemented a
plan that allows police officers to seize
the cars of people arrested for driving
with blood alcohol levels of .10 or
higher. As "specifically established"
exceptions to search and seizure law,
such seizures are considered
constitutional. Are you in favor of this
method of controlling drunk drivers?
What might be some of the practical
problems that New York police officers
will encounter while enforcing this
policy? (NYT Pictures/William Lopez)

Searches Incidental to an Arrest.   The most frequent exception to the
warrant requirement involves **searches incidental to arrests,** so-called because
nearly every time police officers make an arrest, they also search the suspect. As
long as the original arrest was based on probable cause, these searches are valid
for two reasons, established by the United States Supreme Court in *United States v.
Robinson* (1973):[41]

1 The need for a police officer to find and confiscate any weapons a suspect
may be carrying.

2 The need to protect any evidence on the suspect's person from being
destroyed.

Law enforcement officers are, however, limited in the searches they may make
during an arrest. These limits were established by the United States Supreme
Court in *Chimel v. California* (1969).[42] In that case, police arrived at Chimel's
home with an arrest warrant but not a search warrant. Even though Chimel
refused their request to "look around," the officers searched the entire three-
bedroom house for nearly an hour, finding stolen coins in the process. Chimel
was convicted of burglary and appealed, arguing that the evidence of the coins
should have been suppressed.

The United States Supreme Court held that the search was unreasonable. In
doing so, the Court established guidelines as to the acceptable extent of searches
incidental to an arrest. Primarily, the Court ruled that police may search any
area within the suspect's "immediate control" to confiscate any weapons or evidence that the suspect could destroy. The Court found, however, that there was
no justification:

> for routinely searching rooms other than that in which the arrest occurs—or, for
> that matter, for searching through all desk drawers or other closed or concealed
> areas in that room itself. Such searches, in the absence of well-recognized excep-
> tions, may be made only under the authority of a search warrant.

The exact interpretation of the "area within immediate control" has been left to
individual courts, but in general it has been taken to mean the area within the
reach of the arrested person. Thus, the Court is said to have established the
"arm's reach doctrine" in its *Chimel* decision.

**Searches with Consent. Consent
searches,** the second most common type of
warrantless searches, take place when individuals give law enforcement officers permission to
search their persons, homes, or belongings. (For
an overview of the circumstances under which
warrantless searches are allowed, see *Mastering
Concepts—Exceptions to the Requirement That Officers Have a Search Warrant.*) The consent must,
however, be voluntary. If a person has been
physically threatened or otherwise coerced into
giving consent, the search is invalid.[43] The standard for consent searches was set in *Schneckcloth
v. Bustamonte* (1973),[44] in which, after being
asked, the defendant told police officers to "go
ahead" and search his car. A packet of stolen
checks found in the trunk was ruled valid evidence because the driver consented to the search.

Critics of consent searches hold that such
searches are rarely voluntary because most citizens are intimidated by police and will react to a

MASTERING CONCEPTS

Exceptions to the Requirement That Officers Have a Search Warrant

In many circumstances, it would be impractical for police officers to leave a crime scene, go to a judge, and obtain a search warrant before conducting a search. Therefore, under a number of circumstances a search warrant is not required.

Exception	Circumstance Not Requiring a Warrant
Incident to Lawful Arrest	Police officers may search the area within immediate control of a person after they have arrested him or her.
Consent	Police officers may search a person without a warrant if that person voluntarily agrees to be searched and has the legal authority to authorize the search.
Stop and Frisk	Police officers may frisk, or "pat down," a person if they suspect that the person may be involved in criminal activity or pose a danger to those in the immediate area.
Hot Pursuit	If police officers are in "hot pursuit" or chasing a person they have probable cause to believe committed a crime, and that person enters a building, the officers may search the building without a warrant.
Automobile Exception	If police officers have probable cause to believe that an automobile contains evidence of a crime, they may, in most instances, search the vehicle without a warrant.
Plain View	If police officers are legally engaged in police work and happen to see evidence of a crime in "plain view," they may seize it without a search warrant.
Abandoned Property	Any property, such as a hotel room that has been vacated or contraband that has been discarded, may be searched and seized by police officers without a warrant.
Border Searches	Law enforcement officers on border patrol do not need a warrant to search vehicles crossing the border.
Inevitable Discovery	Evidence that has been illegally obtained (without the necessary warrant) may be admitted as evidence if the prosecution can prove that it would have "inevitably" been found by lawful means.

request for permission to make a search as if it were an order.[45] Furthermore, most citizens are unaware that they have the option not to comply with a request for a search. Thus, if a police officer asks to search a citizen's car after issuing a speeding ticket, the citizen is well within her or his rights to refuse. According to the United States Supreme Court's ruling in *Ohio v. Robinette* (1996),[46] however, the Fourth Amendment does not require a police officer to inform citizens that they are "free to go" after an initial stop when no arrest is involved. Thus, an officer can obtain consent to search from someone who is free to leave without ever informing the person that he or she is in fact free to go. The significance of this ruling is underscored by data presented by prosecutors during the *Robinette* ruling: in the two years leading up to the case, four hundred Ohio drivers were convicted of narcotics offenses that resulted directly from search requests that could have been denied but were not.[47]

INFOTRAC®
COLLEGE EDITION

Keyword: electronic surveillance

High-Risk Searches and Seizures

In situations in which a search-and-seizure operation is considered to be particularly dangerous, police officials may use Special Weapons and Tactics (SWAT) teams to execute warrants. SWAT teams are trained to handle high-risk situations, and often use high-destruction weaponry and tactics. Almost every federal law enforcement agency and approximately 90 percent of municipal police departments serving communities with populations greater than 50,000 have SWAT units for support.[48]

A SWAT team makes a forcible entry into a hotel room in Fresno, California, on May 4, 2002. While searching the room earlier in the day, local police officers were surprised by a man with a pistol. Why would a SWAT team be used under these circumstances? Do you think this is a "reasonable" way to conduct a search and seizure? (AP Photo/The Fresno Bee, David Hunter)

INFOTRAC®
COLLEGE EDITION

Keyword: automobile searches

Typically, a SWAT team will make the initial entry. After the site has been secured, another police officer will serve the actual warrant. Although the safest method of entry is often for the agents to knock on the front door and announce their presence, in some situations that would place them in unreasonable danger. Thus, in many of these cases, SWAT teams conduct "dynamic entries," which may entail breaking down a door or window or using explosives to blow a hole in the wall.[49]

While many law enforcement experts believe that SWAT teams are necessary to deal with predicaments beyond the scope of "regular" police officers, others find some of their tactics troubling. The sight of law enforcement officers dressed in black and carrying machine guns, along with the knowledge that SWAT teams train with U.S. Armed Forces units, leads to worries of the *militarization* of police forces.[50] Furthermore, as you learned earlier in this chapter, searches and seizures must be conducted "reasonably"—a concept that seems at odds with the violent nature of SWAT team actions.

Searches of Automobiles

Though the *Chimel* case limited the scope of searches and seizures incident to an arrest in most circumstances, the United States Supreme Court has not been as restrictive concerning searches in arrests involving automobile passengers. In *New York v. Belton* (1981),[51] the Court held that when police officers lawfully arrested a person driving a car, they could legally make a warrantless search of the car's entire front and back compartments. This expansive interpretation of "the area within immediate control" is indicative of the Court's lenient view of automobile searches.

The "Movable Vehicle Exception."

In *Carroll v. United States* (1925),[52] the United States Supreme Court ruled that the law would distinguish among automobiles, homes, and persons in questions involving police searches. In the years since *Carroll,* the Court has established that the Fourth Amendment does not require police to obtain a warrant to search automobiles or other movable vehicles when they have probable cause to believe that a vehicle contains contraband or evidence of criminal activity.[53] The reasoning behind such leniency is straightforward: requiring a warrant to search an automobile places too heavy a burden on police officers. By the time the officers could communicate with a judge and obtain the warrant, the suspects could drive away and destroy any evidence. Consequently, the United States Supreme Court has consistently held that someone in a vehicle does not have the same reasonable expectation of privacy as someone at home or even in a phone booth.

A number of rulings increased police powers in these situations. *Mimms v. Pennsylvania* (1977)[54] established that police officers who stopped a car for a traffic violation could legally order the driver out of the vehicle. In *Whren v. United States* (1996),[55] the United States Supreme Court ruled that the "true" motivation of police officers in making traffic stops was irrelevant as long as they had probable cause to believe that a traffic law had been broken. In other words, police may stop a car they believe to be transporting drugs in order to issue a speeding citation. The fact that the officers are using the speeding ticket as a pretext to search for drugs (and would not have stopped the driver otherwise) does not matter, as long as the driver actually was speeding. One year later, in *Maryland v. Wilson* (1997),[56] the Court further expanded police power by ruling that an officer may order passengers as well as the driver out of a car during a traffic stop; the Court reasoned that the danger to an officer is increased when there is a passenger in the automobile.

Searches of Luggage in Automobiles. Note that the rules governing searches incidental to an arrest apply to automobile searches. So, if a police officer has not made a custodial arrest and does not have reasonable suspicion that a crime has been or is about to be committed, that officer cannot search a car she or he has stopped.[57] In practice, however, this is rarely a problem for law enforcement agents. As mentioned earlier, the United States Supreme Court's *Belton* ruling allows the arresting officer to make a complete search of the inside of an automobile as long as he or she had probable cause to make the arrest.[58]

The Plain View Doctrine

Though police must have probable cause to search luggage in an automobile's trunk, no such protection applies to contraband in *plain view.* For example, suppose a traffic officer pulls over a person for speeding, looks in the driver-side window, and clearly sees what appears to be a bag of heroin resting on the passenger seat. In this instance, under the **plain view doctrine,** the officer would be justified in seizing the drugs without a warrant.

The plain view doctrine was first enunciated by the Supreme Court in *Coolidge v. New Hampshire* (1971).[59] The Court ruled that law enforcement officers may make a warrantless seizure of an item if four criteria are met:

1 The item is positioned so as to be detected easily by an officer's sight or some other sense.

2 The officer is legally in a position to notice the item in question.

3 The discovery of the item is inadvertent; that is, the officer had not intended to find the item.

4 The officer immediately recognizes the illegal nature of the item. No interrogation or further investigation is allowed under the plain view doctrine.

(For a discussion of how the plain view doctrine is being tested by new technology, see *Criminal Justice & Technology—X-Ray Eyes and the Fourth Amendment.*)

A police officer searches a car in front of the Capitol Building in Washington, D.C. According to the United States Supreme Court, under some circumstances the Fourth Amendment to the U.S. Constitution does not require police officers to obtain a warrant before searching an automobile. What is the reasoning behind this "movable vehicle exception"? (Getty Images/Joe Raedle)

INFOTRAC®
COLLEGE EDITION

Keyword: plain view doctrine

THE INTERROGATION PROCESS AND *MIRANDA*

After the Pledge of Allegiance, there is perhaps no recitation that comes more readily to the American mind than the *Miranda* warning:

> You have the right to remain silent. If you give up that right, anything you say can and will be used against you in a court of law. You have the right to speak with an attorney and to have the attorney present during questioning. If you so desire and cannot afford one, an attorney will be appointed for you without charge before questioning.

The *Miranda* warning is not a mere prop. It strongly affects one of the most important aspects of any criminal investigation—the **interrogation,** or questioning of

PLAIN VIEW DOCTRINE
The legal principle that objects in plain view of a law enforcement agent who has the right to be in a position to have that view may be seized without a warrant and introduced as evidence.

INTERROGATION
The direct questioning of a suspect to gather evidence of criminal activity and try to gain a confession.

Criminal Justice & TECHN LOGY

X-Ray Eyes and the Fourth Amendment

Suppose a detective enters a room with a warrant to search for a handgun used in a murder. The weapon is resting on a table and is immediately seized. Hidden in a closed drawer, however, is a packet of heroin. Under the plain view doctrine, the detective would most likely not have the right to search the drawer and seize the heroin. What if that detective could somehow see into the drawer without opening it? How would the plain view doctrine then apply?

A cop with X-ray eyes sounds like something out of a science fiction novel, but in fact courts around the country are already struggling with such situations. Thanks to thermal imagers, also known as forward-looking infrared devices (FLIR), law enforcement agencies now have the ability to look through walls.

Every object with a temperature above absolute zero emits infrared radiation, which cannot be seen by the naked eye. A thermal imager, however, can detect this radiation and project its reading onto a screen. The devices have been most commonly used in missing person searches—with our high body temperature, humans are easy targets for thermal imagers. Only recently have the devices been put to use by law enforcement agencies. Thermal imagers

can be particularly effective in detecting marijuana grown indoors because marijuana plants require considerable heat to survive.

The question for the courts has been whether, in the absence of a warrant, an infrared search of a dwelling is in violation of Fourth Amendment protections of privacy. In one marijuana case, where police used a helicopter fitted with FLIR devices, a Hawaii court ruled that no reasonable expectation of privacy was involved. The court held that the FLIR device measured only heat emanating from the defendant's house and that this "abandoned heat" was not subject to privacy laws because the defendants had not tried to prevent its escape. A Pennsylvania court, ruling on a similar case, rejected the "abandoned heat" justification because thermal imaging allowed the police to see what otherwise would have been hidden to them.

IN THE FUTURE

In 2001, the United States Supreme Court settled the issue by ruling that the use of a thermal imaging device by police was a search and was therefore subject to the Fourth Amendment. The Court's ruling covered not only these devices but also *any* technology that allows police to gain knowledge that would otherwise be impossible to obtain without entering the home. This does not mean that this technology is lost to law enforcement agents, but it does require them to obtain a warrant before using it.

 For more information on the technology described in this box, go to the Crime and Technology feature at http://www.cj.wadsworth.com

---

a suspect from whom the police want to obtain information concerning a crime and perhaps a confession.

The Legal Basis for *Miranda*

The Fifth Amendment guarantees protection against self-incrimination. A defendant's choice not to incriminate himself or herself cannot be interpreted as a sign of guilt by a jury in a criminal trial. A confession, or admission of guilt, is by definition a statement of self-incrimination. How, then, to reconcile the Fifth Amendment with the critical need of law enforcement officers to gain confessions? The answer lies in the concept of *coercion*. When torture or brutality is involved, it is relatively easy to determine that a confession was improperly coerced and is therefore invalid.

Setting the Stage for *Miranda*.   The United States Supreme Court first recognized that a confession could not be physically coerced in a 1936 case concerning a defendant who was beaten and whipped until confessing to a murder.[60] It was not until 1964, however, that the Court specifically recognized that the accused's due process rights should be protected during interrogation. That year, the Court heard the case of *Escobedo v. Illinois*,[61] concerning a convicted murderer who claimed that police had forced incriminating statements from him during interrogation and that this evidence had been portrayed as voluntary during his trial. In *Escobedo,* the Court ruled that the defendant had been denied his Sixth Amendment right to counsel during the interrogation. He therefore had also been denied his Fifth Amendment right against self-incrimination.

The *Miranda* Case. Two years later, the United States Supreme Court expanded on *Escobedo* in its *Miranda* decision,[62] establishing the **Miranda rights** and introducing the concept of what University of Columbia law professor H. Richard Uviller called *inherent coercion;* that is, even if a police officer does not lay a hand on a suspect, the general atmosphere of an interrogation is in and of itself coercive.[63]

Though the *Miranda* case is best remembered for the procedural requirement it spurred, at the time the Court was more concerned about the treatment of suspects during interrogation. (See *CJ in Focus—Landmark Cases: Miranda v. Arizona.*) The Court found that routine police interrogation strategies, such as leaving suspects alone in a room for several hours before questioning them, were inherently coercive. Therefore, the Court reasoned, every suspect needed protection from coercion, not just those who had been physically abused. The *Miranda* warning is a result of this need. In theory, if the warning is not given to a suspect before an interrogation, the fruits of that interrogation, including a confession, are invalid.

When a *Miranda* Warning Is Required

As we shall see, a *Miranda* warning is not necessary under several conditions, such as when no questions are asked of the suspect. Generally, *Miranda* requirements apply only when a suspect is in **custody.** In a series of rulings since *Miranda,* the United States Supreme Court has defined custody as an arrest or a situation in which a reasonable person would not feel free to leave.[64] Consequently, a **custodial interrogation** occurs when a suspect is under arrest or is deprived of her or his freedom in a significant manner. Again, a *Miranda* warning is only required before a custodial interrogation takes place.

When a *Miranda* Warning Is Not Required

A *Miranda* warning is not necessary in a number of situations:

1. When the police do not ask the suspect any questions that are *testimonial* in nature. Such questions are designed to elicit information that may be used against the suspect in court.
2. When the police have not focused on a suspect and are questioning witnesses at the scene of a crime.
3. When a person volunteers information before the police have asked a question.
4. When the suspect has given a private statement to a friend or some other acquaintance. *Miranda* does not apply to these statements so long as the government did not orchestrate the situation.
5. During a stop and frisk, when no arrest has been made.
6. During a traffic stop.[65]

Furthermore, suspects can *waive* their Fifth Amendment rights and speak to a police officer, but only if the waiver is made voluntarily. Silence on the part of a suspect does not mean that his or her *Miranda* protections have been relinquished. To waive their rights, suspects must state—either in writing or orally—that they understand those rights and that they will voluntarily answer questions without the presence of counsel.

Such a waiver is not said to be "voluntary" if the suspect is drugged or otherwise temporarily mentally impaired when it is given. Attorneys for Richard Reid,

MIRANDA RIGHTS
The constitutional rights of accused persons taken into custody by law enforcement officials. Following the United States Supreme Court's decision in *Miranda v. Arizona,* on taking an accused person into custody, the arresting officer must inform the person of certain constitutional rights, such as the right to remain silent and the right to counsel.

CUSTODY
The forceful detention of a person, or the perception that a person is not free to leave the immediate vicinity.

CUSTODIAL INTERROGATION
The questioning of a suspect after that person has been taken in custody. In this situation, the suspect must be read his or her *Miranda* rights before interrogation can begin.

INFOTRAC®
COLLEGE EDITION
Keyword: Miranda rule

Montoun T. Hart answers a question from the media as his mother, Sharon Hart Rhodes, looks on. Hart was acquitted of the mid-1990s murder of a popular high school teacher in New York City in part because the jury did not approve of the harsh tactics used by detectives in "persuading" Hart to admit to the crime. How can the Miranda warning help prevent unreliable admissions by suspects? (AP Photo/David Karp)

CJ in FOCUS

Landmark Cases: *Miranda v. Arizona*

Ernesto Miranda, a produce worker, was arrested in Phoenix, Arizona, in 1963 and charged with kidnapping and rape. After being identified by the victim in a lineup, Miranda was taken into an interrogation room and questioned for two hours by detectives. At no time was Miranda informed that he had a right to have an attorney present. When the police emerged from the session, they had a signed statement by Miranda confessing to the crimes. He was subsequently convicted and

Ernesto Miranda (AP/Wide World)

sentenced to twenty to thirty years in prison. After the conviction was confirmed by the Arizona Supreme Court, Miranda appealed to the United States Supreme Court, claiming that he had not been warned that any statement he made could be used against him, and that he had a right to counsel during the interrogation. The *Miranda* case was one of four examined by the Court that dealt with the question of coercive questioning.

Miranda v. Arizona
United States Supreme Court
384 U.S. 436 (1966)
http://laws.findlaw.com/US/384/436.html

IN THE WORDS OF THE COURT . . .

Mr. Chief Justice WARREN, majority opinion

* * * *

The cases before us raise questions which go to the roots of our concepts of American criminal jurisprudence: the restraints society must observe consistent with the Federal Constitution in prosecuting individuals for crime. More specifically, we deal with the admissibility of statements obtained from an individual who is subjected to custodial police interrogation and the necessity for procedures which assure that the individual is accorded his privilege under the Fifth Amendment to the Constitution not to be compelled to incriminate himself.

* * * *

As for the procedural safeguards to be employed, unless other fully effective means are devised to inform accused persons of their right of silence and to assure a continuous opportunity to exercise it, the following measures are required. Prior to any questioning, the person must be warned that he has a right to remain silent, that any statement he does make may be used as evidence against him, and that he has a right to the presence of an attorney, either retained or appointed. The defendant may waive effectuation of these rights, provided the waiver is made voluntarily, knowingly and intelligently. * * * The mere fact that he may have answered some questions or volunteered some statements on his own does not deprive him of the right to refrain from answering any further inquiries until he has consulted with an attorney and thereafter consents to be questioned.

* * * *

It is obvious that such an interrogation environment is created for no purpose other than to subjugate the individual to the will of his examiner. This atmosphere carries its own badge of intimidation. To be sure, this is not physical intimidation, but it is equally destructive of human dignity. The current practice of incommunicado interrogation is at odds with one of our Nation's most cherished principles—that the individual may not be compelled to incriminate himself. Unless adequate protective devices are employed to dispel the compulsion inherent in custodial surroundings, no statement obtained from the defendant can truly be the product of his free choice.

DECISION

The Court overturned Miranda's conviction, stating that police interrogations are, by their very nature, coercive and therefore deny suspects their constitutional right against self-incrimination by "forcing" them to confess. Consequently, any person who has been arrested and placed in custody must be informed of his or her right to be free from self-incrimination and to be represented by counsel during any interrogation. In other words, suspects must be told that they *do not have to* answer police questions. To accomplish this, the Court established the *Miranda* warning, which must be read prior to questioning of a suspect in custody.

FOR CRITICAL ANALYSIS
What is meant by the phrase "coercion can be mental as well as physical"? What role does the concept of "mental coercion" play in Chief Justice Warren's opinion?

For more information and activities related to this case, go to the Landmark Cases feature at http://cj.wadsworth.com/gainescore2e

a British citizen, who allegedly tried to explode a shoe bomb on a transatlantic flight in 2001, claimed that their client's confession was invalid because he was under the influence of a sedative when he waived his *Miranda* rights. A federal judge rejected this claim, noting that almost nine hours had passed between the time Reid was given the sedative and when he was questioned.[66]

To ensure that the suspect's rights are upheld, prosecutors are required to prove by a preponderance of the evidence that the suspect "knowing and intelligently" waived his or her *Miranda* rights.[67] To make the waiver perfectly clear, police will ask suspects two questions in addition to giving the *Miranda* warning:

❶ Do you understand your rights as I have read them to you?

❷ Knowing your rights, are you willing to talk to another law enforcement officer or me?

If the suspect indicates that she or he does not want to speak to the officer, thereby invoking her or his right to silence, the officer must *immediately* stop any questioning.[68] Similarly, if the suspect requests a lawyer, the police can ask no further questions until an attorney is present.[69] The suspect must be clear about this intention, however. In *Davis v. United States* (1994),[70] the United States Supreme Court upheld the interrogation of a suspect after he said, "Maybe I should talk to a lawyer." The Court found that this statement was too ambiguous, stating that it did not want to force police officers to "read the minds" of suspects who make vague declarations.

The Future of *Miranda*

The United States Supreme Court recently made a strong ruling in favor of the continued importance of *Miranda*. In *Dickerson v. United States* (2000),[71] the Court rejected the application of a little-known law passed by Congress in 1968 that allowed police in federal cases to use incriminating statements even if the suspect had not been read the warning. "*Miranda* has become embedded in routine police practice to the point where the warnings have become part of our national culture," wrote Chief Justice William Rehnquist in his opinion. The chief justice added that *Miranda* was a "constitutional rule" that Congress could not overturn by passing a law.[72]

Miranda may eventually find itself obsolete regardless of any decisions made in the courts. A relatively new trend in law enforcement has been for agencies to record interrogations and confessions on videotape, making it more difficult for defense attorneys to claim that their clients were illegally coerced. In New Mexico, officers now carry tape recorders on their waist belts. State laws in Alaska and Minnesota require interrogations to be recorded.[73] Such practices can work in favor of suspects as well. In 1996, a superior court judge in San Diego threw out Delano Wright's confession to being involved in a drive-by shooting after reviewing an interview of Wright conducted by a detective. The judge ruled that Wright, who was charged with first degree murder, had been coerced into confessing by false promises on the part of the detective that Wright would be charged only as a witness.[74] Some scholars have suggested that the videotaping of *all* custodial interrogations would satisfy the Fifth Amendment's prohibition against coercion and in the process render the *Miranda* warning unnecessary.[75]

THE IDENTIFICATION PROCESS

A confession is a form of self-identification; the suspect has identified herself or himself as the guilty party. If police officers are unable to gain a confession, they must use other methods to link the suspect with the crime. In fact, police must do so even if the suspect confesses, as false admissions do occur. Unless police

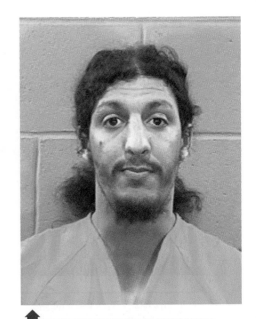

Richard C. Reid, shown here, allegedly tried to set off explosives hidden in his shoes on a flight from Paris, France, to Miami, Florida, on December 22, 2001. Although he confessed to the crime, his attorneys claimed that his waiver of his *Miranda* rights was improper because Reid was under the influence of a sedative at the time. If a suspect is in fact drugged when waiving his *Miranda* rights, why should a court invalidate that waiver? (AP Photo/Plymouth County Jail)

INFOTRAC®
COLLEGE EDITION

Keyword: United States v. Dickerson

"Every prosecutor in the country hated the day it came down . . . but after a decade even those who were strongly [against the ruling] had come to the conclusion, 'Hey, we can live with this.' It would be chaos to ever go back."

—Charles E. Moylan, *former Maryland state's attorney, commenting on* Miranda (1999)

Lineups are one of the primary means police have of identifying suspects. As you can see, in a lineup several people with similar appearances are placed so that a victim or witness can study them. The victim or witness is then asked to point out the one that most closely resembles the person who committed the crime. Lineup identifications are generally considered most valuable if they take place within several hours after the crime has been committed. Why is timing so important with regard to a lineup? (James Shaffer/PhotoEdit)

BOOKING
The process of entering a suspect's name, offense, and arrival time into the police log following her or his arrest.

officers personally witness the commission of the crime, they must establish the identity of the suspect using three basic types of identification procedures:

❶ *Showups,* which occur when a suspect who matches the description given by witnesses is apprehended near the scene of the crime within a reasonable amount of time after the crime has been committed. The suspect is usually returned to the crime scene for possible identification by witnesses.

❷ *Photo arrays,* which occur when no suspect is in custody but the police have a general description of the person. Witnesses and victims are shown "mug shots" of people with police records that match the description. Police will also present witnesses and victims with pictures of people they believe might have committed the crime.

❸ *Lineups,* which entail lining up several physically similar people, one of whom is the suspect, in front of a witness or victim. The police may have each member of the lineup wear clothing similar to that worn by the criminal and say a phrase that was used during the crime. These visual and oral cues are designed to help the witness identify the suspect.

As with the other procedures discussed in this chapter, constitutional law governs the identification process, though some aspects are more tightly restricted than others. The Sixth Amendment right to counsel, for example, does not apply during showups or photo arrays. In showups, the police often need to establish a suspect quickly, and it would be unreasonable to expect them to wait for an attorney to arrive. According to the United States Supreme Court in *United States v. Ash* (1973),[76] however, the police must be able to prove this need for immediate identification, perhaps by showing that it was necessary to keep the suspect from fleeing the state. As for photo arrays, courts have found that any procedure that does not require the suspect's presence does not require the presence of his or her attorney.[77] The lack of an attorney does not mean that police can "steer" a witness toward a positive identification with statements such as "Are you sure this isn't the person you saw robbing the grocery store?" Such actions would violate the suspect's due process rights.

Some observers feel that the standard **booking** procedure—the process of recording information about the suspect immediately after arrest—infringes on a suspect's Fifth Amendment rights. During booking, the suspect is photographed and fingerprinted, and, as we saw in Chapter 5, blood samples may be taken. If these samples lead to the suspect's eventual identification, according to some, they amount to self-incrimination. In *Schmerber v. California* (1966),[78] however, the United States Supreme Court held that such tests are not the equivalent of *testimonial* self-incrimination (where the suspect testifies verbally against himself or herself) and therefore do not violate the Fifth Amendment.

Criminal Justice in Action
Racial Profiling and the Constitution

As noted earlier in this chapter, the Fourth Amendment protects persons against "unreasonable searches and seizures." Nowhere in the Constitution, however, did the framers explain the term *unreasonable.* Thus, the participants in the criminal justice system have been left to find their own coherent and useful definition. Initially, as you will recall, the burden is on the police officer to decide whether his or her actions are reasonable, a decision that—in the absence of a warrant—will be reviewed in a court. In recent years, the question of reasonableness in the context of police stops has become intertwined with the troubling specter of racism in our nation's law enforcement agencies. Are police officers acting reasonably when they determine that there is a greater chance of finding criminal evidence in a vehicle driven by a black or Hispanic motorist than in one with a white driver? The Supreme Court has essentially left this question unanswered, creating a vacuum that has been filled by lawsuits, controversy, and frustration.

BY THE NUMBERS

Though it is often difficult to determine whether an individual officer acted reasonably in a particular situation, patterns of police behavior can provide a clearer picture. Statistics gathered for two recent lawsuits concerning police activity on Interstate 95 seem to point to a serious problem.[79] On a particular stretch of the highway in New Jersey, where 13.5 percent of the vehicles carried an African American occupant, 46.2 percent of the stops were of black motorists.[80] Further south in Maryland, although only 17.5 percent of those violating traffic laws were African American, 72.9 percent of the motorists actually stopped and searched were black.[81]

In both cases, the statistics were seen as proof that the local police were using *racial profiling* in deciding which motorists to stop. Racial profiling occurs when a police action is initiated by the race, ethnicity, or national origin of the suspect, rather than by any evidence or information that the suspect has broken the law. Although it is rare to find a law enforcement agency that has an official policy of racial profiling, many observers feel that the practice is widespread.

THE "RATIONAL DISCRIMINATION" ARGUMENT

This belief is only encouraged by statements such as the one made by Colonel Carl. A. Williams, superintendent of the New Jersey State Police. In answering charges that his officers targeted nonwhite motorists, Williams replied, "Two weeks ago, the president of the United States went to Mexico to talk . . . about drugs. He didn't go to Ireland. He didn't go to England."[82]

In other words, Williams (who subsequently resigned) felt that his officers were justified in stopping nonwhite motorists because they were more likely to be breaking the law. This line of thinking, known as "rational discrimination," relies on statistics that show a correlation between race and crime. Because minorities, the argument goes, are more likely to commit crimes, police are justified in making group distinctions.[83]

David Cole, a professor at Georgetown University Law Center, and John Lamberth, an associate professor of psychology at Temple University, refute the idea of "rational discrimination." If blacks are more likely to be carrying drugs than whites, Cole and Lamberth say, then police should find drugs more often on the African Americans that they stop than on the whites that they stop. This is not the case. In Maryland, for example, the percentages of black and white drivers stopped who actually were in possession of drugs or other contraband were almost equal. Furthermore, in New Jersey, police found contraband on 25 percent of the white drivers, 13 percent of blacks, and only 5 percent of Hispanics.[84]

OPERATION PIPELINE

Given the mistrust of law enforcement agents that racial profiling arouses in minority communities, it

Felix Morka, Lalia Maher, and Ivan Foster are sworn in before testifying at a U.S. Senate Committee hearing on racial profiling in Trenton, New Jersey. (Source needed)

Continued on next page

would seem in society's best interest to eradicate the practice. This may prove difficult, however. As Jerome H. Skolnick has explained, stereotyping is integral to the world of law enforcement. A police officer's job is essentially to investigate behavior that appears to her or him to be out of the ordinary or "different." Race is a very strong cue toward indicating "differences." Consequently, police officers may believe that they are acting "reasonably" in relying on race as an indication of criminal behavior.[85]

Experts also link racial profiling to the aggressive tactics promoted by the federal government to fight the war on drugs. Operation Pipeline, a program started by the Drug Enforcement Administration (DEA) in the 1980s to train local police officers to search for drug traffickers, seems to have encouraged local officers to make distinctions based on race. Among the characteristics identified by the DEA as "tip-offs" of drug couriers: people wearing dreadlocks and cars with two Latino males traveling together.[86] In 1999, the DEA released a "Heroin Trends" report that identified Colombians, Dominicans, Puerto Ricans, and African Americans as "predominant wholesale traffickers" of the drug.[87] So, even as local police are told by their superiors not to take racial characteristics into account, their training seems to place an emphasis on race and ethnicity. "What is your average road trooper to make of all this?" asks one observer.[88]

THE *WHREN* EFFECT

One partial solution to the problem of racial profiling might be to include the race or ethnicity of a suspect in the "reasonableness" calculation under the Fourth Amendment. That is, just as a court will look at the threat of harm to the community or the seriousness of the crime alleged in determining whether an officer acted reasonably in making a warrantless search or seizure, the court should also look at the race of the suspect.[89] After all, the history and purpose of the Fourth Amendment strongly suggest that the framers intended it to be a limitation on discretionary police power.[90] Given that the enforcement of traffic laws involves a great deal of discretion, it would seem that a police officer's subjective views on race would be an important factor in determining the constitutionality of a search and seizure.[91]

The United States Supreme Court, however, rejected this approach in *Whren v. United States* (1996),[92] a case discussed on page 156. In the *Whren* case, the Court ruled that the subjective intentions of the police, including any motives based on racial stereotyping or bias, are irrelevant under Fourth Amendment analysis.[93] As long as there is objective probable cause of a traffic violation, any other reasons for the stop will not be considered. Thus, if a suspect was driving over the speed limit or was not wearing a seat belt, then a police officer's decision to stop that driver

is constitutional, even if there is proof that the "real" reason for the stop was the driver's race.

Why has the Court taken this stance? In general, the Court feels that it is already very difficult to define such terms as *reasonable* and *probable cause*. To try to measure the motivation of a police officer would be more difficult still.[94] The problem, as critics of this approach point out, is that traffic violations are unique in that almost everybody "does it." In the New Jersey study referred to earlier, researchers found that 98.1 percent of the drivers on the highway are committing an offense (mostly speeding) at any given time. In Maryland, the rate of wrongdoing was 93.3 percent.[95] In other words, a police officer has probable cause to stop almost any driver at any time. An officer will almost always have a valid reason for a stop, regardless of the driver's race.

The best method to combat racial profiling would seem to be a commitment to discontinue the practice within law enforcement agencies. Negative publicity generated by lawsuits can act as a "spur" to these policies. In New Jersey, for example, the total number of police stops in the section of Interstate 95 that had come under scrutiny dropped from 440 in 1999 to 281 in 2000. "You have all these investigations and hearings going on," noted one observer, "[and] the troopers don't want to put their necks on the line."[96]

MAKING SENSE OF RACIAL PROFILING

❶ Do you agree with the Supreme Court's reasoning in the *Whren* decision? What might be some of the practical consequences of allowing the suspect's race to be a factor in the "reasonableness" test of the Fourth Amendment?

❷ Recall the "soccer mom" case discussed in the introduction to this chapter. How does Gail Atwater's experience relate to the racial profiling debate?

❸ In the days immediately following the terrorist attacks of September 11, 2001, nearly every suspect stopped and detained by law enforcement agents in connection with the incidents was of Middle Eastern descent. Is this evidence of racial profiling? Is it acceptable under the *Whren* decision? Are law enforcement agents acting "reasonably" in focusing on this segment of the community?

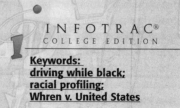

INFOTRAC®
COLLEGE EDITION

Keywords:
driving while black;
racial profiling;
Whren v. United States

KEY TERMS

CHAPTER SUMMARY

① **Outline the four major sources that may provide probable cause.** (a) Personal observation, usually due to an officer's personal training, experience, and expertise; (b) information, gathered from informants, eyewitnesses, victims, police bulletins, and other sources; (c) evidence, which often has to be in plain view; and (d) association, which generally must concern a person with a known criminal background who is seen in a place where criminal activity is openly taking place.

② **Explain the exclusionary rule.** This rule, established federally in *Weeks v. United States* and at the state level in *Mapp v. Ohio,* prohibits the use of illegally seized evidence, or evidence obtained by an unreasonable search and seizure in an inadmissible way.

③ **Distinguish between a stop and a frisk, and indicate the importance of the case *Terry v. Ohio.*** Though the terms *stop* and *frisk* are often used in concert, a stop is the separate act of detaining a suspect when an officer reasonably believes that a criminal activity is about to take place. A frisk is the physical "pat-down" of a suspect. In *Terry v. Ohio,* the United States Supreme Court ruled that an officer must have "specific and articulable" facts before making a stop, but those facts may be "taken together with rational inferences."

④ **List the four elements that must be present for an arrest to take place.** (a) Intent, (b) authority, (c) seizure or detention, and (d) the understanding of the person that he or she has been arrested.

⑤ **Explain under what circumstances officers need not announce themselves before entering a dwelling and under what circumstances arrest warrants are not required.** "No-knock" entries are allowed under exigent circumstances, such as when a suspect is armed and poses a threat of violence; when persons inside the dwelling are destroying evidence or escaping; and when officers believe a felony is being committed. A warrantless arrest can be made if the offense is committed in the presence of an officer or if the officer knows that a crime has been committed and has probable cause to believe that it was committed by a particular suspect.

⑥ **List the four categories of items that can be seized by use of a search warrant.** (a) Items resulting from a crime, such as stolen goods; (b) inherently illegal items; (c) evidence of the crime; and (d) items used in committing crimes.

⑦ **Explain when searches can be made without a warrant.** Searches and seizures can be made without a warrant if they are incidental to an arrest (but they must be reasonable); when they are made with voluntary consent; when they involve the "movable vehicle exception"; when property has been abandoned; and when items are in plain view, under certain restricted circumstances (see *Coolidge v. New Hampshire*).

⑧ **Recite the *Miranda* warning.** You have the right to remain silent. If you give up that right, anything you say can and will be used against you in a court of law. You have the right to speak with an attorney and to have the attorney present during questioning. If you so desire and cannot afford one, an attorney will be appointed for you without charge before questioning.

⑨ **Indicate situations in which a *Miranda* warning is unnecessary.** (a) When no questions that are testimonial in nature are asked of the suspect; (b) when there is no suspect and witnesses in general are being questioned at the scene of a crime; (c) when a person volunteers information before the police ask anything; (d) when a suspect has given a private statement to a friend without the government orchestrating it; (e) during a stop and frisk when no arrests have been made; and (f) during a traffic stop.

⑩ **List the three basic types of police identification.** (a) Showups, (b) photo arrays, and (c) lineups.

QUESTIONS FOR CRITICAL ANALYSIS

1 What are the two most significant legal concepts contained in the Fourth Amendment, and why are they important?

2 Suppose that a police officer stops a person who "looks funny." The person acts strangely, so the police officer decides to frisk him. The officer feels a bulge in the suspect's coat pocket, which turns out to be a bag of cocaine. Would the arrest for cocaine possession hold up in court? Why or why not?

3 What continues to be the best indicator of probable cause in the face of no hard and fast definitions?

4 How does the expression "fruit of the poisoned tree" relate to the issue of searches and seizures?

5 Is it possible for a person legally to be under arrest without an officer indicating to that person that she or he is in fact under arrest? Explain.

6 What is the difference between an arrest warrant and a search warrant?

7 A police officer has an arrest warrant for Jones. He enters Jones's house, presents the warrant, and handcuffs Jones. The officer then searches the house thoroughly and finds what appears to be stolen jewelry in an upstairs bedroom. If you were Jones's defense attorney, what defense would you raise?

SELECTED PRINT AND ELECTRONIC RESOURCES

SUGGESTED READINGS

Leo, Richard A., et al., eds., *The Miranda Debate: Law, Justice, and Policing,* Boston, MA: Northeastern University Press, 1998. This book presents an anthology of key writings on the 1966 *Miranda v. Arizona* ruling. The book is divided into four sections: the first reviews the pre-*Miranda* law of confessions; the second explores the legal and ethical dimensions of the *Miranda* decision; the third examines how the *Miranda* decision works in the real world; and the fourth presents a discussion of challenges to the decision.

Lewis, Anthony, *Gideon's Trumpet,* New York: Vantage Books, 1989. The author goes into the background of the landmark case created by James Earl Gideon. Gideon was in a Florida jail for breaking and entering with intent to commit a misdemeanor. He wrote a letter in pencil to the United States Supreme Court, claiming that his constitutional rights were violated when he was denied the right to have an attorney at his trial. In the end, the Supreme Court agreed. This is the story of one man's improbable battle and the Court's ultimate decision in his favor.

Milovanovic, Dragan, and Katheryn K. Russell, *Petit Apartheid in the U.S. Criminal Justice System: The Dark Figures of Racism,* Durham, NC: Carolina Academic Press, 2001. The authors examine what they believe to be an implicit racially biased criminal justice system in this country. They offer evidence, both statistical and anecdotal, to support their hypothesis.

MEDIA RESOURCES

The Thin Blue Line **(1988)** This documentary painstakingly reproduces key moments in the twenty-month investigation of a wrongfully convicted young drifter named

Randall Adams. Adams was wrongfully convicted of murdering a Dallas police officer named Robert Wood in 1976. During the last few moments of this "docudrama," the chief witness against Adams, David Harris, confesses to murdering Wood. In addition to interviews, the director of this film uses staged reconstructions of Wood's murder. Some people have said this film is more like a waking nightmare than a docudrama.

Critically analyze this film:

1. Provide a general assessment of the police as portrayed in this documentary. Given what you have learned in this chapter about police procedure, do you believe that they followed the letter of the law, or did they allow discretion to supersede their constitutional obligations?

2. A number of those interviewed insinuate that if Robert Wood and his partner had followed department guidelines in handling traffic violations, they would not have placed themselves in such a dangerous position. Do you agree? Why or why not? Also, what does this particular aspect of the film seem to say about the importance of police officers following procedure as opposed to relying on discretion?

3. The Texas jury quickly sentenced Adams to death in his 1977 trial. His sentence, though, was later commuted to life in prison. How might this docudrama be used by opponents of the death penalty?

4. A staff writer for the *Washington Post,* Desson Howe, claimed that this docudrama was "an awesome indictment of America." What did he mean, and do you agree with him?

LOGGING ON

Go to http://cj.wadsworth.com/gainescore2e, and click Hypercontents. There, you will find URLs for the organizations in the following list:

- The **Federal Bureau of Investigtion's** Web site offers a series of articles on subjects covered in this chapter. You will find, for instance, pieces on the exclusionary rule and no-knock entry standard.

- The **dissenting opinion in *Miranda v. Arizona,*** written by Justice White, explores a number of interesting issues concerning police interrogation. Click *Miranda v. Arizona* to read the dissenting opinion.

- Has *Miranda* handcuffed the cops? For insight into the answer, go to the **National Center for Policy Analysis** Web site.

USING THE INTERNET FOR CRIMINAL JUSTICE ANALYSIS

1. Go to InfoTrac College Edition at **http://www.infotrac-college.com/wadsworth/** After you log on, type in: **"could this be the end of fourth amendment protection for motorists?"**

This is an article that analyzes the United States Supreme Court ruling in *Whren v. United States.*

a. What was the main ruling in *Whren v. United States?*

b. Why are subjective intentions so important in this area of criminal procedure?

c. What is the "pretextual" search or seizure?

d. What other cases that the United States Supreme Court decided had to do with this same issue?

e. On what basis did the defendants move to suppress the physical evidence in the case *Whren v. United States?*

f. In the conclusion of this article, what three "problems" does the author see in the *Whren* decision?

2. See Internet Activities 6.1 and 6.2 on the companion Web site for *CJ in Action: The Core.* To get to the activities, go to **http://www.cj.wadsworth.com/gainescore2e,** select the appropriate chapter from the drop down list, then click Internet Activities on the left navigation bar.

NOTES

1. Linda Greenhouse, "Divided Justices Back Full Arrests on Minor Charges," *New York Times* (April 25, 2001), A1.
2. *Atwater v. City of Lago Vista,* 532 U.S. 318 (2001).
3. *Ibid.,* 1557–1558.
4. Jayme S. Walker, "Applying an Understanding of the Fourth Amendment," *The Police Chief* (July 1995), 44–47.
5. *Michigan v. Summers,* 452 U.S. 692 (1981).
6. *Brinegar v. United States,* 338 U.S. 160 (1949).
7. Rolando V. del Carmen, *Criminal Procedure for Law Enforcement Personnel* (Monterey, CA: Brooks/Cole Publishing Co., 1987), 63–64.
8. 500 U.S. 44 (1991).
9. *United States v. Leon,* 468 U.S. 897 (1984).
10. "Jury's Mixed Verdict in Cop Trial," *UPI Online* (April 3, 1998).
11. Karen M. Hess and Henry M. Wrobleski, *Police Operation: Theory and Practice* (St. Paul, MN: West Publishing Co., 1997), 122.
12. 392 U.S. 1 (1968).

13. *Ibid.,* 20.
14. *Ibid.,* 21.
15. 449 U.S. 418 (1981).
16. *Illinois v. Wardlow,* 528 U.S. 119 (2000).
17. *United States v. Arvizu,* 534 U.S. 266 (2002).
18. *United States v. Place,* 462 U.S. 696 (1983).
19. *Minnesota v. Dickerson,* 508 U.S. 366 (1993).
20. *Black's Law Dictionary,* 6th ed. (St. Paul, MN: West Publishing Co., 1990), 109–10.
21. Rolando V. del Carmen and Jeffrey T. Walker, *Briefs of Leading Cases in Law Enforcement,* 2d ed. (Cincinnati, OH: Anderson, 1995), 38–40.
22. *Florida v. Royer,* 460 U.S. 491 (1983).
23. See also *United States v. Mendenhall,* 446 U.S. 544 (1980).
24. del Carmen, *Criminal Procedure,* 97–98.
25. 514 U.S. 927 (1995).
26. Linda J. Collier and Deborah D. Rosenbloom, *American Jurisprudence,* 2d ed. (Rochester, NY: Lawyers Cooperative Publishing, 1995), 122.

27. 495 U.S. 91 (1990).
28. Wayne R. LeFave and Jerold H. Israel, *Criminal Procedure* (St. Paul, MN: West Publishing Co., 1985), 141–44.
29. David Orlin, Jacob Thiessen, Kelli C. McTaggart, Lisa Toporek, and James Pearl, "Warrantless Searches and Seizures," in "Twenty-Sixth Annual Review of Criminal Procedure," *Georgetown Law Journal* 85 (April 1997), 847.
30. 445 U.S. 573 (1980).
31. 451 U.S. 204 (1981).
32. *California v. Greenwood,* 486 U.S. 35 (1988).
33. *Ibid.*
34. 389 U.S. 347 (1967).
35. *Ibid.,* 361.
36. 486 U.S. 35 (1988).
37. *Ibid.*
38. *Coolidge v. New Hampshire,* 403 U.S. 443, 467 (1971).
39. del Carmen, *Criminal Procedure,* 158.
40. *Katz v. United States,* 389 U.S. 347, 357 (1967).

41. 414 U.S. 234–235 (1973).

42. 395 U.S. 752 (1969).

43. *Bumper v. North Carolina,* 391 U.S. 543 (1960).

44. 412 U.S. 218 (1973).

45. Ian D. Midgley, "Just One Question before We Get to *Ohio v. Robinette:* 'Are You Carrying Any Contraband . . . Weapons, Drugs, Constitutional Protections . . . Anything Like That?'" *Case Western Reserve Law Review* 48 (Fall 1997), 173.

46. 519 U.S. 33 (1996).

47. Linda Greenhouse, "Supreme Court Upholds Police Methods in Vehicle Drug Searches," *New York Times* (November 19, 1996), A23.

48. Megan Twohey, "SWATs under Fire," *National Law Journal* (January 1, 2000), 37.

49. Karan R. Singh, "Treading the Thin Blue line: Military Special Operations, Trained SWAT Teams and the Constitution," *William and Mary Bill of Rights Journal* (April 2001), 683.

50. Diane Cecilia Weber, *Warrior Cops: The Ominous Growth of Paramilitarism in American Police Departments; Briefing Paper No. 50* (Washington, D.C.: Cato Institute, 1999).

51. 435 U.S. 454 (1981).

52. 267 U.S. 132 (1925).

53. *United States v. Ross,* 456 U.S. 798, 804–9 (1982); and *Chambers v. Maroney,* 399 U.S. 42, 44, 52 (1970).

54. 434 U.S. 106 (1977).

55. 517 U.S. 806 (1996).

56. 519 U.S. 408 (1997).

57. *Knowles v. Iowa,* 525 U.S. 113 (1998).

58. *New York v. Belton,* 435 U.S. 454 (1981).

59. 403 U.S. 443 (1971).

60. *Brown v. Mississippi,* 297 U.S. 278 (1936).

61. 378 U.S. 478 (1964).

62. *Miranda v. Arizona,* 384 U.S. 436 (1966).

63. H. Richard Uviller, *Tempered Zeal* (Chicago: Contemporary Books, 1988), 188–98.

64. *Orozco v. Texas,* 394 U.S. 324 (1969); *Oregon v. Mathiason,* 429 U.S. 492 (1977); *California v. Beheler,* 463 U.S. 1121 (1983).

65. del Carmen, *Criminal Procedure,* 267–68.

66. Shelley Murphy, "U.S. Judge Rules Confession Wasn't Drug Influenced," *Boston Globe* (June 23, 2002), A8.

67. *Moran v. Burbine,* 475 U.S. 412 (1986).

68. *Michigan v. Mosley,* 423 U.S. 96 (1975).

69. *Fare v. Michael C.,* 442 U.S. 707, 723–4 (1979).

70. 512 U.S. 452 (1994).

71. 530 U.S. 428 (2000).

72. *Ibid.,* 443.

73. William A. Geller, *Videotaping Interrogations and Confessions* (Washington, D.C.: U.S. Department of Justice, March 1993), 1–11.

74. Anne Krueger, "Coerced Confession: The Law Says NO," *San Diego Union & Tribune* (April 21, 1996), A1.

75. Paul G. Cassell, "The Grand Illusion of *Miranda*'s Defenders," *Northwestern University Law Review* 90 (1996), 1118–24.

76. 413 U.S. 300 (1973).

77. *United States v. Barker,* 988 F.2d 77, 78 (9th Cir. 1993).

78. 384 U.S. 757 (1966).

79. *State v. Soto,* 734 A.2d 350 (1996); and *Wilkins v. Maryland State Police* (available at www.aclu.org/court/mspet.html).

80. Tracey Maclin, "Race and the Fourth Amendment," *Vanderbilt Law Review* 51 (March 1998), 347.

81. *Ibid.,* 349.

82. Quoted in Jackson Toby, "'Racial Profiling' Doesn't Prove Cops Are Racist," *Wall Street Journal* (March 11, 1999), A22.

83. Dinesh D'Souza, *The End of Racism: Principles for a Multiracial Society* (New York: Free Press, 1995), 284.

84. David Cole and John Lamberth, "The Fallacy of Racial Profiling," *New York Times* (May 13, 2001), 13.

85. Jerome H. Skolnick, *Justice without Trial: Law Enforcement in Democratic Society,* 3d ed. (New York: Macmillan, 1994).

86. David Kocieniewski, "U.S. Wrote Outline for Race Profiling, New Jersey Argues," *New York Times* (November 29, 2000), A1.

87. *Ibid.*

88. *Ibid.*

89. Randall Kennedy, *Race, Crime and Law* (New York: Pantheon Books, 1997), 144–45.

90. Leonard W. Levy, *Original Intent and the Framers' Constitution* (New York: Macmillan, 1988), 221.

91. John Hart Ely, *Democracy and Distrust* (Cambridge: Harvard University Press, 1980), 97.

92. 517 U.S. 806 (1996).

93. *Ibid.,* 813.

94. *Draper v. United States,* 358 U.S. 333 (1959).

95. Maclin, 377.

96. Iver Peterson, "Data Show Sharp Drop in Turnpike Searches," *New York Times* (April 24, 2001), B1.

CHAPTER 7
CHALLENGES TO EFFECTIVE POLICING

CHAPTER OUTLINE

Chapter Objectives

After reading this chapter, you should be able to:

1. Explain what is involved in background checks of prospective police officers.

2. Identify the five basic values of the police subculture.

3. Explain what stressors are and list some of those found in police work.

4. Indicate some of the guidelines for the use of nondeadly force in most states.

5. Identify the three traditional forms of police corruption.

6. Explain what an ethical dilemma is and name the four categories of ethical dilemmas typically facing a police officer.

7. List the three types of police accountability systems and indicate which one is least important.

INTRODUCTION
Learning Hard Lessons in Los Angeles

For residents of Los Angeles, the videotape brought back ugly memories. Broadcast by local television stations on July 7, 2002, it showed Jeremy Morse, a white police officer, smashing a handcuffed black teenager named Donovan Jackson into a patrol car, and then proceeding to punch him in the face several times as other officers looked on. More than a decade earlier, another amateur video, one showing four police officers beating African American motorist Rodney King, played a decisive role in a series of riots that left fifty-four people dead and more than two thousand injured, and caused about $1 billion in damages.[1]

Jackson's beating very well could have sparked similar anger. He was a special education student with no arrest record who had been pulled over because the license plate on the car he was driving had expired. Yet, three days following the incident, exactly one protester was stationed outside the city hall of Inglewood, a city with a large African American population near Los Angeles International Airport where the incident took place. It appears that local politicians had learned a great deal since 1991, when Los Angeles officeholders seemed reluctant to criticize police action toward King. Mayor Roosevelt Dorn immediately condemned Officer Morse's actions, and within days the city of Inglewood, the Los Angeles County Sheriff's Department, the local district attorney, the FBI, and the U.S. Department of Justice were investigating the incident.[2]

Of course, we would prefer that law enforcement officers never use violence or deadly force, whether justified or not. Reality, however, is not quite so tidy. Society expects law enforcement officers to uphold the law while at the same time embodying the law, but the average police officer—even in a small, rural town—faces on-the-job situations that most Americans cannot imagine. As James Fyfe of Temple University explains, by telling police officers that we expect them to eradicate crime, we are putting them in a "no-win war." Like some soldiers in such combat, Fyfe adds, "they commit atrocities."[3]

In this chapter, we will examine some of these "atrocities," such as police brutality and corruption. We will also consider the possible causes of police misconduct and review the steps that are being taken to ensure that it does not characterize law enforcement actions in the future. As these issues are discussed, it is important to remember that, in the words of one police administrator, "cops are not from another planet. Their backgrounds, their weaknesses, are the same as any other human beings. They are not descended from Planet Honest. We get them from Earth."[4]

Donovan Jackson, left and his father Koby Chavis discuss an incident in which Inglewood, California, police officers beat Jackson during a routine traffic stop on July 6, 2002. (AP Photo/Krista Niles)

RECRUITMENT AND TRAINING: BECOMING A POLICE OFFICER

In 1961, police expert James H. Chenoweth commented that the methods used to hire police officers had changed little since 1829 when the Metropolitan Police of London was created.[5] The past forty years, however, have seen a number of improvements on the original model. Efforts have been made to diversify police rolls, and recruits in most police departments undergo a substantial array of tests and screens—discussed below—to determine their aptitude. Furthermore, annual starting salaries of up to $40,000, along with the opportunities offered by an interesting profession in the public service field, have attracted a wide variety of applicants to police work.

Go to the Stories from the Street feature at http://www.cj.wadsworth.com/gainescore2e to hear Larry Gaines tell insightful stories related to this chapter and his experiences in the field.

Basic Requirements

The selection process involves a number of steps, and each police department has a different method of choosing candidates. (See Figure 7.1.) Most agencies, however, require at a minimum that a police officer:

- Be a U.S. citizen.
- Not have been convicted of a felony.
- Have or be eligible to have a driver's license in the state where the department is located.
- Be at least twenty-one years of age.

Beyond these minimum requirements, police departments usually engage in extensive background checks, including drug tests; a review of the applicant's educational, military, and driving records; credit checks; interviews with spouses, acquaintances, and previous employers; and a Federal Bureau of Investigation (FBI) search to determine whether the applicant has been convicted of any criminal acts.[6]

FIGURE 7.1
Becoming a Police Officer

In their efforts to hire highly qualified future law enforcement officers, most police departments have recruits pass through a lengthy selection process before hiring. The employment procedures of the Albuquerque (New Mexico) Police Department, shown on the right below, are fairly typical of the procedures followed by law enforcement organizations across the nation.

Most police departments also have a number of factors that automatically disqualify a person from employment. The list on the left, provided by the Amarillo (Texas) Police Department, is also fairly representative of national trends.

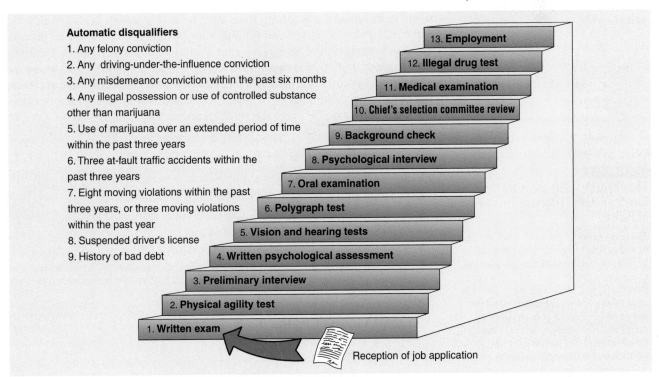

Automatic disqualifiers
1. Any felony conviction
2. Any driving-under-the-influence conviction
3. Any misdemeanor conviction within the past six months
4. Any illegal possession or use of controlled substance other than marijuana
5. Use of marijuana over an extended period of time within the past three years
6. Three at-fault traffic accidents within the past three years
7. Eight moving violations within the past three years, or three moving violations within the past year
8. Suspended driver's license
9. History of bad debt

13. **Employment**
12. **Illegal drug test**
11. **Medical examination**
10. **Chief's selection committee review**
9. **Background check**
8. **Psychological interview**
7. **Oral examination**
6. **Polygraph test**
5. **Vision and hearing tests**
4. **Written psychological assessment**
3. **Preliminary interview**
2. **Physical agility test**
1. **Written exam**

Reception of job application

Sources: Amarillo Police Department, Albuquerque Police Department.

"Police officers possess awesome powers. They perform their duties under hazardous conditions and with the vigilant public eye upon them. Police officers are permitted only a margin of error in judgment under conditions that impose high degrees of physical and mental stress. Their general responsibility to preserve peace and enforce the law carries with it the power . . . to use force—even deadly force."

—*United States Civil Rights Commission report* (1981)

On the Web

If you want more information on how a police academy operates, you can find a link to the home page of the Oakland (California) Police Academy on the Hypercontents page for this chapter at http://www.cj.wadsworth.com/gainescore2e.

Police agencies generally require certain physical attributes in applicants: normally, they must be able to pass a physical agility or fitness test.

Age is also a factor, as few departments will accept candidates younger than twenty-one years of age or older than forty-five. In some departments, the applicant must take a polygraph (lie-detector) exam in conjunction with the background check. The results of the polygraph exam are often compared to the information from the background check to ensure that the applicant has not been deceptive. According to one study, around 20 percent of the nearly 70,000 persons who apply for police jobs annually are rejected because they lied during the screening process.[7]

Testing of Applicants

It would be difficult to find a profession that puts potential employees through a more strenuous series of tests than law enforcement. To start with, almost every police applicant must take a written examination, either the civil service examination or one designed by the department. The written exam attempts to measure the applicant's knowledge of basic information and ability to comprehend certain situations. The exam may also cover subjects such as mathematical ability and writing skills. The written examination is generally pass/fail, and the applicant must pass it to continue with the employment process.

After the written examination, the applicant usually moves on to *physical agility tests.* In the past, these tests have focused on the candidate's basic strength and endurance. In recent years, however, the tests have concentrated more on job-related physical skills that are necessary for the day-to-day work of a police officer. Consequently, many of the tests entail obstacle courses that approximate chasing after a fleeing suspect or jumping over a chain-link fence. (See Figure 7.2 for an example.)

Requirements for height, weight, and physical ability have historically been used to discourage recruitment of women. Following a series of court cases that successfully challenged these tests as discriminatory, most departments now measure recruits against other applicants of the same gender and general body size.[8] For example, to qualify for the Providence (Rhode Island) police department, a 25-year-old, 180-pound man must be able to bench-press 178 pounds, while a 25-year-old, 140-pound woman must be able to bench-press 83 pounds. Because women tend to be more flexible than men, a 32-year-old man must be able to reach half an inch beyond his toes in the "sit-and-reach" test, whereas a 32-year-old woman must reach 3.3 inches beyond her toes.[9] The topic of recruiting both women and minority police candidates, as well as the importance of having a diverse police force, will be discussed at length in the feature *Criminal Justice in Action—Diversity in the Police Work Force* at the end of the chapter.

FIGURE 7.2

The Physical Agility Exam for the Henrico County (Virginia) Division of Police

Those applying for the position of police officer at the Henrico County (Virginia) Division of Police must finish this physical agility exam within 3 minutes, 30 seconds. During the test, applicants are required to wear the equipment (with a total weight of between 9 and 13 pounds) worn by patrol officers, which includes (1) the police uniform, (2) leather gun belt, (3) firearm, (4) baton, (5) portable radio, and (6) ballistics vest.

1. Applicant begins test seated in a police vehicle, door closed, seat belt fastened.
2. Applicant must exit vehicle and jump or climb a six-foot barrier.
3. Applicant then completes a one-quarter mile run or walk, making various turns along the way (to simulate a pursuit run).
4. Applicant must jump a simulated five-foot culvert/ditch.
5. Applicant must drag a "human simulator" (dummy) weighing 175 pounds a distance of 50 feet (to simulate a situation in which an officer is required to pull or carry an injured person to safety).
6. Applicant must draw his or her weapon and fire five rounds with the strong hand and five rounds with the weak hand.

Source: Henrico County Division of Police.

Educational Requirements

One of the most dramatic differences between today's police recruits and those of several generations ago is their level of education. In the 1920s, when August Vollmer began promoting the need for higher education in police officers, few had attended college. By the 1990s, 65 percent of police officers had some college credits and 25 percent were college graduates.[10] Today, 83 percent of all local police departments require at least a high school diploma, and 8 percent require a degree from a two-year college.[11] Recruits with college or university experience are generally seen as having an advantage in hiring and promotion.[12]

Not all police observers believe, however, that education is a necessity for police officers. In the words of one police officer, "effective street cops learn their skills on the job, not in a classroom."[13] By emphasizing a college degree, say some, police departments discourage those who would make solid officers but lack the education necessary to apply for positions in law enforcement.

Training

A candidate may be in top physical condition, have a college degree and an impeccable background, and exhibit the perfect personality to be a law enforcement officer, but still be woefully unprepared for police work. Almost every state requires that police recruits pass through a training period during which they are taught the basics of police work and are under constant observation by superiors. The training period usually has two components: the police academy and field training. On average, local police departments require 599 hours of training—395 hours in a classroom and 204 hours in the field.[14]

The *police academy,* run by either the state or a police agency, provides recruits with a controlled, militarized environment in which they receive their introduction to the world of the police officer. They are taught the laws of search, seizure, arrest, and interrogation; how and when to use weapons; the procedures of securing a crime scene and interviewing witnesses; first aid; self-defense; and other essentials of police work. Academy instructors evaluate the recruits' performance and send intermittent progress reports to police administrators. (See the feature *Careers in Criminal Justice* on the next page.)

Field training takes place outside the confines of the police academy. A recruit is paired with an experienced police officer known as a field training officer (FTO). The goal of field training is to help rookies apply the concepts they have learned in the academy "to the streets," with the FTO playing a supervisory role to make sure that nothing goes awry. According to many, the academy introduces recruits to the formal rules of police work, but field training gives the rookies their first taste of the informal rules. In fact, the initial advice to recruits from some FTOs is along the lines of "O.K., kid. Forget everything you learned in the academy. You're in the real world now." Nonetheless, the academy is a critical component in the learning process, as it provides rookies with a road map to the job.

"US VERSUS THEM": POLICE SUBCULTURE

"Us versus them": these words are often a recruit's introduction to **police subculture,** a broad term used to describe the basic assumptions and values

FIELD TRAINING
The segment of a police recruit's training in which he or she is removed from the classroom and placed on the beat, under the supervision of a senior officer.

POLICE SUBCULTURE
The values and perceptions that are shared by members of a police department and, to a certain extent, by all law enforcement agents. These values and perceptions are shaped by the unique and isolated existence of the police officer.

Adam Kasanof at Columbia University, where he studied Latin before becoming a New York City police officer. Although police work is still not considered an intellectual activity, the ranks of departments across the country are more highly educated than at any time in this nation's history. Many officers such as Kasanof are graduates from "elite" schools. They are sometimes considered "eggheads with a shield" by fellow officers. Members of academia also question the life of a cop for an Ivy Leaguer; one of Kasanof's professors called him a "saintly madman." What stereotypes of the police profession do these attitudes reflect? (NYT Pictures/Edward Keating)

Careers in Criminal Justice

Peter John Mantello,
Training Coordinator for the Vermont Criminal Justice Training Council

Imagine that you are a high school student and observe a "bully" who "picked" a fight with a mentally challenged person whom the bully flipped on his back. While everybody was laughing at the incident, you stood there and did absolutely nothing to help the mentally challenged person. Two years later this mentally challenged person was killed during a robbery at a gas station where he worked. This true-life incident seared my heart with the desire to serve in the police profession. I started by getting a bachelor of arts degree in sociology/ criminal justice, and I am now in the process of completing a master's in educational leadership. You should never stop learning in the police profession.

My experience in the police profession has covered thirteen years. In 1986, I enlisted in the U.S. Army as a military policeman and spent three

years stationed in the Republic of Panama. The experience of an overseas assignment really prepared me for the profession. In March 1989, I was hired as a full-time police professional for the town of Woodstock, Vermont. Because of the size of the department, my duties varied from patrol officer involved in juvenile services to conducting sexual abuse investigations as a corporal. I left Woodstock in 1995 and was hired as a training specialist in the Vermont Criminal Justice Training Council. In 1996, I was promoted to a training coordinator with primary duties in basic training for full-time and part-time police professionals for certifications in the state of Vermont. Vermont is a rural state and unique because it has only one police academy that all officers (whether they are from a municipality, county, or other state agency) attend for state certification. My primary responsibilities are coordinating, scheduling, instructing (my expertise is in physical training, use of force, and firearms), and supervising police candidates in a thirteen-week residential program that certifies officers to enforce the law and service the community.

I train police candidates to be role models for their communities and have tactical awareness. Today, if a candidate "wants in" the police profession he or she needs to have a commitment to service, a sense of humility, a disciplined lifestyle, and a proactive thinking mind. If they do not have the right attitude, then discipline and motivation are key factors that develop those attitudes in the candidates. Police professionals are leaders who need to lead by example and be genuinely concerned with the community that they serve. As one instructor once told me, "You lead people—you manage things." To teach police candidates to develop those traits trainers must challenge them mentally and physically. My biggest challenge and fulfillment as a training coordinator is leading and motivating police candidates to be leaders in their community.

Go to the
Careers in Criminal Justice Interactive CD for more
profiles in the field of
criminal justice.

INFOTRAC®
COLLEGE EDITION

Keyword: police personality

SOCIALIZATION
The process through which a police officer is taught the values and expected behavior of the police subculture.

that permeate law enforcement agencies and are taught to new members of a law enforcement agency as the proper way to think, perceive, and act.[15] Every organization has a subculture, with values shaped by the particular aspects and pressures of that organization. In the police subculture, those values are formed in an environment characterized by danger, stress, boredom, and violence.

The Core Values of Police Subculture

From the first day on the job, rookies begin the process of **socialization**, in which they are taught the values and rules of police work. This process is aided by a number of rituals that are common to the law enforcement experience. Police theorist Harry J. Mullins believes that the following rituals are critical to the police officer's acceptance, and even embrace, of police subculture:

- Attending a recruit academy.
- Working with a senior officer, who passes on the "lessons" of police work and life to the younger officer.
- Making the initial felony arrest.

- Using force to make an arrest for the first time.
- Using or witnessing deadly force for the first time.
- Witnessing major traumatic incidents for the first time.[16]

Each of these rituals makes it clear to the police officer that this is not a "normal" job. The only other people who can understand the stresses of police work are fellow officers, and consequently law enforcement officers tend to insulate themselves from civilians. Eventually, the insulation breeds mistrust, and the police officer develops an "us versus them" outlook toward those outside the force.[17]

One group of researchers described the police subculture as having five basic values:

1 Only a police officer can understand the "true" nature of police work. No one else—from lawyers to politicians to civilians—has any concept of the day-to-day challenges facing an officer.

2 The police officer is the only real crime fighter.

3 The courts have placed too many restrictions on police operations; to fight crime effectively, the police officer is forced to bend, if not break, these rules.

4 The public is fickle when it comes to police work. Civilians are quick to criticize a police officer's actions unless they need help from one themselves.

5 Loyalty is the highest virtue among police officers because everybody else is "out to get" the police and make their job more difficult.[18]

In sum, these core values create what sociologist William Westly called the **blue curtain,** also known as the "blue wall of silence" or simply "the code."[19] This curtain separates the police from the civilians they are meant to protect.

Police Cynicism

Though people become involved in police work for many different reasons, a common theme among young recruits is that they want to "serve society." This idealism tends to dissipate when the new officer is confronted with a public that seems hostile or indifferent and a justice system that appears to routinely allow criminals to go free. Slowly, the idealism is replaced with cynicism.[20]

A cynic is someone who universally distrusts human motives and expects nothing but the worst from human behavior. **Police cynicism** is characterized by a rejection of the ideals of truth and justice—the very values that an officer is sworn to uphold.[21] As cynical police officers lose respect for the law, they replace legal rules with those learned in the police subculture, which are believed to be more reflective of "reality." The implications for society can be an increase in police misconduct, corruption, and brutality.[22]

For those law enforcement officers who believe most strongly in the ideals of police work, cynicism can come as a reaction not to external forces, but to internal ones. Seeing fellow officers engage in obvious misconduct, and yet be encouraged by superiors, can quickly turn an officer into a cynic. The cynicism is exacerbated by a feeling of helplessness—to report another officer's wrongdoing is a severe breach of the blue wall of silence. As one officer said:

> If you were to challenge somebody for something that was going on, they would say: "Listen, if the supervisor isn't saying anything, what the hell are you interjecting for? What are you, a rat?" You've gotta work with a lot of these guys. You go on a gun job, the next thing you know, you got nobody following you up the stairs.[23]

The officer's statement highlights one of the reasons why police subculture resonates beyond department walls—he has basically admitted that he will not report wrongdoing by his peers. In this manner, police subculture influences the actions of police officers, sometimes to the detriment of society. In the next two

*"*The police subculture permits and sometimes demands deception of courts, prosecutors, defense attorneys, and defendants.*"*

—Jerome Skolnick, *professor of law,* University of California at Berkeley (1966)

BLUE CURTAIN
A metaphorical term used to refer to the value placed on secrecy and the general mistrust of the outside world shared by many police officers.

POLICE CYNICISM
The suspicion that citizens are weak, corrupt, and dangerous. This outlook is the result of a police officer being constantly exposed to civilians at their worst and can negatively affect the officer's performance.

New York police carry the casket of fellow officer Dominick Pezzulo, who was one of the nearly eighty law enforcement agents killed in the September 11, 2001, terrorist attacks on the World Trade Center. Why were so many police officers in a position of danger when the two towers collapsed shortly after being struck by hijacked commercial airplanes? What are some of the occupational threats that police officers face on a daily basis? (AP Photo/Beth A. Keiser)

sections, we will examine two areas of the law enforcement work environment that help create police subculture and must be fully understood if the cynical nature of police subculture is ever to be changed: (1) the danger of police work and (2) the need for police officers to establish and maintain authority.[24]

THE PHYSICAL AND MENTAL DANGERS OF POLICE WORK

Vincent Pupo, Jr., and his partner Robert Insalaco, members of the Erie (New York) County Sheriff's Department, knocked on the door of Paul Olson, a suspected arsonist. When the door opened, Olson stood before the officers completely naked. In a moment of shock, neither noticed that Olson was holding a .44 Magnum, which he pointed at Deputy Insalaco. Olson shot the officer in the face, killing him.[25]

Police officers face the threat of physical harm every day. According to the U.S. Department of Justice, police have one of the most dangerous jobs in the United States (along with taxi drivers, private security guards, and prison guards), with 306 of every 1,000 officers targets of nonfatal violence each year.[26] In 2001–2002, almost 370 police officers were killed in the line of duty. (See Figure 7.3.)

Occupational Safety

In a sense, the greatest threat to law enforcement officers is not an armed criminal or a speeding car, but their own level of awareness, or lack thereof.[27] Police tactician Charles Remsberg believes that officers have five general states of awareness, from condition white to condition red (see Figure 7.4).[28] Condition white, in which officers have slipped into the complacency of a routine, can be fatal, as in the case of Officers Pupo and Insalaco. The ideal mental state for an officer in Remsberg's spectrum is condition yellow: alert, but relaxed.

Training is a crucial aspect of officer safety. For example, every law enforcement officer should receive specific guidance on how to handle people who are intoxicated. A recent study by the Behavioral Sciences Unit of the FBI found that more than three-fourths of those interviewed who had killed a law enforcement officer were under the influence of alcohol, drugs, or both at the time of the homicide.[29] Officers need training in how to recognize the signs of intoxication (such

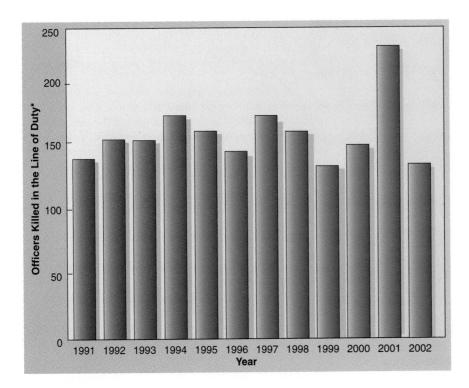

FIGURE 7.3

Police Officers Killed on Duty, 1991-2001

The Officer Down Memorial Page (www.odmp.org) has recorded the name of every law enforcement officer killed in the United States since 1794. The site provides information such as the name, city, and cause of death for all officers who died in the line of the duty.

*Causes of death include assault (shootings and stabbings), as well as heart attacks, drowning, automobile accidents, and so on. Note that the 2001 figures include seventy-one police officers killed as a direct result of the September 11, 2001, terrorist attacks.

Source: Officer Down Memorial Page.

as slurred speech and belligerence) and the "warning flags" of when an intoxicated person is about to become violent (for example, subject's hands not visible, subject in or near a motor vehicle).[30]

Stress

In the months after his partner's death, Officer Pupo continually played the "What If" game. "What if I had been faster with my gun?" he would ask himself. "What if we had waited for more officers? What if I had been standing on his side?" Eventually, Pupo found the best way he could deal with his guilt was by drinking.

Law enforcement officers are 300 percent more likely to suffer from alcoholism than the average American.[31] The average life expectancy of a police officer is fifty-seven years, compared to seventy-one for the general public—a statistic that can be attributed to police officers' top ranking among professions in rates of heart disease, hypertension, and diabetes.[32] The social isolation police officers must deal with also leads to one of the highest divorce rates of any job, which adds to stress. According to the U.S. Bureau of Labor Statistics, policing is one of the ten most stressful occupations in the country, along with firefighting, driving a taxi, and being a surgeon.[33]

INFOTRAC®
COLLEGE EDITION

Keywords: police and stress

FIGURE 7.4

The Awareness Spectrum

As you see here, the awareness spectrum for police officers has five stages, or conditions. According to the spectrum's creator, the ideal mental state for an officer is condition yellow.

| **Condition Black** State of panic, perhaps blacked out or even dead | **Condition Red** Continual feeling of nervous worry | **Condition Orange** State of alarm | **Condition Yellow** Relaxed, but alert and aware of surroundings | **Condition White** Unaware of surroundings, not paying attention to environment |

Source: Adapted from Charles Remsberg, *The Tactical Edge: Surviving High-Risk Patrol* (Northbrook, IL: Calibre Press, 1986), 47–51.

The Balancing Act:
How Aggressive Is Too Aggressive?

Early on a February morning several years ago in the Bronx, four police officers, all members of the elite Street Crime unit, shot and killed a West African immigrant named Amadou Diallo whom they mistakenly believed had threatened them with a gun. In the aftermath of the incident, the crime-fighting tactics employed by the New York Police Department (NYPD) came under intense scrutiny. Since his election in 1993, then–Mayor Rudy Giuliani had ordered the police force to aggressively carry out the "broken windows" policy of cracking down on quality-of-life crimes such as public drunkenness and loitering (see Chapter 5). Part of this "zero tolerance" approach included a drastic increase in the number of stop and frisks, often for minor violations such as public beer drinking and loud radio playing.

Critics contend that these tactics have encouraged police officers to be too aggressive. Every day, nineteen New York City residents file official grievances against police officers for improper behavior, including excessive force. The city pays out more than $20 million each year in compensation as a result. There are also assertions that the police unfairly target New York's minority communities. More than 60 percent of all those stopped by the NYPD's Street Crime unit at the time of the Diallo shooting were African Americans or Latinos.

As many New Yorkers are aware, however, while the aggressive tactics have appeared to lead to abuses and tragic mistakes, they have also appeared to reduce crime. By performing significantly more stop and frisks, police officers seized a huge number of illegally owned firearms. At the same time, the number of murders committed with firearms in the city dropped from 1,605 in 1991 to 375 in 1999. Total murders decreased from more than 2,000 to 667 over that same time period. Getting guns off the street was the top priority of the Street Crime unit.

As nearly every major U.S. city has adopted some, if not most, of New York's "zero tolerance" policies, the debate over where the line should be drawn between aggressive law enforcement and civil rights is taking on national significance. Indeed, over the past several years the federal government has convicted more than two hundred police officers nationwide for civil rights violations. "The challenge to develop an aggressive patrol that is not murderous or excessive is a constant puzzle," says Columbia University Law School Professor H. Richard Uviller.

FOR CRITICAL ANALYSIS
At what point should police authority to use force be curtailed, even if it can be proved that such force is an important factor in reducing violent crime?

STRESSORS
The aspects of police work and life that lead to feelings of stress.

Police Stressline, which provides law enforcement officers with tips on managing stress, also offers a window into the challenges of police work. For a link to this Web site, go to the Hypercontents page for this chapter at http://www.cj.wadsworth.com/ gainescore2e.

The conditions that cause stress—such as worries over finances, relationships, and so on—are known as **stressors.** Each profession has its own set of stressors, but police are particularly vulnerable to occupational pressures and stress factors. In the months following the September 11, 2001, terrorist attacks, the New York Police Department ordered all 55,000 employees to attend mental health counseling to deal with the strain caused by those events.[34] (To learn more about a career as a police psychologist, go to the *Careers in Criminal Justice Interactive CD* and click on the Career Rolodex.) In general, stress factors for police include the following:

1. The constant fear of becoming a victim of violent crime.
2. Exposure to violent crime and its victims.
3. The need to comply with the law in nearly every job action.
4. Lack of community support.
5. Negative media coverage.

Police face a number of internal pressures as well, such as limited opportunities for career advancement, excessive paperwork, and low wages and benefits.[35] The unconventional hours of shift work can also place pressure on an officer's private life and contribute to a lack of sleep. Each of these is a primary stressor associated with police work.[36]

AUTHORITY AND THE USE OF FORCE

If the police subculture is shaped by the dangers of the job, it often finds expression through authority. The various symbols of authority that decorate a police officer—including the uniform, badge, nightstick, and firearm—establish the power she or he holds over civilians. At the same time, many police officers feel that authority does not necessarily bring respect. Even though citizens may defer to the powers vested in the officer by the state, they do not respect the person who wears the uniform or carries the badge. Therefore, the manner in which police officers use their authority ultimately determines whether they are respected.

For better or for worse, both police officers and civilians tend to equate terms such as *authority* and *respect* with the ability to use force. Near the turn of the twentieth century, a police officer stated that his job was to "protect the good people and treat the crooks rough."[37] Implicit in the officer's statement is the idea that to do the protecting, he had to do some roughing up as well. This attitude toward the use of force is still with us today. Indeed, it is generally accepted that not only is police use of force inevitable, but that police officers who are unwilling to use force in certain circumstances cannot do their job effectively.[38] (See the feature *CJ in Focus—The Balancing Act: How Aggressive Is Too Aggressive?*)

The "Misuse" of Force

The Department of Justice estimates that law enforcement officers threatened to use force or used force in encounters with more than 421,000 Americans in 1999.[39] (See Figure 7.5.) Of course, police officers are often justified in using force to protect themselves or other citizens. At the same time, few observers would be naïve enough to believe that police are *always* justified in the use of force. How, then, is "misuse" of force to be defined?

One attempt to qualify excessive force that has been lauded by legal scholars, if not necessarily by police officers, was offered by the Christopher Commission. Established in Los Angeles in 1992 after the beating of African American motorist Rodney King, the commission advised that "an officer may resort to force only where he or she faces a credible threat, and then may only use the minimum amount necessary to control the subject."[40]

The Phoenix Study.   Terms such as *credible* and *necessary* are, of course, quite subjective, rendering such definitions too vague to be practical. To better understand the subject, the Phoenix (Arizona) Police Department, in a partnership with Rutgers University and Arizona State University, implemented a study to measure how often police officers used force. The results showed that police

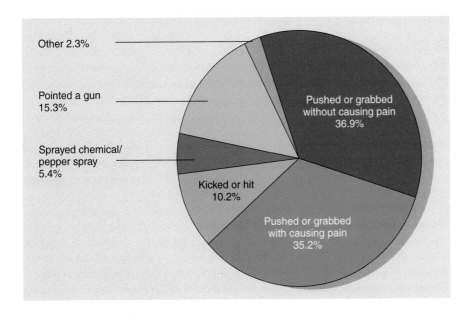

Other 2.3%

Pointed a gun
15.3%

Sprayed chemical/
pepper spray
5.4%

Pushed or grabbed
without causing pain
36.9%

Kicked or hit
10.2%

Pushed or grabbed
with causing pain
35.2%

FIGURE 7.5

The Use of Force by Police against Suspects

Of the 421,714 people who reported forceful behavior on the part of the police in 1999, about 22.5 percent said that force was threatened but not actually used. When force was used, as you can see, about 72 percent of the time it involved pushing and grabbing.

Source: Bureau of Justice Statistics, *Contacts between Police and the Public* (Washington, D.C.: U.S. Department of Justice, February 2001), 25.

used some form of "physical force"—defined as any "weaponless tactic" (such as kicking or shoving) or the threatened or actual use of any weapon—in 22 percent of the surveyed arrests.[41] The study also examined the predictors of force; that is, the factors that were present in the situations where force was used. As one might expect, the study found that the best predictor of police use of force was the suspect's use of force.[42]

The Misuse of Force and Minorities. In its guidelines for the use of deadly force by undercover officers, the New York Police Department warns its officers not to be victims of symbolic opponent syndrome, defined as a "preconceived notion that places suspects into a 'BAD GUY' category because of race, nationality, grooming or mode of dress."[43] The warning may seem self-evident, but it addresses a clear problem in law enforcement today. The Department of Justice reports that in 1999 police officers were almost three times more likely to use force when coming in contact with African Americans than with whites and more than twice as likely with Latinos as with whites.[44] Furthermore, Malcolm D. Holmes of the University of Wyoming has determined that in some of the nation's largest cities blacks and Latinos are significantly more likely to file civil rights complaints alleging police brutality than are whites.[45]

Legal Restrictions on the Use of Force during Arrest

To comply with the various, and not always consistent, laws concerning the use of force during arrest, a police officer must first understand that there are two kinds of force: *nondeadly force* and *deadly force.* Each category has its own set of legal conditions.

Nondeadly Force. Most of the use of force by law enforcement officers comes under the category of *nondeadly force,* or force that is not likely to result in the serious injury or death of the subject. In most states, the use of nondeadly force is regulated by the concept of **reasonable force,** which holds that the use of nondeadly force is allowed when a reasonable person would assume that such force was necessary. In a Pennsylvania case, for example, a jury ruled that two police officers had used reasonable force in handcuffing a seventy-four-year-old disabled man. Although the incident left the man with injuries that required hospitalization, the jury agreed with the defense's argument that the police had to use force because the subject struggled to avoid being handcuffed.[46]

To provide some guidelines for nondeadly force, most states have indicated the circumstances in which such force is acceptable:

1 To prevent the escape of a fleeing felony suspect.
2 To retake a suspect after an escape attempt.
3 To overcome an offender's resistance to a lawful arrest.
4 To protect the officer from bodily injury.
5 To protect the suspect, other persons, or property from harm.[47]

The United States Supreme Court attempted to clarify the definition of "reasonable" force in *Graham v. Connor* (1989),[48] ruling that "not every push or shove" violates a suspect's constitutional rights to due process even if, in retrospect, the situation does not seem to have warranted force.

Deadly Force. Some observers believe that the use of force should be based on the idea of a *use of force continuum.* On one end of the continuum, cooperation by the suspect results in the officer using no force, whereas at the other end dangerous noncooperation by the suspect can bring about maximum force.[49] Otherwise known as **deadly force,** this is force that an objective officer realizes

REASONABLE FORCE
The degree of force that is appropriate to protect the police officer or other citizens and is not excessive.

DEADLY FORCE
Force applied by a police officer that is likely or intended to cause death.

Justified Force?

THE FACTS

Just after midnight, New York City police officers Sean, Ken, Rich, and Ed were riding through a high-crime area in an unmarked car when they saw African immigrant Amadou acting "suspiciously" in front of a building (which turned out to be his home). Sean and Ed, in street clothes, got out of the car and walked toward Amadou. They identified themselves as police officers and told Amadou to keep his hands where they could see them. According to their testimony, instead Amadou "darted into" the building, then reached into his pocket and produced a dark object. Sean shouted "Gun!" and the four officers began firing at Amadou, who fell to the ground almost immediately. Sean walked up to the prone body and searched for the weapon, but found only a wallet in Amadou's hand. Sean tried to revive Amadou with CPR, but he had already died of nineteen bullet wounds.

THE LAW

The Supreme Court has ruled that cases involving the use of police force should be decided by observing all the circumstances surrounding the incident and then determining whether the police officer was "reasonable" in the use of force. In other words, would a reasonable police officer in this officer's shoes have been justified in using force?

YOUR DECISION

Sean, Ken, Rich, and Ed have been charged with Amadou's murder. Are they guilty, or, under the circumstances, were they justified in firing at Amadou?

[To see how a jury in Albany, New York, decided this case, go to Example 7.1 in Appendix A.]

will place the subject in direct threat of serious injury or death. (See the feature *You Be the Judge—Justified Force?*)

Limits on the use of deadly force by law enforcement officers were set by the United States Supreme Court in *Tennessee v. Garner* (1985).[50] The case involved fifteen-year-old Edward Garner and Memphis (Tennessee) police officers Elton Hymon and Leslie Wright. Officers Hymon and Wright answered a call for service and were told by a woman that she had heard glass breaking in a neighboring home. While Wright radioed for back-up, Hymon went behind the home to investigate. He saw Garner running across the backyard and yelled, "Police! Halt!" Garner, unarmed with ten dollars that he had stolen from the house in his pocket, ignored the order and began to climb the backyard fence. Hymon proceeded to shoot Garner in the back of the head, killing him. Hymon testified that when he fired his weapon, he believed the boy was about to escape; Hymon said that he had been trained to shoot to keep a suspect from fleeing. At the time, Tennessee's *fleeing felon* law allowed police officers to apprehend fleeing suspects in this manner. The state appellate court ruled that Hymon's act was within the law's limits.[51]

In reviewing the case, the United States Supreme Court was not concerned with the actions of Officer Hymon, who had followed the law. Instead, the Court scrutinized the Tennessee statute itself, ultimately finding it unconstitutional:

> When the suspect poses no immediate threat to the officer and no threat to others, the use of deadly force is unjustified. . . . It is not better that all felony suspects die than that they escape.[52]

The Court's ruling forced twenty-three states to change their fleeing felon laws. It did not, however, completely eliminate police discretion in such situations: police officers may use deadly force if they have probable cause to believe that the fleeing suspect poses a threat of serious injury or death to the officers or others. In essence, the Court recognized the impossibility of creating guidelines to cover every eventuality. Police officers must be able to make split-second decisions without worrying about the legal ramifications. The Court tried to clarify this concept four years later in the *Graham v. Connor* case (discussed earlier) by stating that the use of any force should be judged by the "reasonableness of the moment."

INFOTRAC®
COLLEGE EDITION

Keyword: deadly force

Criminal Justice & TECHNOLOGY

The "Glock on Steroids" Approach

According to the FBI, police are involved in about four hundred justifiable homicides each year. Even though these killings only occur when the officer is required to use force to protect himself or herself or a third party, law enforcement officials realize that each such incident can damage relations with the community. Furthermore, police officers may hesitate to use deadly force even when justified, for fear of the repercussions.

In an attempt to alleviate these worries, more than 1,500 law enforcement agencies now use the Advanced Taser M26, a form of nonlethal stun gun that police call a "Glock on Steroids." When an officer pulls the trigger on an M26, which looks like a regular handgun, two quarter-inch darts attached to electrical wires are propelled up to twenty-one feet. Once the darts snag the target's clothes or become embedded in his or her skin, a five-second jolt of electricity is automatically discharged. The current attacks the target's central nervous system, paralyzing him or her for up to ninety seconds.

Some human rights groups have called for a ban on these types of weapons, wanting more research to be conducted on how the weapon's electrical charge affects the human body. These groups point out that since 1996, six people have died after being shot with a stun gun. Supporters of the nonlethal weapon counter that drug use by the target was the main cause of death in each of these cases, and point to an overwhelming success of the guns in most jurisdictions. The Los Angeles Police Department, for example, has used various types of stun guns approximately 5,600 times over the past three decades, and no serious injuries have been linked to these weapons.

Clay Winn, of TASER International, demonstrates the company's Advanced M26 nonlethal "stun gun." (AP Photo/Joe Cavaretta)

IN THE FUTURE

A research company in San Diego, California, is in the process of perfecting the latest line of nonlethal stun guns. Called the Anti-Personnel Beam Weapon (APBW), the device uses ultraviolet radiation to send an electrical current through the air toward the target. Like the electrical charge of the M26, this current freezes muscle contraction, causing paralysis. The APBW has a range of about one hundred feet, and the same company is working on a similar device that would disable automobile engines.

Finally, in 2001 the Court dismissed an excessive force claim arising from an altercation between two military police officers and an animal rights activist during an appearance by then-vice president Al Gore in San Francisco. Even though the officers' behavior may have been unreasonable under existing law (they pushed the activist, who was sixty years old and wearing a leg brace, to the ground), reasonable officers could have made the same mistake under similar circumstances (the need for heightened security to protect the vice president).[53] In practice, these decisions have made it difficult for police actions to be judged "unreasonable" in retrospect, unless those actions were clearly and unnecessarily violent. (To learn more about "stun guns," which may lessen the amount of deadly force needed in police work, see the feature *Criminal Justice & Technology— The "Glock on Steroids" Approach.*)

POLICE CORRUPTION

Police corruption has been a concern since the first organized American police departments. As you recall from Chapter 4, a desire to eradicate, or at least limit, corruption was one of the motivating factors behind the reform movement of policing. For general purposes, **police corruption** can be defined as the misuse of authority by a law enforcement officer "in a manner designed to produce personal gain."[54] Corrupt police officers fall into two categories: "grass eaters" and "meat eaters." "Grass eaters" are involved in passive corruption; they simply accept the payoffs and opportunities that police work can provide. As the name implies, "meat eaters" are more aggressive in their quest for personal gain, initiating and going to great lengths to carry out corrupt schemes.

POLICE CORRUPTION
The abuse of authority by a law enforcement officer for personal gain.

Types of Corruption

Certain forms of corruption have been endemic to police work since its inception. These traditional forms of corruption include:

1 *Bribery,* in which the police officer accepts money or other forms of payment in exchange for "favors," which may include allowing a certain criminal activity to continue or misplacing a key piece of evidence before a trial. Related to bribery are *payoffs,* in which an officer demands payment from an individual or a business in return for certain services.

2 *Shakedowns,* in which an officer attempts to coerce money or goods from a citizen or criminal.

3 *Mooching,* in which the police officer accepts free "gifts" such as cigarettes, liquor, or services in return for favorable treatment of the gift giver.

"Who will protect the public when the police violate the law?"

—Ramsey Clark, *former U.S. attorney general (1986)*

Between 1993 and 2000, the number of local, state, and federal law enforcement officers in federal prison rose nearly 600 percent to 668.[55] Perhaps the most visible corruption scandal of the last decade was touched off when Rafael Perez, an officer in a Los Angeles Police Department (LAPD) antigang unit, was arrested for stealing cocaine from an evidence locker. Perez proceeded to admit to a number of other crimes and implicated others members of the unit. Eventually, in 2000, the evidence of widespread corruption forced the LAPD to accept a federal consent degree, placing part of its operations under the watch of the U.S. Department of Justice.[56]

Corruption in Police Subculture

There is no single reason that police corruption occurs. In covering corrupt behavior by a group of Miami police officers known as the Miami River Cops, journalist John Dorschner targeted some of the factors that lead to unethical behavior, including a lack of proper training, a lack of supervision, and the fact that most officers can double or triple their salaries through corrupt activities.[57]

Lawrence Sherman identifies several stages in the moral decline of police officers.[58] In the first stage, the officers accept minor gratuities, such the occasional free meal from a restaurant on their beats. These gratuities gradually evolve into outright bribes, in which the officers receive the gratuity for overlooking some violation. For example, a law officer may accept pay from a bar owner to ensure that the establishment is not investigated for serving alcohol to minors. In the final stage, officers no longer passively accept bribes, but actively seek them out, to the point where the officers may even force the other party to pay for unwanted police services. This stage often involves large amounts of money and may entail protection of or involvement in drug, gambling, or prostitution organizations.

INFOTRAC®
COLLEGE EDITION

Keyword: police corruption

The insulating effects of police subculture also contribute to corruption by making it difficult to uncover. The Knapp Commission highlighted the "code of silence" that exists in police departments, a code that brands anybody within the department who exposes corrupt behavior as a traitor. "The rookie who comes into the department," it was noted, "is faced with the situation where it is easier for him to become corrupt than to remain honest."[59]

POLICE ETHICS

Police corruption is intricately connected with the ethics of law enforcement officers. **Ethics** has to do with fundamental questions of the fairness, justice, rightness, or wrongness of any action. Given the significant power that police officers hold, society expects very high standards of ethical behavior from them. These expectations are summed up in the *Police Code of Conduct,* which was developed by the International Association of Chiefs of Police in 1989 (see Figure 7.6).

To some extent, the *Police Code of Conduct* is self-evident: "A police officer will not engage in acts of corruption or bribery." In other aspects, it is idealistic, perhaps unreasonably so: "Officers will never allow personal feelings, animosities, or friendships to influence official conduct." The police working environment—rife with lying, cheating, lawbreaking, and violence—often does not allow for such ethical absolutes.[60]

Ethical Dilemmas

Some police actions are obviously unethical, such as the behavior of a Pennsylvania officer who paid a woman he was dating $500 to pretend to be an eyewitness in a murder trial. The majority of ethical dilemmas that a police officer will face are not so clear-cut. Joycelyn M. Pollock and Ronald F. Becker, both members of the Criminal Justice Department at Southwest Texas State University, define an ethical dilemma as a situation in which law enforcement officers:

- Do not know the right course of action;
- Have difficulty doing what they consider to be right; and/or
- Find the wrong choice very tempting.[61]

These ethical dilemmas can occur often in police work, and it is how an officer deals with them that determines to what extent he or she is behaving ethically. (For further discussion of the difficult ethical situations that police officers face, see the feature *CJ in Focus—A Question of Ethics: The Dirty Harry Problem* on page 186.)

Elements of Ethics

Pollock and Becker, both of whom have extensive experience as ethics instructors for police departments, further identify four categories of ethical dilemmas, involving discretion, duty, honesty, and loyalty.[62]

- *Discretion.* The law provides rigid guidelines for how police officers must act and how they cannot act, but it does not offer guidelines for how officers *should* act in many circumstances.[63] As mentioned in Chapter 4, police officers often use discretion to determine how they should act, and ethics play an important role in guiding discretionary actions.

- *Duty.* The concept of discretion is linked with **duty,** or the obligation to act in a certain manner. Society, by passing laws, can make a police officer's duty more clear and, in the process, help eliminate discretion from the

INFOTRAC®
COLLEGE EDITION

Keyword: police ethics

ETHICS
The rules or standards of behavior governing a profession; aimed at ensuring the fairness and rightness of actions.

DUTY
The moral sense of a police officer that she or he should apply authority in a certain manner.

FIGURE 7.6
The *Police Code of Conduct*

All law enforcement officers must be fully aware of the ethical responsibilities of their position and must strive constantly to live up to the highest possible standards of professional policing. The International Association of Chiefs of Police believes it important that police officers have clear advice and counsel available to assist them in performing their duties consistent with these standards, and has adopted the following ethical mandates as guidelines to meet these ends.

PRIMARY RESPONSIBILITIES OF A POLICE OFFICER

A police officer acts as an official representative of government who is required and trusted to work within the law. The officer's powers and duties are conferred by statute. The fundamental duties of a police officer include serving the community, safeguarding lives and property, protecting the innocent, keeping the peace and ensuring the rights of all to liberty, equality and justice.

PERFORMANCE OF THE DUTIES OF A POLICE OFFICER

A police officer shall perform all duties impartially, without favor or affection or ill will and without regard to status, sex, race, religion, political belief or aspiration. All citizens will be treated equally with courtesy, consideration and dignity.

Officers will never allow personal feelings, animosities or friendships to influence official conduct. Laws will be enforced appropriately and courteously and, in carrying out their responsibilities, officers will strive to obtain maximum cooperation from the public. They will conduct themselves in appearance and deportment in such a manner as to inspire confidence and respect for the position of public trust they hold.

DISCRETION

A police officer will use responsibly the discretion vested in his position and exercise it within the law. The principle of reasonableness will guide the officer's determinations, and the officer will consider all surrounding circumstances in determining whether any legal action shall be taken.

Consistent and wise use of discretion, based on professional policing competence, will do much to preserve good relationships and retain the confidence of the public. There can be difficulty in choosing between conflicting courses of action. It is important to remember that a timely word of advice rather than arrest—which may be correct in appropriate circumstances—can be a more effective means of achieving a desired end.

USE OF FORCE

A police officer will never employ unnecessary force or violence and will use only such force in the discharge of duty as is reasonable in all circumstances.

The use of force should be used only with the greatest restraint and only after discussion, negotiation and persuasion have been found to be inappropriate or ineffective. While the use of force is occasionally unavoidable, every police officer will refrain from unnecessary infliction of pain or suffering and will never engage in cruel, degrading or inhuman treatment of any person.

CONFIDENTIALITY

Whatever a police officer sees, hears or learns of that is of a confidential nature will be kept secret unless the performance of duty or legal provision requires otherwise.

Members of the public have a right to security and privacy, and information obtained about them must not be improperly divulged.

INTEGRITY

A police officer will not engage in acts of corruption or bribery, nor will an officer condone such acts by other police officers.

The public demands that the integrity of police officers be above reproach. Police officers must, therefore, avoid any conduct that might compromise integrity and thus undercut the public confidence in a law enforcement agency. Officers will refuse to accept any gifts, presents, subscriptions, favors, gratuities or promises that could be interpreted as seeking to cause the officer to refrain from performing official responsibilities honestly and within the law. Police officers must not receive private or special advantage from their official status. Respect from the public cannot be bought; it can only be earned and cultivated.

COOPERATION WITH OTHER POLICE OFFICERS AND AGENCIES

Police officers will cooperate with all legally authorized agencies and their representatives in the pursuit of justice.

An officer or agency may be one among many organizations that may provide law enforcement services to a jurisdiction. It is imperative that a police officer assist colleagues fully and completely; with respect and consideration at all times.

PERSONAL-PROFESSIONAL CAPABILITIES

Police officers will be responsible for their own standard of professional-performance and will take every reasonable opportunity to enhance and improve their level of knowledge and competence.

Through study and experience, a police officer can acquire the high level of knowledge and competence that is essential for the efficient and effective performance of duty. The acquisition of knowledge is a never-ending process of personal and professional development that should be pursued constantly.

PRIVATE LIFE

Police officers will behave in a manner that does not bring discredit to their agencies or themselves.

A police officer's character and conduct while off duty must always be exemplary, thus maintaining a position of respect in the community in which he or she lives and serves. The officer's personal behavior must be beyond reproach.

Source: International Association of Chiefs of Police. Web site: www.theiacp.org/.

CJ in FOCUS

A Question of Ethics: The Dirty Harry Problem

Do the ends justify the means? This is one of the most difficult and complex questions of ethics, and one that is particularly crucial for police officers. Should they take steps that they know to be illegal in order to achieve a positive goal?

In addressing this moral dilemma, the University of Delaware's Carl B. Klockars turns to one of the most popular police dramas of all time, the 1971 film *Dirty Harry*. In this movie, Detective Harry Callahan, played by Clint Eastwood, faces a situation in which a young girl has been kidnapped by a psychotic killer named Scorpio. Demanding $200,000 in ransom, Scorpio has buried the girl alive, leaving her just a few hours' worth of oxygen. Callahan manages to find Scorpio, and in his efforts to learn the location of the girl, he shoots and then tortures the kidnapper. Although Callahan eventually gets the information out of Scorpio, it is too late. By the time he finds the girl, she has suffocated.

Assuming for argument's sake that Callahan was able to save the girl, would he have been justified in taking such drastic measures? After all, Callahan, like all officers, took an oath to obey the U.S. Constitution, which certainly does not permit the torture of suspects. Following proper procedure, Callahan should have arrested Scorpio and advised him of his right to an attorney. If Scorpio had exercised his right, the attorney would certainly have reminded him of his right to

remain silent, and Callahan would have had no chance to save the little girl. In fact, Callahan committed a crime himself by assaulting Scorpio. Given all these factors, was the detective justified in doing what he did in order to save a life? According to Klockars:

> [The] core scene in *Dirty Harry* should only be understood as a dramatic example of a far more common problem: real, everyday, routine situations in which police officers know they can only achieve good ends by employing dirty means. Each time a police officer considers deceiving a suspect into confessing by telling him that his fingerprints were found at the scene or that a conspirator has already confessed, each time a police officer considers adding some untrue details to his account of probable cause to legitimate a crucial stop or search [he or she] faces a Dirty Harry Problem.

Klockars calls the effects of the Dirty Harry problem on police officers "devastating." On the one hand, if the officers decide not to use dirty means, they must face the consequences: perhaps a suspect the officers know is guilty will be set free to commit further crimes. On the other hand, if the officers do abandon rules and procedures to serve the law, they are essentially breaking the very laws that they took an oath to uphold. The Dirty Harry problem, Klockars says, makes policing the most "morally corrosive occupation."

FOR CRITICAL ANALYSIS
Are police ever justified in using unlawful methods, whatever good may be ultimately achieved? What do you believe is the proper solution to the Dirty Harry problem?

> *"Duties are not performed for duty's sake, but because their neglect would make the man uncomfortable. A man performs but one duty—the duty of contenting his spirit, the duty of making himself agreeable to himself."*
>
> —Mark Twain, *American novelist* (1906)

decision-making process. But an officer's duty will not always be obvious, and ethical considerations can often supplement "the rules" of being a law enforcement agent.

- *Honesty.* Of course, honesty is a critical attribute for an ethical police officer. A law enforcement agent must make hundreds of decisions in a day, and most of them require him or her to be honest in order to properly do the job.

- *Loyalty.* What should a police officer do if he or she witnesses a partner using excessive force on a suspect? The choice often sets loyalty against ethics, especially if the officer does not condone the violence.

Although there is no easy "formula" to guide police officers through ethical challenges, Linda S. Miller of the Midwest Regional Community Policing Institute and Karen M. Hess of Normandale Community College have come up with three questions that can act as personal "checks" for police officers. Miller and Hess suggest that officers, when considering a particular action, ask themselves:

1. Is it legal?
2. Is it balanced?
3. How does it make me feel about myself?[64]

POLICE ACCOUNTABILITY

Even in a police department with excellent recruiting methods, state-of-the-art ethics and discretionary training programs, and a culturally diverse work force that nearly matches the make-up of the community, the problems discussed earlier in this chapter are bound to occur. The question then becomes—given the inevitability of excessive force, corruption, and other misconduct—*who shall police the police?*

Internal Investigations

"The minute the public feels that the police department is not investigating its own alleged wrongdoing well, the police department will not be able to function credibly in even the most routine of matters" says Sheldon Greenberg, a professor of police management at Johns Hopkins University.[65] The mechanism for these investigations within a police department is the **internal affairs unit (IAU).** In many smaller police departments, the police chief conducts internal affairs investigations, while midsize and large departments will have a team of internal affairs officers.

As much as police officers may resent internal affairs units, most realize that it is preferable to settle disciplinary matters in-house. The alternatives may be worse. Police officers are criminally liable for any crimes they might commit. In 1999, for example, ex–New York City police officer Justin Volpe received a thirty-year prison sentence for sodomizing Haitian immigrant Abner Louima with a broomstick. City and state governments can also be held civilly liable for wrongdoing by their police officers. The city of New York paid Louima approximately $7 milion to settle a police brutality lawsuit. By some estimates, the city of Los Angeles could wind up paying $100 million to settle lawsuits springing from its most recent scandals.[66]

Citizen Oversight

In the early 1990s, the Denver Police Department had created a "gang list" of potential criminals. Much to the dismay of many community leaders, the "gang list" was composed primarily of minorities. In response to public outrage, the city's Public Safety Review Commission (PSRC) held hearings on the matter. As a result of the PSRC's actions, the Denver police eliminated nearly half the names on the list and changed their methods of labeling people as gang members.[67]

The PSRC is an example of an external procedure for handling citizens' complaints known as **citizen oversight.** In this process, citizens—people who are not sworn officers and, by inference, not biased in favor of law enforcement officers—review allegations of police misconduct or brutality. According to Samuel Walker, nearly one hundred cities now operate some kind of review procedure by an independent body.[68] For the most part, citizen review boards can only recommend action to the police chief or other executive. They do not have the power to discipline officers directly. Although police officers generally resent this intrusion of civilians, most studies have shown that civilian review boards are not widely successful in their efforts to convince police chiefs to take action against their subordinate officers.[69]

Michael Cox successfully sued the city of Boston following an incident in which he was mistaken for a suspect and severely beaten by members of the city's police force. (Boston Globe Photo)

Criminal Justice in Action

Diversity in the Police Work Force

At the opening of this chapter, we discussed the role community dissatisfaction with the local police played in racial unrest in Los Angeles. In Los Angeles, as well as many other major American metropolitan areas, the minority composition of the police force is significantly less than that of the populace—a discrepancy that fueled the sense of powerlessness among the city's African Americans. In this *Criminal Justice in Action,* we will look at efforts to increase racial and gender diversity in the police work force, a process that has been slow but not altogether unsuccessful.

CHANGING THE FACE OF AMERICAN POLICING

For many years, the typical American police officer was white and male. As recently as 1968, the National Advisory Commission on Civil Disorders found that African Americans represented only 5 percent of all sworn officers in the United States.[70] Only within the past twenty-five years has this inconsistency been addressed, and only within the past decade have many police departments been actively trying to recruit women, African Americans, Hispanics, Asian Americans, and other minorities.

To be sure, these steps were not taken without external pressure. The 1964 Civil Rights Act and its 1972 amendments guaranteed minorities and women equal access to jobs in law enforcement, and the Equal Employment Opportunity Act of 1972 set the stage for affirmative action in hiring and promotion. Court decisions also played a role in the transformation of the American police force. As a result of the United States Supreme Court decisions in *Griggs v. Duke Power Company* (1971)[71] and *Abermarle Paper Company v. Moody* (1975),[72] police departments could be found in violation of federal law if their hiring and promotion policies were tainted by racial discrimination.

Not all diversity efforts in law enforcement agencies have been ordered by legislators and the courts. Many departments, particularly those in urban areas, have realized that a culturally diverse police force can offer a number of benefits, including improved community relations and higher levels of service. The results of these changing attitudes, though still insufficient in the view of many observers, can be seen in the latest available figures on women and minorities in law enforcement agencies, which are summarized in Figure 7.7.

THE SLOW PROCESS

The integration of African Americans and other minorities into the nation's police forces has been a slow process. Chicago hired its first black police officer in 1872, but by 1930, African Americans made up only 2 percent of the city's force. That same year, blacks accounted for 4 percent of police officers in Philadelphia, 2 percent in Pittsburgh, and less than 1 percent in such major cities as New York and Cleveland.[73]

These numbers changed with the implementation of affirmative action, but it would be a mistake to see minority representation on police forces solely in terms of the traditional justification for this policy. In general, affirmative action programs strive to increase opportunities for African Americans as a remedy for past injustices. In police departments, the programs have also sought to improve the overall effectiveness of the force.

For example, after a series of racially motivated riots in 1967, Detroit decided to institute quotas to increase its ratio of black police officers—which had been 5 percent in a city that was more than 50 percent African American. In a court case challenging the constitutionality of these quo-

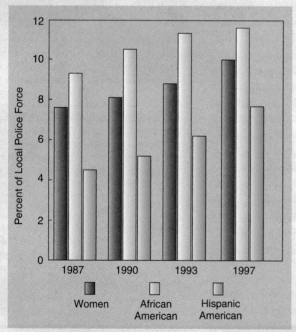

FIGURE 7.7

Minorities and Women as Law Enforcement Agents

Percent of Local Police Force (y-axis: 0, 2, 4, 6, 8, 10, 12)

x-axis: 1987, 1990, 1993, 1997

Legend: Women, African American, Hispanic American

Source: Bureau of Justice Statistics, *Local Police Departments—1997* (Washington, D.C.: U.S. Department of Justice, February 2000), 4.

tas, the city argued that it needed a representative police force to fulfill its duties to the citizens of Detroit. The court agreed, noting that the presence of a "mostly white police force in minority communities can be a 'dangerous irritant' which can trigger" a destructive response.[74] In 1986, United States Supreme Court Justice John Paul Stevens concurred, stating that police administrators "might reasonably conclude that an integrated police force could develop a better relationship with the community and thereby do a more effective job of maintaining law and order than a force composed of white officers."[75]

MINORITIES IN LEADERSHIP POSITIONS

To a certain extent, the increase in minority representation in local police forces shown in Figure 7.7 is also present in leadership positions. In the past three decades, African Americans have been appointed as police commissioners or chiefs in some of the nation's largest police departments. The list includes William Hart (Detroit), Benjamin Ward (New York City), and Willie Williams (Los Angeles). Smaller cities are also becoming more open to minority leadership of their police forces, with African Americans taking control of police departments in Tacoma (Washington), Evansville (Indiana), and Portsmouth (Virginia) in 1998. Other minorities are seeing progress as well: in 1996, Fred Lau became the first Asian American appointed as police chief in the history of the San Francisco Police Department, and in 2000 Raul Martinez became the first Hispanic police chief in Miami.

Despite these hirings, the problems historically faced by minority police officers remain unresolved. First, the extensive programs to recruit minority officers have not been as successful as many observers had hoped. This has been attributed to a lack of aggressiveness on the part of police recruiters and the continuing negative view of law enforcement in minority communities, which discourages African Americans and Hispanics from applying for the jobs.[76]

POLICE DIVERSITY IN BOSTON AND NEW YORK

As can be seen by the different experiences of the Boston and New York police departments, a number of factors contribute to the success or failure of a city's attempts to integrate its police force. In the 1970s, both Boston and New York had similarly low percentages of African Americans on their police forces. Today, 24 percent of the police officers in Boston are black men or women—a percentage that is actually higher than black representation overall in the city. In New York, by contrast, only 14 percent of the police force is African American—slightly more than half of the city's African American make-up.[77]

What accounts for this difference? First, Boston's hiring standards are more conducive to minority representation. That city accepts high school graduates as recruits, while New York requires two years of college, a requirement that serves to disproportionately disqualify minorities. Furthermore, in 1994 Boston enacted an ordinance that requires all municipal employees to be city residents, making it more likely that the racial and ethnic composition of the police department will mirror that of the city. New York has no residency requirement. Finally, and perhaps most important, the starting salary for a Boston police officer is about $40,000, compared to $31,000 in New York. Becoming a police officer is, in the words of one observer, "the best job in Boston for someone with a high school diploma."[78]

Police administrators in Boston have also made a special effort to avoid the bureaucratic pitfalls that can limit diversity. While New York's civil service test often keeps minority officers from being promoted, Boston Police Commissioner Paul F. Evans found a loophole in his state's rules that allows "special skills" to overcome low test scores. Using language as a special skill, Evans has hired eleven Creole-speaking Haitians, as well as officers fluent in Chinese, Vietnamese, and Spanish. Calling himself a "practical person," Evans says, "Having African-American and Hispanic and Vietnamese officers, people of different backgrounds and cultures who can conduct comfortable interviews with crime victims and can infiltrate crime rings that aren't white—the need for that is just common sense."[79]

WOMEN IN POLICING

Since the formation of the earliest police departments in the nineteenth century, policing has been seen as "man's work"—only men were considered to have the physical strength necessary to deal with the dangers of the street.[80] Statistically, the advance of women into police work has been even slower than that of minorities. The first female to serve in a police department was Lola Baldwin of Portland, Oregon, who was hired in 1905 to protect women and children from drunks during the Lewis and Clark Exposition. The first full-time female police officer was Alice Stebbin Wells, who joined the Los Angeles Police Department in 1910. By 1946, only 141 out of 417 American cities had any policewomen at all, and it was not until 1968 that a city—Indianapolis—had two female patrol officers on the force.[81]

Though the legal barriers to employment have for the most part fallen, policewomen still must contend with a number of on-the-job issues. In 2001, twelve female police officers in Grand Rapids, Michigan, filed a lawsuit that enumerated many of these issues. The lawsuit alleged that:

- Female officers were not given their own rest rooms, changing rooms, and showers.
- Supervisors and other male officers made inappropriate, derogatory, and degrading comments of a sexual nature.
- Female officers were inappropriately touched.
- Female officers were not provided with back-up support in the field.

Continued on next page

CJ in Action: Diversity in the Police Work Force *continued*

Mark Jheng, right, looks over an application for the New York Police Department (NYPD). Like many of the nation's law enforcement agencies, the NYPD has stepped up efforts to recruit minorities. (AP Photo/Kathy Willens)

• Female officers were passed over for promotion and advancement.[82]

Policewomen are also under "constant pressures to demonstrate their competence and effectiveness vis-à-vis their male counterparts," says criminologist Susan Martin.[83] One female police officer describes her experience:

I got to a call. They send another male officer and then another male officer. The attitude is—get a *guy*. I'm there with the one male officer and when the other guy shows up, the first male officer says to the second, this is right in front of me—"I'm glad you came."[84]

A number of studies have shown, however, that policewomen can be as effective as men in most situations, and often more so. Citizens appear to prefer dealing with a female police officer rather than a male during service calls—especially those that involve domestic violence.[85] In general, policewomen are less aggressive and more likely to reduce the potential for a violent situation by relying on verbal skills rather than their authority as law enforcement agents.[86] According to a study conducted by the National Center for Women & Policing, payouts in civil lawsuits for cases of brutality and misconduct involving male officers exceed those involving female officers by a ratio of 43 to 1.[87]

MAKING SENSE OF DIVERSITY IN POLICE EMPLOYMENT

1 Many police departments are adjusting their strength requirements to accommodate female recruits. Do you believe this is an acceptable strategy for increasing the number of female police officers?

2 What effect would you expect high-profile incidents of police use of force against minorities to have on a police department's efforts to diversify? What steps could a police department take to lessen the impact of these incidents with regard to recruiting minorities?

3 Under what circumstances might a female police officer be more effective than a male police officer?

INFOTRAC®
COLLEGE EDITION

Keyword: women police

KEY TERMS

blue curtain 175

citizen oversight 187

deadly force 180

duty 184

ethics 184

field training 173

internal affairs unit (IAU) 187

police corruption 183

police cynicism 175

police subculture 173

reasonable force 180

socialization 174

stressors 178

CHAPTER SUMMARY

❶ **Explain what is involved in background checks of prospective police officers.** In addition to making sure that applicants meet the minimum requirements of citizenship, no prior felony record, and ability to get a driver's license, most police departments engage in checks that include drug tests; review of educational, military, and driving records; credit checks; FBI searches; and interviews with spouses and previous employers.

❷ **Identify the five basic values of the police subculture.** (a) Only a police officer can understand the "true" nature of police work; (b) she or he is the only real crime fighter; (c) to fight crime effectively, police officers must bend or break the rules imposed by the courts; (d) civilians criticize the police unless they need help; and (e) loyalty among police officers is the highest virtue because everyone else is "out to get" them.

❸ **Explain what stressors are and list some of those found in police work.** Stressors are any conditions that cause stress. In police work, stressors include (a) the fear of becoming a victim of violent crime, (b) exposure to violent crimes and victims, (c) a need to comply with the law in every job action, (d) lack of community support, (e) negative media coverage, (f) excessive paperwork, and (g) unconventional hours of shift work.

❹ **Indicate some of the guidelines for the use of nondeadly force in most states.** Force is accept-

able in the following circumstances: (a) preventing the escape of a fleeing felony suspect, (b) retaking a suspect after an escape attempt, (c) overcoming an offender's resistance to a lawful arrest, (d) when protecting the officer from bodily injury, and (e) when protecting the suspect, other persons, or property from harm.

❺ **Identify the three traditional forms of police corruption.** The three traditional forms are bribery, shakedowns, and mooching.

❻ **Explain what an ethical dilemma is and name the four categories of ethical dilemmas typically facing a police officer.** An ethical dilemma is a situation in which police officers (a) do not know the right course of action; (b) have difficulty doing what they consider to be right; and/or (c) find the wrong choice very tempting. The four types of ethical dilemmas involve (a) discretion, (b) duty, (c) honesty, and (d) loyalty.

❼ **List the three types of police accountability systems and indicate which one is least important.** The three ways of keeping the police accountable are (a) internal investigations, (b) civil liability, and (c) citizen oversight, such as civilian review boards. Civilian review boards have been the least effective. The presence of civil liability often forces internal affairs units to act in a swift and dramatic way.

QUESTIONS FOR CRITICAL ANALYSIS

❶ In what sense have police departments' physical standards been used to discriminate against women?

❷ What are the various experiences that rookie police officers undergo that make them aware they are not in a "normal" job?

❸ What is the end result of the police subculture on police officers?

❹ What is the greatest threat to a police officer's physical safety?

❺ Why is the average life expectancy of a police officer almost fifteen years less than that of the general public?

❻ Have the most recent United States Supreme Court decisions on the use of deadly force made it easier to ascertain when police actions can be judged "unreasonable"?

SELECTED PRINT AND ELECTRONIC RESOURCES

SUGGESTED READINGS

Brown, Edward S., *A Badge without Blemish: Avoiding Police Corruption,* Kearney, NE: Morris Pub., 1997. This slim volume (only fifty-seven pages) provides some personal reflections on the author's eight years of service as a police officer for the City of Atlanta Police Department. The author contends that the greatest challenge facing law enforcement agencies is how to "resurrect" enthusiasm in their officers.

Champion, Dean J., *Police Misconduct in the United States: A Reference Handbook,* Santa Barbara, CA: ABC-CLIO Publishing, 2001. This comprehensive study of police misconduct may lead the reader to believe that police personnel engage only in improper activities, which is never the case. A good reference source, nonetheless.

Delattre, Edwin J., *Character and Cops: Ethics in Policing,* Washington, D.C.: AIE Press, 2002. This far-reaching study looks at ethical and unethical police behavior and asks, "Why?" Why do some cops exhibit incredible heroism while others seem to personify the worst in human nature? Why is a good cop a good cop and why is a bad cop a bad cop? The author explores the numerous factors that seem to affect ethics in the criminal justice system, including the many conflicting pressures placed on police officers by the society they are sworn to serve.

MEDIA RESOURCES

***Training Day* (2001)** Jake Hoyt (Ethan Hawke) is a young officer with the Los Angeles Police Department. This film tells the story of Hoyt's first day on the job after being pro-moted to an elite narcotics unit. The assignment is a dream come true for the ambitious Hoyt, but his training partner, Alonzo Harris, turns out to be a nightmare. Played by Denzel Washington, Harris introduces Hoyt to a disturbing vision of "life on the street," where the only way to catch the bad guys is to become one of them. As Hoyt becomes more deeply involved in his partner's various corrupt schemes, he is forced to consider the possibility that ideals such as "truth" and "justice" have no place in the career he has chosen for himself.

Critically analyze this film:

1. List the various forms of corruption in which Harris is involved. Would he be characterized as a "grass eater" or a "meat eater"?

2. Discuss the ways in which Harris "socializes" Hoyt to the demands of narcotics work. Despite the fact that Harris is an unsympathetic character, does any of his advice to Hoyt ring true?

3. What evidence of the "blue wall of silence" do you see in this film?

4. Why is it significant that the film is set in Los Angeles and focuses on wrongdoing within that city's police department? What measures has the federal government taken in Los Angeles and other cities with high levels of police corruption?

LOGGING ON

Go to http://cj.wadsworth.com/gainescore2e, and click Hypercontents. There, you will find URLs for the organizations in the following list:

- If you want to find **Web pages about police corruption**, all you need to do is type into your favorite search engine the words "police corruption." Do this and then determine which of these Web pages is credible. What would make you believe that the stories presented are in fact real?

- The **Atlanta Police Department** posts its Code of Ethics on the Web.

- The largest police union in the country is the **International Brotherhood of Police Officers.**

USING THE INTERNET FOR CRIMINAL JUSTICE ANALYSIS

INFOTRAC®
COLLEGE EDITION

1. The use of deadly force by police personnel has given rise to a relatively new phenomenon called "suicide by cop." Police officers are becoming aware that they are sometimes delivering death to individuals who have suicidal tendencies. The average person, unaware of the victim's motives, blames the police for failing to make a reasonable effort to subdue the suspect without using deadly force. Read an article from the *FBI Law Enforcement Bulletin* by first accessing your InfoTrac College Edition at **http://www.infotrac-college.com/wadsworth/** After you log on, type in the words: **"suicide by cop."** Read the article and answer the following questions:

a. Give some examples of potential "suicide-by-cop" instances.

b. What are some hidden forms of suicide that do not involve police shootings?

c. What were the demographic characteristics of most suicide-by-cop incidents that were examined in this article?

d. Do you believe that suicide by cop constitutes a large percentage of police shootings? Why or why not?

2. See Internet Activities 7.1 and 7.2 on the companion Web site for *CJ in Action: The Core.* To get to the activities, go to **http://www.cj.wadsworth.com/gainescore2e**, select the appropriate chapter from the drop down list, then click Internet Activities on the left navigation bar.

NOTES

1. "Inspector Morse Strikes Again," *Economist* (July 13, 2002), 27.

2. James Sterngold, "Lessons from '92 Keep an Angry City Calm," *New York Times* (July 11, 2002), A14.

3. Gordon Witkin, "When the Bad Guys Are Cops," *U.S. News & World Report* (September 11, 1995), 22.

4. David Remnick, "The Crime Buster," *New Yorker* (February 24 and March 3, 1997), 103.

5. James H. Chenoweth, "Situational Tests: A New Attempt at Assessing Police Candidates," *Journal of Criminal Law, Criminology and Police Science* 52 (1961), 232.

6. Thomas H. Wright, "Pre-Employment Background Investigations," *FBI Law Enforcement Bulletin* 60 (1991), 16.

7. Frank Horvath, "Polygraphic Screening Candidates for Police Work in Large Police Agencies in the United States: A Survey of Practices, Policies, and Evaluative Comments," *American Journal of Police* 12 (1993), 67–86.

8. For an exhaustive overview of these cases, see Sonja A. Soehnel, "Sex Discrimination in Law Enforcement and Corrections Employment," *American Law Reports,* 1997 Supplement (Rochester: Lawyers Co-operative Publishing Company, 1997), 31.

9. Marion Davis, "They Came, They Saw and They Perspired," *Providence Journal-Bulletin* (March 31, 1998), C1.

10. David L. Carter and Allen D. Sapp, "College Education and Policing: Coming of Age," *FBI Law Enforcement Bulletin* 61 (1992), 8.

11. Bureau of Justice Statistics, *Local Police Departments—1997* (Washington, D.C.: U.S. Department of Justice, February 2000), 5.

12. Alan Vodicka, "Educational Requirements for Police Recruits," *Law and Order* 42 (1994), 91.

13. D. P. Hinkle, "College Degree: An Impractical Prerequisite for Police Work," *Law and Order* (July 1991), 105.

14. Bureau of Justice Statistics, *Local Police Departments—1997,* 5.

15. Edgar H. Schein, *Organizational Culture and Leadership* (San Francisco: Josey-Bass, 1985), 9.

16. Harry J. Mullins, "Myth, Tradition, and Ritual," *Law and Order* (September 1995), 197.

17. John Van Maanen, "Observations on the Making of a Policeman," *Human Organization* 32 (1973), 407–18.

18. Malcolm Sparrow, Mark Moore, and David Kennedy, *Beyond 911: A New Era For Policing* (New York: Basic Books, 1990), 51.

19. William Westly, *Violence and the Police: A Sociological Study of Law, Custom, and Morality* (Cambridge, MA: MIT Press, 1970).

20. Arthur Neiderhoffer, *Behind the Shield: The Police in Urban Society* (Garden City, NY: Doubleday, 1967).

21. Wallace Graves, "Police Cynicism: Causes and Cures," *FBI Law Enforcement Bulletin* (June 1996), 16–21.

22. Robert Regoli, *Police in America* (Washington, D.C.: R. F. Publishing, 1977).

23. Bob Herbert, "A Cop's View," *New York Times* (March 15, 1998), 17.

24. Jerome H. Skolnick, *Justice without Trial: Law Enforcement in a Democratic Society* (New York: Wiley, 1966), 44.

25. James Hibberd, "Police Psychology," *On Patrol* (Fall 1996), 26.

26. Bureau of Justice Statistics, *Workplace Violence, 1992–1996* (Washington, D.C.: U.S. Department of Justice, July 1998), 3.

27. Greg Connor, "Improving Officer Perception," *Law and Order* (March 1992), 39–40.

28. Charles Remsberg, *The Tactical Edge: Surviving High-Risk Patrol* (Northbrook, IL: Calibre Press, 1986), 47–51.

29. Cited in Gerald W. Garner, "Drunk and Deadly," *Police* (July 1997), 50.

30. *Ibid.*

31. Hibberd, 27.

32. "Dispatches," *On Patrol* (Summer 1996), 25.

33. Les Krantz, *Job-Rated Almanac* (New York: World Almanac, 1998).

34. Richard Lezin Jones, "New York Police Officers Face Counseling on September 11 Events," *New York Times* (November 30, 2001), A1.

35. Gail A. Goolsakian, et al., *Coping with Police Stress* (Washington, D.C.: National Institute of Justice, 1985).

36. J. L. O'Neil and M. A. Cushing, *The Impact of Shift Work on Police Officers* (Washington, D.C.: Police Executive Research Forum, 1991), 1.

37. Lawrence M. Friedman, *Crime and Punishment in American History* (New York: Basic Books, 1993), 362.

38. Jerome H. Skolnick and James J. Fyfe, *Above the Law: Police and Excessive Use of Violence* (New York: Free Press, 1993), 37.

39. Bureau of Justice Statistics, *Contacts between Police and the Public* (Washington, D.C.: U.S. Department of Justice, February 2001), 25.

40. Independent Commission on the Los Angeles Police Department, *Report of the Independent Commission on the Los Angeles Police Department* (1991), ix.

41. Joel Garner, John Buchanan, Tom Schade, and John Hepburn, *Research in Brief: Understanding the Use of Force By and Against the Police* (Washington, D.C.: Office of Justice Programs, November 1996), 5.

42. *Ibid.*, 1.

43. Cited in Peter Noel, "'I Thought He Had a Gun,'" *Village Voice* (July 13, 1998), 41.

44. Bureau of Justice Statistics, *Contacts between Police and the Public*, 24.

45. Malcolm D. Holmes, "Minority Threat and Police Brutality: Determinants of Civil Rights Criminal Complaints in U.S. Municipalities," *Criminology* 38 (May 2000), 361.

46. Elliot Grossman, "Officers Didn't Brutalize Disabled Vet," *Allentown Morning Call* (February 22, 1997), B11.

47. Rolando V. del Carmen, *Criminal Procedure for Law Enforcement Personnel* (Monterey, CA: Brooks/Cole Publishing Co., 1987), 107–8.

48. 490 U.S. 386 (1989).

49. Greg Connor, "Use of Force Continuum: Phase II," *Law and Order* (March 1991), 30–35.

50. 471 U.S. 1 (1985).

51. Grossman, B11.

52. 471 U.S. 11 (1985).

53. *Saucier v. Katz*, 121 S.Ct. 2151 (2001).

54. Herman Goldstein, *Police Corruption: A Perspective on Its Nature and Control* (Washington, D.C.: Police Foundation, 1975), 3.

55. Richard A. Serrano, "Bad Cops Caught in Crackdown," *Los Angeles Times* (June 6, 2000), A1.

56. Todd S. Purdum, "Los Angeles Agrees to Changes for Police," *New York Times* (September 21, 2000), A14.

57. J. Dorschner, "Police Deviance: Corruption and Controls," in *Critical Issues in Policing, Contemporary Readings*, ed. Roger G. Dunham and Geoffrey P. Albert (Prospect Heights, IL: Waveland Press, 1989), 249–85.

58. Lawrence W. Sherman, "Becoming Bent: Moral Careers of Corrupt Policemen," in *Police Corruption*, Lawrence W. Sherman, ed., 191–208.

59. Knapp Commission, *Report on Police Corruption* (New York: Brazilier, 1973).

60. Jocelyn M. Pollock-Byrne, *Ethics in Crime and Justice: Dilemmas and Decisions* (Pacific Grove, CA: Brooks/Cole Publishing Co., 1989), 84–86.

61. Jocelyn M. Pollock and Ronald F. Becker, "Ethics Training Using Officers' Dilemmas," *FBI Law Enforcement Bulletin* (November 1996), 20–28.

62. *Ibid.*

63. Peter K. Manning, *Police Work: The Social Organization of Policing* (Cambridge, MA: MIT Press, 1977), 100–1.

64. Linda S. Miller and Karen M. Hess, *Police in the Community: Strategies for the 21st Century*, 2d ed. (Belmont, CA: Wadsworth Publishing, 1998), 81.

65. Quoted in Jennifer Dukes and Loren Keller, "Can Police Be Police to Selves?" *Omaha World-Herald* (February 22, 1998), 1A.

66. V. Dion Hayes and Don Terry, "3 LAPD Officers Guilty of Conspiracy," *Chicago Tribune* (November 16, 2000), 3.

67. "Curfew Crackdown: Toughened Limits Gain Popularity, Controversy," *Denver Post* (June 26, 1994), A1.

68. Quoted in "Demands Grow for Oversight of Small-City Police by Civilians," *Grand Rapids Press* (April 5, 1998), A6.

69. Hazel Glenn Beh, "Municipal Liability for Failure to Investigate Citizen Complaints Against Police," *Fordham Urban Law Journal* 25 (Winter 1998), 209.

70. National Advisory Commission on Civil Disorder, *Report* (Washington, D.C.: U.S. Government Printing Office, 1968), Chapter 11.

71. 401 U.S. 424 (1971).

72. 422 U.S. 405 (1975).

73. Samuel Walker, *Popular Justice* (New York: Oxford University Press, 1980), 243.

74. *Detroit Police Officers' Association v. Young*, 608 F.2d 671, 675 (6th Cir. 1979).

75. *Wygant v. Jackson Board of Education*, 476 U.S. 314 (1986).

76. George F. Cole, *The American System of Criminal Justice*, 5th ed. (Pacific Grove, CA: Brooks/Cole, 1998), 291.

77. C. J. Chivers, "From Court Order to Reality: A Diverse Boston Police Force," *New York Times* (April 4, 2001), A1.

78. *Ibid.*

79. *Ibid.*

80. D. C. Hale and C. L. Bennett, "Realities of Women in Policing: An Organizational Cultural Perspective," in *Women, Law, and Social Control* (Boston: Allyn & Bacon, 1995), 41–54.

81. Friedman, 364–65.

82. Barton Deiters, "3 Women, Man Join Lawsuit Against GR Police Department," *Grand Rapids Press* (March 27, 2001), A14.

83. Susan Martin, "Women Police and Stress," *Police Chief* 50 (1983), 107–9.

84. Susan Fletcher, *Breaking & Entering: Women Cops Talk about Life in the Ultimate Men's Club* (New York: HarperCollins, 1995), 196.

85. Lewis J. Sherman, "An Evaluation of Policewomen in Patrol in a Suburban Environment," *Journal of Police Science and Administration* 3 (1975), 434–38.

86. Patricia W. Lunnenbourg, *Women Police Officers: Current Career Profiles* (Springfield, IL: Charles C Thomas, 1989).

87. Katherine Spillar, *Gender Differences in the Cost of Police Brutality and Misconduct* (Los Angeles: National Center for Women & Policing, September 5, 2000).

CHAPTER 8
COURTS AND THE QUEST FOR JUSTICE

Chapter Objectives

After reading this chapter, you should be able to:

1. Define jurisdiction and contrast geographical and subject-matter jurisdiction.

2. Explain the difference between trial and appellate courts.

3. Outline the several levels of a typical state court system.

4. Outline the federal court system.

5. Explain briefly how a case is brought to the Supreme Court.

6. List and describe the members of the courtroom work group.

7. List the different names given to public prosecutors and the general powers that they have.

8. Contrast the prosecutor's roles as an elected official and as a crime fighter.

9. Delineate the responsibilities of defense attorneys.

INTRODUCTION
The Devil's Day in Court

As Susan Mosser spoke in the federal district court in Sacramento, California, she stared straight at Ted Kaczynski. Mosser described hearing the blast of the package bomb sent by Kaczynski that, nearly four years earlier, had driven nails and razor blades through her husband's body, killing him instantly. "Please, your honor, make his sentence bullet-proof, bomb-proof, if you will," Mosser said, addressing Judge Garland E. Burrell, Jr. "Lock him so far down so that when he does die, he'll be closer to Hell. That's where the devil belongs."

Mosser's voice was not the only one heard that day as Judge Burrell considered the sentencing for Kaczynski—also known as the "Unabomber"—who had pleaded guilty to charges stemming from a seventeen-year mail bombing campaign that left three dead and twenty-two wounded. Other victims spoke, including one who said he would not "have shed a single tear" if Kaczynski, who evaded the death sentence through a plea bargain, had been executed. The federal prosecutors, representing the American people, claimed that Kaczynski was not a crusader against technology, as he had portrayed himself, but a petulant murderer driven by the desire for "personal revenge." Judge Burrell, after sentencing the defendant to four life terms plus thirty years in prison, said Kaczynski had "committed unspeakable and monstrous crimes for which he shows utterly no remorse." Even the Unabomber himself had a chance to speak, claiming that the prosecution had improperly discredited his political beliefs and urging people to reserve judgment on him "until all the facts are available."[1]

Despite the length of the sentence, many observers felt that justice had not been served in Kaczynski's case. For such crimes, they argued, he should have been put to death. Others countered that, as we shall discuss in Chapter 10, no one should be executed, no matter how heinous his or her crimes. Clearly, the definition of justice is elusive. Famed jurist Roscoe Pound characterized justice as society's demand "that serious offenders be convicted and punished," while at the same time "the innocent and the unfortunate are not oppressed."[2] We can expand this noble, if idealistic, definition. Citizens expect their courts to discipline the guilty, provide deterrents for illegal activities, protect individual civil liberties, and rehabilitate criminals—all simultaneously.

Over the course of the next three chapters, we shall examine these lofty goals and the extent to which they can be reached. The Unabomber case, at the top of the wedding cake model described in Chapter 1, offered a chance for all the principal elements of the criminal justice system to participate in the quest for justice. As will become clear, the American court system does not always provide such luxuries.

Theodore John Kaczynski, known to Americans as the "Unabomber," is led into federal court in Sacramento, California. (AP Photo/John Youngbear)

THE BASIC PRINCIPLES OF THE AMERICAN JUDICIAL SYSTEM

One of the most often cited limitations of the American judicial system is its complex nature. In truth, the United States does not have a single judicial system, but fifty-one different systems—one for each state and the federal government. As each state has its own unique judiciary with its own set of rules, some of which may be in conflict with the federal judiciary, it is helpful at this point to discuss the basics—jurisdiction, trial and appellate courts, and the dual court system.

Go to the Stories from the Street feature at http://www.cj. wadsworth.com/gainescore2e to hear Larry Gaines tell insightful stories related to this chapter and his experiences in the field.

Jurisdiction

In Latin, *juris* means "law," and *diction* means "to speak." Thus, **jurisdiction** literally refers to the power "to speak the law." Before any court can hear a case, it must have jurisdiction over the persons involved in the case or its subject matter. The jurisdiction of every court, even the United States Supreme Court, is limited in some way. One limitation is geographical. Generally, a court can exercise its authority over residents of a certain area. A state trial court, for example, normally has jurisdictional authority over crimes committed in a particular area of the state, such as a county or a district. A state's highest court (often called the state supreme court) has jurisdictional authority over the entire state, and the United States Supreme Court has jurisdiction over the entire country. (For a global perspective on this issue, see the feature *CJ in Focus—The Balancing Act: Jurisdiction and the International Criminal Court* on the following page.)

Jurisdiction over subject matter also acts as a limitation on the types of cases a court can hear. State court systems include courts of *general* (unlimited) *jurisdiction* and courts of *limited jurisdiction*. Courts of general jurisdiction have no restrictions on the subject matter they may address, and therefore deal with the most serious felonies and civil cases. Courts of limited jurisdiction, also known as lower courts, handle misdemeanors and civil matters under a certain amount, usually $1,000. To alleviate caseload pressures in lower courts, many states have created special subject-matter courts that only dispose of cases involving a specific crime. For example, a number of jurisdictions have established drug courts to handle an overload of illicit narcotics arrests, and California has created twelve courts that deal specifically with domestic violence offenders.

The architecture of courthouses reflects the mood of the societies that construct them. In the past, architects have emphasized ideals of citizen participation in constructing noble yet unthreatening courthouses. Boston's new $228 million federal courthouse reflects the crime control concerns of today's society. Judging from the photo provided here, what are the values exhibited through the architectural structure of the building? Do you agree with one critic that it represents the "architecture of paranoia"? (Photo courtesy of Steve Rosenthal)

Trial and Appellate Courts

Another distinction is between courts of original jurisdiction and courts of appellate, or review, jurisdiction. Courts having *original jurisdiction* are courts of the first instance, or **trial courts.** Almost every case begins in a trial court. It is in this court that a trial (or a guilty plea) takes place, and the judge imposes a sentence if the defendant is found guilty. Trial courts are primarily concerned with *questions of fact.* That is, they are designed to determine exactly what events occurred that are relevant to questions of the defendant's guilt or innocence.

Courts having *appellate jurisdiction* act as reviewing courts, or **appellate courts.** In general, cases can be brought before appellate courts only on appeal by one of the parties in the trial court. Note that because of constitutional protections against being tried twice for the same crime, prosecutors who lose in

JURISDICTION
The authority of a court to hear and decide cases within an area of the law or a geographical territory.

TRIAL COURTS
Courts in which most cases usually begin and in which questions of fact are examined.

APPELLATE COURTS
Courts that review decisions made by lower courts, such as trial courts. Also known as courts of appeals.

CJ in F CUS

The Balancing Act: Jurisdiction and the International Criminal Court

The United States has a long history of supporting international prosecution of the most heinous of crimes. In 1946, the United States was the guiding force behind the Nuremberg Trials, which established that individuals could be convicted for war crimes and crimes against humanity. (The trials resulted in Nazi leaders being found guilty of the extermination of millions of Jews.) Over the past decade, the United States has provided financial and evidentiary support for international tribunals to punish the instigators of the genocide in Rwanda and the Balkans. Yet, when the International Criminal Court (ICC)—the world's first permanent court for the prosecution of war criminals—was created on April 11, 2002, the United States refused to take part.

This decision earned the United States a great deal of international criticism, especially from the nations of the European Union. For the Bush administration, however, it was a matter of jurisdiction. The ICC assumes jurisdiction over acts of genocide, crimes against humanity, and war crimes committed by individuals regardless of nationality. In theory, this means that any American, from a high-ranking government official to soldiers in the field, could be accused of committing a crime against humanity by the court's chief prosecutor. Because the United States is presently the world's only superpower, with military operations in dozens of countries at any one time, the administration worries that Americans will be easy targets for frivolous accusations. Furthermore, as some constitutional scholars have pointed out, the ICC does not provide for a trial by jury, as guaranteed to any American charged with committing a crime by the Bill of Rights.

Supporters of the ICC counter that the United States overestimates the risks of seeing its citizens hauled before

The United States chair remains empty during the first meeting of the International Criminal Court at United Nations headquarters in New York City on September 3, 2002. (AP Photo/Shawn Baldwin)

the court, as the court's jurisdiction is only "secondary"; that is, the court will only prosecute in situations in which the home country of the accused is unable or unwilling to do so. Regardless of this argument, the United States has insisted that it will not cooperate with the ICC unless Americans are given immunity from its jurisdiction, a request that has been rejected by most participating nations.

FOR CRITCAL ANALYSIS
Do you agree with the Bush administration's position against the ICC? Which is more important—protecting the rights of Americans (to trial by jury, for example), or cooperating with the international community in fighting the crimes over which the ICC has jurisdiction?

OPINION
A statement by the court expressing the reasons for its decision in a case.

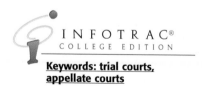

INFOTRAC
COLLEGE EDITION

Keywords: trial courts, appellate courts

criminal trial court *cannot* appeal the verdict. An appellate court does not use juries or witnesses to reach its decision. Instead, its judges make a decision on whether the case should be *reversed* and *remanded,* or sent back to the court of original jurisdiction for a new trial. Appellate judges present written explanations for their decisions, and these **opinions** of the court are the basis for a great deal of the precedent in the criminal justice system.

It is important to understand that appellate courts do not determine the defendant's guilt or innocence—they generally only make judgments on questions of procedure. In other words, they are concerned with *questions of law* and normally accept the facts as established by the trial court. An appeals court will rarely question a jury's decision. Instead, the appellate judges will review the manner in which the facts and evidence were provided to the jury and rule on whether errors were made in the process.

FIGURE 8.1
The Dual Court System

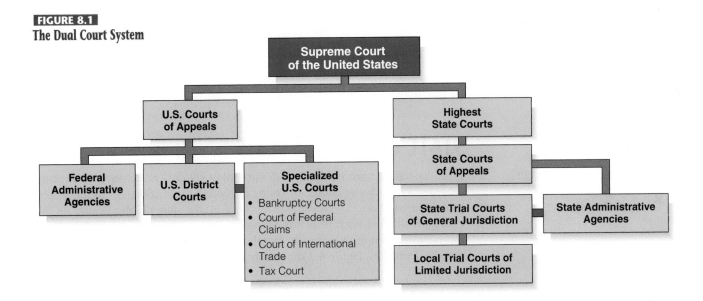

The Dual Court System

Like many other aspects of American government, the structure of the judicial system was the result of a compromise. During the framing of the U.S. Constitution, two camps emerged with different views on the courts. The Anti-Federalists, interested in limiting the power of the federal government, wanted the Supreme Court to be the only *national* court, with the states handling the majority of judicial work. The Federalists, dedicated to ensuring that the states did not have too much power, wanted all cases to be heard in federal courts. Both sides eventually made concessions, and the outcome is reflected in the **dual court system** that we have today (see Figure 8.1).[3]

Federal and state courts both have limited jurisdiction. Generally stated, federal courts deal with acts that violate federal law, and state courts deal with acts that violate state law. The distinction is not, however, always clear. A number of crimes—such as kidnapping and transportation of narcotics—are deemed illegal by both federal and state statutes, and persons accused of such crimes can be tried in either court system. In these instances, federal and state prosecutors must

DUAL COURT SYSTEM
The separate but interrelated court system of the United States, made up of the courts on the national level and the courts on the state level.

In 1977, Ira Einhorn, left, was convicted in Pennsylvania of the bludgeoning murder of his girlfriend, Holly Maddux. Einhorn, pictured here with his wife Annika Flodin-Einhorn and his lawyer Dominique Delthil, had already fled the United States at the time of his trial, and was found guilty *in absentia*. Why did France, where Einhorn relocated, refuse to extradite him to the United States until 2001, nearly a quarter of a century after Maddux's death? How does the concept of jurisdiction apply to the Einhorn case? (AP Photo/ Bob Edme)

decide among themselves who will handle the case—a decision based on a number of factors, including the notoriety of the crime and the relative caseloads of the respective court systems. Often, the prosecutors will "steer" a suspect toward the harsher penalty. Thus, if the punishment for a particular crime is more severe under federal law than state law, then law enforcement officials may decide to try the defendant in federal court (and vice versa).

STATE COURT SYSTEMS

INFOTRAC®
COLLEGE EDITION

Keyword: state courts

Typically, a state court system includes several levels, or tiers, of courts. State courts may include (1) lower courts, or courts of limited jurisdiction, (2) trial courts of general jurisdiction, (3) appellate courts, and (4) the state's highest court. As previously mentioned, each state has a different judicial structure, in which different courts have different jurisdictions, but there are enough similarities to allow for a general discussion. Figure 8.2 shows a typical state court system.

FIGURE 8.2
The Typical State Court System

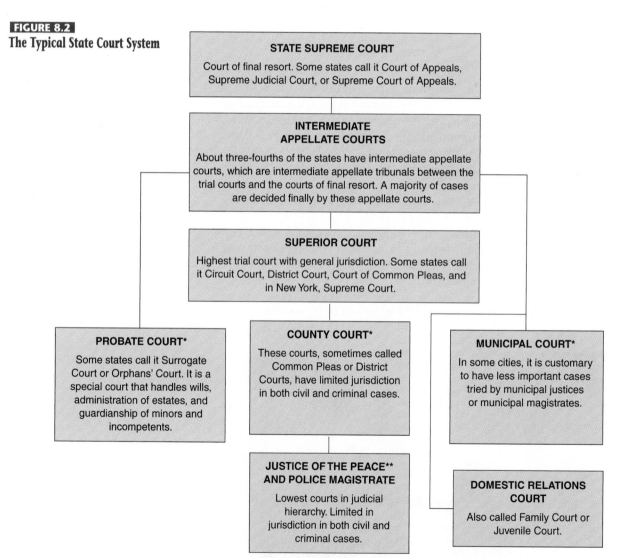

STATE SUPREME COURT

Court of final resort. Some states call it Court of Appeals, Supreme Judicial Court, or Supreme Court of Appeals.

INTERMEDIATE APPELLATE COURTS

About three-fourths of the states have intermediate appellate courts, which are intermediate appellate tribunals between the trial courts and the courts of final resort. A majority of cases are decided finally by these appellate courts.

SUPERIOR COURT

Highest trial court with general jurisdiction. Some states call it Circuit Court, District Court, Court of Common Pleas, and in New York, Supreme Court.

PROBATE COURT*

Some states call it Surrogate Court or Orphans' Court. It is a special court that handles wills, administration of estates, and guardianship of minors and incompetents.

COUNTY COURT*

These courts, sometimes called Common Pleas or District Courts, have limited jurisdiction in both civil and criminal cases.

MUNICIPAL COURT*

In some cities, it is customary to have less important cases tried by municipal justices or municipal magistrates.

JUSTICE OF THE PEACE** AND POLICE MAGISTRATE

Lowest courts in judicial hierarchy. Limited in jurisdiction in both civil and criminal cases.

DOMESTIC RELATIONS COURT

Also called Family Court or Juvenile Court.

*Courts of special jurisdiction, such as probate, family, or juvenile, and the so-called inferior courts, such as common pleas or municipal courts, may be separate courts or may be part of the trial court of general jurisdiction.
**Justices of the peace do not exist in all states. Their jurisdiction varies greatly from state to state when they do exist.

Limited Jurisdiction Courts

Most states have local trial courts that are limited to trying cases involving minor criminal matters, such as traffic violations, prostitution, and drunk and disorderly conduct. Although these minor courts usually keep no written record of the trial proceedings and cases are decided by a judge rather than a jury, defendants have the same rights as those in other trial courts. The majority of all minor criminal cases are decided in these lower courts. Limited jurisdiction courts can also be responsible for the preliminary stages of felony cases. Arraignments, bail hearings, and preliminary hearings often take place in these lower courts.

General Jurisdiction Trial Courts

State trial courts that have general jurisdiction may be called county courts, district courts, superior courts, or circuit courts. In Ohio, the name is the Court of Common Pleas; in New York, it is the Supreme Court; and in Massachusetts, the Trial Court. (The name sometimes does not correspond with the court's functions. For example, in New York the trial court is called the Supreme Court, whereas in most states the supreme court is the state's highest court.) General jurisdiction courts have the authority to hear and decide cases involving many types of subject matter, and they are the setting for criminal trials (discussed in Chapter 9).

State Courts of Appeals

Every state has at least one court of appeals (known as an appellate, or reviewing, court), which may be an intermediate appellate court or the state's highest court. About half of the states have intermediate appellate courts. The highest appellate court in a state is usually called the supreme court, but in both New York and Maryland, the highest state court is called the court of appeals. The decisions of each state's highest court on all questions of state law are final. Only when issues of federal law or constitutional procedure are involved can the United States Supreme Court overrule a decision made by a state's highest court.

THE FEDERAL COURT SYSTEM

The federal court system is basically a three-tiered model consisting of (1) U.S. district courts (trial courts of general jurisdiction) and various courts of limited jurisdiction, (2) U.S. courts of appeals (intermediate courts of appeals), and (3) the United States Supreme Court.

Unlike state court judges, who are usually elected, federal court judges—including the justices of the Supreme Court—are appointed by the president of the United States, subject to the approval of the Senate. All federal judges receive lifetime appointments (because under Article III of the Constitution they "hold their offices during Good Behavior").

U.S. District Courts

On the lowest tier of the federal court system are the U.S. district courts, or federal trial courts. These are the courts in which cases normally involving federal laws begin, and a judge or jury decides the case (if it is a jury trial). Every state has at least one federal district court, and there is one in the District of Columbia. The number of judicial districts varies over time, primarily owing to population changes and corresponding caseloads. Currently, there are ninety-four judicial districts. The federal system also includes other limited jurisdiction trial courts, such as the Tax Court and the Court of International Trade.

On the Web

The Washtenaw County (Michigan) Trial Court Web site takes you inside the operating procedure of a trial court, as well as introducing you to the people that work there. For a link to this Web site, go to the Hypercontents page for this chapter at http://www.cj.wadsworth.com/gainescore2e.

FIGURE 8.3
Geographical Boundaries of the Federal Circuit Courts of Appeals

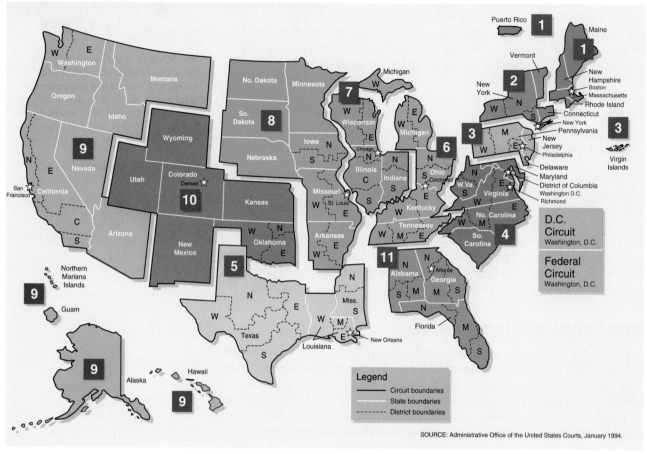

SOURCE: Administrative Office of the United States Courts, January 1994.

U.S. Courts of Appeals

In the federal court system, there are thirteen U.S. courts of appeals—also referred to as U.S. circuit courts of appeals. The federal courts of appeals for twelve of the circuits hear appeals from the district courts located within their respective judicial circuits (see Figure 8.3). The Court of Appeals for the Thirteenth Circuit, called the Federal Circuit, has national appellate jurisdiction over certain types of cases, such as cases involving patent law and cases in which the U.S. government is a defendant. The decisions of the circuit courts of appeals are final unless a further appeal to the United States Supreme Court is pursued and granted.

The United States Supreme Court

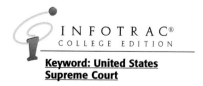

INFOTRAC®
COLLEGE EDITION

Keyword: United States
Supreme Court

Although it reviews fewer than 0.05 percent of the cases decided in the United States each year, the decisions of the United States Supreme Court profoundly affect our lives. The impact of Court decisions on the criminal justice system is equally far reaching: *Gideon v. Wainwright* (1963)[4] established every American's right to be represented by counsel in a criminal trial; *Miranda v. Arizona* (1966)[5] transformed pretrial interrogations; *Furman v. Georgia* (1972)[6] ruled the death penalty was unconstitutional; and *Gregg v. Georgia* (1976)[7] spelled out the conditions under which it could be allowed. As you have no doubt noticed from references in this textbook, the Court has addressed nearly every important facet of criminal law.

The Supreme Court "makes" criminal justice policy in two important ways: through judicial review and through its authority to interpret the law. *Judicial review* refers to the power of the Court to determine whether a law or action by the other branches of the government is constitutional. For example, in the late 1980s Congress and several state legislatures passed laws criminalizing the act of burning the U.S. flag. In two separate decisions—*Texas v. Johnson* (1989)[8] and *United States v. Eichman* (1990)[9]—the Court invalidated these laws as unconstitutional on the ground that they violated First Amendment protection of freedom of expression.

As the final interpreter of the Constitution, the Court must also determine the meaning of certain statutory provisions when applied to specific situations. Deciding what the framers of the Constitution or a legislative body meant by a certain phrase or provision is never easy, and inevitably, at least to some extent, the personal attributes of the justices come into play during the process. For example, those justices who oppose the death penalty for ideological reasons have tended to interpret the Eighth Amendment prohibition against "cruel and unusual punishment" as sufficient constitutional justification to outlaw the execution of criminals by the state.[10]

Jurisdiction of the United States Supreme Court. The Supreme Court consists of nine justices—a chief justice and eight associate justices. The Court has original, or trial, jurisdiction only in rare instances (set forth in Article III, Section 2, of the Constitution). In other words, only rarely does a case originate at the Supreme Court level. Most of the Court's work is as an appellate court. The Supreme Court has appellate authority over cases decided by the U.S. courts of appeals, as well as over some cases decided in the state courts when federal questions are at issue.

Which Cases Reach the United States Supreme Court? There is no absolute right to appeal to the United States Supreme Court. Although thousands of cases are filed with the Supreme Court each year, on average the Court hears fewer than one hundred. With a **writ of *certiorari*** (pronounced sur-shee-uh-*rah*-ree), the Supreme Court orders a lower court to send it the record of a case for review. A party can petition the Supreme Court to issue a writ of *certiorari,* but whether the Court will do so is entirely within its discretion.

United States Supreme Court Decisions. Like all appellate courts, the United States Supreme Court normally does not hear any evidence. The Court's decision in a particular case is based on the written record of the case and the written arguments (briefs) that the attorneys submit. The attorneys also present **oral arguments**—arguments presented in person rather than on paper—to the Court, after which the justices discuss the case in *conference.* The conference is strictly private—only the justices are allowed in the room.

When the Court has reached a decision, the chief justice, if in the majority, assigns the task of writing the Court's opinion to one of the justices. When the chief justice is not in the majority, the most senior justice voting with the majority assigns the writing of the Court's opinion. The opinion outlines the reasons for the Court's decision, the rules of law that apply, and the decision.

Often, one or more justices who agree with the Court's decision may do so for different reasons than those outlined in the majority opinion. These justices may write **concurring opinions** setting forth their own legal reasoning on the issue. Frequently, one or more justices disagree with the Court's conclusion. These

The United States Supreme Court tends to be associated with the philosophy of its chief justice. Accordingly, since William Rehnquist (see above) took over the position in 1975, the "Rehnquist Court" is seen as adopting his conservative views. Specifically, the Rehnquist Court has voted to narrow the scope of civil rights laws and increase the powers of the states at the expense of the federal government. At the same time, however, the Rehnquist Court has championed free speech, upheld abortion rights, and protected the legal rights of homosexuals against local ordinances. Examine the record of the Rehnquist Court on criminal matters to determine whether it has followed a crime control or due process philosophy. (Reuters/Win McNamee/Archive Photos)

WRIT OF *CERTIORARI*
A request from a higher court asking a lower court for the record of a case. In essence, the request signals the higher court's willingness to review the case.

ORAL ARGUMENTS
The verbal arguments presented in person by attorneys to an appellate court. Each attorney presents reasons why the court should rule in his or her client's favor.

CONCURRING OPINIONS
Separate opinions prepared by judges who support the decision of the majority of the court but who want to make or clarify a particular point or to voice disapproval of the grounds on which the decision was made.

DISSENTING OPINIONS
Separate opinions in which judges disagree with the conclusion reached by the majority of the court and expand on their own views about the case.

DOCKET
The list of cases entered on a court's calendar and thus scheduled to be heard by the court.

INFOTRAC®
COLLEGE EDITION

Keyword: Judges

"A judge is not supposed to know anything about the facts . . . until they have been presented in evidence and explained to him at least three times."

—Lord Chief Justice Parker, *British judge* (1961)

justices may write **dissenting opinions** outlining the reasons why they feel the majority erred. Although a dissenting opinion does not affect the outcome of the case before the Court, it may be important later. In a subsequent case concerning the same issue, a justice or attorney may use the legal reasoning in the dissenting opinion as the basis for an argument to reverse the previous decision and establish a new precedent.

JUDGES IN THE COURT SYSTEM

United States Supreme Court justices are the most visible and best-known American jurists, but in many ways they are unrepresentative of the profession as a whole. Few judges enjoy three-room office suites fitted with a fireplace and a private bath, as do the Supreme Court justices. Few judges have four clerks to assist them. Few judges get a yearly vacation that stretches from July to September. Most judges, in fact, work at the lowest level of the system, in criminal trial courts, where they are burdened with overflowing caseloads and must deal daily with the detritus of society.

One thing a Supreme Court justice and a criminal trial judge in any small American city do have in common is the expectation that they will be just. Of all the participants in the criminal justice system, no single person is held to the same high standards as the judge. From her or his lofty perch in the courtroom, the judge is counted on to be "above the fray" of the bickering defense attorneys and prosecutors. When the other courtroom contestants rise at the entrance of the judge, they are placing the burden of justice squarely on the judge's shoulders.

The Roles and Responsibilities of Trial Judges

One of the reasons that judicial integrity is considered so important is the amount of discretionary power a judge has over the court proceedings. As you can see in Figure 8.4, nearly every stage of the trial process includes a decision or action to be taken by the presiding judge.

Before the Trial. In the procedural processes that occur before the trial the judge takes on the role of the *negotiator*.[11] As most cases are decided through plea bargains rather than through trial proceedings, the judge often offers his or her services as a negotiator to help the prosecution and the defense "make a deal." The amount at which bail is set is often negotiated as well. Throughout the trial process, the judge usually spends a great deal of time in his or her *chambers,* or office, negotiating with the prosecutors and defense attorneys.

During the Trial. When the trial starts, the judge takes on the role of *referee.* In this role, she or he is responsible for seeing that the trial unfolds according to the dictates of the law and that the participants in the trial do not overstep any legal or ethical bounds. In this role, the judge is expected to be neutral, determining the admissibility of testimony and evidence on a completely objective basis. The judge also acts as a *teacher* during the trial, explaining points of law to the jury. If the trial is not a jury trial, then the judge must also make decisions concerning the guilt or innocence of the defendant. If the defendant is found guilty, the judge must decide on the length of the sentence and the type of sentence.

The Administrative Role. Judges are also *administrators;* that is, they are responsible for the day-to-day functioning of their courts. A primary administrative task of a judge is scheduling. Each courtroom has a **docket,** or calendar of cases, and it is the judge's responsibility to keep the docket current. This entails not only scheduling the trial, but also setting pretrial motion dates and deciding whether to grant attorneys' requests for *continuances,* or additional time to pre-

FIGURE 8.4

The Role of the Judge in the Criminal Trial Process

In the various stages of a felony case, judges must undertake the actions described here.

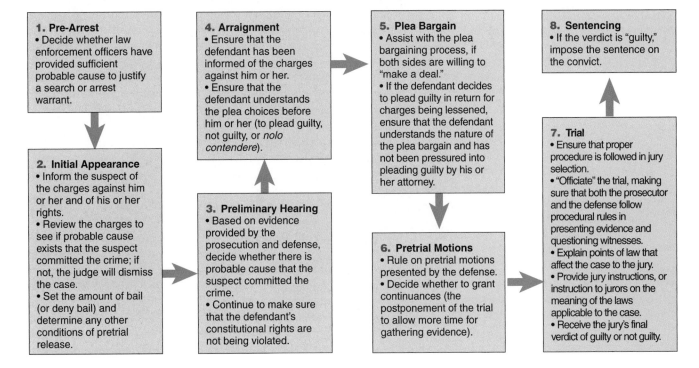

1. Pre-Arrest
• Decide whether law enforcement officers have provided sufficient probable cause to justify a search or arrest warrant.

2. Initial Appearance
• Inform the suspect of the charges against him or her and of his or her rights.
• Review the charges to see if probable cause exists that the suspect committed the crime; if not, the judge will dismiss the case.
• Set the amount of bail (or deny bail) and determine any other conditions of pretrial release.

3. Preliminary Hearing
• Based on evidence provided by the prosecution and defense, decide whether there is probable cause that the suspect committed the crime.
• Continue to make sure that the defendant's constitutional rights are not being violated.

4. Arraignment
• Ensure that the defendant has been informed of the charges against him or her.
• Ensure that the defendant understands the plea choices before him or her (to plead guilty, not guilty, or *nolo contendere*).

5. Plea Bargain
• Assist with the plea bargaining process, if both sides are willing to "make a deal."
• If the defendant decides to plead guilty in return for charges being lessened, ensure that the defendant understands the nature of the plea bargain and has not been pressured into pleading guilty by his or her attorney.

6. Pretrial Motions
• Rule on pretrial motions presented by the defense.
• Decide whether to grant continuances (the postponement of the trial to allow more time for gathering evidence).

7. Trial
• Ensure that proper procedure is followed in jury selection.
• "Officiate" the trial, making sure that both the prosecutor and the defense follow procedural rules in presenting evidence and questioning witnesses.
• Explain points of law that affect the case to the jury.
• Provide jury instructions, or instruction to jurors on the meaning of the laws applicable to the case.
• Receive the jury's final verdict of guilty or not guilty.

8. Sentencing
• If the verdict is "guilty," impose the sentence on the convict.

pare for a case. Judges must also keep track of the immense paperwork generated by each case and manage the various employees of the court. In some instances, judges are even responsible for the budget of their courtroom.[12]

Selection of Judges

In the federal court system, all judges are appointed by the president and confirmed by the Senate. It is difficult to make a general statement about how judges are selected in the state court system, however, because the procedure varies widely from state to state. In some states, such as Delaware, all judges are appointed by the governor and confirmed by the upper chamber of the state legislature. In other states, such as Arkansas, **partisan elections** are used to choose judges. In these elections, a political party such as the Republicans or the Democrats openly supports the candidate for a judgeship. States that conduct **nonpartisan elections** do not require the candidate to affiliate herself or himself with a political party. Figure 8.5 on page 206 shows the variety in the procedures for selecting judges.

In 1940, Missouri became the first state to combine appointment and election. This is called *merit selection*. Today, a number of states have adopted merit selection, also known as the **Missouri Plan,** as the primary method of choosing judges. The Missouri Plan consists of three basic steps:

● When a vacancy on the bench arises, candidates are nominated by a nonpartisan committee of citizens.

● The names of the three most qualified candidates are sent to the governor or executive of the state judicial system, and that person chooses who will be the judge.

● A year after the new judge has been installed, a "retention election" is held so that voters can decide whether the judge deserves to keep the post.[13]

The goal of the Missouri Plan is to eliminate partisan politics from the selection procedure, while at the same time giving the citizens a voice in the process. (For

PARTISAN ELECTIONS
Elections in which candidates are affiliated with and receive support from political parties; the candidates are listed in conjunction with their party on the ballot.

NONPARTISAN ELECTIONS
Elections in which candidates are presented on the ballot without any party affiliation.

MISSOURI PLAN
A method of selecting judges that combines appointment and election. Under the plan, the state governor or another government official selects judges from a group of nominees chosen by a nonpartisan committee. After a year on the bench, the judges face a popular election to determine whether the public wishes to keep them in office.

FIGURE 8.5
Methods of Judicial Selection in the Fifty States

Most states use a variety of methods to select their judges, with different procedures in different jurisdictions. The information presented here, therefore, identifies the predominant method in each state.

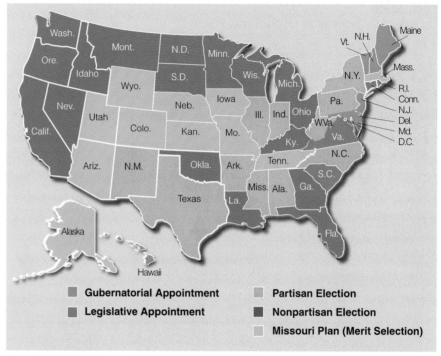

- ■ Gubernatorial Appointment
- ■ Legislative Appointment
- ■ Partisan Election
- ■ Nonpartisan Election
- ■ Missouri Plan (Merit Selection)

Source: Bureau of Justice Statistics, *State Court Organization 1998* (Washington, D.C.: U.S. Department of Justice, June 2000), 34–48.

Judge Carol J. Vigil of Tesuque Pueblo, New Mexico, listens to the plea of a juvenile accused of violating his parole. Vigil was elected to her post in November of 1998, in the process becoming the first female Native American judge in the state's history. What are some of the benefits of electing judges? What are some of the drawbacks of this method of deciding who sits on the bench? (AP Photo/Sarah Marton/*The New Mexican*)

a review of the different selection processes, see *Mastering Concepts—The Selection of Federal and State Judges.*)

Another criticism of the Missouri Plan is that the members of the selection committees, who are mostly white, upper-class attorneys, nominate mostly white, upper-class attorneys. (See *The Diversity Challenge—The Benefits of Branching Out on the Bench* on page 208.)

Judicial Ethics

The question of judicial accountability is complicated by the gulf between what the public expects of judges and what the law expects of judges. The public wants judges to administer justice, while the law demands that they make sure proper legal procedures and rules have been followed. Sometimes, such as when a judge must overturn a conviction he or she knows to be justified because tainted evidence contributed to the jury's finding, proper judicial conduct leads to what we would call injustice—setting a guilty person free. In other words, for judges, proper behavior does not necessarily lead to justice, a concept many citizens have a difficult time accepting.

During the nineteenth century, the American public showed little enthusiasm for formal regulation of judicial conduct—as long as judges were competent, their ethics and honesty were of secondary concern.[14] It was not until the 1920s, when the entire criminal justice system was being reformed, that the American Bar Association (ABA) created the first code to regulate judicial behavior. The ABA's Canons of Judicial Ethics was updated in 1972 and 1990, and today the Model Code of Judicial Conduct forms the basis for judicial conduct codes in forty-seven states and the District of Columbia.[15]

The essence of the Code of Judicial Conduct is to prevent conduct that would "tend to reduce public confidence in the integrity and impartiality of the judiciary."[16] Consequently, the judicial ethics codes frown on not only obviously illegal and corrupt activities such as bribery but also personal conduct that is lawful yet

MASTERING CONCEPTS

The Selection of Federal and State Judges

Federal Judges

The president nominates a candidate to the U.S. Senate.

↓

The Senate Judiciary Committee holds hearings concerning the qualifications of the candidate and makes its recommendation to the full Senate.

↓

The full Senate votes to confirm or reject the president's nomination.

State Judges

Partisan Elections
Judicial candidates, supported by and affiliated with political parties, place their names before the voters for consideration for a particular judicial seat.

↓

The electorate votes to decide who will retain or gain the seat.

Executive Appointment
The governor nominates a candidate to the state legislature.

↓

The legislature votes to confirm or reject the governor's nomination.

Nonpartisan Elections
Judicial candidates, not supported by or affiliated with political parties, place their names before the voters for consideration for a particular judicial seat.

↓

The electorate votes to decide who will retain or gain the seat.

Missouri Plan
A nominating commission provides a list of worthy candidates.

↓

An elected official (usually the governor) chooses from the list submitted by the commission.

↓

A year later, a "retention election" is held to allow voters to decide whether the judge will stay on the bench.

---

gives the appearance of impropriety. Rhode Island, for example, saw two successive state supreme court chief justices resign because of **judicial misconduct.** The first, Chief Justice Thomas Fay, stepped down because of allegations that he used his position to help a relative and friends, and the second, Chief Justice Joseph Bevilacqua, was under investigation for associating with organized crime figures.

THE COURTROOM WORK GROUP

Television dramas often depict the courtroom as a battlefield, with prosecutors and defense attorneys spitting fire at each other over the loud and insistent protestations of a frustrated judge. Consequently, many people are somewhat disappointed when they witness a real courtroom at work. Rarely does anyone raise his or her voice, and the courtroom professionals appear—to a great extent—to be cooperating with each other. In Chapter 7, we discussed the existence of a police subculture, based on the shared values of law enforcement agents. A courtroom subculture exists as well, centered on the **courtroom work group.** The most important feature of any work group is that it is a *cooperative* unit, whose members establish shared values and methods that help the group efficiently reach its goals. Though cooperation is not a concept usually associated with criminal courts, it is in fact crucial to the adjudication process.[17]

Members of the Courtroom Work Group

The courtroom work group is made up of those individuals who are involved with the defendant from the time she or he is arrested until sentencing. The most

INFOTRAC®
COLLEGE EDITION
Keyword: judicial conduct

JUDICIAL MISCONDUCT
A general term describing behavior that diminishes public confidence in the judiciary. This behavior includes obviously illegal acts, such as bribery, and conduct that gives the appearance of impropriety, such as consorting with known felons.

COURTROOM WORK GROUP
The social organization consisting of the judge, prosecutor, defense attorney, and other court workers. The relationships among these persons have a far-reaching impact on the day-to-day operations of any court.

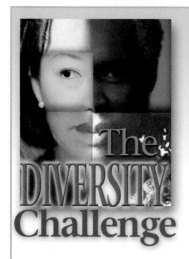

The Benefits of Branching Out on the Bench

The judiciary of the United States is, as one observer notes, "overwhelmingly white, male, and upper-middle class." Only 6 percent of Georgia's state judges are African American, compared to 28 percent of the state's population—a disproportionality mirrored in state and federal courtrooms across the country. Of the 108 justices who have served on the United States Supreme Court, only two have been women (Sandra Day O'Connor [1981]–present] and Ruth Bader Ginsburg [1993–present]), and two have been African American (Thurgood Marshall [1970–1991] and Clarence Thomas [1991–present]).

Traditionally, efforts to diversify American judges by race and ethnicity have been met with resistance from those who insist that judges must be impartial, so by definition it makes no difference whether a judge is African American, Asian American, Hispanic American, or white. Sherrilyn A. Ifill of the University of Maryland School of Law rejects this argument. She believes that "diversity on the bench" can only enrich our judiciary by introducing a variety of voices and perspectives into what are perhaps the most powerful positions in the criminal justice system. By the same token, Ifill credits the lack of diversity in many trial and appeals courts with a number of harmful consequences, such as more severe sentences for minority youths than for white youths who have committed similar crimes, disproportionate denial of bail to minority offenders, and the disproportionate imposition of the death penalty on minority defendants accused of killing white victims.

It should be noted, however, that expectations of how a particular group will act do not always match reality. Many people believe, for example, that female judges are more compassionate than their male counterparts. The evidence coming from the Harris County (Texas) courthouse, one of the few in the country where a majority of the judges—twelve of twenty-one—are women, does not support this stereotype. Since 1976, Harris County has been responsible for sixty-three executions, more than Florida, which ranks third among states in total executions over the time period.

FOR CRITICAL ANALYSIS

Do we want our judges to be "color-blind," or would we rather they bring their cultural background and experiences onto the bench with them? Explain your answer.

---

prominent members are the judge, the prosecutor, and the defense attorney (the latter two will be discussed in detail in the next chapter). Three other court participants complete the work group:

1 The *bailiff of the court* is responsible for maintaining security and order in the judge's chambers and the courtroom. Bailiffs lead the defendant in and out of the courtroom and attend to the needs of the jurors during the trial. A bailiff, often a member of the local sheriff's department but sometimes an employee of the court, also delivers summonses in some jurisdictions.

2 The *clerk of the court* has an exhausting list of responsibilities. Any plea, motion, or other matter to be acted on by the judge must go through the clerk. The large amount of paperwork generated during a trial, including transcripts, photographs, evidence, and any other records, is maintained by the clerk. The clerk also issues subpoenas for jury duty and coordinates the jury selection process. In the federal court system, judges select clerks, while state clerks are either appointed or, in nearly a third of the states, elected. (To learn more about a career in a similar position—court administrator—go to the *Careers in Criminal Justice Interactive CD* and click on the Career Rolodex.)

3 *Court reporters* record every word that is said during the course of the trial. They also record any *depositions,* or pretrial question-and-answer sessions in which a party or a witness answers an attorney's questions under oath.

Video Profile of Gordon Alavao, Court Reporter

The Judge in the Courtroom Work Group

The judge is the dominant figure in the courtroom and therefore exerts the most influence over the values and norms of the work group. A judge who runs a "tight ship" follows procedure and restricts the freedom of attorneys to deviate from regulations, while a *"laissez-faire"* judge allows more leeway to members of the work group.

Although preeminent in the work group, a judge must still rely on other members of the group. To a certain extent, the judge is the least informed member of the trio; like a juror, the judge learns the facts of the case as they are presented by the attorneys. If the attorneys do not properly present the facts, then the judge is hampered in making rulings. Furthermore, if a judge deviates from the norms of the work group—by, for example, refusing to grant continuances—the other members of the work group can "discipline" the judge. Defense attorneys and prosecutors can request further continuances, fail to produce witnesses in a timely matter, and slow down the proceeding through a general lack of preparedness. The delays caused by such acts can ruin a judge's calendar—especially in large courts—and bring pressure from the judge's superiors.

The Prosecution

Criminal cases are tried by **public prosecutors,** who are employed by the government. The public prosecutor in federal criminal cases is called a U.S. attorney. In cases tried in state or local courts, the public prosecutor may be referred to as a *prosecuting attorney, state prosecutor, district attorney, county attorney,* or *city attorney.* Given their great autonomy, prosecutors are generally considered the most dominant figures in the American criminal justice system. In some jurisdictions, the district attorney is the chief law enforcement officer, with broad powers over police operations. Prosecutors have the power to bring the resources of the state against the individual and hold the legal keys to meting out or withholding punishment.[18] Ideally, this power is balanced by a duty of fairness and a recognition that the prosecutor's ultimate goal is not to win cases, but to see that justice is done. In *Berger v. United States* (1935), Justice George Sutherland called the prosecutor

> in a peculiar and very definite sense the servant of the law, the twofold aim of which is that guilt shall not escape or innocence suffer. He may prosecute with earnestness and vigor—indeed, he should do so. But, while he may strike hard blows, he is not at liberty to strike foul ones. It is as much his duty to refrain from improper methods calculated to produce a wrongful conviction as it is to use every legitimate means to bring about a just one.[19]

The Office of the Prosecutor. When acting as an *officer of the law* during a criminal trial, there are limits on the prosecutor's conduct, as we shall see in the next chapter. During the pretrial process, however, prosecutors hold a great deal of discretion in deciding the following:

① Whether an individual who has been arrested by the police will be charged with a crime.

② The level of the charges to be brought against the suspect.

③ If and when to stop the prosecution.[20]

There are more than eight thousand prosecutor's offices around the country—serving state, county, and municipal jurisdictions. Even though the **attorney general** is the chief law enforcement officer in any state, she or he has limited (and in some states, no) control of prosecutors within the state's boundaries.

Each jurisdiction has a chief prosecutor who is sometimes appointed but more often elected. As an elected official, he or she typically serves a four-year term, though in some states, such as Alabama, the term is six years. In small jurisdictions, the chief prosecutor has several assistants. In larger ones, the chief prosecutor may administer numerous *assistant prosecutors,* many of whom he or she will rarely meet. (See the feature *Careers in Criminal Justice.*) Assistant prosecutors—for the most part young attorneys recently graduated from law school—

INFOTRAC®
COLLEGE EDITION

Keyword: prosecutor

PUBLIC PROSECUTORS
Individuals, acting as trial lawyers, who initiate and conduct cases in the government's name and on behalf of the people.

ATTORNEY GENERAL
The chief law officer of a state; also, the chief law officer of the nation.

Careers in Criminal Justice

My name is John G. Esmerado. I am an assistant prosecutor in Elizabeth, New Jersey, for the County of Union. Union County is comprised of twenty-one independent townships with a population of approximately one-half million. Our county lies across the river from New York City. In my office there is the prosecutor, the chief law enforcement officer of the county, and fifty-five assistant prosecutors.

I first became interested in the field of prosecution when I was in high school. In ninth grade I read Harper Lee's *To Kill a Mockingbird.* After reading the book, I wanted to be like Atticus Finch. I wanted to be a lawyer who helped people. In eleventh grade, I participated in a high school mock trial program. Our attorney adviser was a former assistant prosecutor. From her I learned for the first time the role of a prosecutor. I was intrigued. I applied to a nearby Catholic university, Seton Hall, and majored in American history. I sought to learn everything I could about the world. I took courses on a variety of liberal arts and business topics. More and more I felt drawn to

John Esmerado,

Assistant Prosecutor

being a prosecutor, to pursue the truth and to aid people in crisis. I graduated college with honors and applied to Seton Hall University Law School. After receiving early acceptance, I took all the criminal law courses offered by the school. By my third year, I secured a part-time position as a law clerk in the Union County Prosecutor's Office appellate section. I wrote and argued numerous motions.

On graduation and the day after I sat for the New Jersey Bar exam, I started full-time at the prosecutor's office. In March of 1993, I was sworn in as a full-time assistant prosecutor. Since then I have tried fifty-six jury trials and worked in the appellate section, the juvenile and family court section, and pre-indictment plea screening and now work full-time on a trial team. Twice a month, I try a case. I have litigated everything from murder to robbery, sexual assault, police misconduct, drug distribution, prostitution, and aggravated assault.

My current responsibilities are two-fold. Primarily, I represent the state of New Jersey at trial. With a detective staff, I investigate crime by interviewing witnesses, searching out evidence, and asking people questions in court to establish beyond a reasonable doubt that a defendant committed a crime. Trial work is incredibly fun. It requires vast amounts of pretrial preparation. Once it starts, however, it

moves at lightning speed. Trials are strategic chess games of facts and law as well as all-out mental combat, a blitzkrieg of sorts, to find the truth. My secondary responsibility is to act as legal adviser to the police. Many times during the week and periodically in the early morning hours while the world sleeps, detectives call to discuss problematic cases. They arrest someone and are not clear what the appropriate charges are. I listen to the facts and authorize certain complaints and ask the detectives to pursue additional facts to help make the case stronger for trial.

In summary, I am glad to have a job that provides an outlet for my desire to do good. Sometimes, when I am working late at night, for free, on a case, I say to myself, this is the greatest job in the world. I receive a salary to find the truth. I help people in crisis, people subject to violence, confront their attackers and ultimately bring some form of closure. Truth, justice, and the American way, a job far too important to leave to Superman cartoons, is the job of the prosecutor every day in and out of court.

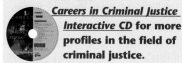

Go to the
***Careers in Criminal Justice
Interactive CD* for more
profiles in the field of
criminal justice.**

may be assigned to particular sections of the organization, such as criminal prosecutions in general or areas of special prosecution, such as narcotics or gang crimes. (See Figure 8.6 for a typical prosecutor's office.)

The Prosecutor as Elected Official.　The chief prosecutor's autonomy is not complete: as an elected official, she or he must answer to the voters. (There are exceptions: U.S. attorneys are nominated by the president and approved by the Senate, and chief prosecutors in Alaska, Connecticut, Rhode Island, New Jersey, and the District of Columbia are either appointed or hired as members of the attorney general's office.) The prosecutor may be part of the political machine; in many jurisdictions the prosecutor must declare a party affiliation and is expected to reward fellow party members with positions in the district attorney's office if elected. The post is often seen as a "steppingstone" to higher political office, and many prosecutors have gone on to serve in legislatures or as

FIGURE 8.6
The Baltimore City State's Attorney's Office

```
                              ┌─────────────────┐
                              │ State's Attorney│
                              └─────────────────┘
         ┌──────────────────────┐        ┌──────────────────┐
         │ Executive Assistant  │        │  Police Liaison  │
         └──────────────────────┘        └──────────────────┘
    ┌────────────────────────┐        ┌───────────────────────────┐
    │  Deputy for Operations │        │ Deputy for Administration │
    └────────────────────────┘        └───────────────────────────┘
```

Deputy for Operations		Deputy for Administration	
General Felony Division	Collateral Non-Support	Fiscal Officer	Administrative Officer
Central Booking Intake Facility	Collateral Non-Support	Homicide Division	Research & Develop. Division
District Courts		F.I.V.E. Division	Management Information Systems
Domestic Violence		Economic Crimes Division	Sex Offenses Division
		Child Abuse Division	Narcotics
			Auto Forfeiture Unit
		Community Services Division	
		Family Bereavement Center	Witness Security

Source: Baltimore City State's Attorney's Office

judges. Arlen Specter, a Republican senator from Pennsylvania; Ron Castille, who sits on the state's supreme court; and former Philadelphia mayor Ed Rendell all served as Philadelphia district attorneys early in their careers.

The Prosecutor as Crime Fighter. One of the reasons the prosecutor's post is a useful first step in a political career is that it is linked to crime fighting. Thanks to savvy public relations efforts and television police dramas such as *Law and Order*—with its opening line "In the criminal justice system, the people are represented by two separate yet equally important groups: the police who investigate crime and the district attorneys who prosecute the offenders"—prosecutors are generally seen as law enforcement agents. Indeed, the prosecutors and the police do have a symbiotic relationship. Prosecutors rely on police to arrest suspects and gather sufficient evidence, and police rely on prosecutors to convict those who have been apprehended.

The Defense Attorney

The media provide most people's perception of defense counsel: the idealistic public defender who nobly serves the poor; the "ambulance chaser"; or the celebrity attorney in the $3,000 suit. These stereotypes, though not entirely fictional, tend to obscure the crucial role that the **defense attorney** plays in the criminal justice system. Most persons charged with crimes have little or no knowledge of criminal procedure. Without assistance, they would be helpless against a government prosecutor. By acting as a staunch advocate for her or his client, the defense attorney (ideally) assures that the government proves every point against that client beyond a reasonable doubt, even for cases that do not go to trial. In sum, the defense attorney provides a counterweight against the state in our adversary system. (See the feature *Criminal Justice & Technology—The Myth of Fingerprints* on the following page.)

Former Congressman Bob Barr, right, a Republican from Georgia's 7th district, was the U.S. attorney for the Northern District of Georgia before being elected to that post in 1994. Give several reasons why ex-prosecutors are often attractive candidates for positions in state or federal government. (AP Photo/ Ric Feld)

DEFENSE ATTORNEY
The lawyer representing the defendant.

Criminal Justice & TECHNOLOGY

The Myth of Fingerprints?

As we saw in Chapter 5, for nearly a century police and prosecutors have relied on fingerprints as a powerful tool to link suspects to crimes. Today, however, defense attorneys are challenging this traditional weapon of forensic science, saying that it is not really "scientific" at all.

When forensic scientists compare a fingerprint lifted from a crime scene and one taken from a suspect, they are looking for "points of similarity." Today, these experts will usually declare a match if there are between eight and sixteen points of similarity between the two samples. Many defense attorneys claim that this method is flawed. First, prints found at crime scenes tend to be incomplete, which means that examiners do not compare whole fingerprints but rather fragments of the same fingerprints. So while it may be true that no two fingerprints are alike, it also may *not* be true that fragments of fingerprints are always similar or identical. Second, fingerprint evidence found at crime scenes requires treatment with chemicals or illumination with ultraviolet light to make it clear enough to work with. Is it scientifically acceptable to compare this "altered" print with a "clean" one obtained from a suspect in controlled circumstances?

Fingerprint misidentifications are rare, but not unheard of. In 1999, Richard Jackson was cleared of a murder conviction when it was found that three examiners had erroneously matched his fingerprints to those taken from the

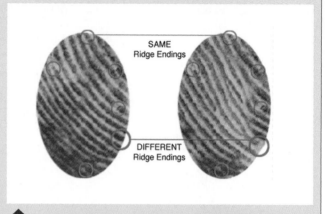

These two fingerprints were taken from different people. Still, they have five common points of similarity.

crime scene. Furthermore, defense attorneys are finding it easier to negotiate favorable plea bargains for their clients when the prosecution's only evidence is a fingerprint.

IN THE FUTURE

In 2002, a federal judge in Philadelphia ruled for the first time that fingerprint experts could not testify that a suspect's prints *conclusively* matched those found at a crime scene. The decision is expected to spur defense attorneys to become even more aggressive in challenging fingerprint evidence. In any event, DNA testing (see Chapter 5) may eventually do to fingerprinting what fingerprinting did to the Bertillon system, a nineteenth-century identification process that matched eleven bodily measurements, facial features, scars, tattoos, and birthmarks. In other words, DNA testing may make fingerprinting obsolete.

The Responsibilities of the Defense Attorney. The Sixth Amendment right to counsel is not limited to the actual criminal trial. In a number of instances, the Supreme Court has held that defendants are entitled to representation as soon as their rights may be denied, which, as we have seen, includes the custodial interrogation and lineup identification procedures.[21] Therefore, the primary responsibility of the defense attorney is to represent the defendant at the various stages of the custodial process, such as arrest, interrogation, lineup, and arraignment. Other responsibilities include:

- Investigating the incident for which the defendant has been charged.
- Communicating with the prosecutor, which includes negotiating plea bargains.
- Preparing the case for trial.
- Submitting defense motions, including motions to suppress evidence.
- Representing the defendant at trial.
- Negotiating a sentence, if the client has been convicted.
- Determining whether to appeal a guilty verdict.[22]

One question that has troubled defense attorneys and legal ethicists is whether a lawyer has a duty to defend a client he or she knows to be guilty. This debate is addressed in the feature *Criminal Justice in Action—Legal Ethics on Trial: Defending the Guilty* at the end of this chapter. (To learn more about a career as a paralegal, a crucial position in the office of any attorney, go to the *Careers in Criminal Justice Interactive CD* and click on the Career Rolodex.)

The Public Defender. Generally speaking, there are two different types of defense attorneys: (1) private attorneys, who are hired by individuals, and (2) **public defenders,** who work for the government. The distinction is not absolute, as many private attorneys hire out as public defenders, too. The modern role of the public defender was established by the Supreme Court's interpretation of the Sixth Amendment in *Gideon v. Wainwright* (1963).[23] The Court ruled that no defendant can be "assured a fair trial unless counsel is provided for him," and therefore the state must provide a public defender to those who cannot afford to hire one for themselves. Subsequently, the Court extended this protection to juveniles in *In re Gault* (1967)[24] and those faced with imprisonment for committing misdemeanors in *Argersinger v. Hamlin* (1972).[25] The impact of these decisions has been substantial: approximately three out of every four inmates in state prisons and jails were represented by publicly paid counsel.[26]

The Attorney-Client Relationship

To defend a client effectively, a defense attorney must have access to all the facts concerning the case, including those that may be harmful to the defense. To promote the unrestrained flow of information between the two parties, laws of **attorney-client privilege** have been constructed. These laws require that communications between a client and his or her attorney be kept confidential, unless the client consents to disclosure. The scope of this privilege is not all encompassing, however. In *United States v. Zolin* (1989),[27] the Supreme Court ruled that attorneys may disclose the contents of a conversation with a client if the client has provided information concerning a crime that has yet to be committed.

The implied trust between an attorney and her or his client is not usually in question when the attorney has been hired directly by the defendant—as an "employee," the attorney well understands her or his duties. Relationships between public defenders and their clients, however, are often marred by suspicion on both sides. As Northwestern University's Jonathan D. Casper discovered while interviewing indigent defendants, many of them feel a certain amount of respect for the prosecutor. Like police officers, prosecutors are just "doing their job" by trying to convict the defendant. In contrast, the defendants' view of their own attorneys can be summed up in the following exchange between Casper and a defendant:

> Did you have a lawyer when you went to court the next morning?
> No, I had a public defender.[28]

This attitude is somewhat understandable. Given the caseloads that most public defenders carry, they may have as little as five or ten minutes to spend with a client before appearing in front of a judge. How much, realistically, can a public defender learn about the defendant in that time?[29] Furthermore, the defendant is well aware that the public defender is being paid by the same source as the prosecutor and the judge. "Unabomber" Ted Kaczynski acted on impulses felt by many defendants when he requested the right to defend himself, complaining that his public counsel was "supping from the same trough" as the prosecution.[30]

The situation handcuffs the public defenders as well. With so little time to spend on each case, they cannot validate the information provided by their clients. If the defendant says he or she has no prior offenses, the public defender often has no choice but to believe the client. Consequently, many public defenders later find that their clients have deceived them. In addition to the low pay and high pressures of the job, a client's lack of cooperation and disrespect can limit whatever satisfaction a public defender may find in the profession.[31]

"**Look at the stakes. In civil law, if you screw up, it's just money. Here, it's the client— his life, his time in jail— and you never know how much time people have in their life.**"

—*Criminal defense attorney* Stacey Richman (2001)

Video Profile of Whitney Leigh, former Deputy Public Defender

PUBLIC DEFENDERS
Court-appointed attorneys who are paid by the state to represent defendants who are unable to hire private counsel.

ATTORNEY-CLIENT PRIVILEGE
A rule of evidence requiring that communications between a client and his or her attorney be kept confidential, unless the client consents to disclosure.

Criminal Justice in Action

Legal Ethics on Trial: Defending the Guilty

One of the most prominent aspects of the judicial system described in this chapter and the next is the amount of power it places in the hands of lawyers. They decide the course of the trial, which evidence to provide, what witnesses to call, whether to plea bargain, and so on. In countries that favor an "inquisitorial system," including most European nations, this is not the case. The inquisitorial system places power with judges; they decide what evidence will be admitted to court and who will interview witnesses. Lawyers, for the most part, act as investigators and provide information for the judge. These differing roles for lawyers seem to breed different perspectives on the legal profession. French *avocats,* for example, are generally held in high esteem, while in the United States, lawyer bashing can get so fierce that the president of the California Bar Association demanded that lawyer jokes be considered hate crimes.[32] In this *Criminal Justice in Action* feature, we examine one attribute of the American system that seems to inspire a great deal of mistrust toward lawyers, particularly defense attorneys.

Strong Feelings against Lawyers Have a Long History

Disdain for the members of the legal profession is nothing if not enduring. At the end of the sixteenth century, Shakespeare wrote a play in which a character exhorted his colleagues to "kill all the lawyers." Four hundred years later, the very same words were used as the title of a film. This general enmity seems to be based on the perception that legal practitioners are deeply dishonest.

A great deal of this mistrust is based on the presumption that lawyers will do anything in the interests of their clients. To a certain extent, the ideals of our judicial system promote this view. In a classic statement, the British attorney Lord Brougham asserted:

[A]n advocate, in the discharge of his duty, knows but one person in all the world, and that person is his client. To save the client by all means and expedients, and at all hazards and costs to other persons, and among them, himself, is his first and only duty; and in performing this duty he must not regard the alarm, the torments, the destruction which he may bring upon others.[33]

When Lord Brougham made this statement in 1820, he was serving as defense attorney to the very popular Queen Caroline, who was charged with having engaged in an adulterous relationship with a courtier before ascending to the throne. The ethical issues he raises may not be so clear to a defense attorney today, especially one who is working on behalf of a client she or he suspects, or knows, is guilty.

The "Truth" of the Courtroom

It is a question many defense attorneys come to dread: How can you defend a client you know is guilty? Many nonlawyers seem to sympathize with the premise of the film *Devil's Advocate,* in which Satan is a senior partner in a law firm that specializes in representing the rich and the guilty. If defense attorneys are not doing the "devil's work" in defending the guilty, the popular line of thought goes, then certainly they are breaking some moral or legal rule.

Many legal scholars disagree. Just as a physician is morally obliged to treat a patient even if that patient may go on to do harm, they say, a defense attorney is morally obliged to represent a client who may have committed or will possibly commit a crime. This obligation is based on every American citizen's constitutional right to counsel, protection against self-incrimination, and, most important, presumption of innocence. Because the burden of proof is on the government, the framers of the Constitution saw fit to provide the accused with an ally. Indeed, as legal expert Murray L. Schwartz noted, "If lawyers refuse to represent defendants who they believe are guilty, the right of a defendant to be represented by counsel is eliminated and with it the entire traditional criminal trial."[34]

Furthermore, defense attorneys, as advocates, have a responsibility not to interject their own personal opinions into the process. Theoretically, no absolute "truth" exists in a courtroom. Instead, "truth" emerges through a process in which the prosecution and defense present their cases and a judge or jury decides questions of guilt and innocence.[35]

Privileged Confessions

Practical reasons also compel an attorney to defend a client who may be guilty. Attorney-client privilege, for example, rests on the assumption that a free flow of information between the two parties is crucial to providing a solid defense. This privilege must cover all attorney-client communications, including those that suggest the client's guilt, as well as confessions. If, on hearing any statement that points toward guilt, the defense lawyer either uses the statement to help the prosecution convict the client or tries to resign from the case, the attorney-client privilege is rendered meaningless.[36]

Ralf Panitz, left, and his attorney, Geoffrey Fieger, listen as a verdict is handed down finding Panitz guilty of second degree murder in the death of his ex-wife Nancy Campbell-Panitz. The crime took place hours after Nancy, Ralf, and Ralf's present wife Eleanor appeared on a television show about secret mistresses. (AP Photo/Mike Diemer)

If such behavior on the part of defense attorneys became commonplace, notes legal expert John Kaplan, lawyers would be forced to give their clients the equivalent of *Miranda* warnings before representing them.[37] That is, lawyers would have to make clear what clients could or could not say in the course of preparing for trial, because any incriminatory statements might be used against them in court. Such a development would have serious ramifications for the criminal justice system.

ON A PERSONAL LEVEL

Although most defense lawyers are aware of constitutional, theoretical, and practical arguments in favor of defending guilty clients, it can be a difficult task. In the words of one prominent defense attorney:

> [I]f you're a decent human being and you've been a victim of crime yourself and you have family members that have been victims of crime, you feel tremendous turmoil. We're supposed to say, "It's not our job to worry about society, and everyone is entitled to a defense." That's all true, at an intellectual level, but at an emotional level, this takes a terrible toll, which is why some lawyers don't want to know if their clients are guilty.[38]

Sometimes, the decision to uphold client confidentiality can have tragic results, as in the situation surrounding the case of *Frank v. Magnum* (1915).[39] In that trial, Leo Frank had been convicted of murder and sentenced to life in prison. After Frank had been imprisoned, a client of attorney Arthur Powell admitted to Powell that he, and not Frank, had committed the murder in question. Powell decided not to divulge this information, and other inmates

eventually lynched Frank in prison. Afterward, an anguished Powell said, "I could not have revealed the information the client had given me in the confidential relationship, without violating my oath as an attorney. . . . Such is the law; I did not make the law; but it is my duty and the court's duty to obey the law, so long as it stands."[40]

MAKING SENSE OF DEFENDING THE GUILTY

1 Do you agree that a defense attorney is morally obliged to represent a client who may have committed or will possibly commit a crime? Explain your answer.

2 What would be the consequences if public defenders could decide not to represent certain defendants because of their presumed guilt?

3 Consider the following hypothetical situation. Ms. Franks agrees to represent Mr. Smith in his upcoming trial for attempted murder. Three days after this agreement, Mr. Smith tells Ms. Franks that he is responsible for a different murder for which Mr. Jones was found guilty and is currently in prison. What should Ms. Franks do?

KEY TERMS

attorney-client privilege 213

attorney general 209

appellate courts 197

concurring opinions 203

courtroom work group 208

defense attorney 211

dissenting opinions 204

docket 204

dual court system 199

judicial misconduct 208

jurisdiction 197

Missouri plan 205

nonpartisan elections 205

opinion 198

oral arguments 203

partisan elections 205

public defenders 213

public prosecutors 209

trial courts 197

writ of *certiorari* 203

CHAPTER SUMMARY

1 **Define jurisdiction and contrast geographical and subject-matter jurisdiction.** Jurisdiction relates to the power of a court to hear a particular case. Courts are typically limited in geographical jurisdiction, for example, to a particular state. Some courts are restricted in subject matter, such as a small claims court, which can hear only cases involving civil matters under a certain amount.

2 **Explain the difference between trial and appellate courts.** Trial courts are courts of the first instance, where a case is first heard. Appellate courts review the proceedings of a lower court. Appellate courts do not have juries.

3 **Outline the several levels of a typical state court system.** (a) At the lowest level are courts of limited jurisdiction, (b) next are trial courts of general jurisdiction, (c) then appellate courts, and (d) finally, the state's highest court.

4 **Outline the federal court system.** (a) At the lowest level are the U.S. district courts in which trials are held, as well as various minor federal courts of limited jurisdiction; (b) next are the U.S. courts of appeals, otherwise known as circuit courts of appeal; and (c) finally, the United States Supreme Court.

5 **Explain briefly how a case is brought to the Supreme Court.** Cases decided in U.S. courts of appeals, as well as cases decided in the highest state courts (when federal questions arise), can be appealed to the United States Supreme Court. If at least four justices approve of a case filed with the Supreme Court, the Court will issue a writ of *certiorari*, ordering the lower court to send the Supreme Court the record of the case for review.

6 **List and describe the members of the courtroom work group.** (a) The judge; (b) the prosecutor, who brings charges in the name of the people (the state) against the accused; (c) the defense attorney; (d) the bailiff, who is responsible for maintaining security and order in the judge's chambers and the courtroom; (e) the clerk, who accepts all pleas, motions, and other matters to be acted on by the judge; and (f) court reporters, who record what is said during a trial as well as at depositions.

7 **List the different names given to public prosecutors and the general powers that they have.** At the federal level, the prosecutor is called the U.S. attorney. In state and local courts, the prosecutor may be referred to as the prosecuting attorney, state prosecutor, district attorney, county attorney, or city attorney. Prosecutors in general have the power to decide when and how the state will pursue an individual suspected of criminal wrongdoing. In some jurisdictions, the district attorney is also the chief law enforcement officer, holding broad powers over police operations.

8 **Contrast the prosecutor's roles as an elected official and as a crime fighter.** In most instances, the prosecutor is elected and therefore may feel obliged to reward members of her or his party with jobs. To win reelection or higher political office, the prosecutor is dependent on the police, and indeed prosecutors are generally seen as law enforcement agents. Prosecutors, however, generally only pursue cases when they believe there is sufficient legal guilt to obtain a conviction.

9 **Delineate the responsibilities of defense attorneys.** (a) The investigation of the supposed criminal incident; (b) communication with the prosecutor (including plea bargaining); (c) preparation of the case for trial; (d) submission of defense motions; (e) representation of the defendant at trial; (f) negotiation of a sentence after conviction; and (g) appeal of a guilty verdict.

QUESTIONS FOR CRITICAL ANALYSIS

1. Which court has virtually unlimited geographical and subject-matter jurisdiction? Why is this so?

2. How did we end up with a dual court system?

3. Federal judges and justices typically hold office for many years. Why is this so?

4. What are some of the various functions that a judge undertakes during a trial? What function does a judge assume when presiding over a trial that is not a jury trial?

5. Why are public prosecutors considered such powerful figures in the American justice system?

6. Do defense attorneys have an obligation to defend a client they know is guilty? Why or why not?

SELECTED PRINT AND ELECTRONIC RESOURCES

SUGGESTED READINGS

Ball, Howard, *A Defiant Life: Thurgood Marshall and the Persistence of Racism in America,* New York: Crown Publishers, 1998. Author Ball presents Marshall's life as the "story of racism in America," starting with his childhood experiences as part of a middle-class African American family living in Baltimore, Maryland, at the dawn of the twentieth century. Ball proceeds to detail Marshall's many accomplishments in the law, from his role as a civil rights attorney in the landmark 1954 case *Brown v. Board of Education* to his struggles as a liberal on a Supreme Court dominated by a conservative majority.

Baum, Lawrence, *The Supreme Court,* 6th ed., Washington, D.C.: CQ Press, 1998. Written by a noted judicial scholar, this is a comprehensive treatment of the Supreme Court.

Parrish, Michael, et al., *For the People: Inside the Los Angeles County District Attorney's Office, 1850–2000,* Santa Monica, CA: Angel City Press, 2001. The authors present a candid analysis of the problems that face a typical big-city prosecutor's office. The book also relates the details of many famous trials.

MEDIA RESOURCES

***My Cousin Vinny* (1992)** This film stars Joe Pesci (Vinny) as a New Yorker who took six tries to pass the bar exam.

He becomes the defense attorney in Alabama for his cousin, played by Ralph Macchio, and a friend, played by Mitchell Whitfield. These are two innocent college students on their way to school who have been charged with the murder of a convenience store owner. Pesci's character, Vinny, has virtually no legal experience and almost sinks his clients at every turn during the trial. As you watch this movie, concentrate on the relationship among the members of the courtroom work group.

Critically analyze this film:

1. Would you say the small-town Alabama community that acts as the setting for this film is interested in crime control, due process, or rehabilitation as the primary function of the courts? Explain your answer.

2. To the extent that the film allows, describe the court in which the action takes place. Is it a trial or appellate court? Federal or state? What is its jurisdiction?

3. How does Judge Haller exercise his discretion? Why, for example, is Vinny jailed several times?

4. How does Judge Haller fit the description of a judge as *referee* and *teacher?* What appears to be his personal philosophy—is he "big on procedures"? How does this philosophy show itself in his courtroom demeanor?

5. Describe the relationships among the courtroom work group members in this film. Do they appear to be cooperating with each other in the best interests of justice?

LOGGING ON

Go to http://cj.wadsworth.com/gainescore2e, and click Hypercontents. There, you will find URLs for the organizations in the following list:

- If you would like to find information about your state court system, you can go to the **Internet Legal Research Compass** Web site and click on "State Court Locator."

- If you are interested following current controversial cases, or learning about famous cases from the past, you can go to **CourtTV's** Web site.

- For access to information on the **federal court system** in general, go to the home page of the federal courts.

USING THE INTERNET FOR CRIMINAL JUSTICE ANALYSIS

INFOTRAC®
COLLEGE EDITION

1. Go to InfoTrac College Edition at
http://www.infotrac-college.com/wadsworth/
Type in the words **"Running for Judge: How Nonpartisan?"**
This article is from *Campaigns & Elections.* The author examines how to run a campaign for a judge who must run for office as would any other politician. Read the article and answer the following questions:

   a. How many states have an elective system for judges?

   b. How much does a campaign for a judge cost in a large city?

   c. Where do judicial candidates raise the largest amount of campaign funds?

   d. On what issues do judicial candidates attempt to get media attention, and why?

2. See Internet Activities 8.1 and 8.2 on the companion Web site for *CJ in Action: The Core.* To get to the activities, go to **http://www.cj.wadsworth.com/gainescore2e**, select the appropriate chapter from the drop down list, then click Internet Activities on the left navigation bar.

NOTES

1. William Booth, "Kaczynski Sentenced to Four Life Terms," *Washington Post* (May 5, 1998), A1; and Martin Kasindorf, "Bomber's Victims Have Their Say," *USA Today* (May 5, 1998), 3A.

2. Roscoe Pound, "The Administration of Justice in American Cities," *Harvard Law Review* 12 (1912).

3. David W. Neubauer, *America's Courts and the Criminal Justice System,* 5th ed. (Belmont, CA: Wadsworth Publishing Company, 1996), 41.

4. 372 U.S. 335 (1963).

5. 384 U.S. 436 (1966).

6. 408 U.S. 238 (1972).

7. 428 U.S. 153 (1976).

8. 491 U.S. 397 (1989).

9. 496 U.S. 310 (1990).

10. *Callins v. Collins,* 50 U.S. 1141, 1159 (1994) (Blackmun, J., dissenting).

11. Barry R. Schaller, *A Vision of American Law: Judging Law, Literature, and the Stories We Tell* (Westport, CT: Praeger, 1997).

12. Harlington Wood, Jr., "Judiciary Reform: Recent Improvements in Federal Judicial Administration," *American University Law Review* 44 (June 1995), 1557.

13. James E. Lozier, "The Missouri Plan a.k.a. Merit Selection Is the Best Solution for Selecting Michigan's Judges," *Michigan Bar Journal* 75 (September 1996), 918.

14. Shirley S. Abrahamson, *Foreword to Judicial Conduct and Ethics* (Charlottesville, VA: Michie Co., 1990), vi–vii.

15. American Bar Association, *Model Code of Judicial Conduct* (Chicago: ABA, August 1990).

16. ABA Commission on Ethics and Professional Responsibility, Informal Opinion 1468 (1981).

17. Roy B. Fleming, Peter F. Nardulli, and James Eisenstein, *The Craft of Justice: Politics and Work in Criminal Court Communities* (Philadelphia: University of Pennsylvania Press, 1992).

18. Bennett L. Gershman, "Abuse of Power in the Prosecutor's Office," in *Criminal Justice 92/93,* John J. Sullivan and Joseph L. Victor, eds. (Guilford, CT: The Dushkin Publishing Group, 1991), 117–23.

19. 295 U.S. 78 (1935).

20. Celesta Albonetti, "Prosecutorial Discretion: The Effects of Uncertainty," *Law and Society Review* 21 (1987), 291–313.

21. *Gideon v. Wainwright,* 372 U.S. 335 (1963); *Massiah v. United States,* 377 U.S. 201 (1964); *United States v. Wade,* 388 U.S. 218 (1967); *Argersinger v. Hamlin,* 407 U.S. 25 (1972); *Brewer v. Williams,* 430 U.S. 387 (1977).

22. Larry Siegel, *Criminology,* 6th ed. (Belmont, CA: West/Wadsworth Publishing Company, 1998), 487–88.

23. 372 U.S. 335 (1963).

24. 387 U.S. 1 (1967).

25. 407 U.S. 25 (1972).

26. Bureau of Justice Statistics, *Indigent Defense* (Washington, D.C.: U.S. Department of Justice, 1996), 3.

27. 491 U.S. 554 (1989).

28. Jonathan D. Casper, *American Criminal Justice: The Defendant's Perspective* (Englewood Cliffs, NJ: Prentice-Hall, 1972), 101.

29. *Ibid.,* 106.

30. William Finnegan, "Defending the Unabomber," *New Yorker* (March 16, 1998), 61.

31. Anthony Platt and Randi Pollock, "Channeling Lawyers: The Careers of Public Defenders," in *The Potential for Reform in Criminal Justice,* ed. Herbert Jacob (Newbury Park, CA: Sage, 1974).

32. Vicki Torres, "Chief of Bar Association Asks End to Lawyer-Bashing," *Los Angeles Times* (July 6, 1993), A1.

33. Quoted in Charles Fried, "The Lawyer as Friend: The Moral Foundations of the Lawyer-Client Relation," *Yale Law Journal* 85 (1976), 1060.

34. Murray L. Schwartz, *Cases and Materials on Professional Responsibility and the Administration of Criminal Justice* (New York: Council on Legal Education for Professional Responsibility, 1961), 115.

35. David Luban, "The Adversary System Excuse," in *The Good Lawyer: Lawyers' Roles and Lawyers' Ethics,* ed. David Luban (Totowa, NJ: Rowman & Allanheld, 1983), 83.

36. David Rosenthal, "The Criminal Defense Attorney, Ethics and Maintaining Client Confidentiality: A Proposal to Amend Rule 1.6 of the Model Rules of Professional Conduct," *St. Thomas Law Review* 6 (Fall 1993), 153.

37. John Kaplan, "Defending Guilty People," *University of Bridgeport Law Review* 7 (1986), 223.

38. Cheryl Lavin, "Alan Dershowitz Defends Attorneys," *Fort Worth Star-Telegram* (April 4, 1995), 1.

39. 237 U.S. 309 (1915).

40. Quoted in Rosenthal, 153.

CHAPTER 9
PRETRIAL PROCEDURES AND THE CRIMINAL TRIAL

CHAPTER OUTLINE

- **Pretrial Detention: Bail**
- **Establishing Probable Cause**
- **The Prosecutor in Action**
- **Pleading Guilty**
- **Special Features of Criminal Trials**
- **The Trial**
- **The Jury in Action**
- **Appeals**
- **Criminal Justice in Action—Cameras in the Courtroom: Is Justice Served?**

Chapter Objectives

After reading this chapter, you should be able to:

1. Identify the steps involved in the pretrial criminal process.
2. Explain how a prosecutor screens potential cases.
3. List and briefly explain the motivations of the prosecutors, defense attorneys, and defendants to plea bargain.
4. Identify the basic protections enjoyed by criminal defendants in the United States.
5. Contrast challenges for cause and peremptory challenges during *voir dire*.
6. List the standard steps in a criminal jury trial.
7. Explain the difference between testimony and real evidence; between lay witnesses and expert witnesses; and between direct and circumstantial evidence.
8. List the six basic steps of an appeal.

INTRODUCTION
Justice Delayed in Birmingham

On September 15, 1963, four young African American girls were killed by a bomb blast that destroyed a Baptist church in Birmingham, Alabama. Law enforcement agents identified four suspects, including Ku Klux Klansman Thomas E. Blanton, Jr. Charges were never brought against the quartet, however. Prosecutors were convinced that a jury in Alabama in the early 1960s, which would certainly have been all white and all male, would never find the four guilty. It was a low point in race relations in this country and persuaded many Americans that their criminal justice system was inherently unfair.

On May 1, 2001, Blanton, then sixty-two years old, was finally convicted of the bombing by a Birmingham jury and sentenced to four life terms in prison.[1] Because almost all of the evidence at the trial was circumstantial, the prosecution made a concerted effort to choose jurors who would be sympathetic to the plight of the four girls. They polled nearly five hundred residents of the Birmingham area and came up with a hundred-question survey designed to put parents and churchgoers in the jury box.[2] The jury that convicted Blanton included eight whites and four African Americans—none of the whites was male. Blanton's attorney vowed to appeal the verdict on the ground that the prosecution had intentionally kept the jury free of white men. This, he claimed, was unfair.

Fairness is, of course, a crucial component of the criminal trial. Protection against the arbitrary abuse of power is at the heart of the U.S. Constitution. In the criminal justice system, the right to a criminal trial before a jury is one means of assuring this protection. For many, the fairness exhibited in criminal trials inspires faith in the system as a whole.[3]

Fairness, however, is not easily defined. The criminal trial is basically a fact-finding process, but how those facts are presented by the prosecution and defense and then deciphered by the jury adds a measure of uncertainty to the process. For example, in 1984 Curtis Kyles was arrested in connection with the murder of Delores Dye. New Orleans police found Dye's purse in the front seat of Kyles's car, the murder weapon behind Kyles's stove, and ammunition that matched the bullet that killed Dye in his car and in his dresser.

Fourteen years later, after five criminal trials, Kyles was released. Kyles's attorneys had been able to produce enough evidence of the *possibility* that their client was framed to cause three hung juries (in which a verdict could not be reached) and one United States Supreme Court reversal. After the final trial, prosecutors insinuated that the trial process had been too fair to Kyles, placing procedural and legal concerns above those of justice for his victim and society at large.[4]

In this chapter, we will examine the events leading up to a criminal trial in the United States, as well as the trial itself. These processes are the backbone of America's *adversary system,* in which the prosecution and the defense treat each other as adversaries, with the guilt or innocence of the defendant the "prize" to be won or lost at the end of the battle.

Thomas Blanton, Jr., is led out of a Birmingham, Alabama, courtroom on May 1, 2001, after being convicted for the bombing murder of four African American girls in 1963. (AP Photo/ Dave Martin)

PRETRIAL DETENTION: BAIL

After an arrest has been made, the first step toward determining the suspect's guilt or innocence is the **initial appearance.** During this brief proceeding, a magistrate (see Chapter 8) informs the defendant of the charges that have been brought against him or her and explains his or her constitutional rights—particularly, the right to remain silent (under the Fifth Amendment) and the right to be represented by counsel (under the Sixth Amendment). At this point, if the defendant cannot afford to hire a private attorney, a public defender may be appointed, or private counsel may be hired by the state to represent the defendant. As the U.S. Constitution does not specify how soon a defendant must be brought before a magistrate after arrest, it has been left to the judicial branch to determine the timing of the initial appearance.

In misdemeanor cases, a defendant may decide to plead guilty and be sentenced during the initial appearance. Otherwise, the magistrate will usually release those charged with misdemeanors on their promise to return at a later date for further proceedings. For felony cases, however, the defendant is not permitted to make a plea at the initial appearance, because a magistrate's court does not have jurisdiction to decide felonies. Furthermore, in most cases the defendant will be released only if she or he posts **bail**—an amount of money paid by the defendant to the court and retained by the court until the defendant returns for further proceedings. Defendants who cannot afford bail are generally kept in a local jail or lockup until the date of their trial, though many jurisdictions are searching for alternatives to this practice because of overcrowded incarceration facilities.

The Purpose of Bail

Historically, the main purpose of bail has been to ensure the appearance of the defendant at trial without detention. In the United States, bail is provided for under the Eighth Amendment. The amendment does not, however, guarantee the right to bail. Instead, it states that "excessive bail shall not be required." This has come to mean that in all cases except those involving a capital crime (where bail is often prohibited), the amount of bail required must be reasonable compared with the seriousness of the wrongdoing. It *does not* mean that the amount of bail must be within the defendant's ability to pay.

Setting Bail

There is no uniform system for pretrial detention; each jurisdiction has its own *bail tariffs,* or general guidelines concerning the proper amount of bail. For misdemeanors, the police usually follow a preapproved bail schedule created by local judicial authorities. In felony cases, the primary responsibility to set bail lies with the judge. Figure 9.1 on the next page shows typical bail amounts.

Extralegal factors may also play a part in bail setting. University of New Orleans political scientist David W. Neubauer has identified three contexts that may influence a judge's decision-making process:[5]

1. *Uncertainty.* To some extent, predetermined bail tariffs are unrealistic, given that judges are required to set bail within forty-eight hours of arrest. It is often difficult to get information on the defendant in that period of time, and even if a judge can obtain a "rap sheet," or list of prior arrests ("priors"), she or he will probably not have an opportunity to verify its accuracy. Due to this uncertainty, most judges have no choice but to focus primarily on the seriousness of the crime in setting bail.

Go to the Stories from the Street feature at http://www.cj. wadsworth.com/gainescore2e to hear Larry Gaines tell insightful stories related to this chapter and his experiences in the field.

"**Unless th(e) right to bail before trial is preserved, the presumption of innocence, secured only after centuries of struggle, would lose its meaning.**"

—Fred M. Vinson, *United States Supreme Court chief justice* (1951)

Video Profile of Chris Harrington, Pretrial Services Officer

INITIAL APPEARANCE
An accused's first appearance before a judge or magistrate following arrest; during the appearance, the defendant is informed of the charges, advised of the right to counsel, told the amount of bail, and given a date for the preliminary hearing.

BAIL
The amount or conditions set by the court to ensure that an individual accused of a crime will appear for further criminal proceedings. If the accused person provides bail, whether in cash or by means of a bail bond, then she or he is released from jail.

FIGURE 9.1

Average Bail Amounts for Various Misdemeanors and Felonies

These figures represent the median bail figures for the seventy-five largest counties in the nation.

Offense	Median Bail Amount
Murder	$250,000
Rape	$30,000
Robbery	$25,000
Assault	$10,000
Weapons offense	$10,000
Burglary	$8,000
Drug offense	$7,500
Theft	$3,500

Source: Adapted from Bureau of Justice Statistics, *Federal Defendants in Large Urban Counties* (Washington, D.C.: U.S. Department of Justice, 2001), Table 16, page 18.

FIGURE 9.2

The Likelihood of Pretrial Release

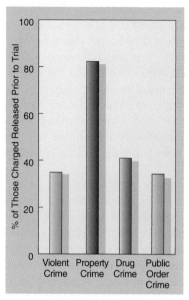

Source: Adapted from the Bureau of Justice Statistics, *Compendium of Federal Justice Statistics, 1999* (Washington, D.C.: U.S. Department of Justice, 2001), 41.

❷ *Risk.* There is no way of knowing for certain whether a defendant released on bail will return for his or her court date, or whether he or she will commit a crime while free. Judges are aware of the criticism they will come under from police groups, prosecutors, the press, and the public if a crime is committed during that time. Consequently, especially if she or he is up for reelection, a judge may prefer to "play it safe" and set a high bail to detain a suspect or refuse outright to offer bail when legally able to do so. In general, risk aversion also dictates why those who have committed violent crimes are less likely to be released prior to trial than those who have committed property crimes (see Figure 9.2). In the minds of many judges, someone who is under suspicion of stealing a television is much less of a risk than someone who is under suspicion of murder.

❸ *Overcrowded jails.* As we will discuss in detail in Chapter 12, many of the nation's jails are overcrowded. This may force a judge to make a difficult distinction between those suspects she or he believes must be detained and those who might need to be detained. To save jail space, a judge might be more lenient in setting bail for members of the latter group.[6]

Gaining Pretrial Release

Earlier, we mentioned that many jurisdictions are looking for alternatives to the bail system. One of the most popular options is **release on recognizance (ROR).** This is used when the judge, based on the advice of trained personnel, decides that the defendant is not at risk to "jump" bail and does not pose a threat to the community. The defendant is then released with the understanding that he or she will return at the time of the trial.

Those suspected of committing a felony are, however, rarely released on recognizance. These defendants may post, or pay, the full amount of the bail in cash to the court. The money will be returned when the suspect appears for trial. Given the large sums involved, and the relative lack of wealth of many criminal defendants, a defendant can rarely post bail in cash. Another option is to use personal property as collateral. These *property bonds* are also rare because most courts require property valued at double the bail amount. Thus, if bail is set at $5,000, the defendant (or the defendant's family and friends) will have to produce a piece of property valued at $10,000.

If unable to post bail with cash or property, a defendant may arrange for a **bail bondsperson** to post a bail bond on the defendant's behalf. The bondsperson, in effect, promises the court that he or she will turn over to the court the full amount of bail if the defendant fails to return for further proceedings. The defendant usually must give the bondsperson a certain percentage of the bail (often 10 percent) in cash. This amount, which is often not returned to the defendant later, is considered payment for the bondsperson's assistance and assumption of risk.

RELEASE ON RECOGNIZANCE (ROR)
A judge's order that releases an accused from jail with the understanding that he or she will return for further proceedings of his or her own will; used instead of setting a monetary bond.

BAIL BONDSPERSON
A businessperson who agrees, for a fee, to pay the bail amount if the accused fails to appear in court as ordered.

In Macon, Georgia, bounty hunter Cedric Miller takes aim at Stan Bernard Rouse. Miller, a former Macon narcotics cop, is often paid substantial sums by bail bondspeople to capture bond-jumping clients. (Beau Cabell, *The Macon Telegraph*)

Depending on the amount of the bail bond, the defendant may also be required to sign over to the bondsperson rights to certain property (such as a car, a valuable watch, or other asset) as security for the bond.

Bail Reform

In the 1960s, as various researchers produced empirical proof that pretrial detention increased the odds of conviction and led to longer sentences, reformers began to point out that this created an imbalance of justice between the wealthy and the poor.[7] Those who could afford to post bail were convicted less frequently and spent less time in jail than those who could not. Furthermore, the conditions in pretrial detention centers were considerably worse than the conditions in prison, and the cost of maintaining these centers was becoming prohibitive.

In response to these concerns, Congress passed the Bail Reform Act of 1966.[8] Though the new law did not place statutory restrictions on the discretionary powers of federal judges, it did strongly suggest that judges implement a wide range of "conditions of release" for suspects who qualified.[9] The Bail Reform Act of 1966 was criticized for concentrating on ways of increasing pretrial release, while failing to give judges the ability to detain suspects who posed a danger to the community.[10] Although judges have always had the *de facto* power to do just that by setting prohibitively high bails for dangerous defendants, thirty states have passed **preventive detention** laws that allow judges to deny bail to suspects with prior records of violence or nonappearance for trial. The Bail Reform Act of 1984 similarly states that federal offenders can be held without bail to assure "the safety of any other person and the community."[11]

Critics of the 1984 act believe that it violates the U.S. Constitution by allowing the freedom of a citizen to be restricted before he or she has been proved guilty in a court of law. For many, the act also brings up the troubling issue of *false positives*—erroneous predictions that defendants, if given pretrial release, would commit a crime, when in fact they would not.[12] (See the feature *CJ in Focus—The Balancing Act: Innocent on Bail?* on page 224.) In *United States v. Salerno* (1987),[13] however, the Supreme Court upheld the act's premise. Chief Justice William Rehnquist wrote that preventive detention was not a "punishment for dangerous individuals" but a "potential solution to a pressing social problem." Therefore, "there is no doubt that preventing danger to the community is a legitimate . . . goal."

On the Web

The Professional Bail Agents of the United States Web site is designed to help bail bondspersons to be more competent and effective. Action Bail Bonds's home page provides insight on how a bail bond agency operates. For links to both Web sites, go to the Hypercontents page for this chapter at http://www.cj.wadsworth.com/gainescore2e.

INFOTRAC®
COLLEGE EDITION

Keywords: bail bondsmen, bounty hunters

PREVENTIVE DETENTION
The retention of an accused person in custody due to fears that she or he will commit a crime if released before trial.

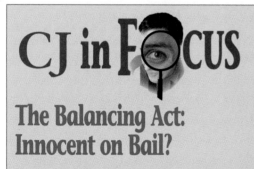

CJ in FOCUS

The Balancing Act: Innocent on Bail?

Sylvia Hernandez was stabbed to death in Austin, Texas, by Leonard Saldana, her common law husband. Saldana, it turned out, had been arrested a month earlier for violating a court order to keep away from Hernandez. He had been jailed nineteen times in ten years, including four times for assaults involving domestic violence and once for violating a protective court order concerning a different woman. When he murdered Hernandez, Saldana was free on $4,000 bail.

In retrospect, Saldana should not have been released for such a small amount, given his background. Concern over such situations has convinced three-fifths of the states and the federal government to pass laws that allow judges to confine suspects before trial without bail if there is a threat of harm to the community. Civil libertarians, however, believe such preventive detention laws unjustly sacrifice the individual's right to be presumed innocent to a generally unsubstantiated government interest in pretrial detention.

Supreme Court Justice Thurgood Marshall, in his dissent in the case in which the Bail Reform Act of 1984 was upheld, wrote that the denial of due process in such judicial decisions was "consistent with the usage of tyranny and the excesses of what bitter experience teaches us to call the police state."

The main criticism of preventive detention is that it presumes a certain ability to predict future criminal activity on the basis of past activity (a presumption that is usually not allowed in criminal trials). Criminologist Charles Ewing has concluded that statistical predictions about violent criminal behavior are "much more likely to be wrong than right." Some observers believe preventive detention will be used indiscriminately by judges who do not want to risk being criticized for freeing a suspect who goes on to commit a crime while out on bail. Furthermore, though it is possible to measure how many suspects eligible to be detained under these laws committed violent crimes after being released (between 5 and 10 percent, according to recent studies), it is not possible to determine how many of those who *were* detained would *not* have committed crimes if freed.

FOR CRITICAL ANALYSIS
Given the relatively low rate of criminal activity by suspects who have been released pending trial, are preventive detention laws justified?

ESTABLISHING PROBABLE CAUSE

INFOTRAC®
COLLEGE EDITION

Keyword: probable cause

Once the initial appearance has been completed and bail has been set, the prosecutor must establish *probable cause;* that is, the prosecutor must prove that a crime was committed and link the defendant to that crime. There are two formal procedures for establishing probable cause at this stage of the pretrial process: preliminary hearings and grand juries.

The Preliminary Hearing

During the **preliminary hearing,** the defendant appears before a judge or magistrate who decides whether the evidence presented is sufficient for the case to proceed to trial. Normally, every person charged by warrant has a right to this hearing within a reasonable amount of time after his or her initial arrest[14]— typically, no later than ten days if the defendant is in custody or within thirty days if he or she has gained pretrial release.

The preliminary hearing is conducted in the manner of a minitrial. Typically, a police report of the arrest is presented by a law enforcement officer, supplemented with evidence provided by the prosecutor. Because the burden of proving probable cause is relatively light (compared to proving guilt beyond a reasonable doubt), prosecutors rarely call witnesses during the preliminary hearing, saving them for the trial. During this hearing, the defendant has a right to be represented by counsel, who may cross-examine witnesses and challenge any evidence offered by the prosecutor. In most states, defense attorneys can take advantage of the preliminary hearing to begin the process of **discovery,** in which they are entitled to have access to any evidence in the possession of the prosecution relating to the case. Discovery is considered a keystone in the adver-

PRELIMINARY HEARING
An initial hearing in which a magistrate decides if there is probable cause to believe that the defendant committed the crime with which he or she is charged.

DISCOVERY
Formal investigation prior to trial. During discovery, the defense uses various methods to obtain information from the prosecution to prepare for trial.

sary process, as it allows the defense to see the evidence against the defendant prior to making a plea.

The preliminary hearing often seems rather perfunctory, although in some jurisdictions, it replaces grand jury proceedings. It usually lasts no longer than five minutes, and the judge or magistrate rarely finds that probable cause does not exist. In one study, only 2 percent of the cases were dismissed by the judicial official at this stage in the process.[15] For this reason, defense attorneys commonly advise their clients to waive their right to a preliminary hearing. Once a judge has ruled affirmatively on probable cause, the defendant is bound over to the grand jury in many jurisdictions. If the grand jury believes there are grounds for a trial, it issues an indictment. In other jurisdictions, the government prosecutor issues an **information,** which replaces the police complaint as the formal charge against the defendant for the purposes of a trial.

The Grand Jury

The federal government and about half of the states require a grand jury to make the decision as to whether a case should go to trial. A **grand jury** is a group of citizens called to decide whether probable cause exists. Grand juries are *impaneled,* or created, for a period of time usually not exceeding three months. During that time, the grand jury sits in closed (secret) session and hears only evidence presented by the prosecutor—the defendant cannot present evidence at this hearing. The prosecutor presents to the grand jury whatever evidence the state has against the defendant, including photographs, documents, tangible objects, the testimony of witnesses, and other items. If the grand jury finds that probable cause exists, it issues an **indictment** against the defendant. Like an information in a preliminary hearing, the indictment becomes the formal charge against the defendant.

Because the grand jury is given only one version of the facts—the prosecution's—it is likely to find probable cause. Defendants are indicted at a rate of nearly 99.5 percent.[16] In the words of one observer, a grand jury would indict a "ham sandwich" if the government asked it to do so.[17]

THE PROSECUTOR IN ACTION

Once police have charged a defendant with committing a crime, prosecutors can prosecute the case as it stands, reduce or increase the initial charge, file additional charges, or dismiss the case. Indeed, the discretion of a prosecutor when it comes to charging a person with having committed a crime is far ranging. It is not, however, entirely correct to say such powers are unlimited. Controls are indirect and informal, but they do exist.[18]

Case Attrition

Prosecutorial discretion includes the power *not* to prosecute cases. Figure 9.3 depicts the average outcomes of one hundred felony arrests in the United States. As you can see, of the one hundred arrestees brought before the district attorney, only thirty-five were prosecuted, and only twenty–three of these prosecutions led to incarceration. Consequently, only 36 percent of adults arrested for a felony sees the inside of a prison or jail cell. This phenomenon is known as **case attrition,** and it is explained in part by prosecutorial discretion.

According to Figure 9.3, about half of those adult felony cases brought to prosecutors by police are dropped, or dismissed through a *nolle prosequi;* that is, the district attorney chooses not to prosecute. Why are these cases "nolled"? In the section on law enforcement, you learned that the police do not have the resources to arrest every lawbreaker in the nation. Similarly, district attorneys do not have

---

I N F O T R A C®
COLLEGE EDITION
Keyword: grand jury

"Let me tell you, you can paint pictures and get people indicted for just about anything."

—Alfonse D'Amato, *former U.S. senator from New York* (1996)

INFORMATION
The formal charge against the accused issued by the prosecutor after a preliminary hearing has found probable cause.

GRAND JURY
The group of citizens called to decide whether probable cause exists to believe that a suspect committed the crime with which she or he has been charged.

INDICTMENT
A charge or written accusation, issued by a grand jury, that probable cause exists to believe that a named person has committed a crime.

CASE ATTRITION
The process through which prosecutors, by deciding whether or not to prosecute each person arrested, effect an overall reduction in the number of persons prosecuted. As a result, the number of persons convicted and sentenced is much smaller than the number of persons arrested.

FIGURE 9.3
Following One Hundred Felony Arrests: The Criminal Justice Funnel

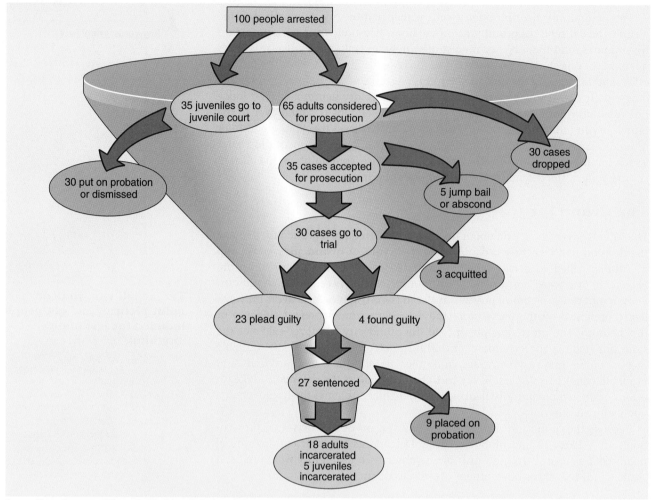

Source: Brian Reaves and Pheny Smith, *Felony Defendants in Large Urban Counties, 1992* (Washington D.C.: Bureau of Justice Statistics, 1995).

the resources to prosecute every arrest. They must choose how to distribute their scarce resources. In some cases, the decision is made for them, such as when police break procedural law and negate important evidence. This happens rarely—less than 1 percent of felony arrests are dropped because of the exclusionary rule, and almost all of these are the result of illegal drug searches.[19]

Most prosecutors have a *screening process* for deciding when to prosecute and when to "noll." This process varies a bit from jurisdiction to jurisdiction, but most prosecutors consider several factors in making the decision:

- The most important factor in deciding whether to prosecute is not the prosecutor's belief in the guilt of the suspect, but whether there is *sufficient evidence for conviction.*[20] If prosecutors have strong physical evidence and a number of reliable and believable witnesses, they are quite likely to prosecute.

- Prosecutors also tend to establish *case priorities.* In other words, everything else being equal, a district attorney will prosecute a rapist instead of a jaywalker because the former presents a greater threat to society than does the latter. A prosecutor will also be more likely to prosecute someone with an extensive record of wrongdoing than a first-time offender. Often, in coordination with the police, a district attorney's office will target a single area of crime, such as drug use or drunk driving.

- Sometimes a case is dropped even when it involves a serious crime and a wealth of evidence exists against the suspect. These situations usually involve *uncooperative victims.* For example, violent offenses committed by one member of a family against another member are difficult to prosecute because the victim is often unwilling to cooperate. Despite legislative and law enforcement attempts to protect victims of domestic violence (discussed at more length in Chapter 4), prosecutors are three times more likely to drop charges after arrests for intrafamily violence than for violence between strangers.[21]

- *Unreliability of victims* can also affect a charging decision. If the victim in a rape case is a crack addict and a prostitute, while the defendant is the chief executive officer of a large corporation, prosecutors may be hesitant to have a jury decide which one is more trustworthy.

- A prosecutor may be willing to drop a case, or reduce the charges, against a *defendant who is willing to testify against other offenders.* In New Jersey, for example, prosecutors are allowed to waive mandatory sentencing laws for low-level drug traffickers who agree to "snitch," or give the police information on major narcotics suppliers.[22]

Rolando Cruz, right, spent twelve years in prison for a rape/murder he did not commit. When he was released by a judge's order, attention turned toward the efforts made by Illinois state prosecutors to see that Cruz died in the electric chair. Following an official investigation, three of the prosecutors in the Cruz case were indicted for conspiracy and obstruction of justice. A grand jury decided that the three prosecutors had purposefully lied and fabricated evidence in their zealous advocacy of Cruz's guilt. In 1999, however, a Chicago jury found all three not guilty of the charges. (AP Photo/ Beth A. Keiser)

Furthermore, in certain situations the "interests of justice" do not seem to warrant aggressive prosecutorial action. For example, pop singer George Michael was arrested for committing an unspecified "lewd act" in a park in Beverly Hills, California. The crime carries a penalty of up to six months in jail, but the district attorney's office instead fined Michael $810, ordered him to perform eighty hours of community service, and forbade him to return to the park.

Prosecutorial Charging and the Defense Attorney

For the most part, there is little the defense attorney can do when the prosecutor decides to charge a client. If a defense attorney feels strongly that the charge has been made in violation of the defendant's rights, he or she can, however, submit *pretrial motions* to the court requesting that a particular action be taken to protect his or her client. Pretrial motions include the following:

1. Motions to suppress evidence gained illegally.
2. Motions for a change of venue because the defendant cannot receive a fair trial in the original jurisdiction.
3. Motions to invalidate a search warrant.
4. Motions to dismiss the case because of a delay in bringing it to trial.
5. Motions to obtain evidence that the prosecution may be withholding.

As we shall soon see, defense attorneys sometimes use these pretrial motions to pressure the prosecution into offering a favorable deal for their clients.

PLEADING GUILTY

Based on the information (delivered during the preliminary hearing) or indictment (handed down by the grand jury), the prosecutor submits a motion to the court to order the defendant to appear before the trial court for an **arraignment.** Due process of law, as guaranteed by the Fifth Amendment, requires that a criminal defendant be informed of the charges brought against her or him and be

ARRAIGNMENT
A court proceeding in which the suspect is formally charged with the criminal offense stated in the indictment. The suspect enters a plea (guilty, not guilty, *nolo contendere*) in response.

NOLO CONTENDERE
Latin for "I will not contest it." A criminal defendant's plea, in which he or she chooses not to challenge, or contest, the charges brought by the government. Although the defendant may still be sentenced or fined, the plea neither admits nor denies guilt.

PLEA BARGAINING
The process by which the accused and the prosecutor work out a mutually satisfactory conclusion to the case, subject to court approval. Usually, plea bargaining involves the defendant's pleading guilty to a lesser offense in return for a lighter sentence.

INFOTRAC®
COLLEGE EDITION

Keyword: plea bargaining

On September 9, 1998, Jeremy Strohmeyer pleaded guilty to kidnapping, molesting, and strangling a seven-year-old girl in the Primadonna casino outside of Las Vegas. The plea bargain was made with the express purpose of avoiding the death penalty. "For the sake of his parents, he chose to be assured he would live," said Leslie Abramson, Strohmeyer's attorney. Cases such as this one invariably lead to criticism of plea bargaining as a means for criminals to "get off" with light sentences. In contrast, how does the practice benefit the criminal justice system? (AP Photo/Lennox McLendon)

offered an opportunity to respond to those charges. The arraignment is one of the ways in which due process requirements are satisfied by criminal procedure law.

At the arraignment, the defendant is informed of the charges and must respond by pleading not guilty or guilty. In some but not all states, the defendant may also enter a plea of **nolo contendere,** which is Latin for "I will not contest it." The plea of *nolo contendere* is neither an admission nor a denial of guilt. (The consequences for someone who pleads guilty and for someone who pleads *nolo contendere* are the same in a criminal trial, but the latter plea cannot be used in a subsequent civil trial as an admission of guilt.) Most frequently, the defendant pleads guilty to the initial charge or to a lesser charge that has been agreed on through *plea bargaining* between the prosecutor and defendant. If the defendant pleads guilty, no trial is necessary, and the defendant is sentenced based on the crime he or she has admitted committing.

Plea Bargaining in the Criminal Justice System

Plea bargaining usually takes place after the arraignment and before the beginning of the trial. In its simplest terms, it is a process by which the accused, represented by the defense counsel, and the prosecutor work out a mutually satisfactory disposition of the case, subject to court approval.

In *Santobello v. New York* (1971),[23] the United States Supreme Court held that plea bargaining "is not only an essential part of the process but a highly desirable part for many reasons." Many observers would agree, but with ambivalence. They understand that plea bargaining offers the practical benefit of saving court resources, but question whether it is the best way to achieve justice.[24] Given the pressures placed on the court system, many participants conclude that plea bargaining is, in fact, an ethically acceptable means of determining the defendant's fate.

Motivations for Plea Bargaining

Given the high rate of plea bargaining—see Figure 9.4—it follows that the prosecutor, defense attorney, and defendant each have strong reasons to engage in the practice.

Prosecutors and Plea Bargaining. In most cases, a prosecutor has a single goal after charging a defendant with a crime: conviction. If a case goes to trial, no matter how certain a prosecutor may be that a defendant is guilty, there is always a chance that a jury or judge will disagree. Plea bargaining removes this risk. Furthermore, the prosecutorial screening process described earlier in the chapter is not infallible. Sometimes, a prosecutor will find that the evidence against the accused is weaker than first thought or will uncover new information that changes the complexion of the case. In these situations, the prosecutor may decide to drop the charges or, if he or she still feels that the defendant is guilty, turn to plea bargaining to "save" a questionable case.

The prosecutor's role as an administrator also comes into play. She or he may be interested in the quickest, most efficient manner to dispose of caseloads, and plea bargains reduce the time and money spent on each case. Personal philosophy can affect the proceedings as well. A prosecutor who feels that a mandatory minimum sentence for a particular crime, such as marijuana possession, is too strict may plea bargain in order to lessen the penalty. Similarly, some prosecutors will consider plea bargaining only in certain instances—for burglary and theft, for example, but not for more serious felonies such as rape and murder.[25]

Rates of Plea Bargaining

As you can see, most convictions are gained when the defendant pleads guilty. The numbers used here refer to convictions in cases terminating in federal courts between October 1, 1998, and September 30, 1999.

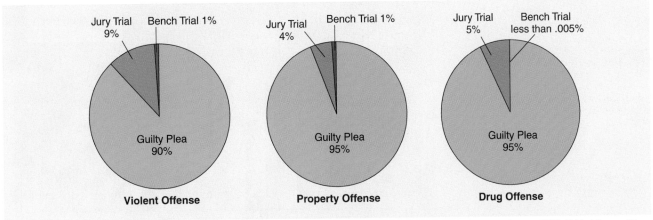

Source: Adapted from Bureau of Justice Statistics, *Compendium of Federal Justice Statistics, 1999* (Washington, D.C.: U.S. Department of Justice, 2001), Table 4.2, page 56.

Defense Attorneys and Plea Bargaining. Political scientist Milton Heumann has said that the most important thing that a defense attorney learns is that "most of his clients are guilty."[26] Given this stark reality, favorable plea bargains are often the best a defense attorney can do for clients, aside from helping them to gain acquittals. Some have suggested that defense attorneys have other, less savory motives for convincing a client to plead guilty, such as a desire to increase profit margins by quickly disposing of cases[27] or a wish to ingratiate themselves with the other members of the courtroom work group by showing their "reasonableness."[28] In other cases, a defense attorney may want to go to trial, even though it is not in the client's best interest, to win publicity or gain work experience.[29]

Defendants and Plea Bargaining. The plea bargain allows the defendant a measure of control over his or her fate. When Unabomber Ted Kaczynski accepted the government's plea bargain for life imprisonment, against the wishes of his defense counsel, he did so because he wanted to spare himself a trial that would have focused on his mental health.[30] The benefits of plea bargaining are tangible. As Figure 9.5 on page 230 shows, defendants who plea bargain receive lighter sentences on average than those who are found guilty at trial.

Courts do take precautions to assure that defendants are not unduly pressured into accepting a plea bargain. Many jurisdictions require that the accused sign a form stating that he or she agrees to the plea bargain and waives the right to trial.

Going to Trial

The pretrial process does not inexorably lead to a guilty plea. Just as prosecutors, defense attorneys, and defendants have reasons to negotiate, they may also be motivated to take a case to trial. If either side is confident in the strength of its arguments and evidence, it will obviously be less likely to accept a plea bargain. Both prosecutors and defense attorneys may favor a trial to gain publicity, and sometimes public pressure after an extremely violent or high-profile crime will force a chief prosecutor (who is, remember, normally an elected official) to take a weak case to trial. Also, some defendants may insist on their right to a trial, regardless of their attorney's advice. Later in this chapter, we will examine what happens to the 10 percent of indictments that do lead to the courtroom.

"I pleaded guilty on second degree murder because they said there is too much evidence, but I ain't shot no man, but I take the fault for the other man. . . . I just pleaded guilty because they said if I didn't they would gas me for it, and that is all."

—Henry Alford, *who claimed that he pleaded guilty to a murder charge only because he faced the threat of the death penalty if the case went to trial (1970)*

FIGURE 9.5
Sentencing Outcomes for Guilty Pleas

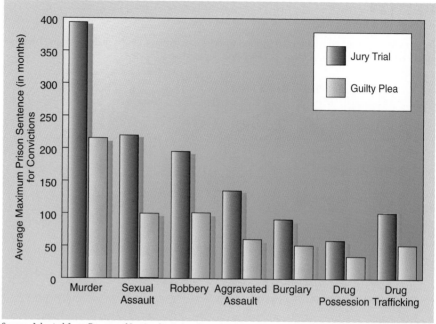

FIGURE 9.5
Sentencing Outcomes for Guilty Pleas

Source: Adapted from Bureau of Justice Statistics, *State Court Sentencing of Convicted Felons, 1998* (Washington, D.C.: U.S. Department of Justice, 2001), Table 4.5.

"[O]ur fundamental principles of justice declare that the defendant is as innocent on the day before his trial as he is on the morning after his acquittal."

—Thurgood Marshall, *United States Supreme Court associate justice* (1987)

INFOTRAC®
COLLEGE EDITION

Keywords:
speedy, trial;
Sixth Amendment

SPECIAL FEATURES OF CRIMINAL TRIALS

Criminal trial procedures reflect the need to protect criminal defendants against the power of the state by providing them with a number of rights. Many of the significant rights of the accused are spelled out in the Sixth Amendment, which reads, in part, as follows:

> In all criminal prosecutions, the accused shall enjoy the right to a speedy and public trial, by an impartial jury of the State and the district wherein the crime shall have been committed, . . . and to be informed of the nature and cause of the accusation; to be confronted with the witnesses against him; to have compulsory process for obtaining witnesses in his favor; and to have the Assistance of Counsel for his defense.

In this section, we will examine the aspects of the criminal trial that make it unique, beginning with two protections explicitly stated in the Sixth Amendment: the right to a speedy trial by an impartial jury. (For a discussion of how televising trials might affect a defendant's Sixth Amendment rights, see the feature *Criminal Justice in Action—Cameras in the Courtroom: Is Justice Served?* at the end of this chapter.)

A "Speedy" Trial

As you have just read, the Sixth Amendment requires a speedy trial for those accused of a criminal act. The reason for this requirement is obvious: depending on various factors, the defendant may lose his or her right to move freely and may be incarcerated prior to trial. Also, the accusation that a person has committed a crime jeopardizes that person's reputation in the community. If the defendant is innocent, the sooner the trial is held, the sooner his or her innocence can be established in the eyes of the court and the public.

The Speedy Trial Act of 1974[31] (amended in 1979) specifies time limits for those in the federal court system. This act requires:

❶ No more than thirty days between arrest and indictment.

❷ No more than ten days between indictment and arraignment.

3 No more than sixty days between arraignment and trial.

Federal law allows extra time for hearings on pretrial motions, mental competency examinations, and other procedural actions.

Note that when discussing issues of a "speedy trial," the primary issue is the time period between the arrest and the beginning of the actual trial, not the length of the trial itself. Indeed, most trials are completed relatively quickly, as you can see in Figure 9.6.

The Role of the Jury

The Sixth Amendment also states that anyone accused of a crime shall be judged by "an impartial jury." In *Duncan v. Louisiana* (1968),[32] the United States Supreme Court solidified this right by ruling that in all felony cases, the defendant is entitled to a **jury trial.** The Court has, however, left it to the individual states to decide whether juries are required for misdemeanor cases.[33] If the defendant waives her or his right to trial by jury, a **bench trial** takes place in which a judge decides questions of legality and fact, and no jury is involved.

The predominant American jury consists of twelve persons, and in most jurisdictions, jury verdicts in criminal cases must be *unanimous* for **acquittal** or conviction; that is, all twelve jurors must agree that the defendant is innocent or guilty. There are some exceptions, however. About half of the states allow fewer than twelve persons on criminal juries, though the United States Supreme Court has struck down attempts to use juries with fewer than six members.[34] Furthermore, five states—Oklahoma, Texas, Oregon, Montana, and Louisiana—permit nonunanimous trial verdicts, though none allows more than three dissenting votes for convictions by twelve-person juries.

The Privilege against Self-Incrimination

In addition to the Sixth Amendment, which specifies the protections we have just discussed, the Fifth Amendment to the Constitution also provides important safeguards for the defendant. The Fifth Amendment states that no person "shall be compelled in any criminal case to be a witness against himself." Therefore, a defendant has the right *not* to testify at a trial if to do so would implicate him or her in the crime. Witnesses may also refuse to testify on this ground. For example, if a witness, while testifying, is asked a question and the answer would reveal her or his own criminal wrongdoing, the witness may "take the Fifth." In other words, she or he can refuse to testify on the ground that such testimony may be self-incriminating. This rarely occurs, however, as witnesses are often granted immunity before testifying, meaning that no information they disclose can be used to bring criminal charges against them. Witnesses who have been granted immunity cannot refuse to answer questions on the basis of self-incrimination.

It is important to note that not only does the defendant have the right to "take the Fifth," but also that the decision to do so should not prejudice the jury in the prosecution's favor. The United States Supreme Court came to this controversial decision while reviewing *Adamson v. California* (1947),[35] a case involving the convictions of two defendants who had declined to testify in their own defense against charges of robbery, kidnapping, and murder. The prosecutor in *Adamson* frequently and insistently brought this silence to the notice of the jury in his closing argument, insinuating that if the pair had been innocent, they would not have been afraid to testify. The Court ruled that such tactics effectively invalidated the Fifth Amendment by using the defendants' refusal to testify against them. Now judges are required to inform the jury that an accused's decision to remain silent cannot be held against him or her. (For a look at the right to remain silent in Great Britain, see the feature *Cross-National CJ Comparison: The British Right to Remain Silent* on the following page.)

FIGURE 9.6
The Length of Criminal Trials in U.S. District Courts
Because many of the trials in the public eye last for weeks, one could easily get the impression that trials are lengthy undertakings. As you see here, that is not true in most cases.

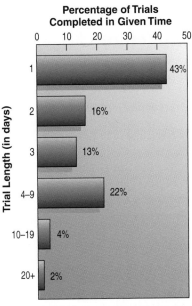

Percentage of Trials Completed in Given Time

Trial Length (in days):
- 1: 43%
- 2: 16%
- 3: 13%
- 4–9: 22%
- 10–19: 4%
- 20+: 2%

Source: Bureau of Justice Statistics, *Sourcebook of Criminal Justice Statistics, 1997* (Washington, D.C.: U.S. Department of Justice, 1998), 417–18.

INFOTRAC® COLLEGE EDITION
Keyword: Fifth Amendment

JURY TRIAL
A trial before a judge and a jury.

BENCH TRIAL
A trial conducted without a jury, in which a judge makes the determination of the defendant's guilt or innocence.

ACQUITTAL
A declaration following a trial that the individual accused of the crime is innocent in the eyes of the law and thus absolved from the charges.

Under current court interpretations of the Fifth Amendment and because of the *Miranda* ruling, when police officers question a suspect, the suspect can remain silent. No adverse inference may be drawn from the suspect's refusal to speak to police or to testify at trial. Thus, under current law, a defendant's refusal to take the stand could be interpreted negatively by everyone in the country—except by the twelve jurors.

Great Britain has had its own version of the Fifth Amendment (no person "shall be compelled in any criminal case to be a witness against himself"). Since a 1994 act of Parliament, however, at trial an adverse inference *may* be drawn from the defendant's refusal to speak when questioned by the police. In Britain, at each arrest, the arresting officer tells the suspect that he or she need not say anything, but "it may harm your defense if you do not mention when questioned something which you later rely on in court." In plain words, silence may be used as evidence of guilt in Britain.

FOR CRITICAL ANALYSIS
Should juries be made aware that a defendant has refused to answer a relevant question? What impact would allowing silence to be used as evidence have on American criminal trials?

On the Web

A group of college students has put together a Web site that addresses the most important aspects of the criminal trial in the United States. For a link to this highly informative site, go to the Hypercontents page for this chapter at **http://www.cj.wadsworth.com/gainescore2e**.

INFOTRAC®
COLLEGE EDITION

Keyword: jury size

BEYOND A REASONABLE DOUBT
The standard used to determine the guilt or innocence of a person charged with a crime. To be guilty of a crime, a suspect must be proved guilty "beyond and to the exclusion of a reasonable doubt."

The Presumption of a Defendant's Innocence

A presumption in criminal law is that a defendant is innocent until proved guilty. The burden of proving guilt falls on the state (the public prosecutor). Even if a defendant did in fact commit the crime, she or he will be "innocent" in the eyes of the law unless the prosecutor can substantiate the charge with sufficient evidence to convince a jury (or judge in a bench trial) of the defendant's guilt.[36]

A Strict Standard of Proof

In a criminal trial, the defendant is not required to prove his or her innocence. As mentioned, the burden of proving the defendant's guilt lies entirely with the state. Furthermore, the state must prove the defendant's guilt **beyond a reasonable doubt;** that is, the prosecution must show that, based on all the evidence, the defendant's guilt is clear and unquestionable. In *In re Winship* (1970),[37] a case involving the due process rights of juveniles, the United States Supreme Court ruled that the Constitution requires the reasonable doubt standard because it reduces the risk of convicting innocent people and therefore reassures Americans of the law's moral force and legitimacy.

This high standard of proof in criminal cases reflects a fundamental social value—the belief that it is worse to convict an innocent individual than to let a guilty one go free. The consequences to the life, liberty, and reputation of an accused person from an erroneous conviction for a crime are enormous, and this has been factored into the process. Placing a high standard of proof on the prosecutor reduces the margin of error in criminal cases (at least in one direction).

Jury Selection

The initial step in a criminal trial involves choosing the jury. The main goal of jury selection is to produce a cross section of the population in the jurisdiction where the crime was committed. Sometimes, a defense attorney may argue that his or her client's trial should be moved to another community to protect against undue prejudice. Judges, mindful of the intent of the Constitution, are hesitant to grant such pretrial motions.

Besides having to live in the jurisdiction where the case is being tried, there are very few restrictions on eligibility to serve on a jury. State legislatures generally set the requirements, and they are similar in most states. For the most part, jurors must be

1 Citizens of the United States.

2 Over eighteen years of age.

3 Free of felony convictions.

4 Of the necessary good health to function in a jury setting.

5 Sufficiently intelligent to understand the issues of a trial.

The **master jury list**, sometimes called the *jury pool*, is made up of all the eligible jurors in a community. This list is usually drawn from voter registration lists or driver's license rolls, which have the benefit of being easily available and timely.

After this list has been established, the next step in gathering a jury is to draw together the **venire** (Latin for "to come"). The *venire* is composed of all those people who are notified by the clerk of the court that they have been selected for jury duty. Those selected to be part of the *venire* are ordered to report to the courthouse on the date specified by the notice.

Voir Dire.   At the courthouse, prospective jurors are gathered, and the process of selecting those who will actually hear the case begins. This selection process is not haphazard. The court ultimately seeks jurors who are free of any biases that may affect their willingness to listen to the facts of the case impartially. To this end, both the prosecutor and the defense attorney have some input into the ultimate make-up of the jury. Each attorney questions prospective jurors in a proceeding known as **voir dire** (old French for "to tell the truth").[38] During *voir dire*, jurors are required to provide the court with a significant amount of personal information, including their home address, marital status, employment status, arrest record, and life experiences.

The *voir dire* process involves both written and oral questioning of potential jurors. Attorneys fashion their inquiries in such a manner as to uncover any biases on the parts of prospective jurors and to find persons who might identify with the plights of their respective sides. As one attorney noted, though a lawyer will have many chances to talk to a jury as a whole, *voir dire* is his only chance to talk with the individual jurors.[39]

Challenges for Cause.   During *voir dire,* the attorney for each side may exercise a certain number of challenges to prevent particular persons from serving on the jury. Both sides can exercise two types of challenges: challenges "for cause" and peremptory challenges.

If a defense attorney concludes that a prospective juror is unfit to serve, the attorney may exercise a **challenge for cause** and request that that person not be included on the jury. Attorneys must provide the court with a sound, legally justifiable reason for why potential jurors are "unfit" to serve. For example, jurors can be challenged for cause if they are mentally incompetent or are proved to have a prior link—be it personal or financial—with the defendant or victim.

Jurors can also be challenged if they are outwardly biased in some way that would prejudice them for or against the defendant. The United States Supreme Court has ruled that individuals may be legally excluded from a jury in a capital case if they would under no circumstances vote for a guilty verdict if it carried the death penalty.[40] At the same time, potential jurors cannot be challenged for cause if they have "general objections" or have "expressed conscientious or religious scruples" against capital punishment.[41] The final responsibility for deciding whether a potential juror should be excluded rests with the judge, who may choose not to act on an attorney's request.

When juries are presented with compelling evidence, they can make their decision quickly. The photo above was shown as an exhibit in the 1999 murder trial of John William King, who was charged with dragging an African American named James Byrd, Jr., to his death behind a pickup truck. Jurors were shown a number of photos of images tattooed on King's body, including one that showed a black man hanging from a tree. The jury found King guilty after deliberating for only 150 minutes.

Do you agree with prosecutors that the intricate racist, satanic, and neo-Nazi tattoos covering King's body helped prove motive, intent, and state of mind? Or do you agree with the defense attorney who said that the tattoos do not necessarily make King a racist? (© Jasper County District Attorney's Office, AP Photo)

MASTER JURY LIST
The list of citizens in a court's district from which a jury can be selected; often compiled from voter registration lists, driver's license lists, and other sources.

VENIRE
The group of citizens from which the jury is selected.

VOIR DIRE
The preliminary questions that the trial attorneys ask prospective jurors to determine whether they are biased or have any connection with the defendant or a witness.

CHALLENGE FOR CAUSE
A *voir dire* challenge for which an attorney states the reason why a prospective juror should not be included on the jury.

PEREMPTORY CHALLENGES
Voir dire challenges to exclude potential jurors from serving on the jury without any supporting reason or cause.

> "A jury consists of twelve persons chosen to decide who has the better lawyer."
>
> —Robert Frost,
> *American poet* (1874–1963)

INFOTRAC®
COLLEGE EDITION

Keyword: Batson v. Kentucky

Peremptory Challenges. Each attorney may also exercise a limited number of **peremptory challenges.** These challenges are based *solely* on an attorney's subjective reasoning; that is, the attorney is usually not required to give any legally justifiable reason for wanting to exclude a particular person from the jury. Because of the rather random nature of peremptory challenges, each state limits the number that an attorney may utilize: between five and ten for felony trials (depending on the state) and ten and twenty for capital trials (also depending on the state). Once an attorney's peremptory challenges are used up, he or she must accept forthcoming jurors, unless a challenge for cause can be used.

Jury Science. A great deal of what has been called "jury folklore" has come to surround the use of peremptory challenges. According to this folklore, defense attorneys favor Jewish people, who are seen to have played the historical role of victims. Some prosecutors see jurors of Scandinavian or German descent as more willing to punish a perceived wrongdoer. Stockbrokers are considered useful for the prosecution, musicians are not, and so on.[42]

Though this folklore still exists, it is increasingly being accompanied by the phenomenon of *jury science,* which replaces guesses and intuition with a "scientific process" for determining the biases—conscious or subconscious—of the members of the jury pool. Generally, as in the trial of Thomas Blanton discussed in the chapter introduction, this science is carried out by consultants who determine the "ideal" juror profile for their client and direct the attorney to use peremptory or for-cause challenges to shape the jury accordingly.[43]

Race and Gender Issues in Jury Selection. The Sixth Amendment guarantees the right to an *impartial* jury. But, as researcher Jeremy W. Barber notes, it is in the best interests of neither the defense nor the prosecution attorneys to seek an impartial jury.[44] In fact, the goal of their peremptory challenges is to create a *partial* jury—partial, that is, toward or against the defendant. If the jury turns out to be impartial, it may be that the efforts of the two sides have balanced each other out.

For many years, prosecutors used their peremptory challenges as an instrument of *de facto* segregation in juries. Prosecutors were able to keep African Americans off juries in cases in which an African American was the defendant. The argument that African Americans—or members of any other minority group—would be partial toward one of their own was tacitly supported by the United States Supreme Court.

The Court invalidated this practice in 1986 with *Batson v. Kentucky.*[45] In this case, the Court declared that the equal protection clause prohibits prosecutors from using peremptory challenges to strike possible jurors on the basis of race. Under *Batson,* the defendant must prove that the prosecution's use of a peremptory challenge was racially motivated.

In *J.E.B. v. Alabama* (1994),[46] the United States Supreme Court extended *Batson* to cover gender bias in jury selection. The case was a civil suit for paternity and child support brought by the state of Alabama. Prosecutors used nine of their ten challenges to remove men from the jury, while the defense made similar efforts to remove women. When challenged, the state defended its actions on what it called the rational belief that men and women might have different views on the issues of paternity and child support. The Court held this to be unconstitutional under the equal protection clause.

THE TRIAL

Once the jury members are seated, the judge swears in the jury and the trial itself can begin.

Mr. FRAWLEY: I would like to start by showing you a photograph so that you can have a face to go with some of the names that you're going to be hearing throughout this trial.

This photograph is of Sherri Dally and her family. That's Michael Dally, the other adult in the picture, and Max and Devon. Max is the younger one. On the date that Sherri was killed, . . . Max was six. And Devon, he had just turned eight a couple months before.

You will learn that children were Sherri's life.

Aside from her own, she ran a day-care center out of her home.

And beyond that, the other focus of Sherri's life was Michael Dally. They had been married for fourteen years.

Michael Dally was the only male that Sherri had ever dated.

And what the evidence is going to show is that the defendant, Diana Haun, wanted to take Sherri Dally's place.

FIGURE 9.7
The Opening Statement

Sherri Dally of Ventura, California, was kidnapped from a parking lot and later killed. Prosecutors charged Diana Haun with the murder, alleging that she was in love with Dally's husband and wanted to "replace" her. In his opening statements, Deputy District Attorney Michael Frawley immediately attempts to humanize Dally for the jury, with the ultimate purpose of making her murder all the more worthy of harsh punishment.

Opening Statements

Attorneys may choose to open the trial with a statement to the jury, though they are not required to do so. In these **opening statements,** the attorneys give a brief version of the facts and the supporting evidence that they will present during the trial. Because some trials can drag on for weeks or even months, it is extremely helpful for jurors to hear a summary of what will unfold. In short, the opening statement is a kind of "road map" that describes the destination that each attorney hopes to reach and outlines how she or he plans to reach it.

The opening statement is also the first opportunity for the prosecution and defense to put their "spin" on the events being addressed in the trial. As you can read in Figure 9.7, the attorneys will often employ dramatic language in an immediate attempt to win the jury over to their side.

The Role of Evidence

Once the opening statements have been made, the prosecutor begins the trial proceedings by presenting the state's evidence against the defendant. Courts have complex rules about what types of evidence may be presented and how the evidence may be brought out during the trial. **Evidence** is anything that is used to prove the existence or nonexistence of a fact. For the most part, evidence can be broken down into two categories: testimony and real evidence. **Testimony** consists of statements by competent witnesses. **Real evidence,** presented to the court in the form of exhibits, includes any physical items—such as the murder weapon or a blood-stained piece of clothing—that affect the case. (Given the huge amount of testimony and evidence that can accumulate during a trial, efforts are being made to "streamline" the trial process. To learn more, see the feature *Criminal Justice & Technology—The Electronic Courtroom* on page 236.)

Testimonial Evidence. A person who is called to testify on factual matters that would be understood by the average citizen is referred to as a **lay witness.** If asked about the condition of a victim of an assault, for example, a lay witness could relate certain facts, such as "she was bleeding from her forehead" or "she lay unconscious on the ground for several minutes." A lay witness could not, however, give information about the medical extent of the victim's injuries, such as whether she suffered from a fractured skull or internal bleeding. Coming from a lay witness, such testimony would be inadmissible. When the matter in question requires scientific, medical, or technical skill beyond the scope of the average person, prosecutors and defense attorneys may call an **expert witness** to the stand. The expert witness is an individual who has professional training,

OPENING STATEMENTS
The attorneys' statements to the jury at the beginning of the trial. Each side briefly outlines the evidence that will be offered during the trial and the legal theory that will be pursued.

EVIDENCE
Anything that is used to prove the existence or nonexistence of a fact.

TESTIMONY
Verbal evidence given by witnesses under oath.

REAL EVIDENCE
Evidence that is brought into court and seen by the jury, as opposed to evidence that is described for a jury.

LAY WITNESS
A witness who can truthfully and accurately testify on a fact in question without having specialized training or knowledge; an ordinary witness.

EXPERT WITNESS
A witness with professional training or substantial experience qualifying her or him to testify on a certain subject.

Criminal Justice & TECHNOLOGY

The Electronic Courtroom

"Never forget that the human race with technology is like an alcoholic with a barrel of wine," wrote "Unabomber" Ted Kaczynski in his manifesto "Industrial Society and Its Future." Taking the analogy one step further, Kaczynski could have expected to see a great deal of "drunkenness" in the high-tech courtroom in Sacramento, California, where his trial was slated to take place. Courtrooms across the country are increasingly employing technological features with the ultimate goal of making the trial process faster and more efficient.

Beyond the Paperless Trial

For several years, members of the courtroom work group have had access to technology that allows them to avoid the drawbacks of the paper-driven trial. Using digital imaging, they can store thousands of pages of testimony and evidence, photographs, blueprints, maps, and graphics on CD-ROMs and hard drives. With portable computers, attorneys can easily access these data and, in some cases, present them to judges and jurors on large screens. Even with the new tools, however, most courtrooms are not as efficient as they could be. If one side's equipment is not compatible with that of the other side or with the system used

by the court, then each side must install its own apparatus, a time-consuming and expensive process. With this in mind, federal officials are experimenting with the totally media integrated courtroom.

Under the floor of this electronic courtroom, cabling connects video, audio, and real-time transcription equipment to terminals at both lawyers' work areas and the judge's bench. Branching out from a central control panel, the system converts data to a format that can be displayed on sixteen different monitors around the courtroom, including one for each juror. A special monitor on the witness stand allows the witness to use a light pen to highlight areas of a document as both the document and the additions appear on the courtroom's screens.

One of the many benefits of this integrated system is the ease with which information can be passed to the jurors, most of whom are used to receiving information from a television screen. It also helps attorneys, who can download "live" transcriptions of testimony for easy recall later in the trial without having to rely on a court reporter to find and read back certain passages. Judges benefit as well: a "kill switch" will enable them to turn off jury monitors while deciding whether evidence contested by the prosecution or defense is admissible.

IN THE FUTURE

Only five federal courtrooms in the United States can boast this level of technological integration. The cost—$150,000 for the equipment alone—assures that the electronic courtroom will not be a reality in most state courts for some years to come.

---

advanced knowledge, or substantial experience in a specialized area, such as medicine, computer technology, or ballistics.

Direct versus Circumstantial Evidence.   Two types of testimonial evidence may be brought into court: direct evidence and circumstantial evidence. **Direct evidence** is evidence that has been witnessed by the person giving testimony. "I saw Bill shoot Chris" is an example of direct evidence. **Circumstantial evidence** is indirect evidence that, even if believed, does not establish the fact in question but only the degree of likelihood of the fact. In other words, circumstantial evidence can create an inference that a fact exists.

Suppose, for example, that the defendant owns a gun that shoots bullets of the type found in the victim's body. This circumstantial evidence, by itself, does not establish that the defendant committed the crime. Combined with other circumstantial evidence, however, it may do just that. For instance, if other circumstantial evidence indicates that the defendant had a motive for harming the victim and was at the scene of the crime when the shooting occurred, the jury might conclude that the defendant committed the crime.

Relevance.   Evidence will not be admitted in court unless it is relevant to the case being considered. **Relevant evidence** is evidence that tends to prove or disprove a fact in question. Forensic proof that the bullets found in a victim's body were fired from a gun discovered in the suspect's pocket at the time of arrest, for example, is certainly relevant. The suspect's prior record, showing a convic-

DIRECT EVIDENCE
Evidence that establishes the existence of a fact that is in question without relying on inference.

CIRCUMSTANTIAL EVIDENCE
Indirect evidence that is offered to establish, by inference, the likelihood of a fact that is in question.

RELEVANT EVIDENCE
Evidence tending to make a fact in question more or less probable than it would be without the evidence. Only relevant evidence is admissible in court.

tion for armed robbery ten years earlier, is, as we shall see in the next section, irrelevant to the case at hand and in most instances will be ruled inadmissible by the judge.

Prejudicial Evidence. Evidence may be excluded if it would tend to distract the jury from the main issues of the case, mislead the jury, or cause jurors to decide the issue on an emotional basis. In American trial courts, this rule precludes prosecutors from using prior purported criminal activities or actual convictions to show that the defendant has criminal propensities or an "evil character."[47]

This concept is codified in the Federal Rules of Evidence, which state that evidence of "other crimes, wrongs, or acts is not admissible to prove the character of a person in order to show action in conformity therewith." Such evidence is allowed only when it does not apply to character construction and focuses instead on "motive, opportunity, intent, preparation, plan, knowledge, identity, or absence of mistake or accident."[48]

Though this legal concept has come under a great deal of criticism, it is consistent with the presumption of innocence standards discussed earlier. Presumably, if a prosecutor is allowed to establish that the defendant has shown antisocial or even violent character traits, this will prejudice the jury against the defendant.

The Prosecution's Case

Because the burden of proof is on the state, the prosecution is generally considered to have a more difficult task than the defense. The prosecutor attempts to establish guilt beyond a reasonable doubt by presenting the *corpus delicti* ("body of the offense" in Latin) of the crime to the jury. The *corpus delicti* is simply a legal term that refers to the substantial facts that show a crime has been committed. By establishing such facts through the presentation of evidence, the prosecutor hopes to convince the jury of the defendant's guilt.

Witnesses are crucial to establishing the prosecutor's case against the defendant. The prosecutor will call witnesses to the stand and ask them questions pertaining to the sequence of events that the trial is addressing. This form of questioning is known as **direct examination.** During direct examination, the prosecutor will usually not be allowed to ask *leading questions*—questions that might suggest to the witness a particular desired response. A leading question might be something like "So, Mrs. Williams, you noticed the defendant threatening the victim with a broken beer bottle?" If Mrs. Williams answers "yes" to this question, she has, in effect, been "led" to the conclusion that the defendant was, in fact, threatening with a broken beer bottle. (A properly worded query would be, "Mrs. Williams, please describe the defendant's manner toward the victim during the incident.") The fundamental purpose behind testimony is to establish what actually happened, not what the trial attorneys would like the jury to believe happened.

When interviewing a witness, both the prosecutor and the defense attorney will make sure that the witness's statements are based on the witness's own knowledge and not hearsay. **Hearsay** can be defined as any testimony given in court about a statement made by someone else.[49] Literally, it is what someone heard someone else say. For the most part, hearsay is not admissible as evidence.[50] It is excluded because the listener may have misunderstood what the other person said, and without the opportunity of cross-examining the originator of the statement, the misconception cannot be challenged.

The job of the prosecution is to remove any traces of doubt concerning the defendant's guilt. This task can prove more difficult when the alleged crime took place many years earlier, as was the case in the 2002 trial of Kenneth K. Behrel, the longtime chaplain of the St. James School near Hagerstown, Maryland. Behrel was eventually found guilty of sexually molesting a male student in the early 1980s. A key piece of evidence in Behrel's trial was a black footlocker containing pornography that his victim had described to police officers. Is this footlocker direct evidence or circumstantial evidence of any wrongdoing? (AP Photo/Dennis Grundman)

DIRECT EXAMINATION
The examination of a witness by the attorney who calls the witness to the stand to testify.

HEARSAY
An oral or written statement made by an out-of-court declarant that is later offered in court by a witness (not the declarant) concerning a matter before the court. Hearsay usually is not admissible as evidence.

It is extremely rare for a defendant to be convicted of first degree, or premeditated, murder when neither the body of the victim nor a murder weapon can be found. About sixty people have been convicted of murder without the body of the victim, including Thomas Capano, above, who was found guilty of killing his lover. The circumstantial evidence in the case, including an admission by Capano's brother that the two had dumped a body seventy miles off the New Jersey coast on the night of the murder, was sufficient for the jury to deliver a guilty verdict and recommend the death penalty. Why do you think the body of the victim has been so important in establishing that a defendant is guilty beyond a reasonable doubt? (AP Photo/Tim Shaffer)

Cross-Examination

After the prosecutor has directly examined her or his witnesses, the defense attorney is given the chance to question the same witnesses. The Sixth Amendment states that "In all criminal prosecutions, the accused shall enjoy the right . . . to be confronted with witnesses against him." In practical terms, this gives the accused, through his or her attorneys, the right to cross-examine witnesses. **Cross-examination** refers to the questioning of an opposing witness during trial, and both sides of a case are allowed to do so.

Cross-examination allows the attorneys to test the truthfulness of opposing witnesses and usually entails efforts to create doubt in the jurors' minds that the witness is reliable. Cross-examination is also linked to the problems presented by hearsay evidence. When a witness offers hearsay, the person making the original remarks is not in the court and therefore cannot be cross-examined. If such testimony were allowed, the defendant's Sixth Amendment right to confront witnesses against him or her would be violated.

After the defense has cross-examined a prosecution witness, the prosecutor may want to reestablish any reliability that might have been lost. The prosecutor can do so by again questioning the witness, a process known as *redirect examination.* Following the redirect examination, the defense attorney will be given the opportunity for *recross-examination,* or to ask further questions of prosecution witnesses. Thus, each side has two opportunities to question a witness. The attorneys need not do so, but only after each side has been offered the opportunity will the trial move on to the next witness or the next stage.

The Defendant's Case

After the prosecutor has finished presenting evidence against the defendant, the defense attorney may offer the defendant's case. Because the burden is on the state to prove the accused's guilt, the defense is not required to offer any case at all. It can simply "rest" without calling any witnesses or producing any real evidence and ask the jury to judge the merits of the case on what it has seen and heard from the prosecution.

Creating a Reasonable Doubt. Defense lawyers most commonly defend their clients by attempting to expose weaknesses in the prosecutor's case. Remember that if the defense attorney can create reasonable doubt concerning the client's guilt in the mind of just a single juror, the defendant has a good chance of gaining an acquittal or at least a hung jury. Even in cases in which the defendant's guilt seems obvious, the defense may be able to create doubt through cross-examination, calling its own witnesses, and attacking the prosecution's evidence. Defense lawyers for Theodore J. Kaczynski, the Unabomber, were faced with a daunting task: a great deal of evidence in their client's Montana cabin pointed to his sending mail bombs to sixteen targets. Nevertheless, they were still confident that they could induce reasonable doubt. There were no eyewitnesses to any of the attacks and no known accomplices—all of the evidence against the defendant was circumstantial. The prosecution could prove without a doubt that Kaczynski made bombs, but that did not necessarily make him the Unabomber.

Other Defense Strategies. The defense can choose among a number of strategies to generate reasonable doubt in the jurors' minds. It can present an *alibi defense,* by submitting evidence that the accused was not at or near the scene of the crime at the time the crime was committed. Another option is to attempt an *affirmative defense,* by presenting additional facts to the ones offered by the prosecution. Possible affirmative defenses, which we discussed in detail in Chapter 3, include the following:

CROSS-EXAMINATION
The questioning of an opposing witness during trial.

1 Self-defense

2 Insanity

3 Duress

4 Entrapment[51]

"I'm trusting in the Lord and a good lawyer."

—Oliver North, *U.S. marine officer, after being indicted for obstruction of justice (1986)*

With an affirmative defense strategy, the defense attempts to prove that the defendant should be found not guilty because of extenuating circumstances surrounding the crime. An affirmative strategy can be difficult to carry out because it forces the defense to prove the veracity of its own evidence, not simply disprove the evidence offered by the prosecution.

The defense is often willing to admit that a certain criminal act took place, especially if the defendant has already confessed. In this case, the primary question of the trial becomes not whether the defendant is guilty, but what the defendant is guilty of. In these situations, the defense strategy focuses on obtaining the lightest possible penalty for the defendant. This strategy is responsible for the high percentage of proceedings that end in plea bargains.

Rebuttal and Surrebuttal

After the defense closes its case, the prosecution is permitted to bring new evidence forward that was not used during its initial presentation to the jury. This is called the **rebuttal** stage of the trial. When the rebuttal stage is finished, the defense is given the opportunity to cross-examine the prosecution's new witnesses and introduce new witnesses of its own. This final act is part of the *surrebuttal.*

Closing Arguments

In their **closing arguments,** the attorneys summarize their presentations and argue one final time for their respective cases. In most states, the defense attorney goes first, and then the prosecutor. (In Kentucky, Colorado, and Missouri, the order is reversed.) An effective closing argument includes all of the major points that support the government's or the defense's case. It also emphasizes the shortcomings of the opposing party's case. Jurors will view a closing argument with some skepticism if it merely recites the central points of a party's claim or defense without also responding to the unfavorable facts or issues raised by the other side. Of course, neither attorney wants to focus too much on the other side's position, but the elements of the opposing position do need to be acknowledged and their flaws highlighted.

THE JURY IN ACTION

After closing arguments, the outcome of the trial is in the hands of the jury. Before the jurors begin their deliberations, the judge gives the jury a **charge,** summing up the case and instructing the jurors on the rules of law that apply to the issues in the case. These charges, also called jury instructions, are usually prepared during a special *charging conference* involving the judge and the trial attorneys. In this conference, the attorneys suggest the instructions they would like to see be sent to the jurors, but the judge makes the final decision as to the charges submitted.[52] If the defense attorney disagrees with the charges sent to the jury, he or she can enter an objection, thereby setting the stage for a possible appeal.

The judge usually begins by explaining basic legal principles such as the need to find the defendant guilty beyond a reasonable doubt. Then, the jury instructions narrow to the specifics of the case at hand, and the judge explains to the jurors what facts the prosecution must have proved in order to convict. If the defense strategy centers on an affirmative defense such as insanity or entrapment,

REBUTTAL
Evidence given to counteract or disprove evidence presented by the opposing party.

CLOSING ARGUMENTS
Arguments made by each side's attorney after the cases for the plaintiff and defendant have been presented.

CHARGE
The judge's instructions to the jury following the attorneys' closing arguments; the charge sets forth the rules of law that the jury must apply in reaching its decision, or verdict.

Terry Nichols was convicted on December 23, 1997, of conspiracy and eight counts of involuntary manslaughter in the 1995 bombing of the Oklahoma City federal building. When the twelve jurors began deliberating Nichols's fate, however, their first vote was 10–2 for acquittal. "I couldn't believe it," recalled juror Tim Burge, who initially voted to convict. "I was like, man, did I miss something here or what." It took six days of heated arguments, which left some of the jurors in tears, before a compromise verdict was worked out in which the defendant was acquitted of more serious murder and weapons-related counts. How does this case show the strengths and/or weaknesses of the jury system? (AP Photo/Orlin Wagner)

VERDICT
A formal decision made by the jury.

HUNG JURY
A jury whose members are so irreconcilably divided in their opinions that they cannot reach a verdict. In this situation, the judge may order a new trial.

APPEAL
The process of seeking a higher court's review of a lower court's decision for the purpose of correcting or changing the lower court's judgment or decision.

DOUBLE JEOPARDY
To twice place at risk (jeopardize) a person's life or liberty. The Fifth Amendment to the U.S. Constitution prohibits a second prosecution for the same criminal offense.

the judge will discuss the relevant legal principles that the defense must have proved to obtain an acquittal. The final segment of the charges discusses possible verdicts. These always include "guilty" and "not guilty," but some cases also allow for the jury to find "guilt by reason of insanity" or "guilty but mentally ill." Juries are often charged with determining the seriousness of the crime as well, such as deciding whether a homicide is murder in the first degree, murder in the second degree, or manslaughter.

Jury Deliberation

After receiving the charge, the jury begins its deliberations. Jury deliberation is a somewhat mysterious process, as it takes place in complete seclusion. In extreme cases, the judge will order that the jury be *sequestered,* or isolated from the public, during the trial and deliberation stages of the proceedings. Sequestion is used when deliberations are expected to be lengthy, or the trial is attracting a great amount of interest and the judge wants to keep the jury from being unduly influenced. Juries are usually sequestered in hotels and kept under the watch and guard of officers of the court. (For information on a courtroom participant who oversees sequestering and many other aspects of the trial, see the feature *Careers in Criminal Justice.*)

The Verdict

Once it has reached a decision, the jury issues a **verdict.** The most common verdicts are guilty and not guilty, though as we have seen, juries may signify different degrees of guilt if instructed to do so. Following the announcement of a guilty or not guilty verdict, the jurors are discharged, and the jury trial proceedings are finished. (See Figure 9.8 for a review of the steps of a jury trial.)

When a jury in a criminal trial is unable to agree on a unanimous verdict—or a majority in certain states—it returns with no decision. This is known as a **hung jury.** After the trauma of a trial, a hung jury is often unsatisfactory to the participants of the trial. When a high-profile case ends with a hung jury, as occurred in the first trial of Oklahoma City bombing (April 19, 1995) co-conspirator Terry Nichols, there is a predictably high level of disapproval in the press concerning the jury's inability to come to a decision.

APPEALS

Even if a defendant is found guilty, the trial process is not necessarily over. In our criminal justice system, a person convicted of a crime has a right to appeal. An **appeal** is the process of seeking a higher court's review of a lower court's decision for the purpose of correcting or changing the lower court's judgment. Any defendant who loses a case in a trial court cannot automatically appeal the conviction, however. The defendant normally must first be able to show that the trial court acted improperly on a question of law. Common reasons for appeals include the introduction of tainted evidence by the prosecution or faulty jury instructions delivered by the trial judge.

Double Jeopardy

The appeals process is available only to the defense. If a jury finds the accused not guilty, the prosecution cannot appeal to have the decision reversed. To do so would infringe on the defendant's Fifth Amendment rights against multiple trials for the same offense. This guarantee against being tried a second time for the same crime is known as protection from **double jeopardy.**

Careers in Criminal Justice

Collins E. Ijoma,

Trial Court Administrator

I moved to the United States from Nigeria in 1976 to complete my college education majoring in accounting and business administration. I earned a master's degree in public administration from Seton Hall University in 1982 with a concentration in public budgeting and finance. I was immensely interested in public service but was not particularly aware of the judiciary as a potential employer. My first job in the court system was by accident rather than design. After completing a graduate internship with the Essex County government, I had the opportunity to seek permanent employment with the county-funded judiciary. I was first employed in the Trial Court Administrator's Office in Newark, New Jersey, as the court finance officer in 1983. Much of my education in court administration was gained through the Institute for Court Management of the National Center for State Courts. I pur-

sued this program of professional development from 1984 through 1991 when I graduated as a fellow of ICM.

As the trial court administrator, I serve principally as the chief administrative officer to the largest trial and municipal court system in New Jersey. We provide technical and managerial support to the court (over sixty superior court judges and thirty-six municipal court judges) on such matters as personnel, program development, caseflow, resources, and facilities management. This description may sound highfalutin considering that most people can only describe a court in terms of a judge, one or two courtroom staff, and a few other employees associated with the visible activities in the courthouse. Obviously, there is a lot more going on behind the scenes that the average citizen is not aware of. For example, besides directing caseflow for the four major divisions (criminal, civil, family, and probation), the work involved in managing personnel programs for more than 1,200 employees, information systems and technology infrastructure, maintaining records of proceedings, coordination of transcription, grand and petit jury operations,

and court interpreting, to mention but a few examples, is enormous. The modern court needs dedicated professionals in each of these areas.

One thing that keeps me going and enthused about this profession is the resolve and dedication of our judges and staff. The family division embraces a host of issues, and in some cases those who seek help are hurting and desperate. The court may be their only hope. We are also actively engaged in pursuing new ways to offer and manage dispute resolution. Some of these include drug courts to give nonviolent drug offenders a chance at rehabilitation rather than going to jail, complimentary dispute resolution to reach more satisfactory conclusions in less time and at a lower cost to litigants, and creative uses of volunteers to assist in the work of the court and create a positive connection to the community.

Go to the *Careers in Criminal Justice Interactive CD* for more profiles in the field of criminal justice.

FIGURE 9.8
The Steps of a Jury Trial

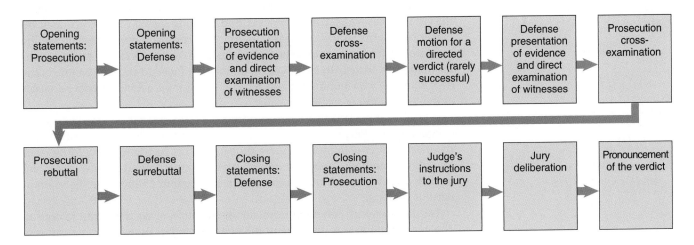

On May 6, 2002, Court of Appeals Chief Judge Judith S. Kaye and Judge Howard A. Levine enter the New York State Court of Appeals to hear arguments as to whether Darrel K. Harris should be executed by the state. The Court of Appeals eventually overturned Harris's death sentence. Six of the seven judges found that he had been unfairly forced to choose between exercising his constitutional rights under the Fifth and Sixth Amendments, or pleading guilty to a lesser charge that was not punishable by execution. How does Harris's case show the important role that appeals courts play in the criminal justice system? (AP Photo/Jim McKnight)

INFOTRAC®
COLLEGE EDITION

Keywords:
jury deliberation;
double jeopardy

"Appeal: In law, to put the dice into the box for another throw."

—Ambrose Bierce, *American author*
(c. 1900)

The basic idea of the double jeopardy clause, in the words of United States Supreme Court Justice Hugo Black, is that the state should not be allowed to

> make repeated attempts to convict an individual for an alleged offense, thereby subjecting him to embarrassment, expense and ordeal and compelling him to live in a continuing state of anxiety and insecurity, as well as enhancing the possibility that even though innocent he may be found guilty.[53]

Today, some observers are arguing that certain defendants are being unfairly subjected to the embarrassment, expense, ordeal, and anxiety against which Justice Black warned.[54] Though it remains true that a defendant may not be retried on the same criminal charge, that person can be the target of a civil suit following participation in a criminal trial. For example, in 1995, after a criminal trial, a jury acquitted O. J. Simpson of the murders of his ex-wife Nicole Brown Simpson and Ron Goldman. Sixteen months later, however, Simpson lost a civil wrongful death suit brought by the families of the victims, was found *liable* for the murders, and was ordered to pay damages of $33.5 million. This is not considered double jeopardy because the second suit involved a civil claim, not a criminal one. Therefore, Simpson, or anybody else in the same situation, has not been charged with committing the same *crime* twice.

The Appeal Process

There are two basic reasons for the appeal process. The first is to correct an error made during the initial trial. The second is to review policy. Because of this second function, the appellate courts are an important part of the flexible nature of the criminal justice system. When existing law has ceased to be effective or no longer reflects the values of society, an appellate court can effectively change the law through its decisions and the precedents that it sets.[55] A classic example was the *Miranda v. Arizona* decision, which, although it failed to change the fate of the defendant (he was found guilty on retrial), had a far-reaching impact on custodial interrogation of suspects.

It is also important to understand that once the appeal process begins, the defendant is no longer presumed innocent. The burden of proof has shifted, and the defendant is obligated to prove that her or his conviction should be overturned. The method of filing an appeal differs slightly among the fifty states and the federal government, but the six basic steps are similar enough to be summarized in Figure 9.9.

For the most part, defendants are not required to exercise their right to appeal. The one exception is in the case of the death sentence. Given the seriousness of

1. Within a specific period of time—usually between thirty and ninety days—the defendant must file a **notice of appeal**. This is a short written statement outlining the basis of the appeal.

2. The appellant, or losing party in the lower court, must then **transfer the trial court record to the appellate court.** This record includes items of the case file, including exhibits, and a transcript of the testimony.

3. Next, **the briefs must be filed**. A brief is a written argument that presents the party's legal arguments and precedents to support these arguments. Both the appellant and the winning prosecutorial team must submit briefs to the appellate court.

4. The briefs are followed by **oral arguments**, in which attorneys from both sides appear before the appellate court panel to state their positions. In oral arguments, the judge or judges ask questions of the attorneys to clarify certain points or voice a particular disagreement.

5. After the oral arguments, the judges retire to **deliberate the case**. After a decision has been made, one or more of the judges prepare the written opinion. (This process is described in Chapter 8 in more detail.) A judge who disagrees with the majority opinion may write a dissenting opinion.

6. Finally, the court holds a **disposition** in which it announces the next step for the case. The court can uphold the decision of the lower court, or it can modify the lower court decision by changing a part of it but not the whole. The lower court's decision can be reversed, or set aside, or the appellate court can reverse and remand the case, meaning that the lower court's decision is overturned and the matter is sent back for further proceedings. Or, the appellate court may simply remand the case without overturning it.

FIGURE 9.9
The Steps of an Appeal

capital punishment, the defendant is required to appeal the case, regardless of his or her wishes.

Habeas Corpus

The 1980s and early 1990s saw a rise in a postconviction process known as *habeas corpus* (Latin for "you have the body"). *Habeas corpus* is a judicial order that literally commands a corrections official to bring a prisoner before a federal court so that the court can hear the person's claim that he or she is being held illegally. A writ of *habeas corpus* differs from an appeal in several respects. First, it can be filed only by someone who is imprisoned. Second, it can address only constitutional issues, not technical errors. Thus, an inmate can file a *habeas corpus* petition claiming that the conditions of her or his imprisonment constitute cruel and unusual punishment, but not that the judge provided the jury with improper instructions during the trial.

The most aggressive move to limit *habeas corpus* review in recent years has come from Congress. In 1996, motivated by the politically popular goal of shortening the time between conviction and execution in death penalty cases, Congress passed the Anti-Terrorism and Effective Death Penalty Act, which placed a one-year time limit on filing a *habeas corpus* petition and restricted a federal court's ability to overturn a state court's criminal conviction.[56] Many observers felt that the United States Supreme Court would not uphold this legislation in the event that it was challenged on the basis that Article I of the Constitution limits Congress's ability to suspend *habeas corpus*.[57]

The Court was given the chance to do so almost immediately when Georgia inmate Ellis Wayne Felker challenged the new law, claiming it unconstitutionally limited the appeals of convicted murderers. Felker had been found guilty of rape and murder in 1983 and sentenced to die, but he had managed to elude the death penalty through *habeas corpus* petitions. In a unanimous decision, the Court rejected Felker's claim and upheld the act,[58] setting the stage for further erosion of *habeas corpus* in the future.

On the Web

In 1998, attorneys for convicted murderer Karla Faye Tucker filed a last-minute writ of *habeas corpus* in an attempt to save their client from her scheduled execution. For a link to view a copy of this writ at CourtTV's Web site, go to the Hypercontents page for this chapter at <u>http://www.cj.wadsworth.com/ gainescore2e</u>.

INFOTRAC®
COLLEGE EDITION
Keyword: habeas corpus

HABEAS CORPUS
An order that requires corrections officials to bring an inmate before a court or a judge and explain why he or she is being held in prison.

Criminal Justice in Action

Cameras in the Courtroom: Is Justice Served?

German physicist Werner Heisenberg once commented that the act of observation changes the thing that is being observed. Heisenberg was referring to Albert Einstein's theories of space and time, but this principle may also be applied to the criminal trial. In this chapter, we have discussed many of the guidelines for the trial process contained in the U.S. Constitution. The framers, however, would have been hard pressed to envision CourtTV and the modern media storm that surrounds high-profile cases. Consequently, the decision to televise or not to televise rests with individual judges. As we close this chapter, we will examine two crucial questions: (1) Does the act of televising trials change them? (2) Even if it does, should the practice continue to be allowed?

A Right or a Wrong?

The issue of media in the courtroom has been debated since the 1935 trial of Bruno Hauptman, who was charged with kidnapping and murdering the baby of aeronautic pioneer Charles Lindbergh. After the disruption caused by 120 photographers at the trial, the presiding judge banned all cameras from the courtroom, and the American Bar Association moved to remove journalists permanently from court proceedings. In the 1981 case of *Chandler v. Florida*,[59] the Supreme Court ruled that states had free rein to set their own regulations concerning cameras in the courtroom.

Those who favor cameras in the courtroom point to the First Amendment's guarantee of freedom of the press. They argue that viewers have a right of access to the trial process and that this scrutiny will make the system more accountable to the public. Also, a televised trial is, in the words of one proponent, "the ultimate civics lesson" and contributes to Americans' overall understanding of the criminal justice system.[60]

Opponents of televised trials counter that the presence of cameras infringes on the defendant's right to a fair trial. The participants in a trial, they claim, will modify their behavior if they are aware that they are on television. These opponents insist that even the slightest change in behavior by a judge, attorney, witness, or juror damages the entire process of justice.[61]

The Simpson Shadow

As in so many areas of the criminal justice system, the example of the 1995 O. J. Simpson trial has come to dominate the debate on televised trials. Attorneys from both sides came under criticism for grandstanding before the cameras, as did Los Angeles Superior Court Judge Lance Ito. Yet in the years prior to the Simpson trial, sensational court proceedings were routinely televised. It is estimated that 62 percent of the public watched some part of the trial of Lorena Bobbit for mutilating her husband in 1994. Similar ratings were garnered for the Menendez brothers trial for killing their parents (53 percent), the Rodney King police brutality trial (81 percent), and the William Kennedy Smith rape trial (55 percent).[62]

The decision of whether a trial will be televised is, for the most part, the domain of the presiding judge. Only two states, South Dakota and Mississippi, completely prohibit television cameras in the courtroom.[63] In the years immediately following the Simpson trial, judges were much more reluctant to allow the proceedings to be televised. As the Simpson trial recedes into memory, however, judges and legislators are revisiting the issue. In 2000, for example, Justice Joseph Teresi of the New York Supreme Court struck down that state's ban on the televising of trials as unconstitutional under the First Amendment. In his ruling, Teresi argued that broadcasting the trial of four white police officers accused of shooting African immigrant Amadou Diallo would contribute to public understanding of the judicial system and enhance public confidence in the courts.[64]

That same year, Senator Charles Grassley (R-Iowa) introduced a bill designed to, in his words, "let the sun shine in our federal courts."[65] The bill, if passed, would allow federal judges to decide on a case-by-case basis whether to allow media coverage of their trials. Currently, federal

The trial of Lyle Menendez, pictured, and his brother Erik for the murder of their parents was watched by millions of Americans on television. (AP Photo/Nick Ut)

courts, including the United States Supreme Court, generally do not allow their proceedings to be televised, though some are doing so on an experimental basis.

SUPPORT FOR A "CAMERA-FREE ZONE"

Many in the judicial community remain skeptical about the televising of trials, however. When Los Angeles Superior Court Judge James Ideman declared his courtroom a "camera-free zone" for the trial of Symbionese Liberation Army fugitive Sara Jane Olson in 2000, he cited worries that the nearly two hundred witnesses set to appear would become targets of harassment if their faces were to appear on television. (In 2001, Olson pleaded guilty to two charges of attempted murder during jury selection.) A few months earlier, the Oklahoma Court of Criminal Appeals blocked the televising of hearings for convicted Oklahoma bombing co-conspirator Terry Nichols on the ground that the cameras would violate Nichols's due process rights.

Many critics of televised trials share the Oklahoma court's concern that televised trials may be unfair to the defendant. A study conducted by the Federal Judicial Center found that the presence of cameras makes witnesses more nervous than they would be otherwise and, in many cases, makes witnesses less willing to appear in court.[66] The study also found that attorneys and witnesses often feel obligated to "play the camera," thereby changing their behavior. United States Supreme Court Justice David H. Souter, in arguing against the presence of cameras in the Court, attested to television's effect on the judge. As a state judge in New Hampshire, Souter admitted, he altered his behavior when he knew he was going to appear on the evening news.[67]

Others believe that, by its nature, television is not the proper medium for trials. After all, the purpose of television is to entertain, while the purpose of a criminal trial is to determine the guilt or innocence of the accused. Indeed, viewers may actually lose confidence in the court system if the particular trial they are watching does not have the "happy ending" they have come to expect from most television shows.[68]

TWO RIGHTS IN CONFLICT?

Many see the issue of televised trials as a conflict between the media's right to freedom of the press and the defendant's right to a fair trial. In 1941, Justice Hugo Black commented that "free speech and fair trials are two of the most cherished policies of our civilization, and it would be a trying task to choose between them."[69]

If such a choice must be made, argues legal scholar Taffiny L. Smith, the right to a fair trial must carry more weight.[70] Smith points out that the United States Supreme Court, in *Richmond Newspapers, Inc. v. Virginia* (1980),[71] ruled that the media's right of access to trials is not absolute and may be subject to reasonable limitations. These limitations come in the form of judicial discretion.

Furthermore, though a judge has an inherent right to set the courtroom off-limits to television cameras, she or he may not exclude the print media from the proceedings. That *would* deny the media freedom of the press.

Proponents of televised trials argue that it is precisely this judicial discretion that allows the rights of the press and the trial to coexist. If a judge sees media coverage contaminating the trial, he or she can take several steps to remedy it, including the following:

- Sequestering the jurors, or isolating them from contact with the public or the media during the course of the trial. Officers of the court control the flow of information to jurors while they are sequestered, keeping them from being unduly influenced by media reports on the trial.
- Ordering a *change of venue,* in which the trial is transferred to a new location. A judge will take this step if the publicity and interest in a case in its original jurisdiction are so intense that the judge believes the defendant cannot receive a fair trial in that area.
- Placing a *gag order* on the participants in the trial.

If a judge believes any of these efforts to secure a fair trial has been compromised, she or he can take dramatic action. For example, in DeKalb County, Georgia, a judge declared a mistrial after one of the witnesses violated a direct order by watching testimony on television.[72]

Just because the O. J. Simpson case was handled poorly, the proponents contend, the public should not be denied the benefits of seeing a criminal trial in progress. The Massachusetts murder trial of British *au pair* Louise Woodward—which was televised—is held up as an example of a judge (Hiller B. Zobel) successfully keeping the media frenzy outside the courtroom. "The legal system is the public's legal system," said one of Zobel's peers. "Who are we to say that we can work in an isolated little courtroom with a select few people who can stand in line to get in? If 100 people can see it, then why can't the rest of the world see it? The public should have access. Simple as that."[73]

MAKING SENSE OF CAMERAS IN THE COURTROOM

1 What steps could courts take to prevent judges, attorneys, and jurors from changing their behavior because of the camera's presence?

2 Do you think certain types of trials should never be broadcast? For example, those involving sex crimes or children?

3 In the Diallo trial mentioned above, the proceedings were moved from New York City to Albany, New York, because of the racially charged atmosphere surrounding the trial. In such a situation, how might televising a trial lessen the chances of civil unrest following an unpopular verdict?

KEY TERMS

acquittal   231

appeal   240

arraignment   227

bail   221

bail bondsperson   222

bench trial   231

beyond a reasonable doubt   232

case attrition   225

challenge for cause   233

charge   239

circumstantial evidence   236

closing arguments   239

cross-examination   238

direct evidence   236

direct examination   237

discovery   224

double jeopardy   240

evidence   235

expert witness   235

grand jury   225

habeas corpus   243

hearsay   237

hung jury   240

indictment   225

information   225

initial appearance   221

jury trial   231

lay witness   235

master jury list   233

nolo contendere   228

opening statements   235

peremptory challenges   234

plea bargaining   228

preliminary hearing   224

preventive detention   223

real evidence   235

rebuttal   239

release on recognizance (ROR)   222

relevant evidence   236

testimony   235

venire   233

verdict   240

voir dire   233

CHAPTER SUMMARY

1 Identify the steps involved in the pretrial criminal process. (a) Suspect taken into custody or arrested; (b) initial appearance before a magistrate, at which time the defendant is informed of his or her constitutional rights and a public defender may be appointed or private counsel may be hired by the state to represent the defendant; (c) the posting of bail or release on recognizance; (d) preventive detention, if deemed necessary to ensure the safety of other persons or the community, or regular detention, if the defendant is unable to post bail; (e) preliminary hearing (minitrial), at which the judge rules on whether there is probable cause and the prosecutor issues an information; or in the alternative (f) grand jury hearings, after which an indictment is issued against the defendant if the grand jury finds probable cause; (g) arraignment, in which the defendant is informed of the charges and must respond by pleading not guilty or guilty (or in some cases *nolo contendere*); and (h) plea bargaining.

2 Explain how a prosecutor screens potential cases. (a) Is there sufficient evidence for conviction? (b) What is the priority of the case? The more serious the alleged crime, the higher the priority. The more extensive the defendant's criminal record, the higher the priority. (c) Are the victims cooperative? Violence against family members often yields uncooperative victims; therefore, these cases are rarely prosecuted. (d) Are the victims reliable? (e) Might the defendant be willing to testify against other offenders?

3 List and briefly explain the motivations of the prosecutors, defense attorneys, and defendants to plea bargain. Prosecutors may decide to plea bargain because it assures them of gaining a conviction. Defense attorneys often see plea bargains as opportunities to secure a lesser punishment for their client, or perhaps to quickly wrap up a case. Defendants benefit from plea bargains by receiving lighter sentences than they would if found guilty at trial.

4 Identify the basic protections enjoyed by criminal defendants in the United States. According to the Sixth Amendment, a criminal defendant has the right to a speedy and public trial by an impartial jury in the physical location where the crime was committed. Additionally, a person accused of a crime must be informed of the nature of the crime and be confronted with the witnesses against him or her. Further, the accused must be able to summon witnesses in her or his favor and have the assistance of counsel.

5 Contrast challenges for cause and peremptory challenges during *voir dire*. A challenge for cause occurs when an attorney provides the court with a legally justifiable reason why a potential juror should be excluded; for example, because the juror does not speak English. In contrast, peremptory challenges do not require any justification by the attorney and are usually limited to a small number. They cannot, however, be based, even implicitly, on race or gender.

6 List the standard steps in a criminal jury trial. (a) Opening statements by the prosecutor and the defense attorney; (b) presentation of evidence, usually in the form of questioning by the prosecutor, known as direct examination; (c) cross-examination by the defense attorney of the same witnesses; (d) at the end of the prosecutor's presentation of evidence, motion for a directed verdict by the defense (also called a motion for judgment as a matter of law in the federal courts), which is normally denied by the judge; (e) presentation of the defendant's case, which may include placing the defendant on the stand and direct examination of the defense's witnesses; (f) cross-examination by the prosecutor; (g) after the defense closes its case, rebuttal by the prosecution, which may involve new evidence that was not used initially by the prosecution; (h) cross-examination of the prosecution's new witnesses by the defense and introduction of new witnesses of its own, called the surrebuttal; (i) closing arguments by both the defense and the prosecution; (j) the charging of the jury by the judge, during which the judge sums up the case and instructs the jurors on the rules of law that apply; (k) jury deliberations; and (l) presentation of the verdict.

❼ Explain the difference between testimony and real evidence; between lay witnesses and expert witnesses; and between direct and circumstantial evidence. Testimony consists of statements by competent witnesses, whereas real evidence includes physical items that affect the case; a lay witness is an "average person," whereas an expert witness speaks with the authority of one who has professional training, advanced knowledge, or substantial experience in a specialized area; direct evidence is evidence presented by witnesses as opposed to circumstantial evidence, which can create an inference that a fact exists, but does not directly establish the fact.

❽ List the six basic steps of an appeal. (a) The filing of a notice of appeal; (b) the transfer of the trial court records to the appellate court; (c) the filing of briefs; (d) the presentation of oral arguments; (e) the deliberation of the appellate judges who then prepare a written opinion; and (f) the announcement of the judges—upholding the decision of the lower court, modifying part of the decision, reversing the decision, or reversing and remanding the decision to the trial court.

QUESTIONS FOR CRITICAL ANALYSIS

❶ What are the arguments against preventive detention?

❷ What is the distinction between a preliminary hearing and an initial appearance?

❸ What is case attrition, and why does it occur?

❹ Is plea bargaining inevitable?

❺ Under what circumstances may evidence be excluded?

❻ What are the arguments for and against televising criminal trials?

SELECTED PRINT AND ELECTRONIC RESOURCES

SUGGESTED READINGS

Heumann, Milton, *Plea Bargaining: The Experiences of Prosecutors, Judges, and Defense Attorneys,* Chicago: University of Chicago Press, Reprint Edition, 1981. This classic treatise on plea bargaining is both amusing and informative. It gives realistic accounts of the institutional roles and norms that are relevant to the plea bargaining universe. Lawyers and judges speak their piece about this necessary aspect of the criminal justice system.

Kurland, Michael, *How to Try a Murder: The Handbook for Armchair Lawyers,* New York: Macmillan General Reference, 1998. In spite of its title, this book explains the details of a criminal trial. The author examines the powers of judges and juries. He looks at defense strategies as well as prosecutors' tactics while examining each stage of the criminal trial.

Williams, Daniel R., *Executing Justice: An Inside Account of the Case of Mumia Abu-Jamal,* New York: St. Martin's Press, 2001. This book concerns the murder case of an activist-journalist. The murder trial is dissected by the defendant's death-row defense lawyer. The author questions how justice is served in high-profile cases.

MEDIA RESOURCES

12 Angry Men **(1957)** This classic movie is a primer on what *not* to do when deliberating as a juror, but it is great to watch. One juror (Henry Fonda) applies the correct legal standard of requiring proof beyond a reasonable doubt. He is the only juror who will not accept the prosecution's case. He continues questioning the rest of the jurors during deliberations and one by one causes them to examine the facts presented at the trial. The jurors show their prejudices and weaknesses throughout the movie.

Critically analyze this film:

1. The jury is all male. Why?

2. Why did the jurors want a quick decision?

3. Is juror #8, Davis (played by Henry Fonda), truly certain of the boy's innocence?

4. Explore some of the prejudices of the jurors. Do you think any of them could have been excluded by for-cause exemptions?

LOGGING ON

Go to http://cj.wadsworth.com/gainescore2e, **and click Hypercontents.** There, you will find URLs for the organizations in the following list:

- The **ThinkQuest Internet Challenge Library** allows you to follow a fictional criminal case through the courts. The site also contains a glossary of terms used in criminal law, images of actual forms that are filled out during the course of an arrest, a search engine for landmark United States Supreme Court criminal law cases, and a series of controversial criminal law issues.

- The **American Civil Liberties Union** (ACLU) has long acted as a guardian of Americans' civil liberties. You can learn about some of the constitutional questions raised by various criminal laws and procedures at the ACLU's Web site.

- **FindLaw** provides access to each state's criminal code.

USING THE INTERNET FOR CRIMINAL JUSTICE ANALYSIS

INFOTRAC®
COLLEGE EDITION

1. Go to your InfoTrac College Edition at **http://www.infotrac-college.com/wadsworth/**. After you log on, type in the words: **"Hiding the identity of potential jurors"**

   In highly charged criminal cases, the identity of jurors is kept secret. Jurors are hidden from the press, and no cameras are allowed in the court. This is what occurred during the case of *United States v. McVeigh* in April 1997.

   a. What did the case concern? Why was it so important to the media?

   b. What does it mean when a case is tried by an "anonymous" jury?

   c. What does it mean when a judge "seals all records"?

   d. What was the two-part type of *voir dire?* Is such a two-part *voir dire* common?

   e. What is the historical basis of public jury selection in the United States?

   f. In what case did the United States Supreme Court rule that *voir dire* normally has to be open to the public?

   g. Why is the author of this article presumably so concerned about anonymous juries?

2. See Internet Activities 9.1 and 9.2 on the companion Web site for *CJ in Action: The Core.* To get to the activities, go to **http://www.cj.wadsworth.com/gainescore2e**, select the appropriate chapter from the drop down list, then click Internet Activities on the left navigation bar.

NOTES

1. Jeffrey Gettleman, "A Racist Jailed, a City Healed," *Los Angeles Times* (May 3, 2001), A5.

2. Kevin Sack, "Research Guided Jury Selection in Bombing Trial," *New York Times* (May 3, 2001), A12.

3. National Advisory Commission on Criminal Justice Standards and Goals, *Courts* (Washington, D.C.: U.S. Government Printing Office, 1973), 66.

4. Pamela Coyles, "Fifth Murder Trial a Mistrial," *New Orleans Times-Picayune* (February 18, 1998), A1.

5. David W. Neubauer, *America's Courts and the Criminal Justice System,* 5th ed. (Belmont, CA: Wadsworth Publishing Company, 1996), 179–81.

6. Roy Flemming, C. Kohfeld, and Thomas Uhlman, "The Limits of Bail Reform: A Quasi Experimental Analysis," *Law and Society Review* 14 (1980), 947–76.

7. Esmond Harmsworth, "Bail and Detention: An Assessment and Critique of the Federal and Massachusetts Systems," *New England Journal on Criminal and Civil Confinement* 22 (Spring 1996), 213.

8. 18 U.S.C. Section 3146(b) (1966).

9. Harmsworth, 213.

10. Thomas C. French, "Is It Punitive or Is It Regulatory?" *University of Toledo Law Review* 20 (Fall 1988), 189.

11. 18 U.S.C. Sections 3141–3150 (Supp. III 1985).

12. Douglas Mossman, "Assessing Predictions of Violence: Being Accurate about Accuracy," *Journal of Consulting and Clinical Psychology* 62 (1994), 783.

13. 481 U.S. 739 (1987).

14. *Gerstein v. Pugh,* 420 U.S. 103 (1975).

15. David W. Neubauer, *Criminal Justice in Middle America* (Morristown, NJ: General Learning Press, 1974).

16. Thomas P. Sullivan and Robert D. Nachman, "If It Ain't Broke, Don't Fix It: Why the Grand Jury's Accusatory Function Should Not Be Changed," *Journal of Criminal Law and Criminology* 75 (1984), 1050, citing *Statistical Report of U.S. Attorney's Offices, Fiscal Year 1984,* 2.

17. New York Court of Appeals Judge Sol Wachtler, quoted in David Margolik, "Law Professor to Administer Courts in State," *New York Times* (February 1, 1985), B2.

18. Mirjan R. Damaska, *The Faces of Justice and State Authority* (New Haven, CT: Yale University Press, 1986), 483–87.

19. Barbara Boland, Paul Mahanna, and Ronald Scones, *The Prosecution of Felony Arrests, 1988* (Washington, D.C.: Bureau of Justice Statistics, 1992).

20. *Ibid.*

21. Brian Forst, Frank Leahy, Jean Shirhall, Herbert Tyson, Eric Wish, and John Bartolemo, *Arrest Convictability as a Measure of Police Performance* (Washington, D.C.: Institute for Law and Social Research, 1981).

22. Kathy B. Carter, "Court Orders Statewide Drug Penalties, Ending County Disparities," *Newark Star-Ledger* (February 20, 1998), 46.

23. 404 U.S. 257 (1971).

24. Fred C. Zacharias, "Justice in Plea Bargaining," *William and Mary Law Review* 39 (March 1998), 1121.

25. Albert W. Alschuler, "The Prosecutor's Role in Plea Bargaining," *University of Chicago Law Review* 36 (1968), 52.

26. Milton Heumann, *Plea Bargaining: The Experiences of Prosecutors, Judges, and Defense Attorneys* (Chicago: University of Chicago Press, 1978), 58.

27. Albert W. Alschuler, "The Defense Attorney's Role in Plea Bargaining," *Yale Law Journal* 84 (1975), 1200.

28. Stephen J. Schulhofer, "Plea Bargaining as Disaster," *Yale Law Journal* 101 (1992), 1987.

29. Kevin Cole and Fred C. Zacharias, "The Agony of Victory and the Ethics of Lawyer Speech," *Southern California Law Review* 69 (1996), 1660–63.

30. William Glaberson, "Kaczynski Avoids a Death Sentence with Guilty Plea," *New York Times* (January 23, 1998), A1.

31. 18 U.S.C. Section 3161.

32. 391 U.S. 145 (1968).

33. *Blanton v. Las Vegas,* 489 U.S. 538 (1989).

34. *Ballew v. Georgia,* 435 U.S. 223 (1978).

35. 332 U.S. 46 (1947).

36. Barton L. Ingraham, "The Right of Silence, the Presumption of Innocence, the Burden of Proof, and a Modest Proposal," *Journal of Criminal Law and Criminology* 85 (1994), 559–95.

37. 397 U.S. 358 (1970).

38. *Black's Law Dictionary,* 6th ed. (St. Paul, MN: West Publishing Co., 1990), 1575.

39. James L. Gilbert, Stuart A. Ollanik, and David A. Wenner, "Overcoming Juror Bias in Voir Dire," *Trial* (July 1997), 42–46.

40. *Lockhart v. McCree,* 476 U.S. 162 (1986).

41. *Witherspoon v. Illinois,* 391 U.S. 510 (1968).

42. Jeremy W. Barber, "The Jury Is Still Out," *American Criminal Law Review* 31 (Summer 1994) 1225–52.

43. Diane Burch Beckham, "The Art of the Voir Dire: Is It Really a Science?" *New Jersey Law Journal* (July 5, 1990), 5.

44. Barber, "The Jury Is Still Out."

45. 476 U.S. 79 (1986).

46. *J.E.B. v. Alabama ex rel T.B.,* 511 U.S. 127 (1994).

47. Thomas J. Reed, "Trial by Propensity: Admission of Other Criminal Acts Evidenced in Federal Criminal Trials," *University of Cincinnati Law Review* 50 (1981), 713.

48. *Ibid.*

49. Jay L. Hack, "Declaration against Penal Interest: Standards of Admissibility under an Emerging Majority Rule," *Boston University Law Review* 56 (1976), 148.

50. Emily F. Duck, "The Williamson Standard for the Exception to the Rule against Hearsay for Statements against Penal Interest," *Journal of Criminal Law and Criminology* 85 (Spring 1995), 1084–113.

51. Neubauer, *America's Courts and the Criminal Justice System,* 254.

52. Roger LeRoy Miller and Mary S. Urisko, *West's Paralegal Today* (St. Paul, MN: West Publishing Co., 1995), 443.

53. *Green v. United States,* 355 U.S. 184 (1957).

54. Donald A. Dripps, "The Continuing Decline in Finality in Criminal Law," *Trial* (April 1997), 78–79.

55. Neubauer, *America's Courts and the Criminal Justice System,* 331.

56. 28 U.S.C. Section 2254(d)(1).

57. F. Martin Tieber, "Federal *Habeas Corpus* Law and Practice—The Antiterrorism and Effective Death Penalty Act of 1996," *Michigan Bar Journal* 77 (January 1998), 50.

58. *Felker v. Turpin,* 518 U.S. 1051 (1996).

59. 949 U.S. 560 (1981).

60. Claire Papanastasiou, "Cameras in the Courtroom," *The Massachusetts Lawyer* (December 15, 1997), B1.

61. Taffiny L. Smith, "The Distortion of Criminal Trials through Televised Proceedings," *Law and Psychology Review* 21 (Spring 1997), 257.

62. Dan Trigoboff, "Court Coverage Hindered by O. J. Backlash?" *Broadcasting & Cable* (June 23, 1997), 24.

63. Radio and Television News Directors' Association.

64. Dan Trigoboff, "Judge Affirms Cameras in New York Courtroom," *Broadcast & Cable* (January 31, 2000), 37.

65. "Bill to Open Courtroom to Cameras Opposed by Judiciary, Key Lawmaker," *Associated Press Newswires* (September 6, 2000).

66. Statement of Chief Judge Edward R. Becker on Behalf of the Judicial Conference of the United States before the Senate Judiciary Subcommittee on Administrative Oversight and the Courts, September 6, 2000.

67. Jim Gordon, "No Camera Fans Here," *News Photographer* (May 1, 1996), 4.

68. Neil Postman, *Amusing Ourselves to Death: Public Discourse in an Age of Show Business* (New York: Viking Press, 1985), 87.

69. *Bridges v. California,* 314 U.S. 252 (1941).

70. Smith, 257.

71. 448 U.S. 555 (1980).

72. Celia Sibley, "Sandlin Ruling: Eye Is on Courtroom Cameras," *Atlanta Journal and Atlanta Constitution* (July 19, 1997), B2.

73. Papanastasiou, B1.

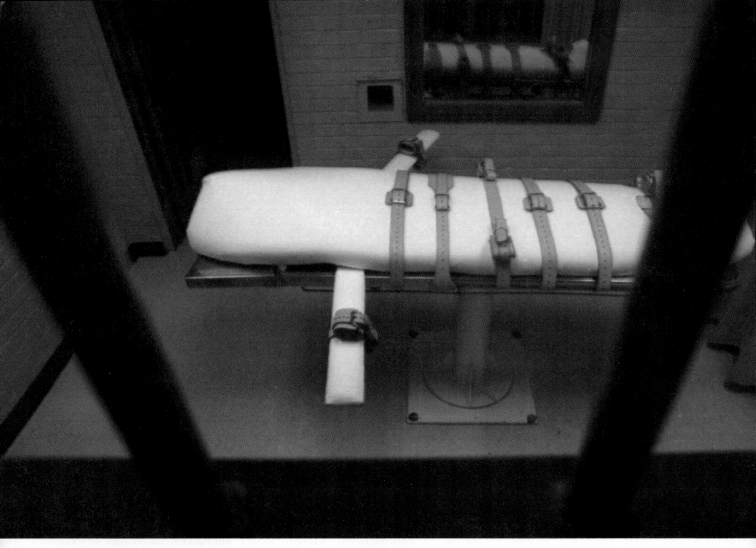

CHAPTER 10
PUNISHMENT AND SENTENCING

Chapter Objectives

After reading this chapter, you should be able to:

1. List and contrast the four basic philosophical reasons for sentencing criminals.

2. Contrast indeterminate with determinate sentencing.

3. Explain why there is a difference between a sentence imposed by a judge and the actual sentence carried out by the prisoner.

4. List the six forms of punishment.

5. Explain some of the reasons why sentencing reform has occurred.

6. Contrast sentencing guidelines with mandatory sentencing guidelines.

7. Describe the main issues of the death penalty debate.

INTRODUCTION
Dealing with Drunk Driving

On July 2, 2000, Gary Lewis Kohlenburg was pulled over by police on the very same Maryland road where, twenty years earlier, he had killed a married couple in a drunk driving accident. The officers smelled alcohol on his breath, and he admitted to having drunk four or five beers. Kohlenburg was eventually sentenced to eighteen months' probation and required to undergo treatment for alcoholism.[1] This was Kohlenburg's third drunk driving conviction since he caused the fatal accident.

Given that drunk driving accidents are the leading cause of death in the United States for people under the age of thirty-one and account for more than 40 percent of all traffic fatalities, one might ask, why are repeat offenders such as Kohlenburg given a second, third, and, in some cases, twentieth chance? In other words, how much should we punish drunk drivers? Because each state has authority to pass its own drunk driving laws, this question has at least fifty different answers. Some jurisdictions have tough laws—in New York City, police can confiscate the automobiles of drunk drivers.[2] In Texas, a judge can sentence a multiple offender to prison.[3] A number of states, however, classify drunk driving as a misdemeanor, which in many cases assures that the offender will see no jail time.

The question is further clouded by studies that show that a higher probability of being caught is a much better deterrent to drunk driving than the severity of the punishment.[4] Does that mean, then, that jurisdictions should

abandon efforts to "get tough" on drunk drivers and instead focus on increasing the police presence on the roads?

As the uncertainty surrounding drunk driving shows, punishment and sentencing present some of the most complex issues of the criminal justice system. One scholar has even asserted that:

> There is no such thing as "accurate" sentencing; there are only sentences that are more or less just, more or less effective. Nothing in the recent or distant history of sentencing reform suggests that anything approaching perfection is attainable.[5]

In this chapter, we will discuss the various attempts to "perfect" the practice of sentencing over the past century and explore the ramifications of these efforts for the American criminal justice system. Whereas previous chapters have concentrated on the prosecutor and defense attorney, this one will spotlight the judge and his or her role in making the sentencing decision. We will particularly focus on recent national and state efforts to limit judicial discretion in this area, a trend that has had the overall effect of producing harsher sentences for many offenders. Finally, we will examine the issues surrounding the death penalty, a controversial subject that forces us to confront the basic truth of sentencing: the way we punish criminals says a great deal about the kind of people we are.[6]

The wreck of a car that had been carrying one of the more than 17,000 people killed each year in this country by drunk drivers. (AP Photo/Sarah Martone)

Stories from the Street

Go to the Stories from the Street feature at http://www.cj.wadsworth.com/gainescore2e to hear Larry Gaines tell insightful stories related to this chapter and his experiences in the field.

THE PURPOSE OF SENTENCING

Professor Herbert Packer has said that punishing criminals serves two ultimate purposes: the "deserved infliction of suffering on evil doers" and "the prevention of crime."[7] Even this straightforward assessment raises several questions. How does one determine the sort of punishment that is "deserved"? How can we be sure that certain penalties "prevent" crime? Should criminals be punished solely for the good of society, or should their well-being also be taken into consideration? Sentencing laws indicate how any given group of people has answered these questions, but do not tell us *why* they were answered in that manner. To understand why, we must first consider the four basic philosophical reasons for sentencing—retribution, deterrence, incapacitation, and rehabilitation.

Retribution

The oldest and most common justification for punishing someone is that he or she "deserved it"—as the Old Testament states, "an eye for an eye and a tooth for a tooth." Under a system of justice that favors **retribution,** a wrongdoer who has freely chosen to violate society's rules must be punished for the infraction. Retribution relies on the principle of **just deserts,** which holds that the severity of the punishment must be in proportion to the severity of the crime. Retributive justice is not the same as *revenge*. Whereas revenge implies that the wrongdoer is punished only with the aim of satisfying a victim or victims, retribution is more concerned with the needs of society as a whole.

> "Men are not hanged for stealing horses, but that horses may not be stolen."
>
> —Marquis de Halifax, *Political Thoughts and Reflections* (1750)

Deterrence

The concept of **deterrence** (as well as incapacitation and rehabilitation) takes the opposite approach: rather than seeking only to punish the wrongdoer, the goal of sentencing should be to prevent future crimes. By "setting an example," society is sending a message to potential criminals that certain actions will not be tolerated. Jeremy Bentham, a nineteenth-century British reformer who first articulated the principles of deterrence, felt that retribution was counterproductive because it does not serve the community. He believed that a person should be punished only when doing so was in society's best interests and that the severity of the punishment should be based on its deterrent value, not on the severity of the crime.[8]

Deterrence can take two forms: general and specific. The basic idea of *general deterrence* is that by punishing one person, others will be dissuaded from committing a similar crime. *Specific deterrence* assumes that an individual, after being punished once for a certain act, will be less likely to repeat that act because she or he does not want to be punished again.[9] Both forms of deterrence have proved problematic in practice. General deterrence assumes that a person commits a crime only after a rational decision-making process, in which he or she implicitly weighs the benefits of the crime against the possible costs of the punishment. This is not necessarily the case, especially for young offenders who tend to value the immediate rewards of crime over the possible future consequences.[10] Specific deterrence, for its part, seems to be contradicted by the fact that a relatively small number of habitual offenders are responsible for the majority of certain criminal acts.[11]

Incapacitation

"Wicked people exist," said James Q. Wilson. "Nothing avails except to set them apart from innocent people."[12] Wilson's blunt statement summarizes the justification for **incapacitation** as a form of punishment. As a purely practical matter, incarcerating criminals guarantees that they will not be a danger to society,

RETRIBUTION
The philosophy that those who commit criminal acts should be punished based on the severity of the crime and that no other factors need be considered.

JUST DESERTS
A sanctioning philosophy based on the assertion that criminals deserve to be punished for breaking society's rules. The severity of the punishment should be determined by no other factor than the severity of the crime.

DETERRENCE
The strategy of preventing crime through the threat of punishment. Assumes that potential criminals will weigh the costs of punishments versus the benefits of the criminal act; therefore, punishments should be severe.

INCAPACITATION
A strategy for preventing crime by detaining wrongdoers in prison, thereby separating them from the community and reducing criminal opportunities.

at least for the length of their prison terms. To a certain extent, the death penalty is justified in terms of incapacitation, as it prevents the offender from committing any future crimes.

Several studies have pointed to the effectiveness of incapacitation as a crime prevention tool. Criminologist Isaac Ehrlich of the University of Chicago estimated that a 1 percent increase in sentence length will produce a 1 percent decrease in crime rates.[13] Another Chicago professor, Steve Levitt, has noticed a trend that further supports incapacitation: violent crime rates rise in communities where inmate litigation over prison overcrowding has forced the early release of some inmates and a subsequent drop in the prison population.[14]

Incapacitation as a theory of punishment suffers from several weaknesses, however. Unlike retribution, it offers no proportionality with regard to a particular crime. Giving a burglar a life sentence would certainly assure that she or he would not commit another burglary; does that justify such a severe penalty? Furthermore, incarceration protects society only until the criminal is freed. Many studies have shown that, on release, offenders may actually be more likely to commit crimes than before they were imprisoned.[15] In that case, incapacitation may increase the likelihood of crime, rather than diminish it.

Rehabilitation

For most of the past century, **rehabilitation** has been seen as the most "humane" goal of punishment. This line of thinking reflects the view that crime is a "social phenomenon" caused not by the inherent criminality of a person, but by factors in that person's surroundings. By removing wrongdoers from their environment and intervening to change their values and personalities, the rehabilitative model suggests, criminals can be "treated" and possibly even "cured" of their proclivities toward crime. (See on the next page the feature *Criminal Justice & Technology—A Cure for the Brain.*)

As will become clear over the course of this chapter, the American criminal justice system is currently in the process of rejecting many of the precepts of rehabilitation in favor of "get tough" retributive, deterrent, and incapacitating sentencing strategies. When a recent poll asked whether the government should focus its resources toward rehabilitation or punishment of criminals, nearly 60 percent of the respondents chose the punishment option. Only 27 percent identified rehabilitation as a priority.[16] It would be a mistake, however, to separate these four philosophies. For the most part, a society's overall sentencing direction is influenced by all four theories, with political and social factors determining which one is predominant at any given time.

THE STRUCTURE OF SENTENCING

Philosophy not only is integral to explaining *why* we punish criminals, but also influences *how* we do so. The history of criminal sentencing in the United States has been characterized by shifts in institutional power among the three branches of the government. When public opinion moves toward more severe strategies of retribution, deterrence, and incapacitation, *legislatures* have responded by asserting their power over determining sentencing guidelines. In contrast, periods of rehabilitative justice are marked by a transfer of this power to the *judicial* and *administrative* branches.

Legislative Sentencing Authority

Because legislatures are responsible for making law, these bodies are also initially responsible for passing the criminal codes that determine the length of sentences.

State-sanctioned executions continue to be controversial. These protesters, whose number swelled to over three hundred, demonstrate against the death penalty at San Quentin Prison on February 8, 1999. California Governor Gray Davis refused to spare convicted double murderer Jay Siripongs in spite of an eleventh-hour plea by Pope John Paul II. Siripongs's lawyers had unsuccessfully appealed to the U.S. Court of Appeals in San Francisco and the United States Supreme Court. (AP Photo/Rich Pedroncelli)

REHABILITATION
The philosophy that society is best served when wrongdoers are not simply punished, but provided the resources needed to eliminate criminality from their behavioral pattern.

A Cure for the Brain

The methods that have been used to "cure" convicts of their criminal and antisocial behavior have always reflected the latest scientific beliefs. Of course, methods that seemed to be on the cutting edge of medical research in the past now appear hopelessly outdated, and even barbaric. In the eighteenth and nineteenth centuries, inmates would be whipped, burned, and starved to encourage positive behavior. In the twentieth century, treatment included spraying criminals with needlelike jets of water, forced hypothermia caused by swaddling in refrigerated blankets, electroshock therapy, and even lobotomies.

Today, the treatment of criminal behavior as a medical problem is dominated by the use of pyschotropic drugs. Convicts whose crimes have been linked to schizophrenia are treated with drugs such as Clozaril, Risperdal, and Zyprexa. Many of the nation's prison doctors prescribe the antidepressants Prozac, Paxil, and Wellbutrin. Because drug and alcohol abuse is so closely related to criminal activity, many inmates who suffer from such problems are treated with drugs such as Revia, which has been shown to lessen the negative effects of these addictions. The extent of this treatment is considerable. In Maine, for example, about a quarter of all prisoners receive psychotropic drugs.

Indeed, the success of some of these drugs has raised interesting questions. What if a person suffers from a personality or depressive disorder and commits a murder while under the influence of his or her illness? Then, that person is presumably "cured" through the use of drugs. Should the punishment be any less? Almost every court that has addressed these issues has responded with a resounding "no" (as long as the person was not legally insane at the time of the crime, as we saw in Chapter 3).

IN THE FUTURE

Scientists are now combining the study of genetic predisposition to crime (discussed in Chapter 2) and the use of psychotropic drugs not only to "treat" criminal behavior, but also to prevent it. In 2002, researchers from the United States and England discovered a gene mutation that predisposes some males to violent behavior, especially if they were abused as children. The findings suggest that youths diagnosed with this mutation could be given drugs to counter its effects, thereby lessening their chances of growing up to be criminals.

INFOTRAC®
COLLEGE EDITION

Keyword: sentencing

INDETERMINATE SENTENCING
An indeterminate term of incarceration in which a judge determines the minimum and maximum terms of imprisonment. When the minimum term is reached, the prisoner becomes eligible to be paroled.

DETERMINATE SENTENCING
A period of incarceration that is fixed by a sentencing authority and cannot be reduced by judges or other corrections officials.

"GOOD TIME"
A reduction in time served by prisoners based on good behavior, conformity to rules, and other positive actions.

Indeterminate Sentencing.   For most of the twentieth century, goals of rehabilitation dominated the criminal justice system, and legislatures were more likely to enact **indeterminate sentencing** policies. Penal codes with indeterminate sentences set a minimum and maximum amount of time that a person must spend in prison. For example, the indeterminate sentence for aggravated assault could be three to nine years, or six to twelve years, or twenty years to life. Within these parameters, a judge can prescribe a particular term, after which an administrative body known as the *parole board* decides at what point the offender is to be released. A prisoner is aware that he or she is eligible for *parole* as soon as the minimum time has been served and that good behavior can further shorten the sentence.

Determinate Sentencing.   Disillusionment with the ideals of rehabilitation has led to **determinate sentencing,** or fixed sentencing. As the name implies, in determinate sentencing an offender serves exactly the amount of time to which she or he is sentenced (minus "good time," described below). For example, if the legislature deems that the punishment for a first-time armed robber is ten years, then the judge has no choice but to impose a sentence of ten years, and the criminal will serve ten years minus good time before being freed.

"Good Time" and Truth-in-Sentencing.   Often, the amount of time prescribed by a judge bears little relation to the amount of time the offender actually spends behind bars. In states with indeterminate sentencing, parole boards have broad powers to release prisoners once they have served the minimum portion of their sentence. Furthermore, all but four states offer prisoners the opportunity to reduce their sentences by doing **"good time"**—or behaving well—as determined by prison administrators. (See Figure 10.1 for an idea of the effects of good time regulations and other early-release programs.)

Most Serious Conviction Offense	Average Prison Sentence (in months)	Estimated Time in Prison (in months)	% Expected to Be Served
Murder/manslaughter	192	106	53
Rape	124	79	58
Robbery	197	55	52
Aggravated assault	62	39	59
Burglary	73	36	44
Drug trafficking	64	29	42

FIGURE 10.1
Average Sentence Length and Estimated Time to Be Served in State Prison

Source: Bureau of Justice Statistics, *Sourcebook of Criminal Justice Statistics, 1999* (Washington, D.C., 2000), page 528, Table 6.53.

Sentence-reduction programs promote discipline within a correctional institution and reduce overcrowding; therefore, many prison officials welcome them. The public, however, may react negatively to news that a violent criminal has served a shorter term than ordered by a judge and pressure elected officials to "do something." In Illinois, for example, some inmates were serving less than half their sentences by receiving a one-day reduction in their term for each day of "good time." Under pressure from victims' groups, the state legislature passed a **truth-in-sentencing law** that requires murderers and others convicted of serious crimes to complete at least 85 percent of their sentences with no time off for good behavior.[17] Today, forty states have instituted some form of truth-in-sentencing laws, though the future of such statutes is in doubt due to numerous challenges on constitutional grounds and the pressure of overflowing prisons.

Judicial Sentencing Authority

Determinate sentencing is a direct encroachment on the long-recognized power of judges to make the final decision on sentencing. Historically, the judge bore most of the responsibility for choosing the proper sentence within the guidelines set by the legislature.[18] In the twentieth century, this power was reinforced by the rehabilitative ethic. Each offender, it was believed, has a different set of problems and should, therefore, receive a sentence tailored to her or his particular circumstances. Legislators have generally accepted a judge as the most qualified person to choose the proper punishment.

Between 1880 and 1899, seven states passed indeterminate sentencing laws, and in the next dozen years, another twenty-one followed suit. By the 1960s, every state in the nation allowed its judges the freedom of operating under an indeterminate sentencing system.[19] In the 1970s, however, criticism of indeterminate sentencing began to grow. Marvin E. Frankel, a former federal district judge in New York, gained a great deal of attention when he described sentencing authority as "unchecked" and "terrifying and intolerable for a society that professes devotion to a rule of law."[20] As we shall see, the 1980s and 1990s saw numerous attempts on both the state and federal level to limit this judicial discretion.

Administrative Sentencing Authority

Parole is a condition of early release in which a prisoner is released from a correctional facility but is not freed from the legal custody and supervision of the state. Generally, after an inmate has been released on parole, he or she is supervised by a parole officer for a specified amount of time. The decision of whether to parole an inmate lies with the parole board. Parole is a crucial aspect of the criminal justice system and will be discussed in detail in Chapter 13.

"During a guilty-plea colloquy, a defendant was asked by the judge if he understood all the rights he was waiving by pleading guilty. 'Judge,' the man responded, 'the only right I'm interested in is the right sentence.'"

—David Racher, *Philadelphia Daily News* (1990)

TRUTH-IN-SENTENCING LAWS
Legislative attempts to assure that convicts will serve approximately the terms to which they were initially sentenced.

MASTERING CONCEPTS   Who Has the Responsibility to Determine Sentences?

Three different sentencing authorities determine the amount of time a person who has been convicted of a felony will spend in prison: legislatures, judges, and officials of the executive branch. The process through which these three groups influence the sentencing process is summarized below.

First Step: Legislators Pass Laws

Federal and state legislators are responsible for creating and updating the criminal codes that define how the law will punish those who commit crimes. Legislatures specify the terms of imprisonment in two different ways:

- By passing *indeterminate sentencing laws.* These laws designate a maximum and minimum amount of time that a person who commits a specific crime must spend in prison—one to three years, five to ten years, and so on.
- By passing *determinate sentencing laws.* These laws designate a fixed amount of time that a person who commits a specific crime must spend in prison—seven years, for example, instead of five to ten.

If lawmakers feel that the other two bodies—judges and officials of the executive branch—are being too lenient in their sentencing decisions, they can pass truth-in-sentencing laws that require convicts to serve the amount of time indicated in criminal codes.

Second Step: Judges Impose Sentences

Judges have the authority to choose among the sentencing options provided by legislatures. They are expected to consider all of the circumstances that surround a case and decide the length of the sentence based on these circumstances. (There are a few exceptions to this judicial authority. Only a jury, for example, can decide whether to impose the death penalty.)

Third Step: Executive Officials Set the Date of Release

Although judges impose the sentence, officials of the executive branch are responsible for deciding the extent to which a prisoner will serve his or her entire sentence. Most prisoners do not serve their maximum possible terms of imprisonment. Parole boards, appointed in most states by the governor, decide whether an inmate is eligible for *parole*—the conditional release of a prisoner before his or her sentence has been served. Executive officials also determine whether an inmate will have his or her sentence reduced because of *"good time,"* which is awarded for good behavior and participation in various treatment, vocational, and educational programs. (Remember, however, that legislatures can restrict parole and good time provisions.)

For now, it is important to understand the role rehabilitation theories play in *administrative sentencing authority.* The formation in 1910 of the U.S. Parole Commission and similar commissions in the fifty states implied that the judge, though a legal expert, was not trained to determine when an inmate had been rehabilitated. Therefore, the sentencing power should be given to experts in human behavior, who were qualified to determine whether a convict was fit to return to society.[21] The recent repudiation of rehabilitation principles has not spared these administrative bodies; since 1976, fourteen states and the federal government have abolished traditional parole for their prisoners.[22] (See *Mastering Concepts—Who Has the Responsibility to Determine Sentences?.*)

INDIVIDUALIZED JUSTICE AND THE JUDGE

During the pretrial procedures and the trial itself, the judge's role is somewhat passive and reactive. She or he is a primarily a "procedural watchdog," assuring that the rights of the defendant are not infringed on while the prosecutor and defense attorney dictate the course of action.

At a traditional sentencing hearing, however, the judge is no longer an arbiter between parties; she or he is now called on to exercise the ultimate authority of the state in determining the defendant's fate.

From the 1930s to the 1970s, when theories of rehabilitation held sway over the criminal justice system, indeterminate sentencing practices were guided by the theory of "individualized justice." Just as a physician gives specific treatment to individual patients depending on their particular health needs, the hypothesis goes, a judge needs to consider the specific circumstances of each individual offender in choosing the best form of punishment. Taking the analogy one step further, just as the diagnosis of a qualified physician should not be questioned, a qualified judge should have absolute discretion in making the sentencing decision. *Judicial discretion* rests on the assumption that a judge should be given ample leeway in determining punishments that fit both the crime and the criminal.[23] As we shall see later in the chapter, the growth of determinate sentencing has severely restricted judicial discretion in many jurisdictions.

Forms of Punishment

Within whatever legislative restrictions apply, the sentencing judge has a number of options when it comes to choosing the proper form of punishment. These sentences, or *dispositions*, include:

1. *Capital punishment.* Reserved normally for those who commit first degree murder under aggravated circumstances, capital punishment, or the death penalty, is a sentencing option in thirty-eight states and in federal courts.

2. *Imprisonment.* Whether for the purpose of retribution, deterrence, incapacitation, or rehabilitation, a common form of punishment in American history has been imprisonment. In fact, it is currently so common that judges—and legislators—are having to take factors such as prison overcrowding into consideration when making sentencing decisions. The issues surrounding imprisonment will be discussed in Chapters 12 and 13.

3. *Probation.* One of the effects of prison overcrowding has been a sharp rise in the use of probation, in which an offender is permitted to live in the community under supervision and is not incarcerated. Probation is covered in Chapter 11. Alternative sanctions (also discussed in Chapter 11) combine probation with other dispositions such as electronic monitoring, house arrests, boot camps, and shock incarceration.

4. *Fines.* Fines can be levied by judges in addition to incarceration and probation or independently of other forms of punishment. When a fine is the full extent of the punishment, it usually reflects the judge's belief that the offender is not a threat to the community and does not need to be imprisoned or supervised. In some instances, mostly involving drug offenders, a judge can order the seizure of an offender's property, such as his or her home.

5. *Restitution and community service.* Whereas fines are payable to the government, restitution and community service are seen as reparations to the injured party. *Restitution* is a direct payment to the victim or victims of a crime; community service consists of "good works"—such as cleaning up highway litter or tutoring disadvantaged youths—that benefit the entire community.

6. *Restorative justice.* Where the offender has committed a less serious crime, many judges are turning to restorative justice to provide a remedy. At the heart of restorative justice is the apology. So, for example, a judge in Texas required a teenager who had vandalized thirteen schools to go to each school and apologize to the students and faculty.[24] In many such cases,

This is a photo of Luis Felipe, who was sentenced to life in solitary confinement by federal Judge John S. Martin, Jr., in the fall of 1997. Such individualized justice was based on Felipe's role as founder of the New York chapter of the Almighty Latin Kings and Queens Nation. Felipe, already in jail, had ordered murders by writing to his lieutenants on the outside. Judge Martin even forbade Felipe to be visited by anyone except his lawyers and close relatives. Because Felipe has no close relatives, only his lawyers can visit. What legal arguments might Felipe's lawyers use to appeal his harsh sentence? (Lisa Terry/Getty Images)

PRESENTENCE INVESTIGATIVE REPORT
An investigative report on an offender's background that assists a judge in determining the proper sentence.

victims appreciate the expression of remorse, and offenders are thankful for a chance to "set things right."[25] Restorative justice focuses more on "healing" the harm that a crime does to individual relationships and the community than on punishing the offender.

In some jurisdictions, judges have a great deal of discretionary power and can impose sentences that do not fall into any of these categories. In Illinois, for example, Kane County Judge Donald Hudson agreed to a convicted child molester's request to undergo surgical castration in penance for his crime.[26] Though a number of state legislatures are considering making this punishment mandatory for certain sex offenders, it is still considered cruel and unusual punishment in most jurisdictions.

The Sentencing Process

The decision of how to punish a wrongdoer is the end result of what Yale Law School professor Kate Stith and federal appeals court judge José A. Cabranes call the "sentencing ritual."[27] The two main participants in this ritual are the judge and the defendant, but prosecutors, defense attorneys, and probation officers also play a role in the proceedings. Individualized justice requires that the judge consider all the relevant circumstances in making sentencing decisions. Therefore, judicial discretion is often tantamount to *informed* discretion—without the aid of the other members of the courtroom work group, the judge would not have sufficient information to make the proper sentencing choice.

On the Web

For a link to the U.S. Sentencing Commission's Web site, go to the Hypercontents page for this chapter at http://www.cj.wadsworth.com/gainescore2e.

The Presentence Investigative Report.   For judges operating under various states' indeterminate sentencing guidelines, information in the **presentence investigative report** is a valuable component of the sentencing ritual. Compiled by a probation officer, the report describes the crime in question, notes the suffering of any victims, and lists the defendant's prior offenses (as well as any alleged but uncharged criminal activity). The report also contains a range of personal data such as family background, work history, education, and community activities—information that is not admissible as evidence during trial. In putting together the presentence investigative report, the probation officer is supposed to gain a "feel" for the defendant and communicate these impressions of the offender to the judge.[28]

The Prosecutor and Defense Attorney.   To a certain extent, the adversarial process does not end when the guilt of the defendant has been established. Both the prosecutor and the defense attorney are interviewed in the course of preparing the presentence investigative report, and both will try to present a version of the facts consistent with their own sentencing goals. The defense attorney in particular has a duty to make sure that the information contained in the report is accurate and not prejudicial toward his or her client. Depending on the norms of any particular courtroom work group, prosecutors and defense attorneys may petition the judge directly for certain sentences. Note that this process is not always adversarial. As we saw in Chapter 9, in some instances the prosecutor will advocate leniency and may join the defense attorney in requesting a short term of imprisonment, probation, or some form of intermediate sanction.[29]

Factors of Sentencing

The sentencing ritual strongly lends itself to the concept of individualized justice.[30] With inputs—sometimes conflicting—from the prosecutor, attorney, and probation officer, the judge can be reasonably sure of getting the "full picture" of the crime and the criminal. In making the final decision, however, most judges consider two factors above all others: the seriousness of the crime and any mitigating or aggravating circumstances.

The Seriousness of the Crime.

As would be expected, the seriousness of the crime is the primary factor in a judge's sentencing decisions. The more serious the crime, the harsher the punishment, for society demands no less. (See Figure 10.2.) Each judge has his or her own methods of determining the seriousness of the offense. Many judges simply consider the "conviction offense"; that is, they base their sentence on the crime for which the defendant was convicted.

Other judges—some mandated by statute—focus instead on the **"real offense"** in determining the punishment. The "real offense" is based on the actual behavior of the defendant, regardless of the official conviction. For example, through a plea bargain, a defendant may plead guilty to simple assault when in fact he hit his victim in the face with a baseball bat. A judge, after reading the presentence investigative report, could decide to sentence the defendant as if he had committed aggravated assault, which is the "real" offense. Though many prosecutors and defense attorneys are opposed to "real offense" procedures, which can render a plea bargain meaningless, there is a growing belief in criminal justice circles that they bring a measure of fairness to the sentencing decision.[31]

Mitigating and Aggravating Circumstances.

Consider the case of Marcos Mascarenas of Questa, New Mexico, who was responsible for the death of his six-month-old son by "shaken baby syndrome." Mascarenas had an intelligence quotient (IQ) of 90 and purportedly was not aware of the harm he was doing when he shook the baby. The judge in his case, Peggy Nelson, expressed frustration that she was forced to sentence the defendant to prison for a minimum of twelve years under state law. Because of his lack of mental capacity, the judge felt that Mascarenas did not deserve the punishment he received. In many situations, circumstances surrounding the crime may prompt a judge to adjust a sentence so that it more accurately reflects the totality of the crime. Judge Nelson considered Mascarenas's lack of mental capacity a mitigating circumstance, and given the opportunity, she would have given him a lesser punishment. There are other **mitigating circumstances,** or those circumstances that allow a lighter sentence to be handed down. They can be defined to include a defendant's youth or the fact that the defendant was coerced into committing the crime. In contrast, **aggravating circumstances** such as a prior record, blatant disregard for safety, or the use of a weapon can lead a judge to inflict a harsher penalty than might otherwise be the case (see Figure 10.3 on the next page).

Judicial Philosophy.

Most states spell out mitigating and aggravating circumstances in statutes, but there is room for judicial discretion in applying the law to particular cases. Judges are not uniform, or even consistent, in their opinions concerning which circumstances are mitigating or aggravating. One judge may believe a fourteen-year-old is not fully responsible for his or her actions, while another may believe teenagers should be treated as adults. Those judges who support rehabilitative theories of criminal justice have been found to give more lenient sentences than those who are governed by goals of deterrence and incapacitation.[32] Furthermore, judges can have different philosophies with regard to different crimes, handing down, for example, harsh penalties for domestic abusers while showing leniency toward drug offenders.

FIGURE 10.2

Average Maximum Sentences for Selected Crimes

Crime	Average Maximum Sentence (in months)
Murder	270
Sexual assault	92
Robbery	93
Aggravated assault	45
Burglary	39
Drug trafficking	37
Drug possession	21

Source: Bureau of Justice Statistics, *State Court Sentencing of Convicted Felons, 1998* (Washington, D.C.: U.S. Department of Justice, 2001), Table 2.6.

"REAL OFFENSE"
The actual offense committed, as opposed to the charge levied by a prosecutor as the result of a plea bargain. Judges who make sentencing decisions based on the real offense are often seen as undermining the plea bargain process.

MITIGATING CIRCUMSTANCES
Any circumstances accompanying the commission of a crime that may justify a lighter sentence.

AGGRAVATING CIRCUMSTANCES
Any circumstances accompanying the commission of a crime that may justify a harsher sentence.

FIGURE 10.3
Aggravating and Mitigating Circumstances

AGGRAVATING CIRCUMSTANCES

- An offense involved multiple participants and the offender was the leader of the group.

- A victim was particularly vulnerable.

- A victim was treated with particular cruelty for which an offender should be held responsible.

- The offense involved injury or threatened violence to others committed to gratify an offender's desire for pleasure or excitement.

- The degree of bodily harm caused, attempted, threatened, or foreseen by an offender was substantially greater than average for the given offense.

- The degree of economic harm caused, attempted, threatened, or foreseen by an offender was substantially greater than average for the given offense.

- The amount of contraband materials possessed by the offender or under the offender's control was substantially greater than average for the given offense.

MITIGATING CIRCUMSTANCES

- An offender acted under strong provocation, or other circumstances in the relationship between the offender and the victim were extenuating.

- An offender played a minor or passive role in the offense or participated under circumstances of coercion or duress.

- An offender, because of youth or physical or mental impairment, lacked substantial capacity for judgment when the offense was committed.

Source: ABA Standards for Criminal Justice Sentencing (Washington, D.C.: American Bar Association, 1994), 47, 52–53.

Inconsistencies in Sentencing

For some, the natural differences in judicial philosophies, when combined with a lack of institutional control, raise important questions. Why should a bank robber in South Carolina receive a different sentence than a bank robber in Michigan? Even federal indeterminate sentencing guidelines seem overly vague: a bank robber can receive a prison term from one day to twenty years, depending almost entirely on the judge.[33] Furthermore, if judges have freedom to use their discretion, do they not also have the freedom to misuse it?

Purported improper judicial discretion is often the first reason given for two phenomena that plague the criminal justice system: sentencing disparity and sentencing discrimination. Though the two terms are often used interchangeably, they describe different statistical occurrences—the causes of which are debatable.

Sentencing Disparity.   Justice would seem to demand that those who commit similar crimes should receive similar punishments. **Sentencing disparity** occurs when this expectation is not met in one of three ways:

① Criminals receive similar sentences for different crimes of unequal seriousness.

② Criminals receive different sentences for similar crimes.

③ Mitigating or aggravating circumstances have a disproportionate effect on sentences. Prosecutors, for example, reward drug dealers who inform on their associates with lesser sentences. As a result, low-level drug sellers, who have no information to trade for reduced sentences, often spend more time in prison than their better-informed employers.[34]

Sentencing Discrimination.   Sentencing disparity is often attributed to circumstances that go beyond the reach of human motive. Such is not the case with sentencing discrimination. **Sentencing discrimination** occurs when disparities can be attributed to extralegal variables such as the defendant's gender, race, or economic standing. At first glance, racial discrimination would seem to be rampant in sentencing practices. Research by Cassia Spohn and David Holleran of the

I N F O T R A C®
COLLEGE EDITION

Keywords:
sentencing disparity;
sentencing discrimination

SENTENCING DISPARITY
A situation in which those convicted of similar crimes do not receive similar sentences.

SENTENCING DISCRIMINATION
A situation in which the length of a sentence appears to be influenced by a defendant's race, gender, economic status, or other factor not directly related to the crime he or she committed.

University of Nebraska at Omaha suggests that minorities pay a "punishment penalty" when it comes to sentencing.[35] In Chicago, Spohn and Holleran found that convicted African Americans were 12.1 percent more likely to go to prison than convicted whites, and convicted Hispanics were 15.3 percent more likely. In Miami, Hispanics were 10.3 percent more likely to be imprisoned than either blacks or whites.[36] Nationwide, in 2000 nearly half of all inmates in state and federal prisons were African American, even though that minority group makes up only about 13 percent of the country's population.[37] (For a discussion of trends in sentencing women, see the feature *Criminal Justice in Action—The Gender Factor* at the end of this chapter.)

This police photograph shows Brian Stewart, who was charged with injecting his son with blood infected with the AIDS virus because Stewart allegedly wanted to avoid paying child support. To make the punishment fit the crime, Circuit Judge Ellsworth Cundiff on January 8, 1999, imposed the maximum sentence that he could: life in prison. The judge then told Stewart that such a sentence was "far too lenient." Will Stewart necessarily spend his entire life behind bars? (Reuters/HO/Getty Images)

Daniel Leroy Crocker is shown here at his sentencing at the Johnson County Court House in Olathe, Kansas. Crocker had confessed to smothering nineteen-year-old Tracy Fesquez in 1979 after sexually assaulting the sleeping woman. Crocker was sentenced in 1999 to only twenty years in prison and will be eligible for parole in just ten years. This lenient sentence was based on the fact that he was never a suspect in the case. Rather, he eventually admitted to the murder, based on his religious faith. Three members of the victim's family urged in court that Crocker be given a life sentence. Should the reason Crocker voluntarily confessed affect his sentence? (AP Photo/Jeff Roberson)

SENTENCING REFORM

Judicial discretion, then, appears to be a double-edged sword. Although it allows judges to impose a wide variety of sentences to fit specific criminal situations, it appears to fail to rein in a judge's subjective biases, which leads to disparity and perhaps discrimination. Critics of judicial discretion believe that its costs (the lack of equality) outweigh its benefits (providing individualized justice). As Columbia law professor John C. Coffee noted:

> If we wish the sentencing judge to treat "like cases alike," a more inappropriate technique for the presentation could hardly be found than one that stresses a novelistic portrayal of each offender and thereby overloads the decisionmaker in a welter of detail.[38]

In other words, Professor Coffee feels that judges are given too much information in the sentencing process, making it impossible for them to be consistent in their decisions. It follows that limiting judicial discretion would not only simplify the process but lessen the opportunity for disparity or discrimination. Since the 1970s, this attitude has spread through state and federal legislatures, causing more extensive changes in sentencing procedures than in any other area of the American criminal justice system over that time period.

Beginnings of Reform

Research efforts in the mid-1970s laid the groundwork for sentencing reform. Particularly influential was the Twentieth Century Fund report developed by a task force of twelve criminal justice experts. The task force introduced the idea of **presumptive sentencing.** Revising ideas of determinate sentencing, the report urged lawmakers to legislate sentences that were "presumed" to be fair for any given crime category, restricting the court's discretion to finding aggravating or mitigating circumstances.[39]

PRESUMPTIVE SENTENCING
A sentencing strategy in which legislators set the average sentence that should be served for any particular crime, leaving judges with the ability to shorten or lengthen the sentence based on the circumstances of each case.

The Sentencing Project has news publications and a search engine. For a link to its Web site, go to the Hypercontents page for this chapter at http://www.cj.wadsworth.com/ gainescore2e.

Around the same time, Dr. Robert Martinson and several colleagues released an exhaustive study that seemed to prove that efforts to rehabilitate prisoners were generally unsuccessful.[40] Politicians on both sides seized on Martinson's report as an excuse to reject the idea of rehabilitating criminals and reestablish the ideals of determinate sentencing. Conservatives, believing judges, on the whole, to be too lenient, wished to limit their discretionary powers. Liberals—led by Senator Edward Kennedy (D-Mass.), who called sentencing a "national scandal" that leads to "massive injustice"[41]—felt the only way to eliminate the evils of sentencing disparity was to remove judicial bias from the process. Supported by a public alarmed by dramatic increases in violent crime, politicians moved sharply away from the notion of "treating" prisoners and toward the goal of punishing them.

Sentencing Guidelines

As the rehabilitative model came under criticism, so did its manifestations; indeterminate sentencing discretion, parole, probation, and "good time" credit became scapegoats for a failed system.[42] In an effort to reinstate determinacy into the sentencing process, many states and the federal government turned to **sentencing guidelines,** which require judges to dispense legislatively determined sentences based on factors such as the seriousness of the crime and the offender's prior record.

State Sentencing Guidelines.
In 1978, Minnesota became the first state to create a Sentencing Guidelines Commission with a mandate to construct and monitor the use of a determinate sentencing structure. The Minnesota Commission left no doubt as to the philosophical justification for the new sentencing statutes, stating unconditionally that retribution was its primary goal.[43] Today, seventeen states employ some form of sentencing guidelines with similar goals.

In general, these guidelines remove discretionary power from state judges by turning sentencing into a mathematical exercise. Members of the courtroom work group are guided by a *grid,* which helps them determine the proper sentence.

Federal Sentencing Guidelines.
In 1984, Congress passed the Sentencing Reform Act (SRA),[44] paving the way for federal sentencing guidelines that went into effect in 1987. Similar in many respects to the state guidelines, the SRA also eliminated parole for federal prisoners and severely limited early release from prison due to good behavior.[45] Furthermore, the act changed the sentencing role of U.S. probation officers. No longer would they be allowed to "suggest" the terms of punishment in presentence investigative reports. Instead, they are simply called on to calculate the presumptive sentence based on the federal sentencing guidelines grid.[46]

INFOTRAC®
COLLEGE EDITION

Keyword: federal sentencing guidelines

SENTENCING GUIDELINES
Legislatively determined guidelines that judges are required to follow when sentencing those convicted of specific crimes. These guidelines limit judicial discretion.

DEPARTURE
A stipulation in many federal and state sentencing guidelines that allows a judge to adjust his or her sentencing decision based on the special circumstances of a particular case.

Judicial Departures.
Even in their haste to limit a judge's power, legislators realized that sentencing guidelines could not be expected to cover every possible criminal situation. Therefore, both state and federal sentencing guidelines allow an "escape hatch" of limited judicial discretion known as a **departure.** The SRA has a proviso that a judge may "depart" from the presumptive sentencing range if there are aggravating or mitigating circumstances present that are not adequately covered in the guidelines. For example, suppose two men are involved in the robbery of a liquor store, and during court proceedings it becomes clear that one of them forced his partner to take part in the crime by threatening physical harm. In this case, a federal judge could reduce the accomplice's sentence because he committed the crime under "duress," a factor that is not accounted for in the sentencing guidelines.[47]

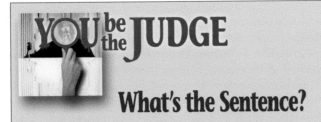

YOU be the JUDGE

What's the Sentence?

THE FACTS

Twenty-three-year-old law school student Angela attended the rehearsal dinner for a friend's wedding. At the event, she took part in a series of toasts. Driving back to her home in Seattle, Washington, in her Porsche, Angela ran a red light and collided with another vehicle. The occupant of the other car suffered a broken neck. Angela had a blood alcohol level of 0.16 percent (the legal limit was 0.10 percent at the time and has since been lowered to 0.08 percent) and pled guilty to vehicular assault.

THE LAW

Under Washington State's Sentencing Reform Act (SRA), vehicular assault is considered a "violent offense" and cate-

gorized as a "most serious" Level IV felony. Under the SRA presumptive sentencing guidelines, Angela, who had no previous offense, could be sentenced to between three and nine months in jail.

YOUR DECISION

Angela's lawyer presented the trial court with a number of arguments aimed at lowering her sentence, including her lack of a prior record, her history of charitable work, her sincere sense of regret, and her family background, which made it unlikely she would commit any further crimes. What sentence would you give Angela?

[To see how the Washington trial court ruled in this case, go to Example 10.1 in Appendix A.]

Judges do not, however, have unlimited access to departures. Any such decision must be justified in writing, and both the prosecution and the defense may appeal a judicial departure. In 1989, the Court of Appeals for the First Circuit ruled that departures must be measured on the basis of the circumstances and facts of the case and the reasonableness of the judge's decision.[48] (See the feature *You Be the Judge—What's the Sentence?*.)

Mandatory Sentencing Guidelines

In response to continuing disparities in sentencing decisions, politicians (urged on by their constituents) have passed sentencing laws increasingly contrary to the idea of individualized justice. These **mandatory** (minimum) **sentencing guidelines** further limit a judge's power to deviate from determinate sentencing laws by setting firm standards for certain crimes. Forty-six states have mandatory sentencing laws for crimes such as selling drugs, driving under the influence of alcohol, and committing any crime with a dangerous weapon. In Alabama, for example, any person caught selling drugs must spend at least two years in prison, with five years added to the sentence if the sale takes place within three miles of a school or housing project.[49] Similarly, Congress has set mandatory minimum sentences for more than one hundred crimes, mostly drug offenses.

Habitual offender laws are a form of mandatory sentencing that have proved increasingly popular over the past decade. Also known as "three strikes and you're out" laws, these statutes require that any person convicted of a third felony must serve a lengthy prison sentence. The crime does not have to be of a violent or dangerous nature. Under Washington's habitual offender law, for example, a "persistent offender" is automatically sentenced to life if the third felony offense happens to be "vehicular assault" (a automobile accident that causes injury), unarmed robbery, or attempted arson, among other lesser felonies.[50] Today, twenty-six states and the federal government employ "three strikes" statutes, with varying degrees of severity.

The Supreme Court paved the way for these "three strikes" laws when it ruled in *Rummel v. Estelle* (1980)[51] that Texas's habitual offender statute did not

> *"Those who repeatedly assault our citizens, terrorize our elderly, and prey upon our children must pay a severe price."*
>
> —Pete Wilson, *former California governor* (1996)

MANDATORY SENTENCING GUIDELINES
Statutorily determined punishments that must be applied to those who are convicted of specific crimes.

HABITUAL OFFENDER LAWS
Statutes that require lengthy prison sentences for those who are convicted of multiple felonies.

Outside a federal building in Los Angeles, activist Corey Nasario sits inside a makeshift cell to protest the thousands of California prisoners who have been jailed under the state's "three strikes" law. The vast majority of these prisoners have never committed a violent crime, yet they will spend from twenty-five years to life behind bars. What are the arguments for and against the contention that such "three strikes" laws violate the Eighth Amendment's prohibition of cruel and unusual punishment? (AP Photo/Damian Dovaganes)

> *"The calculated killing of a human being by the State involves, by its very nature, a denial of the executed person's humanity."*
>
> —William Brennan, *United States Supreme Court associate justice* (1972)

CAPITAL PUNISHMENT
The use of the death penalty to punish wrongdoers for certain crimes.

constitute "cruel and unusual punishment." Basically, the Court gave each state the freedom to legislate such laws in the manner that it deems proper. This had led to some "fine-tuning" of state statutes. California, for example, had a strict "three strikes" law that in its first seven years saw more than 7,000 felony offenders receive sentences of between twenty-five years and life. Eighty percent of the criminals sentenced under this law had committed nonviolent crimes such as drug use and petty thievery.[52]

In 2002, the United States Supreme Court agreed to hear two challenges to California's "three strikes" law, one brought by a man who was sentenced to twenty-five years in prison for stealing golf clubs and the other by a shoplifter who received a fifty-year term for taking $25 worth of videotapes.[53] The Court's decision on these cases will rest on whether such punishments violate the Eighth Amendment's prohibition of cruel and unusual punishment, and could have a broad impact on all "three strikes"–type laws in the country.

CAPITAL PUNISHMENT— THE ULTIMATE SENTENCE

"You do not know how hard it is to let a human being die," Abraham Lincoln (1809–1865) once said, "when you feel that a stroke of your pen will save him." Despite these misgivings, during his four years in office Lincoln approved the execution of 267 soldiers, including those who had slept at their posts.[54] Our sixteenth president's ambivalence toward **capital punishment** is reflected in America's continuing struggle to reconcile the penalty of death with the morals and values of society. Capital punishment has played a role in sentencing since the earliest days of the Republic and—having survived a brief period of abolition between 1972 and 1976—continues to enjoy public support.

Still, few topics in the criminal justice system inspire such heated debate. Death penalty opponents such as legal expert Stephen Bright wonder if "there comes a time when a society gets beyond some of the more primitive forms of punishment."[55] They point out that two dozen countries have abolished the death penalty since 1985, and the United States is the only Western democracy that continues the practice. Critics also claim that a process whose subjects are chosen by "luck and money and race" cannot serve the interests of justice.[56] Proponents believe that the death penalty serves as the ultimate deterrent for violent criminal behavior and that the criminals who are put to death are the "worst of the worst" and deserve their fate.

Today, more than 3,700 convicts are living on "death row" in American prisons. In 2000 and 2001, 151 were executed, a number that pales in comparison to execution rates from earlier in the twentieth century, but represents a high point over the past twenty-five years (see Figure 10.4). As legislators pass laws that increase the circumstances under which death can be sentenced, and prosecutors become more aggressive in seeking the harshest penalty, capital punishment appears likely to play a larger role in the sentencing process in the future. Thus, the questions that surround the death penalty—Is it fair? Is it humane? Does it deter crime?—will continue to inflame both its supporters and its detractors.

FIGURE 10.4
Executions in the United States, 1930 to Present

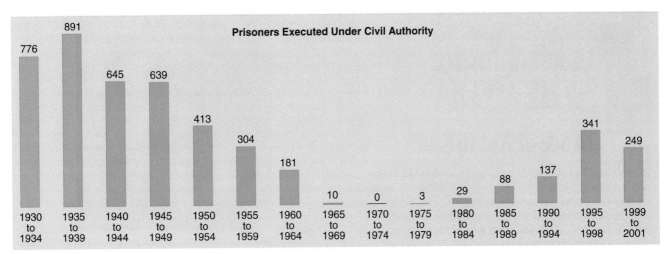

Prisoners Executed Under Civil Authority

1930 to 1934	776
1935 to 1939	891
1940 to 1944	645
1945 to 1949	639
1950 to 1954	413
1955 to 1959	304
1960 to 1964	181
1965 to 1969	10
1970 to 1974	0
1975 to 1979	3
1980 to 1984	29
1985 to 1989	88
1990 to 1994	137
1995 to 1998	341
1999 to 2001	249

Source: Death Penalty Information Center.

Methods of Execution

When the young United States adopted the practice of capital punishment from England, it also adopted the methods of the mother country. These methods included drawing and quartering and boiling the convict alive. In the nineteenth century, the practice of hanging replaced these techniques on the ground that they were too "barbaric." Indeed, the history of capital punishment in America is marked with attempts to make the act more humane. The 1890s saw the introduction of electrocution as a less painful method of execution than hanging, and in 1890 William Kemmler became the first American to die in an electric chair (for murdering his mistress) in Auburn Prison, New York. (The last public execution in the United States took place in Missouri in 1937, though the argument for restarting this tradition occasionally takes the public stage. See the feature *Criminal Justice & the Media—To See or Not to See?* on the following page.)

Even though Nevada introduced lethal gas as an even more humane method of capital punishment in 1924, the "chair" was the primary form of execution until the 1980s. In 1982, Texas became the first state to use lethal injection, and today this method dominates executions in the United States.[57] In this process, the condemned convict is usually given a sedative, which is followed by a combination of lethal drugs administered intravenously.

The Death Penalty and the Supreme Court

In part, these attempts to provide a "kinder, gentler" mode of execution reflect capital punishment's relationship with the U.S. Constitution. In 1890, William Kemmler challenged his sentence to die in New York's new electric chair on the ground that electrocution infringed on his Eighth Amendment rights against cruel and unusual punishment.[58] Kemmler's challenge is historically significant in that it did not challenge the death penalty *itself* as being cruel and unusual, but only the method by which it was carried out. In ruling against Kemmler, the United States Supreme Court stated, "Punishments are cruel when they involve torture or a lingering death; but the punishment of death is not cruel."[59] Thus, the Court set a standard that it has followed to this day. No *method* of execution has ever been found to be unconstitutional by the United States Supreme Court.

On the Web

The Death Penalty Information Center offers a great deal of information on capital punishment in the United States today. For a link to its Web site, go to the Hypercontents page for this chapter at **http://www.cj.wadsworth.com/ gainescore2e.**

INFOTRAC®
COLLEGE EDITION

Keyword: death penalty

Criminal Justice & THE MEDIA

To See or Not to See?

When Timothy McVeigh, found guilty for the Oklahoma City bombing (April 19, 1995), requested that his execution be televised, many Americans treated the idea with scorn and derision. Television programming, they argued, is already oversaturated with both fictional and, increasingly, real violence. Furthermore, images of such events are already readily available in our culture. *The Green Mile,* a 1999 film starring Tom Hanks that was nominated for an Academy Award, graphically depicts three executions. In 2001, Georgia officials released an eleven-minute audiotape of actual executions in their state. Furthermore, high-profile capital punishment cases such as McVeigh's receive intense media coverage, which seems to show everything but the convict's death.

There is, however, a good deal of support for televising executions from both supporters and critics of the death penalty. Proponents believe that public viewing of executions adds to their deterrent value. Opponents believe that by "hiding" executions, the government prevents people from seeing how gruesome they really are. These critics are convinced that if the public were allowed to witness these events, support for the death penalty would drop dramatically.

Evidence to uphold such a theory is hard to find, however. In fact, human curiosity seems to drive large numbers of people to horrific events, whether they are televised or not. In 1837, when support for capital punishment was as high as it is today, 20,000 spectators gathered in Philadelphia to watch the hanging of pirate James Moran. More than 160 years

The electric chair was the sole method of capital punishment in Florida from 1922 until July 8, 1999. On that day, the execution of convicted murderer Allen Lee Davis, shown above, turned grisly when the chair's current caused a significant amount of blood to flow from his nose during the electrocution. Critics of the electric chair hoped that Davis's macabre death would finally convince the United States Supreme Court that the method ran counter to the U.S. Constitution's prohibition of "cruel and unusual punishment." To head off any possible legal problems, in January 2000, Florida Governor Jeb Bush signed a bill that gave the state's death-row inmates the choice between dying by lethal injection or in the electric chair. Why might Davis's extensive nosebleeding have signified to the Court that execution by electric chair is unconstitutional? (AP Photo/Florida Department of Corrections)

later, in 1999, Florida Supreme Court Justice Leander J. Shaw, Jr., placed photos of the electrocution of Allen Lee "Tiny" Davis on the court's Web site to highlight the brutality of the electric chair. (The photos showed Davis hemorrhaging blood from his nose onto his white prison shirt.) The site received so many hits in such a short period of time that it crashed.

Furman v. Georgia. For nearly eight decades following its decision regarding Kemmler, the Court was silent with regard to capital punishment. Then, in *Furman v. Georgia* (1972),[60] the Court ruled that, as *administered,* the death penalty was cruel and unusual. By a 5–4 margin, the Court essentially agreed that the death penalty violated the Eighth Amendment. Only two of those in the majority (Justices Marshall and Brennan), however, were willing to state that capital punishment was blatantly unconstitutional. The other three (Justices Douglas, Stewart, and White) took the narrower view that the sentence was unconstitutional as practiced by the states. Justice Potter Stewart was particularly eloquent on the subject, stating that the sentence of death was so arbitrary as to be comparable to "being struck by lightning."[61] (See the feature *CJ in Focus—Landmark Cases:* Furman v. Georgia.) In its decision, therefore, the Court did not rule that the death penalty inherently violated the Eighth Amendment's protection

CJ in F☉CUS

Landmark Cases: *Furman v. Georgia*

Three cases were brought before the United States Supreme Court regarding the death penalty and the assertion that racial biases inherent in the system rendered the practice "cruel and unusual." The lead case concerned William Henry Furman, who was sentenced to death for killing a man during a burglary in Savannah, Georgia. For the first time, in *Furman v. Georgia,* the Supreme Court in a 5–4 vote ruled that all existing death penalty statutes were unconstitutional under the Eighth Amendment because they were being applied arbitrarily and inconsistently.

Furman v. Georgia
United States Supreme Court
408 U.S. 238 (1972)
http://laws.findlaw.com/US/408/238.html

IN THE WORDS OF THE COURT . . .

Mr. Justice BRENNAN, concurring

* * * *

At bottom, then, the Cruel and Unusual Punishments Clause prohibits the infliction of uncivilized and inhuman punishments. The State, even as it punishes, must treat its members with respect for their intrinsic worth as human beings. A punishment is "cruel and unusual," therefore, if it does not comport with human dignity.

* * * *

In determining whether a punishment comports with human dignity, we are aided also by a * * * principle inherent in the Clause—that the State must not arbitrarily inflict a severe punishment. This principle derives from the notion that the State does not respect human dignity when, without reason, it inflicts upon some people a severe punishment that it does not inflict upon others.* * * Although there are no exact figures available, we know that thousands of murders and rapes are committed annually in States where death is an authorized punishment for those crimes. However the rate of infliction is characterized—as "freakishly" or "spectacularly" rare, or simply as rare—it would take the purest sophistry to deny

that death is inflicted in only a minute fraction of these cases. * * * When the punishment of death is inflicted in a trivial number of the cases in which it is legally available, the conclusion is virtually inescapable that it is being inflicted arbitrarily. Indeed, it smacks of little more than a lottery system. * * * No one has yet suggested a rational basis that could differentiate in those terms the few who die from the many who go to prison. Crimes and criminals simply do not admit of a distinction that can be drawn so finely as to explain, on that ground, the execution of such a tiny sample of those eligible. * * * In other words, our procedures are not constructed to guard against the totally capricious selection of criminals for the punishment of death.

* * * *

Death is an unusually severe and degrading punishment; there is a strong probability that it is inflicted arbitrarily; its rejection by contemporary society is virtually total; and there is no reason to believe that it serves any penal purpose more effectively than the less severe punishment of imprisonment.

DECISION

The Court held that the death penalty, as carried out by the states, was cruel and unusual punishment and therefore violated the Eighth Amendment. Later, however, in *Gregg v. Georgia,* the Court reinstated capital punishment, ruling that by following certain procedures when sentencing a convict to be executed, the states could satisfy Eighth Amendment requirements.

FOR CRITICAL ANALYSIS

How does the fact that the death penalty is rarely carried out lend itself to Justice Brennan's argument that it is arbitrary and therefore cruel and unusual punishment?

 For more information and activities related to this case, go to the Landmark Cases feature at http://cj.wadsworth.com/gainescore2e

against cruel and unusual punishment or the Fourteenth Amendment's guarantee of due process, only that it did so as practiced by the states. So, although *Furman* invalidated the death penalty for over six hundred offenders on death row at the time, it also provided the states with a window of opportunity to bring their death penalty statutes up to constitutional standards.

The Bifurcated Process. As a result, a number of states adopted a two-stage, or *bifurcated,* procedure for capital cases. In the first stage, a jury must

INFOTRAC®
COLLEGE EDITION

Keyword: death penalty moratorium

Gary Gilmore is led to a Provo, Utah, court on December 1, 1976. Less then two months later, Gilmore became the first American executed under a new bifurcated system adopted by a number of states in the mid-1970s. Why did the U.S. Supreme Court put a halt to executions in this country in 1972? (AP Photo/Ron Barker)

"Let's do it."

—convicted murderer Gary Gilmore, *shortly before his execution by a Utah firing squad (1977)*

GREAT DEBATES

"Just deserts" or "official sanction to a climate of violence"? Capital punishment is one of the most controversial topics in the American criminal justice system. For an in-depth look at both sides of the death penalty issue, go to the Great Debates feature on the text's companion Web site at **http://www.cj.wadsworth. com/gainescore2e**.

determine the guilt or innocence of the defendant for a crime that has statutorily been determined to be punishable by death. If the defendant is found guilty, the jury reconvenes in the second stage and considers all relevant evidence in order to decide whether the death sentence is in fact warranted. Therefore, even if a jury were to find the defendant guilty of a crime, such as first degree murder, that *may be* punishable by death, in the second stage it could decide that the circumstances surrounding the crime justified only a punishment of life in prison.

In *Gregg v. Georgia* (1976),[62] the United States Supreme Court ruled in favor of Georgia's new bifurcated process, establishing a "road map" for all states to follow that would assure them protection from lawsuits based on Eighth Amendment grounds. On January 17, 1977, Gary Mark Gilmore became the first American executed (by Utah) under the new laws, and today thirty-eight states and the federal government have capital punishment laws based on the guidelines established by *Gregg*.

Debating the Sentence of Death

Of the topics covered in this textbook, few inspire the passion of argument that can be found concerning the death penalty. Many advocates believe that execution is "just deserts" for those who commit heinous crimes. In the words of Ernest van den Haag, death is the "only fitting retribution for murder that I can think of."[63] Opponents worry that retribution is simply another word for vengeance, and that "the use of the death penalty by the state will increase the acceptance of revenge in our society and will give official sanction to a climate of violence."[64]

Those advocates of the death penalty who wish to demonstrate that the practice benefits society often turn to the idea of deterrence. In other words, they believe that by executing convicted criminals, the system will discourage potential criminals from committing similar violent acts. (They also point out that execution is the ultimate form of incapacitation: those violent criminals who are put to death will certainly not repeat their crimes.) Studies that attempt to prove the deterrent effect of the death penalty on the overall crime rate are quite controversial, however, and have been rejected by many members of the criminal justice community.

Fallibility. Many observers feel that if a system of capital punishment is to exist, it must be *infallible;* that is, the system must never execute someone who is not actually guilty. In fact, between 1976, when the Supreme Court reinstated capital punishment, and 2001, ninety-eight American men and women who had been convicted of capital crimes and sentenced to death were later found to be innocent. Over that same time period, 795 executions took place, meaning that for every eight convicts put to death since *Gregg,* one death-row inmate has been found innocent.[65]

There are several explanations for this relatively high ratio of error in capital cases. First, police and prosecutors are often under a great deal of public pressure to solve violent crimes and may be overzealous in arresting and prosecuting suspects. Such was the case with Rolando Cruz, who spent a decade on Illinois's death row for the rape and murder of a ten-year-old girl. Even after another man named Brian Dugan confessed to the crime and DNA testing linked Dugan to the crime scene, prosecutors still insisted that Cruz was the culprit. Only after a police officer admitted that he lied under oath concerning Cruz's "confession" was Cruz declared not guilty.[66]

Outright lying by persons involved in capital cases contributes to false convictions. Professors Hugo Bedau of Tufts University and Michael Radelet of the University of Florida found that one-third of wrongful capital convictions resulted from "jailhouse snitches" who perjured themselves by telling the court that they overheard a confession by the defendant. In addition, false confessions and faulty eyewitness identifications were found to be responsible for two of every seven wrongful convictions.[67] The single factor that contributes the most to the criminal justice system's fallibility, however, is widely believed to be unsatisfactory legal representation. Many states refuse to allocate adequate funds for public defenders, meaning that poor capital defendants are often provided with inexperienced or incompetent counsel. Alabama, for example, pays its lawyers just $40 an hour, with a cap of $1,000, to prepare for a capital trial and $60 an hour for work in court.[68] (By comparison, private lawyers receive as much as $500 an hour.)

Arbitrariness.   The chances of a defendant being found guilty in a capital trial seem to rely heavily not only on who is defending her or him, but also on where she or he committed the crime. As Figure 10.5 shows, a convict's chances of being executed are strongly influenced by geography. Six southern states (Texas, Georgia, Virginia, Florida, Louisiana, and Missouri) account for nearly two-thirds of all death sentences, while twelve states and the District of Columbia do not provide for capital punishment within their borders. Therefore, a person on trial for first degree murder in New Mexico has a much better chance of avoiding execution than someone who has committed the same crime in Texas.

During a special session of the Nebraska legislature held in November of 2002, Omaha Senator Ernie Chambers argues a point. The legislature voted 38–7 to give juries the duty to decide whether the aggravating circumstances in first degree murder cases warrant the sentence of death. The legislature also rejected a measure to introduce lethal injection as a means of execution, leaving it the only state that relies solely on electrocution to carry out the death penalty. (AP Photo)

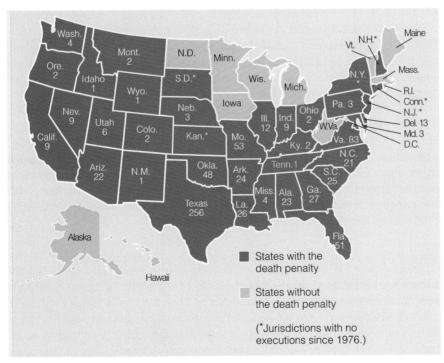

FIGURE 10.5
Number of Executions by State, 1976–2001

Wash. 4
Mont. 2
N.D.
Minn.
Vt.
N.H.*
Maine
Ore. 2
Idaho 1
S.D.*
Wis.
Mich.
N.Y.*
Mass.
Wyo. 1
Neb. 3
Iowa
Ohio 2
Pa. 3
R.I.
Conn.*
Nev. 9
Utah 6
Colo. 2
Ill. 12
Ind. 9
W.Va.
N.J.*
Del. 13
Calif. 9
Kan.*
Mo. 53
Ky. 2
Va. 83
Md. 3
D.C.
Ariz. 22
N.M. 1
Okla. 48
Ark. 24
Tenn. 1
N.C. 21
S.C. 25
Texas 256
La. 26
Miss. 4
Ala. 23
Ga. 27
Fla. 51
Alaska
Hawaii

■ States with the death penalty

■ States without the death penalty

(*Jurisdictions with no executions since 1976.)

Source: Death Penalty Information Center.

Prizefighter Rubin "Hurricane" Carter was convicted in 1966 of a triple murder in New Jersey and sentenced to life. In 1985, he was exonerated. Today, he heads the Association in Defense of the Wrongly Convicted. At one conference he stated, "There is no separation between being on death row or being held unjustly for the rest of your life. Prison is death." What might be the cost to society if no sentences of life imprisonment were ever handed out? (AP Photo/Barry Thumma)

*"***We didn't feel she should get the death penalty. When you're on Death Row, you're there so long with nothing to bother you. In jail, she'll be with murderers and rapists. We thought the death penalty would be too easy for her.***"*

—Jodi Dotts, *explaining her decision to ask the prosecutor not to seek capital punishment for her daughter's killer (1999)*

On July 3, 1982, Mumia Abu-Jamal was convicted of first degree murder in the death of Philadelphia police officer Daniel Faulkner and sentenced to death. Over the past two decades, Abu-Jamal's case has raised numerous questions concerning race and capital punishment. For a link to a Web site dedicated to Abu-Jamal's innocence, and to one dedicated to his guilt, go to the Hypercontents page for this chapter at **http://www.cj.wadsworth.com/ gainescore2e.**

Despite the bifurcated process required by *Furman,* therefore, a certain amount of arbitrariness appears to remain in the system. Comparing the number of murders known by police to the number of executions carried out between 1979 and 1996, the chances of a murderer being executed are approximately 1,000 to 1.[69]

Discriminatory Intent and the Death Penalty.   Whether or not capital punishment is imposed arbitrarily, claim some observers, it is not done without bias. Of the 4,220 prisoners executed in the United States between 1930 and 1996, 53 percent were African American, even though that minority group made up between 10 and 15 percent of the national population during that time span.[70] Today, nearly 43 percent of all inmates on death row are black; thus, the black proportion of the death-row population is more than triple the black proportion of the general population.[71] Another set of statistics continues to be problematic. African Americans are approximately four times more likely to receive the death penalty if their victim is white than if he or she is black.[72] A study of death penalty cases in North Carolina found that the odds of receiving a death sentence for convicts of any race increased three and a half times if the victim was white rather than black.[73]

In *McCleskey v. Kemp* (1987),[74] the defense attorney for an African American sentenced to death for killing a white police officer used similar statistics to challenge Georgia's death penalty law. A study of 2,000 Georgia murder cases showed that although African Americans were the victims of six out of every ten murders in the state, over 80 percent of the cases in which death was imposed involved murders of whites.[75] In a 5–4 decision, the United States Supreme Court rejected the defense's claims, ruling that statistical evidence did not prove discriminatory intent on the part of Georgia's lawmakers.

The Immediate Future of the Death Penalty

A very significant event in the recent history of the capital punishment debate took place in January 2000, when Governor George Ryan of Illinois halted all executions in his state. Ryan, formerly a death penalty supporter, put the moratorium into effect after Anthony Porter, who had spent nearly sixteen years on the state's death row for a double murder, was found innocent and released two

Andy Hulette testifies at the 2002 trial of his former roommate Shane Ragland in a Lexington, Kentucky, courtroom. Ragland was eventually convicted of first degree murder in the 1994 sniper death of Trent DiGiuro, a University of Kentucky football player. Prosecutors had asked that Ragland receive the death penalty. What impact did the fact that Ragland was tried and convicted in Kentucky have on his chances of being executed? In what states is it most likely that a person convicted of murder will receive the death penalty? (AP Photo/Frank Anderson, Pool)

days before his scheduled execution. Porter was the thirteenth death-row convict to be exonerated in Illinois since 1977. "People are starting to understand that there's a possibility that innocent people are going to be put to death," said Ryan of his decision. "I don't think anyone wants that on their hands or their consciences."[76] (On January 11, 2003, just two days before the end of his term, Ryan commuted all Illinois 167 death sentences to prison terms of life or less, the largest emptying of a state death row in the history of the United States.)

In 2002, the United States Supreme Court took its own significant step by deciding, in the case of *Atkins v. Virginia,* that the Eighth Amendment ban on cruel and unusual punishment prohibits the execution of the mentally retarded.[77] The decision kept Virginia from putting Daryl Atkins—who has an IQ of 59—to death, and stayed the execution of 160 other death-row inmates with IQs of less than 70.

That same year, three justices (Justice John Paul Stevens, Justice Ruth Bader Ginsberg, and Justice Stephen Breyer) called for the Court to address the issue of whether convicts should be put to death for crimes they committed while juveniles.[78] In addition, the Senate Judiciary Committee endorsed a bill that would establish minimum standards for lawyers defending indigents who have been sentenced to death. The proposed bill would also make access to DNA testing easier for those on death row.[79]

It is important to note, however, that proposals to ban capital punishment are still rare. A Gallup poll taken in 2002 showed that 72 percent of the public still supports the death penalty, the highest level of approval since 1995.[80] Furthermore, prosecutors are still aggressively seeking the punishment, as reflected in a nationwide death-row population that is growing by 100 to 150 convicts a year. The tenor of the death penalty debate appears to have shifted. The main focus now is on how the sentence of death can be more fairly administered—and no longer on the morality of executions.

On the Web

Northwestern University School of Law in Chicago operates a clinic in which students are given the opportunity to work on death penalty cases. To learn more about the program, find a link to its Web site on the Hypercontents page for this chapter at http://www.cj.wadsworth.com/ gainescore2e.

Criminal Justice in Action

The Gender Factor

As has been noted throughout this chapter, many observers believe that race plays a large role in the criminal justice system's decisions concerning who gets punished and for how long. Statistically, however, the most important characteristic when it comes to sentencing is gender. Women, on the whole, are not punished as harshly as men, and in many instances the differences are striking. In this *Criminal Justice in Action* feature, we will examine the "gender gap" and discuss some of the reasons why it exists.

THE DRASTIC RISE IN FEMALE OFFENDERS

As was noted in Chapter 1, women account for a small fraction of this country's criminal offenders. Only 11 percent of the national jail population and 6 percent of the national prison population are female, and in 2001 only 23 percent of all arrests involved women.[81] These statistics, however, fail to convey the startling rate at which the female presence in the criminal justice system has been increasing. In 1970, there were about 6,000 women in federal and state prisons; today, there are nearly 100,000. During the 1990s, the number of women incarcerated in this country doubled,[82] and the number of women arrested increased by 30 percent.

There is little support in the academic community for any idea that the basic nature of American women has changed over the past thirty years. Freda Adler, a professor of criminal justice at Rutgers University, uses the "liberation hypothesis" to partially explain the increase in female arrestees and inmates.[83] This theory holds that as women become more and more equal in society as a whole, their opportunities to commit crimes will increase as well. "You can't embezzle if you're not near funds," Professor Adler notes. "You can't get involved in a fight at the bar if you're not allowed in the bar."[84] Criminologist Meda Chesney-Lind believes that the "get tough" attitude among politicians and law enforcement agencies has been the main contributor to increased rates of female criminality. "Simply put," she says, "it appears that the criminal justice system is now more willing to incarcerate women."[85]

WOMEN AND THE "WAR ON DRUGS"

A closer look at the offenses for which women are sent to prison and jail supports Chesney-Lind's thesis. The vast majority of women are prosecuted for nonviolent crimes, usually drug-related offenses. In fact, drug offenses account for nearly two-thirds of the women sent to federal prison each year (violent crimes account for only about

2 percent).[86] The habitual offender statutes and mandatory sentences for drug crimes that have accompanied the "war on drugs" have been particularly influential. In the 1980s, many of the women now in prison would not have been arrested or would have received light sentences for their drug-related wrongdoing.

When women do commit violent crimes, the patterns are distinct as well. Research conducted by social psychologists Angela Browne and Kirk R. Williams shows that when women do kill, the victim is usually an intimate male partner. Moreover, a woman is likely to kill in response to physical aggression or threats of physical aggression by her partner.[87]

THE "NEW FEMALE CRIMINAL"

As the last sentence suggests, not only are the criminal patterns of women distinct from those of their male counterparts, but the reasons behind the crime are different as well. According to Jane Roberts Chapman, the "new female criminal" is a single mother with children, who commits property crimes out of need or abuses drugs as an avenue of escape from her difficult situation.[88] Four-fifths of all female prisoners are mothers, and nearly 30 percent describe themselves as the "primary care giver" of their children (meaning they do not have a partner to share the responsibility).[89] Chapman predicts that if the number of single mothers below the poverty line increases, female crime rates will rise accordingly.

Using information found in presentencing investigative reports, feminist criminologist Kathleen Daly has identified several distinct pathways to crime that women follow.[90] The *harmed-and-harming woman,* for example, suffered from abuse and neglect as a child, which in turn led her to "act out" and be labeled a "problem child." As an adult, this woman reacts to difficult situations with violence. The *battered woman,* in contrast, does not necessarily have a history of childhood abuse, but uses violence to defend herself against an abusive partner. Similarly, the *drug-connected woman* does not have a criminal past, but has become involved in a relationship—either with a partner or with a child—characterized by drug use. A drug-connected woman might, for example, let her son use their home as a place to sell drugs or turn to street crime to support a boyfriend or husband's drug habit.

THE CHIVALRY EFFECT

Few people would argue that race or ethnicity should be a factor in sentencing decisions. The system should be "color-blind." But what about women—should the system be "gender-blind" as well? On a policy level, at least, Congress answered that question in the Sentencing Reform Act of 1984, which emphasized the ideal of gender-neutral sentencing.[91] In practice, however, this is not the case. Women who are convicted of crimes are less likely to go to prison than men, and those who are incarcerated serve shorter sentences. One study attributes these differences to the elements of female criminality: in property crimes, women are usually accessories, and in violent crimes, women are usually reacting to physical abuse. In both cases, the mitigating circumstances would lead to lesser punishment.[92] Wider evidence suggests, however, that the *chivalry effect,* a theory that women are treated more leniently than men, plays a large part in the decisions of prosecutors, judges, and juries.

Data compiled by the U.S. Sentencing Commission show that prosecutors are more likely to offer women beneficial plea bargains.[93] Several self-reported studies have shown that judges may treat female defendants more "gently" than male ones, and that judges are influenced by mitigating factors such as marital status and family background with women that they would ignore with men.[94] As for juries, their leniency toward women can be most clearly seen in death penalty cases. Though women account for 13 percent of all murder arrests, they represent only 1.5 percent of those prisoners on death row. According to Karen Jo Koonan, an Oakland (California) jury consultant, jurors do not want to believe that a woman, in her role as nurturer, could also be a cold-blooded killer.[95]

IS CHIVALRY DEAD?

There are signs, however, that some of these attitudes are changing. Overall, chivalry appears to be dying. Twenty-five years ago, almost two-thirds of all women sentenced in federal court were given probation, and, as mentioned before, the female presence in prison was negligible.[96] Between 1976 and 1997, only one woman was executed in the United States; since 1998, eight have been put to death. And, it must be noted, the chivalry effect was never in effect for African American women. In Florida, for example, black women are nine times more likely to be sentenced as habitual offenders for drug-related offenses than white women.[97]

Is there an argument to be made in favor of the chivalry effect? In fact, some observers are now supporting judicial leniency for women and claim that gender-neutral sentencing exacts a heavy price on society. By separating increasing numbers of nonviolent female offenders from their children, the sentencing guidelines often shift the cost of caring for these children to the taxpayer through social service programs.[98] Furthermore, by increasing the chances that the children themselves will have emotional problems due to lack of an active parent, such laws increase the probability that these children will become delinquent. Instead of sending nonviolent offenders who are pregnant or have children

In 1990, teen-age lovers Douglas Christopher Thomas and Jessica Wiseman (right) shot and killed her parents. Wiseman was sent to a juvenile detention center and released in 1997. Thomas, in contrast, wound up in an adult prison and was executed by the state of Virginia in 2000. Is this necessarily evidence of a gender disparity in sentencing? Does it matter that Wiseman was fourteen years old and Thomas was seventeen years old at the time of the crime? (AP Photo, *Newport News Daily Press*)

to jail or prison, the argument goes, the correctional system should place them in community-based programs where they can continue to care for their offspring.

MAKING SENSE OF THE GENDER GAP IN PUNISHMENT AND SENTENCING

1 Do you believe that sentencing should be gender neutral? What are the arguments for and against giving women more lenient sentences for nonviolent crimes?

2 To what extent should a judge consider the motivation behind a crime committed by a woman (self-defense, did it for boyfriend, and so on) as a mitigating circumstance? What might be the result if judges did this more often?

3 Give some reasons to explain why so few women are on death row. Why do you think society seems to be uncomfortable with the idea of sentencing a woman to be executed? Do you think that there are some crimes a woman could commit that a judge or jury might be more likely to punish with the death sentence?

INFOTRAC®
COLLEGE EDITION

Keyword: female offenders

KEY TERMS

aggravating circumstances 259

capital punishment 264

departure 262

determinate sentencing 254

deterrence 252

"good time" 254

habitual offender laws 263

incapacitation 252

indeterminate sentencing 254

just deserts 252

mandatory sentencing guidelines 263

mitigating circumstances 259

presentence investigative report 258

presumptive sentencing 261

"real offense" 259

rehabilitation 253

retribution 252

sentencing discrimination 260

sentencing disparity 260

sentencing guidelines 262

truth-in-sentencing law 255

CHAPTER SUMMARY

❶ List and contrast the four basic philosophical reasons for sentencing criminals. (a) Retribution, (b) deterrence, (c) incapacitation, and (d) rehabilitation. Under the principle of retributive justice, the severity of the punishment is in proportion to the severity of the crime. Punishment is an end in itself. In contrast, the deterrence approach seeks to prevent future crimes by setting an example. Such punishment is based on its deterrent value and not necessarily on the severity of the crime. The incapacitation theory of punishment simply argues that a criminal in jail cannot impose further harm on society. In contrast, the rehabilitation theory believes that criminals can be rehabilitated in the appropriate prison environment.

❷ Contrast indeterminate with determinate sentencing. Indeterminate sentencing follows from legislative penal codes that set minimum and maximum amounts of incarceration time; determinate sentencing carries a fixed amount of time, although this may be reduced for "good time."

❸ Explain why there is a difference between a sentence imposed by a judge and the actual sentence carried out by the prisoner. Although judges may decide on indeterminate sentencing, thereafter it is parole boards that decide when prisoners will be released after the minimum sentence is served.

❹ List the six forms of punishment. (a) Capital (death sentence), (b) imprisonment, (c) probation, (d) fines, (e) restitution and community service, and (f) restorative justice.

❺ Explain some of the reasons why sentencing reform has occurred. One reason is sentencing dis-

parity, which has been seen on a geographic basis and on a courtroom basis (due to a particular judge's philosophy). Sentencing discrimination has also occurred on the basis of defendants' gender, race, or economic standing. An additional reason for sentencing reform has been a general desire to "get tough on crime."

❻ Contrast sentencing guidelines with mandatory sentencing guidelines. At the state level, courtroom work groups are guided by a grid, which determines the proper sentence. Starting in 1987, a similar grid system was put into place at the federal level. In response to judges' continued departures from such sentencing guidelines, federal and state legislatures have instituted mandatory (minimum) sentencing guidelines, which limit a judge's discretion for certain classes of crimes, such as selling drugs. The most stringent guideline is represented by "three strikes and you're out" laws, which require any person convicted of a third felony to serve a lengthy prison sentence without the possibility of parole.

❼ Describe the main issues of the death penalty debate. Many of those who favor capital punishment believe that it is "just deserts" for the most violent of criminals. Those who oppose it see the act as little more than revenge. There is also disagreement over whether the death penalty acts as a deterrent. The relatively high number of death-row inmates who have been found innocent has raised questions about the fallibility of the process, while certain statistics seem to show that execution is rather arbitrary. Finally, many observers see capital punishment as being used unfairly with regard to members of minority groups.

QUESTIONS FOR CRITICAL ANALYSIS

1. How can punishing a wrongdoer be reconciled with the concept of rehabilitation?

2. How does the limitation of "good time" along with fixed sentencing make a prison warden's job more difficult?

3. What single fact will probably lead to a reduction in truth-in-sentencing laws as well as a reduction in mandatory minimum sentencing laws?

4. What restricts judicial discretion in sentencing in many jurisdictions?

5. How do "real offense" procedures effectively render plea bargains almost meaningless?

6. What are some of the arguments that proponents of the death penalty offer in its favor? What are some of the arguments that opponents offer against it?

SELECTED PRINT AND ELECTRONIC RESOURCES

SUGGESTED READINGS

Banner, Stuart, *The Death Penalty: An American History,* Cambridge, MA: Harvard University Press, 2002. Banner, a law professor at Washington University in St. Louis, Missouri, chronicles the record of capital punishment in this country. He shows how a number of different factors—including public opinion, the press, politics, and an evolving concept of "justice"—have influenced how and why we execute wrongdoers in the United States. The author provides a wealth of interesting anecdotes to round out the history of the death penalty, including an explanation of how dissection of the dead convict was once viewed as punishment beyond the grave.

Lovegrove, Austin, *The Framework of Judicial Sentencing: A Study in Legal Decision Making,* Cambridge, MA: Cambridge University Press, 1997. This book looks at how judges think when they sentence multiple offenders. The author tries to determine the strategies that judges develop to help them apply sentencing law in each case. From interviews with judges, the author tries to develop a standardized framework of judicial sentencing.

Stith, Kate, and José A. Cabranes, *Fear of Judging: Sentencing Guidelines in the Federal Courts,* Chicago: University of Chicago Press, 1998. This book presents an accessible explanation of how federal sentencing guidelines work. The authors argue against such guidelines. They would prefer that a common law of sen-

tencing be used instead. They point out that federal judges exercised wide discretion in criminal sentencing for more than two centuries. All this changed in 1987 when federal sentencing guidelines went into effect. The authors believe that the sentencing guidelines have failed to address inequities in sentencing.

MEDIA RESOURCES

Dead Man Walking **(1995)** This film is about a religious woman who becomes the spiritual adviser of a convicted murderer on death row. Sister Helen (Susan Sarandon) faces an angry community and the victims' anguished parents. The film examines the challenge of bringing fairness, honor, and a voice from the victims' families to the process.

Critically analyze this film:

1. Both those in favor and those against the death penalty have said that this film supports their views. How is this possible?

2. In the film, Susan Sarandon's character, Sister Helen Prejean, visits the parents of the two teenagers who allegedly were murdered by Sean Penn's character, Matthew Poncelet. The movie viewer sees that at least one couple seeks retribution. What do these scenes indicate to you about the interjection of victims' rights into the sentencing process?

LOGGING ON

Go to http://cj.wadsworth.com/gainescore2e, and click Hypercontents. There, you will find URLs for the organizations in the following list:

- If you want to find out more about truth-in-sentencing laws, you should visit the Web site of the **Bureau of Justice Statistics (BJS).** The BJS has published a document called "Truth in Sentencing in State Prisons," which describes the development and use of truth-in-sentencing laws and presents data on the growing numbers of states not using them.

- The amount of information concerning the death penalty on the Web can be overwhelming. **Derechos Human Rights** offers a useful, if not exhaustive, list of links to death penalty sites.

USING THE INTERNET FOR CRIMINAL JUSTICE ANALYSIS

INFOTRAC®
COLLEGE EDITION

1. Go to InfoTrac College Edition at **http://www.infotrac-college.com/wadsworth/.** After you log on, go to the article entitled: **"Individual and Contextual Influences on Sentencing Lengths"** Then go to: **"Thou shall not kill any nice people."** This article, from the *American Criminal Law Review,* examines the problems associated with victim impact statements in capital sentencing.

a. Summarize the Supreme Court decision in *Payne v. Tennessee.*

b. How did the Supreme Court's decisions in *Booth v. Maryland* and *South Carolina v. Gathers* differ from its decision in *Payne v. Tennessee?*

c. In *Payne v. Tennessee,* did all of the Supreme Court justices agree with the opinion?

d. According to the article, how many states utilize victim impact statements in their capital sentencing hearings?

2. See Internet Activities 10.1 and 10.2 on the companion Web site for *CJ in Action: The Core.* To get to the activities, go to **http://www.cj.wadsworth.com/gainescore2e,** select the appropriate chapter from the drop down list, then click Internet Activities on the left navigation bar.

NOTES

1. "Man Sentenced for Third Drunken Driving Conviction since Causing Fatal Crash," *Associated Press Newswires* (March 30, 2001).

2. N.Y. Veh. & Traf. Law Section 1192 (McKinney 1999).

3. Tex. Parks & Wild. Code Ann. Sections 12.204, 12.405, 77.020(c).

4. Bruce L. Benson, David W. Rasmussen, and Brent D. Mast, "Deterring Drunk Driving Fatalities: An Economics of Crime Perspective," *International Journal of Law and Economics* (June 1999), 222.

5. David Yellen, "Just Deserts and Lenient Prosecutors: The Flawed Case for Real Offense Sentencing," *Northwestern University Law Review* 91 (Summer 1997), 1434.

6. Brian Forst, "Prosecution and Sentencing," in *Crime,* James Q. Wilson and Joan Petersilia, eds. (San Francisco: ICS Press, 1995), 386.

7. Herbert L. Packer, "Justification for Criminal Punishment," in *The Limits of Criminal Sanction* (Palo Alto, CA: Stanford University Press, 1968), 36–37.

8. Jeremy Bentham, *An Introduction to the Principles of Morals and Legislation 1789* (New York: Hafner Publishing Corp., 1961).

9. Forst, 376.

10. John J. DiIulio, Jr., "Help Wanted: Economists, Crime and Public Policy," *Journal of Economic Perspectives* 10 (1996), 3, 16–17.

11. Sue T. Reid, *Crime and Criminology,* 7th ed. (New York: Holt, Rinehart, and Winston, 1995), 352.

12. James Q. Wilson, *Thinking about Crime* (New York: Basic Books, 1975), 235.

13. Isaac Ehrlich, "Participation in Illegitimate Activities: A Theoretical and Empirical Investigation," *Journal of Political Economy* 81 (May/June 1973), 521–64.

14. Steve Levitt, "The Effect of Prison Population Size on Crime Rates," *Quarterly Journal of Economics* 111 (May 1996), 319.

15. Todd Clear, *Harm in Punishment* (Boston: Northeastern University Press, 1980).

16. Jurg Gerber and Simone Engelhardt-Greer, "Just and Painful: Attitudes Toward Sentencing Criminals," in Timothy J. Flanagan and Dennis R. Longmire, eds., *Americans View Crime and Justice; A National Public Opinion Survey* (Thousand Oaks, CA: Sage, 1996), 72.

17. Gregory W. O'Reilly, "Truth-in-Sentencing, Illinois Adds Yet Another Layer of 'Reform' to Its Complicated Code of Corrections," *Loyola University of Chicago Law Journal* (Summer 1996), 986, 999–1000.

18. Arthur W. Campbell, *Law of Sentencing* (Rochester, NY: Lawyers Co-operative Publishing Co., 1978), 9.

19. Marvin Zalman, "The Rise and Fall of the Indeterminate Sentence," *Wayne Law Review* 24 (1977), 45, 52.

20. Marvin E. Frankel, *Criminal Sentences: Law without Order* (New York: Hill & Wang, 1972), 5.

21. Jessica Mitford, *Kind and Usual Punishment* (New York: Alfred A. Knopf, 1973), 80–83.

22. Bureau of Justice Statistics, *Truth in Sentencing in State Prisons* (Washington, D.C.: Department of Justice, 1999).

23. Paul W. Keve, *Crime Control and Justice in America: Searching for Facts and Answers* (Chicago: American Library Association, 1995), 77.

24. Haya El Nasser, "Paying for Crime with Shame," *USA Today* (June 25, 1996), 1A.

25. Mark S. Umbreit, *Victim Meets Offender: The Impact of Restorative Justice and Mediation* (Monsey, N.Y.: Criminal Justice Press, 1994), 2.

26. Gary Wisby, "Child Molester Has Castration Surgery," *Chicago Sun-Times* (January 21, 1998), 9.

27. Kate Stith and José A. Cabranes, "Judging under the Federal Sentencing Guidelines," *Northwestern University Law Review* 91 (Summer 1997), 1247.

28. Stephen A. Fennell and William N. Hall, "Due Process at Sentencing: An Empirical and Legal Analysis of the Disclosure of Presentence Reports in Federal Courts," *Harvard Law Review* 93 (1980), 1666–68.

29. Stith and Cabranes, 1247.

30. Andrew Von Hirsch, *Doing Justice: The Choice of Punishments* (New York: Hill and Wang, 1976), 98.

31. Julie R. O'Sullivan, "In Defense of the U.S. Sentencing Guidelines Modified Real-Offense System," *Northwestern University Law Review* 91 (1997), 1342.

32. Brian Forst and Charles Wellford, "Punishment and Sentencing: Developing Sentencing Guidelines Empirically from Principles of Punishment," *Rutgers Law Review* 33 (1981).

33. 18 U.S.C. Section 2113(a) (1994).

34. Alfred Blumstein, Jacqueline Cohen, Susan Martin, and Michael Tonry, *Research on Sentencing: The Search for Reform,* vol. 1 (Washington, D.C.: National Academy Press, 1983), 7–8.

35. Cassia Spohn and David Holleran, "The Imprisonment Penalty Paid by Young, Unemployed Black and Hispanic Male Offenders," *Criminology* 35 (2000), 281.

36. Ibid., 297.

37. Bureau of Justice Statistics, *Prisoners in 2001* (Washington, D.C.: U.S. Department of Justice, 2002), 12.

38. John C. Coffee, "Repressed Issues of Sentencing," *Georgetown Law Journal* 66 (1978), 987.

39. Twentieth Century Fund Task Force on Criminal Sentencing, *Fair and Certain Punishment* (New York: McGraw-Hill, 1976).

40. Robert Martinson, "What Works?— Questions and Answers about Prison Reform," *Public Interest* 35 (Spring 1974), 22.

41. Edward Kennedy, "Introduction to Symposium on Sentencing," *Hofstra Law Review* 1 (1978), 1.

42. Francis A. Allen, *The Decline of the Rehabilitative Ideal* (New Haven, CT: Yale University Press, 1981), 8.

43. J. S. Bainbridge, Jr., "The Return of Retribution," *ABA Journal* (May 1985), 63.

44. Sentencing Reform Act of 1984, Pub. L. No. 98-473, 98 Stat. 1987 [codified as amended at 18 U.S.C. Sections 3551–3742 and 28 U.S.C. Sections 991–998 (1988)].

45. Julia L. Black, "The Constitutionality of Federal Sentences Imposed under the Sentencing Reform Act of 1984 after *Mistretta v. United States,*" *Iowa Law Review* 75 (March 1990), 767.

46. Roger Haines, Kevin Cole, and Jennifer Wole, *Federal Sentencing Guidelines Handbook* (New York: McGraw-Hill, 1994), 3.

47. Michael S. Gelacak, Ilene H. Nagel, and Barry L. Johnson, "Departures under the Federal Sentencing Guidelines: An Empirical and Jurisprudential Analysis," *Minnesota Law Review* 81 (December 1996), 299.

48. *United States v. Diaz-Villafane,* 874 F.2d 43, 49 (1st Cir. 1989).

49. Alabama Code 1975 Section 20-2-79.

50. Washington Rev. Code Ann. Sections 9.94A.030.

51. 445 U.S. 263 (1980).

52. California Department of Corrections study, cited in Carl Ingram, "Serious Crime Falls in State's Major Cities," *Los Angeles Times* (March 13, 1996), A3.

53. Joan Biskupic, "Supreme Court to Hear 'Three Strikes' Case," *USA Today* (April 2, 2002), 3A.

54. Walter Berns, "Abraham Lincoln (book review)," *Commentary* (January 1, 1996), 70.

55. Comments made at the Georgetown Law Center, "The Modern View of Capital Punishment," *American Criminal Law Review* 34 (Summer 1997), 1353.

56. David Bruck, quoted in Bill Rankin, "Fairness of the Death Penalty Is Still on Trial," *Atlanta Constitution & Journal* (July 29, 1997), A13.

57. Stephen Trombley, *The Execution Protocol: Inside America's Capital Punishment Industry* (New York: Crown Publishers, 1992), 73.

58. Larry C. Berkson, *The Concept of Cruel and Unusual Punishment* (Lexington, MA: Lexington Books, 1975), 43.

59. *In re Kemmler,* 136 U.S. 447 (1890).

60. 408 U.S. 238 (1972).

61. 408 U.S. 309 (1972) (Stewart, concurring).

62. 428 U.S. 153 (1976).

63. Ernest van den Haag, "The Ultimate Punishment: A Defense," *Harvard Law Review* 99 (1986), 1669.

64. *The Death Penalty: The Religious Community Calls for Abolition* (pamphlet published by the National Coalition to Abolish the Death Penalty and the National Interreligious Task Force on Criminal Justice, 1988), 48.

65. Death Penalty Information Center, 2002.

66. Joseph F. Shapiro, "The Wrong Men on Death Row," *U.S. News & World Report* (November 9, 1998), 26.

67. Hugo Adam Bedau and Michael L. Radelet, "Miscarriages of Justice in Potentially Capital Cases," *Stanford Law Review* 40 (1987), 21–23.

68. Sara Rimer, "Questions of Death Row Justice for Poor People in Alabama," *New York Times* (March 1, 2000), A1.

69. John J. DiIulio, "Abolish the Death Penalty, Officially," *Wall Street Journal* (December 15, 1997), A23.

70. Scott Shepherd, "More Blacks Agreeing with Death Penalty," *Fresno Bee* (April 18, 1998), A6.

71. Death Penalty Information Center, 2002.

72. Janice Joseph, "Young, Black, and Sentenced to Die: Black Males and the Death Penalty," *Challenge: A Journal of Research on African American Men* 7 (December 1996), 68.

73. Isaac Utah and John Charles Boger, *Race and the Death Penalty in North Carolina* (Raleigh, NC: The Common Sense Foundation, 2001).

74. 481 U.S. 279 (1987).

75. David C. Baldus, George Woodworth, and Charles A. Pulaski, *Equal Justice and the Death Penalty: A Legal and Empirical Analysis* (Boston: Northeastern University Press, 1990), 140–97, 306.

76. Toni Locy, "Push to Reform Death Penalty Growing," *USA Today* (February 20, 2001), 5A.

77. 122 S.Ct. 2242 (2002).

78. Adam Liptak, "3 Justices Call for Reviewing Death Sentences for Juveniles," *New York Times* (August 30, 2002), A1.

79. David Stout, "Bill to Prevent Errant Executions Gains in Senate," *New York Times* (July 19, 2002), A10.

80. Roger Simon, "Not a Suitable Punishment," *U.S. News & World Report* (July 8, 2002), 9.

81. Federal Bureau of Investigation, *Crime in the United States, 2001* (Washington, D.C.: U.S. Department of Justice, 2002), 239.

82. Bureau of Justice Statistics, *Prisoners in 2000* (Washington, D.C.: U.S. Department of Justice, 2000), 6.

83. Freda Adler, *Sisters in Crime: The Rise of the New Female Criminal* (New York: McGraw-Hill, 1975), 95.

84. Barry Yeoman, "Violent Tendencies: Crime by Women Has Skyrocketed in Recent Years," *Chicago Tribune* (March 15, 2000), 3.

85. Meda Chesney-Lind, "Patriarchy, Prisons, and Jails: A Critical Look at Trends in Women's Incarceration," *Prison Journal* (Spring/Summer 1991), 57.

86. Bureau of Justice Statistics, *Sourcebook of Criminal Justice Statistics* (Washington, D.C.: U.S. Department of Justice, 1998), 505.

87. Angela Browne and Kirk R. Williams, "Exploring the Effect of Resource Availability and the Likelihood of Female-Perpetrated Homicides," *Law and Society Review* 23 (1989), 75–94.

88. Jane Roberts Chapman, *Economic Realities and Female Crimes* (Lexington, MA: Lexington Books, 1980).

89. Stefanie Fleischer Seldin, "A Strategy for Advocacy on Behalf of Women Offenders," *Columbia Journal of Gender and Law* 1 (1995), 1.

90. Kathleen Daly, "Women's Pathways to Felony Court: Feminist Theory of Lawbreaking and Problems of Representation," *Review of Law and Women's Studies* 2 (1992), 11–52.

91. 28 U.S.C. Section 991 (1994).

92. Clarice Feinmen, *Women in the Criminal Justice System*, 3d ed. (Westport, CT: Praeger, 1994), 35.

93. Ilene H. Nagel and Barry L. Johnson, "The Role of Gender in a Structured Sentencing System: Equal Treatment, Policy Choices, and the Sentencing of Female Offenders under the United States Sentencing Guidelines," *Journal of Criminal Law and Criminology* 85 (1994), 181–90.

94. Darrell Steffensmeir, John Kramer, and Cathy Streifel, "Gender and Imprisonment Decisions," *Criminology* 31 (1993), 411.

95. Quoted in Raymond Smith, "Death Penalty Rare for Women," *Press-Enterprise* (Riverside, California) (July 30, 1998), A12.

96. Elizabeth F. Moulds, "Chivalry and Paternalism: Disparities of Treatment in the Criminal Justice System," in *Women, Crime, and Justice*, ed. Susan Datesman and Frank Scarpitti (New York: Oxford University Press, 1980), 286–87.

97. Charles Crawford, "Sentencing in Florida," *Criminology* 38 (February 2000), 277.

98. Myrna S. Raeder, "Gender and Sentencing: Single Moms, Battered Women, and Other Sex-Based Anomalies in the Gender-Free World of the Federal Sentencing Guidelines," *Pepperdine Law Review* 20 (1993), 14.

CHAPTER 11
PROBATION AND COMMUNITY CORRECTIONS

CHAPTER OUTLINE

- **The Justification for Community Corrections**
- **Probation: Doing Time in the Community**
- **Intermediate Sanctions**
- **Criminal Justice in Action—Boot Camps: Do They Work?**

Chapter Objectives

After reading this chapter, you should be able to:

1. Explain the justifications for community-based corrections programs.

2. Explain several alternative sentencing arrangements.

3. Specify the conditions under which an offender is most likely to be denied probation.

4. Describe the three general categories of conditions placed on a probationer.

5. Explain the three stages of probation revocation.

6. List the five sentencing options for a judge besides imprisonment and probation.

7. Contrast day reporting centers with intensive supervision probation.

8. List the three levels of home monitoring.

279

INTRODUCTION

A Light Rap for Eminem

On April 10, 2001, rap star Marshall Mathers III, also known as Eminem, pleaded guilty to carrying a concealed weapon. The charge arose from an incident nearly a year earlier in which Mathers had struck a man he believed had been kissing his wife outside a Warren, Michigan, nightclub. Although this particular crime carries a maximum sentence of five years in prison under state law, Macomb County Circuit Court Judge Antonio Viviano sentenced Mathers to two years' probation, fined him $2,500, and ordered him to undergo counseling and drug treatment.[1]

Mathers's sentence sparked skepticism, as many felt he had been "let off easy" because of his fame and his high-priced defense attorney. In fact, Judge Viviano was hardly breaking new ground. Defendants who plead guilty to crimes far more serious than carrying a concealed weapon are routinely given probation in this country. A system that initially gave judges the discretion to show leniency to first-time, minor offenders increasingly allows those who have committed serious crimes to serve their time in the community rather than in a prison or jail. Nearly one of every five probationers in the United States has been convicted of a violent felony such as homicide, rape, or assault.[2] Ironically, this increase can be partly attributed to the "get tough" approach to crime that has emerged in public policy. Campaigns to crack down on drunk drivers, the "war on drugs," harsher sentencing statutes, and severe limitations on judicial discretion have placed a great amount of pressure on the American corrections infrastructure. Even with unprecedented rates of prison and jail construction, there is simply not enough space to incarcerate all of the new criminals. The result: more than 3 million adults are under the supervision of state and federal probation organizations—a figure growing at a rate of 3 percent each year.[3]

There is little question that our corrections system is suffering from "probation overload." In many cities, adult probation caseloads top 500 per probation officer. In Los Angeles, six out of every ten probationers are tracked solely by computer.[4] Consequently, judges and correctional officials are increasingly turning to intermediate sanctions such as intensive supervision programs, fines, boot camps, electronic monitoring, and home confinement to alleviate the pressure on both incarceration facilities and probation rolls. As widespread as these community-based punishments have become, however, they have not been completely accepted by the public. Numerous opinion polls show that a majority of Americans consider any punishment besides imprisonment a "slap on the wrist."

In this chapter, we will discuss the strengths and weaknesses of probation and other community sanctions, as well as efforts to make these sentencing alternatives more efficient and more palatable to the electorate. Given the scarcity of prison resources, decisions made today concerning community-based punishment will affect the criminal justice system for decades to come.

In April 2001, rapper Eminem (born Marshall Mathers III) reacts with relief after being sentenced to two years' probation for carrying a concealed weapon. (AP Photo/Paul Sancya, Pool)

280

THE JUSTIFICATION FOR COMMUNITY CORRECTIONS

In the court of popular opinion, retribution and crime control take precedence over community-based correctional programs. America, says University of Minnesota law professor Michael Tonry, is preoccupied with the "absolute severity of punishment" and the "widespread view that only imprisonment counts."[5] Mandatory sentencing guidelines and "three strikes" laws are theoretically opposed to community-based corrections.[6] To a certain degree, correctional programs that are administered in the community are considered a less severe, and therefore less worthy, alternative to imprisonment.

Reintegration

Supporters of probation and intermediate sanctions reject such views as not only shortsighted, but also contradictory to the aims of the corrections system. A very small percentage of all convicted offenders have committed crimes that warrant capital punishment or life imprisonment—most, at some point, will return to the community. Consequently, according to one group of experts, the task of the corrections system

> includes building or rebuilding solid ties between the offender and the community, integrating or reintegrating the offender into community life—restoring family ties, obtaining employment and an education, securing in the larger sense a place for the offender in the routine functioning of society.[7]

Considering that some studies have shown higher recidivism rates for offenders who are subjected to prison culture, a frequent justification of community-based corrections is that they attempt to reintegrate the offender into society.

Reintegration has a strong theoretical basis in rehabilitative theories of punishment. An offender is generally considered to be "rehabilitated" when he or she no longer represents a threat to other members of the community and therefore is believed to be fit to live in that community. In the context of this chapter and the next two, it will also be helpful to see reintegration as a process through which corrections officials such as probation and parole officers provide the offender with incentives to follow the rules of society. In doing so, the corrections system must constantly balance the rights of the individual offender against the rights of law-abiding members of the community. (See the feature *CJ in Focus—The Balancing Act: "Jason's Law" and Compromised Justice* on page 282.)

Diversion

Another justification for community-based corrections, based on practical considerations, is **diversion.** As you are already aware, most criminal offenses fall into the category of "petty," and it is practically impossible, as well as unnecessary, to imprison every offender for every offense. Community-based corrections are an important means of diverting criminals to alternative modes of punishment so that scarce incarceration resources are consumed by only the most dangerous criminals. In his "strainer" analogy, corrections expert Paul H. Hahn likens this process to the workings of a kitchen strainer. With each "shake" of the corrections "strainer," the less serious offenders are diverted from incarceration. At the end, only the most serious convicts remain to be sent to prison.[8]

The diversionary role of community-based punishments has become more pronounced as prisons and jails have filled up over the past three decades. Probationers now account for nearly two-thirds of all adults in the American corrections systems (see Figure 11.1 on page 282). According to the U.S. Department of Justice, on any single day, nearly 2 percent of all adult citizens are under probation supervision.[9]

Go to the Stories from the Street feature at http://www.cj.wadsworth.com/gainescore2e to hear Larry Gaines tell insightful stories related to this chapter and his experiences in the field.

REINTEGRATION
A goal of corrections that focuses on preparing the offender for a return to the community unmarred by further criminal behavior.

DIVERSION
In the context of corrections, a strategy to divert those offenders who qualify away from prison and jail and toward community-based and intermediate sanctions.

CJ in FOCUS

The Balancing Act: "Jason's Law" and Compromised Justice

When the Roberts family learned that a man named Callahan had been released from a Massachusetts county jail after only three months, under the condition that he wear an electronic monitoring bracelet, they were outraged. A year earlier, a drunk Callahan had killed twenty-one-year-old Jason Roberts in an automobile accident. Callahan had been sentenced to thirty months in jail, with eighteen months suspended. The Roberts family felt that Sheriff John Flood, who made the decision to release Callahan, had betrayed their trust and the trust of the community.

Community-based corrections represent a compromise society makes with certain wrongdoers. Theoretically, society benefits by saving scarce incarceration space for truly dangerous criminals and by giving supposedly low-risk offenders the opportunity to reintegrate into the community. These utilitarian justifications, however, often fail to counterbalance the cold, hard facts of an incident such as Jason Roberts's death. Given that we cannot predict criminal activity,

inevitably some convicts being supervised outside prison or jail will commit crimes, and some of those crimes will be violent. In any given year, offenders in community corrections programs are responsible for more than 10,000 murders and nearly 40,000 robberies, along with tens of thousands of other crimes. For the victims of these acts, the scales of justice appear to be heavily weighted in favor of the individual offender and against the best interests of society.

In response to the Callahan incident, the Massachusetts legislature considered passing "Jason's Law," which would have prohibited sheriffs from transferring inmates sentenced to prisons or jails into programs such as house arrest and electronic monitoring. The Massachusetts Sheriff's Association strongly protested the bill, arguing that its members use an objective classification system to determine who is eligible for community supervision. Furthermore, noted critics of the bill, existing local corrections facilities were already overcrowded, and the county in question did not have the financial resources to incarcerate all convicts: the cost of keeping an inmate in jail for a year is $35,000, compared to only $6,000 for electronic monitoring.

FOR CRITICAL ANALYSIS
Should victims and victims' families such as the Roberts family have a say in whether criminals are sentenced to community-based corrections?

PROBATION
A criminal sanction in which a convict is allowed to remain in the community rather than be imprisoned as long as she or he follows certain conditions set by the court

PROBATION: DOING TIME IN THE COMMUNITY

As Figure 11.1 shows, **probation** is the most common form of punishment in the United States. Although it is administered differently in various jurisdictions, probation can be generally defined as

> the legal status of an offender who, after being convicted of a crime, has been directed by the sentencing court to remain in the community under the supervision of a probation service for a designated period of time and subject to certain conditions imposed by the court or by law.[10]

FIGURE 11.1

Probation in American Corrections

As you can see, the number of Americans on probation almost quadrupled between 1980 and 2001 (matching the growth rate of prison and jail populations).

Source: Bureau of Justice Statistics, *Probation and Parole in the United States, 2001* (Washington, D.C.: U.S. Department of Justice, 2002), 1.

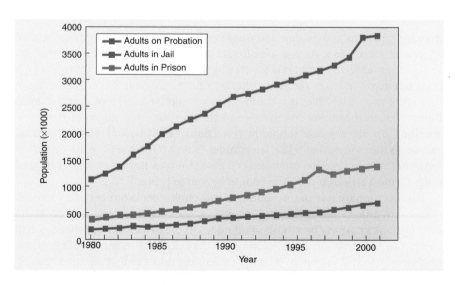

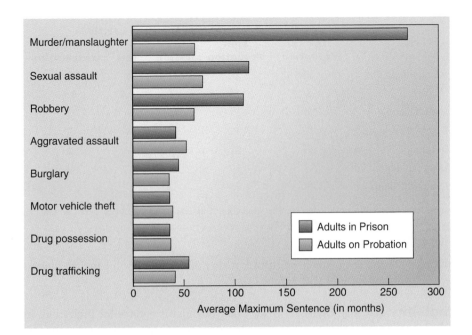

FIGURE 11.2
Average Length of Sentence: Prison versus Probation

As you can see, the average probation sentence is shorter than the average prison sentence for most crimes.

Source: Adapted from Bureau of Justice Statistics, *Felony Sentences in the State Courts, 1998* (Washington, D.C.: U.S. Department of Justice, 2001), 4.

The theory behind probation is that certain offenders, having been found guilty of a crime, can be more economically and humanely treated by placing them under controls while still allowing them to live in the community.

Sentencing Choices and Probation

Probation is basically an "arrangement" between sentencing authorities and the offender. In traditional probation, the offender agrees to follow certain terms for a specified amount of time in return for serving the sentence in the community. One of the primary benefits for the offender, besides not getting sent to a correctional facility, is that the length of the probationary period is usually considerably shorter than the length of a prison term (see Figure 11.2).

The "traditional" form of probation is not, however, the only arrangement that can be made. A judge can forgo probation altogether by handing down a **suspended sentence.** A suspended sentence places no conditions or supervision on the offender. He or she remains free for a certain length of time, but the judge keeps the option of revoking the suspended sentence and remanding the offender to prison or jail if circumstances call for such action.

Alternative Sentencing Arrangements.
Judges can also combine probation with incarceration. Such sentencing arrangements include:

- *Split sentences.* In **split sentence probation,** also known as *shock probation,* the offender is sentenced to a specific amount of time in prison or jail, to be followed by a period of probation.

- *Shock incarceration.* In this arrangement, an offender is sentenced to prison or jail with the understanding that after a period of time, she or he may petition the court to be released on probation. Shock incarceration is discussed more fully later in the chapter.

- *Intermittent incarceration.* Intermittent incarceration requires that the offender spend a certain amount of time each week, usually during the weekend, in a jail, workhouse, or other government institution.

Such arrangements have become more popular with judges, as they combine the "treatment" aspects of probation with the "punishment" aspects of incarceration.

INFOTRAC®
COLLEGE EDITION

Keyword: probation

SUSPENDED SENTENCE
A judicially imposed condition in which an offender is sentenced after being convicted of a crime, but is not required to begin the sentence immediately. The judge may revoke the suspended sentence and remit the offender to prison or jail if he or she does not follow certain conditions.

SPLIT SENTENCE PROBATION
A sentence that consists of incarceration in a prison or jail, followed by a probationary period in the community.

	Percentage of Felony Convictions				
	Straight Probation	Split Probation	Prison	Jail	No Incarceration
All offenses	30	28	31	9	2
Murder	3	10	86	0.5	0.5
Sexual assault	16	32	46	4	2
Aggravated assault	27	31	31	9	2
Burglary	23	31	37	7	2
Drug possession	33	29	24	12	2
Drug trafficking	27	27	32	12	2

Source: Adapted from Bureau of Justice Statistics, *State Court Sentencing of Convicted Felons, 1998* (Washington, D.C.: U.S. Department of Justice, 2001), Table 3.2, page 24.

According to the Department of Justice, nearly 30 percent of all convicted felons receive split sentences.[11] (See Figure 11.3.)

Eligibility for Probation. Not every offender is eligible for probation. In Bell County, Texas, for example, juries can recommend probation only for assessed prison sentences of ten years or less. Generally, research has shown that offenders are most likely to be denied probation if they:

- Are convicted on multiple charges.
- Were on probation or parole at the time of the arrest.
- Have two or more prior convictions.
- Are addicted to narcotics.
- Seriously injured the victim of the crime.
- Used a weapon during the commission of the crime.[12]

As might be expected, the chances of a felon being sentenced to probation are highly dependent on the seriousness of the crime he or she has committed (see Figure 11.4).

Conditions of Probation

As part of the decision to sentence an offender to probation, a judge may also set conditions of probation. These conditions represent a "contract" between the judge and the offender, in which the latter agrees that if she or he does not follow certain rules, probation may be revoked. The probation officer usually recommends the conditions of probation, but judges also have the power to set any terms they believe to be necessary.

This power is far-reaching, and a judge's personal philosophy is often reflected in the probation conditions that are set. In *In re Quirk* (1998),[13] for example, the United States Supreme Court upheld the ability of a Louisiana trial judge to impose church attendance as a condition of probation. Though judges have a great deal of discretion in setting the conditions of probation, they do operate under several guiding principles. First, the conditions must be related to the dual purposes of probation, which most federal and state courts define as (1) the rehabilitation of the probationer and (2) the protection of the community. Second, the conditions must not violate the U.S. Constitution; that is, probationers are generally entitled to the same constitutional rights as prisoners.[14] Of course, probationers do give up certain constitutional rights when they consent to the terms of probation; most probationers, for example, agree to spot checks of their homes for contraband such as drugs or weapons, and they therefore have a diminished expectation of privacy.

In 2001, Mohammed Haroon Ali, pictured here, was sentenced to sixty-four years in prison for the first degree murder of his girlfriend Tracey Biletnikoff. Three years before the killing, Ali pleaded guilty to felony kidnapping and threatening bodily injury in an incident involving a former girlfriend. Instead of being sent to prison for these crimes, however, Ali was sentenced to probation. How does a case such as Ali's leave the probation system open to criticism? (AP Photo/Courtesy of San Mateo Police Department via San Mateo County Times)

Obviously, probationers who break the law are very likely to have their probation revoked. Other, less serious infractions may also result in revocation. The conditions placed on a probationer fall into three general categories:

- *Standard conditions,* which are imposed on all probationers. These include reporting regularly to the probation office, notifying the agency of any change of address, not leaving the jurisdiction without permission, and remaining employed.

- *Punitive conditions,* which usually reflect the seriousness of the offense and are intended to increase the punishment of the offender. Such conditions include fines, community service, restitution, drug testing, and home confinement (discussed later).

- *Treatment conditions,* which are imposed with the goal of helping the offender with a condition that may contribute to his or her criminal activity. Data show that more than 40 percent of probationers were required to seek drug or alcohol treatment as part of their sentence, and an additional 18 percent were ordered to seek other kinds of treatment such as anger-control therapy.[15] (Figure 11.5 shows the most common conditions for adult felony probationers.)

The Probation Officer

The probation officer has two basic roles. The first is investigative and consists of conducting the presentence investigation (PSI), which was discussed in Chapter 10. The second is supervisory and begins as soon as the offender has been sentenced to probation. In smaller probation agencies, individual officers perform both tasks. In larger jurisdictions, the trend has been toward separating the responsibilities, with investigating officers handling the PSI and *line officers* concentrating on supervision. (For insight into this role, see the feature *Careers in Criminal Justice* on the following page.)

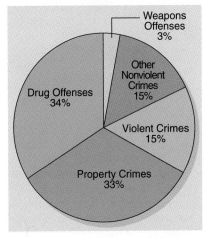

FIGURE 11.4

Adults on Probation by Felony Conviction Type

As you see here, the majority of adults on probation were convicted of property crimes or drug offenses.

Source: Adapted from Bureau of Justice Statistics, *State Court Sentencing of Convicted Felons, 1998* (Washington, D.C.: U.S. Department of Justice, 2001), Table 3.6, page 33.

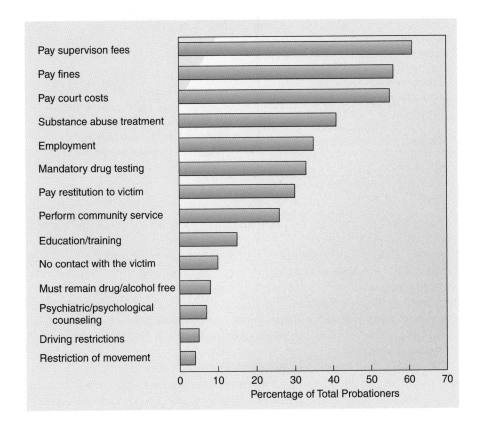

FIGURE 11.5

Special Conditions Imposed on Probationers

Source: Bureau of Justice Statistics, *Characteristics of Adults on Probation, 1995* (Washington, D.C.: U.S. Department of Justice, December 1997), 7.

Careers in Criminal Justice

Scott T. Ballock

U.S. Probation Officer

Uncertain about my future at the beginning of my sophomore year, I stumbled into an Introduction to Criminal Justice course at Indiana University and quickly became fascinated with the work of professionals in this field. The only difficulty was deciding which route to go; there were so many possibilities and they all seemed fun and interesting. Throughout the rest of my undergraduate and graduate programs, I set out to get a closer look at each career path and volunteered variously at the local jail, probation office, police department, courthouse, and different social services agencies. I rode along with police officers, interviewed prison administrators, and met with attorneys and judges. My time spent with these people provided me with a more realistic picture of each profession than I had received through my education. Ultimately, the field of probation and parole appeared to provide the best fit for my interests and goals.

As a federal probation officer, I work for the United States District Court in the District of Nevada (Las Vegas Office). U.S. Probation Officers serve as officers of the court and as agents of the U.S. Parole Commission. We are responsible for the supervision of all persons conditionally released to the community by the courts, the Parole Commission, the Federal Bureau of Prisons, and military authorities. Being released "conditionally" to the community means that in exchange for allowing an offender to remain in the community, the court expects him or her to meet certain standards and goals. These include remaining law abiding and drug free, working, supporting family, repaying victims, perhaps performing volunteer work for the community, and making other improvements in his or her life.

Supervising offenders in the community, our mission is to execute the court's sentence, control risk, and promote law-abiding behavior. In order to meet these goals, probation officers must become very knowledgeable about offenders' activities and lifestyles. We do so by meeting with them on a regular basis in the community, conducting unannounced home inspections, speaking regularly with their families, friends, neighbors, and employers, and—when necessary—conducting surveillance or warrantless searches of their homes and vehicles.

I am often asked whether probation officers are law enforcement officers or social workers. We are both. Responsible for protecting the public, we are also charged with promoting positive change among our probationers and parolees. Half of our day may be spent following an offender through the city to learn if he is engaged in illegal activities, while the second half is spent counseling offenders, helping them prepare a résumé, or referring them to local social service agencies for further assistance. Our dual role is an especially challenging aspect of the job.

We recognize that a prison sentence is a very costly proposition, to both the offender and the community. A decision to send or return a person to a prison setting is a serious matter, and great lengths are taken to first effect positive change. I think even those we supervise come to realize this. It's not infrequent that a person I've spent months trying to help, and who ultimately fails and is sent back to prison, extends his hand to thank me for trying—even as he's being led away by the U.S. Marshals.

Go to the
Careers in Criminal Justice Interactive CD **for more profiles in the field of criminal justice.**

INFOTRAC®
COLLEGE EDITION

Keyword: probation officer

Supervisory policies vary and are often a reflection of whether the authority to administer probation services is *decentralized* (under local, judicial control) or *centralized* (under state, administrative control). In any circumstance, however, certain basic principles of supervision apply. Starting with a preliminary interview, the probation officer establishes a relationship with the offender. This relationship is based on the mutual goal of both parties: the successful completion of the probationary period. Just because the line officer and the offender have the same goal, however, does not mean that probation is necessarily marked by excessive cooperation.

The ideal probation officer–offender relationship is based on trust. In reality, this trust does not often exist. Any incentive an offender might have to be completely truthful with a line officer is marred by one simple fact: self-reported wrongdoing can be used to revoke probation. Even probation officers whose primary mission is to rehabilitate are under institutional pressure to punish their clients for violating conditions of probation. One officer deals with this situation by telling his clients

> that I'm here to help them, to get them a job, and whatever else I can do. But I tell them too that I have a family to support and that if they get too far off track, I can't afford to put my job on the line for them. I'm going to have to violate them.[16]

In the absence of trust, most probation officers rely on their **authority** to guide an offender successfully through the sentence. An officer's authority, or ability to influence a person's actions without resorting to force, is based not only on her or his power to revoke probation, but also on a number of lesser sanctions. For example, if a probationer fails to attend a required alcohol treatment program, the officer can place him or her in a "lock-up," or detention center, overnight. To be successful, a probation officer must establish this authority early in the relationship; it is the primary tool in persuading the probationer to behave in a manner acceptable to the community.[17]

Juvenile Court Probation Officer Michael J. Manteria, left, consults with a probationer at the Hampden County Hall of Justice in Springfield, Massachusetts. The ideal probation officer-probationer relationship is based on trust, but often probation officers must rely on their authority to do their jobs correctly. Why is trust often so difficult to achieve between probation officers and offenders?
(AP Photo/Springfield Union-News, Michael Gordon)

Revocation of Probation

The probation period can end in one of two ways. Either the probationer successfully fulfills the conditions of the sentence, or the probationer misbehaves and probation is revoked, resulting in a prison or jail term. The decision of whether to revoke after a **technical violation**—such as failing to report a change of address or testing positive for drug use—is often a "judgment call" by the probation officer and therefore the focus of controversy.

Revocation Trends.   In the past, a technical violation almost always led to revocation. Today, many probation officers will take that step only if they believe the technical violation in question represents a danger to the community. At the same time, the public's more punitive attitude, along with improved drug-testing methods, has increased the number of conditions that probationers are placed under, and consequently the odds that they will violate one of those conditions. To a certain extent, these two trends have negated each other: since 1987 there has been almost no change in the percentage (between 75 and 80 percent) of offenders who successfully complete their probation terms.[18]

The reasons why probationers do not successfully complete their terms have shifted, however. The percentage of probationers with special conditions related to drug abuse has more than doubled since 1987.[19] Not surprisingly, the number of probationers caught and punished for using drugs has risen as well.[20]

The Revocation Process.   Probationers do not enjoy the same rights as other members of society. In *Griffin v. Wisconsin* (1987),[21] the United States Supreme Court ruled that probationers have only "conditional liberty" that is dependent "on observance of special restrictions." As long as the restrictions assure that a probationer works toward rehabilitation and does not harm the community, the Court allows the probationer's privacy to be restricted in a manner it would not accept otherwise.

"I try to get in the field two to three nights a week to see my offenders. It's really the only way to stop trouble before it happens. Otherwise, it's a free-for-all."

—Kevin Dudley, *Salt Lake City probation officer* (1997)

INFOTRAC®
COLLEGE EDITION

Keyword: probation revocation

AUTHORITY
The power designated to an agent of the law over a person who has broken the law.

TECHNICAL VIOLATION
An action taken by a probationer that, although not criminal, breaks the terms of probation as designated by the court; can result in the revocation of probation and a return to prison or jail.

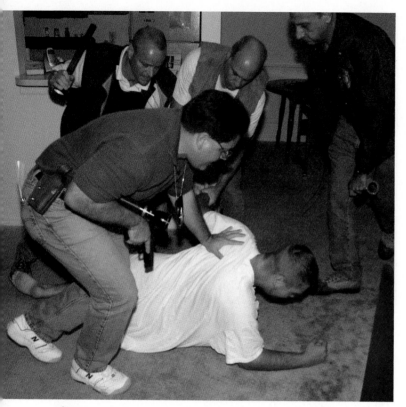

Three probation officers and a sheriff's deputy take down a probation violator during a roundup in Tampa, Florida. When an offender violates the terms of probation, his or her status can be revoked, and he or she can be sent to jail or prison. This is often a "judgment call" by the probation officer. What might be some reasons that a probation officer would not revoke an offender's probation even though that person has committed a violation? (AP Photo/Chris O'Meara)

The Court has not stripped probationers of all due process rights. In *Mempa v. Rhay* (1967),[22] the Court ruled that probationers were entitled to an attorney during the revocation process. Then, in *Morrissey v. Brewer* (1972) and *Gagnon v. Scarpelli* (1973),[23] the Court established a three-stage procedure by which the "limited" due process rights of probationers must be protected in potential revocation situations:

- *The preliminary hearing.* In this appearance before a "disinterested person" (often a judge), the facts of the violation or arrest are presented, and it is determined whether probable cause for revoking probation exists. This hearing can be waived by the probationer.

- *The revocation hearing.* During this hearing, the probation agency presents evidence to support its claim of violation, and the probationer can attempt to refute this evidence. The probationer has the right to know the charges being brought against him or her. Furthermore, probationers can testify on their own behalf and present witnesses in their favor, as well as confront and cross-examine adverse witnesses. A "neutral and detached" body must hear the evidence and rule in favor of the probation agency or the offender.

- *Revocation sentencing.* If the presiding body rules against the probationer, then the judge must decide whether to impose incarceration and for what length of time. In a revocation hearing dealing with technical violations, the judge will often reimpose probation with stricter terms or intermediate sanctions.

In effect, this is a "bare-bones" approach to due process. Most of the rules of evidence that govern regular trials do not play a role in revocation hearings. Probation officers are not, for example, required to read offenders *Miranda* rights when questioning them about crimes that may have been committed during probation. In *Minnesota v. Murphy* (1984),[24] the United States Supreme Court ruled that a meeting between probation officer and client does not equal custody, and therefore the Fifth Amendment protection against self-incrimination does not apply.

INTERMEDIATE SANCTIONS

During the 1960s and 1970s, many probation departments experimented with smaller caseloads under a management program known as *intensive supervision probation (ISP)*. These programs were discontinued when research showed that offenders in ISP had similar rearrest rates and more technical violations than those under regular supervision.[25] ISP was resurrected by the state of Georgia in 1982, however, with a different mandate. The state, experiencing prison crowding and a limited corrections budget, saw ISP as an alternative sanction for offenders who would have otherwise gone to prison. Georgia's version of ISP has been adopted in some measure by all fifty states, and it is at the vanguard of a movement to use **intermediate sanctions** to a greater degree in the American corrections system.

Many observers feel that the most widely used sentencing options—imprisonment or probation—fail to reflect the immense diversity of crimes and criminals. Intermediate sanctions provide a number of additional sentencing options for

INTERMEDIATE SANCTIONS
Sanctions that are more restrictive than probation and less restrictive than imprisonment. Intended to alleviate pressure on overcrowded corrections facilities and understaffed probation departments.

those wrongdoers who require stricter supervision than that supplied by probation, but for whom imprisonment would be unduly harsh and counterproductive.[26] The intermediate sanctions discussed in this section are designed to match the specific punishment and treatment of an individual offender with a corrections program that reflects that offender's situation.

Dozens of different variations of intermediate sanctions are handed down each year. To cover the spectrum succinctly, two general categories of such sanctions will be discussed in this section: those administered primarily by the courts and those administered primarily by probation departments, including day reporting centers, ISP programs, shock incarceration, and home confinement. Remember that none of these sanctions are exclusive: they are often combined with imprisonment and probation, and with each other.

Judicially Administered Intermediate Sanctions

The lack of sentencing options is most frustrating for the person who, in most cases, does the sentencing: the judge. Consequently, when judges are given the discretion to "color" a punishment with intermediate sanctions, they will often do so. Besides imprisonment and probation (and, to a lesser extent, other intermediate sanctions), a judge has five sentencing options:

1 Fines

2 Community service

3 Restitution

4 Forfeiture

5 Pretrial diversion programs

Fines, community service, and restitution were discussed in Chapter 10. In the context of intermediate sanctions, it is important to remember that these punishments are generally combined with incarceration or probation. For that reason, some critics feel the retributive or deterrent impact of such punishments is severely limited. Many European countries, in contrast, rely heavily on fines as the sole sanctions for a variety of crimes.

Forfeiture. In 1970, Congress passed the Racketeer Influenced and Corrupt Organizations Act (RICO) in an attempt to prevent the use of legitimate business

On the Web

The Corrections Connection acts as a clearinghouse for information concerning the corrections industry. For a link to its Web site, go to the Hypercontents page for this chapter at **http://www.cj.wadsworth.com/gainescore2e.**

Two gang members perform their court-ordered community service under the watchful eye of a supervisor. Community service is one of a number of intermediate sanctions used to punish offenders instead of probation or incarceration. Why might corrections officials support the increased use of intermediate sanctions? (PhotoEdit/Phil McCarten)

Judges and prosecutors may, in certain cases, give offenders the chance to attend pretrial diversion programs. Offered by care-giving facilities such as the community substance abuse center pictured here, these programs provide a chance to treat the causes behind criminal behavior without sending the offender to prison or jail. Do pretrial diversion programs "punish" offenders? If not, can they be justified as part of the corrections system? (PhotoEdit/ Jeff Greenberg)

enterprises as shields for organized crime.[27] As amended, RICO and other statutes give judges the ability to implement forfeiture proceedings in certain criminal cases. **Forfeiture** refers to a process by which the government seizes property gained from or used in criminal activity. For example, if a person is convicted for smuggling cocaine into the United States from South America, a judge can order the seizure of not only the narcotics, but also the speedboat the offender used to deliver the drugs to a pickup point off the coast of South Florida. In *Bennis v. Michigan* (1996),[28] the United States Supreme Court ruled that a person's home or car could be forfeited even if the owner was unaware that it was connected to illegal activity.

Pretrial Diversion Programs.   Not every criminal violation requires the courtroom process. Consequently, some judges have the discretion to order an offender into a **pretrial diversion program** during the preliminary hearing. (Prosecutors can also offer an offender the opportunity to join such a program in return for reducing or dropping the initial charges.) These programs represent an "interruption" of the criminal proceedings and are generally reserved for young or first-time offenders who have been arrested on charges of illegal drug use, child or spousal abuse, or sexual misconduct. Pretrial diversion programs usually include extensive counseling, often in a treatment center. If the offender successfully follows the conditions of the program, the criminal charges are dropped.

Day Reporting Centers

First used in Great Britain, **day reporting centers** are mainly tools to reduce jail and prison overcrowding. Although the offenders are allowed to remain in the community, they must spend all or part of each day at a reporting center. To a certain extent, being sentenced to a day reporting center is an extreme form of supervision. With offenders under a single roof, they are much more easily controlled and supervised.

Day reporting centers are also instruments of rehabilitation. Many house treatment programs for drug and alcohol abusers and provide counseling for a number of psychological problems (such as depression) and anger management. Many of those found guilty in the Roanoke (Virginia) Drug Court, for example,

FORFEITURE
The process by which the government seizes private property attached to criminal activity.

PRETRIAL DIVERSION PROGRAM
An alternative to trial offered by a judge or prosecutor, in which the offender agrees to participate in a specified counseling or treatment program in return for withdrawal of the charges.

DAY REPORTING CENTER
A community-based corrections center to which offenders report on a daily basis for purposes of treatment, education, and incapacitation.

are ordered to participate in a year-long day reporting program. At the center, offenders meet with probation officers, submit to urine tests, and attend counseling and education programs, such as parenting and life-skills classes. After the year has passed, if the offender has completed the program to the satisfaction of the judge and found employment, the charges will be dropped.[29]

Intensive Supervision Probation

As stated previously, **intensive supervision probation (ISP)** offers a more restrictive alternative to regular probation, with higher levels of face-to-face contact between offenders and officers, drug testing, and electronic surveillance. Different jurisdictions have different methods of determining who is eligible for ISP. In New Jersey, for example, violent offenders may not be placed in the program, while a majority of states limit ISP to those who do not have prior probation violations. The frequency of officer-client contact also varies widely. A Rand study of fourteen ISP sites found that offenders in Contra Costa County, California, had 2.7 contacts per month, compared to 22.8 contacts per month in Waycross, Georgia.[30]

Intensive supervision has two primary functions: (1) to *divert* offenders from overcrowded prisons or jails, and (2) to place these offenders under higher levels of *control,* as befits the risk they pose to the community. Researchers have had difficulty, however, in determining whether ISP is succeeding in these two areas. Any diversion benefits of ISP programs have tended to be offset by the stricter sentencing guidelines discussed in Chapter 10.[31] Furthermore, a number of studies have found that ISP clients have higher violation rates than traditional probationers.[32] One theory is that ISP "causes" these high failure rates—greater supervision increases the chances that an offender will be caught breaking conditions of probation. Despite its questionable performance, ISP is viable in today's political landscape because it satisfies the public's desire for stricter controls on convicts, while providing intermediate sanctions options for judges, prosecutors, and corrections administrators.

Shock Incarceration

Before the concept of intermediate sanctions was widely recognized in the criminal justice community, "Scared Straight" programs were used by some jurisdictions with the express purpose of deterring further criminal activity by juveniles and first-time offenders. The original Scared Straight was developed by the Lifers Group at Rahway State Prison (now East Jersey State Prison) in New Jersey in the mid-1970s. Consisting of about forty inmates serving sentences from twenty-five years to life, the Lifers Group would oversee juvenile offenders who had not yet been incarcerated but were considered "at risk" during a short stint (between 30 and 120 days) in the prison. The hope, as the program's name indicates, was that by getting a taste of the brutalities of daily prison life, the offender would be shocked into a crime-free existence.

A form of **shock incarceration,** Scared Straight programs generally fell out of favor in the 1980s, though several states, including Nevada, still employ them. Critics contended that the programs seemed to have no discernible effect on recidivism rates and thus needlessly exposed minor offenders to mental and physical cruelties from hardened criminals.[33]

Today, corrections officials are turning toward programs such as Colorado's "Shape-Up" and Idaho's DETOUR. These programs assign a juvenile offender to an adult "partner" who is serving a prison term. The juvenile spends a day in prison with the partner; then, the adult offender, the juvenile offender, and the juvenile's family meet together. A coordinator of DETOUR believes that these programs are more effective because they are not merely trying to scare already hardened juvenile offenders. Instead, he sees DETOUR as an educational

> "I've had a lot of people come up to me from the past, asking me to do things. When I see them, it's like, no can't do that, don't talk to me no more because my PO [probation officer] is shadowing me. Look, I don't like police officers or probation officers, I do what I got to do and that's all."
>
> —Vanessa Martinez, *probationer convicted of attempted murder* (1997)

INTENSIVE SUPERVISION PROBATION (ISP)
A punishment-oriented form of probation in which the offender is placed under stricter and more frequent surveillance and control than regular probation by probation officers with limited caseloads.

SHOCK INCARCERATION
A short period of incarceration that is designed to deter further criminal activity by "shocking" the offender with the hardships of imprisonment.

BOOT CAMP
A correctional facility based on militaristic principles of discipline and physical conditioning; reserved primarily for juvenile and first-time offenders serving terms of less than six months, with the ultimate goal of deterring further criminal behavior.

HOME CONFINEMENT
A community-based sanction in which offenders serve their terms of incarceration in their homes.

ELECTRONIC MONITORING
A technique of probation supervision in which the offender's whereabouts, though not his or her actions, are kept under surveillance by an electronic device; often used in conjunction with home confinement.

program.[34] The concept appears to work; Colorado's juvenile corrections department reports an 86 percent success rate for Shape-Up.[35]

The precepts of shock incarceration have not disappeared, however. In fact, this particular form of intermediate sanctioning has prospered with the rapid, and controversial, proliferation of **boot camps**. (For an in-depth discussion of the controversy surrounding this form of shock incarceration, see the feature *Criminal Justice in Action—Boot Camps: Do They Work?* at the end of this chapter.)

Home Confinement and Electronic Monitoring

Various forms of **home confinement**—in which offenders serve their sentence not in a government institution but at home—have existed for centuries.

For purposes of general law enforcement, home confinement was impractical until relatively recently. After all, one could not expect offenders to "promise" to stay at home, and the manpower costs of guarding them were prohibitive. In the 1980s, however, with the advent of **electronic monitoring**, or using technology to "guard" the prisoner, home confinement became more viable. Today, all fifty states and the federal government have home monitoring programs.

The Levels of Home Monitoring and Their Benefits. Home monitoring has three general levels of restriction:

1. *Curfew,* which requires offenders to be in their homes at specific hours each day, usually at night.

2. *Home detention,* which requires that offenders remain home at all times, with exceptions being made for education, employment, counseling, or other specified activities such as the purchase of food or, in some instances, attendance at religious ceremonies.

3. *Home incarceration,* which requires the offender to remain home at all times, save for medical emergencies.

Under ideal circumstances, home confinement serves many of the goals of intermediate sanctions. It protects the community. It saves public funds and space in correctional facilities by keeping convicts out of institutional incarceration. It meets public expectations of punishment for criminals. Uniquely, home confinement also recognizes that convicts, despite their crimes, play important roles in the community, and allows them to continue in those roles. An offender, for example, may be given permission to leave confinement to care for elderly parents.

Types of Electronic Monitoring. According to some reports, the inspiration for electronic monitoring was a *Spiderman* comic book in which the hero was trailed by the use of an electronic device on his arm. In 1979, a New Mexico judge named Jack Love, having read the comic, convinced an executive at Honeywell, Inc., to begin developing similar technology to supervise convicts.[36]

Two major types of electronic monitoring have grown out of Love's initial concept. The first is a "programmed contact" program, in which the offender is contacted periodically by telephone or beeper to verify his or her whereabouts. Verification is obtained via a computer that uses voice or visual identification techniques or by requiring the offender to enter a code in an electronic box when called. The second is a "continuously signaling" device, worn around the convict's wrist, ankle, or neck. A transmitter in the device sends out a continuous signal to a "receiver-dialer" device located in the offender's dwelling. If the receiver device does not detect a signal from the transmitter, it informs a central computer, and the police are notified.[37] (For advances in this field, see the feature *Criminal Justice & Technology—Satellite Tracking: The Next Step in Electronic Monitoring.*)

Offenders who are confined to their homes are often monitored by an electronic device that fits around the ankle. A transmitter in the device sends a continuous signal to a receiver, also located within the home. If this signal is broken—that is, the offender moves outside the range of the device—the police are automatically notified. What are some of the drawbacks of this form of electronic monitoring? (PhotoEdit/Tony Freeman)

Criminal Justice & TECHNOLOGY

Satellite Tracking: The Next Step in Electronic Monitoring

As we have already discussed, all intermediate sanctions entail a certain amount of risk. In electronic monitoring, as with other sanctions, this risk is compounded by the fact that the success of the program depends on the offender's commitment to "play by the rules." If the offender decides to leave the area of confinement, the signaling device will emit an alarm, alerting the police of the infraction but giving them no clues as to where the person is going.

A new breakthrough in electronic monitoring may provide the solution to this problem. Pro Tech Monitoring, Inc., a Palm Harbor (Florida) company, has developed a system that uses federal government satellites to monitor an offender's movements from above. Under this system, each subject will carry a "smart box" along with an ankle bracelet. The "smart box" contains a tracking device and is programmed with information about the offender's geographical restrictions. A satellite monitors the offender's movements and notifies the police if she or he violates conditional boundaries. So, for example, if a pedophile approaches an "off-limits" junior high school, the satellite warning system would alert police of the person's present location.

IN THE FUTURE
As satellite tracking technology becomes more advanced, corrections agencies will have the ability to keep an "electronic eye" on convicts at all times, calling up a visual image whenever necessary.

Widening the Net

As mentioned above, most of the convicts chosen for intermediate sanctions are low-risk offenders. From the point of view of the corrections official doing the choosing, this makes sense. Such offenders are less likely to commit crimes and attract negative publicity. This selection strategy, however, appears to invalidate one of the primary reasons intermediate sanctions exist: to reduce prison and jail populations. If most of the offenders in intermediate sanctions programs would otherwise have received probation, then the effect on these populations is nullified. Indeed, studies have shown this to be the case.[38]

At the same time, such selection processes broaden the reach of the corrections system. In other words, they increase rather than decrease the amount of control the state exerts over the individual. Suppose a person is arrested for a misdemeanor such as shoplifting and, under normal circumstances, would receive probation. With access to intermediate sanctions, the judge may add a period of home confinement to the sentence. Critics contend that such practices **widen the net** of the corrections system by augmenting the number of citizens who are under the control and surveillance of the state and also *strengthen the net* by increasing the government's power to intervene in the lives of its citizens.[39]

WIDEN THE NET
The criticism that intermediate sanctions designed to divert offenders from prison actually increase the number of citizens who are under the control and surveillance of the American corrections system.

Criminal Justice in Action
Boot Camps: Do They Work?

One might say that the American corrections system is "between a rock and a hard place." On the one hand, prisons and jails do not have enough space for all the offenders being arrested by law enforcement agencies. On the other hand, as noted throughout this chapter, community corrections and intermediate sanctions, while lessening the pressure on prisons and jails, are regarded as insufficiently "tough" by many citizens and public officials. In this *Criminal Justice in Action* feature, we will examine what would seem to be the perfect corrections option—a "tough" intermediate sanction known as the boot camp.

Boot camps rely on tough, militaristic discipline to steer young and first-time offenders away from a criminal lifestyle. (AP Photo/Las Cruces Sun-News, Vladimir Chaloupka)

BEYOND PUNISHMENT

You are nothing and nobody, fools, maggots, dummies, mothers, and you have just walked into the worst nightmare you ever dreamed. I don't like you. I have no use for you, and I don't give a f*** who you are on the street. This is my acre, hell's half acre, and it matters not one damn to me whether you make it here or get tossed out into the general prison population, where, I promise you, you won't last three minutes before you're somebody's wife. Do you know what that means, tough guys?[40]

Such was the welcome a group of inmates received on arriving at boot camp. A form of shock incarceration, boot camp programs are modeled after military basic training, emphasizing strict discipline, manual labor, and physical training. Boot camps provide a short term of incarceration—usually between three and six months—for young, first-time offenders. The idea is that the program's intense nature makes it as punitive as a longer prison term. But boot camps promise more than punishment. They are designed to instill self-discipline, self-responsibility, and self-respect, thereby lessening the chances that the offender will return to crime on release.

The first boot camp program appeared in Georgia in 1983. Within ten years, fifty-nine similar programs were operating in twenty-nine states.[41] An important reason for this rapid growth has been public acceptance of boot camps.[42] In contrast to generally negative feelings about probation, a recent survey found that 78 percent of the respondents had a positive impression of boot camps as a form of alternative sanctioning. Boot camps seem to reflect commonly held beliefs that offenders should receive strict punishment, while also offering the chance of rehabilitation within a confined space. Politicians, not wanting to appear soft on crime, have reacted to this support by earmarking funds to construct new camps. After a two-decade-long honeymoon period, however, many criminal justice participants are questioning whether boot camps deliver on all of their promises.

THE BENEFITS OF BOOT CAMP

Offenders are sent to boot camps either by the sentencing judge or by an official within the corrections agency. (In four states, the decision is made by a probation or parole officer.)[43] Though eligibility varies across jurisdictions (see Figure 11.6), most boot camps are restricted to young (though not necessarily juvenile) first-time offenders. In

Eligibility Requirements of Boot Camps in the United States

1. Offender Status
Boot camps are for the most part limited to first-time, nonviolent offenders.

2. Age
States differ in their age requirements, as these examples show:

- Oklahoma: Under 25 years
- Illinois: Ages 17 to 29
- New York: Age 30 or under
- Kansas: Ages 18 to 25
- Maryland: Under 32 years
- California: Age 40 or under
- Tennessee: Ages 17 to 29

3. Sentence Length
As one of the primary goals of boot camps is to reduce prison overcrowding, those who are sent to boot camps are generally diverted from prison. Consequently, many states have specific requirements concerning the prison sentences that boot "campers" must have received. In Maryland, for example, boot camps are restricted to offenders who have been sentenced for no longer than 10 years and who have at least 9 months remaining on their sentences. Illinois requires offenders to have been sentenced for up to 5 years and Tennessee for up to 6 years.

Source: John K. Zachariah, "Correctional Boot Camps: A Tough Intermediate Sanction—Chapter 2," in *An Overview of Boot Camp Goals, Components, and Results* (Washington, D.C.: National Institute of Justice, 1996).

most cases, attending a boot camp is a voluntary decision, and the offender can leave at any time and finish the sentence in a jail or prison.

The McNeil Island camp in Washington State is typical of such programs. Approximately 125 inmates, aged eighteen to twenty-eight, spend eight hours a day doing menial labor such as pulling weeds and painting the ferries that travel to and from the island. This work is supplemented by a number of seminars, including adult education, anger management, planning for life after the program, and victim awareness. Inmates also receive drug-abuse counseling and other treatments. The dropout rate from McNeil Island is 30 percent, even though completion of the four-month program can reduce a prison term by as much as a year.[44]

Besides the benefits for individual inmates, supporters of boot camps believe the programs are advantageous to society in three ways:

1. By reducing prison and jail overcrowding.
2. By saving costs associated with prison and jail terms.
3. By lowering recidivism rates among offenders.

The explanations behind these three supposed benefits are fairly straightforward. First, inmates placed in boot camps do not take up space in prisons and jails. Second, even though the average yearly costs of housing an inmate in a boot camp and in a prison are comparable, the term of a boot camp is much shorter and therefore less costly. Third, through improved self-discipline and treatment programs, inmates will change their behavior and therefore be less likely to commit further crimes on release from the camp.

EVIDENCE TO THE CONTRARY

Few observers doubt that the boot camp experience is a positive one for those who complete it—inmates learn valuable life skills and receive treatment, options often not available in prisons and jails.[45] Statistical benefits have also been reported: the state of Illinois estimates that boot camp graduates have a recidivism rate of 21 percent, as compared to 34 percent for those on probation or those who have served time behind bars.[46]

Criminologists, however, are wary of claims that boot camps are fulfilling their mandates. A number of long-term studies seem to show that although boot camps do not have a negative impact, they are not a panacea for the ills of the corrections system. One of the earliest surveys of boot camp graduates, compiled in Louisiana, found no difference in recidivism rates between boot campers and convicts who were confined in traditional correctional facilities.[47] A national study by the Koch Crime Institute showed that recidivism among those who attended boot camp ranged from 64 to 75 percent, slightly higher than for those juveniles who were sentenced to adult prisons.[48] The most extensive study of boot camps, evaluating programs in seven states, concluded that the overall effect of boot camps on recidivism was negligible.[49]

COMMON CRITICISMS

Similar doubts are raised concerning boot camps' ability to reduce costs and prison overcrowding. Researcher Dale G. Parent notes that when calculating the amount saved by sending inmates to boot camps instead of to prison, officials tend to account only for the goods consumed by offenders, such as food, clothing, and health care. These short-term savings amount to only a few dollars a day. To achieve substantial, long-term savings, prison populations must be reduced to the point where a cellblock or even an entire facility can be closed.[50] This has yet to occur.

Parent uses similar arguments to counteract claims that boot camps reduce prison and jail overcrowding. First of all, boot camps suffer from the net-widening effect discussed earlier in the chapter; that is, the offenders sent to boot camps would most likely have been given probation if intermediate sanctions did not exist. Even when specific steps are taken to avoid "net widening," the results are negligible. When the New York State Department of Correctional Services designed its boot camps, all inmates were chosen

Continued on next page

CJ in Action: Boot Camps: Do They Work? *continued*

from incoming prison populations—no net widening was possible. In its first five years, the department estimated that it had reduced the state's prison rolls by 1,540 inmates. During that same period, however, the prison rolls grew from 41,000 to 58,000, overwhelming the small gains made by the boot camps. To have an effect on either costs or overcrowding, Parent concludes, boot camp populations would have to be increased significantly, which would lessen their ability to treat individual offenders.[51]

THE FUTURE OF BOOT CAMPS

Boot camps have raised other concerns. Working in a boot camp can be a demanding task, and some observers believe staff stress and burnout contribute to verbal and physical intimidation of offenders.[52] Sometimes, these intimidation tactics break the bounds of legality. In Houston, for example, five drill instructors were indicted on felony charges after choking and beating inmates with their fists, feet, and broomsticks. When fourteen-year-old Anthony Hayes died after being exposed to 111-degree temperatures for five hours at an Arizona boot camp on July 1, 2001, it was the thirtieth "camper" death at such a program in the past two decades.[53] After her daughter died of dehydration in a Florida boot camp, one woman echoed the thoughts of many observers: "either regulate this industry or abolish it."[54]

Given the continued popular support for boot camps, it seems highly unlikely that they will be abolished. As long as the media portray these programs as "tough on prisoners," the political appeal of boot camps will continue to be high.[55] Some observers have gone as far as to suggest that corrections officials are aware of the drawbacks of boot camps, but are willing to take advantage of their popularity in order to receive government funding for these operations.[56] If this is indeed the strategy, it appears to be working. California alone received more than $1 billion in federal funds between 1995 and 2000 for alternative sentencing programs such as boot camps.

MAKING SENSE OF BOOT CAMPS

❶ Recall the four basic philosophical reasons for sentencing from Chapter 10—retribution, deterrence, incapacitation, and rehabilitation. How does each one apply to boot camps? In practice, which one seems to receive the most emphasis? Why?

❷ What are the strengths of boot camps when compared to probation? What are the weaknesses of boot camps when compared to probation?

❸ Some observers believe correctional boot camps can never be as effective as military boot camps because a person at a military boot camp is usually there voluntarily. Do you agree? What difference should that make?

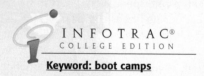

INFOTRAC®
COLLEGE EDITION

Keyword: boot camps

KEY TERMS

authority 287

boot camp 292

day reporting centers 290

diversion 281

electronic monitoring 292

forfeiture 290

home confinement 292

intensive supervision
    probation (ISP) 291

intermediate sanctions 288

pretrial diversion program 290

probation 282

reintegration 281

shock incarceration 291

split sentence probation 283

suspended sentence 283

technical violation 287

widen the net 293

CHAPTER SUMMARY

❶ Explain the justifications for community-based corrections programs. The first justification involves reintegration of the offender into society. Reintegration restores family ties, encourages employment and education, and secures a place for the offender in the routine functioning of society. The other justification involves diversion; by diverting criminals to alternative modes of punishment, further overcrowding of jail and prison facilities can be avoided.

❷ Explain several alternative sentencing arrangements. In addition to a suspended sentence, which is in fact a judicial reprieve, there are three general types of sentencing arrangements: (a) split sentence probation, in which the judge specifies a certain time in jail or prison followed by a certain time on probation; (b) shock incarceration, in which a judge sentences an offender to be incarcerated, but allows that person to petition the court to be released on probation; and (c) intermittent incarceration, in which an offender spends a certain amount of time each week in jail or in a halfway house or another government institution.

❸ Specify the conditions under which an offender is most likely to be denied probation. The offender (a) has been convicted of multiple charges, (b) was on probation or parole when arrested, (c) has two or more prior convictions, (d) is addicted to narcotics, (e) seriously injured the victim of the crime, or (f) used a weapon while committing the crime.

❹ Describe the three general categories of conditions placed on a probationer. (a) Standard conditions, such as requiring that the probationer notify the agency of a change of address, not leave the jurisdiction without permission, and remain employed; (b) punitive conditions, such as restitution,

community service, and home confinement; and (c) treatment conditions, such as required drug or alcohol treatment.

❺ Explain the three stages of probation revocation. (a) The preliminary hearing, which usually takes place before a judge, during which the facts of the probation violation are presented; (b) the revocation hearing, during which the claims of the violation are presented as well as any refutation by the probationer; and (c) revocation sentencing, during which a judge decides what to do with the probationer convicted of violating the terms of probation.

❻ List the five sentencing options for a judge besides imprisonment and probation. (a) Fines, (b) community service, (c) restitution, (d) forfeiture, and (e) pretrial diversion programs.

❼ Contrast day reporting centers with intensive supervision probation. In a day reporting center, the offender is allowed to remain in the community, but must spend all or part of each day at the reporting center. While at the center, offenders meet with probation officers, submit to drug tests, and attend counseling and education programs. In contrast, with intensive supervision probation (ISP), more restrictions are imposed, and there is more face-to-face contact between offenders and probation officers. ISP may also include electronic surveillance.

❽ List the three levels of home monitoring. (a) Curfew, which requires that the offender be at home during specified hours; (b) home detention, which requires that the offender be at home except for education, employment, and counseling; and (c) home incarceration, which requires that the offender be at home at all times except for medical emergencies.

QUESTIONS FOR CRITICAL ANALYSIS

1 What is the major reason that probationers account for nearly two-thirds of all adults in the American corrections system?

2 Why don't probationers have all constitutionally defined due process rights during revocation procedures?

3 Is the small number of probation officers a reason that recidivism is high?

4 What is the purpose of day reporting centers?

5 What does the term "widening the net" mean, and why is it important today?

6 What benefits are attributed to boot camps, and what is the evidence to support these proposed benefits?

SELECTED PRINT AND ELECTRONIC RESOURCES

SUGGESTED READINGS

Anderson, David C., *Sensible Justice: Alternatives to Prison*, New York: New Press, 1998. The author examines a range of probation-based supervision and rehabilitation programs, all of which involve no time in prison. He goes through the options in ascending order of severity. They range from community service, to daily reporting, all the way to boot camps. He examines the various options in the context of how different jurisdictions have applied them.

Anderson, James F., et al., *Boot Camps: An Intermediate Sanction*, Lanham, MD: University Press of America, 1999. The authors examine the theory and practice of boot camps throughout the United States. They offer criticisms of the concept as well as suggestions on how it might be applied for better results.

Festervan, Earlene, *Survival Guide for New Probation Officers*, Lanham, MD: American Correctional Association, 2000. This no-nonsense guide for new probation officers was sponsored by the 20,000-member, 125-year-old American Correctional Association. The author presents pointers on what to look out for and how to mentally prepare for the worst.

MEDIA RESOURCES

Good Will Hunting (1997) Will Hunting, played by Matt Damon, is a complex character. On the one hand, he is a tough kid from Boston who regularly finds himself in trouble with the law. On the other hand, he is a genius with a photographic memory. His mental capacity is uncovered by Professor Lambeau (Stellan Skargard), a professor at the Massachusetts Institute of Technology, where Hunting works as a janitor. Lambeau offers Hunting a path out of his blue-collar existence, but the genius janitor, scared of the challenges a new life might present, refuses. Then, fate steps in. Hunting is involved in a street brawl and faces serious prison time for striking a police officer. Lambeau makes a deal with the criminal justice system, persuading the judge to give Hunting probation if he agrees to attend therapy sessions with counselor Sean McGuire (Robin Williams).

Critically analyze this film:

1. Describe how Professor Lambeau takes advantage of the probation system.

2. What are some of the reasons that a real judge might not consider probation given the circumstances surrounding Will Hunting's arrest?

3. What are the conditions of Hunting's probation?

4. Given what you've read in this chapter, how realistic is Hunting's probationary situation?

5. At what points in the film could Hunting's probation be revoked?

LOGGING ON

Go to http://cj.wadsworth.com/gainescore2e, **and click Hypercontents.** There, you will find URLs for the organizations in the following list:

- A number of private companies have become involved in intermediate sanctions. One of them— **LCA, Inc.**—operates a Web site that gives detailed information on its services, including the technology of home detention systems.

- The **National Criminal Justice System Information Center** has gathered a large amount of data on boot camps and their effectiveness, or lack thereof.

● The **National Center on Institutions and Alternatives** has created a Community Based Alternatives Initiative in order to explore creative approaches to punishment and sentences.

USING THE INTERNET FOR CRIMINAL JUSTICE ANALYSIS

INFOTRAC®
COLLEGE EDITION

1. Go to your InfoTrac College Edition at **http://www. infotrac-college.com/wadsworth/**. After you log on, type in the words: **Forging a police-probation alliance**

Probation officers can work with police officers, even though there often seem to be rivalries between the two agencies. In this article you will read about a number of police departments that have established collaboration with local probation officers. Read the article and answer the following questions:

a. Why does the author believe that the police cannot solve numerous crime and public order problems without forming partnerships with other resources?

b. What did the ride-a-long program in Greenville, Texas, involve?

c. How is a bulletin board utilized in such a partnership arrangement?

d. What benefits did the Greenville Police Department realize from the partnership with probation officers?

e. List the five suggested improvements in a police-probation partnership. In your mind, which is the most important, and why?

2. See Internet Activities 11.1 and 11.2 on the companion Web site for *CJ in Action: The Core.* To get to the activities, go to **http://www.cj.wadsworth.com/gainescore2e**, select the appropriate chapter from the drop down list, then click Internet Activities on the left navigation bar.

NOTES

1. Laura Potts, "Eminem's Sentence: Two Years Probation for Concealed Weapons Charge," *Tulsa World* (April 11, 2001), 4.

2. Bureau of Justice Statistics, *Characteristics of Adults on Probation, 1995* (Washington, D.C.: U.S. Department of Justice, December 1997), 1.

3. *Ibid.*

4. John J. DiIulio, Jr., and Joseph P. Tierny, "An Easy Ride for Felons on Probation," *New York Times* (August 29, 2000), A27.

5. Michael Tonry, *Sentencing Matters* (New York: Oxford Press, 1996), 28.

6. Todd Clear and Anthony Braga, "Community Corrections," in *Crime,* James Q. Wilson and Joan Petersilia, eds. (San Francisco: ICS Press, 1995), 444.

7. Corrections Task Force of the President's Commission on Law Enforcement and Administration of Justice (1967).

8. Paul H. Hahn, *Emerging Criminal Justice: Three Pillars for a Proactive Justice System* (Thousand Oaks, CA: Sage Publications, 1998), 106–8.

9. Bureau of Justice Statistics, *Characteristics of Adults on Probation, 1995,* 1.

10. Paul W. Keve, *Crime Control and Justice in America* (Chicago: American Library Association, 1995), 183.

11. "National Report on Probationers Says Half Got Split Sentences," *Corrections Journal* (December 22, 1997), 7.

12. Joan Petersilia and Susan Turner, *Prison versus Probation in California: Implications for Crime and Offender Recidivism* (Santa Monica, CA: Rand Corporation, 1986).

13. 97 U.S. 1143 (1998).

14. Neil P. Cohen and James J. Gobert, *The Law of Probation and Parole* (Colorado Springs, CO: Shepard's/McGraw-Hill, 1983), Section 5.01, at 183–4; Section 5.03, at 191–2.

15. "National Report on Probationers Says Half Got Split Sentences," *Corrections Journal* (December 22, 1997), 7.

16. Carl B. Klockars, Jr., "A Theory of Probation Supervision," *Journal of Criminal Law, Criminology, and Police Science* 63 (1972), 551.

17. Hahn, 116–18.

18. Bureau of Justice Statistics, *Special Report, Federal Offenders under Community Supervisions, 1987–1996* (Washington, D.C.: U.S. Department of Justice, August 1998), Table 6, page 5.

19. *Ibid.,* 4.

20. *Ibid.,* 6.

21. 483 U.S. 868, 874 (1987).

22. 389 U.S. 128 (1967).

23. *Morrissey v. Brewer,* 408 U.S. 471 (1972); *Gagnon v. Scarpelli,* 411 U.S. 778 (1973).

24. 465 U.S. 420 (1984).

25. Robert M. Carter and Leslie T. Wilkins, "Caseloads: Some Conceptual Models," in *Probation, Parole, and Community Corrections,* ed. Robert M. Carter and Leslie T. Wilkins (New York: Wiley & Sons, 1976), 391–401.

26. Norval Morris and Michael Tonry, *Between Prison and Probation: Intermediate Punishments in a Rational Sentencing System* (Oxford, UK: Oxford University Press, 1990).

27. 18 U.S.C. Sections 1961–1968.

28. 516 U.S. 442 (1996).

29. Laurence Hammck, "Drug Court to Recognize Those Who've Stayed Clean," *Roanoke Times & World News* (May 31, 1998), B1.

30. Joan Petersilia and Susan Turner, *Intensive Supervision for High-Risk Probationers: Findings from Three California Experiments* (Santa Monica, CA: Rand Corporation, 1990).

31. Betsy Fulton, Edward J. Latessa, Amy Stichman, and Lawrence F. Travis, "The State of ISP: Research and Policy Implications," *Federal Probation* (December 1997), 65.

32. Peter Jones, "Expanding the Use of Non-Custodial Sentencing Options: An Evaluation of the Kansas Community Corrections Act," *Howard Journal* 29 (1990), 114–29.

33. Dale Parent, *Shock Incarceration: An Overview of Existing Programs* (Washington, D.C.: U.S. Department of Justice, 1989).

34. Candice Chung, "Cigarette Money Will Fund Juvenile Program," *Idaho Statesman* (May 9, 1997), 2B.

35. *Ibid.*

36. Josh Kurtz, "New Growth in a Captive Market," *New York Times* (December 31, 1989), 12.

37. Jeff Potts, "American Penal Institutions and Two Alternative Proposals for Punishment," *South Texas Law Review* (October 1993), 443.

38. Michael Tonry and Mary Lynch, "Intermediate Sanctions" in *Crime and Justice,* vol. 20, ed. Michael Tonry (Chicago: University of Chicago Press, 1996), 99.

39. Dennis Palumbo, Mary Clifford, and Zoann K. Snyder-Joy, "From Net Widening to Intermediate Sanctions: The Transformation of Alternatives to Incarceration from Benevolence to Malevolence," in *Smart Sentencing: The Emergence of Intermediate Sanctions,* ed. James M. Byrne, Arthur Lurigio, and Joan Petersilia (Newbury Park, CA: Sage, 1992), 231.

40. Quoted in Doris L. Mackenzie and Claire Souryal, "A 'Machiavellian' Perspective on the Development of Boot-Camp Prison: A Debate," *University of Chicago Roundtable* 2 (1995), 435.

41. "A Tough Intermediate Sanction," in *Correctional Boot Camps: A Tough Intermediate Sanction,* ed. Doris L. MacKenzie and Eugene E. Hebert (Washington, D.C.: National Institute for Justice, 1996).

42. Sarah Glazer, "Juvenile Justice," *CQ Researcher 4* (1994), 180.

43. United States General Accounting Office, *Prison Boot Camps: Short-Term Prison Costs Reduced, but Long-Term Impact Uncertain* (Washington, D.C.: U.S. General Accounting Office, 1993), 16.

44. Deborah Sharp, "Boot Camps—Punishment and Treatment," *Corrections Today* (June 1, 1995), 81.

45. "A Tough Intermediate Sanction."

46. Sharp, 81.

47. Doris L. MacKenzie and Dale Parent, "Shock Incarceration and Prison Crowding in Louisiana," *Journal of Criminal Justice* 19 (1991), 231.

48. Brent Zaehringer, *Juvenile Boot Camps: Cost and Effectiveness vs. Residential Facilities* (Topeka, KS: Koch Crime Institute, 1998).

49. Doris L. MacKenzie and Claire Souryal, *Multisite Evaluation of Shock Incarceration, Evaluation Report* (Washington, D.C.: National Institute of Justice, 1994).

50. Dale G. Parent, "Boot Camps and Prison Crowding," in *Correctional Boot Camps: A Tough Intermediate Sanction,* ed. Doris L. MacKenzie and Eugene E. Hebert (Washington, D.C.: National Institute for Justice, 1996).

51. *Ibid.*

52. L. R. Acorn, "Working in a Boot Camp," *Corrections Today* (October 1991), 110.

53. Michael Janofsky, "Arizona Boot Camp Where Boy Died Re-opens," *New York Times* (September 7, 2001), A10.

54. Mareva Brown, "4 Moms Rip Youth Boot Camps," *Sacramento Bee* (March 18, 1998), A1.

55. Adam Nossiter, "As Boot Camps for Criminals Multiply, Skepticism Grows," *New York Times* (December 18, 1993), 37.

56. Mackenzie and Souryal, "A 'Machiavellian' Perspective."

CHAPTER 12
PRISONS AND JAILS

CHAPTER OUTLINE

- **A Short History of American Prisons**
- **The Prison Population Bomb**
- **Types of Prisons**
- **Prison Administration**
- **The Emergence of Private Prisons**
- **Jails**
- **The Consequences of Our High Rates of Incarceration**
- **Criminal Justice in Action—The End of the Line: Supermax Prisons**

Chapter Objectives

After reading this chapter, you should be able to:

1 Contrast the Pennsylvania and the New York penitentiary theories of the 1800s.

2 List the factors that have caused the prison population to grow dramatically in the last several decades.

3 List and briefly explain the four types of prisons.

4 Summarize the distinction between jails and prisons, and indicate the importance of jails in the American correctional system.

5 Indicate some of the consequences of our high rates of incarceration.

INTRODUCTION
The Largest Corrections System in the World

Sir Henry Alfred McCardie, the famed English jurist, once said, "Trying a man is easy, as easy as falling off a log, compared with deciding what to do with him when he has been found guilty."[1] In the American criminal justice system, to a certain extent, the decision has been simplified: many of the guilty go behind bars. The United States has the largest corrections system in the world. One out of every 142 Americans is in a federal or state prison or in a local jail.[2] According to the U.S. Department of Justice, the number of inmates in American prisons and jails passed the 2 million mark in late 2001.[3] Despite comparable crime rates, the United States incarcerates five times as many of its citizens as Canada does, and seven times as many as most European democracies.[4] In fact, after Russia, the United States has the highest incarceration rate in the "first" world.

For the most part, this high rate is a product of the past thirty-five years. From the 1920s until 1970, America's incarceration rates remained fairly stable at 110 per 100,000. Over the past three and a half decades the jail and prison population of the United States increased by nearly 600 percent. There is, it must be noted, some evidence that the nation's incarceration population is beginning to stabilize. When the number of state prisoners increased by only 0.4 percent in 2001, it was the lowest annual increase in the past twenty-eight years.[5] Some corrections experts believe that this "leveling off" is a result of the decline in crime rates in the 1990s: with fewer people committing crimes, fewer people will go to prison. Others point to a number of new state laws under which those convicted of drug possession are sent to treatment programs rather than prison or jail.

One year does not make a trend, however. The American corrections system remains a massive institution. Throughout the course of this textbook, we have discussed many of the social and political factors that help explain the prison population "boom" of the past thirty years.

In this chapter and the next, we turn our attention to the incarceration system itself. This chapter focuses on the history and organizational structures of prisons (which generally hold those who have committed serious felonies for long periods of time) and jails (which generally hold those who have committed less serious felonies and misdemeanors, and those awaiting trial, for short periods of time). Though the two terms are often used interchangeably, prisons and jails are two very different institutions, each with its own responsibilities and its own set of seemingly unsolvable problems.

Inside Tutwiler Women's Prison in Wetumpka, Alabama, a handful of the two million inmates incarcerated in the United States pass time.
(AP Photo/Kevin Glackmeyer)

A SHORT HISTORY OF AMERICAN PRISONS

Today, we view prisons as instruments of punishment; the loss of freedom imposed on inmates is society's retribution for the crimes they have committed. This has not always been the function of incarceration. The prisons of eighteenth-century England, known as "bridewells" after London's Bridewell Palace, actually had little to do with punishment. These facilities were mainly used to hold debtors or those awaiting trial, execution, or banishment from the community. (In many ways, as shall be made clear, these facilities resemble the modern jail.) Prisoners rarely spent a great deal of time in confinement. Indeed, given the filthy conditions of early prisons, they could not have survived long-term imprisonment without succumbing to disease.

Given the practices of the time, the English did not particularly need prisons. English courts generally imposed one of two sanctions on convicted felons: they turned them loose or they executed them.[6] (To be sure, most felons were released, pardoned either by the court or the clergy after receiving a whipping or a branding.) Consequently, when a series of sturdy, clean prisons began springing up in the last quarter of the eighteenth century, they were seen as part of a large-scale reform of the English criminal justice system. Believing that "small crimes lead to great," the reformers wanted to rehabilitate wrongdoers as well as punish them and urged the use of prisons as places where inmates could be "cured" of their evil ways through religious instruction and the discipline of hard labor.[7]

The correctional system in the American colonies differed very little from that of their motherland. If anything, colonial administrators were more likely to use corporal punishment than their English counterparts, and the death penalty was not uncommon in early America. The one dissenter was William Penn, who adopted the "Great Law" in Pennsylvania in 1682. Based on Quaker ideals of humanity and rehabilitation, this criminal code forbade the use of torture and mutilation as forms of punishment; instead, felons were ordered to pay restitution of property or goods to their victims. If the felons did not have sufficient property to make restitution, they were placed in a prison, which was primarily a "workhouse."[8] The death penalty was still allowed under the "Great Law," but only in cases of premeditated murder. Penn proved to be an exception, however, and the path to reform was much slower in the colonies than in England.

Walnut Street Prison: The First Penitentiary

On Penn's death in 1718, the "Great Law" was rescinded in favor of a harsher criminal code, similar to those of the other colonies. At the time of the American Revolution, however, the Quakers were instrumental in the first wide swing of the incarceration pendulum from punishment to rehabilitation. In 1776, Pennsylvania passed legislation ordering that offenders be reformed through treatment and discipline rather than simply beaten or executed.[9] Several states, including Massachusetts and New York, quickly followed Pennsylvania's example.

Under pressure from the renowned Quaker Dr. Benjamin Rush, Pennsylvania continued its reformist ways by opening the country's first **penitentiary** in a wing of Philadelphia's Walnut Street Jail in 1790. Based on the ideas of the British reformer John Howard, the penitentiary operated on the assumption that silence and labor provided the best hope of rehabilitating the criminal spirit. Remaining silent would force the prisoners to think about their crimes, and eventually the weight of conscience would lead to repentance. At the same time, enforced labor would attack the problem of idleness—regarded as the main cause of crime by penologists of the time.[10] Consequently, inmates at Walnut Street were isolated from one another in solitary rooms and kept busy with constant menial chores.

Eventually, the penitentiary at Walnut Street succumbed to the same problems that continue to plague institutions of confinement: overcrowding and excessive

Go to the Stories from the Street feature at http://www.cj. wadsworth.com/gainescore2e to hear Larry Gaines tell insightful stories related to this chapter and his experiences in the field.

> "In one corrupt and corrupting assemblage were to be found the disgusting objects of popular contempt, besmeared with filth from the pillory—the unhappy victim of the lash . . . the half naked vagrant—the loathsome drunkard—the sick suffering from various bodily pains, and too often the unaneled malefactor."
>
> —Robert Vaux, *describing Pennsylvania jails* (1776)

PENITENTIARY
An early form of correctional facility that emphasized separating inmates from society and from each other so that they would have an environment in which to reflect on their wrongdoing and ponder their reformation.

FIGURE 12.1
The Eastern Penitentiary

The Eastern Penitentiary opened in 1829 with the controversial goal of changing the behavior of inmates instead of merely punishing them. An important component of this goal was the layout of the facility. As you can see, the Eastern Penitentiary was designed in the form of a "wagon wheel," known today as the radial style. The back-to-back cells in each "spoke" of the wheel faced outward from the center to limit contact between inmates. About 300 prisons worldwide have been built based on this design.

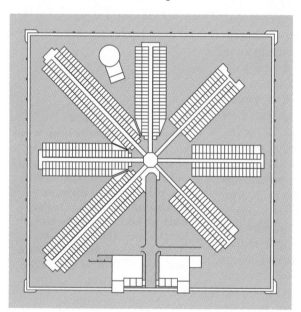

SEPARATE CONFINEMENT
A nineteenth-century penitentiary system developed in Pennsylvania in which inmates were kept separate from each other at all times, with daily activities taking place in individual cells.

CONGREGATE SYSTEM
A nineteenth-century penitentiary system developed in New York in which inmates were kept in separate cells during the night but worked together in the daytime under a code of enforced silence.

costs. As an influx of inmates forced more than one person to be housed in a room, silence became a nearly impossible condition. By the early 1800s, officials could not find work for all of the convicts, so many were left idle.

The Great Penitentiary Rivalry: Pennsylvania versus New York

The apparent lack of success at Walnut Street did little to dampen enthusiasm for the penitentiary concept. Throughout the first half of the nineteenth century, a number of states reacted to prison overcrowding by constructing new penitentiaries. Each state tended to have its own peculiar twist on the roles of silence and labor, and two such systems—those of Pennsylvania and New York—emerged to shape the debate over the most effective way to run a prison.

The Pennsylvania System. After the failure of Walnut Street, Pennsylvania constructed two new prisons: the Western Penitentiary near Pittsburgh (opened in 1826) and the Eastern Penitentiary in Cherry Hill, near Philadelphia (1829). The Pennsylvania system took the concept of silence as a virtue to new extremes. Based on the idea of **separate confinement**, these penitentiaries were constructed with back-to-back cells facing both outward and inward. (See Figure 12.1 for the layout of the original Eastern Penitentiary.) To spare each inmate from the corrupting influence of the others, prisoners worked, slept, and ate alone in their cells. Their only contact with other human beings came in the form of religious instruction from a visiting clergyman or prison official.[11]

The New York System. If Pennsylvania's prisons were designed to transform wrongdoers into honest citizens, those in New York focused on obedience. When New York's Newgate Prison (built in 1791) became overcrowded, the state authorized the construction of Auburn Prison, which opened in 1816. Auburn initially operated under many of the same assumptions that guided the penitentiary at Walnut Street. Solitary confinement, however, seemed to lead to an inordinate amount of sickness, insanity, and even suicide among inmates, and it was abandoned in 1822. Nine years later, Elam Lynds became warden at Auburn and instilled the **congregate system,** also known as the Auburn system. Like Pennsylvania's separate confinement system, the congregate system was based on silence and labor. At Auburn, however, inmates worked and ate together, with silence enforced by prison guards.[12]

If either state can be said to have "won" the debate, it was New York. The Auburn system proved more popular, and a majority of the new prisons built during the first half of the nineteenth century followed New York's lead, though mainly for economic reasons rather than philosophical ones. New York's penitentiaries were cheaper to build because they did not require so much space. Furthermore, inmates in New York were employed in workshops, whereas those in Pennsylvania toiled alone in their cells. Consequently, the Auburn system was better positioned to exploit prison labor in the early years of widespread factory production.

The Reformers and the Progressives

The Auburn system did not go unchallenged. During the landmark 1870 meeting of the National Prison Association (forerunner of today's American Correctional Association) in Cincinnati, Ohio, a group of penal reformers contended that existing prisons did not provide sufficient incentive for inmate reformation. Arguing that fixed sentences, imposed silence, and isolation did nothing to improve the prisoners, the reformers proposed that instead penal institutions should offer the "carrot" of early release as a prime tool for rehabilitation. Echoing the views of the Quakers a century earlier, the reformers presented an ideology that would heavily influence American corrections for the next century.

The Elmira Reformatory. On his appointment as superintendent at New York's Elmira Reformatory in 1876, Zebulon Brockway put the concepts of this "new penology" into practice. "It cannot be too often stated," Brockway insisted, "that prisoners are of inferior class and that our prison system is intended for treatment of defectives." These defectives, he felt, could be cured through "scientifically directed bodily and mental exercises."[13] Designed for first-time felons between the ages of sixteen and thirty, the Elmira Reformatory had no fixed sentences. The institution's administrators had the final say on when an inmate could be released, so long as the time served did not exceed the maximum sentence prescribed by law.[14]

At Elmira, good behavior was rewarded by early release, and misbehavior was punished with extended time under a three-grade system of classification. On entering the institution, a wrongdoer was assigned a grade of 2. If the inmate followed the rules and completed work and school assignments, after six months he would be moved up to grade 1, the necessary grade for release. If, however, the inmate broke institutional rules or otherwise failed to cooperate, he would be lowered to grade 3. A grade 3 inmate needed to behave properly for three months before he could return to grade 2 and begin to work toward grade 1 and eventual release.[15]

The Progressives. Although Brockway and his reforming peers had largely disappeared by 1900, their theories had a great influence on the Progressive movement that came into prominence in the first two decades of the twentieth century. The Progressive movement was linked to the positivist school, which was discussed in Chapter 2. The Progressives believed criminal behavior was caused by social, economic, and biological factors, and therefore a corrections system should have a goal of treatment, not punishment. The Progressives were largely responsible for the spread of indeterminate sentences, probation, community sanctions, and parole in the first half of the twentieth century.

They also trumpeted the **medical model** of prisons, which held that institutions should offer a variety of programs and therapies to cure inmates of their "ills," whatever the root causes. The "glory years" of the medical model and the ideals of rehabilitation came in the decade after the end of World War II in 1945. The general postwar optimism applied to the nation's criminals as well—a society that had defeated the Axis powers in Europe and the Pacific could certainly "cure" the "disease" of criminality.[16] At the forefront of the rehabilitation movement in these years was a commitment to behavior modification programs ranging from group therapy to shock therapy to psychotherapy. Holding out the possibility of a "cure" for inmates, the American corrections system eased its more punitive aspects. Capital punishment, for example, dropped significantly from prewar levels.[17]

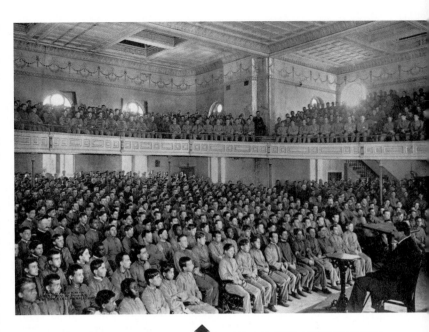

Inmates of Elmira State Prison in New York attend a presentation at the prison auditorium. Zebulon Brockway, the superintendent at Elmira, believed that criminals were an "inferior class" of human being and should be treated as society's defectives. Thus, mental exercises designed to improve the inmates' minds were part of the prison routine at Elmira. To what extent do you believe that treatment should be a part of the incarceration of criminals? (Corbis)

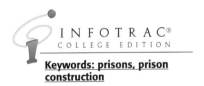

INFOTRAC®
COLLEGE EDITION

Keywords: prisons, prison construction

MEDICAL MODEL
A model of corrections in which the psychological and biological roots of an inmate's criminal behavior are identified and treated.

The Reassertion of Punishment

Even though the Progressives had a great influence on the corrections system as a whole, their theories had little impact on the prisons themselves, many of which had been constructed in the nineteenth century and were impervious to change. More important, prison administrators usually did not agree with the Progressives and their followers, so the day-to-day lives of most inmates varied little from the congregate system of Auburn Prison.

Academic attitudes began to shift toward the prison administrators in the mid-1960s. The publication of Robert Martinson's famous "What Works?" essay in 1974 provided critics of the medical model with statistical evidence that rehabilitation efforts did nothing to lower recidivism rates.[18] This is not to say that Martinson's findings went unchallenged. A number of rebuttals arguing that rehabilitative programs could be successful appeared immediately after the publication of "What Works?"[19] In fact, Martinson himself retracted most of his claims in a little-noticed article published five years after his initial report.[20] Attempts by Martinson and others to "set the record straight" went largely unnoticed, however, as a sharp rise in crime in the early 1970s led many criminologists and politicians to champion "get tough" measures to deal with criminals they now considered "incurable." By the end of the 1980s, the legislative, judicial, and administrative strategies that we have discussed throughout this text had positioned the United States for an explosion in inmate populations and prison construction unparalleled in the nation's history.

THE PRISON POPULATION BOMB

The number of Americans in prison or jail has more than doubled since 1985 and has continued to rise at an annual rate of about 4 percent (see Figure 12.2). In fact, the 1.6 percent increase between 2000 and 2001 was the lowest increase since 1972. These numbers are not only dramatic, but also, say some observers, inexplicable, given the overall crime picture in the United States. In the 1990s, violent and property crime rates dropped; yet the number of inmates continued to rise. According to accepted theory, rising incarceration rates should be the result of a rise in crime, leaving one expert to comment that America's prison population is "defying gravity."[21] (See the feature *CJ in Focus—Myth versus Reality: Does Placing Criminals in Prison Reduce Crime?*)

FIGURE 12.2

The Inmate Population of the United States

The total number of inmates in custody in the United States has risen from 744,208 in 1985 to 1,965,495 in 2001.

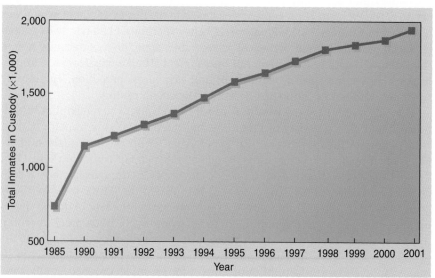

Source: Adapted from Bureau of Justice Statistics, *Prison and Jail Inmates of Midyear 2001* (Washington, D.C.: U.S. Department of Justice, 2002), Table 1, page 2.

CJ in F⊙CUS

Myth versus Reality: Does Placing Criminals in Prison Reduce Crime?

Violent crime rates in the United States have been stable or declining in recent years. At the same time, as Figure 12.3 shows, the rate at which Americans have been imprisoned has climbed precipitously. The correlation between these two trends has become a subject of much discussion among crime experts.

The Myth

A popular view of incarceration is that "a thug in jail can't shoot your sister." Obviously, a prison inmate is incapable of doing any further harm to the community. By extension, then, as the number of criminals behind bars increases, the crime rate should drop accordingly.

The Reality

Numerous studies have shown that this is not always the case. A study released in 2000 by the Sentencing Project, a research group in Washington, found that states that increased the number of prison inmates the most in the 1990s actually had less reduction in crime than those states with below-average increases in incarceration over the same

time period. Louisiana has had the highest incarceration rates in the nation and also one of the highest rates of violent crime. At the other extreme, North Dakota has had both the lowest incarceration rates and the lowest crime rates. Such statistics may show that other factors (particularly the social factors discussed in Chapter 2) play a more significant role in crime rates than the number of criminals who are incapacitated.

One theory offered to explain the apparent lack of negative correlation between rates of imprisonment and crime in general is the "replacement" hypothesis. Most crimes, especially those related to drug sales, are committed by groups of co-offenders, not by a single criminal. Consequently, when one member of the group is arrested, the criminal activity does not stop. Instead, the group merely recruits somebody else to take his or her place. Furthermore, there is widespread support for the idea that some inmates become hard-core criminals only after being exposed to prison culture and commit more crimes after being released from prison than they would have if they had never gone there in the first place.

Few observers would suggest that imprisonment rates have no effect on crime rates. Instead, criminologists seem to be cautioning that the relationship between the prison population and crime rates is not fully understood, and that public policymakers should not make laws on the assumption that more prisoners equals less crime.

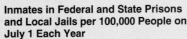

FOR CRITICAL ANALYSIS
What other factors could explain the lack of positive correlation between incarceration rates and crime rates?

FIGURE 12.3
Comparing Crime Rates and Incarceration Rates

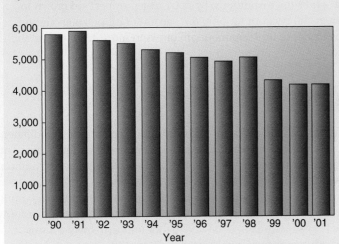

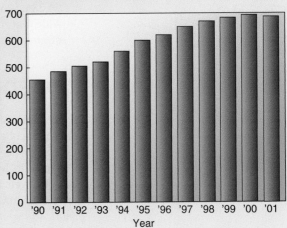

Sources: Federal Bureau of Investigation and Bureau of Justice Statistics

Security measures—including television surveillance, pat-downs, and the constant attention of correctional officers in towers (pictured above)—dominate the lives of inmates in maximum-security prisons. How do guard towers contribute to the overall security of a prison facility? What might be some of the limitations of the guard tower as a security device? (PhotoEdit/ A. Ramsey)

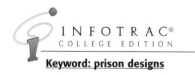

INFOTRAC®
COLLEGE EDITION
Keyword: prison designs

Alfred Blumstein of Carnegie Mellon University attributes much of the growth in the number of Americans behind bars to the enhancement and stricter enforcement of the nation's drug laws. Since 1980, he points out, the rate of incarceration for drug arrests in the United States has risen 1,000 percent, and there are more Americans in prison or jail for drug offenses today than there were for all offenses in the early 1970s.[22] Although there are 400,000 more violent offenders incarcerated in this country today than in 1980, the proportion of violent offenders behind bars actually dropped 12 percent over that time period. But in every year of the 1990s, more people were put in prison for drug crimes than for violent crimes.[23]

Other reasons for the growth in incarceration populations include:

- *Increased probability of incarceration.* Simply stated, the chance of someone who is arrested going to prison today is much greater than it was twenty years ago. Most of this growth took place in the 1980s, when the likelihood of incarceration after arrest increased fivefold for drug offenses, threefold for weapons offenses, and twofold for crimes such as sexual assault, burglary, auto theft, and larceny. These trends leveled off in the 1990s, though those arrested for murder, sexual assault, and weapons offenses still have a greater chance of going to prison or jail today than they did fifteen years ago.[24]

- *Inmates serving more time for each crime.* After the Sentencing Reform Act of 1984 (see Chapter 10), the length of time served by federal convicts for their crimes rose significantly. Since the law went into effect, the average time served by inmates in federal prisons has climbed from 15 months to 25 months—a 67 percent increase.[25] State sentencing reform statutes and "truth-in-sentencing" laws have had similar consequences. In the thirty-two states that require their inmates to serve at least 85 percent of their sentence, for example, violent offenders are expected to spend an average of fifteen months more in prison than violent offenders in states without such laws.[26]

- *Revocation of community-based sanctions.* As we discussed in Chapter 11, increased control over offenders supervised in the community has led to increased rates of their rearrest. From 1985 to 1997—a period when the corrections system continued to readjust its sights from rehabilitation to punishment, deterrence, and incapacitation—a parolee became 33 percent more likely to be returned to prison or jail for violating her or his parole.[27]

- *Rising incarceration rates of women.* In 1981, 14,000 women were prisoners in federal and state institutions; by 2001, the number had grown to 94,336. Women still account for only 6.7 percent of all prisoners nationwide, but their rates of imprisonment are growing more rapidly than those of men.[28]

TYPES OF PRISONS

Prison administrators have long been aware of the need to separate different kinds of offenders. In federal prisons, this led to a system with six levels based on the security needs of the inmates, from level 1 facilities with the lowest amount of security to level 6 with the harshest security measures. To simplify matters, most observers refer to correctional facilities as being one of three levels—minimum, medium, and maximum. A fourth level—the supermaximum-security prison, known as the "supermax"—is relatively rare and extremely controversial due to its hyperharsh methods of punishing and controlling the most dangerous prisoners. (See the feature *Criminal Justice in Action—The End of the Line: Supermax Prisons* at the end of this chapter.)

Maximum-Security Prisons

In a certain sense, the classification of prisoners today owes a debt to the three-grade system developed by Zebulon Brockway at the Elmira Penitentiary, discussed earlier in the chapter. Once wrongdoers enter a corrections facility, they are constantly graded on behavior. Those who serve good time, as we have seen, are often rewarded with early release. Those who compile extensive misconduct records are usually housed, along with violent and repeat offenders, in **maximum-security prisons.** The names of these institutions—Folsom, San Quentin, Sing Sing, Attica—conjure up foreboding images of concrete and steel jungles, with good reason.

Maximum-security prisons are designed with full attention to security and surveillance. In these institutions, inmates' lives are programmed in a militaristic fashion to keep them from escaping or from harming themselves or the prison staff. About a quarter of the prisons in the United States are classified as maximum security, and these institutions house about 16 percent of the country's prisoners. Maximum-security prisons tend to be large—holding more than a thousand inmates—and they have similar features. The entire operation is usually surrounded by concrete walls that stand 20 to 30 feet high and have also been sunk deep into the ground to deter tunnel escapes; fences reinforced with razor-ribbon barbed wire that can be electrically charged may supplement or replace the walls. The prison walls are studded with watchtowers, from which guards armed with shotguns and rifles survey the movement of prisoners below. The designs of these facilities, though similar, are not uniform. Though correctional facilities built using the radial design pioneered by the Eastern State Penitentiary still exist, several other designs have become prominent in more recently constructed institutions. For an overview of these designs, including the radial design, see Figure 12.4 on the following page.

Medium- and Minimum-Security Prisons

Medium-security prisons hold about 35 percent of the prison population and minimum-security prisons 49 percent. Inmates at **medium-security prisons** have for the most part committed less serious crimes than those housed in

Video Profiles of Ney Lawson, Deputy Chief of Corrections; Dr. Claire D'Agostino, Corrections Treatment

MAXIMUM-SECURITY PRISON
A correctional institution designed and organized to control and discipline dangerous felons, as well as prevent escape, with intense supervision, cement walls, and electronic, barbed-wire fences.

MEDIUM-SECURITY PRISON
A correctional institution that houses less dangerous inmates than a maximum-security facility, and therefore uses less restrictive measures to avoid violence and escapes.

FIGURE 12.4 **Prison Designs**

The Radial Design

The radial design has been utilized since the early nineteenth century. The "wagon wheel"–like form of the structure was created with the dual goals of separation and control. Inmates are separated from each other in their cells on the "spokes" of the wheel, and prison officials can control the activities of the inmates from the control center in the "hub" of the wheel.

The Courtyard Style

In the courtyard-style prison, a courtyard replaces the transportation function of the "pole" in the telephone-pole prison. The prison buildings form a square around the courtyard, and to get from one part of the facility to another, the inmates go across the courtyard. In a number of these facilities, the recreational area, mess hall, and school are located in the courtyard.

The Telephone-Pole Design

The main feature of the telephone-pole design is a long central corridor that serves as a means for transporting inmates from one part of the facility to another. Branching off from this main corridor are the functional areas of the facility: housing, food services, workshops, treatment program rooms, and so on. Prison officials survey the entire facility from the central "pole" and can shut off the various "arms" when necessary for security reasons. The majority of maximum-security prisons in the United States were constructed using this design blueprint.

The Campus Style

Some of the newer minimum-security prisons have adopted the campus style, a style that had previously been used in correctional facilities for women and juveniles. Like a college campus, housing units are scattered among functional units such as the dining room, recreation area, and treatment centers. The benefit of the campus style is that individual buildings can be used for different functions, making the operation more flexible. Due to concerns that the campus style provides less security than the other designs discussed, it remains for the most part the design of choice for medium- and minimum-security prisons.

Source: Text adapted from Todd R. Clear and George F. Cole, *American Corrections,* 4th ed. (Belmont, CA: Wadsworth Publishing Company, 1997), 255–56.

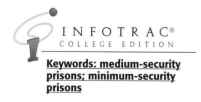

INFOTRAC®
COLLEGE EDITION

Keywords: medium-security prisons; minimum-security prisons

maximum-security prisons and are not considered high risks to escape or to cause harm. Consequently, medium-security institutions are not designed for control to the same extent as maximum-security prisons and have a more relaxed atmosphere. These facilities also offer more educational and treatment programs and allow for greater contact between inmates. Medium-security prisons are rarely walled, relying instead on high fences. Prisoners have more freedom of movement within the structures, and the levels of surveillance are much lower. Living quarters are less restrictive as well—many of the newer medium-security prisons provide dormitory housing.

A **minimum-security prison** seems at first glance to be more like a college campus than an incarceration facility. Most of the inmates at these institutions are first-time offenders, nonviolent, and well behaved and include a high percentage of white-collar criminals. Indeed, inmates are often transferred to minimum-security prisons as a reward for good behavior in other facilities. Therefore, security measures are lax compared even to medium-security prisons. Unlike medium-security institutions, minimum-security prisons do not have armed guards. Prisoners are allowed amenities such as television sets and computers in their rooms, they enjoy freedom of movement, and they are allowed off prison grounds for educational or employment purposes to a much greater extent than those held in more restrictive facilities. Some critics have likened minimum-security prisons to "country clubs," but in the corrections system, everything is relative. A minimum-security prison may seem like a vacation spot when compared to the horrors of Sing Sing, but it still represents a restriction of personal freedom and separates the inmate from the outside world.

Inmates in the medium-security section of Nevada's High Desert Prison hone their computer skills and learn new languages at the on-site prison school. (AP Photo/Lennox McLendon)

PRISON ADMINISTRATION

The security level of the institution generally determines the specific methods by which a prison is managed. There are, however, general goals of prison administration, summarized by Charles Logan as follows:

> The mission of a prison is to keep prisoners—to keep them in, keep them safe, keep them in line, keep them healthy, and keep them busy—and to do it with fairness, without undue suffering and as efficiently as possible.[29]

Considering the environment of a prison—an enclosed world inhabited by people who are generally violent, angry, and would rather be anywhere else—Logan's mission statement may be slightly Utopian. A prison staff must supervise the daily routines of hundreds or thousands of inmates, a duty that includes providing them with meals, education, vocational programs, and different forms of leisure. The smooth operation of this supervision is made more difficult—if not, at times, impossible—by budgetary restrictions, overcrowding, and continual inmate turnover.

The implications of mismanagement are severe. While studying a series of prison riots, sociologists Bert Useem and Peter Kimball found that breakdowns in managerial control commonly preceded such acts of mass violence.[30] During the 1970s, for example, conditions in the State Penitentiary in New Mexico deteriorated significantly; inmates who had become well organized and comfortable with their daily routines increasingly became the targets of harsh treatment from the prison staff, while at the same time a reduction in structured activities left prison life "painfully boring."[31] The result, in 1980, was one of the most violent prison riots in the nation's history. (To learn how new monitoring systems are helping prison administrators manage and control prison populations, see the feature *Criminal Justice & Technology—The Electronic Head Count* on page 312.)

In some respects, the management structure of a prison is similar to that of a police department, as discussed in Chapter 5. Both systems rely on a hierarchical (top-down) *chain of command* to increase personal responsibility (see Figure 12.5 on page 313). Both assign different employees to specific tasks, though prison managers have much greater direct control over their subordinates than do police managers. The main difference is that police departments have a *continuity of purpose* that is sometimes lacking in prison organizations. All members of a police force are, at least theoretically, working to reduce crime and apprehend criminals. In a prison, this continuity is less evident. An employee in the prison

MINIMUM-SECURITY PRISON
A correctional institution designed to allow inmates, most of whom pose low security risks, a great deal of freedom of movement and contact with the outside world.

Criminal Justice & TECHNOLOGY

The Electronic Head Count

In Chapter 11, we saw how monitoring devices have changed the face of community corrections. Similar technology, though not as widespread, is beginning to have an equally dramatic effect on prison management. Called TSI PRISM, the monitoring equipment acts as a high-tech head count: Inmates wear bracelets, while corrections officers wear small, pagerlike devices. Guided by a series of radio transmitters and receivers, the system is able to pinpoint the location of inmates and guards within twenty feet. Every two seconds, radio signals "search out" where each inmate and guard is, and relay this information to a central computer. Onscreen the inmate shows up as a yellow dot and the corrections officer as a blue dot on a grid of the prison. Administrators can quickly determine which inmates and officers are represented by each dot, and all movements are stored in a database for future reference, if necessary. "It completely revolutionizes a prison because you know where everyone is—not approximately but exactly where they are," says an official at the National institute of Justice.

In 2002, a new maximum-security juvenile prison in Michigan was outfitted with PRISM. The hope is that PRISM will end the "guessing games" that inevitably follow charges of assault—either physical or sexual—by one juvenile against another. With its tracing abilities, the system will allow corrections officials to immediately determine whether the accuser is telling the truth. "It's almost like having a videotape" of the attack, noted one official, "because you

Vincent Campos (above), a correctional officer at Calipatria state prison in California, monitors inmates using the TSI PRISM system. Inmates (left) wear electronic wrist bands so their movements can be tracked at all times. (AP Photos/Fred Greaves)

can track who was there." The bracelet is also tamper resistant, so if an inmate tries to remove it or damage it in any way, an alarm is immediately sent to the central computer system.

IN THE FUTURE

Electronic monitoring experts predict that systems such as PRISM will soon be "customized" to fit the needs of any specific prison population. So, for example, if officials are aware that two rival gangs exist, PRISM can be programmed to trigger an alarm when individual gang members come in close contact with each other. The bracelets could also be linked to satellite tracking systems, helping track down escaped convicts who manage to get outside the boundaries of the prison's radio transmitters.

Video Profile of Ana Ramirez-Palmer, Warden

WARDEN
The prison official who is ultimately responsible for the organization and performance of a correctional facility.

laundry service and one who works in the visiting center have little in common. In some cases, employees may even have cross-purposes: a prison guard may want to punish an inmate, while a counselor in the treatment center may want to rehabilitate her or him.

Consequently, a strong hierarchy is crucial for any prison management team that hopes to meet Logan's expectations. As Figure 12.5 shows, the **warden** (also known as a superintendent) is ultimately responsible for the operation of a prison. He or she oversees deputy wardens, who in turn manage the various organizational lines of the institution. The custodial employees, who deal directly with the inmates and make up more than half of a prison's staff, operate under a militaristic hierarchy, with a line of command passing from the deputy warden

FIGURE 12.5
FIGURE 12.5
Organizational Chart for a Typical Correctional Facility

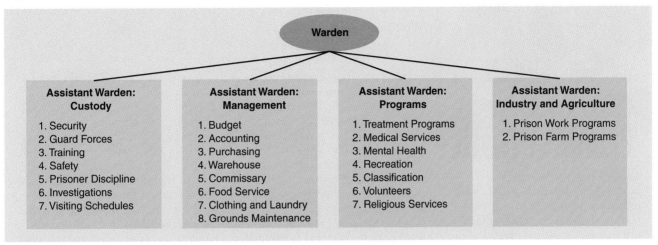

Warden

Assistant Warden: Custody
1. Security
2. Guard Forces
3. Training
4. Safety
5. Prisoner Discipline
6. Investigations
7. Visiting Schedules

Assistant Warden: Management
1. Budget
2. Accounting
3. Purchasing
4. Warehouse
5. Commissary
6. Food Service
7. Clothing and Laundry
8. Grounds Maintenance

Assistant Warden: Programs
1. Treatment Programs
2. Medical Services
3. Mental Health
4. Recreation
5. Classification
6. Volunteers
7. Religious Services

Assistant Warden: Industry and Agriculture
1. Prison Work Programs
2. Prison Farm Programs

to the captain to the corrections officer. (See the *Careers in Criminal Justice* feature on the next page to learn more about the responsibilities of a warden.)

THE EMERGENCE OF PRIVATE PRISONS

In addition to all the other pressures placed on wardens and other prison administrators, they must operate within a budget assigned to them by an overseeing governmental agency. The great majority of all prisons are under the control of federal and state governments. The Federal Bureau of Prisons (BOP), part of the U.S. Department of Justice, operates nearly one hundred prisons. The executive branch of each state is responsible for state prisons and, in some instances, jails. In the nineteenth century, not all correctional facilities were under the control of the state. In fact, the entire Texas prison system was privately operated from 1872 to the late 1880s. For most of the twentieth century, however, **private prisons,** or prisons run by private business firms to make a profit, could not be found in the United States.

That is certainly not the case today. With corrections exhibiting all appearances of, in the words of one observer, "a recession-proof industry," the American business community eagerly entered the market in the late 1980s and 1990s.[32] Thirteen private corrections firms operate nearly two hundred facilities across the United States. The two largest corrections companies, Prison Realty Trust and Wackenhut Corrections Corporation, are contracted to supervise nearly 85,000 inmates. In 1997, the BOP awarded the first contract paying a private company to operate one of its prisons—Wackenhut received $88 million to run the Taft Correctional Institution in Taft, California.[33] At midyear 2001, 94,938 prisoners in the United States were being held in private facilities, up nearly 5 percent from the year before.[34]

PRIVATE PRISONS
Correctional facilities operated by private corporations instead of the government, and therefore reliant on profit for survival.

Corrections Corporation of America (CCR) constructed the McRae Correctional Facility (pictured here) in McRae, Georgia, at a cost of $45 million. The state of Georgia, however, told CCR that it had no inmates for the 1,524-bed medium-security prison, thus delaying its scheduled 2001 opening. Why might a state not want to send its inmates to a privately run prison? (AP Photo)

Careers in Criminal Justice

Penny Lucero
Warden

As warden of the New Mexico Women's Correctional Facility, I have executive oversight of the management and operation of the nation's first privately managed, multicustody state prison. I became interested in corrections as a result of the employment opportunities made available with the state. When I entered the job market, I had received my undergraduate degree in psychology and completed work toward my graduate degree from New Mexico State University.

My corrections career began in 1981 with the New Mexico Department of Corrections, where I held a series of progressively more responsible positions, including training officer, ACA accreditation manager, and chief classification officer. In 1985, I became the first woman to be promoted to the rank

of assistant warden at a male prison in New Mexico. In order to expand my experience to include juvenile corrections, I took the position of deputy superintendent at the Youth Diagnostic Center and New Mexico Girls' School.

Although I left corrections for a while to manage my own business, I realized that my true career had become corrections. Being my own boss had its "pros," but the "cons" had won my heart; I wanted to dedicate my energy, expertise, and leadership to corrections. Fortunately, Corrections Corporation of America was opening the new women's prison in Grants, and I was quickly recruited as a member of the management team. Joining this team of experienced corrections professionals is what I claim to be the catalyst that propelled me to the highest executive level of institutional leadership. The management team included three well-established professionals: two retired wardens from the New Mexico system and one nationally recognized warden of a female prison. All three became friends and mentors, always encouraging me to excel.

As warden, I consider my major responsibilities to be maintaining a healthful, positive, safe, and mutually respectful environment for staff and inmates; establishing a working relationship with outside communities in order to assist with public education about offenders and the mutual benefit of working with them on release; participating in civic and professional organizations and encouraging the staff to do so; ensuring that the New Mexico Women's Correctional Facility meets established national correctional standards; and staying current on new management, program, and technology trends that can assist me in maintaining the standards of excellence established at the facility.

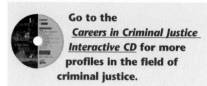

Go to the *Careers in Criminal Justice Interactive CD* for more profiles in the field of criminal justice.

INFOTRAC®
COLLEGE EDITION

Keyword: private prisons

JAIL
A facility, usually operated by county government, used to hold persons awaiting trial or those who have been found guilty of misdemeanors.

JAILS

Although prisons and prison issues dominate the public discourse on corrections, there is an argument to be made that jails are the dominant penal institutions in the United States. In general, a prison is a facility designed to house people convicted of felonies for lengthy periods of time, while a **jail** is authorized to hold pretrial detainees and offenders who have committed misdemeanors. On any given day, more than 630,000 inmates are in jail in this country, and approximately 7 million Americans spend at least a day in jail each year. Yet jail funding is often the lowest priority for the tight budgets of local governments, leading to severe overcrowding and other dismal conditions.[35]

Many observers see this negligence as having far-reaching consequences for criminal justice. Jail is often the first contact that citizens have with the corrections system. It is at this point that treatment and counseling have the best chance to deter future criminal behavior.[36] By failing to take advantage of this opportunity, says Professor Frank Zimring of the Earl Warren Legal Institute at the University of California at Berkeley, corrections officials have created a situation in which "today's jail folk are tomorrow's prisoners."[37]

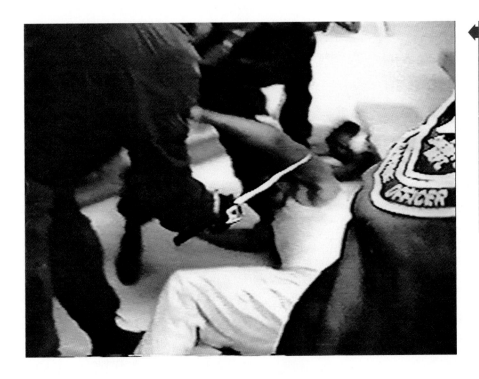

Local sheriffs' deputies strike an inmate of the Brazoria County Detention Center in Clute, Texas, with a baton. After viewing the video from which this scene was taken, the FBI began an investigation into possible civil rights violations at the jail. Guard-on-inmate violence is only one of the problems plaguing the nation's jails, others being inmate-on-inmate violence, poor living conditions, and inadequate health care facilities. Yet jail issues do not receive nearly the same attention as prison issues. Why might this be the case? (AP Photo/*The Brazosport Facts*)

The Function of Jails

Until the eighteenth century, all penal institutions existed primarily to hold those charged with a crime until their trial. Although jails still serve this purpose, they have evolved to play a number of different roles in the corrections system. According to the Department of Justice, these roles include the following:

- Holding those convicted of misdemeanors.
- Receiving individuals pending arraignment and holding them while awaiting trial (if they cannot post bail), conviction, or sentencing.
- Temporarily detaining juveniles pending transfer to juvenile authorities.
- Holding the mentally ill pending transfer to health facilities.
- Detaining those who have violated conditions of probation or parole and those who have "jumped" bail.
- Housing inmates awaiting transfer to federal or state prisons.
- Operating community-based corrections programs such as home confinement and electronic monitoring.

Increasingly, jails are also called on to handle the overflow from saturated state and federal prisons. In Texas, for example, corrections officials were recently forced to rent a thousand county jail cells to house inmates for whom no space was available in state prisons.[38]

According to sociologist John Irwin, the unofficial purpose of the jail is to manage society's "rabble," so-called because

> [they] are not well integrated into conventional society, they are not members of conventional social organizations, they have few ties to conventional social networks, and they are carriers of unconventional values and beliefs.[39]

In Irwin's opinion, "rabble" who act violently are arrested and sent to prison. The jail is reserved for merely offensive rabble, whose primary threat to society lies in their failure to conform to its behavioral norms. This concept has been used by some critics of American corrections to explain the disproportionate number of poor and minority groups who may be found in the nation's jails at any time.

On the Web

For a link to the home page of Wackenhut Corrections Corporation, one of the largest private corrections corporations in the world, go to the Hypercontents page for this chapter at **http://www.cj.wadsworth.com/ gainescore2e**.

GREAT DEBATES

Why privatize prisons? Proponents claim that private facilities can be run more cheaply and efficiently than public ones. Opponents assert that in trying to "cut corners" to save costs, administrators at private prisons deny inmates important guarantees of safety and general well-being. For more information on this debate, go to the Great Debates feature on the text's companion Web site at **http://www.cj.wadsworth. com/gainescore2e**

FIGURE 12.6 The Characteristics of America's Jail Population

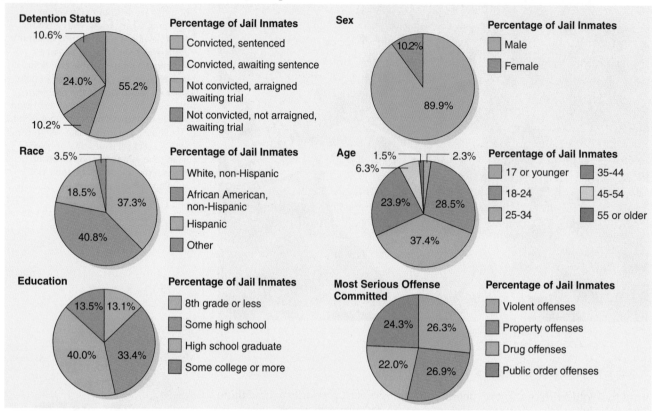

Source: Bureau of Justice Statistics, *Profile of Jail Inmates 1996* (Washington, D.C.: U.S. Department of Justice, April 1998), 1–4.

The Jail Population

Almost 90 percent of jail inmates in the United States are male. As in other areas of corrections, however, women are becoming more numerous. Since 1990, the adult female jail population has grown at an annual rate of 6.3 percent, compared to 3.8 percent for males.[40] Jails also follow the general corrections pattern in that a disproportionate number of their inmates are members of minority groups. (For an overview of the characteristics of the jail population, see Figure 12.6.)

Pretrial Detainees. As you can see in Figure 12.6, a significant number of those detained in jails technically are not prisoners. They are **pretrial detainees** who have been arrested by the police and are unable to post bail. Pretrial detainees are, in many ways, walking legal contradictions. According to the U.S. Constitution, they are innocent until proven guilty. At the same time, by being incarcerated while awaiting trial, they are denied a number of personal freedoms and are subjected to the poor conditions of many jails. In 1979, the United States Supreme Court rejected the notion that this situation is inherently unfair by refusing to give pretrial detainees greater legal protections than sentenced jail inmates have.[41]

Sentenced Jail Inmates. According to the Department of Justice, about 65 percent of those in jail have been convicted of their current charge.[42] In other words, they have been found guilty of a crime, usually a misdemeanor, and sentenced. The typical jail term lasts between thirty and ninety days, and rarely does a prisoner spend more than one year in jail for any single crime. Often, a judge will credit the length of time the convict has spent in detention waiting for trial—known as **time served**—toward his or her sentence. This practice acknowledges two realities of jails:

PRETRIAL DETAINEES
Individuals who cannot post bail after arrest and are therefore forced to spend the time prior to their trial incarcerated in jail.

TIME SERVED
The period of time a person denied bail has spent in jail prior to his or her trial. If the suspect is found guilty and sentenced to a jail or prison term, the judge will often lessen the duration of the sentence based on the amount of time served as a pretrial detainee.

① Terms are generally too short to allow the prisoner to gain any benefit (that is, rehabilitation) from the jail's often limited or nonexistent treatment facilities. Therefore, the jail term can serve no other purpose than to punish the wrongdoer. (Judges who believe jail time can serve purposes of deterrence and incapacitation may not agree with this line of reasoning.)

② Jails are chronically overcrowded, and judges need to clear space for new offenders.

Other Jail Inmates. Pretrial detainees and misdemeanants make up the vast majority of the jail population. As mentioned earlier, jail inmates also include felons either waiting for transfer or assigned to jails because of prison overcrowding, probation and parole violators, the mentally ill, and juveniles. In addition, jails can hold those who require incarceration but do not "fit" anywhere else. A material witness or an attorney in a trial who refuses to follow the judge's instructions may, for example, be held in contempt of court and sent to jail.

THE CONSEQUENCES OF OUR HIGH RATES OF INCARCERATION

For many observers, especially those who support the crime control theory of criminal justice, America's high rate of incarceration has contributed significantly to the drop in the country's crime rates.[43] At the heart of this belief is the fact, which we covered in Chapter 2, that most crimes are committed by a relatively small number of repeat offenders. Numerous studies have tried to corroborate this viewpoint, with varying results—estimates of the number of crimes committed each year by habitual offenders range from 3 to 187.[44] If one accepts the higher appraisal, each year a repeat offender spends in prison prevents a significant number of criminal acts.

Criminologists, however, note the negative consequences of America's growing prison and jail population. For one, incarceration can have severe social consequences for communities and the families that make up those communities. When a parent is imprisoned, her or his children will often suffer financial hardships, reduced supervision and discipline, and a general deterioration of the family structure.[45] These factors are used to explain the fact that children of convicts are more likely to become involved in delinquent behavior. Our high rates of incarceration also deny one of the basic rights of American democracy—the right to vote—to a certain segment of the citizenry. (A number of states and the federal government disenfranchise, or take away the ability to vote, from those convicted of felonies. Some states do not, however.) This has a disproportionate impact on minority groups who are disproportionately imprisoned, weakening their voice in the democratic debate.[46] Many observers find such consequences unacceptable, especially if they feel, as does Kathleen Auerhahn of the University of California at Riverside, that "incarceration-focused" approaches to reducing crime are "ineffective [or] at the very least inefficient."[47]

Whether the American incarceration situation is "good" or "bad" depends to a large extent on one's personal philosophy. In the end, it is difficult to do a definitive cost-benefit analysis for each person incarcerated, weighing the benefits of preventing crimes that might (or might not) have been committed by an inmate against the costs to the convict's family and society. One thing that can be stated with some certainty is that, given the present political and social atmosphere, the increase in correctional facilities and inmates will continue in the foreseeable future.

> "To assert in any case that a man must be absolutely cut off from society because he is absolutely evil amounts to saying that society is absolutely good, and no one in his right mind will believe this today."
>
> —Albert Camus, *French author* (1961)

About half a million children in the United States, including the three pictured below, can see their mothers only by visiting them in prison or jail. What are some of the possible consequences of this separation? (AP Photo/Kathy Willens)

Criminal Justice in Action

The End of the Line: Supermax Prisons

On Easter Sunday, 1993, inmates at a maximum-security prison in Lucasville, Ohio, seized control of an entire cell block and held it for eleven days. During the extended rioting, one correctional officer and nine inmates were killed; afterward the state spent nearly $80 million on prison repairs, investigations, and lawsuits. The Easter riot had a profound effect on the state's prison system. Within five years, Ohio had added seven new penal institutions and doubled the budget of the Department of Rehabilitation and Corrections. The centerpiece of the new efforts was the Ohio State Penitentiary in Youngstown. At its opening in the spring of 1998, the Youngstown facility was celebrated by officials as the nation's latest **supermax** (short for supermaximum-security) **prison.** In this *Criminal Justice in Action* feature, we will examine these "intense" corrections facilities, condemned by critics as inhuman and lauded by supporters as the ultimate in "get tough" incarceration.

"THE WORST OF THE WORST"

Supermax prisons are reserved for the "worst of the worst." Inmates generally are not sent to such facilities by a court; instead, commitment to a supermax prison is usually the result of misbehavior within a penal institution. The murder or attempted murder of a fellow inmate was the most common reason for commitment to the BOP's U.S. Penitentiary Administrative Maximum (ADX) in Florence, Colorado.

The main purpose of a supermax prison is to strictly control the inmates' movement, thereby limiting (or eliminating) situations that could lead to breakdowns in discipline. The conditions in California's Security Housing Unit (SHU) at Pelican Bay State Prison are representative of most supermax institutions. Prisoners are confined to their one-person cells for twenty-two and a half hours each day under video camera surveillance; they receive meals through a slot in the door. The cells measure 8 by 10 feet in size and are windowless. No decorations of any kind are permitted on the white walls.[48]

For the ninety minutes each day the inmates are allowed out of their cells (compared to twelve to sixteen hours in regular maximum-security prisons), they may either shower or exercise in an enclosed, concrete "yard" covered by plastic mesh. Prisoners are strip-searched before and after leaving their cells, and placed in waist restraints and handcuffs on their way to and from the "yard" and showers. They can have a limited number of books or magazines in their cells and, if they can afford it, a television or radio.[49]

Removing the most violent and problematic inmates from the general prison population is seen as a key to modern prison management. Because those inmates transferred to supermax facilities are more likely to be impulsive and unpredictable and to have a gang affiliation, their absence is believed to create a safer environment for other inmates and the correctional staff. Furthermore, prison administrators use the supermax as a disciplinary tool—problematic inmates may change their behavior if they fear being transferred.[50]

MARION—THE FIRST SUPERMAX

The precursor of today's supermax was San Francisco's Alcatraz Prison. Opening in 1932 on Alcatraz Island in San Francisco Bay, the maximum-security prison was populated by the most dangerous and disruptive federal convicts.

Alcatraz Prison, pictured here in 1934. Located on an island in San Francisco Bay, it housed some of the most dangerous and notorious convicts of the day, including Chicago gangster Al Capone. (AP Photo)

Alcatraz was closed in 1963—mainly due to the expense of operating an island prison. For most of the next two decades, the BOP used the **dispersion** model for placing the most hazardous inmates; that is, the department dispersed its "hard-core" offenders to various federal prisons around the country, hoping the general inmate population would assimilate them.[51]

By the late 1970s, it became apparent that this strategy was not functioning as planned. The "hard cores" continued to act violently, endangering other inmates and correctional employees. Then, in October 1983, two staff members and an inmate were murdered within a week at the federal prison in Marion, Illinois. Prison officials instituted a **lockdown,** in which all inmates are confined to their cells, and social activities such as meals, recreational sports, and treatment programs are canceled. Lockdowns are considered temporary, "cooling-off" measures, but officials at Marion decided to leave the conditions in effect indefinitely, creating the first supermax prison. The supermax is based on the model of **consolidation:** all high-risk inmates are placed in a single institution, which is administered with a focus on complete control.[52]

The New-Generation Supermax

At first, the consolidation model led federal and state officials to construct supermax facilities on existing prison grounds. Over the past decade, however, the trend has been toward building new penal institutions, expressly designed with the goals of the supermax in mind. The Closed Maximum Security Correctional Center (CMAX) in Tamms, Illinois, for example, is designed around inmate housing pods. Each pod contains sixty cells on two levels, arranged around a control station with complete visual access. CMAX is designed so that an inmate never leaves his pod; medical facilities, library cells, and recreational areas are located within its boundaries.

All inmate movement in the pod takes place on the lower level, while armed security staff patrol the upper level. These guards can see through the upper-level flooring grid, allowing them to closely monitor any activity below. Furthermore, officials can control circulation by sealing off portions of the facility at will.[53] These new-generation supermax prisons also strive to limit contact between staff and inmates through technology. Automatic doors, intercoms, and electronic surveillance cameras have reduced the exposure of guards to inmates at most of the new facilities.

Senseless Suffering?

Many prison officials support the proliferation of supermax prisons because they provide increased security for the most dangerous inmates. Observers believe that as the inmate population becomes aware of these new facilities, their harsh reputation will deter convicts from misbehaving for fear of transfer to a supermax.

The supermax has aroused a number of criticisms, however. Amnesty International and other human rights groups assert that the facilities violate international standards of proper treatment for prisoners. Other opponents point out that inmates are provided minimal due process protections during the transfer process. An inmate has no right to an attorney while being considered for a transfer, and the decision to send someone to a supermax cannot be appealed. Because this decision is made by an administrative—and not a judicial or legislative—body, in *Sandin v. Conner* (1995),[54] the United States Supreme Court ruled only that such a

Continued on next page

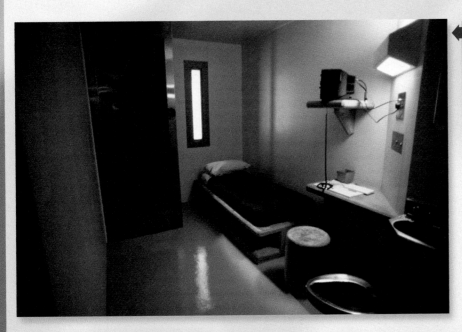

A typical supermax prison cell at the ADX outside Florence, Colorado. The cell is 8 feet 8 inches × 12 feet 3 inches, and contains a stainless steel mirror and a 12-inch black-and-white television set, as well as a concrete desk, stool, and bed that are permanently fixed to the floor. The small window has no view. (Bob Daemmrich/Corbis Sygma)

CJ in Action: Supermax Prisons *continued*

move must not impose an "atypical and significant hardship on the inmate in relation to the ordinary incidents of prison life." As yet, no court has found that the conditions in a supermax constitute such a hardship.[55]

Other observers believe not only that those conditions are atypical and significant, but that they violate Eighth Amendment protections against cruel and unusual punishment. The negative effects of solitary confinement on a prisoner's psyche are considerable, and supermax facilities are structured to keep their inmates isolated at all times. After studying inmates at California's Pelican Bay, a Harvard University psychiatrist found that 80 percent suffered from what he called "SHU [security housing unit] syndrome"; after spending a certain amount of time at the facility, the inmates either exhibited new signs of mental instability, or their existing conditions were exacerbated.[56] In *Madrid v. Gomez* (1995),[57] U.S. District Judge Thelton Henderson found that Pelican Bay violated its inmates' Eighth Amendment rights, writing that "dry words on paper cannot adequately capture the senseless suffering" of the convicts.

Despite his harsh sentiments, Judge Henderson's ruling only forced the supermax to improve medical care and had no discernible effect on the operation of the facility. Indeed, it does not appear that the American courts will pose a threat to the operation of these institutions. According to the National Institute of Corrections, supermax prisons are the fasting-growing type of prison in the United States, and house more than 16,000 inmates.[58]

MAKING SENSE OF SUPERMAX PRISONS

① Explain the thinking behind the dispersion and consolidation models of dealing with highly dangerous inmates. Why is the supermax prison considered to be an example of the consolidation model?

② Summarize the arguments for and against the supermax prison. Which side do you fall on, and why?

③ Do you feel that supermax prisons infringe on inmates' Eighth Amendment right to be free from "cruel and unusual punishment"? What other information about how supermax prisons are operated might you need to know before you answer?

SUPERMAX PRISON
A correctional facility reserved for those inmates who have extensive records of misconduct in maximum-security prisons; characterized by extremely strict control and supervision over the inmates, including extensive use of solitary confinement.

DISPERSION
A corrections model in which high-risk inmates are spread throughout the general prison population, in the hopes that they will be absorbed without causing misconduct problems.

LOCKDOWN
A disciplinary action taken by prison officials in which all inmates are ordered to their quarters and nonessential prison activities are suspended.

CONSOLIDATION
A corrections model in which the inmates who pose the highest security risk are housed in a single facility to separate them from the general prison population.

INFOTRAC®
COLLEGE EDITION

Keyword: supermax prisons

KEY TERMS

congregate system 304

consolidation 320

dispersion 320

jail 314

lockdown 320

maximum-security prison 309

medical model 305

medium-security prison 309

minimum-security prison 311

penitentiary 303

pretrial detainees 316

private prisons 313

separate confinement 304

supermax prison 320

time served 316

warden 312

CHAPTER SUMMARY

1 Contrast the Pennsylvania and the New York penitentiary theories of the 1800s. Basically, the Pennsylvania system imposed total silence on its prisoners. Based on the concept of separate confinement, penitentiaries were constructed with back-to-back cells facing both outward and inward. Prisoners worked, slept, and ate alone in their cells. In contrast, New York used the congregate system; silence was imposed, but inmates worked and ate together.

2 List the factors that have caused the prison population to grow dramatically in the last several decades. (a) The enhancement and stricter enforcement of the nation's drug laws; (b) increased probability of incarceration; (c) inmates serving more time for each crime; (d) revocation of community-based sanctions; and (e) rising incarceration rates for women.

3 List and briefly explain the four types of prisons. (a) Maximum-security prisons, which are designed mainly with security and surveillance in mind. (b) Medium-security prisons, which offer considerably more educational and treatment programs and allow more contact between inmates. Such prisons are rarely walled, but rather are surrounded by high fences. (c) Minimum-security prisons, which permit prisoners to have television sets and computers and often allow them to leave the grounds for educational and employment purposes. (d) Supermaximum-security (supermax) prisons, in which prisoners are confined to one-person cells for up to twenty-two and a half hours per day under constant video camera surveillance.

4 Summarize the distinction between jails and prisons, and indicate the importance of jails in the American correctional system. Generally, a prison is for those convicted of felonies who will serve lengthy periods of incarceration, whereas a jail is for those who have been convicted of misdemeanors and will serve less than a year of incarceration. A jail also (a) receives individuals pending arraignment and holds them while awaiting trial, conviction, or sentencing; (b) temporarily holds juveniles pending transfer to juvenile authorities; (c) holds the mentally ill pending transfer to health facilities; (d) detains those who have violated probation or parole and those who have "jumped" bail; and (e) houses those awaiting transfer to federal or state prisons. Approximately 7 million Americans spend time in jail each year, and jail populations are growing at about 4.4 percent per year.

5 Indicate some of the consequences of our high rates of incarceration. (a) Some people believe that the reduction in the country's crime rate is a direct result of increased incarceration rates; (b) others believe that high incarceration rates are having increasing negative social consequences, such as financial hardships, reduced supervision and discipline of children, and a general deterioration of the family structure when one parent is in prison; and (c) more money spent on prisons has taken away money for other public services, such as education.

QUESTIONS FOR CRITICAL ANALYSIS

1 Explain the benefit of nonfixed sentences coupled with the possibility of early release.

2 How did the Elmira Reformatory classify prisoners? How did the system work?

3 Crime rates are falling, yet prison rates are rising rapidly. Why?

4 The chain of command in prisons and police departments appears quite similar, yet there is a big difference. What is it?

5 Why are jails so important in the American corrections system?

6 In the first two decades after the closing of Alcatraz, what method did the Bureau of Prisons use in dealing with its most dangerous inmates? Was the method successful?

SELECTED PRINT AND ELECTRONIC RESOURCES

SUGGESTED READINGS

Glenn, Lon, *The Largest Hotel Chain in Texas: Texas Prisons,* Burnet, TX: 2001. Though a semibiography, this book chronicles what the author claims is the destruction of the best prison system in the world.

Kerle, Kenneth E., *American Jails: Looking to the Future,* Boston: Butterworth-Heinemann, 1998. The author is the co-founder of the American Jail Association and editor of the magazine *American Jails.* He looks at the jail system and contrasts it with the prison system. He examines overcrowding and other issues. He also predicts what will happen to prisons in the future.

Sifakis, Carl, *The Encyclopedia of American Prisons,* New York: Checkmark Books, 2003. Sifakis mixes history, statistics, and anecdotes to give a complete analysis of the American prison system. The author also presents the viewpoints of various corrections experts, as well as detailed information on individual facilities, to fill out this valuable overview.

MEDIA RESOURCES

***Escape from Alcatraz* (1979)** According to legend, Alcatraz Prison, located on Alcatraz Island in San Francisco Bay, was escape proof. Indeed, during the thirty-one years that Alcatraz was operational, nobody did manage to escape; that is, most people are pretty sure that nobody managed to escape. This film tells the story of Frank Morris (played by Clint Eastwood), a bank robber who may indeed have been able to find his way out of the prison and off the island. Shot on location, the film strives to give a realistic picture of life at Alcatraz while at the same time providing a dramatic setting for Morris's efforts at escape.

Critically analyze this film:

1. How would you describe the prison environment within Alcatraz?

2. The prison was built to hold really dangerous prisoners. Does the film give the impression that those are the only types of prisoners there? Why or why not?

3. What kind of tight security at Alcatraz was evident in the movie?

4. Describe the use of solitary confinement in Alcatraz, both as a punishment and as a way of life.

5. How much privacy was available for prisoners in their cells?

LOGGING ON

Go to http://cj.wadsworth.com/gainescore2e, and click Hypercontents. There, you will find URLs for the organizations in the following list:

- **Corrections.com** calls itself "the official home of corrections." Their Web site is certainly a valuable resource for information on the corrections industry.

- In 1829, **Eastern State Penitentiary** in Philadelphia was opened as a place for "confinement and soli-tude with labor." Today, it is a prison museum, and its Web site offers a number of interesting historical and educational features.

- If you would like information on **Alcatraz,** another famous penal institution located in the middle of San Francisco Bay, check out its Web site.

USING THE INTERNET FOR CRIMINAL JUSTICE ANALYSIS

1. Go to your InfoTrac College Edition at http://www.infotrac-college.com/wadsworth/. After you log on, type in the words: **To the max: Supermax facilities provide prison administrators with more options.**

This is an article about the design and administration of supermax facilities. Read the article and answer the following questions:

a. When you click on the photo on the left-hand margin about halfway down the article, what are some of the characteristics that you see from the aerial view of the Florence, Colorado, supermax prison?

b. Why is it misleading to label supermax facilities as "lockdown" institutions?

c. What is the distinction between the dispersion and the consolidation models of handling extremely dangerous inmates?

d. What are the benefits of the disperson model?

e. What are the benefits of the consolidation model?

f. What was the best-known consolidation model institution at the federal level, and why?

g. What do the initials "ADX" stand for?

h. Are inmates in supermax prisons, such as in Florence, Colorado, given any choice in programs and services?

2. See Internet Activities 12.1 and 12.2 on the companion Web site for *CJ in Action: The Core.* To get to the activities, go to **http://www.cj.wadsworth.com/gainescore2e**, select the appropriate chapter from the drop down list, then click Internet Activities on the left navigation bar.

NOTES

1. Quoted in Claud Mullins, *Crime and Psychology* (London: Methuen, 1943), 142.

2. Bureau of Justice Statistics, *Prison and Jail Inmates at Midyear 2001* (Washington, D.C.: U.S. Department of Justice, 2002), 1.

3. *Ibid.*, 1.

4. Kenneth F. Schoen and Julie Peterson, "How Powerful Is Prison as a Crime Fighting Tool?" *Perspectives* (Summer 1996), 32.

5. *Prison and Jail Inmates at Midyear 2001,* 1.

6. James M. Beattie, *Crime and the Courts in England 1660–1800* (Princeton, NJ: Princeton University Press, 1986), 506–7.

7. George Fisher, "The Birth of the Prison Retold," *Yale Law Journal* 104 (April 1995), 1235.

8. Samuel Walker, *Popular Justice* (New York: Oxford University Press, 1980), 11.

9. Michael Meranze, *Laboratories of Virtue: Punishment, Revolution, and Authority in Philadelphia, 1760–1835* (Chapel Hill, NC: University of North Carolina Press, 1996), 55.

10. Negley K. Teeters, *The Cradle of the Penitentiary: The Walnut Street Jail at Philadelphia, 1773–1835* (Philadelphia: Pennsylvania Prison Society, 1955), 30.

11. Negley K. Teeters and John D. Shearer, *The Prison at Philadelphia's Cherry Hill* (New York: Columbia University Press, 1957), 142–43.

12. Henry Calvin Mohler, "Convict Labor Policies," *Journal of the American Institute of Criminal Law and Criminology* 15 (1925), 556–57.

13. Zebulon R. Brockway, "The American Reformatory," in *Correction Contexts: Contemporary and Classical Readings,* James W. Marquart and Jonathan R. Sorenson, eds. (Los Angeles: Roxbury Publishing Co., 1997), 68.

14. Alan H. Dershowitz, "Indeterminate Sentencing: Letting the Therapy Fit the Crime," *University of Pennsylvania Law Review* 123 (1974), 313–14.

15. Zebulon Brockway, *Fifty Years of Prison Service* (Montclair, NJ: Patterson Smith, 1969), 400–1.

16. American Correctional Association, *The American Prison: From the Beginning* (College Park, MD: American Correctional Association, 1983), 279.

17. Lawrence Friedman, *Crime and Punishment in American History* (New York: Basic Books, 1993), 316.

18. Robert Martinson, "What Works? Questions and Answers about Prison Reform," *Public Interest* 35 (Spring 1974), 22.

19. See Ted Palmer, "Martinson Revisited," *Journal of Research on Crime and Delinquency* (1975), 133; and Paul Gendreau and Bob Ross, "Effective Correctional Treatment: Bibliotherapy for Cynics," *Crime & Delinquency* 25 (1979), 499.

20. Robert Martinson, "New Findings, New Views: A Note of Caution Regarding Sentencing Reform," *Hofstra Law Review* 7 (1979), 243.

21. Fox Butterfield, "'Defying Gravity,' Inmate Population Climbs," *New York Times* (January 19, 1998), A10.

22. *Ibid.*

23. Cait Murphy, "Crime and Punishment," *Fortune* (April 30, 2001), 128.

24. Allen J. Beck, "Growth, Change, and Stability in the U.S. Prison Population, 1980–1995," *Corrections Management Quarterly* (Spring 1997), 9–10.

25. *Ibid.*, 12.

26. Bureau of Justice Statistics, *Truth in Sentencing in State Prisons* (Washington, D.C.: U.S. Department of Justice, 1999), 7.

27. *Ibid.*, 4.

28. Bureau of Justice Statistics, *Prison and Jail Inmates at Midyear 2001,* 5.

29. Charles H. Logan, "Well Kept: Comparing Quality of Confinement in a Public and Private Prison," *Journal of Criminal Law and Criminology* 83 (1992), 580.

30. Bert Useem and Peter Kimball, *Stages of Siege: U.S. Prison Riots, 1971–1986* (New York: Oxford University Press, 1989).

31. Bert Useem, "Disorganization and the New Mexico Prison Riot of 1980," *American Sociology Review* 50 (1985), 685.

32. "A Recession-Proof Industry," *Economist* (November 15, 1997), 28.

33. "BOP Awards First Contract for a Privatized Prison," *Corrections Journal* (August 7, 1997), 3.

34. Bureau of Justice Statistics, *Prison and Jail Inmates at Midyear 2001,* 1.

35. Paul Katsampes, "Jail Megatrends," *Corrections Management Quarterly* (Winter 1997), 64–66.

36. Arthur Wallenstein, "Jail Crowding: Bringing the Issue to the Corrections Center Stage," *Corrections Today* (December 1996), 76–81.

37. Quoted in Butterfield, "Defying Gravity."

38. "State to Rent County Jails for Inmates," *UPI Online* (February 5, 1998).

39. John Irwin, *The Jail: Managing the Underclass in American Society* (Berkeley, CA: University of California Press, 1985), 2.

40. Bureau of Justice Statistics, *Prison and Jail Inmates at Midyear 2001,* 9.

41. *Bell v. Wolfish,* 441 U.S. 520 (1979).

42. Bureau of Justice Statistics, *Prison and Jail Inmates at Midyear 2001,* 9.

43. John Dilulio and Charles Logan, "Ten Deadly Myths about Crime and Punishment," in *Restoring Responsibility in Criminal Justice,* 2d ed., Robert J. Bidinotto, ed. (Irvington-on-Hudson, NY: Foundation for Economic Education, 1996).

44. Franklin E. Zimring and Gordon Hawkins, *Incapacitation: Penal Confinement and the Restraint of Crime* (New York: Oxford University Press, 1995), 38, 40, 145.

45. Todd R. Clear and Dina R. Rose, "A Thug in Jail Can't Shoot Your Sister: The Unintended Consequences of Incarceration," paper presented to the American Sociological Association (August 18, 1996).

46. Alice E. Harvey, "Ex-Felon Disenfranchisement and Its Influence on the Black Vote: The Need for a Second Look," *University of*

Pennsylvania Law Review 142 (January 1994), 1145.

47. Kathleen Auerhahn, "Selective Incapacitation," *Criminology* 37 (1999), 728.

48. Scott N. Tachiki, "Intermediate Sentences in Supermax Prisons Based on Alleged Gang Affiliations," *California Law Review* (July 1995), 1115.

49. "Facts about Pelican Bay's SHU," *California Prisoner* (December 1991).

50. Jeffrey Endicott, Jerry Berge, and Gary McCaughtry, "Prison Wardens Push for

'Supermax' Prison," *Wisconsin State Journal* (February 12, 1996), 5A.

51. Gregory L. Hershberger, "To the Max," *Corrections Today* (February 1998), 55.

52. *Ibid.*, 55–56.

53. Robert A. Sheppard, Jeffrey G. Geiger, and George Welborn, "Closed Maximum Security: The Illinois Supermax," *Corrections Today* (July 1996), 4.

54. 515 U.S. 472 (1995).

55. "Supermax Placement Raises New Concerns about Due Process," *Correctional Law*

Reporter (October/November 1997), 1–2, 45–46.

56. Robert Perkinson, "Shackled Justice: Florence Federal Penitentiary and the New Politics of Punishment," *Social Justice* 21 (Fall 1994), 117–23.

57. 889 F.Supp. 1146 (1995).

58. National Institute of Corrections, *Supermax Housing: A Survey of Current Practice* (Longmont, CO: National Institute of Corrections Information Center, March 1997), 4–7.

CHAPTER 13
BEHIND BARS:
THE LIFE OF AN INMATE

CHAPTER OUTLINE

Chapter Objectives

After reading this chapter, you should be able to:

1. Explain the concept of prison as a total institution.

2. Describe the possible patterns of inmate behavior, which are driven by the inmate's personality and values.

3. Indicate some of the reasons for violent behavior in prisons.

4. List and briefly explain the six general job categories among correctional officers.

5. Contrast the hands-off doctrine of prisoner law with the hands-on approach.

6. List the concepts on which parole is based.

7. Contrast probation, parole, mandatory release, pardon, and furlough.

8. Describe truth-in-sentencing laws and their goals.

9. Describe typical conditions of parole.

10. Indicate typical release conditions for a paroled child molester.

INTRODUCTION
The "No Frills" Movement

In 2000, about 250 inmates rioted in California's Pelican Bay State Prison, leaving more than 30 injured after being stabbed or slashed with homemade weapons and 16 shot—one fatally—by correctional officers. One observer blamed the violence on the lack of "meaningful activities" for inmates, leaving them little to do but concentrate on group rivalries and hostility.[1]

Today's penal institutions have been described as characterized by "grindingly dull routine interrupted by occasional flashes of violence and brutality."[2] A "no frills" movement in political thought and prison management has moved to eliminate comforts from inmates' existence.[3] Five states have banned weightlifting in their prisons, and others have barred televisions, radios, adult magazines, hot pots, and, to the chagrin of correctional officers, cigarettes. The pleasures, as they were, of food and dress are also under attack: Texas prisoners have dined on "vita-pro," a tasteless soybean-based meat product, while Mississippi inmates are required to wear color-coded, zebra-striped uniforms.[4]

Life behind bars has long been predicated on the principle of least eligibility, which holds that the least advantaged members of outside society should lead a better existence than any person living in prison or jail.[5] As the "no frills" movement shows, the idea that incarceration is not punishment enough, and that daily life itself must be an arduous trial for prisoners, is particularly popular at the moment. In recent polls, as many as 82 percent of Americans believe life in prison is too easy. Many critics, however, feel that the treatment of prisoners has become increasingly inhumane and, indeed, unconstitutional. At one point in the 1990s, thirty-five states were under federal court order to improve living conditions in their penal institutions.[6]

In this chapter, we look at these living conditions and the factors that influence the quality of life in America's prisons and jails. To that end, we will discuss the ramifications of violence in prison, the role played by correctional officers, efforts by prisoners and prisoners' rights advocates to improve the conditions, and several other issues that are at the forefront of prison debate today. To start, we must understand the forces that shape prison culture and how those forces affect the overall operation of the correctional facility.

Pelican Bay State Prison in Crescent City, California, where inmates rioted with fatal results in 2000. (AP Photo/Nick Baker/*The Daily Triplicate*)

PRISON CULTURE

Any institution—whether a school, a bank, or a police department—has an organizational culture; that is, a set of values that help the people in the organization understand what actions are acceptable and what actions are unacceptable.[7] According to a theory put forth by the influential sociologist Erving Goffman, prison cultures are unique because prisons are **total institutions** that encompass every aspect of an inmate's life. Unlike a student or a bank teller, a prisoner cannot leave the institution or have any meaningful interaction with outside communities. Others arrange every aspect of daily life, and all prisoners are required to follow this schedule in exactly the same manner.[8]

Inmates develop their own *argot*, or language (see Figure 13.1). They create their own economy, which, in the absence of currency, is based on the barter of valued items such as food, contraband, and sexual favors. They establish methods of determining power, many of which, as we shall see, involve violence. Isolated and heavily regulated, prisoners create a social world that is, out of both necessity and design, separate from the outside world.[9]

Go to the Stories from the Street feature at <ins>http://www.cj.wadsworth.com/gainescore2e</ins> to hear Larry Gaines tell insightful stories related to this chapter and his experiences in the field.

Who Is in Prison?

The culture of any prison is heavily influenced by its inmates; their values, beliefs, and experiences in the outside world will be reflected in the social order that exists behind bars. In Chapter 2, we noted that a majority of Americans commit at least one crime that could technically send them to prison. In reality,

TOTAL INSTITUTION
An institution, such as a prison, that provides all of the necessities for existence to those who live within its boundaries.

FIGURE 13.1 **Prison Slang**

Ace-duce. Best friend.

All day. Life sentence, as in "he's doing all day."

Big bitch. A felon who has been convicted under habitual criminal laws that carry a mandatory life sentence.

Catch a ride. To ask a friend with drugs to get you high, as in "Hey, man, can I catch a ride?"

Catch a square. To prepare to fight, as in "you'd better catch a square."

Chi-mo, also chester, baby-raper, short eyes. Child molester.

Click up. To join a gang.

Deck. Pack of cigarettes.

Ding. A term of derision for a mentally deranged prisoner.

Fish. A new arrival who does not yet know the rules of the prison culture.

Gangster, or monster. HIV/AIDS. As in "watch out for that guy, he's got the gangster."

Hacks, also hogs, snouts, pigs, cops, bulls, screws. Correctional officers.

Herb. Weak inmate.

The hole. Solitary confinement.

Jigger. An inmate who stands watch while an illegal act is taking place.

Luv, luv. Doing well, as in "living luv, luv."

Mule. A person who smuggles drugs into the correctional facility.

Nazi low rider. A member of a white prison gang.

Old school. A prisoner who is seen as having values from the "old days" in prisons, when more respect was given to fellow prisoners.

On the leg. A prisoner who is seen as being overly friendly with prison staff.

Pepsi generation. The newer, younger inmates who are seen as having no respect for the old school ways of the prison.

Pitcher. A sexually aggressive, dominant inmate.

Playing on ass. Gambling without having any cash, as in "if you lose, it's your ass."

Punk. A derogatory term referring to a homosexual or weak-willed person.

Rapo. Anyone imprisoned on a sex offense.

Riding leg. An inmate who is friendly with staff in order to receive preferential treatment.

Split your wig. A quick punch to the head.

Stick. A marijuana joint.

T-jones. An inmate's mother or parents, as in "I got a letter from my T-jones."

Wolf ticket. To "talk tough" without the will to back it up, as in, "he's selling wolf tickets," or "he's making a lot of noise but doesn't have the guts to stand up for himself."

Prisoners also use rhyming slang in order to make their conversations confusing to newcomers or outsiders. In rhyming slang, "bees and money" could mean "honey," "oh my dear" could mean "beer," and so on.

Sources: Adapted from much larger glossaries found at <ins>www.halcyon.com/scripts/dante/cgi-pvt</ins> and <ins>www.wco.com/~aerick/lingo.htm</ins>.

FIGURE 13.2
Offenders in Prison

These figures show the changing proportion of inmates, based on crimes committed, in state correctional facilities in the United States between 1985 and 2000.

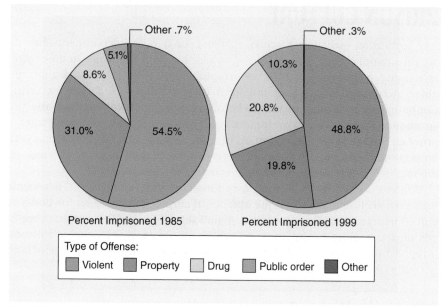

Sources: Bureau of Justice Statistics, *Correctional Population in the United States, 1995* (Washington, D.C.: U.S. Department of Justice, June 1997), Table 1.2, page 10; and Bureau of Justice Statistics, *Prisoners in 2001* (Washington, D.C.: U.S. Department of Justice, 2000), Table 17, page 13.

*"I know not whether Laws be right
Or whether Laws be wrong;
All that we know who live in gaol
Is that the wall is strong;
And that each day is like a year,
A year whose days are long."*

—Oscar Wilde, *Irish playwright, author* (1898)

slightly more than 5 percent will be confined in a state or federal prison during their lifetimes. That percentage is considerably higher for male members of minority groups: statistically, nearly 30 percent of African American males and 16 percent of Hispanic males will be imprisoned at some point in their lives.[10]

The prison population is not static. The past two decades have seen the incarceration rates of women and minority groups rise sharply. Furthermore, the crimes of inmates have changed over that period. Figure 13.2 shows that inmates are increasingly likely to have been convicted on drug charges, and less likely to have been convicted of a violent or property crime.

Among age groups, persons aged eighteen to twenty-four account for the highest percentage of new admissions to prison, approximately 30 percent.[11] The median age of the prison population is twenty-nine, though that number is expected to rise in the near future. Because of determinate sentences, long terms, and more restrictive release policies, criminal justice experts are predicting that inmates over the age of fifty will comprise 33 percent of the total prison population by 2010, compared to just under 10 percent today.[12] Education also appears to be a determinant in who goes to prison. Over 60 percent of inmates failed to earn a high school diploma, and fewer than one in ten have attended college.[13]

Adapting to Prison Society

On arriving at prison, each convict attends an orientation session and receives a "Resident's Handbook." The handbook provides information such as meal and official count times, disciplinary regulations, and visitation guidelines. The norms and values of the prison society, however, cannot be communicated by the staff or learned from a handbook. As first described by Donald Clemmer in his classic 1940 work, *The Prison Community,* the process of **prisonization**—or adaptation to the prison culture—advances as the inmate gradually understands what constitutes acceptable behavior in the institution, as defined not by the prison officials but by other inmates.[14]

In studying prisonization, criminologists have focused on two areas: how prisoners change their behavior to adapt to life behind bars, and how life behind bars has changed because of inmate behavior. (For an example of how the oppo-

PRISONIZATION
The socialization process through which a new inmate learns the accepted norms and values of the prison population.

Criminal Justice & THE MEDIA

Prison Chic

If inmates import cultural attitudes from outside life into the prison, there is mounting evidence that they are in the export business as well. According to Richard Stratton, the editor of *Prison Life*, "the prison culture [is] spilling out and becoming the popular culture." Stratton offers the examples of rap music and tattoos, both of which are rooted in prison communities and have been adopted by the culture at large. Another popular export has been the fashion statement known as "sagging," in which adolescent boys wear baggy pants slung low around their hips, intentionally exposing their underwear and covering their shoes.

The origins of sagging can be found in the common prison policy of denying inmates the use of belts, which can be used either as a weapon or as a means to commit suicide by hanging. Without belts, the prisoners' pants tend to sag. The style first caught on among rap musicians, whose exposure through MTV and other media outlets brought the practice to a wider audience. "Sagging" holds an obvious appeal for youths—"If it will upset [adults], they'll wear it," says a psychologist who specializes in adolescent behavior.

Many adults who are offended by the fashion sit on school boards, and baggy pants have been banned in numerous districts because of gang associations. The issue has even led to a lawsuit. In *Bivens v. Albuquerque* (1995), the plaintiff tried to overturn such a ban by arguing that by wearing baggy pants he was expressing his African American urban identity. The judge ruled in favor of the New Mexico school district, reasoning that sagging was a widespread trend followed by hundreds of thousands of young men across the nation; therefore, the plaintiff could not be sending a particularized message that deserved constitutional protection.

Baggy pants may not be the last prison fashion trend. When Alabama recently brought back chain gangs, the state corrections department began receiving outside requests for the white pants, shirt, and caps worn by inmates on the gangs.

site process occurs as well, see the feature *Criminal Justice & the Media—Prison Chic*.) Sociologist John Irwin has identified several patterns of inmate behavior, each one driven by the inmate's personality and values:

1 Professional criminals adapt to prison by "doing time." In other words, they follow the rules and generally do whatever is necessary to speed up their release so they can continue their chosen careers.

2 Some convicts, mostly state-raised youths or those frequently incarcerated in juvenile detention centers, are more comfortable inside prison than outside. These inmates serve time by "jailing," or establishing themselves in the power structure of prison culture.

3 Other inmates take advantage of prison resources such as libraries or drug-treatment programs by "gleaning," or working to improve themselves to prepare for a return to society.

4 Finally, "disorganized" criminals exist on the fringes of prison society. These inmates may have mental impairments or low levels of intelligence and find it impossible to adapt to prison culture on any level.[15]

The process of categorizing prisoners has a theoretical basis, but it serves a practical purpose as well, allowing administrators to reasonably predict how different inmates will act in certain situations. An inmate who is "doing time" generally does not present the same security risk as one who is "jailing."

The Changing Prison Code

The best evidence that prison culture has changed can be found in the shifts that have taken place in the traditional **prison code.** In the early studies of prisoner culture, researchers found that an unwritten set of rules guided inmate conduct. A prisoner's standing among his or her peers was determined by whether he or

PRISON CODE
A system of social norms and values established by inmates to regulate behavior within the correctional institution.

FIGURE 13.3

The Prison Code

According to many studies of prison life done from the 1940s to the 1970s, inmates lived by an unwritten code. The tenets of the code, which are listed here, stressed reliability, toughness, and a social structure in which individual inmates avoided conflict with each other.

- Never rat on a con.
- Do your own time.
- Don't interfere with the interests of other inmates.
- Mind your own business.
- Don't have a loose lip.
- Be tough.

- Be a man.
- Don't exploit inmates.
- Be sharp.
- Keep off a man's back.
- Don't put a guy on the spot.
- Be loyal to your class.
- Be cool.

Source: Gresham Sykes and Sheldon Messinger, "The Inmate Social System," in *Theoretical Studies in the Social Organization of the Prison*, ed. R. Cloward et al. (New York: Social Science Research Council, 1970), 6–10.

I N F O T R A C®
COLLEGE EDITION

Keyword: prison code

she followed the prison code; those who failed to do so were rejected by the institutional society. The two most important tenets of the code were "never rat on a con" and "do your own time"—in other words, never inform on another inmate and don't interfere in another inmate's affairs (see Figure 13.3).[16]

During the era when the code dominated prison culture (generally encompassing the three decades following World War II), prisons were repressive but relatively safe. In contrast, one observer calls the modern institution an "unstable and violent social jungle."[17] There has been an influx of youthful inmates and drug offenders who are seen as being only "out for themselves" and unwilling to follow any code that preaches collective values. With the formation of racial gangs in prison, the traditional prison code has been replaced by one in which the shared values of gang loyalties are preeminent; as we shall see, inmate-on-inmate violence has risen accordingly.[18]

PRISON VIOLENCE

A prison is a dangerous place to live. Although homicide rates in prison are about half the civilian homicide rate,[19] the prison culture is predicated on violence. Prison guards use the threat of violence (and, at times, its reality) to control the inmate population. Among the prisoners, violence is used to establish power and dominance. Often, this violence leads to death. About 100 inmates are murdered by fellow inmates each year, and about 26,000 inmate-on-inmate assaults take place annually.

Gangs such as the Crips (a member of which is shown here), the Aryan Brotherhood, the Bloods, and Barrio Azteca function within prison walls and add to the overall levels of violence in correctional facilities. What factors make prisons susceptible to gang activity? (Photo courtesy of Cable News Network, Inc.)

The worry among prisoners' rights advocates is that inmate violence has become so common that Americans—especially American judges—will come to see it as inevitable. This line of thinking would practically absolve prison officials from the responsibility to take measures to limit violent behavior.[20] In *Farmer v. Brennan* (1994),[21] the United States Supreme Court stated that being assaulted in prison is not "part of the penalty criminal offenders pay for their offenses against society." Increasingly, however, the reality of prison life suggests otherwise.

Violence in Prison Culture

In the prison code era, with its emphasis on "noninterference," the prison culture did not support inmate-on-inmate violence. Prison "elders" would themselves punish any of their peers who showed a proclivity toward assaulting fellow inmates. Today, in contrast, violence is used to establish the prisoner hierarchy by separating the powerful from the weak. Humboldt State University's Lee H. Bowker has identified several other reasons for violent behavior:

Criminal Justice & TECHNOLOGY

The Drugbuster

According to a recent study, about 57 percent of all prisoners had used drugs within thirty days prior to their arrest. Experience has taught prison administrators that, given the addictive nature of many illegal drugs, inmates will go to great lengths to continue their pattern of substance abuse even behind bars (where drug use is, of course, prohibited). In December 2001, for example, random testing by officials in the Nebraska penitentiary system found that almost 6 percent of inmates tested positive for drug use.

Experts have long known that visitors smuggle drugs into prisons and jails. Most facilities do not have the personnel or the budget to subject every visitor to an intense body search, a precaution which was thought to be the only way to significantly reduce the flow of contraband. Over the past few years, however, an number of federal prisons have seen drug use among the inmate population plummet after corrections officers began using a device called an ion scanner on visitors. Before entering a facility, each visitor has his or her hands and pockets vacuumed. The filter from the vacuum is then placed in the scanner, and its contents are heated up and analyzed. Using technology called ion spectrometry, the machine is programmed to detect trace ele-

ments of marijuana, cocaine, methamphetamines, and other illegal drugs that may be in the filter. According to its manufacturer, the ion scanner is so powerful that it can detect the equivalent of a packet of sugar dissolved into an Olympic-sized swimming pool. Visitors who "test positive" are not arrested or detained; rather, they are not allowed to proceed into the facility.

Critics of the ion scanner say the device is *too* good. It can pick up minute amounts of drugs that a visitor may have come into contact with simply by using a gas pump, a public doorknob, or even a dollar bill that was previously "tainted" with drug particles. As far as many prison officials are concerned, however, the results speak for themselves. In Nebraska, just six months after implementing the scanners, drug use dropped by more than 80 percent. A federal prison in Tucson, Arizona, saw positive prisoner drug tests fall by two-thirds after randomly scanning visitors. The technology has been so successful that by 2003, more than thirty federal prisons featured ion scanners.

IN THE FUTURE
Ion spectrometry has proven to be just as effective in picking up drug residue in mail as on a person. The problem, again, is that the scanner is so effective in finding tiny amounts of an illegal drug that it might not give corrections officials "reasonable cause" to open inmates' mail.

For more information on the technology described in this box, go to the Crime and Technology feature at http://www.cj.wadsworth.com

---

- It provides a deterrent against being victimized, as a reputation for violence may eliminate an inmate as a target of assault.

- It enhances self-image in an environment that does not respect other attributes, such as intelligence.

- In the case of rape, it gives sexual relief.

- It serves as a means of acquiring material goods through extortion or outright robbery.[22]

The **deprivation model** can be used to explain the high level of prison violence. According to this model, the stressful and oppressive conditions of prison life lead to aggressive behavior on the part of inmates. When conditions such as overcrowding worsen, prison researcher Stephen C. Light found that inmate misconduct often increases.[23] In these circumstances, the violent behavior may not have any express purpose—it may just be a means of relieving tension.[24] (One thing that many inmates are deprived of while incarcerated is easy access to illegal drugs. To learn how prison officials combat efforts to smuggle drugs into their facilities, see the feature *Criminal Justice & Technology—The Drugbuster*.)

Riots

The deprivation model is helpful, though less convincing, in searching for the roots of collective violence. As far back as the 1930s, Frank Tannenbaum noted that harsh prison conditions can cause tension to build among inmates until it eventually explodes in the form of mass violence.[25] Living conditions in prisons

DEPRIVATION MODEL
A theory that inmate aggression is the result of the frustration inmates feel at being deprived of freedom, consumer goods, sex, and other staples of life outside the institution.

On the Web

An inside look at the Anderson County Jail in Clinton, Tennessee, is provided by the facility's Jail Cam. For a link to its Web site, go to the Hypercontents page for this chapter at http://cj.wadsworth.com/gainescore2e.

RELATIVE DEPRIVATION
The theory that inmate aggression is caused when freedoms and services that the inmate has come to accept as normal are decreased or eliminated.

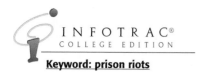

Keyword: prison riots

"**I've seen seven stabbings, about six bashings and three self-mutilations. Two hangings, one attempted hanging, any number of overdoses. And that's only me, in just 70 days.**"

—Anonymous jail inmate (1998)

are fairly constant, however, so how can the seemingly spontaneous outbreak of prison riots be explained?

Researchers have addressed these inconsistencies with the concept of **relative deprivation,** a theory that focuses on the gap between what is expected in certain situations and what is achieved. Peter C. Kratcoski has argued that because prisoners enjoy such meager privileges to begin with, any further deprivation can spark disorder.[26] A number of criminologists, including Bert Useem in his studies made in the wake of the riot at the Penitentiary of New Mexico in 1980, have noted that collective violence occurs in response to heightened measures of security at corrections facilities.[27] Thus, the violence occurs in response to an additional reduction in freedom for inmates, who enjoy very little freedom to begin with.

Rape

In contrast to riots, the problem of sexual assault in prisons receives very little attention from media sources. This can be partly attributed to the ambiguity of the subject: that rape occurs in prisons and jails is undisputed, but determining exactly how widespread the problem is has proved difficult. Prison officials, aware that any sexual contact is prohibited in penal institutions, are often unwilling to provide realistic figures for fear of negative publicity. Even when they are willing, they may be unable to do so. Most inmates are ashamed of being rape victims and refuse to report instances of sexual assault. Consequently, it has been difficult to come up with consistent statistics for sexual assault in prison. While research published in *The Prison Journal* found that about 7 percent of all inmates in four states had been sexually assaulted,[28] self-reported data gathered by the Human Rights Watch revealed that one in three inmates reported being raped.[29]

Whatever the figures, prison rape, like all rape, is considered primarily an act of violence rather than sex. Inmates subject to rape ("punks") are near the bottom of the prison power structure and, in some instances, may accept rape by one particularly powerful inmate in return for protection from others.[30] Raped inmates often suffer from rape trauma syndrome and a host of other psychological ailments including suicidal tendencies. Many prisons do not offer sufficient medical treatment for rape victims, nor does the prison staff take the necessary measures to protect obvious targets of rape—young, slightly built, nonviolent offenders. (For a discussion of the issue as it relates to institutions that house female inmates, see *The Diversity Challenge—Inside a Women's Prison.*) Furthermore, corrections officials are rarely held liable for inmate-on-inmate violence.

CORRECTIONAL OFFICERS AND DISCIPLINE

Under model circumstances, the presence of correctional officers—the standard term used to describe prison guards—would mitigate the levels of violence in American correctional institutions. To a large extent, this is indeed the case; without correctional officers, the prison would be a place of anarchy. But in the highly regulated, oppressive environment of the prison, correctional officers must use the threat of violence, if not actual violence, to instill discipline and keep order. Thus, the relationship between prison staff and inmates is marked by mutual distrust. Consider the two following statements, the first made by a correctional officer and the second by a prisoner:

[My job is to] protect, feed, and try to educate scum who raped and brutalized women and children . . . who, if I turn my back, will go into their cell, wrap a blanket around their cellmate's legs, and threaten to beat or rape him if he doesn't give sex, carry contraband, or fork over radios, money, or other goods willingly. And they'll stick a shank in me tomorrow if they think they can get away with it.[31]

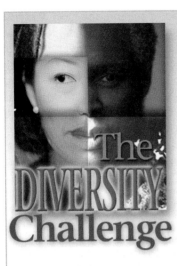

Inside a Women's Prison

The problem of sexual assault also exists in women's prisons, but the reported aggressor is more likely to be a male correctional officer than another inmate. Several reports by the human rights group Amnesty International have found that sexual misconduct—from rape to consensual sex—is a growing problem in America's prisons for women. In 2000, for example, forty prison staff members from several women's prisons in California were under investigation for sexual misconduct. Furthermore, studies have shown that many female inmates who may have been victims of mistreatment by correctional officers do not report the incidents for fear of reprisal. Although many states are passing laws to better protect their female prisoners, Amnesty International reports that six states—Alabama, Minnesota, Oregon, Utah, Vermont, and Wisconsin—still have no laws prohibiting sexual misconduct by prison staff.

The organization believes that one way to better protect female inmates would be to staff women's prisons with only female correctional officers, as is done in many other Western countries. A number of prison experts agree, noting that the world of the women's prison is significantly different from that of the men's prison and should be treated accordingly. The prisonization process in female institutions, for example, relies on tightly knit cliques of prisoners that mimic the traditional family structure. The more experienced convicts adopt the role of the "father" or "mother" and act as parent-figures for younger, inexperienced "sons" or "daughters."

Homosexuality also manifests itself in the women's prison through the formation of another traditional family mode: the monogamous couple. In general, sex between inmates plays a different role in women's prisons than in men's prisons. In the latter, rape is considered an act of aggression and power rather than sex, and "true" homosexuals are relegated to the lower rungs of the social hierarchy. By contrast, women who engage in sexual activity in prison are not automatically labeled homosexual, and lesbians are not hampered in their social climbing efforts.

FOR CRITICAL ANALYSIS
What might be the benefits of having only female correctional officers in women's prisons? By the same token, what might be some of the drawbacks of having female correctional officers working in men's prisons? Note that the Supreme Court does not allow states to discriminate because of gender in hiring officers for either type of institution, but does let states preclude women from "contact positions," such as those that require the officer to conduct a body search of male inmates, and vice versa.

> The pigs in the state and federal prisons . . . treat me so violently, I cannot possibly imagine a time I could ever have anything but the deepest, aching, searing hatred for them. I can't begin to tell you what they do to me. If I were weaker by a hair, they would destroy me.[32]

It may be difficult for an outsider to understand the emotions that fuel such sentiments. French philosopher Michael Foucault points out that discipline, both in prison and in the general community, is a means of social organization as well as punishment.[33] Discipline is imposed when a person behaves in a manner that is contrary to the values of the dominant social group. Correctional officers and inmates have different concepts of the ideal structure of prison society, and, as the two quotations above demonstrate, this conflict generates intense feelings of fear and hatred, which often lead to violence.

INFOTRAC®
COLLEGE EDITION

Keyword: correctional officers

Rank and Duties of Correctional Officers

The custodial staff at most prisons is organized according to four general ranks—captain, lieutenant, sergeant, and officer. In keeping with the militaristic model, captains are primarily administrators who deal directly with the warden on custodial issues. Lieutenants are the disciplinarians of the prison, responsible for policing and transporting the inmates. Sergeants oversee platoons of officers in specific parts of the prison, such as various cell blocks or workspaces.

Lucien X. Lombardo, professor of sociology and criminal justice at Old Dominion University, has identified six general job categories among correctional officers.[34]

One benefit of the prison boom has been economic, as prisons infuse money and jobs into the regions where they are located. These regions are often rural and poor. In upstate New York's North County, for example, the average worker earns about $18,000 a year; the correctional officers at North County's Clinton Prison, shown above, earn an average of $36,000. Working as a correctional officer is one of the few ways that residents of North County who do not have a college degree can enjoy a middle-class life. Furthermore, as prisons are recession proof, job security among correctional officers is higher than in most other local industries. Why, despite these benefits, does the profession of correctional officer continue to have a negative image? (Andrew Lichtenstein/ Corbis Sygma)

Video Profiles of Darlene Gordon, Correctional Officer, and Donald Pappa, Corrections Counselor

Block Officers.   In Lombardo's opinion, the most demanding job assignment is that of the block officer. This employee may supervise the cell blocks of as many as four hundred inmates, as well as the correctional officers on block guard duty. During the day, the job is a hectic combination of security, housekeeping, and human services. At night, when the convicts are confined to their cells, block officers must maintain continuous inspections to assure that no self-destructive behavior is taking place.

In general, the block officer is responsible for the "well-being" of the inmates. In addition to making sure that inmates do not harm themselves or other prisoners, the block officer also acts as somewhat of a camp counselor, dispensing advice and seeing that inmates understand and follow the rules of the facility. Finally, because the block officer comes in daily close contact with prisoners, she or he is most likely to be the target of inmate violence when it erupts.

Work Detail Supervisors.   In many penal institutions, the inmates work in the cafeteria, the prison store, the laundry, or other areas. Work detail supervisors oversee small groups of inmates as they perform their jobs. In general, the atmosphere in these work groups is more relaxed than in the cell blocks. The inmates and their supervisor are actively working toward the same goal—to complete the assignment—and therefore can develop a solidarity that does not exist in the cell blocks. If an inmate and work supervisor find themselves on the same detail for an extended period of time, they may even develop a friendly personal relationship, though it would be based on the parent-child model rather than a relationship of two equals.[35]

Industrial Shop and School Officers.   These officers perform maintenance and security functions in educational and workshop programs. Their primary responsibility is to make sure that inmates are on time for these programs and that attendance requirements are followed. The officers must also make sure that the inmates are not disruptive during the sessions and that they do not steal items from the workshop or classroom.

Yard Officers.   Officers who work the prison yard usually have the least seniority, befitting the assignment's reputation as dangerous and stressful. Unlike the cell blocks, programs, and work details, which are strictly organized, the prison yard is a place of relative freedom for the inmates. Consequently, yard officers must be constantly on alert for breaches in prison discipline or regulations. If collective violence occurs, yard officers run the highest chance of being injured, taken hostage, or even killed.

Tower Guards.   Previously, a wall post was considered the worst assignment in the prison. Tower guards spend their entire shifts, which usually last eight hours, in their isolated, silent posts high above the grounds of the facility. While keeping watch with a high-powered rifle, they communicate only through walkie-talkies. As prison violence has become more commonplace, however, the tower guard, being "above" any real danger, has become a more coveted position. Correctional officers now feel the benefits of safety outweigh the loneliness that comes with the job.

Administrative Building Assignments.   Officers who hold administrative building assignments are in even less personal danger than tower guards and therefore hold the most desired job assignments. These officers provide security at prison gates, oversee visitation procedures, act as liaisons for civilians, and

Careers in Criminal Justice

Robert M. Lucas

Corrections Facility Commander

My interest in the corrections field grew out of the need to be involved in solving problems associated with crime and punishment. I began my career as a law enforcement deputy. On completion of my undergraduate studies I sought experience in the counseling and programs aspect of detention. Ultimately I became interested in the management of jails and decided to become a sworn detention officer. My career path has given me a unique perspective from having experience in three major components of criminal justice: law enforcement, detention, and programs. Throughout my career I have continued my education as a corrections professional; my accomplishments include a master of arts degree in criminal justice from the University of South Florida, and I am a graduate of the Southern Police Institute's Administrative Officers Course.

I am currently assigned as a facility commander in a 1,714-bed direct-supervision jail. The facility is divided into two factions: housing and central intake. Central intake encompasses all facets of booking as well as the classification and records bureau. There is a combined total of approximately 300 sworn and civilian employees assigned to this multidimensional command and responsible for the processing and booking of over 62,000 inmates in 1998. Additionally, my command must ensure that inmates make all required court appearances and that all transfers or releases are proper and within established releasing standards. My most important duties are ensuring that staff are properly trained, that they are assigned to functions which guarantee security is maintained at the highest level, and that all inmates are treated in accordance with local, state, and federal standards.

I feel the qualities essential to the corrections field are those common to most fields such as a desire to perform at a high level of standards, a commitment to personal growth through change and development, and facing each task as a challenge as opposed to a problem. The management and operation of any detention facility is taxing, and it challenges the abilities, knowledge, and experience of those in supervisory roles. Staff are expected to fulfill a number of roles and encounter any number of problems or emergencies daily. The jail practitioner of today must be well versed in all aspects of the jail operation and applicable laws and standards, and be able to address problems associated with expanding inmate populations, construction needs, and specialized inmate categories.

Go to the *Careers in Criminal Justice Interactive CD* **for more profiles in the field of criminal justice.**

handle administrative tasks such as processing the paperwork when an inmate is transferred from another institution. Because such assignments involve contact with the public, the officers are often chosen for their public relations skills as well as any other talents they may have. (See the feature *Careers in Criminal Justice*.)

Discipline

As Erving Goffman noted in his essay on the "total institution," in the general society adults are rarely placed in a position where they are "punished" as a child would be.[36] Therefore, the strict disciplinary measures imposed on prisoners come as something of a shock and can provoke strong defensive reactions. Correctional officers who must deal with these responses often find that disciplining inmates is the most difficult and stressful aspect of their job.

The prisoners' manual lists the types of behavior that can result in disciplinary action. An institutional disciplinary committee decides the sanctions for specific types of misconduct. These sanctions include loss of privileges such as visiting and recreational opportunities for minor infractions, as well as more serious punishments for major infractions. The most severe sanction is punitive segregation, also known as solitary confinement or sensory deprivation, in which the inmate is isolated in a cell known as "the hole." This punishment is considered so debilitating

On the Web

The U.S. Department of Labor offers information about a career as a correctional officer. For a link to its Web site, go to the Hypercontents page for this chapter at **http://cj.wadsworth.com/ gainescore2e.**

FIGURE 13.4

Use of Force Guidelines

Between 1994 and 1998, twelve inmates in California's maximum-security prisons were killed and thirty-two more were injured by correctional officers using firearms to break up fights. During that same time period, in all of the other states combined only six inmates were shot and killed by correctional officers. In response to public pressure over what were seen as overly brutal control tactics, the California Department of Corrections issued these use of force guidelines, which went into effect in 1999.

1. Deadly force, defined as "any use of force that is likely to result in death," will only be used when it is reasonably needed to:
   - Defend the employee or other persons from an immediate threat of death or great bodily injury.
   - Prevent an escape.
   - Stop acts such as riots or arson that constitute an immediate jeopardy to institutional security and, because of their magnitude, are likely to result in escapees or the death of other persons.

2. A firearm shall not be discharged if there is reason to believe that persons other than the intended target may be injured.

3. Deadly force is not intended to stop fist fights.

Source: California Department of Corrections.

that most facilities—initially fearful that the courts would find long periods of total deprivation "cruel and unusual" under the Eighth Amendment—have placed a twenty-day limit on the length of the confinement. Prison officials can, if they so choose, remove the inmate for a short period of time and then return him or her to the hole, effectively sidestepping the restrictions.

This is not to say that the judicial system has greatly restricted disciplinary actions in prison. For the most part, correctional officers are given the same discretionary powers as police officers (discussed in Chapter 5) to use their experience to determine when force is warranted. In *Whitley v. Albers* (1986),[37] the United States Supreme Court held that the use of force by prison officials violates an inmate's Eighth Amendment protections only if the force amounts to "the unnecessary and wanton infliction of pain." Excessive force can be considered "necessary" if the legitimate security interests of the penal institution are at stake. Consequently, an appeals court ruled that when officers at a Maryland prison formed an "extraction team" to remove the leader of a riot from his cell, beating him in the process, the use of force was justified given the situation.[38]

In contrast, in *Hudson v. McMillan* (1992)[39] the United States Supreme Court ruled that minor injuries suffered by a convict at the hands of a correctional officer following an argument did violate the inmate's rights, because there was no security concern at the time of the incident. To protect themselves from lawsuits, many corrections departments have developed codes to help guide correctional officers in the proper use of force (see Figure 13.4).

> "[C]ourts are ill equipped to deal with the increasingly urgent problems of prison administration and reform. Judicial recognition of that fact reflects no more than a healthy sense of realism."
>
> —Lewis Powell, *United States Supreme Court associate justice* (1974)

PROTECTING PRISONERS' RIGHTS

The general attitude of the law toward inmates is summed up by the Thirteenth Amendment to the U.S. Constitution:

> Neither slavery nor involuntary servitude, except as a punishment for crime whereof the party shall have been duly convicted, shall exist within the United States.

In other words, inmates do not have the same guaranteed rights as other Americans. For most of the nation's history, courts have followed the spirit of this amendment by applying the **"hands-off" doctrine** of prisoner law. This (unwritten) doctrine assumes that the care of inmates should be left to prison officials and that it is not the place of judges to intervene in penal administrative matters.

The prison code flourished during the "hands-off" period; prisoners, unable to count on any outside forces to protect their rights, needed an internal social structure that would allow them to do so themselves. In the 1960s, as disenfranchised groups from all parts of society began to insist on their constitutional rights, prisoners did so as well. The prisoners' rights movement demanded, and received,

INFOTRAC®
COLLEGE EDITION

Keyword: prisoners' rights

"HANDS-OFF" DOCTRINE
The unwritten judicial policy that favors noninterference by the courts in the administration of prisons and jails.

fuller recognition of prisoners' rights and greater access to American courts. It would be difficult, however, to label the movement a complete success. As one observer notes, "conditions of confinement in many American prisons have deteriorated during the same time period in which judicial recognition and concern for prisoners' legal rights dramatically increased."[40]

The "Hands-On" Approach

The end of the "hands-off" period can be dated to the United States Supreme Court's decision in *Cooper v. Pate* (1964).[41] In this case, Cooper, an inmate at the Illinois State Penitentiary, filed a petition for relief under the Civil Rights Act of 1871, stating that he had a First Amendment right to purchase reading material about the Black Muslim movement. The Court, overturning rulings of several lower courts, held that the act did protect the constitutional rights of prisoners. This decision effectively allowed inmates to file civil lawsuits under Title 42 of the United States Code, Section 1983—known simply as Section 1983—if they felt that a prison or jail was denying their civil rights. An inmate who has been beaten by a correctional officer, for example, can bring a Section 1983 suit against the penal institution for denial of Eighth Amendment protection from cruel and unusual punishment.

Symbolically, the United States Supreme Court's declaration in *Wolff v. McDonnell* (1974)[42] that "[t]here is no iron curtain drawn between the Constitution and the prisons of this country" was just as significant as the *Cooper* ruling. It represented to civil rights lawyers that the Court would no longer follow the "hands-off" doctrine. The case had practical overtones as well, establishing that prisoners have a right to the following basic due process procedures when being disciplined by a penal institution:

- A fair hearing.
- Written notice at least twenty-four hours in advance of the hearing.
- An opportunity to speak at the hearing (though not to be represented by counsel during the hearing).
- An opportunity to call witnesses (unless doing so jeopardizes prison security).
- A written statement detailing the final decision and reasons for that decision.

Indeed, the prisoners' rights movement can count to its credit a number of legal decisions that have increased protection of inmates' constitutional rights. (See Figure 13.5 for a summary of the key United States Supreme Court decisions.)

Limiting Prisoners' Rights

Despite these successes, not all proponents of prisoners' rights feel that the courts have entirely abandoned the "hands-off" doctrine. Instead, they believe that by

- *Cruz v. Beto* **(405 U.S. 319 [1972]).** Prisoners cannot be denied the right to practice their religion, even if that religion is not one of the "standard" belief systems in the United States. In this case, the inmate who had been denied the opportunity to practice was a Buddhist.
- *Procunier v. Martinez* **(416 U.S. 396 [1974]).** Correctional officials can censor an inmate's mail only when such censorship is necessary to maintain prison security.
- *Wolff v. McDonnell* **(418 U.S. 539 [1974]).** Prisoners have due process rights when they are faced with disciplinary action that may place them in segregation or add time to their sentences. The rights include the right to a hearing, an opportunity to speak at the hearing, and an opportunity to call witnesses (unless doing so would threaten prison security).
- *Hutto v. Finney* **(437 U.S. 678 [1978]).** Solitary confinement that lasts for more than thirty days is cruel and unusual punishment.

FIGURE 13.5

The United States Supreme Court in the 1970s: Expanding Prisoners' Rights

In these cases, the United States Supreme Court recognized inmates' rights to freedom of religion, freedom of expression, due process, and protection from cruel and unusual punishment.

Michael Blucker filed a lawsuit, charging that prison officials at the Menard Correctional Center in Illinois failed to protect him from being sexually assaulted while he was an inmate at the facility. A jury found that five members of the prison staff were not liable for Blucker's pain and suffering. How would the concepts of "simple negligence" and "deliberate indifference" apply to Blucker's case and its outcome? (Ted Dargan/*St. Louis Post-Dispatch*)

"DELIBERATE INDIFFERENCE"
A standard that must be met by inmates trying to prove that their Eighth Amendment rights were violated by a correctional facility. It occurs when prison officials are aware of harmful conditions of confinement but fail to take steps to remedy those conditions.

"IDENTIFIABLE HUMAN NEEDS"
The basic human necessities that correctional facilities are required by the Constitution to provide to inmates. Beyond food, warmth, and exercise, the court system has been unable to establish exactly what these needs are.

establishing standards of "deliberate indifference" and "identifiable human needs," court rulings have merely provided penal institutions with legally acceptable methods of denying prisoners' constitutional protections.

"Deliberate Indifference."   In the 1976 case *Estelle v. Gamble*,[43] the United States Supreme Court established the **"deliberate indifference"** standard. Specifically, Justice Thurgood Marshall wrote that prison officials violated a convict's Eighth Amendment rights if they deliberately failed to provide him or her with necessary medical care. At the time, the decision was hailed as a victory for prisoners' rights. Defining the term *deliberate* has proved difficult, however. Does it mean that prison officials "should have known" that an inmate was placed in harm's way, or does it mean that prison officials purposefully placed the inmate in harm's way?

In subsequent decisions, the Court appears to have accepted the latter interpretation. In ruling on two separate 1986 cases, for example, the Court held that "simple negligence" was not acceptable grounds for a Section 1983 civil suit, and that a prison official's behavior was actionable only if it was done "maliciously or sadistically for the very purpose of causing harm."[44] Since it is quite difficult to prove in court a person's state of mind, the "deliberate negligence" standard has become a formidable one for prisoners to meet.

In *Wilson v. Seiter* (1991),[45] for example, Pearly L. Wilson filed a Section 1983 suit alleging that certain conditions of his confinement—including overcrowding; excessive noise; inadequate heating, cooling, and ventilation; and unsanitary bathroom and dining facilities—were cruel and unusual. The United States Supreme Court ruled against Wilson, stating that he had failed to prove that these conditions, even if they existed, were the result of "deliberate indifference" on the part of prison officials. Three years later, in a case concerning a transsexual inmate who was placed in the general population of a federal prison and subsequently beaten and raped, the Court narrowed the definition of "deliberate" even further. Though ruling in favor of the inmate, it held that the prison official must both be aware of the facts that create a potential for harm and also *draw the conclusion* that those facts will lead to harm.

"Identifiable Human Needs."   The *Wilson* decision created another standard for determining Eighth Amendment violations that has drawn criticism from civil rights lawyers. It asserted that a prisoner must show that the institution has denied her or him a basic human need such as food, warmth, or exercise.[46] The Court failed, however, to mention any other needs besides these three, forcing other courts to interpret **"identifiable human needs"** for themselves. Taking a similar slant, in *Sandin v. Conner* (1995),[47] the Court ruled that inmates have rights to due process in disciplinary matters only when the punishment imposes "atypical or significant hardships in relation to ordinary incidents of prison life." Using this standard, inmates transferred to supermax prisons do not have the right to a hearing because the conditions in a supermax (discussed in Chapter 12) are not atypical. They are merely extreme.

Limiting Prisoner Litigation

The prisoners' rights movement has also been slowed by federal and state legislation to limit the number of Section 1983 lawsuits inmates can file. During the early 1990s, politicians and the media took up the issue of "frivolous prison lawsuits." Though a small percentage of these lawsuits are valid, the majority cannot be defended on constitutional grounds. One Colorado inmate, for example, claimed that by confiscating his pornographic mail, prison officials were denying him his right to "obtain a doctorate in obstetrics-gynecology."[48] Such cases invariably found their way into the media, angering the public.

As most prisoner lawsuits are filed *pro se*—without the aid of an attorney—they are subject to screening by judges (or, often, their law clerks), who can dismiss a case if they feel it is frivolous. Of the nearly 40,000 prisoner lawsuits filed annually in the early 1990s, 95 percent were found to be "without merit" and never even reached the preliminary trial stage.[49] Mindful of the enormous toll this screening process took on the courts, Congress passed the Prison Litigation Reform Act (1996), which, among other things, placed strict limits on the number of cases an inmate can file in federal court. It also forced prisoners to pay their own court costs.[50] Within a year after the act was passed, Section 1983 cases filed by inmates in federal courts dropped 90 percent.[51] Prisoners began to file their claims in state courts, providing many states with an incentive to adopt laws similar to the federal statute.

> "**Number one, a prison needs to be a place they want to get out of and don't want to come back to. If it's not more difficult in prison than it is out, you're beating your head against the wall in the effort against [repeat offenders].**"
>
> —Wayne Garner, *Commissioner of the Georgia Department of Corrections* (1998)

PAROLE AND RELEASE FROM PRISON

An important fact to remember about inmates, note supporters of prison work, is that almost all of them will at some point be returned to the community. In fact, every year about 600,000 inmates will leave prison.[52] One of the great challenges facing prison administrators is to prepare their charges for "life on the outside." With that goal in mind, prisons offer a number of self-improvement programs for inmates. For many of these inmates, a successful adjustment following release is predicated on finding and keeping employment. Two main obstacles to achieving this goal are lack of education and a lack of employable skills. Consequently, many penal institutions offer programs in these areas. They also offer therapy programs to help inmates overcome emotional or psychological problems that may direct them toward criminal activity.

Though little empirical research exists to support the claim, many criminal justice experts suspect that inmates attend prison programs not for self-improvement but to secure an early release.[53] This can be accomplished in two ways. First, many penal institutions offer prisoners incentives to take part in the programs. Inmates in the Orange County Jail (Florida), for example, earn eleven days of *good-time credit* for every month they successfully complete a program. As was discussed in Chapter 10, inmates receive these credits—which allow time to be subtracted from their terms—for obeying prison rules, working within the prison, and other laudable activities.

Second, inmates believe that by participating in prison programs, they can impress parole boards and increase their chances of early release by **parole,** or the *conditional* release of a prisoner after a portion of his or her sentence has been served. Parole allows the corrections system to continue to supervise an offender who is no longer incarcerated. As long as parolees follow the conditions of their parole, they are allowed to finish their terms outside the prison. If parolees break the terms of their early release, however, they face the risk of being returned to a penal institution.

According to Todd R. Clear and George F. Cole, parole is based on three concepts:

❶ *Grace.* The prisoner has no right to be given an early release, but the government has granted her or him that privilege.

❷ *Contract of consent.* The government and the parolee enter into an agreement whereby the latter agrees to abide by certain conditions in return for continued freedom.

❸ *Custody.* Technically, though no longer incarcerated, the parolee is still the responsibility of the state. Parole is an extension of corrections.[54] (The phonetic and administrative similarities between probation and parole can be confusing. See *Mastering Concepts—Probation versus Parole* on the following page for clarification.)

INFOTRAC®
COLLEGE EDITION

Keyword: parole

PAROLE
The conditional release of an inmate before his or her sentence has expired. The remainder of the sentence is served in the community under the supervision of correctional officers, and the offender can be returned to incarceration if he or she breaks the conditions of parole, as determined by a parole board.

MASTERING CONCEPTS	**Probation versus Parole**	

Probation and parole have many aspects in common. In fact, probation and parole are so similar that many jurisdictions combine them into a single agency. There are, however, some important distinctions between the two systems, as noted below.

	PROBATION	**PAROLE**
Basic Definition	An alternative to imprisonment in which a person who has been convicted of a crime is allowed to serve his or her sentence in the community subject to certain conditions and supervision by a probation officer.	An early release from a correctional facility as determined by an administrative body (the parole board), in which the convicted offender is given the chance to spend the remainder of his or her sentence under supervision in the community.
Timing	The offender is sentenced to a probationary term in place of a prison or jail term. If the offender breaks the conditions of probation, he or she is sent to prison or jail. Therefore, probation occurs *before* imprisonment.	Parole is a form of early release. Therefore, parole occurs *after* an offender has spent time behind bars.
Authority	Probation falls under the domain of the judiciary. In other words, judges make the decision whether to send a convicted offender to prison or jail or to give her or him a sentence of probation. If a person violates the terms of probation, a judge ultimately decides whether she or he should be sent to a correctional facility as punishment.	Parole falls under the domain of an administrative body (often appointed by an executive such as a state governor) known as the parole board. The parole board determines whether the prisoner is qualified for early release, and under which conditions he or she will be allowed to remain in the community. When a parolee violates the conditions of parole, the parole board must decide whether to send him or her back to prison. (Although they can be asked to make recommendations to the parole board, judges generally *are not* involved in the parole decision.)
Characteristics of Offenders	As Todd R. Clear and George F. Cole point out, probationers are normally less involved in the criminal lifestyle. Most of them are first-time offenders who have committed nonviolent crimes.	Many parolees, Clear and Cole note, have spent many months or even years in prison and, besides abiding by conditions of parole, must make the difficult transition to "life on the outside."

Because of these differences, many observers believe that probation and parole should not be combined in the same agency, though limited financial resources will assure that many jurisdictions will continue to do so.

Because of good-time credits and parole, most prisoners do not serve their entire sentence in prison. In fact, the average felon serves only about half of the term handed down by the court.

Other Types of Prison Release

Parole, a conditional release, is the most common form of release, but it is not the only one (see Figure 13.6). Prisoners receive an unconditional release when they have completed the terms of their sentence and no longer require incarceration or supervision. One form of unconditional release is **mandatory release** (also known as "maxing out"), which occurs when an inmate has served the maximum amount of time on the initial sentence, minus reductions for good-time credits.

Another, quite rare unconditional release is a **pardon,** a form of executive clemency. The president (on the federal level) and the governor (on the state level) can grant pardon, or forgive, a convict's criminal punishment. Most states have a board of pardons—affiliated with the parole board—which makes recommendations to the governor in cases where it believes a pardon is warranted.

MANDATORY RELEASE
Release from prison that occurs when an offender has served the length of his or her sentence, with time taken off for good behavior.

PARDON
An act of executive clemency that overturns a conviction and erases mention of the crime from the person's criminal record.

Most pardons involve obvious miscarriages of justice, though sometimes a governor will pardon an individual to remove the stain of conviction from his or her criminal record.

Certain *temporary releases* also exist. Some inmates, who qualify by exhibiting good behavior and generally proving that they do not represent a risk to society, are allowed to leave the prison on **furlough** for a certain amount of time, usually between a day and a week. At times, a furlough is granted because of a family emergency, such as a funeral. Furloughs can be particularly helpful for an inmate who is nearing release and can use them to ease the readjustment period.

Discretionary Release

As you may recall from Chapter 10, corrections systems are classified by sentencing procedure—indeterminate or determinate. Indeterminate sentencing occurs when the legislature sets a range of punishments for particular crimes, and the judge and the parole board exercise discretion in determining the actual length of the prison term. For that reason, states with indeterminate sentencing are said to have systems of **discretionary release.** Until the mid-1970s, all states and the federal government operated in this manner.

Eligibility for Parole. Under indeterminate sentencing, parole is not a right but a privilege. This is a crucial point, as it establishes the terms of the relationship between the inmate and the corrections authorities during the parole process. In *Greenholtz v. Inmates of the Nebraska Penal and Correctional Complex* (1979),[55] the United States Supreme Court ruled that inmates did not have a constitutionally protected right to expect parole, thereby giving states the freedom to set their own standards for determining parole eligibility. In most states that have retained indeterminate sentencing, a prisoner is eligible to be considered for parole release after serving a legislatively determined percentage of the minimum sentence—usually one-half or two-thirds—less any good time or other credits.

Contrary to what is depicted in many films and television shows, a convict does not "apply" for parole. An inmate's case automatically comes up before the parole board a certain number of days—often ninety—before she or he is eligible for parole. The date of eligibility depends on statutory requirements, the terms of the sentence, and the behavior of the inmate in prison. The board has an eligibility report prepared, which provides information on the various factors that must be taken into consideration in making the decision. The board also reviews the case file to acquaint itself with the original crime and conducts an interview with the inmate. At some point before the eligibility date, the entire board, or a subcommittee of the board, votes on whether parole will be granted.

Not all convicts are eligible for parole. Many states have a sentencing system in which offenders who have committed the most serious crimes receive life terms without the possibility of early release. In general, life-without-parole is reserved for those offenders who have done the following:

FIGURE 13.6 **Release from State and Federal Correctional Facilities**

Type of Release	% of All Releases
Parole/mandatory supervision	68
Expiration of sentence	21
Probation*	6
Other	5

*As the second step in a split sentence (see page 283).
Source: Adapted from Bureau of Justice Statistics, *Correctional Populations in the United States, 1997* (Washington, D.C.: U.S. Department of Justice, 2000), Table 5.13.

FURLOUGH
Temporary release from a prison for purposes of vocational or educational training, to ease the shock of release, or for personal reasons.

DISCRETIONARY RELEASE
The release of an inmate into a community supervision program at the discretion of the parole board within limits set by state or federal law.

Peter "Commando Pedro" Langan, shown here as he is escorted by Franklin County (Ohio) sheriff's deputies from the county jail, was found guilty of participating in twenty-two bank robberies over a two-year period. Langan was the leader of the Midwestern Bank Bandits, a white separatist gang that declared itself in opposition to the government. U.S. District Judge John D. Holschuh sentenced Langan to a life sentence without possibility of parole. Do you agree with some observers who believe that life-without-parole is a harsher sentence than the death penalty? Or do you believe that life-without-parole is a humane alternative to the death penalty? (AP Photo/Doral Chenoweth III, *Columbus Dispatch*)

- committed capital, or first degree, murder;
- committed serious offenses other than murder; or
- been defined by statute as habitual, or repeat, offenders, such as those sentenced under "three strikes" laws.[56]

Besides murder, drug offenders and sex offenders are most commonly targeted for life-without-parole. The sentence is fraught with controversy, as many observers, including inmates, feel serving life-without-parole is a crueler punishment than the death penalty.[57] Furthermore, the United States Supreme Court has ruled that when a capital defendant who has been convicted of murder will be ineligible for parole, due process requires the jury to be told of this fact.[58] In other words, the jury must know, in sentencing the defendant, it has a choice between execution and life-without-parole.

The Parole Board.   The cumulated efforts of the police, the courtroom work group, and correctional officials lead to a single question in most cases: When should an offender be released?[59] This is a difficult question and is often left to the **parole board** to answer. When members of the parole board make what in retrospect was a mistake, they quickly draw the attention of the media, the public, and the courts.

According to the American Correctional Association, the parole board has four basic roles:

1 To decide which offenders should be placed on parole.

2 To determine the conditions of parole and aid in the continuing supervision of the parolee.

3 To discharge the offender when the conditions of parole have been met.

4 If a violation occurs, to determine whether parole privileges should be revoked.[60]

Most parole boards are small, made up of five to seven members. In many jurisdictions, board members' terms are limited to between four and six years. The requirements for board members vary. Nearly half the states have no prerequisites, while others require a bachelor's degree or some expertise in the field of criminal justice.

In a system that uses discretionary parole, the actual release decision is made at a **parole grant hearing.** During this hearing, the entire board or a subcommittee reviews relevant information on the convict. Sometimes, but not always, the offender is interviewed. Because the board members have only limited knowledge of each offender, key players in the case are often notified in advance of the parole hearing and asked to provide comments and recommendations. These participants include the sentencing judge, the attorneys at the trial, the victims, and any law enforcement officers who may be involved.[61] After these preparations, the typical parole hearing itself is *very* short—usually lasting just a few minutes.

If parole is denied, the entire process is replayed at the next "action date," which depends on the nature of the offender's crimes and all relevant laws. In 1998, for example, Leslie Van Houten was denied parole for the twelfth time. Van Houten was convicted of murder in 1969 for the role she played in the gruesome Beverly Hills killing of pregnant actress Sharon Tate and six others under the direction of Charles Manson. While in prison, Van Houten—who claims that she played a minimal role in the murders—has earned bachelor's and master's degrees and has never had a disciplinary report filed against her. Families of the victims continue to petition the California Board of Prison Terms to keep her incarcerated, and although the board has said Van Houten's chances improve with each hearing, most observers believe she will never be released. (Manson himself has been

In May 1999, boxer Mike Tyson was released on parole after serving about a third of a one-year prison sentence he had received following a plea of no contest to misdemeanor assault charges stemming from a minor traffic accident. The Maryland Parole Commission voted 5–1 to grant Tyson parole, under the condition that he pass two drug tests a week and undergo anger management treatment for the balance of his sentence. (AP Photo/Lennox McLendon)

PAROLE BOARD
A body of appointed civilians that decides whether a convict should be granted conditional release before the end of his or her sentence.

PAROLE GRANT HEARING
A hearing in which the entire parole board or a subcommittee reviews information, meets the offender, and hears testimony from relevant witnesses to determine whether to grant parole.

denied parole ten times.) In some states, the parole board is required to give written reasons for denying parole, and some jurisdictions give the inmate, prosecution, or victims the option to appeal the board's decision. Many states provide parole boards with legal requirements for parole, designed to give some structure to a process that relies to a great extent on personal discretion.

The Emergence of Mandatory Release

The legitimacy of discretionary release relies to a certain extent on the perception of parole decisions by offenders, victims, and the general public. Like judicial discretion (as we discussed in Chapter 10), parole board discretion is criticized when the decisions are seen as arbitrary and unfair and lead to rampant disparity in the release dates of similar offenders.[62] Proponents of discretionary release argue that parole boards must tailor their decisions to the individual case, but such protestations seem to be undermined by the raw data: research done by the Bureau of Justice Statistics has found that most offenders were serving less than a third of their sentences in the early 1990s.[63]

As Michael Tonry noted, such statistics gave the impression that parole board members "tossed darts at a dartboard" to determine who should be released and when.[64] As a result of this criticism, twenty-seven states have now implemented determinate sentencing systems, which set minimum mandatory terms without possibility of parole. These systems provide for *mandatory release,* in which offenders leave incarceration when their sentences have expired, minus adjustments made for good time.

Truth in Sentencing. The move toward mandatory release has come partly at the urging of the federal government. The federal sentencing guidelines that went into effect in 1987 required those who were convicted in federal courts to serve at least 85 percent of their terms.[65] Federal crime bills in 1994 and 1995 encouraged states to adopt this *truth-in-sentencing* (mentioned previously in Chapter 10) approach by making federal aid for prison construction conditional on the passage of such laws.[66] Many have done just that (see Figure 13.7).

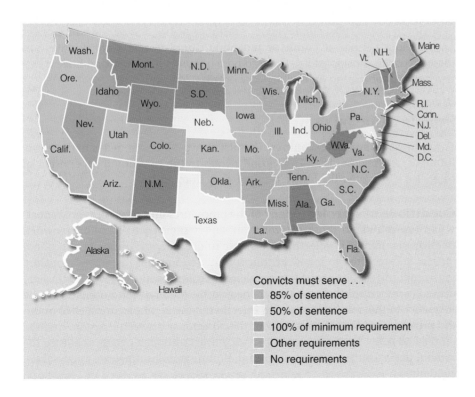

FIGURE 13.7

State Truth-in-Sentencing Requirements

Twenty-nine states and the District of Columbia have adopted federal truth-in-sentencing laws that require convicts to serve at least 85 percent of their sentence before being released.

Source: Adapted from Bureau of Justice Statistics, *Truth in Sentencing in State Prisons* (Washington, D.C.: U.S. Department of Justice, 1999), Table 1.

Convicts must serve . . .

- 85% of sentence
- 50% of sentence
- 100% of minimum requirement
- Other requirements
- No requirements

The Delancey Street residential facility for drug offenders in San Francisco offers nearly five hundred male and female residents the opportunity to kick their habits. What are some of the benefits of these facilities, both for the residents and for society? (AP Photo/Sam Deaner)

PAROLE GUIDELINES
Employed to remove discretion from the parole process, these guidelines attempt to measure the risks of an offender recidivating, and then use these measurements to determine whether early release will be granted and under what conditions.

PAROLE CONTRACT
An agreement between the state and the offender that establishes the conditions under which the latter will be allowed to serve the remainder of her or his prison term in the community.

"Truth in sentencing" is an umbrella term that covers a number of different state and federal statutes. In general, these laws have the following goals:

- To restore "truth" to the sentencing process by eliminating situations in which offenders are released by a parole board after serving less than the minimum term to which they were sentenced.
- To increase the percentage of the term that is actually served in prison, with the purpose of reducing crime by keeping convicts imprisoned for a longer period.
- To control the use of prison space by giving corrections officials the benefit of predictable terms and policymakers advance notice of the impact that sentencing statutes will have on prison populations.[67]

Note that fourteen states and the federal government have officially "abolished" parole. For the most part, however, these states simply emphasize prison terms that are "truthful," not necessarily "longer." Therefore, in Louisiana—noted for its harsh sentencing practices—violent offenders who serve only 50 percent of their terms spend more time in prison than do prisoners in many states that have "abolished" parole.[68]

The decision to switch from indeterminate to determinate sentencing is for the most part a political one, often made after a parolee commits a violent crime. New Jersey, for example, saw a number of these incidents in the mid-1990s. In one, a seven-year-old girl was raped and murdered by a parolee who had been released six weeks earlier. In another, motorcycle gang member Robert "Mudman" Simon, who had been paroled in Pennsylvania several months earlier, shot and killed a New Jersey police officer during a routine traffic stop.[69] As a result, the New Jersey legislature passed the No Early Release Act. Under this law, criminals convicted of first and second degree violent crimes must complete 85 percent of their sentences before becoming eligible for parole.[70]

Parole Guidelines.   One of the most popular methods of ensuring truth in sentencing is the use of **parole guidelines.** Similar to sentencing guidelines (see Chapter 10), parole guidelines attempt to measure a potential parolee's risk of recidivism by considering factors such as the original offense, criminal history, behavior in prison, past employment, substance abuse, and performance under any previous periods of parole or probation. Inmates who score positively in these areas are considered less likely to pose a danger to society and have a better chance of obtaining an early release date.

Parole Supervision

The term *parole* has two meanings. The first, as we have seen, refers to the establishment of a release date. The second relates to the continuing supervision of convicted felons after they have been released from prison.

Conditions of Parole.   Many of the procedures and issues of parole supervision are similar to those of probation supervision. Like probationers, when parolees are granted parole, they are placed under the supervision of correctional officers and required to follow certain conditions. Some of these conditions are fairly uniform. All parolees, for example, must comply with the law, and they are generally responsible for reporting to their parole officer at certain intervals. The frequency of these visits, along with the other terms of parole, are spelled out in the **parole contract,** which sets out the agreement between the state and the paroled offender. Under the terms of the contract, the state agrees to release the inmate under certain conditions, and the future parolee agrees to follow these conditions.

FIGURE 13.8 **Standard Conditions of Parole**

1. Upon my release I will report to my parole officer as directed and follow the parole officer's instructions.

2. I will report to my parole officer in person and in writing whenever and wherever the parole officer directs.

3. I agree that the parole officer has the right to visit my residence or place of employment at any reasonable time.

4. I will seek, obtain and maintain employment throughout my parole term, or perform community service as directed by my parole officer.

5. I will notify my parole officer prior to any changes in my place of residence, in my place of employment, or of any change in my marital status.

6. I will notify my parole officer within 48 hours if at any time I am arrested for any offense.

7. I will not at any time have firearms, ammunition, or any other weapon in my possession or under my control.

8. I will obey all laws, and to the best of my ability, fulfill all my legal obligations, including payment of all applicable child support and alimony orders.

9. I will not leave the state of _____ without prior permission of my parole officer.

10. I will not at any time, use, or have in my possession or control, any illegal drug or narcotic.

11. I will not at any time have contact or affiliation with any street gangs or with any members thereof.

12. Your release on parole is based upon the conclusion of the parole panel that there is a reasonable probability that you will live and remain at liberty without violating the law and that your release is not incompatible with the welfare of society. In the event that you engage in conduct in the future which renders this conclusion no longer valid, then your parole will be revoked or modified accordingly.

Source: Connecticut Board of Parole.

Each jurisdiction has its own standard parole contract, although the parole board can add specific provisions if it sees the need (see Figure 13.8).

Parole Officers.   The correctional agent given the responsibility to supervise parolees is the parole officer. In many respects, the parole officer's relationship with the parolee mirrors that of the probation officer and the probationer (see Chapter 11); in fact, many municipal and state departments of corrections combine the two posts to create probation/parole officers. Parole officers are required to enforce the conditions of parole and initiate revocation hearings when these conditions are not met. Furthermore, a parole officer is expected to help the parolee readjust to life outside the correctional institution by helping her or him find a place to live and a job, and seeing that she or he receives any treatment or rehabilitation that may be necessary.

According to Todd R. Clear of Florida State University and Edward Latessa of the University of Cincinnati, the major role conflict for parole officers is whether to be a law enforcement officer or a social worker.[71] In other words, parole officers are constantly required to choose between the good of the community and the good of the paroled offender. In one study of parole officer stress and burnout, researchers found that more than 60 percent of the officers interviewed felt uncertain about how to balance these two requirements.[72] To be sure, some parole officers focus entirely on protecting the community and see the welfare of the client as a secondary concern. (For an example of this conflict, see the feature *CJ in Focus—The Balancing Act: Cop or Caretaker?* on the next page.)

A growing number of parole experts, however, believe that parole officers should act as agents of change, meaning that they should try not simply to control the offender's behavior but also to change it. This entails that the parole officer establish strong bonds of trust and commitment with the parolee by taking what could be called a parental attitude to the officer-client relationship.[73]

Parole Revocation.   If convicts follow the conditions of their parole until the *maximum expiration date,* or the date on which their sentence ends, then they are discharged from supervision. A large number—about 40 percent, according to the latest research—return to incarceration before their maximum expiration date, most because they were convicted of a new offense or had their parole revoked (see Figure 13.9 on page 346). **Parole revocation** is similar in many aspects to

"Johnny plus alcohol plus women equals trouble."

—*Excerpt from 1976 parole report on Johnny Robert Eggers, who was released on parole five different times before stabbing a female teenager to death in 1994*

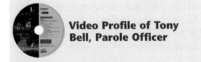

Video Profile of Tony Bell, Parole Officer

PAROLE REVOCATION
When a parolee breaks the conditions of parole, the process of withdrawing parole and returning the person to prison.

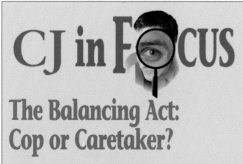

CJ in FOCUS

The Balancing Act: Cop or Caretaker?

When five parole officers burst into the residence in Noble, Oklahoma, they expected to find one Ned Snow, parolee. Snow was wanted for alleged parole violations. Even though Snow did not happen to be at the residence at the time of the "visit," the parole officers, who were accompanied by two local deputies, proceeded to search the house and seize prescription drugs from the women who lived there. Several days later, the parole officers returned to the dwelling, once again to find that Snow was not at home. Snow's wife and mother, to their misfortune, were present. The parole officers proceeded to handcuff the two women and place them in a state vehicle. At this point, Snow arrived in another car, but fled as soon as he saw what was taking place. One of the parole officers commandeered the women's pickup truck and chased Snow at a high speed until the truck's engine blew.

In the aftermath of these events, one of the parole officers involved lost her job and three others were suspended. This was not, however, an isolated incident. To the chagrin of many Oklahoma corrections and law enforcement officials, it represented an internal philosophical debate over the proper role of the state's parole officers. Was their primary purpose to act as surrogate police officers or as social workers concerned mainly with the well-being of their clients?

The parole officers involved in the Snow debacle, along with a number of their colleagues, leaned toward assuming the role of law enforcement officer. In the words of one insider, these officers felt that their job was "to take names and kick asses." According to another officer, "These few guys want to be 120 percent law enforcement and they don't want to do any of the social-work part of it."

A further worry was that this aggressive attitude was denying parolees their constitutional rights. Although parole officers are allowed to conduct unannounced "visits" at the homes and workplaces of parolees, they do not have the authority to conduct searches without a warrant. In the words of one parole officer, parolees "have a right to a search warrant just like everybody else does." In several Oklahoma counties, parole and probation officers have an understanding with local police agencies: if the police suspect a parolee of illegal activity but do not have a warrant to search his or her abode, they will call on the parolee's parole officer to make an unannounced visit and search.

Supporters of "John Wayne–style" parole officers argue that such tactics are needed to protect citizens. Senior Oklahoma probation and parole officer Kris Evans disagrees. "We do have a law enforcement component to our job, but we're not supposed to be out there playing detective," Evans says. "We supervise people on probation or parole, and that's the scope of our employment." He adds, "If you want to go kick in doors, go apply to the OSBI (Oklahoma State Bureau of Investigation) or a local law enforcement agency."

FOR CRITICAL ANALYSIS
What would be some of the consequences if all parole officers focused on the law enforcement aspects of their job rather than its social service responsibilities?

FIGURE 13.9 **Terminating Parole**

As you can see, nearly half of all parolees successfully complete their terms of parole. The rest are either returned to incarceration, transferred, or die while on parole.

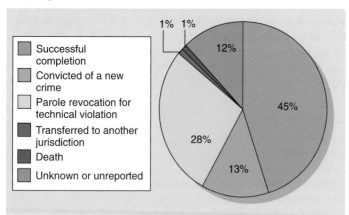

- Successful completion
- Convicted of a new crime
- Parole revocation for technical violation
- Transferred to another jurisdiction
- Death
- Unknown or unreported

1% 1% 12% 45% 13% 28%

Source: Adapted from Bureau of Justice Statistics, *Correctional Populations in the United States, 1997* (Washington, D.C.: U.S. Department of Justice, 2000), Table 6.5, page 130.

probation revocation. If the parolee commits a new crime, then a return to prison is very likely. If, however, the individual breaks a condition of parole, known as a technical violation, the parole authorities have discretion as to whether revocation proceedings should be initiated. An example of a technical violation would be failure to report a change in address to parole authorities. As with probation revocation, many observers believe that those who commit technical violations should not be imprisoned, as they have not committed a crime.

Until 1972, parole officers had the power to arbitrarily revoke parole status for technical violations. A parolee who was returned to prison had little or no recourse. In *Morrissey v. Brewer* (1972),[74] the United States Supreme Court changed this by deciding that a parolee has a "liberty interest" in remaining on parole. In other words, before parolees can be deprived of their liberty, they must be afforded a measure of due process at a parole revocation hearing.

Although this hearing does not provide the same due process protections as a criminal trial, the parolee does have the right to be notified of the charges, to present witnesses, to speak in his or her defense, and to question any hostile witnesses (as long as such questioning would not place them in danger). In the first stage of the hearing, the parole board determines whether there is probable cause that a violation occurred. Then, the board decides whether to return the parolee to prison.

TOO DANGEROUS FOR RELEASE?

In a letter to the Pennsylvania Board of Pardons, Reginald McFadden asked for a chance to show that he could "function normally" among law-abiding citizens. "You have given me these years to reassess my life's values," McFadden wrote, "and as a result, I am a better person." Three months after being granted parole, McFadden was arrested on three charges of murder and suspected of a fourth.[75] Such incidents, rare though they may be, not only lead to questions about the parole system, but also heighten fears of releasing any violent criminal.[76] This mistrust manifests itself in the legal restrictions faced by all convicts, even those who were model prisoners or parolees. In many jurisdictions, convicts do not have the right to hold public office, serve on a jury, own firearms, or adopt children. Perhaps no statutory restrictions better represent society's feeling toward the "dangerous" ex-prisoner than sex offender notification laws, known as "Megan's Laws." (See the feature *Criminal Justice in Action—Protecting the Community from Sex Offenders* at the end of this chapter.)

For many released inmates, however, the inability to serve on a jury or other civil rights restrictions are the least of their worries. For all the hardships of incarceration, it does offer a haven from the day-to-day decisions that characterize life on the outside. Furthermore, the prison environment insulates inmates; a convict released after a long prison term may find common acts such as using an ATM or pumping his or her own gas completely alien.

In prison, according to one inmate, the "rules" of daily life followed by citizens on the outside are turned upside-down:

> An unexpected smile could mean trouble. A man in uniform was not a friend. Being kind was a weakness. Viciousness and recklessness were to be respected and admired.[77]

Consequently, inmates experience a shift in reality while behind bars. In other words, they live differently than do those on the outside. As another long-term inmate commented:

> For most, the prison experience is a one-way ride on a psychological roller coaster—downhill. And the easiest thing to do, in a world where almost everything is an assault against you, is to permit yourself to be defeated by the overwhelming indifference and sense of hopelessness that steals into your daily existence, slowly, almost unnoticeably sapping your drive, your dreams, your ambition, evoking cries from the soul to surrender.[78]

It is understandably difficult for many inmates to readjust to life on the outside after feeling such pressures. A friend of parolee Reginald McFadden's blamed his recidivism on the fact that he "could not handle any of the emotions that come with being set free."[79]

On the Web

Victims' rights groups have become more and more vocal in trying to keep violent criminals from receiving parole. For a link to the Web sites of several of these groups, go to the Hypercontents page for this chapter at **http://cj.wadsworth.com/ gainescore2e.**

Criminal Justice in Action
Protecting the Community from Sex Offenders

In the summer of 1994, seven-year-old Megan Kanka of Hamilton Township, New Jersey, was raped and murdered by a twice-convicted pedophile (an adult sexually attracted to children) who had moved into her neighborhood after being released from prison on parole. As we have seen in this chapter, the actions of one released offender can have far-reaching consequences. The next year, the state passed a series of laws known collectively as the New Jersey Sexual Offender Registration Act, or "Megan's Law."[80] Today, forty-seven states and the federal government have passed their own versions of Megan's Law, which require local law authorities to alert the public when a sex offender has been released in the community. Hailed by victims' rights groups and reviled by civil libertarians, these laws—which are the focus of this *Criminal Justice in Action* feature—have been the topic of much controversy.

ACTIVE AND PASSIVE NOTIFICATION

No two of these laws have exactly the same provisions, but all are designed with the goal of allowing the public to learn the identities of convicted sex offenders living in their midst. The incentive to institute such laws was enhanced in 1996 when Congress passed its own Megan's Law, which requires a state to provide communities with relevant information on sex offenders as a condition of receiving federal anticrime funds.[81] In 2000, Congress passed another law requiring sexual offenders to report their status to college administrations if they are enrolled at the school or if they have a job on campus.[82] By October 2002, all colleges had to give the public access to this information.

In general, these laws demand that a paroled sexual offender notify local law enforcement authorities on taking up residence in a state. This registration process must be renewed every time the parolee changes his or her address. The process of community notification by the authorities has two models. The "active" model requires that they directly notify the community or community representatives. This often takes the form of bulletins or flyers, distributed and posted within a certain distance from the offender's home. In the "passive" model, information on sex offenders must be open and available for public scrutiny. In California, for example, the state has created a CD-ROM that provides the names, photos, and Zip Codes of nearly 64,000 of the state's released sex offenders.[83]

In some instances, convicts must notify authorities themselves. Paroled sex offenders in Georgia are required to present themselves to both the sheriff and the superintendent of the public school district where they plan to reside.[84] Generally, sex offenders are supervised by parole officers and are subject to the same threat of revocation as other parolees. Paroled child molesters usually have the following conditions of release:

- Must have no contact with children under the age of sixteen.
- Must continue psychiatric treatment.
- Must receive permission from their parole officer to change residence.
- Must stay a certain distance from schools or parks where children are present.
- Cannot own toys that may be used to lure children.
- Cannot have a job or participate in any activity that involves children.

In some cases, after release from incarceration, sex offenders must return to the county where they committed their crime.

LEGAL ISSUES

In nearly every jurisdiction, Megan's Laws have been challenged as unconstitutional. The common theme among these court cases is that Megan's Laws represent a form of "punishment" and as such violate state and federal constitutional prohibitions against double jeopardy and cruel and unusual punishment. In other words, by forcing sex offend-

Judge Manuel Banales ordered twenty-one registered sex offenders in Corpus Christi, Texas, to place signs similar to the one pictured here on their front yards. Do you think this unfairly infringes on the privacy rights of the sex offenders? Or, are such steps justified to protect children who live nearby? (AP Photo/ *Corpus Christi Caller–Times,* Paul Iverson)

ers to register in expectation of a crime they have yet to commit, these laws operate in opposition to the principle that persons are innocent until proven guilty. Furthermore, because of the scrutiny that is certain to fall on a pedophile whose past crimes have been broadcast to the community, offenders have filed suit claiming that the laws unconstitutionally invade their privacy.[85]

Most courts have ruled that the notification process in Megan's Laws does not, in fact, constitute "punishment." The Supreme Court of New Jersey, for example, found that although some of the ramifications of the law may indeed be punitive, its intent was remedial and consequently did not violate the state or federal constitution.[86] The New Jersey court also found that the law did infringe on offenders' privacy rights, but held that the need to protect those rights was outweighed by the strong state interest of disclosure.[87] In other words, the offender's right to privacy was not as strong as the public's right to be informed of his or her presence.

Many legal experts are awaiting a United States Supreme Court ruling on notification laws, hoping that it would eliminate some of the confusion and inconsistency that plague the many different state statutes. In 1998, however, the Court refused to hear challenges to the Megan's Laws of New York and New Jersey, effectively allowing individual jurisdictions to continue setting their own notification policies.[88]

GETTING TOUGHER WITH SEX OFFENDERS

Megan's Laws have increased community awareness of the danger of sex offenders—one in twelve of the 24,000 Californians who accessed the sex offender CD-ROM recognized a registrant. Furthermore, notification policies have no doubt forced some offenders to confront their psychological problems and driven them to participate more actively in their own rehabilitation.

Even some supporters are beginning to question the laws, however. Identified offenders often become targets of vigilante action, and sometimes that action is misguided. In New Jersey, for example, a man broke into an apartment and severely beat its occupant after finding the address on the state's sex offender computer bank. The convict had moved, however, and the beating victim was not a former criminal.

Such incidents are rare, but they have been more effective than the constitutional challenges in raising questions in the public mind about Megan's Laws. Why, observers are beginning to ask, is the government releasing people from prison when the state itself considers them so likely to reoffend that the community must be warned of their very presence? To address this problem, sixteen states have passed laws that say, in effect, Megan's laws are not enough. In these states, sexual offenders can be sent to another, noncorrectional facility (such as a psychiatric hospital) after serving their prison or jail terms. By 2000, nearly nine hundred sex offenders were incarcerated for indefinite terms ("from one day to life" in judicial language) under such laws.[89]

In 2001, the state of Washington's Community Protection Act—the model for many other such acts nationwide—withstood a challenge in the United States Supreme Court. The plaintiff, Andre Brigham Young, had been locked up in a health-care facility for twelve years after serving his prison term for rape. Young argued that he was being punished a second time for the same crime, which is unconstitutional under the Fifth Amendment. The Court rejected this argument, stating that Young's commitment to the health facility was a "civil" decision made by the state that did not involve criminal law. Therefore, the Fifth Amendment's prohibition of double jeopardy did not apply.[90]

THE ONLY WAY?

The spread of sex offender laws reflects a dual need among citizens: notification and prevention. In the case of notification, it would appear that these laws can be effective; that is, they can help answer the question: Is my neighbor a sex offender?

As for preventing further sex offenses, the laws may not be as effective as citizens and politicians may hope. The problem is that sex offenders have a high rate of recidivism; according to the Bureau of Justice Statistics, they are "substantially more likely" than other violent criminals to be rearrested for a new violent offense.[91]

Certainly, it would be simple if society could just send all sex offenders to an island and forget about them—simple, but unconstitutional and, ultimately, impossible. Megan's Law and similar legislation, for all the criticism they receive, may represent the best way to protect communities from sex offenders by providing citizens with the means to protect themselves.

MAKING SENSE OF SEX OFFENDER LAWS

1 What are the two "rights" that legislators must weigh in passing Megan's Laws? Do you agree that the rights of the community outweigh the rights of the individual offender? Explain your answer.

2 In New Jersey, housing associations may refuse occupancy to serious sex offenders. Opponents of the law say that released sex offenders have already paid their debt to society and should not be denied the basic necessity of housing. Which side do you agree with, and why?

3 Some states and local communities post lists of convicted sex offenders, with photos, on the Internet. Is this a fair method of notification, or is it too intrusive on the privacy of the felon? Why?

KEY TERMS

CHAPTER SUMMARY

1 **Explain the concept of prison as a total institution.** Though many people spend time in partial institutions—schools, companies where they work, and religious organizations—only in prison is every aspect of an inmate's life controlled, and that is why prisons are called total institutions. Every detail for every prisoner is fully prescribed and managed.

2 **Describe the possible patterns of inmate behavior, which are driven by the inmate's personality and values.** (a) Professional criminals adapt to prison by "doing time" and follow the rules in order to get out quickly. (b) Those who are "jailing" establish themselves within the power structure of prison culture. These are often veterans of juvenile detention centers and other prisons. (c) Those who are "gleaning" are working to improve themselves for return to society. (d) "Disorganized" criminals have mental impairments or low IQs and therefore are unable to adapt to prison culture.

3 **Indicate some of the reasons for violent behavior in prisons.** (a) To separate the powerful from the weak and to establish a prisoner hierarchy; (b) to minimize one's own probability of being a target of assault; (c) to enhance one's self-image; (d) to obtain sexual relief; and (e) to obtain material goods through extortion or robbery.

4 **List and briefly explain the six general job categories among correctional officers.** (a) Block officers, who supervise cell blocks or are on block guard duty; (b) work detail supervisors, who oversee the cafeteria, prison store, and laundry, for example; (c) industrial shop and school officers, who generally oversee workshop and educational programs; (d) yard officers, who patrol the prison yard when prisoners are allowed there; (e) tower guards, who work in isolation; and (f) those who hold administrative building assignments, such as prison gate guards, overseers of visitation procedures, and so on.

5 **Contrast the hands-off doctrine of prisoner law with the hands-on approach.** The hands-off doctrine assumes that the care of prisoners should be left entirely to prison officials and that it is not the place of judges to intervene. In contrast, the hands-on philosophy started in 1964 after the United States Supreme Court decision in *Cooper v. Pate.* Prisoners have been able to file civil lawsuits, called Section 1983 petitions, when they feel their civil rights have been violated.

6 **List the concepts on which parole is based.** (a) Grace, (b) contract of consent, and (c) custody.

7 **Contrast probation, parole, mandatory release, pardon, and furlough.** Probation is an alternative to incarceration. Parole is an early release program for those incarcerated. Mandatory release occurs when the inmate has served the maximum time for her or his initial sentence minus good-time credits. A pardon can be given only by the president or one of the fifty governors. Furlough is a temporary release while in jail or prison.

8 **Describe truth-in-sentencing laws and their goals.** Such laws make more transparent the actual time that a convicted criminal will serve in jail or prison. The goals are (a) to restore "truth" to the sentencing process; (b) to increase the percentage of the term that is actually served in prison in order to reduce crime by keeping convicts "off the streets" for a longer period; and (c) to better control the use of prison space by giving corrections officials predictable terms and policymakers advance notice of potential overcrowding.

9 **Describe typical conditions of parole.** Parolees must not use drugs, not associate with known felons, not change their addresses without notifying authorities, and report to their parole officers at specified intervals. (The latter is usually specified in the parole contract.)

10 **Indicate typical conditions for release for a paroled child molester.** (a) Have no contact with children under the age of sixteen; (b) continue psychiatric treatment; (c) obtain permission from a parole officer to change residence; (d) keep away from schools or parks where children are present; (e) cannot own toys that may be used to lure children; and (f) cannot have a job or participate in any activity that involves children.

QUESTIONS FOR CRITICAL ANALYSIS

1 Why is the principle of least eligibility relevant in today's political environment?

2 How does the deprivation model seek to explain prison violence?

3 What is the most demanding job assignment in the correctional institution hierarchy?

4 What has caused a reduction in the amount of discretion that parole boards have?

5 When a parolee is caught committing a crime, what typically tends to happen, and why?

6 Why do civil libertarians criticize Megan's Laws?

SELECTED PRINT AND ELECTRONIC RESOURCES

SUGGESTED READINGS

Burton-Rose, Daniel, et al., eds., *The Celling of America: An Inside Look at the U.S. Prison Industry,* Monroe, ME: Common Courage Press, 1998. This book is an edited collection of articles written by criminals in prison as well as interviews with them. Two of the coeditors were in prison while the book was being put together. Their message is that the United States seems to be in an era of social vengeance. They describe the prison system as a bleak environment where brutality, substandard medical care, racism, and extremely crowded conditions are common. Many of the prisoners contend that conditions are becoming worse each year.

Conover, Ted, *Newjack,* New York: Random House, 2000. The author, a journalist, describes his experiences as an undercover "newjack," or rookie correctional officer, at Sing Sing prison in Ossining, New York. Early on, a supervisor tells Conover, "You're the zookeeper now. . . . Go run the zoo"; this book explores the implications of this attitude for both correctional officers and prisoners.

Lerner, Jimmy, *You Got Nothing Coming: Notes from a Prison Fish,* New York: Broadway Books, 2002. The author killed a man in Las Vegas, and, after being convicted of voluntary manslaughter, he is now serving time in the Nevada state prison system. A memoir of Lerner's first year behind bars, this book is a lively, graphic, and often funny recounting of what it's like to be a newcomer in prison.

MEDIA RESOURCES

***The Farm: Angola, U.S.A.* (1998)** This is a black-and-white documentary depicting the day-to-day life in the Louisiana State Penitentiary at Angola, the largest maximum-security prison in the country. Angola is a former slave plantation turned into a maximum-security "lifer" penitentiary. The facility houses almost five thousand inmates. More than 85 percent of those who enter Angola will never leave. *The Farm* was nominated for an Oscar for best feature documentary in 1999.

Critically analyze this film:

1. Do you see evidence of any sort of "prison code" at Angola? What aspects of "prisonization" (page 328) are evident?

2. How does the prospect of spending one's life behind bars color virtually every scene in the film?

3. Of the six inmates who are chronicled in different stages of their life sentences, how many believe they stand a good chance of making it out of Angola?

4. Warden Burl Cain said, "If we keep their despair down and their hopes up, they won't try to escape." How can the inmates' hopes be kept up?

5. The Italian newspaper *Corriere della Sera* describes Angola as "America's Gulag." Why do you think the paper refers to Angola this way, and what does the term *Gulag* mean?

LOGGING ON

Go to http://cj.wadsworth.com/gainescore2e, and click Hypercontents. There, you will find URLs for the organizations in the following list:

• Many groups are active in trying to change prison conditions. One such group—the **Prison Activist Resource Center**—has established an instructive Web site with departments such as *Prison Issues, Prison News,* and *Activist/Advocacy Groups.*

• Founded in 1870, the **American Correctional Association** is an organization that believes that the object of punishment should be the "moral regeneration" of the prisoner.

• If you want to know more about the language of the inmate, go to the **Correctional Officers Guide to Prison Slang**.

USING THE INTERNET FOR CRIMINAL JUSTICE ANALYSIS

INFOTRAC®
COLLEGE EDITION

1. Go to your InfoTrac College Edition at **http://www.infotrac-college.com/wadsworth/**. After you log on, type the words: **"Moderating probation and parole officer attitudes to achieve desired outcomes."** This is an article from *The Prison Journal*. It is based on a study of how to moderate parole officer attitudes to improve the effectiveness of correctional intervention. Basically, the conclusion is that a comprehensive training and development program must be instituted to instill in parole officers the supervision attitudes that are most conducive to promoting offender change. After you read the article, answer the following questions:

a. What is the "seemingly inherent conflict between treatment and control"?

b. Of the eight principles of effective intervention for parole officers, which one appears to be the most important, and why?

c. How did the study find out about parole officers' attitudes?

Read Table 1, which gives "The Subjective Role Scale."

d. Which questions seem most important, and why?

2. See Internet Activities 13.1 and 13.2 on the companion Web site for *CJ in Action: The Core*. To get to the activities, go to **http://www.cj.wadsworth.com/gainescore2e**, select the appropriate chapter from the drop down list, then click Internet Activities on the left navigation bar.

NOTES

1. Seth Rosenfield, "Agency Wants Outside Probe of Prison Riot," *San Francisco Examiner* (February 27, 2000), D4.
2. Norval Morris, "The Contemporary Prison: 1965—Present," in *The Oxford History of Prisons: The Practice of Punishment in Western Society,* ed. Norval Morris and David J. Rothman (New York: Oxford University Press, 1995), 227.
3. Peter Finn, "No-Frills Prisons and Jails: A Movement in Flux," *Federal Probation* (September 1996), 35.
4. Kenneth Adams, "A Bull Market in Corrections," *The Prison Journal* (December 1996), 465, 467.
5. Edward W. Sieh, "Less Eligibility: The Upper Limits of Penal Policy," *Criminal Justice Policy Review* 3 (1989), 159.
6. Richard Lacayo, "The Real Hard Cell," *Time* (September 4, 1995), 31.
7. Gregory Moorhead and Ricky W. Griffin, *Organizational Behavior*, 2d ed. (Boston: Houghton Mifflin, 1989), 497.
8. Erving Goffman, "On the Characteristics of Total Institutions," in *Asylums: Essays on the Social Situation of Mental Patients and Other Inmates* (New York: Doubleday, 1961), 6.
9. Justin Brooks, "How Can We Sleep While the Beds Are Burning: The Tumultuous Prison Culture of Attica Flourishes in American Prisons Twenty-Five Years Later," *Syracuse Law Journal* 47 (1996), 159.
10. Bureau of Justice Statistics, *Lifetime Likelihood of Going to State or Federal Prison* (Washington, D.C.: U.S. Department of Justice, March 1997), 1.
11. Craig Perkins, *National Corrections Reporting Program 1992* (Washington, D.C.: U.S. Department of Justice, 1994).
12. Connie L. Neeley, Laura Addison, and Delores Craig-Moreland, "Addressing the Needs of Elderly Offenders," *Corrections Today* (August 1997), 120.
13. Perkins, *National Corrections Reporting Program 1992*.
14. Donald Clemmer, *The Prison Community* (Boston: Christopher, 1940).
15. John Irwin, *Prisons in Turmoil* (Boston: Little, Brown, 1980), 67.
16. Gresham M. Sykes and Sheldon Messinger, "The Inmate Social System," in *Theoretical Studies in the Social Organization of the Prison,* ed. Richard A. Cloward (New York: Social Science Research Council, 1960), 6–10.
17. Robert Johnson, *Hard Time: Understanding and Reforming the Prison,* 2d ed. (Belmont, CA: Wadsworth Publishing Company, 1996), 133.
18. Jocelyn Pollock, "The Social World of the Prisoner," in *Prisons: Today and Tomorrow,* Jocelyn Pollock, ed. (Gaithersburg, MD: Aspen Publishers, 1997), 246–59.
19. Michael Puisis, "Update on Public Health in Correctional Facilities," *Western Journal of Medicine* (December 1, 1998).
20. Anders Kaye, "Dangerous Places: The Right to Self-Defense in Prison and Prison Conditions," *University of Chicago Law Review* 63 (Spring 1996), 693.
21. 511 U.S. 825 (1994).
22. Lee H. Bowker, *Prison Victimization* (New York: Elsevier, 1981), 31–33.
23. Stephen C. Light, "The Severity of Assaults on Prison Officers: A Contextual Analysis," *Social Science Quarterly* 71 (1990), 267–84.
24. Lee H. Bowker, "An Essay on Prison Violence," in *Prison Violence in America,* Michael Braswell, Steven Dillingham, and Reid Montgomery, Jr., eds. (Cincinnati, OH: Anderson Publishing Co., 1985), 7–18.
25. Frank Tannenbaum, *Crime and Community* (Boston: Ginn & Co., 1938).
26. Randy Martin and Sherwood Zimmerman, "A Typology of the Causes of Prison Riots and an Analytical Extension to the 1986 Virginia Riot," *Justice Quarterly* 7 (1990), 711–37.
27. Bert Useem, "Disorganization and the New Mexico Prison Riot of 1980," *American Sociological Review* 50 (1985), 677–88.
28. Robert W. Dumond, "Inmate Sexual Assault," *Prison Journal* 80 (December 2000), 407.
29. Human Rights Watch, "World Report 2000—United States."
30. Mary Dallao, "How to Make Your Facility Safer," *Corrections Today* (December 1996), 101.
31. Quoted in John J. Dilulio, Jr., *No Escape: The Future of American Corrections* (New York: Basic Books, 1991), 268.
32. Jack Henry Abbott, *In the Belly of the Beast* (New York: Vintage Books, 1991), 54.
33. Michael Foucault, *Discipline and Punish: The Birth of the Prison* (New York: Pantheon Books, 1977), 128.
34. Lucien X. Lombardo, *Guards Imprisoned: Correctional Officers at Work* (Cincinnati, OH: Anderson Publishing Co., 1989), 51–71.
35. Ben M. Crouch, "The Book vs. the Boot: Two Styles of Guarding in a Southern Prison," in *The Keepers,* Ben M. Couch, ed. (Springfield, IL: Charles C. Thomas, 1980), 207–24.
36. Goffman, 7.
37. 475 U.S. 312 (1986).
38. *Stanley v. Hejirika* (U.S. Court of Appeals for the 4th Circuit, No. 97-62124, 1998).
39. 503 U.S. 1 (1992).
40. Craig Haney, "Psychology and the Limits to Prison Pain," *Psychology, Public Policy, and the Law* 3 (December 1977), 499.
41. 378 U.S. 546 (1964).

42. 418 U.S. 539 (1974).

43. 429 U.S. 97 (1976).

44. *Daniels v. Williams*, 474 U.S. 327 (1986); and *Whitley v. Albers*, 475 U.S. 312 (1986).

45. 501 U.S. 296 (1991).

46. *Ibid.*, 294, 304.

47. 515 U.S. 472 (1995).

48. Genevieve Anton, "Lawmakers Seek to Halt Silly Lawsuits by Prisoners," *Colorado Springs Gazette-Telegraph* (March 22, 1998), NEWS1.

49. Andrew Peyton Thomas, "Rule of Law: Congress Revokes Prisoners' Access to Frivolous Appeals," *Wall Street Journal* (July 3, 1996), A11.

50. Public Law Number 104-34 110 Stat. 1321 (1996).

51. Anton, NEWS1.

52. "Too Many Convicts," *Economist* (August 10, 2002), 9.

53. Ted Palmer, "The Effectiveness of Intervention: Recent Trends and Current Issues," *Crime & Delinquency* 37 (1991), 34.

54. Todd R. Clear and George F. Cole, *American Corrections*, 4th ed. (Belmont, CA: Wadsworth Pubishing Co., 1997), 416.

55. 442 U.S. 1 (1979).

56. Danya W. Blair, "A Matter of Life and Death: Why Life without Parole Should be a Sentencing Option in Texas," *American Journal of Criminal Law* 22 (Fall 1994), 191.

57. Julian H. Wright, Jr., "Life-without-Parole: An Alternative to Death or Not Much of a Life at All?" *Vanderbilt Law Review* 43 (March 1990), 529.

58. *Simmons v. South Carolina*, 512 U.S. 154 (1994).

59. Victoria J. Palacios, "Go and Sin No More: Rationality and Release Decisions by Parole Boards," *South Carolina Law Review* 45 (Spring 1994), 567.

60. William Parker, *Parole: Origins, Development, Current Practices, and Statutes* (College Park, MD: American Correctional Association, 1972), 26.

61. Mike A. Cable, "Limiting Parole: Required Consideration of Statements and Recommendations Received by the Parole Board," *Pacific Law Journal* 28 (Spring 1997), 778.

62. Andrew Von Hirsch and Kathleen J. Hanrahan, *The Question of Parole: Retention, Reform, or Abolition* (Cambridge, MA: Ballinger Publishing Company, 1979), 4.

63. Bureau of Justice Statistics, *Bulletin* (Washington, D.C.: U.S. Department of Justice, January 1995), 2.

64. Michael Tonry, "Twenty Years of Sentencing Reform: Steps Forward, Steps Backward," *Judicature* 78 (January/February 1995), 169.

65. Comprehensive Crime Control Act of 1984, Pub. L. No. 98-473, Section 217(a), 98 Stat. 1837, 2017 (1984), codified as amended at 28 U.S.C. Sections 991–98 (1988).

66. 42 U.S.C.A. Sections 13701–09.

67. Marc Mauer, "The Truth about Truth in Sentencing," *Corrections Today* (February 1, 1996), S1.

68. *Ibid.*

69. Stacey L. Pilato, "New Jersey's No Early Release Act: A Band-Aid Approach to Victims' Pain and Recidivism?" *Seton Hall Legislative Journal* 25 (1997), 357.

70. 1997 New Jersey Sess. Law Serv. 117.

71. Todd R. Clear and Edward Latessa, "Probation Officer Roles in Intensive Supervision: Surveillance versus Treatment," *Justice Quarterly* 10 (1993), 441–62.

72. J. T. Whitehead and C. A. Lindquist, "Job Stress and Burnout among Probation/Parole Officers: Perceptions and Causal Factors," *International Journal of Offender Therapy and Comparative Criminology* 29 (1985), 109–19.

73. Betsy Fulton, Amy Stichman, Lawrence Travis, and Edward Latessa, "Moderating Probation and Parole Officers' Attitudes to Achieve Desired Outcomes," *Prison Journal* (September 1, 1997), 295.

74. 408 U.S. 471 (1972).

75. "Deadly Spree Followed Vote to Give Killer '2nd Chance,'" *Buffalo News* (July 2, 1996), A12.

76. Tim Landis, "Real Time: Truth-in-Sentencing Law Changes Plea Negotiations," *St. Louis Dispatch* (July 11, 1996), 1.

77. Victor Hassine, *Life without Parole: Living in Prison Today*, ed. Thomas J. Bernard and Richard McCleary (Los Angeles: Roxbury Publishing Company, 1996), 12.

78. Wilbert Rideau and Ron Wikberg, *Life Sentences: Rage and Survival behind Bars* (New York: Times Books, 1992), 59–60.

79. "Deadly Spree Followed Vote to Give Killer '2nd Chance,'" A12.

80. NJ.REV.STAT. Section 2C:7-8(c) (1995).

81. Megan's Law, Pub. L. No. 104-145, 110 Stat. 1345 (1996).

82. 20 U.S.C. Section 1094(c)(3)(B) (2000).

83. Carl Ingram, "Megan's Law Works Well to Protect Public, Lungren Says," *Los Angeles Times* (June 13, 1998), A15.

84. Ga. Code Ann. Section 42-9-44.1(b)(1).

85. Tara L. Wayt, "Megan's Law: A Violation of the Right to Privacy?" *Temple Political and Civil Rights Law Review* 6 (Fall 1996/Spring 1997), 139.

86. *Doe v. Poritz*, 662 A.2d 405 (N.J. 1995).

87. *Ibid.*, at 411.

88. Linda Greenhouse, "High Court Refuses to Hear Challenges to Megan's Laws," *New York Times* (February 24, 1998), A1.

89. Carey Goldberg, "In Some States, Sex Offenders Serve More Than Their Time," *New York Times* (April 22, 2001), A1.

90. *Seling v. Young*, 531 U.S. 250 (2001).

91. Lawrence A. Greenfeld, "Sixty Percent of Convicted Sex Offenders Are on Parole or Probation," *Bureau of Justice Statistics News Release* (February 2, 1997).

CHAPTER 14
THE JUVENILE JUSTICE SYSTEM

Chapter Objectives

After reading this chapter, you should be able to:

1. Describe the child saving movement and its relationship to the doctrine of *parens patria*.

2. List the four major differences between juvenile courts and adult courts.

3. Identify and briefly describe the single most important Supreme Court case with respect to juvenile justice.

4. Describe the four primary stages of pretrial juvenile justice procedure.

5. Explain the distinction between an adjudicatory hearing and a disposition hearing.

6. List the four categories of residential treatment programs.

7. Describe the one variable that always correlates highly with juvenile crime rates.

INTRODUCTION
Old Enough to Do the Crime . . .

ike many other states, Florida reacted to a dramatic increase in juvenile crime rates in the late 1980s and early 1990s by "getting tough" on young offenders. One of the "toughest" measures was a mandatory sentencing law that requires juveniles convicted of first degree murder to receive a life sentence with no parole, as adults do. Many Floridians began to question the law in the wake of two murder trials involving teen-age boys.[1] In the first, thirteen-year-old Nathaniel Brazill was charged with killing his English teacher after being sent home for throwing water balloons. In the second, twelve-year-old Lionel Tate was indicted for the death of a six-year-old playmate.[2] Both boys were convicted in 2001 when they were fourteen years old; Tate was sent to prison for life while Brazill was eventually sentenced to twenty-eight years without parole. The Tate case—in which the defendant claimed he was imitating a pro wrestler he had seen on television when the death occurred—seemed particularly severe to observers, considering the tender age of the boy. Judge Joel Lazarus, however, called Tate's actions "cold, callous, and indescribably cruel," and said the sentence was just.[3]

Not all participants in the criminal justice system are so eager to punish. A year before Brazill and Tate were convicted, a state judge in Michigan ruled that Nathaniel Abraham, the youngest American ever charged and convicted for the adult crime of murder, would serve only a seven-year sentence in a juvenile detention center. In sentencing Abraham, who killed a man with a rifle when he was eleven years old, Judge Eugene A. Moore rejected the possibility of a twenty-five-year prison sentence, which he denounced as too harsh.[4]

The different sentencing approaches taken by legislators in Florida and the Michigan judge highlight a debate that goes to the basis of the American juvenile justice system, which has been both hailed as one of the "greatest social inventions of modern times" and criticized for "failing to protect either the legal rights of the juvenile offenders or of the public on whom they prey."[5] The question: Should criminal acts by youths be given the same weight as those committed by adults or seen as "mistakes" that can be "corrected" by the state?

For most of its century-long history, the system was dominated by the latter philosophy; only recently have political trends summarized by the sound bite "old enough to do the crime, old enough to do the time" gained widespread acceptance. Since 1992, forty-four states have changed their laws to make it easier to try juveniles as adults, representing a shift toward harsher measures in a juvenile justice system that generally acts as a "compromise between rehabilitation and punishment, treatment and custody."[6]

In this chapter, we will discuss the successes and failures of this compromise and examine the aspects of the juvenile justice system that differentiate it from the criminal justice system. As you will see, observers on both sides of the "rehabilitation versus punishment" debate find many flaws with the present system; some have even begun to argue for its complete dismantling. Others blame social problems such as poverty, racism, and a culture dominated by images of violence for creating a situation that no government agency or policy can effectively control.[7]

Lionel Tate, right, is taken from the Fort Lauderdale, Florida, courtroom where, in 2001, he was sentenced to life in prison for killing a playmate. (AP Photo/Lou Toman, Pool)

JUVENILE DELINQUENCY
Behavior that is illegal under federal or state law that has been committed by a person who is under an age limit specified by statute.

FIGURE 14.1
Status Offenses

A status offense is an act that, if committed by a juvenile, is considered grounds for apprehension and perhaps state custody. The same act, if committed by an adult, does not warrant law enforcement action.

Status Offenses

1. Smoking cigarettes
2. Drinking alcohol
3. Being truant (skipping school)
4. Disobeying teachers
5. Running away from home
6. Violating curfew
7. Participating in sexual activity
8. Using profane language

INFOTRAC®
COLLEGE EDITION

Keyword: juvenile delinquency

a specified age (see Figure 14.1). In contrast, **juvenile delinquency** refers to conduct that would be criminal if committed by an adult.

Constitutional Protections and the Juvenile Court

Though the ideal of the juvenile court seemed to offer the "best of both worlds" for juvenile offenders, in reality the lack of procedural protections led to many children being arbitrarily punished not only for crimes, but for status offenses. Juvenile judges were treating all violators similarly, which led to many status offenders being incarcerated in the same institutions as violent delinquents. In response to a wave of lawsuits demanding due process rights for juveniles, the United States Supreme Court issued several rulings in the 1960s and 1970s that significantly changed the juvenile justice system.

Kent v. United States.　　The first decision to extend due process rights to children in juvenile courts was *Kent v. United States* (1966).[12] The case concerned sixteen-year-old Morris Kent, who had been arrested for breaking into a woman's house, stealing her purse, and raping her. Because Kent was on juvenile probation, the state sought to transfer his trial for the crime to an adult court (a process to be discussed later in the chapter). Without giving any reasons for his decision, the juvenile judge consented to this judicial waiver, and Kent was sentenced in the adult court to a thirty- to ninety-year prison term. The Supreme Court overturned the sentence, ruling that juveniles have a right to counsel and a hearing in any instance in which the juvenile judge is considering sending the case to an adult court. The Court stated that, in jurisdiction waiver cases, a child receives "the worst of both worlds," getting neither the "protections accorded to adults" nor the "solicitous care and regenerative treatment" offered in the juvenile system.[13]

In re Gault.　　*Kent* provided the groundwork for *In re Gault* one year later. Considered by many the single most important case concerning juvenile justice, *In re Gault* involved a young offender who was arrested for allegedly making a lewd phone call while on probation.[14] (See *CJ in Focus—Landmark Cases: In re Gault*.) In its decision, the Supreme Court held that juveniles are entitled to many of the same due process rights granted to adult offenders, including notice of charges, the right to counsel, the privilege against self-incrimination, and the right to confront and cross-examine witnesses.

Other Important Court Decisions.　　Over the next ten years, the Supreme Court handed down three more important rulings on juvenile court procedure. *In re Winship* (1970)[15] required the government to prove "beyond a reasonable doubt" that a juvenile had committed an act of delinquency, raising the burden of proof from a "preponderance of the evidence." In *Breed v. Jones* (1975),[16] the Court held that the Fifth Amendment's double jeopardy clause prevented a juvenile from being tried in an adult court for a crime that had already been adjudicated in juvenile court. In contrast, *McKeiver v. Pennsylvania* (1971)[17] represented the one instance in which the Court did not move the juvenile court further toward the adult model. It ruled that the Constitution did not give juveniles the right to a jury trial.

DETERMINING DELINQUENCY TODAY

In the eyes of many observers, the net effect of the Supreme Court decisions during the 1966–1975 period was to move juvenile justice away from the ideals of the child savers and toward a formalized system that is often indistinguishable from

CJ in FCUS

Landmark Cases: *In re Gault*

In 1964, fifteen-year-old Gerald Gault and a friend were arrested for making lewd telephone calls to a neighbor in Gila County, Arizona. Gault, who was on probation, was placed under custody with no notice given to his parents. The juvenile court in his district held a series of informal hearings to determine Gault's punishment. During these hearings, no records were kept, Gault was not afforded the right to counsel, and the complaining witness was never made available for questioning. At the close of the hearing, the judge sentenced Gault to remain in Arizona's State Industrial School until the age of twenty-one. The defendant filed a writ of *habeas corpus,* claiming that he had been denied due process rights at his hearing. The Arizona Supreme Court affirmed the dismissal of this writ, ruling that the proceedings did not infringe on Gault's due process rights, a matter eventually taken up by the United States Supreme Court.

In re Gault
United States Supreme Court
387 U.S. 1 (1967)
http://laws.findlaw.com/US/387/1.html

IN THE WORDS OF THE COURT . . .

Mr. Justice FORTAS, majority opinion

* * * *

From the inception of the juvenile court system, wide differences have been tolerated—indeed insisted upon—between the procedural rights accorded to adults and those of juveniles. In practically all jurisdictions, there are rights granted to adults which are withheld from juveniles.

* * * *

Accordingly, the highest motives and most enlightened impulses led to a peculiar system for juveniles, unknown to our law in any comparable context. The constitutional and theoretical basis for this peculiar system is—to say the least—debatable. And in practice, as we remarked in the *Kent* case, the results have not been entirely satisfactory. * * * The absence of substantive standards has not necessarily meant that children receive careful, compassionate, individualized treatment. The absence of procedural rules based upon constitutional principle has not always produced fair, efficient, and effective procedures. Departures from established principles of due process have frequently resulted not in enlightened procedure, but in arbitrariness.

* * * *

Ultimately, however, we confront the reality of that portion of the Juvenile Court process with which we deal in this case. A boy is charged with misconduct. The boy is committed to an institution where he may be restrained of liberty for years. It is of no constitutional consequence—and of limited practical meaning—that the institution to which he is committed is called an Industrial School. The fact of the matter is that, however euphemistic the title, a "receiving home" or an "industrial school" for juveniles is an institution of confinement in which the child is incarcerated for a greater or lesser time. His world becomes "a building with whitewashed walls, regimented routine and institutional hours . . . ." Instead of mother and father and sisters and brothers and friends and classmates, his world is peopled by guards, custodians, state employees, and "delinquents" confined with him for anything from waywardness to rape and homicide. In view of this, it would be extraordinary if our Constitution did not require the procedural regularity and the exercise of care implied in the phrase "due process." Under our Constitution, the condition of being a boy does not justify a kangaroo court.

* * * *

DECISION

The Court held that juveniles were entitled to the basic procedural safeguards afforded by the Fourteenth Amendment, including the right to advance notice of charges, the right to counsel, the right to confront and cross-examine witnesses, and the privilege against self-incrimination. The decision marked a turning point in juvenile justice in this country: no longer would informality and paternalism be the guiding principles of juvenile courts. Instead, due process would dictate the adjudication process, much as in an adult court.

FOR CRITICAL ANALYSIS
What might be some of the negative consequences of the *In re Gault* decision for juveniles charged with committing delinquent acts?

 For more information and activities related to this case, go to the Landmark Cases feature at **http://cj.wadsworth.com/ gainescore2e**

its adult counterpart. But, though the Court has recognized that minors possess certain constitutional rights, it has failed to dictate at what age these rights should be granted and at what age minors are to be held criminally responsible for delinquent actions. Consequently, the legal status of children in the United States varies depending on where they live, with each state making its own policy decisions on the crucial questions of age and competency.

The Age Question

When a six-year-old and a younger friend smothered her three-year-old brother to death with a pillow in Blythe, California, authorities refused to press charges. Under state law, they could have done so if they could prove that the girls knew the "wrongfulness" of their action. The local district attorney said that the system was "not prepared to do anything with kids five or six years old."[18]

Under common law, a child under the age of seven was considered to lack the requisite *mens rea* to commit a crime. (That is, he or she did not possess the mental capacity to understand the consequences of his or her action.) Also under common law, a child between the ages of seven and fourteen could use the defense of infancy (being a minor) to plead innocent. On attaining fourteen years of age, the youth was considered an adult and treated accordingly.[19]

Today, as Figure 14.2 shows, twenty-six states and the District of Columbia do not have age restrictions in prosecuting juveniles as adults. Indeed, many states require juveniles who commit violent felonies such as murder, rape, or armed robbery to be waived to adult courts. When juveniles in a state without such a requirement commit a serious crime, they are given a "limited" sentence, usually meaning they cannot remain incarcerated in juvenile detention centers past their eighteenth or twenty-first birthday.

The Competency Question

One of the precepts of *parens patriae* was the assumption that children are not legally competent and must, in the absence of parental care, be protected by

INFOTRAC®
COLLEGE EDITION
Keyword: juveniles' rights

FIGURE 14.2

The Minimum Age at Which a Juvenile Can Be Tried as an Adult

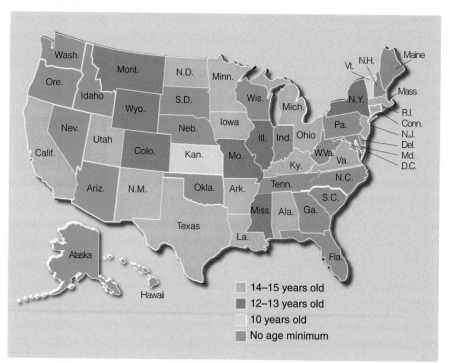

Source: Office of Juvenile Justice and Delinquency Prevention, 2002.

the state. In today's juvenile justice environment, however, the question of a minor's competency to make informed decisions about criminal actions is far more complicated.

Psychological Competency.   Most researchers believe that by the age of fourteen, an adolescent has the same ability to make a competent decision as does an adult.[20] Nevertheless, according to some observers, a juvenile's ability to theoretically understand the difference between "right" and "wrong" does not mean that she or he should be held to the same standards of competency as an adult. Legal psychologist Richard E. Redding believes that:

> adolescents' lack of life experience may limit their real-world decision-making ability. Whether we call it wisdom, judgment, or common sense, adolescents may not have nearly enough.[21]

Juveniles are generally more impulsive, more likely to engage in risky behavior, and less likely to calculate the long-term consequences of any particular action. Furthermore, adolescents are far more likely to respond to peer pressure than are adults. The desire for acceptance and approval may drive them to commit crimes; juveniles are arrested as part of a group at much higher rates than adults.[22]

Legal Competency.   In *Thompson v. Oklahoma* (1988),[23] the United States Supreme Court overturned the death penalty for a juvenile who was fifteen at the time he committed his capital crime. In ruling that such a punishment violated the Eighth Amendment's prohibition against "cruel and unusual punishment," the Court stated that a defendant that young "is not capable of acting with the degree of culpability that can justify the ultimate penalty."[24] One year later, however, the Court upheld the death penalty for sixteen- and seventeen-year-olds in *Stanford v. Kentucky* (1989).[25] Though the Court continued to hold that juveniles were less culpable than adults committing the same crime, it reversed its prior finding that capital punishment for juveniles *always* violates the Constitution. The Court basically gave states permission to determine their own age limits for executions.

PRETRIAL PROCEDURES IN JUVENILE JUSTICE

The first contact between a juvenile and the juvenile justice system (see Figure 14.3 on the next page) is made by a police officer. Even if the officer decides to arrest the juvenile for delinquent behavior, a trial is not automatic. Various decision makers are provided the opportunity to determine how the juvenile justice system will dispose of each case. The offender may be diverted to a social services program or detained in a juvenile lockup facility. In the most serious cases, the youth may even be transferred to adult court. To ensure due process during pretrial procedures, offenders and their families may retain an attorney or have one appointed by the court. The four primary stages of this critical period—intake, diversion, waiver, and detention—are discussed below.

Intake

If, following arrest, a police officer feels the offender warrants the attention of the juvenile justice process, the officer will refer the youth to juvenile court. The juvenile court receives the majority of its respondents from the police, though parents, relatives, welfare agencies, and school officials may also refer juveniles. Once this step has been taken, a complaint is filed with a special division of the

Sniper suspect John Lee Malvo, 17, is escorted from juvenile court in Fairfax, Virginia, on December 4, 2002. Malvo is charged with the shooting of FBI analyst Linda Franklin at a Home Depot store. He and sniper suspect John Allen Muhammad have been accused of killing 13 and wounding five in Alabama, Georgia, Louisiana, Maryland, Virginia, and Washington, D.C. (AP Photo/Lawrence Jackson)

On the Web

The Juvenile Justice Center is a valuable source for juvenile justice information and data. For a link to its Web site, go to the Hypercontents page for this chapter at
http://cj.wadsworth.com/gainescore2e.

FIGURE 14.3 The Juvenile Justice Process

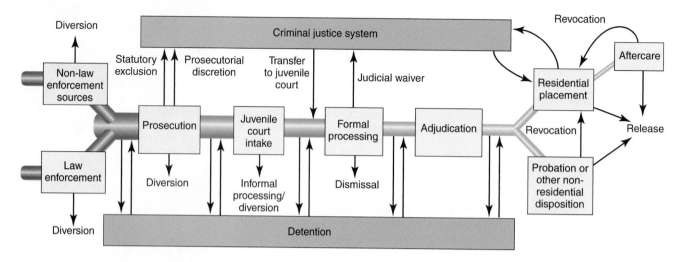

Source: Office of Juvenile Justice and Delinquency Prevention.

INFOTRAC®
COLLEGE EDITION

Keyword: juvenile courts

INTAKE
Following referral of a juvenile to juvenile court by a police officer or other concerned party, the process by which an official of the court must decide whether to file a petition, release the juvenile, or place the juvenile under some other form of supervision.

PETITION
The document filed with a juvenile court alleging that the juvenile is a delinquent or a status offender, and asking the court to either hear the case or transfer it to an adult court.

DIVERSION
The removal of an alleged juvenile delinquent from the formal criminal or juvenile justice system and the referral of that person to a treatment or rehabilitation program.

juvenile court, and the **intake** process begins. During intake, an official of the juvenile court—usually a probation officer, but sometimes a judge—must decide, in effect, what to do with the offender. The screening official has several options during intake.

1 Simply dismiss the case, releasing the offender without taking any further action.

2 Divert the offender to a social services program, such as drug rehabilitation or anger management.

3 File a **petition** for a formal court hearing.

4 Transfer the case to an adult court where the offender will be tried as an adult.

Pretrial Diversion

To a certain extent, the juvenile justice system started as a diversionary program with the goal of diverting children from the punitive adult court to the more rehabilitative juvenile court.[26] By the 1960s, many observers felt that juvenile courts had lost sight of this early mandate and were badly in need of reform. One specific target for criticism was the growing number of status offenders—40 percent of all children in the system—who were being punished even though they had not committed a truly delinquent act.

The idea of diverting certain children, including status and first-time offenders, from the juvenile court system to nonjudicial community agencies was encouraged by the President's Commission on Law Enforcement and Administration of Justice in 1967.[27] Seven years later, Congress passed the Juvenile Justice and Delinquency Prevention (JJDP) Act, which ordered the development of methods "to divert juveniles from the traditional juvenile justice system."[28] Within a few years, hundreds of diversion programs had been put into effect. Today, **diversion** refers to the process of removing low-risk offenders from the formal juvenile justice system by placing them in community-based rehabilitation programs.

Diversion programs vary widely, but fall into three general categories:

1 *Probation.* In this program, the juvenile is returned to the community, but placed under the supervision of a juvenile probation officer. If the youth breaks the conditions of probation, he or she can be returned to the formal juvenile system.

2 *Treatment and aid.* Many juveniles have behavioral or medical conditions that contribute to their delinquent behavior, and many diversion programs offer remedial education, drug and alcohol treatment, and other forms of counseling to alleviate these problems.

3 *Restitution.* In these programs, the offender "repays" her or his victim, either directly or, in the case of community service, symbolically.[29]

Proponents of diversion programs include many labeling theorists (see Chapter 2), who believe that contact with the formal juvenile justice system "labels" the youth a delinquent, which leads to further delinquent behavior.

Transfer to Adult Court

One side effect of diversionary programs is that the youths who remain in the juvenile courts are more likely to be seen as "hardened" and less amenable to rehabilitation.[30] This, in turn, increases the likelihood that the offender will be transferred to an adult court, a process in which the juvenile court waives jurisdiction over the youth. As the American juvenile justice system has shifted away from ideals of treatment and toward punishment, transfer to adult court has been one of the most popular means of "getting tough" on delinquents.

Juveniles are most commonly transferred to adult court through **judicial waiver.** In forty-eight states (excluding New York and Nebraska), the juvenile judge is the official who determines whether jurisdiction over a minor offender should be waived to adult court. The judge formulates this ruling by taking into consideration the offender's age, the nature of the offense, and any criminal history.

Thirty-four states have taken the waiver responsibility out of judicial hands through **automatic transfer,** also known as legislative waiver. In these states, the legislatures have designated certain conditions—usually involving serious crimes such as murder and rape—under which a juvenile case is automatically "kicked up" to adult court. In Rhode Island, for example, a juvenile aged sixteen or older with two prior felony adjudications will automatically be transferred on being accused of a third felony.[31] Ten states allow for **prosecutorial waiver,** in which juvenile court judges are allowed to waive jurisdiction when certain age and offense conditions are met. In general, no matter what the process, those juveniles who commit violent felonies are most likely to be transferred to an adult court (see Figure 14.4).

Detention

Once the decision has been made that the offender will face adjudication in a juvenile court, the intake official must decide what to do with him or her until the start of the trial. Generally, the juvenile is released into the custody of parents or a guardian—most jurisdictions favor this practice in lieu of setting money bail for youths. The intake officer may also place the offender in **detention,** or temporary custody in a secure facility, until the disposition process begins. Once a juvenile has been detained, most jurisdictions require that a **detention hearing** be held within twenty-four hours. During this hearing, the offender has several due process safeguards, including the right to counsel, the right against self-incrimination, and the right to cross-examine and confront witnesses.

In justifying its decision to detain, the court will usually address one of three issues:

JUDICIAL WAIVER
The process in which the juvenile judge, based on the facts of the case at hand, decides that the alleged offender should be transferred to adult court.

AUTOMATIC TRANSFER
The process by which a juvenile is transferred to adult court as a matter of state law. In some states, for example, a juvenile who is suspected of murder is automatically transferred to adult court.

PROSECUTORIAL WAIVER
A procedure in which juvenile court judges have the discretion to transfer a juvenile case to adult court, when certain predetermined conditions as to the seriousness of the offense and the age of the offender are met.

DETENTION
The temporary custody of a juvenile in a state facility after a petition has been filed and before the adjudicatory process begins.

DETENTION HEARING
A hearing to determine whether a juvenile should be detained, or remain detained, while waiting for the adjudicatory process to begin.

FIGURE 14.4 **Felony Arrest Charge for Juveniles Transferred to Adult Criminal Courts**
Two out of every three juveniles transferred to adult criminal court under suspicion of committing a felony were charged with a violent offense. The data shown here were collected in criminal courts located in the seventy-five largest counties in the United States.

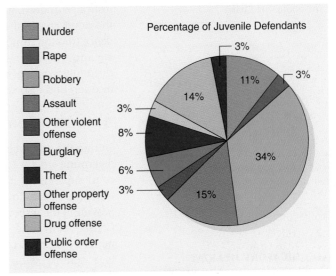

Source: Bureau of Justice Statistics, *Juvenile Felony Defendants in Criminal Courts* (Washington, D.C.: U.S. Department of Justice, September 1998), Table 2, page 2.

1 Whether the child poses a danger to the community.

2 Whether the child will return for the adjudication process.

3 Whether detention will provide protection for the child.

The Supreme Court upheld the practice of preventive detention (see Chapter 9) for juveniles in *Schall v. Martin* (1984)[32] by ruling that youths can be detained if they are deemed a "risk" to the safety of the community or to their own welfare.

On any given day, approximately 250,000 juveniles are held in detention facilities. A continuing concern for juvenile justice experts is that more than 7,600 of these youths are kept in adult jails, where they face dangerous situations caused by overcrowding and the violent and predatory nature of the adult inmates.[33] Because of the poor conditions in these jails and the exposure of minors to physical and sexual abuse from other inmates, reformers have consistently lobbied for separate adult and juvenile detention facilities.

JUVENILES ON TRIAL

Over the past thirty years, the one constant in the juvenile justice system has been change. Supreme Court rulings in the wake of *In re Gault* (1967) have increased the procedural formality and the overriding punitive philosophy of the juvenile court. Diversion policies have worked to remove many status offenders from the juvenile court's jurisdiction, and waiver policies assure that the most violent juveniles are tried as adults. Some observers feel these adjustments have "criminalized" the juvenile court, effectively rendering it indistinguishable both theoretically and practically from adult courts.[34]

Along with a number of his colleagues, law professor Barry C. Feld thinks that the juvenile court has become obsolete and should be abolished. Feld believes the changes noted above have "transformed the juvenile court from its original model as a social service agency into a deficient second-rate criminal court that provides young people with neither positive treatment nor criminal procedural justice."[35] Indeed, juvenile hearings do proceed along many of the same lines as the adult criminal court, with similar due process protections and rules of evidence (though minors do not enjoy the right to a jury trial). As *Mastering Concepts* explains, however, juvenile justice proceedings may still be distinguished from the adult system of criminal justice, and these differences are evident in the adjudication and disposition of the juvenile trial.

Adjudication

During the adjudication stage of the juvenile justice process, a hearing is held to determine whether or not the offender is delinquent or in need of some form of court supervision. Most state juvenile codes dictate a specific set of procedures that must be followed during the **adjudicatory hearing,** with the goal of providing the respondent with "the essentials of due process and fair treatment." Consequently, the respondent in an adjudicatory hearing has the right to notice of charges, counsel, confrontation and cross-examination, and the privilege against self-incrimination.[36] Furthermore, "proof beyond a reasonable doubt" must be established to find the child delinquent. When the child admits guilt—that is, admits to the charges of the initial petition—the judge must ensure that the admission was voluntary.

In a Pensacola, Florida, courtroom, fourteen-year-old Derek King, right, and his thirteen-year-old brother Alex King stand on September 6, 2002, as the jury leaves to begin deliberation in their case. The brothers were charged with first-degree murder for killing their sleeping father with a baseball bat, and thus were eligible to be tried in adult court under state law. The jury found Derek and Alex guilty, a decision later overturned by the judge. (AP Photo/Phil Coale)

INFOTRAC®
COLLEGE EDITION

Keyword: juvenile trials

ADJUDICATORY HEARING
The process through which a juvenile court determines whether there is sufficient evidence to support the initial petition.

The Criminal Justice System versus the Juvenile Justice System

When the juvenile justice system first began in the United States, its participants saw it as being separate from the adult criminal justice system. Indeed, the two systems remain separate in many ways. There are, however, a number of similarities between juvenile and adult justice. In this *Mastering Concepts,* we summarize both the similarities and the differences.

Similarities between Juvenile and Adult Justice Systems

- The right to receive the *Miranda* warning applies to both juveniles and adults.
- Juveniles and adults enjoy similar procedural protection when making an admission of guilt.
- Prosecutors and defense attorneys play equally important roles in the adjudication of adults and juveniles.
- Juveniles and adults have the right to be represented by counsel at the crucial stages of the trial process.
- Juveniles and adults have access to plea bargains.
- Juveniles and adults have the right to a hearing and an appeal.
- The standard of evidence in adult criminal trials and the juvenile delinquency process is proof beyond a reasonable doubt.
- Juveniles and adults can be placed on probation by the judge.
- Juveniles and adults can be held before adjudication if the judge believes them to be a threat to the community.
- Following trial, juveniles and adults can be sentenced to community supervision.

Differences between Juvenile and Adult Justice Systems

- The juvenile justice system is concerned with the rehabilitation of the offender, while the adult justice system is more concerned with punishment.
- Juveniles can be apprehended by law enforcement officers for acts (status offenses) that are not criminal for adults.

- Juvenile wrongdoing is considered a "delinquent act"; adult wrongdoing is considered a "crime."
- Adult criminal proceedings are more formal and regimented than juvenile proceedings.
- Juvenile court proceedings are closed to the public. Adult criminal trials are open to the public.
- Courts may not release identifying information about a juvenile facing delinquency charges to the press, while courts must release information about adults facing criminal charges.
- Parents play a significant role in the juvenile justice process. This is not the case in the criminal justice process.
- Juveniles are released into parental custody, while adults are given the opportunity to post bail when justified.
- In most, but not all, states, juveniles do not have the right to a jury trial. All adults have this right.
- Juveniles can be searched in school without probable cause. No adult can be searched without probable cause.
- A juvenile's delinquency record is sealed when the age of majority is reached. An adult's criminal record is permanent.
- Juveniles cannot be sentenced to county jails or state prisons, institutions that are reserved for adults.
- The juvenile justice system does not have a death penalty. The United States Supreme Court has ruled, however, that the Constitution does not prohibit states from punishing crimes committed by juveniles aged sixteen and seventeen with execution. Capital punishment is not allowed for those under age sixteen.

Source: Larry Siegel and Joseph Senna, *Juvenile Delinquency: Theory, Practice, and Law,* 6th ed. (St. Paul, MN: West Publishing Company, 1997), 446.

The increased presence of defense attorneys in juvenile courts has had a significant impact on juvenile adjudication. (See *Careers in Criminal Justice* on page 366.) Aspects of the adversarial system have become increasingly apparent in juvenile courts, as has the practice of plea bargaining. To a certain extent, however, juvenile trials have retained the informal atmosphere that characterized proceedings prior to the *In re Gault* decision. Respondents and their families often waive the due process rights provided by the Supreme Court at the suggestion of a juvenile probation officer or judge. One study of Minnesota juvenile courts found that no counsel was present in 50 percent of that state's adjudicatory hearings.[37]

At the close of the adjudicatory hearing, the judge is generally required to rule on the legal issues and evidence that have been presented. Based on this ruling, the judge determines whether or not the respondent is delinquent or in need of court supervision. Alternatively, the judge can dismiss the case based on a lack

Careers in Criminal Justice

Grandpa had always said I could talk my way out of the electric chair. So when a friend in college suggested applying to law school, I thought, yes, why not? I attended Seton Hall Law in Newark, New Jersey, where I participated in the Juvenile Justice Clinic for two and a half semesters. This experience representing delinquents, coupled with a childhood of being raised on *Perry Mason,* as well as a law clerkship with a Superior Court judge, helped me to recognize my strong interest in criminal law. The forum of pleading my case in open court seemed like the only place to be.

Following my clerkship, I was hired by the Office of the Public Defender. Working for the P.D. is the fastest way to be in command of your own cases and to appear in court on all kinds of matters, particularly trials. My caseload consisted of clients charged with everything from fourth degree theft to armed robbery. The first year and a

Cathy Wasserman
Public Defender: Juvenile Courts

half, I represented adults. Then I went to the Appellate Section where I wrote briefs for two and a half years. I enjoyed the treasure hunt of looking for the cases to support my arguments. I also enjoyed presenting those arguments to the Appellate Division panels. However, I found I missed being in court on a daily basis and dealing with clients in person. Thus, when the opportunity to transfer to another trial region arose, I grabbed it and began representing juveniles once again.

Every day I enter court prepared to do battle for a youngster who in all likelihood is not cognizant of how at risk his or her freedom is. Initially, my most important responsibility is to interview my client and his or her family to gain their trust, obtain information about the child, and learn their version of the facts in the case. I gather all the evidence provided by the State, review it carefully, and conduct my own investigations. Following a careful review of all the evidence available, weighing all the strengths and weaknesses in the case, and considering whether any trial would be before a judge rather than a jury, I discuss the options, risks, and penalties with my

client. Whether we go to trial or negotiate a plea agreement, my duties are to be an effective attorney for the child. However, once we face a sentence, I must also become a social worker as I attempt to fashion the least restrictive disposition from the myriad of sentencing alternatives. It is this array of options and the court's discretion to impose them which most clearly distinguishes the juvenile system from its adult counterpart.

I am an impassioned advocate for children because I believe most offenders should be allowed to survive childhood and adolescence without permanently damaging their prospects for a positive future. My skills as an attorney and negotiator give my clients the opportunity to rise above their acts, often committed through poor judgment, inexperience, or by succumbing to peer pressure. Occasionally, I make a significant difference in the life of a youngster.

Go to the
Careers in Criminal Justice Interactive CD for more profiles in the field of criminal justice.

of evidence. It is important to remember that finding a child to be delinquent is *not* the same as convicting an adult of a crime. A delinquent does not face the same restrictions, such as those concerning the right to vote and to run for political office, as do adult convicts in some states (discussed in Chapter 13).

Disposition

Once a juvenile has been adjudicated delinquent, the judge must decide what steps will be taken toward treatment and/or punishment. Most states provide for a *bifurcated process* in which a separate **disposition hearing** follows the adjudicatory hearing. Depending on state law, the juvenile may be entitled to counsel at the disposition hearing.

In an adult trial, the sentencing phase is primarily concerned with the "needs" of the community to be protected from the convict. In contrast, a juvenile judge uses the disposition hearing to determine a sentence that will serve the "needs" of the child.[38] For assistance in this crucial process, the judge will order the pro-

DISPOSITION HEARING
Similar to the sentencing hearing for adults, a hearing in which the juvenile judge or officer decides the appropriate punishment for a youth found to be delinquent or a status offender.

bation department to gather information on the juvenile and present it in the form of a **predisposition report.** The report usually contains information concerning the respondent's family background, the facts surrounding the delinquent act, and interviews with social workers, teachers, and other important figures in the child's life.

In keeping with the rehabilitative tradition of the juvenile justice system, many judges have a great deal of discretion in choosing one of several disposition possibilities. Generally, the choice is among incarceration in a juvenile correctional facility, probation, or community treatment. In most cases, seriousness of the offense is the primary factor used in determining whether to incarcerate a juvenile, though history of delinquency, family situation, and the offender's attitude are all relevant.[39] Further research suggests that race plays a significant role in disposition—that minority delinquents are more likely to be incarcerated than their white counterparts.

JUVENILE CORRECTIONS

In general, juvenile corrections is based on the concept of **graduated sanctions**—that is, the severity of the punishment should fit the crime. Consequently, status and first-time offenders are diverted or placed on probation, repeat offenders find themselves in intensive community supervision or treatment programs, and serious and violent offenders are placed in correctional facilities.[40] As society's expectations of the juvenile justice system have changed, so have the characteristics of its corrections programs. In some cities, for example, juvenile probation officers join police officers on the beat. Because the former are not bound by the same search and seizure restrictions as other law enforcement officials, this interdepartmental teamwork provides more opportunities to fight youth crime aggressively. Juvenile correctional facilities are also changing their operations to reflect public mandates that they both reform and punish. Keep in mind as well that as of 2001, 3,147 juveniles were serving time in state adult prisons.[41]

Probation and Residential Treatment Programs

The most common form of juvenile corrections is probation—35 percent of all delinquency cases disposed of by juvenile courts result in conditional diversion. The majority of all adjudicated delinquents (nearly 55 percent) will never receive a disposition more severe than being placed on probation.[42] These statistics reflect a general understanding among juvenile court judges and other officials that removing a child from her or his home should be considered primarily as a last resort.

The organization of juvenile probation is very similar to adult probation (see Chapter 11), and juvenile probationers are increasingly subjected to electronic monitoring and other supervisory tactics. The main difference between the two programs lies in the attitude toward the offender. Adult probation officers have an overriding responsibility to protect the community from the probationer, while juvenile probation officers are expected to take the role of a mentor or a concerned relative in looking after the needs of the child.[43]

When intensive supervision must be instituted, youths can be placed in **residential treatment programs.** These programs, run by either probation departments or social service organizations, provide treatment in a nonsecure living facility. Residential treatment programs can be divided into four categories:

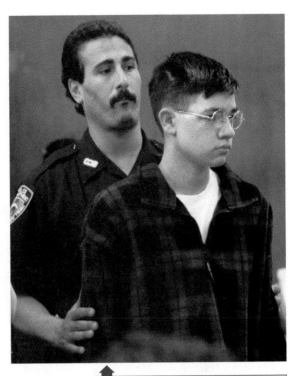

Fifteen-year-old Christopher Vasquez faced murder charges for stabbing Michael McMorrow, a forty-four-year-old man, in New York City's Central Park. The case attracted a great deal of interest because of Vasquez's age and the brutality of the crime—McMorrow was stabbed more than thirty times. Many observers felt that, despite his age, Vasquez should have received the same harsh punishment as would an adult who committed the same crime. In fact, the jury acquitted Vasquez of second degree murder, which would have carried a lifetime prison sentence. Instead he was found guilty of the less serious charge of manslaughter. Do you believe that a wrongdoer's age should be a consideration in determining punishment? (AP Photo/Kathy Willens)

PREDISPOSITION REPORT
A report prepared during the disposition process that provides the judge with relevant background material to aid in the disposition decision.

GRADUATED SANCTIONS
The practical theory in juvenile corrections that a delinquent or status offender should receive a punishment that matches in seriousness the severity of the wrongdoing.

RESIDENTIAL TREATMENT PROGRAMS
Government-run facilities for juveniles whose offenses are not deemed serious.

The State Correctional Institution at Pine Grove, Pennsylvania, offers a juvenile delinquency discussion program while at the same time providing for large numbers of newly admitted violent youth offenders. Here a prison counselor "tells it like it is" to young visitors while in the presence of current inmates. Under what circumstances might such a program work? (AP Photo/Gary Tramontina)

1 *Foster care programs,* in which the juvenile lives with a couple who act as surrogate parents, or with a single person who assumes parental duties.

2 *Group homes,* which generally house between twelve and fifteen youths and provide treatment, counseling, and educational services by a professional staff.

3 *Family group homes,* which combine aspects of foster care and group homes, meaning that a single family, rather than a group of professionals, looks after the needs of the offenders.

4 *Rural programs,* which include wilderness camps, farms, and ranches where between thirty and fifty children are placed in an environment that provides recreational activities and treatment programs.[44]

Nearly 106,000 American youths (up from 30,000 at the end of the 1970s) are incarcerated in public and private juvenile correctional facilities in the United States.[45] Most of these juveniles have committed crimes against people or property, but a significant number (about 16 percent) have been incarcerated because of other factors, such as familial neglect or mental incapacity.

RECENT TRENDS IN JUVENILE DELINQUENCY

When asked, juveniles will admit to a wide range of illegal or dangerous behavior (see Figure 14.5). Have juvenile law enforcement efforts, juvenile courts, and juvenile corrections been effective in controlling and preventing this kind of misbehavior, as well as more serious acts?

To answer this question, many observers turn to the Federal Bureau of Investigation's Uniform Crime Report (UCR), initially covered in Chapter 2. Because the UCR breaks down arrest statistics by age of the arrestee, it has been

FIGURE 14.5

Delinquent and Risky Behavior by High School Students

As you can see, a self-reported survey of high school students reveals a wide array of delinquent and dangerous behavior.

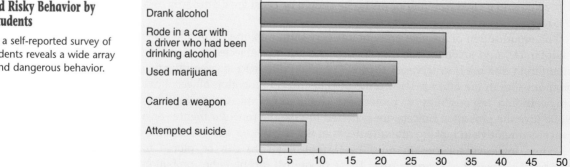

Source: Adapted from Centers for Disease Control and Prevention, *Surveillance Summaries: Youth Risk Behavior Surveillance—United States 2001,* June 28, 2002.

considered the primary source of information on the presence of juveniles in America's justice system. This does not mean, however, that the UCR is completely reliable when it comes to measuring juvenile delinquency. The process measures only those juveniles who were caught and therefore does not accurately reflect all delinquent acts in any given year. Furthermore, it measures the number of arrests but not the number of arrestees, meaning that—due to repeat offenders—the number of actual juveniles could be below the number of juvenile arrests.

Delinquency by the Numbers

With these cautions in mind, UCR findings are quite clear as to the extent of the juvenile delinquency problem in the United States today. In 2001, juveniles accounted for 15.4 percent of violent crime arrests and 16.7 percent of criminal activity arrests in general.[46] According to the 2001 UCR, juveniles were responsible for

- 10.2 percent of all murder arrests;
- 13.6 percent of all aggravated assault arrests;
- 16.8 percent of all forcible rapes;
- 22.6 percent of all weapons arrests;
- 23.6 percent of all robbery arrests;
- 30.4 percent of all property crimes; and
- 12.8 percent of all drug offenses.

Furthermore, although girls cannot compare with their male counterparts in the number of crimes they commit each year, between 1980 and 1997 the number of female juveniles arrested increased by 72 percent, compared to a 30 percent increase in arrests of male juveniles.[47]

The impact of juvenile delinquency on America's overall crime rate cannot be overstated. As Figure 14.6 shows, the ten-year period between 1985 and 1994 saw

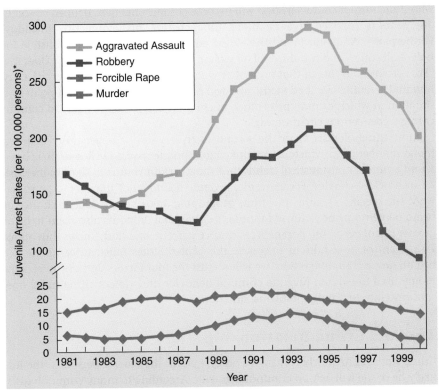

FIGURE 14.6

Arrest Rates of Juveniles, 1981-2000

After rising dramatically from 1985 to 1994, arrest rates for juveniles began to fall.

*Arrests of persons under age 18 per 100,000 persons ages 10 to 17 in the population of the United States.
Source: Office of Juvenile Justice and Delinquency Prevention

a drastic rise in the rate of juvenile arrests. Especially distressing were juvenile violent crime arrest trends: murder arrests alone rose 150 percent over that decade. Further scrutiny of UCR research reveals an especially disturbing trend: the juvenile crime rate rose faster than the overall crime rate. Violent crimes committed by youths rose by over 60 percent in the 1990s, even as the overall violent crime rate dropped.

Is Juvenile Crime Leveling Off?

Just as Figure 14.6 on page 369 paints a bleak picture of the years between 1985 and 1994, it also shows that arrest rates have fallen off in many categories since then. From 1994 to 2001, the number of juveniles arrested for murder dropped about 75 percent, along with decreases of about 60 percent in arrests for robberies, about 33 percent for motor vehicle theft, and about 40 percent for burglary.[48] Furthermore, even though high-profile shootings continue to thrust the issue of school violence to the forefront of the juvenile crime debate, the numbers are promising in that area as well. (For a discussion of a new theory concerning these shootings, see the feature *Criminal Justice in Action—The Bully Problem* at the end of this chapter.) School-associated violent deaths fell 70 percent from the 1992–1993 academic year to the 1999–2000 academic year.[49] So, while the juvenile arrest rates for some crimes, such as fraud, embezzlement, and driving under the influence, are still rising, the overall situation is not as bleak as it was at the height of the youth crime wave in the mid-1990s. (For more information on steps being taken to protect students in school, see the feature *Criminal Justice & Technology— The Electronic Hall Monitor* on the next page.)

FACTORS IN JUVENILE DELINQUENCY

In one of the most influential studies in the field of criminology, Professor Marvin Wolfgang found that 6 percent of all boys in any given cohort (group of persons who share similar characteristics) will become chronic offenders, defined as someone who is arrested five or more times before his eighteenth birthday. Furthermore, Wolfgang found that these chronic offenders were responsible for half of all crimes and two-thirds of all violent crimes within the cohort.[50] Does this "Six Percent Rule" mean that no matter what steps society takes, six out of every hundred juveniles are "bad seeds" and will act delinquently? Or does it point to a situation in which a small percentage of children may be more likely to commit crimes under certain circumstances?

Most criminologists favor the second interpretation. It is generally believed that a number of "risk factors" are linked to delinquent activity. Researchers have found a number of statistical trends that show certain youths to be at higher risk for antisocial behavior. For example, juvenile delinquency appears to be somewhat site specific—youths in certain geographic areas have a higher chance of being perpetrators or victims of murder. High school dropouts also seem to be at greater risk of becoming part of Wolfgang's 6 percent; one study shows that about 70 percent of all adults in prison in the United States failed to complete the twelfth grade.[51] In this section, we will discuss the four factors that are most commonly used to explain juvenile criminal behavior and violent crime rates: age, substance abuse, family problems, and gangs.

The Age-Crime Relationship

Crime statistics are fairly conclusive on one point: the older a person is, the less likely he or she will exhibit criminal behavior. According to many criminologists, particularly Travis Hirschi and Michael Gottfredson, age is the one constant fac-

Criminal Justice & TECHNOLOGY

The Electronic Hall Monitor

Americans are accustomed to being watched. Surveillance cameras are commonplace in banks, stores, office lobbies, and airports. But how about schools? Increasingly, the student hall monitor is being replaced by the electronic eye—or even better, dozens of electronic eyes.

Following the lead of colleagues across the United States, officials at Mansfield High, located just outside of Boston, recently installed fourteen cameras in the school's halls and entryways. A video feed is piped into two television monitors in the school office, allowing administrators to watch and record a great deal of student activity. During their first year of operation, the devices were mainly successful in recording and consequently preventing acts of petty vandalism. Their main purpose, however, is to "create an atmosphere of safety," says principal Peter Deftos. In other words, Deftos and other proponents of using cameras in schools believe they will protect against acts of violence such as occurred in Columbine High School in Colorado in 1999, when two students shot and killed fourteen fellow students and a teacher.

Not everyone is convinced that the cameras can be effective in deterring such shootings. First, because of privacy concerns schools will generally not place cameras in bathrooms or classrooms, thereby severely limiting their scope and effectiveness. Second, just because school officials may be able to see a student with a gun walking down the hall, there is no guarantee that the official will be able to stop that student from committing a crime. In fact, Columbine High was equipped with hall cameras at the time of the tragedy.

Surveillance cameras in Columbine High School in Littleton, Colorado, show Eric Harris, left, and Dylan Klebold during their April 20, 1999, shooting spree in which they killed fourteen students and one teacher. (AP Photo/Jefferson County Sheriff's Department)

IN THE FUTURE

What if not only school officials could monitor the hallways, but also law enforcement officers? *Safewatch* is a real-time video monitoring system that allows the police to view the images from as many as ten cameras at one time on a Web browser. In order to protect student and teacher privacy, systems such as Safewatch remain dormant until activated by a trigger such as a 911 call, somewhat limiting their effectiveness in preventing a student or intruder from initiating a violent event. Because almost all police stations, as well as many police cars, are equipped with computer screens, however, officers responding to a crisis at a school would have the invaluable advantage of an electronic eye on the events within. "We could use the cameras to see inside the building before we sent in officers," said one police official. "It could save lives."

tor in criminal behavior, more important than gender, race, intelligence, or class.[52] Any group of at-risk persons—whether they be high school dropouts or (as we shall see) the children of abusive parents—will commit fewer crimes as they grow older. This process is known as **aging out.**

Another view sees the **age of onset,** or the age at which the youth begins delinquent behavior, as a consistent predictor of future criminal behavior. One study compared recidivism rates between juveniles first judged to be delinquent before the age of fifteen and those first adjudicated delinquent after the age of fifteen. Of the seventy-one subjects who made up the first group, 32 percent became chronic offenders. Of the sixty-five who made up the second group, none became chronic offenders.[53] This research suggests that juvenile justice resources should be concentrated on the youngest offenders, with the goal of preventing crime and reducing the long-term risks for society.

AGING OUT
A term used to explain the fact that criminal activity declines with age.

AGE OF ONSET
The age at which a juvenile first exhibits delinquent behavior. The earlier the age of onset, according to some observers, the greater the chance a person will become a career offender.

> *"My homeboys became my family—the older ones were father figures. Each time I shot someone, each time I put another gun on the set, each time I successfully recruited a combat soldier, I was congratulated by my older homeboys."*
>
> —Sanyka Shakur, *former gang member* (1993)

INFOTRAC®
COLLEGE EDITION

Keywords: juveniles and substance abuse

CHILD ABUSE
Mistreatment of children by causing physical, emotional, or sexual damage without any plausible explanation, such as an accident.

CHILD NEGLECT
A form of child abuse in which the child is denied certain necessities such as shelter, food, care, and love. Neglect is justification for a government agency to assume responsibility for a child in place of the parents or legal guardian.

Substance Abuse

As we have seen throughout this textbook, substance abuse plays a strong role in criminal behavior for adults. The same can certainly be said for juveniles. According to the Office of National Drug Control Policy, nearly 10 million Americans under the age of twenty consume alcohol each year, increasing the probability that they will experience academic problems, drop out of school, or commit acts of vandalism (the willful destruction of property).[54] The health consequences of this level of underage drinking are staggering: alcohol is a factor in between 50 and 65 percent of all teenage suicides, and nearly 2,500 youths are killed each year in alcohol-related automobile crashes.

There are signs that some use of illegal drugs and alcohol is increasing, if slightly. According to the Substance Abuse and Mental Health Services Administration, the rate of illicit drug use in the twelve-to-seventeen age group rose two percent from 2000 to 2001. A similar increase in alcohol use was noted over this time period.[55]

These statistics do not seem to be reflected in arrest rates for drug- and alcohol-related crimes. From 1997 to 2001, for example, juvenile arrests for drunkenness declined 21.1 percent.[56] And, although arrests for drug abuse violations continued to increase until 1997, they decreased 7.2 percent between 1997 and 2001.[57] There is still little doubt, however, that substance abuse plays a major role in juvenile delinquency and crime. A male between the ages of twelve and seventeen who uses drugs is eight times more likely to be arrested for any offense, and a female in that age range who uses drugs is eleven times more likely to be arrested.[58] In fact, many criminologists point out that increases in juvenile violence began in 1985, the same year that marked the start of the recent rise in juvenile arrests for drug use and trafficking.[59]

Child Abuse and Neglect

Abuse by parents also plays a substantial role in juvenile delinquency. **Child abuse** can be broadly defined as the infliction of physical or emotional damage on a child, while **child neglect** refers to deprivations—of love, shelter, food, proper care—children undergo by their parents. A significant portion (estimates can range from 40 percent[60] to 88 percent[61]) of parents who mistreat their children are believed to be under the influence of illegal drugs or alcohol. (See your *Careers CD-ROM* for information on *social workers,* who are trained to alleviate family problems related to juveniles.)

Children in homes characterized by violence or neglect suffer from a variety of physical, emotional, and mental health problems at a much greater rate than their peers.[62] This, in turn, increases their chances of engaging in delinquent behavior. Research done for the Office of Juvenile Justice and Delinquency Prevention by David Huizinga, Rolf Loeber, and Terence Thornberry, for example, recently found that a history of maltreatment increases the chances of a youth being violent by 24 percent.[63] Another survey of violent juveniles showed that 75 percent had suffered severe abuse by a family member, 80 percent had witnessed violence in their home, 33 percent had a sibling with a criminal record, and 25 percent had at least one parent who abused drugs or alcohol.[64]

Cathy Spatz Widom, a professor of criminal justice and psychology at the State University of New York at Albany, compared the arrest records of two groups of subjects—one made up of 908 cases of substantiated parental abuse and neglect and the other made up of 667 children who had not been abused or neglected. Widom found that those who had been abused or neglected were 53 percent more likely to be arrested as juveniles than those who had not.[65]

Gangs

When youths cannot find the stability and support they require in the family structure, they will often turn to their peers. This is just one explanation for why juveniles join **youth gangs.** Although jurisdictions may have varying definitions, for general purposes a youth gang is viewed as a group of three or more persons who (1) self-identify themselves as an entity separate from the community by special clothing, vocabulary, hand signals, and names and (2) engage in criminal activity. Although the first gangs may have appeared at the time of the American Revolution in the 1780s, there have been four periods of major gang activity in American history: the late 1800s, the 1920s, the 1960s, and the 1990s and early 2000s. According to an exhaustive survey of law enforcement agencies, there are probably around 29,000 gangs with more than 780,000 members in the United States.[66]

According to estimates, approximately 3,300 gang-related homicides were committed in 1997, accounting for 18 percent of all homicides committed that year.[67] Statistics also show high levels of gang involvement in aggravated assault, larceny, and motor vehicle theft, while 42 percent of all youth gangs are believed to be involved in drug sales.[68] Furthermore, a recent study of criminal behavior among juveniles in Cleveland found that gang members were considerably more likely to commit crimes than at-risk youths who shared many characteristics with gang members but were not affiliated with any gang (see Figure 14.7).[69] The gang members in Cleveland were also much more likely to own firearms or to have friends who owned firearms.

Guns

The correlation between access to guns and juveniles' homicide rates is striking. The juvenile arrest rate for weapons violations doubled between 1987 and 1993. By 1994, 82 percent of all homicides committed by juveniles involved a handgun. Then, as the homicide rate began to drop, so did the arrest rate for weapons

INFOTRAC®
COLLEGE EDITION

Keyword: youth gangs

YOUTH GANGS
Self-formed groups of youths with several identifiable characteristics, including a gang name and other recognizable symbols, a geographic territory, a leadership structure, a meeting pattern, and participation in illegal activities.

On the Web

For more information on gangs and crime, visit the National Youth Gang Center's home page. To learn about the issues surrounding school violence, go to the Center for the Prevention of School Violence's Web site. For a link to both Web sites, go to the Hypercontents page for this chapter at **http://cj.wadsworth.com/ gainescore2e.**

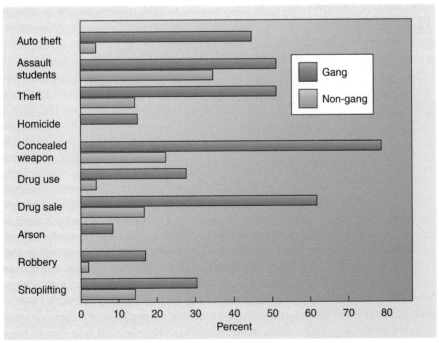

Source: C. Ronald Huff, *Comparing the Criminal Behavior of Youth Gangs and At-Risk Youths* (Washington, D.C.: U.S. Department of Justice, October 1998), 4.

FIGURE 14.7

Comparison of Gang and Non-gang At-Risk Youth Criminal Behavior

Matching gang and nongang youths for age, race, education, and other personal characteristics, C. Ronald Huff found that the gang members were much more likely to commit violent and property offenses.

offenses, and many experts believe that the downward trend in juvenile homicide arrests from 1993 to 1999 can be traced largely to a decline in firearm usage.[70]

Despite these encouraging trends, guns are still widespread in youth culture. A 2000 survey by the Josephson Institute of Ethics found that 47 percent of high school and 22 percent of middle school students said they could obtain a gun if they felt the need.[71] Almost 26,000 juveniles were arrested for gun-related crimes in 2001,[72] and the firearm homicide rate in the United States is more than twice that of Finland, the industrial country with the next highest rate.[73]

KEEPING JUVENILE DELINQUENCY UNDER CONTROL

Though the decrease in juvenile crime over the past few years has been welcome, many criminologists and law enforcement officials have expressed concern that this recent drop in youth crime will lead to a sense of complacency among their colleagues. Any such decline, they believe, should be seen in the context of the immense growth in delinquency since 1985. Furthermore, the factors we have just discussed—substance abuse by adults and adolescents, child abuse and neglect, guns, gang membership—continue to plague juveniles.

The Office of the Surgeon General, which produced a far-reaching report on juvenile violence in 2001, also cautions that the "war against youth crime" has not been won. Even as crime statistics have shown a decrease since 1994, self-reports of violent offending show no decline at all. In other words, when researchers ask juveniles about their violent behavior, the answers suggest that delinquency and youth crime are still quite high, leading the report to conclude that "the rise and fall in arrest rates are set against a backdrop of ongoing violent behavior."[74]

Three general strategies are being put in place to deal with juvenile delinquency—and its possible increase—in the near future. The first, transfer to adult court, was discussed earlier in the chapter and is based on the notion that harsher punishments will deter juvenile crime. The second, known as *social control regulation*, aims to prevent crime by changing behavior without addressing underlying causes. Examples of social control regulation would be

GREAT DEBATES

Some observers feel that popular culture is another "risk factor," and bears some of the blame for delinquent behavior in juveniles. To better understand this controversial issue, go to the Great Debates feature on the text's companion Web site at **http://cj.wadsworth.com/ gainescore2e**.

- *Juvenile curfews,* which restrict the movements of minors during certain hours, usually after dark. Juvenile arrests for curfew violations and loitering increased 64 percent between 1990 and 2000.[75]

- *Parental responsibility statutes,* which make parents responsible in some way for the offenses of their children. At present, forty-two states have enacted these statutes; seventeen of these states hold the parents *criminally* liable for their child's actions, punishing them with fines, community service, and even jail time.

The third method of juvenile prevention can be found in community-based programs that attempt to improve the chances that at-risk youth will not turn to crime. These programs may try to educate children about the dangers of drugs and crime, or they may counsel parents who abuse their children. Today, nearly a thousand private and public groups hold after-school workshops to prevent youth violence. Though the results of community-based efforts are difficult, if not impossible, to measure—it cannot be assumed that children would have become delinquent if they did not participate—they are generally considered a crucial element in keeping youth crime under control.

Criminal Justice in Action

The Bully Problem

From 1997 to 2002, juveniles wielding firearms killed thirty-one students and four teachers on school grounds in the United States. Although, as noted earlier in the chapter, these figures represent only a small percentage of all youth violence, shootings at schools have focused public attention on the problems surrounding juvenile delinquency and crime. As we will discuss in this feature, this attention has led to intense scrutiny of behavior that is as common on school grounds as homicides are rare.

"A Normal Kid"

Students said the noise that echoed through the halls at Santana High School in Santee, California, on the morning of March 5, 2001, sounded like "firecrackers." Instead, it was the sound of shots from a .22 caliber revolver. One of their classmates, a fifteen-year-old named Charles Andrew Williams, had opened fire inside the boys' bathroom, killing two students and injuring thirteen other people.

As investigators looked into Williams's background, a picture of "a normal kid" emerged. Part of that normality, however, was a pattern of taunting by some of his older and larger schoolmates. "He was picked on all the time," said one sophomore at Santana High. "He was picked on because he was one of the scrawniest guys. People called him freak, dork, nerd, stuff like that."[76] The stories of bullying brought back memories of the fatal shootings two years earlier at Columbine High School near Littleton, Colorado. There, two students who claimed to have been mistreated by other students killed fourteen students and a teacher.

Other incidents also seemed to point to a connection between bullying and violent, retaliatory behavior. In 2000, fourteen-year-old Sean Botkin held thirty-two former classmates and a teacher hostage for an hour with a 9-mm handgun. After being persuaded to surrender, he said in a television interview that he was unhappy at being picked on and that, "Using a gun would get their attention more than just walking into school and saying 'I need help,' or something."[77]

Taking on Bullies

The first large-scale national study of bullying in American schools was released about six weeks after the killings at Santana High. Of nearly 16,000 students interviewed, 10.6 percent reported being bullied "sometimes" or "weekly," and 13 percent

admitted to having bullied others. About 6 percent said they had been both the targets of and the perpetrators of bullying. The bullying seemed to be most intense among the younger students: the researchers found that about a quarter of all middle school children had been involved in behavior that included threats, ridicule, name calling, punching, slapping, and taunting.[78]

These figures came as no surprise to many observers, who see bullying as a normal, if unfortunate, aspect of growing up. In the wake of the Columbine High tragedy, however, both schools and legislators have taken measures to, if not eliminate the behavior, at least keep it from leading to violence. Hundreds of schools have instituted "zero tolerance" policies that impose harsh penalties on what in the past might have been seen as unthreatening behavior. A third-grader in Hudson, Ohio, for example, was suspended from school for writing the words "You will die an honorable death" during a fortune-cookie writing project, while a seven-year-old Cincinnati elementary student was suspended for bringing a cap gun on the school bus. Many school authorities have banned the game of dodgeball, which experts say fosters overly aggressive behavior and stigmatizes less athletic students.[79]

In 2001, lawmakers in Colorado passed a law—similar to measures already on the books in several other states,

Continued on next page

Students from Santana High School in Santee, California, gather at a memorial service for two students shot and killed by classmate Charles Andrew Williams in 2001. (AP Photo/Michael Caulfield)

including New Hampshire and Georgia—requiring every school district in the state to draw up a policy aimed at stopping student bullying.[80] That same year, the Washington State Senate passed a bill that would not only prohibit harassment and intimidating behavior at schools but would direct schools to notify the parents of the "bulliers" of their children's behavior.[81]

WARNING SIGNS

But some experts criticize such policies and laws as an oversimplification of the problem of school violence. One clinical psychologist pointed out that if bullying were the actual cause of such incidents, "we would have millions of school shootings each year."[82] Instead, bullying appears to be only one piece of the puzzle, which includes violence and instability in the home, depression, violence in the culture at large, and the availability of firearms.

In fact, the best way to stem school violence seems to be to convince students to take threats of violence by their peers seriously. The weekend before he came to school with the gun, Williams had told several other students and at least one adult about his plans. This is apparently typical behavior in such cases. The U.S. Secret Service found that in almost three-quarters of the thirty-seven school shootings that have taken place in this country since 1974, the shooters told someone what they were going to do.[83] Within three days after the killings at Santana High, eight other juveniles in southern California were arrested when students alerted law enforcement authorities of their plans for "copycat" violence.[84]

THE ILLUSION OF SAFETY?

Why did those to whom Williams had boasted keep silent about his scheme? The answer may lie in a government study that measured fear of crime in schools. The report found that twice as many African American and Hispanic students as white students are afraid of school violence.[85] In particular, the town of Santee, where Santana High is located, has the second lowest crime rate of any jurisdiction in San Diego County.[86] Thus, Williams's classmates may have found it hard to imagine that "it could happen here."

This lack of fear points to a crucial fact concerning school violence: even though minority youths living in low-income, urban areas have much higher rates of victimization, the majority of all school shootings take place in rural or suburban areas and are perpetrated by white students. Since the mid-1990s, when crime at inner-city schools reached its peak, many such schools have hired security guards and adopted other safety measures such as metal detectors. It is highly unlikely, for example, that Williams could have easily carried his gun into Ballou High School, which is located in a high-crime area of Washington, D.C. At Ballou High, students must pass through a metal detec-

> *"You'll never get over it, but you have to try. It's scary that someone might decide to bring a gun tomorrow, maybe, and do the same thing."*
>
> —Sean Kaiser, *senior at Santana High School in Santee, California, where classmate Charles Andrew Williams shot and killed two and wounded thirteen others* (2001)

tor each time they enter the school and are constantly under observation by five security guards.

Another explanation is that guns are not considered as dangerous in rural areas as in metropolitan ones. Whereas a teenager carrying a gun near Ballou High would set off a certain number of warning bells, it is relatively common for rural youths to have firearms for hunting and target practice. Indeed, Williams appeared to have easy access to his father's gun collection, where he obtained the firearm that he eventually used on his classmates.

It seems unlikely, however, that the recent spate of school shootings will change the attitudes of those who live in the "safest" parts of the United States. "There has never been a need for metal detectors here," said a member of the Santee City Council. "We don't even have a gang problem."[87]

MAKING SENSE OF THE BULLY PROBLEM AND SCHOOL VIOLENCE

1 Why might schools in low-crime areas be reluctant to take safety measures such as setting up metal detectors or hiring security guards? Is this reluctance justified?

2 What would be your main concerns if you were to set up a policy against bullying at schools? Do you think any policy or plan could effectively stop such behavior?

3 Do you favor "zero tolerance" plans that punish any hint of violent or illegal behavior at schools? What are the advantages and drawbacks of such plans?

INFOTRAC®
COLLEGE EDITION

Keyword: juvenile crime

KEY TERMS

adjudicatory hearing   364

age of onset   371

aging out   371

automatic transfer   363

child abuse   372

child neglect   372

detention   363

detention hearing   363

disposition hearing   366

diversion   362

graduated sanctions   367

intake   362

judicial waiver   363

juvenile delinquency   358

parens patriae   356

petition   362

predisposition report   367

prosecutorial waiver   363

residential treatment programs   367

status offender   357

youth gangs   373

CHAPER SUMMARY

❶ Describe the child saving movement and its relationship to the doctrine of *parens patriae*. Under the doctrine of *parens patriae,* the state has a right and a duty to care for neglected, delinquent, or disadvantaged children. The child saving movement, based on the doctrine of *parens patriae,* started in the 1800s. Its followers believed that juvenile offenders require treatment rather than punishment.

❷ List the four major differences between juvenile courts and adult courts. (a) No juries, (b) different terminology, (c) limited adversarial relationship, and (d) confidentiality.

❸ Identify and briefly describe the single most important Supreme Court case with respect to juvenile justice. The case was *In re Gault,* decided by the Supreme Court in 1967. In this case a minor was arrested for allegedly making an obscene phone call. His parents were not notified. They were not present during the juvenile court judge's decision-making process. In this case, the Supreme Court held that juveniles are entitled to many of the same due process rights granted to adult offenders, including notice of charges, the right to counsel, the privilege against self-incrimination, and the right to confront and cross-examine witnesses.

❹ Describe the four primary stages of pretrial juvenile justice procedure. (a) Intake—when an official of the juvenile court engages in a screening process to determine what to do with the youthful offender; (b) pretrial diversion—which may consist of probation, treatment and aid, and/or restitution; (c) jurisdictional waiver to an adult court—in which case the youth leaves the juvenile justice system; and (d) some type of detention in which the youth is held until the disposition process begins.

❺ Explain the distinction between an adjudicatory hearing and a disposition hearing. An adjudicatory hearing is essentially the "trial." Defense attorneys may be present during the adjudicatory hearing in juvenile courts in some states. In many states, once adjudication has occurred, there is a separate disposition hearing that is similar to the sentencing phase in an adult court. At this point, the court, often aided by a predisposition report, determines the sentence that serves the "needs" of the child.

❻ List the four categories of residential treatment programs. Foster care, group homes, family group homes, and rural programs such as wilderness camps, farms, and ranches.

❼ Describe the one variable that always correlates highly with juvenile crime rates. The older a person is, the less likely he or she will exhibit criminal behavior. This process is known as aging out. Thus, any group of at-risk persons will commit fewer crimes as they get older.

QUESTIONS FOR CRITICAL ANALYSIS

1 In spite of the constitutional safeguards given to juvenile defendants by the United States Supreme Court decision in *In re Gault,* only 50 percent of juvenile defendants have lawyers. Why?

2 Under what conditions in certain states is a juvenile automatically transferred to the adult court system?

3 The presence of defense attorneys in juvenile courts has led to what changes? In what way have these changes made juvenile courts resemble adult courts?

4 What distinguishes the sentencing phase in juvenile versus adult courts?

5 Why is the age of onset an important factor in predicting juvenile criminal behavior?

6 What has been the relationship between alcohol and drug abuse and juvenile offenders?

7 What has been the statistical relationship between armed gang members and juvenile violent crime?

SELECTED PRINT AND ELECTRONIC RESOURCES

SUGGESTED READINGS

Ayers, Williams, *A Kind and Just Parent: The Children of Juvenile Court,* Boston: Beacon Press, 1997. The author teaches juvenile offenders in the Chicago juvenile court system. He examines the lives of many of his students, who are often from the juvenile temporary detention center, as well as others who are in custody for a longer time. He uses a single school year to structure his portrait of the teen-age residents and those teachers who help them. He offers a sympathetic portrait of those caught up in the juvenile justice system. He claims that society has failed to nurture them.

Clement, Mary, *The Juvenile Justice System: Law and Process,* Boston: Butterworth-Heinemann, 1996. This professor of criminal justice looks at the inner workings of the juvenile justice system. While presenting a complete history of the system, she examines case law as well as research and theories derived from the behavioral sciences. She also examines the constitutional issues of search, seizure, investigation, and interrogation of juveniles.

McCord, Joan, ed., *Juvenile Crime, Juvenile Justice,* Washington, DC: National Academy Press, 2001. The authors present evidence of the importance of child poverty and social decision making that contribute to juvenile crime. Some solutions are offered.

Rodriguez, Joseph, et al., *East Side Stories: Gang Life in East LA,* New York: Powerhouse Cultural Entertainment, 1998. This book presents a collection of essays and photographs, as well as an interview with ex-gang member Luis J. Rodriguez, who is now the author of five books. The rules and codes of gang life are examined and explained. Some have called this the definitive work on the gangs of East Los Angeles.

Sikes, Gini, *8 Ball Chicks: A Year in the Violent World of Girl Gangsters,* New York: Doubleday, 1998. This book presents a riveting account of female gangs in Los Angeles, San Antonio, and Milwaukee. According to the author, "in a world of second-class citizens, they remain third-class." Many of the girl gang members were mothers themselves.

MEDIA RESOURCES

***Bad Boys* (1983)** In one of his first roles, Sean Penn plays Mick O'Brien, a "young punk" looking for trouble. He finds it when he and a buddy attempt to rip off a cache of drugs from a gang headed by Paco Moreno (Esai Morales). The scam goes wrong, and after the dust has settled, Moreno's younger brother is dead. Charged with the boy's murder, O'Brien is sent to a juvenile correctional facility. To get revenge, Moreno rapes O'Brien's girlfriend and winds up in the same facility. Though the inevitable showdown between the two is somewhat forced, the film paints an impressively horrific portrait of life in a juvenile correctional facility.

Critically analyze this film:

1. Describe the juvenile correctional facility in which O'Brien is incarcerated. Is there any evidence of *parens patriae* in its operating philosophy?

2. What treatment programs exist in the facility? Do they seem to have any impact on the juvenile inmates?

3. What values appear to dominate the society within the facility? What implications does this have for the juveniles once they are released?

4. Does this film offer any arguments *against* the idea of treating juvenile offenders as adults?

LOGGING ON

Go to http://cj.wadsworth.com/gainescore2e, and click Hypercontents. There, you will find URLs for the organizations in the following list:

- You can read articles out of the bimonthly online magazine **Juvenilejustice.com.** It targets those involved in youth services, human services, law enforcement, probation, parole, court administration, and staff training.

- The U.S. Department of Justice oversees the **Office of Juvenile Justice and Delinquency Prevention (OJJDP).** The OJJDP provide numerous resources for information concerning the nation's juvenile justice system.

- Another useful Web site is provided by the **Koch Crime Institute,** an independent group that promotes aggressive attempts to find solutions for juvenile offenders.

USING THE INTERNET FOR CRIMINAL JUSTICE ANALYSIS

INFOTRAC®
COLLEGE EDITION

1. Go to your InfoTrac College Edition at **http://www. infotrac-college.com/wadsworth/.** After you log on, type in the words: **Breaking the Cycle of Juvenile Crime.** This article examines research pursuant to actions by the Office of Juvenile Justice and Delinquency Prevention (OJJDP). The article claims that the rates of juvenile offending and victimization are of "crisis" proportions. Specifically, the author believes that there have been failures by neglectful families, schools, communities, and social systems for which adults are responsible. Read the article and answer the following questions:

a. Do the statistics in the first part of the article indicate that juvenile crime is on the rise and is in fact overwhelming the country? Why or why not?

b. What are the key risk factors for becoming a juvenile offender? Which one is most important?

c. This article lists six OJJDP programs and strategies. Which two are the most important, and why?

d. What is the role of the criminal court in this system, according to the author?

2. See Internet Activities 14.1 and 14.2 on the companion Web site for *CJ in Action: The Core.* To get to the activities, go to **http://www.cj.wadsworth.com/gainescore2e**, select the appropriate chapter from the drop down list, then click Internet Activities on the left navigation bar.

NOTES

1. "Teen Murder Trials Spark Debate over Florida Justice," *Star Tribune* (Minneapolis–St. Paul, MN) (May 19, 2001), 16A.

2. "14-year-old Gets Life, No Parole," *Star Tribune* (Minneapolis-St. Paul, MN) (March 10, 2001), 1A.

3. *Ibid.*

4. Keith Bradsher, "Boy Who Killed Gets 7 Years; Judge Says Law Is Too Harsh," *New York Times* (January 14, 2000), A1.

5. Peter W. Greenwood, "Juvenile Crime and Juvenile Justice," in *Crime,* James Q. Wilson and Joan Petersilia, eds. (San Francisco: ICS Press, 1995), 91.

6. Jennifer M. O'Connor and Lucinda K. Treat, "Getting Smart about Getting Tough: Juvenile Justice and the Possibility of Progressive Reform," *American Criminal Law Review* 33 (Summer 1996), 1299.

7. Eric K. Klein, "Dennis the Menace or Billy the Kid: An Analysis of the Role of Transfer to Criminal Court in Juvenile Justice," *American Criminal Law Review* 35 (Winter 1998), 371.

8. Dalia Sussman, "Lock 'Em Up," ABCNews.com, May 8, 2001.

9. *In re Gault,* 387 U.S. 15 (1967).

10. Samuel Davis, *The Rights of Juveniles: The Juvenile Justice System,* 2d ed. (New York: C. Boardman Company, 1995), Section 1.2.

11. Cited in Anthony Platt, *The Child Savers* (Chicago: University of Chicago Press, 1969), 119.

12. 383 U.S. 541 (1966).

13. *Ibid.,* 556.

14. 387 U.S. 1 (1967).

15. 397 U.S. 358 (1970).

16. 421 U.S. 519 (1975).

17. 403 U.S. 528 (1971).

18. Andrew Murr and Karen Springen, "Death at a Very Early Age," *Newsweek* (August 28, 2000), 32.

19. Andrew Walkover, "The Infancy Defense in the New Juvenile Court," *UCLA Law Review* 31 (1984), 509–13.

20. Gary B. Melton, "Toward 'Personhood' for Adolescents: Autonomy and Privacy as Values in Public Policy," *American Psychology* 38 (1983), 99–100.

21. Richard E. Redding, "Juveniles Transferred to Criminal Court: Legal Reform Proposals Based on Social Science Research," *Utah Law Review* (1997), 709.

22. Howard N. Snyder and Melissa Sickmund, *Juvenile Offenders and Victims: A National Report* (Washington, D.C.: U.S. Department of Justice, 1995), 47.

23. 487 U.S. 815 (1988).

24. *Ibid.,* at 822–23.

25. 492 U.S. 361, 371 (1989).

26. Frederick Ward, Jr., "Prevention and Diversion in the United States," in *The Changing Faces of Juvenile Justice,* V. Lorne Stewart, ed. (New York: New York University Press, 1978), 43.

27. President's Commission on Law Enforcement and Administration of Justice, *Task Force Report: Juvenile Delinquency and Youth Crime* (Washington, D.C.: U.S. Government Printing Office, 1967).

28. 42 U.S.C. Sections 5601–5778 (1974).

29. S'Lee Arthur Hinshaw II, "Juvenile Diversion: An Alternative to Juvenile Court," *Journal of Dispute Resolution* (1993), 305.

30. Eric L. Jensen, "The Waiver of Juveniles to Criminal Court: Policy Goals, Empirical Realities, and Suggestions for Change," *Idaho Law Review* 21 (1994), 180.

31. Rhode Island Gen. Laws Section 14-1-7.1 (1994 & Supp. 1996).

32. 467 U.S. 253 (1984).

33. Bureau of Justice Statistics, *Prison and Jail Inmates at Midyear 2001* (Washington, D.C.: U.S. Department of Justice, 2002), 9.

34. Barry C. Feld, "Criminalizing the American Juvenile Court," *Crime and Justice* 17 (1993), 227–54.

35. Barry C. Feld, "Abolish the Juvenile Court," *Journal of Criminal Law and Criminology* 88 (Fall 1997), 68.

36. *In re Gault* 387 U.S. 1 (1967).

37. Barry C. Feld, "Violent Youth and Public Policy: A Case Study of Juvenile Justice Law Reform," *Minnesota Law Review* 79 (May 1995), 965.

38. Barry C. Feld, "The Juvenile Court Meets the Principle of Offense: Punishment, Treatment, and the Difference It Makes," *Boston University Law Review* 68 (1988), 848–49.

39. Lawrence E. Cohen, *Delinquency Dispositions: An Empirical Analysis of Processing Decisions in Three Juvenile Courts* (Washington, D.C.: U.S. Government Printing Office, 1975).

40. Eric R. Lotke, "Youth Homicide: Keeping Perspective on How Many Children Kill," *Valparaiso University Law Review* 31 (Spring 1997), 395.

41. Bureau of Justice Statistics, *Prison and Jail Inmates at Midyear 2001* (Washington, D.C.: U.S. Department of Justice, 2001), 6.

42. Bureau of Justice Statistics, *Sourcebook of Criminal Justice Statistics, 1997* (Washington, D.C.: U.S. Department of Justice, 1998), Table 5.76 at 441.

43. Charles E. Springer, "Rehabilitating the Juvenile Court," *Notre Dame Journal of Law, Ethics, and Public Policy* 5 (1991), 397.

44. Larry Siegel and Joseph Senna, *Juvenile Delinquency*, 6th ed. (St. Paul, MN: West Publishing Co., 1997), 602–4.

45. Melissa Sickmund and Howard N. Snyder, *Juvenile Offenders and Victims: 1999 National Report* (Washington, D.C.: Office of Juvenile Justice and Delinquency Prevention, 1999), 182.

46. Federal Bureau of Investigation, *Crime in the United States, 2001* (Washington, D.C.: U.S. Department of Justice, 2002), Table 38 at 244.

47. Howard N. Snyder, "Law Enforcement and Juvenile Crime," *Juvenile Offenders and Victims: National Report Series Bulletin* (Washington, D.C.: Office of Juvenile Justice and Delinquency Prevention, December 2001), 11–12.

48. Office of Juvenile Justice and Delinquency Prevention.

49. Scott Bowles, "Violence Threatens Schools across U.S.," *USA Today* (March 8, 2001), 3A.

50. Marvin E. Wolfgang, *From Boy to Man, From Delinquency to Crime* (Chicago: University of Chicago Press, 1987).

51. Susan Gaertner, "Three Strikes Against Juvenile Crime: Prevention, Intervention, and Detention, *Prosecutor* (November/ December 1996), 18.

52. Travis Hirschi and Michael Gottfredson, "Age and the Explanation of Crime," *American Journal of Sociology* 89 (1982), 552–84.

53. David P. Farrington, "Offending from 10 to 25 Years of Age," in *Prospective Studies of Crime and Delinquency*, ed. Katherine Teilmann Van Dusen and Sarnoff A. Mednick (Boston: Kluwer-Nijhoff Publishers, 1983), 17.

54. *Combating Underage Drinking, Fact Sheet #75* (Washington, D.C.: Office of Juvenile Justice and Delinquency Prevention, February 1998).

55. Substance Abuse and Mental Health Services Administration, *Summary of Findings from the 2001 National Household Survey on Drug Use* (Washington, D.C.: Department of Health and Human Services, 2002).

56. FBI, *Crime in the United States, 2001*, Table 34, page 240.

57. *Ibid.*

58. U.S. Department of Health and Human Services, Substance Abuse and Mental Health Services Administration, *Substance Use among Women in the United States, Analytic Series A-3* (Rockville, MD: U.S. Department of Health and Human Services, 1997), 8–18.

59. Alfred Blumstein, "Violence by Young People: Why the Deadly Nexus," *National Institute of Justice Journal* 229, (1995), 2–9.

60. *Collaboration, Coordination, and Cooperation: Helping Children Affected by Parental Addiction and Family Violence* (New York: Children of Alcoholics Foundation, 1996).

61. Ching-Tung Lung and Deborah Daro, *Current Trends in Child Abuse Reporting and Fatalities: The Results of the 1997 Annual Fifty State Survey* (Chicago: National Committee to Prevent Child Abuse, 1998).

62. Polly E. Bijur, Matthew Kurzon, Mary Overpeck, and Peter C. Scheidt, "Parental Alcohol Use, Problem Drinking and Child Injuries," *Journal of the American Medical Association* 267 (1992), 3166–71.

63. David Huizinga, Rolf Loeber, and Terence Thornberry, *Urban Delinquency and Substance Abuse* (Washington, D.C.: Office of Juvenile Justice and Delinquency Prevention, 1993).

64. Grover Trask, "Defusing the Teenage Time Bomb," *Prosecutor* (March/April 1997), 29.

65. Cathy Spatz Widom, *The Cycle of Violence* (Washington, D.C.: National Institute of Justice, October 1992).

66. Office of Juvenile Justice and Delinquency Prevention, *1998 Youth Gang Survey* (Washington, D.C.: U.S. Department of Justice, November 2000), Table 9.

67. Office of Juvenile Justice and Delinquency Prevention, *1997 Youth Gang Survey* (Washington, D.C.: U.S. Department of Justice, December 1999), Table 13.

68. Office of Juvenile Justice and Delinquency Prevention, *1998 Youth Gang Survey*, Table 34.

69. C. Ronald Huff, *Comparing the Criminal Behavior of Youth Gangs and At-Risk Youths* (Washington, D.C.: U.S. Department of Justice, October 1998).

70. Office of Juvenile Justice and Delinquency Prevention, *1999 National Report Series: Juvenile Justice Bulletin—Kids and Guns* (Washington, D.C.: U.S. Department of Justice, March 2000), 4.

71. *Ethics of American Youth* (Marina del Ray, CA: Josephson Institute of Ethics, 2001).

72. FBI, *Crime in the United States, 2001,* Table 38, page 244.

73. Office of Juvenile Justice and Delinquency Prevention, *1999 National Report Series: Juvenile Justice Bulletin—Kids and Guns, 4.

74. Delbert Elliot, Norma J. Hatot, Paul Sirovatka, and Blair B. Potter, eds., *Youth Violence: A Report of the Surgeon General* (Washington, D.C.: U.S. Department of Health and Human Services, 2001), Chapter 2, Section 1.

75. Howard Snyder, *Juvenile Arrests 2000* (Washington, D.C.: Office of Juvenile Justice and Delinquency Prevention [forthcoming]).

76. Scott Bowles, "Friends Tell of Picked On But 'Normal' Kid," *USA Today* (March 6, 2001), 4A.

77. Amanda Bower, "Scorecard of Hatred," *Time* (March 19, 2001), 30.

78. Tonja R. Nansel, Mary Overpeck, Ramani S. Pilla, W. June Ruan, Bruce Simons-Morton, and Peter Scheidt, "Bullying Behaviors among U.S. Youth," *Journal of the American Medical Association* 285 (April 25, 2001), 2094.

79. Natalie Angier, "Bully for You: Why Push Comes to Shove," *New York Times* (May 20, 2001), Section 4, Page 1.

80. Nancy Mitchell, "Colorado to Take Bullies by the Horn," *Rocky Mountain News* (October 25, 2001), 4A.

81. David Crary, "Anti-Bullying Programs Gain Favor and Funding," *Seattle Times* (March 11, 2001), A12.

82. Michael Janofsky, "Bill on Student Bullying Is Considered in Colorado," *New York Times* (March 19, 2001), A10.

83. Fox Butterfield, "Tips by Students Result in Arrests at 5 Schools," *New York Times* (March 8, 2001), A16.

84. *Ibid.*

85. National Center for Education Statistics, *Indicators of School Crime and Safety* (Washington, D.C.: U.S. Department of Education, October 2000), Table 13.2.

86. Timothy Egan, "School Shooting Underlines Illusion of Safety," *New York Times* (March 9, 2001), A13.

87. *Ibid.*

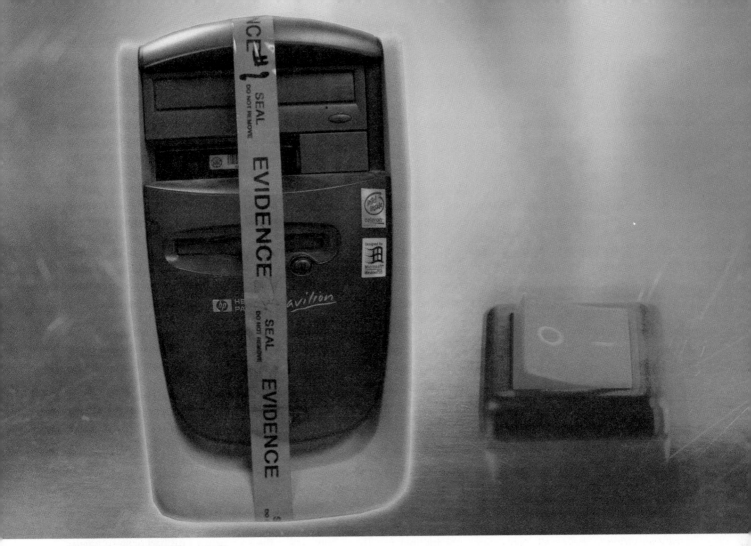

CHAPTER 15
CYBER CRIME

CHAPTER OUTLINE

Chapter Objectives

After reading this chapter, you should be able to:

1. Distinguish a cyber crime from a "traditional" crime.

2. Indicate how the Internet has contributed to increased instances of identity theft.

3. Explain the activities and purposes of most hackers.

4. Outline the three major reasons that the Internet is conducive to juvenile cyber crime.

5. Explain how the Internet has contributed to piracy of intellectual property.

6. Describe the challenges to enforcing online gambling laws.

7. Indicate which federal law enforcement agencies are primarily responsible for preventing and investigating cyber crimes.

8. List two areas in which crime control and civil liberties have conflicted on the Internet.

INTRODUCTION
"Sick" Computers and a Nasty Virus

During the second week of February 2001, millions of computers around the world received what appeared to be a harmless e-mail. "Hi: Check This," read the text line of the message, offering an attachment entitled "AnnaKournikova.jpg.vbs." Though most people deleted the communication, thereby sparing themselves any further trouble, several million users apparently could not resist the temptation to view what they believed to be an electronic photo of the popular Russian tennis star.[1] Instead, by clicking on the attachment they invited a computer virus into their systems. The virus, though doing no permanent damage to a computer's hard drive, did overload mail servers and networks, forcing a time-consuming "clean-up" process before a system could resume operating.

The person who created the Kournikova virus had committed a **computer crime,** which can be defined as any act that is directed against computers and computer parts, that uses computers as instruments of crime, or that involves computers and constitutes abuse.[2] A number of the white-collar crimes discussed in Chapter 1, such as fraud, embezzlement, and the theft of intellectual property, are now committed with the aid of computers and thus are considered computer crimes. In this chapter, we will be using the term **cyber crime,** which covers any criminal activity occurring in the virtual community of the Internet. The Kournikova virus is a prime example of such a crime.

The "location" of cyber crime—cyberspace—raises many new issues in the investigation of crimes and the prosecution of perpetrators. Cyberspace allows users to communicate, provide and receive information, and, increasingly, commit crimes under the cloak of anonymity. Thus, the online environment makes it difficult to identify and prosecute those who commit cyber crimes.[3] The creator of the Kournikova virus, a twenty-year-old Dutchman who went by the online name of "OnTheFly," made things easy by surrendering himself to authorities. The unique nature of the Internet also causes one of the toughest problems in enforcing laws against cyber crimes: the issue of jurisdiction. Although his virus cost individuals and companies all over the world millions of dollars, OnTheFly committed his crime without leaving his room in the small town of Sneek in the Netherlands. Under lenient local law, he was charged with damaging private property and computer programs and then sent home with his parents.[4]

In this final chapter of the textbook, we will examine various types of computer and cyber crimes and the efforts of law enforcement agencies to combat them. We will also look at private methods of fighting such crimes—just as technology provides opportunities for wrongdoers, it also provides individuals with the means to better protect themselves. As you study this chapter, remember that it covers perhaps the most volatile area of the criminal justice system. Three months after the Kournikova virus had been subdued, the "Homepage" virus began appearing on computers worldwide. Experts calculated that the Homepage virus spread four times faster than its Kournikova predecessor.[5]

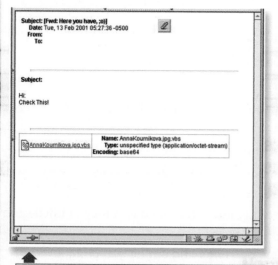

A screen image showing the Anna Kournikova computer virus contained in the attachment to the widely disseminated e-mail "Hi Check This."

COMPUTER CRIME
Any wrongful act that is directed against computers and computer parties, or wrongful use or abuse of computers or software.

CYBER CRIME
A crime that occurs online, in the virtual community of the Internet, as opposed to the physical world.

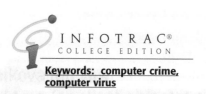

INFOTRAC® COLLEGE EDITION

Keywords: computer crime, computer virus

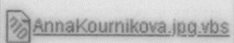
Name: AnnaKournikova.jpg.vbs
Type: unspecified type (application/octet-stream)

CRIME AND THE INTERNET

While the Internet has become an almost unavoidable part of daily life in America only over the past ten years, its history goes back more than four decades. In the late 1950s, the United States government decided that, in order to protect sensitive information, it needed to create a network of computers that were connected to each other. By the 1970s, some of the nation's most prestigious universities were "hooked up," and the early version of the Internet was almost exclusively used by the academic and scientific communities.[6]

Technology such as the "point and click" system and "browsers" allowed easier access to the Internet, and its use began to grow. Currently, there are approximately 600 million Internet users worldwide. Though debate over whether the system should be more regulated continues, the Internet for the most part remains a medium from which people can get information for free, which has contributed significantly to its popularity. A great deal of restricted information is passed from party to party over the Internet as well, and the first cyber crime was "hacking"—or stealing that restricted information.

As the uses of the Internet have become more diverse, so have the criminal activities related to that use. It is very difficult, if not impossible, to tell how much computer crime actually takes place. Often, a person will never know that he or she has been a victim of a computer crime. Furthermore, businesses sometimes do not report such crimes for fear of losing customer confidence.[7] Several agencies do exist, however, that provide reliable information on specific areas of cyber crime, including the Internet Security Alliance, the National Institute for Standards and Technology, and the National Infrastructure Protection Center. We rely on these sources and others for a great deal of the information in this chapter.

Stories from the Street

Go to the Stories from the Street feature at http://www.cj.wadsworth.com/gainescore2e to hear Larry Gaines tell insightful stories related to this chapter and his experiences in the field.

In 2001, National Security Adviser Condoleezza Rice delivers the keynote speech at the Internet Policy Forum in Washington, D.C. Speakers at the forum discussed the security threats to the American people and the nation's economy posed by Internet "hackers" and other cyber criminals. (AP Photo/Ron Edmonds)

CYBER CRIMES AGAINST PERSONS AND PROPERTY

Most cyber crimes are not "new" crimes. Rather, they are existing crimes in which the Internet is the instrument of wrongdoing. When, for example, Michael Ian Campbell sent an e-mail to a Columbine High School student threatening to "finish what [had] begun," he was charged with making a threat across state lines.[8] The charge would have been the same if he had sent the message via regular mail. The challenge for law enforcement is to apply traditional laws, which were designed to protect persons from physical harm or to safeguard their physical property, to crimes committed in cyberspace. Here, we look at several types of activity that constitute "updated" crimes against persons and property— online consumer fraud, cyber theft, and cyber stalking.

Cyber Consumer Fraud

The expanding world of e-commerce (buying and selling that takes place in cyberspace) has created many benefits for consumers. It has also led to some challenging problems, including fraud conducted via the Internet. In general, fraud is any misrepresentation knowingly made with the intention of deceiving another and on which a reasonable person would and does rely to her or his detriment. **Cyber fraud**, then, is fraud committed over the Internet. Scams that were once conducted solely by mail or phone can now be found online, and new technology had led to increasingly more creative ways to commit fraud.[9]

INFOTRAC®
COLLEGE EDITION

Keywords: computer fraud

CYBER FRAUD
Any misrepresentation knowingly made over the Internet with the intention of deceiving another and on which a reasonable person would and does rely to his or her detriment.

FIGURE 15.1 Fraudulent Activities Online

In 2001, the Internet Fraud Complaint Center referred 49,711 complaints to law enforcement agencies. As the graph shows, the largest number of these referrals concerned auction fraud.

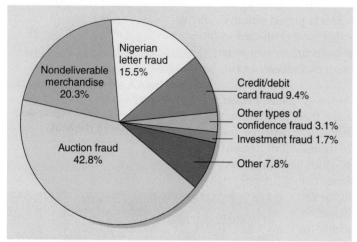

Nigerian letter fraud 15.5%

Nondeliverable merchandise 20.3%

Credit/debit card fraud 9.4%

Other types of confidence fraud 3.1%

Investment fraud 1.7%

Auction fraud 42.8%

Other 7.8%

Source: Internet Fraud Complaint Center, *Internet Fraud Report*, January 1, 2001–December 31, 2001 (Washington, D.C.: Federal Bureau of Investigation and National White Collar Crime Center, 2002), 5.

On the Web

The Privacy Rights Clearinghouse provides information on identity theft and other online violations of privacy. For a link to its Web site, go to the Hypercontents page for this chapter at http://cj.wadsworth.com/gainescore2e.

INFOTRAC®
COLLEGE EDITION

Keywords: cyber theft, computer crime

IDENTITY THEFT
The theft of identity information, such as name, driver's license number, or Social Security number. The information is then usually used to access the victim's financial resources.

No one knows the full extent of cyber fraud. Indications are that the practice is increasing with the growing use of the Internet. In 2000, the Federal Bureau of Investigation (FBI) and the National White Collar Crime Center formed the Internet Fraud Complaint Center (IFCC). In its first six months of operation, the IFCC received nearly 20,000 complaints and referred more than a quarter of them to law enforcement agencies for possible investigation.[10] The IFCC received complaints involving total losses of $17.8 million in 2001.[11]

Online Auction Fraud. As you can see from Figure 15.1, online auction fraud is the most widely reported form of consumer fraud on the Internet. In its most basic form, online auction fraud is a simple process. A person puts up an expensive item for auction on either a legitimate or a fake auction site, and then refuses to send the product after receiving payment. Or, as a variation, the wrongdoer may provide the purchaser with an item that is worth less than the one offered in the auction.[12]

Online Retail Fraud. Somewhat similar to online auction fraud is online retail fraud, in which consumers directly pay (without bidding) for items that are never delivered. Because most online consumers will purchase items only from reputable, brand name sites, criminals have had to take advantage of some of the complexities of cyberspace to lure unknowing customers.

Again, though determining the actual extent of online sales fraud is difficult, the anecdotal evidence suggests it is a substantial problem. In 2001, the FBI arrested a fraud ring of more than sixty persons believed to have cheated more than 56,000 consumers out of nearly $120 million. The fraud included charging entry fees to nonexistent online "shopping malls" and bogus investment schemes (discussed later in the chapter).[13] Soon after the tragic terrorist attacks on the World Trade Center in September 2001, numerous online solicitations for funds to help the more than three thousand families who lost loved ones flooded the Web. Many, if not most, of these were fraudulent. Perhaps the most widespread and long-running Internet fraud is the "Nigerian letter fraud scam." In this scheme, targets are sent e-mails promising them a percentage if they will send money to help fictitious officials from the African country transfer millions of nonexistent dollars to Western banks. In 2002, victims worldwide delivered over $100 million to these criminals.[14]

Cyber Theft

In cyberspace, thieves are not subject to the physical limitations of the "real" world. A thief can steal data stored in a networked computer with network access from anywhere on the globe. Only the speed of the connection and the thief's computer equipment limit the quantity of data that can be stolen.

Identity Theft. This freedom has led to a marked increase in **identity theft**, which has been called the "crime of the new millennium."[15] Identity theft occurs when the wrongdoer steals a form of identification—such as a name, date of birth, or Social Security number—and uses the information to access the victim's financial resources. This crime existed to a certain extent before widespread use of the Internet. Thieves would "steal" calling-card numbers by watching people using public telephones, or they would rifle through garbage to find bank account or credit-card numbers. The identity thief would then use the calling-card or credit-card number or withdraw funds from the victim's account until the theft was discovered.

The Internet has, however, turned identity theft into perhaps the fastest-growing financial crime in the United States.[16] Primarily, it provides those who steal information off-line with an easy medium for using items such as stolen credit-card numbers or e-mail addresses while protected by anonymity. Also, frequent Web surfers may be providing a wealth of information about themselves without knowing it. Many Web sites use "cookies" to collect data on those who visit their sites. The data can include the areas of the site the user visits and the links the user clicks on. Furthermore, Web browsers often store information such as the consumer's name and e-mail address. Finally, every time a purchase is made online, the item is linked to the purchaser's name, allowing Web retailers to amass a database of who is buying what.[17]

Targeting Private Accounts. As more consumers are discovering, information that can be collected can be stolen. An estimated 500,000 Americans are victims of identity theft each year.[18] Perhaps the most dramatic case involved Abraham Abdallah, a busboy in Brooklyn, New York. When he was arrested, Abdallah had a cache of information on the four hundred richest people in America, including the Social Security numbers, bank account information, credit-card numbers, and mother's maiden names of Steven Spielberg, Martha Stewart, and Oprah Winfrey. Abdallah allegedly sent an e-mail pretending to be the founder of a large insurance company and directing that $10 million be transferred to a fraudulent private account from these individuals' private accounts.[19] (See Figure 15.2 on page 386 for information on how to avoid being the target of identity theft.)

Cyber Stalking

California passed the first stalking law in 1990, in response to the murders of six women by men who had harassed them. The law made it a crime to harass or follow a person while making a "credible threat" that puts the person in reasonable fear for her or his safety or the safety of the person's immediate family.[20] Most other states have enacted similar stalking laws. Generally speaking, about half the states have stalking laws that require a physical act, such as following the victim. **Cyber stalking,** however, involves stalkers who find their victims through Internet chat rooms, Usenet groups or other bulletin boards, and e-mail.[21] None of these communications requires that the stalker physically "follow" his or her prey. Though many of the stalking laws *could* apply in cyberspace because of the broad meaning of "harassment," they were not created with the Internet in mind.

This "loophole" in stalking statutes may contribute to the perception that cyber stalking is less threatening than physical stalking. In fact, cyber stalking shares many of the same characteristics of physical stalking and in some respects can be *more* threatening. While it takes a great deal of effort to physically stalk someone, it is relatively easy to harass a victim with electronic messages. Furthermore, the possibility of personal confrontation may discourage a stalker from actually following his or her victim. This disincentive is removed in cyberspace. Finally, there is always the possibility that a cyber stalker will eventually pose a physical threat to his or her target.[22]

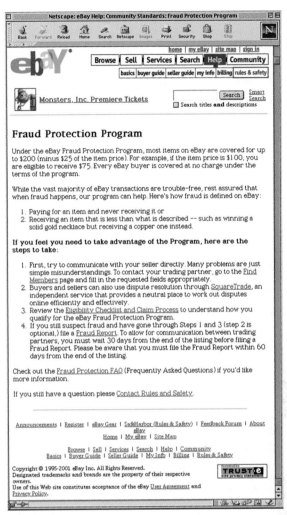

The online auction service eBay offers a Fraud Protection Program, shown here, that reimburses customers up to $200 (minus $25 of the price) for items not received or received in a damaged condition. eBay also provides rating histories of its buyers and sellers, allowing users to avoid those with poor records. Are these effective safeguards against auction fraud on eBay? What steps might a fraudulent seller take to avoid detection?

Keywords: identity theft

CYBER STALKING
The crime of stalking, committed in cyberspace. Generally, stalking consists of harassing a person and putting that person in reasonable fear for his or her safety or the safety of the person's immediate family.

FIGURE 15.2 Eight Steps toward Preventing Identity Theft

1. **Share information only when necessary.** Make sure that you give out your credit-card number and/or Social Security number only to a party that has a legitimate need for this information. Also, give out this information only if you are relatively sure that the other party is trustworthy.

2. **Be cautious about providing identity information in public.** Be on the lookout for "shoulder surfers" when entering account information at an automated teller machine or dialing a calling-card number on a public telephone. Also, do not put private information on something that can be easily observed, such as a key chain.

3. **Do not carry unnecessary identification in a purse or wallet.** The primary means that thieves gain personal information is through the theft of these items.

4. **Secure your mailbox.** The second most successful means for thieves to obtain personal information is through stolen mail.

5. **Secure information on your personal computer.** Again, specific information such as credit-card or Social Security numbers should be given out only to legitimate

enterprises on the Internet, and only when you can be sure that the site is secure. Also, you should install firewall software on your computer. This software isolates the computer system from the rest of the Internet, thus preventing unauthorized access to personal data.

6. **Shred all nonessential material containing identity information.** Any material such as credit-card statements, canceled checks, bank statements, or even junk mail with personal information should be destroyed before it is placed in the trash.

7. **Remove your name from mailing lists.** This reduces the number of commercial entities with access to your identity information. To opt out of many direct-mail lists, write the Direct Marketing Association, DMA Preference Service, P.O. Box 9008, Farmingdale, NY, 11735-9008 or visit www.e-mps.org.

8. **Review financial statements.** Review all credit-card statements for accuracy. Also, pay attention to billing cycles. A missed bill may mean that the document has been stolen.

Source: Sean B. Hoar, "Identity Theft: The Crime of the New Millennium," *United States' Attorney's USA Bulletin* (March 2001).

On the Web

Cyberangels is an organization designed to assist people who need help online—whether they are being cyberstalked, harassed, or otherwise victimized by cyber criminals. For a link to its Web site, go to the Hypercontents page for this chapter at http://cj.wadsworth.com/gainescore2e.

CYBER CRIMES IN THE BUSINESS WORLD

Just as cyberspace can be a dangerous place for consumers, it presents a number of hazards for businesses that wish to offer their services on the Internet. The same circumstances that enable companies to reach a wide number of consumers also leave them susceptible to cyber crime. The improper use of stolen credit cards online, for example, could cost businesses around the world more than $15 billion a year by 2005.[23]

Credit-Card Crime on the Web

In the previous section, credit-card theft was mentioned in connection with identity fraud. An important point to note, however, is that stolen credit cards are much more likely to "hurt" merchants than the consumer from whom the card or card number has been appropriated. In most cases, the legitimate holders of credit cards are not held responsible for the costs of purchases made with a stolen number. That means the financial burden must be borne either by the merchant or by the credit-card company. Almost all of these companies require merchants to cover these costs—especially if the address to which the goods are sent does not match the billing address of the credit card.[24]

Companies take further risks by "storing" their customers' credit-card numbers. In doing so, companies provide quicker service; the consumer can make a purchase by providing a code or clicking on a particular icon without entering the lengthy card number. These data warehouses are, as one can imagine, quite tempting to cyber thieves. In 2000, an unknown person copied the credit-card numbers of more than 300,000 customers of CD Universe, an online music store. The thief then threatened to post the numbers on an open site unless the company paid $100,000. When CD Universe refused to cooperate with this extortion attempt, some of its customers' credit-card numbers did in fact turn up on a Web site that could be accessed by any Web surfer.[25]

Hackers

The person who "broke into" CD Universe's database to steal the credit-card numbers is known as a hacker. A **hacker** is someone who uses one computer to break into another. Hackers who break into computers without authorization often commit cyber theft. In most cases, however, a hacker's principal aim is to prove how smart she or he is by gaining access to others' password-protected computers and causing data errors. The Dutchman who created the Kournikova virus—discussed in the chapter introduction—falls under this category of "show-off" hacker. Indeed, it appears that he had no concept of the damage that his virus would cause.[26]

The Scope of the Problem. It is difficult to know just how frequently hackers succeed in breaking into databases across the United States. The Computer Crime and Security Survey polled 503 companies and large government institutions and found that 90 percent had experienced security breaches through computer-based means in 2001. Eighty percent suffered financial losses because of the breaches, costing nearly $300 million to correct.[27] The number of hacking incidents reported to Carnegie Mellon University's Cert Coordination Center reached 52,658 that same year, up from 9,859 in 1999.[28]

The actual number of hacking victims is probably much larger. The FBI estimates that only 25 percent of all corporations that suffer such security breaches report the incident to a law enforcement agency. The main reasons for failing to report appear to be fear and shame. The company's officials may feel that admitting to a breach either would reveal a certain degree of incompetence or would erode shareholder confidence and affect company stock prices.[29]

Though hackers are sometimes romanticized as youthful rebels, they cause significant damage. A destructive program such as the Kournikova virus often overloads a company's computer system, making not only e-mail but also many other functions impossible until it is "cleaned out" of the system. This cleansing process can cost between $100,000 and $5 million a day, depending on the size of the company affected.[30] One computer consulting firm estimated that viruses cost the world economy more than $13 billion in 2001.[31]

Juvenile Cyber Crime. In 2000, a series of "hack attacks" were launched at some of the largest Internet companies, including Amazon.com and eBay. The sites either froze or significantly slowed down, costing the parent companies nearly $2 billion in damages. While the FBI was searching for the hacker, one of its investigation chiefs joked that the companies' computer systems were so vulnerable that any fifteen-year-old with technological know-how could break into them.[32]

As it turned out, the FBI agent was only a year off. The culprit was a sixteen-year-old Canadian high school dropout who was working as a kitchen worker in Montreal when he was arrested. The teenager, who went by the moniker of Mafiaboy, had uploaded software programs on Web sites in Europe and South Korea, from which he bombarded the American companies with e-mails. (To see how easy it is to wreak havoc on the Internet, see the feature *Criminal Justice & Technology—Scriptkiddies and the "Do It Yourself" Web Attack* on page 388.)

According to Assistant U.S. Attorney Joseph V. DeMarco, it should come as no surprise that Mafiaboy could cause so much damage. DeMarco believes that there are three main reasons why cyber crime is clearly suited to the habits and limitations of juveniles:

- *The enormous technological capacities of personal computers.* Most juvenile delinquents will never commit crimes more serious than shoplifting and other forms of petty theft. Advanced computer equipment and software, however, give these youth the ability to carry out complex criminal fraud

Abraham Abdallah, a busboy in Brooklyn, New York, was arrested in 2001 after allegedly perpetrating the largest identity theft in the history of the Internet, discussed on page 385. Using a public library computer and a Web-enabled mobile phone, Abdallah accessed the private bank accounts of some of the wealthiest people in the United States. Taking advantage of information published in *Forbes* magazine, Abdallah was able to obtain some of his targets' Social Security numbers and gain access to their brokerage accounts. What are some other methods used to "steal" a person's identity? (AP Photo/NYPD)

INFOTRAC®
COLLEGE EDITION
Keywords: juvenile hackers

HACKER
A person who uses one computer to break into another.

Criminal Justice & TECHNOLOGY

Scriptkiddies and the "Do It Yourself" Web Attack

After the mayor of Sneek in the northern Netherlands discovered that one of his constituents—a twenty-year-old who goes by the Web name OnTheFly—was responsible for the "Anna Kournikova" e-mail worm, he promptly offered the young man a job with the city's information technology department. "It is obvious," the mayor said, "that [he] is very capable."

Experienced hackers scoffed at the mayor's comments. "A five-year-old can do what he did," said one. In fact, OnTheFly is known in the world of cyberspace as a "scriptkiddy," or someone who creates a virus by following directions from a "kit" taken from the Internet. The kit that OnTheFly used to create "Kournikova" was the VBS Worm Generator. (Technically, a "virus" is a program that infects other programs, while a "worm" is a program that copies itself. Both can travel through cyberspace via e-mail.) This particular kit has been downloaded at least 15,000 times.

One observer compared creating a virus or worm from a kit to making brownies from a mix, "only easier." In essence, the scriptkiddy need only fill in the answers to a series of questions, such as the desired date for the virus to be released, the subject line of the e-mail message, and so forth. The program even has a box that can be checked next to "erase hard disk." All the person needs to do is check that box, and if an e-mail recipient opens the attachment, his or her hard drive will be erased. "To do this stuff is utterly trivial," said Peter G. Neumann, a scientist at a technological consulting firm. "Every other kid can do it."

Various screen shots of the VBS Worm Generator, used by OnTheFly to create the Kournikova virus.

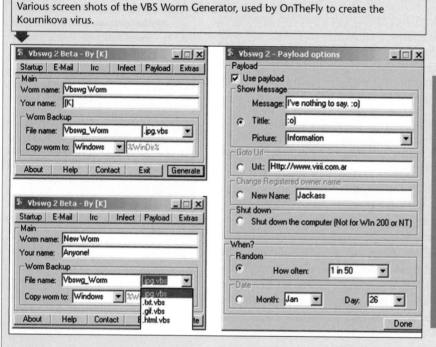

IN THE FUTURE

About 50,000 viruses are floating through the Internet, with hundreds more being created every day. A minuscule proportion of those—perhaps 0.03 percent—will ever do any damage, so the threat posed by scriptkiddies is relatively small. Experts are concerned, however, that someone may create a "supervirus," which would have the ability to attack certain components of a computer and spawn variations of itself to avoid detection and destruction. "[E]very year the situation gets worse," says one observer. "The Internet is just too complex to secure."

> "There is a segment in society that views the unleashing of computer viruses as a challenge, a game. Far from it; it is a serious crime."
>
> —Robert J. Cleary, *lead prosecutor for the U.S. Attorney's office, New Jersey* (1997)

and hacking schemes without leaving their bedrooms. Thus, computer technology has given juveniles the ability to "commit offenses that are disproportionate to their age." In addition, nearly 76 percent of all children have access to the Internet, either at home, at school, or through a library.[33]

● *The anonymity of the Internet.* The physical world denies juveniles the ability to commit many crimes. It would be very difficult, for example, for a fifteen-year-old to run a fraudulent auction in the flesh. The Internet, however, allows young people to depict themselves as adults, thereby opening up a number of criminal possibilities that would otherwise be denied. Furthermore, the lack of a driver's license or the wealth necessary to travel does not limit a juvenile cyber delinquent's ability to commit far-reaching offenses, as we saw in the case of Mafiaboy.

● *The acceptance of hacking in youth culture.* A recent poll of nearly 50,000 elementary and middle school students conducted by Scholastic, Inc., found that nearly half of them did not consider hacking to be a crime.[34] Thus, DeMarco believes, there is an ethical "deficit" when it comes to youth and computer crimes: juveniles who would never consider robbery or burglary are not troubled by the prospect of committing cyber crimes.[35]

Online Securities Fraud

The Securities and Exchange Commission (SEC) reports that it receives between 200 and 300 complaints each day concerning possible securities fraud online.[36] This form of fraud involves investment scams that occur in cyberspace. Buyers and sellers of securities such as stocks have always relied heavily on outside information in making their investment decisions. As we have seen, the Internet is an ideal environment for those who wish to manipulate information.

Cyberspace provides a wealth of information to investors, including tens of thousands of online chat rooms in which participants praise or criticize certain securities. These chat rooms are perfectly tailored for "pumping and dumping" schemes, in which a person who has purchased a particular stock heavily promotes ("pumps up") that stock—thereby creating a great demand for it and driving up its price—and then sells ("dumps") it. The most famous case in this area involved another juvenile, fifteen-year-old Jonathan Lebed of New Jersey. Using numerous false names to hide his identity, Lebed flooded stock-related chat rooms, particularly at Yahoo!'s finance boards, with messages touting the virtues of stocks he had recently purchased. The resourceful teenager even arranged a system in which his broker would sell his overvalued stocks while he was in school. In 2000, the SEC forced Lebed to return nearly $300,000 in gains plus interest.[37]

A number of other forms of securities fraud are also common in cyberspace. "Cybersmear" schemes are similar to "pump and dump" schemes, except the goal is to disparage a stock in order to drive its price down (speculators who have sold a stock short profit when its price declines). In several cases, the person trying to manipulate a stock price has released an official-looking but fake press release giving false information about a company. (In 2000, a fictitious press release posted by twenty-three-year-old college student Mark Jakob caused the total market valuation of Internet Wire to fall by $2.4 billion.) There have even been instances in which individuals have sold securities for nonexistent companies online. As the number and types of online securities frauds increase, the SEC is attempting to keep pace by expanding its Office of Internet Enforcement, staffed by several hundred employees.

Pirating Intellectual Property Online

Most people think of wealth in terms of houses, land, cars, stocks, and bonds. Wealth, however, also includes **intellectual property,** which consists of the products that result from intellectual, creative processes. The government provides various forms of protection for intellectual property such as copyrights and patents. These protections ensure that a person who writes a book or a song or creates a software program is financially rewarded if that product is sold in the marketplace.

Intellectual property such as books, films, music, and software is vulnerable to "piracy"—the unauthorized copying and use of the property. In the past, copying intellectual products was time consuming, and the quality of the pirated copies was clearly inferior. In today's online world, however, things have changed. Simply clicking a mouse can now reproduce millions of unauthorized copies, and pirated duplicates of copyrighted works obtained via the Internet are often exactly the same as the original, or close to it.

In 2001, Jonathan Lebed became the first minor charged with securities fraud by the Securities and Exchange Commission (SEC). According to the SEC, Lebed used brokerage accounts set up by his father to buy cheap stocks. He then flooded Internet chat groups with misleading information intended to bolster the worth of these stocks (for example: "Next stock to gain 1,000 percent!"). When the price of each stock hit a certain level, Lebed would sell it, earning as much as $74,000 on a single trade. Why is this kind of activity known as "pumping and dumping"? (NYT Picture/Katy Grannan)

On the Web

The FBI and the National White Collar Crime Center maintain a joint Web site for people wishing to report Internet fraud. For a link to its Web site, go to the Hypercontents page for this chapter at http://cj.wadsworth.com/ gainescore2e.

INTELLECTUAL PROPERTY
Property resulting from intellectual, creative processes.

"Sadly, there is a common misperception among many—especially many young people—that crimes committed online are not as serious as more traditional crimes."

—John Ashcroft, *attorney general of the United States* (2001)

INFOTRAC®
COLLEGE EDITION

Keywords: online pornography, cyber crime

The Business Software Alliance estimates that over a third of all business software is pirated, costing software makers about $12 billion in 2000.[38] The International Federation of the Phonographic Industry believes that 36 percent of recorded music is pirated.[39] Much of the piracy of intellectual property, especially software and music, is deemed "altruistic." People give away or share intellectual property not to make money but because they want to be generous or are part of a community of like-minded "traders."

Is there any current solution to the increasing problem of the piracy of intellectual property via the Internet? The simple answer is no. Some private companies offer online "digital detective" software that uses special search tools called "spiders" or "robots" to monitor the Web for sites containing copyrighted works. In the United States, pirates can be prosecuted under the No Electronic Theft Act[40] and the Digital Millennium Copyright Act.[41] Global efforts are also under way to protect intellectual property.

CYBER CRIMES AGAINST THE COMMUNITY

One of the greatest challenges cyberspace presents for law enforcement is how to enforce laws governing activities that are prohibited under certain circumstances but are not always illegal. Such laws generally reflect the will of the community, which recognizes behavior as acceptable under some circumstances and unacceptable under others. Thus, while it is legal in many areas to sell a pornographic video to a fifty-year-old, it is never legal to sell the same item to a fifteen-year-old. Similarly, placing a bet on a football game with a bookmaker in Las Vegas, Nevada, is legal, but placing a bet on a football game with a bookmaker in Cleveland, Ohio, is not. Of course, in cyberspace it is often impossible to know whether the customer buying porn is fifty or fifteen, or if the person placing the bet is from Las Vegas or Cleveland.

Online Pornography

The Internet has been a boon to the pornography industry. According to estimates, the online sex industry generates over $1 billion each year.[42] Though no general figures are available, the Internet has undoubtedly also been a boon to those who produce and sell child pornography, or any material "depicting sexually explicit conduct involving a child."[43] As we have seen with other cyber crimes, the Internet is conducive to child pornography for a number of reasons:

- *Speed.* The Internet is the fastest means of sending visual material over long distances. Child pornographers can deliver their material faster and more securely online than through regular mail.

- *Security.* Any illegal material that is placed in the hands of a mail carrier is inherently in danger of being discovered. This risk is significantly reduced with e-mail. Furthermore, Internet sites that offer child pornography can protect their customers with passwords, which keep random "Web surfers" (or law enforcement agents) from stumbling onto the site or chat room.

- *Anonymity.* Obviously, anonymity is the most important protection offered by the Internet for sellers and buyers of child pornography, as it is for any person engaged in illegal behavior in cyberspace.[44]

Because of these three factors, courts and lawmakers have had a difficult time controlling the dissemination of obscenity and child pornography via the Internet. In 1996, Congress first attempted to protect minors from pornographic materials on the Internet by passing the Communications Decency Act (CDA).[45]

Steven J. DiPietro, a police officer with the Connecticut State Police Computer Crimes and Electronic Evidence Unit in Meriden, Conn., talks about his work. The unit has seen a major increase in work with the emergence of the Internet as a conduit for child pornography. The unit's yearly caseload surged from 103 cases in 1999 to about 580 in 2001. About 300 cases were reported in the first half of 2002. The department issued warnings to children and parents after the May 20 death of Christina Long, a 13-year-old Danbury cheerleader who was allegedly strangled by a 25-year-old man she met on the Internet. (AP Photo/Journal Inquirer, Leslloyd F. Alleyne Jr.)

Later in the chapter, when we examine the issue of civil rights and the Internet, we will discuss the United States Supreme Court's reaction to this law and other attempts to regulate cyberspace.

Gambling in Cyberspace

In general, gambling is illegal. All states have statutes that regulate gambling—defined as any scheme that involves the distribution of property by chance among persons who have paid valuable consideration for the opportunity (chance) to receive the property. In some states, certain forms of gambling, such as casino gambling or horse racing, are legal. Many states also have legalized state-operated lotteries, as well as lotteries (such as bingo) conducted for charitable purposes. A number of states also allow gambling on Native American reservations.

One of the challenges facing both federal and state governments today is how to enforce gambling laws in an online environment. Now, virtually any person, even a fourteen-year-old with a credit card, can play blackjack or other gambling games on the Internet. Given that approximately 4.5 million Americans admit to having gambled online, and that nearly nine hundred Internet casinos are currently in operation, the questions raised by online gambling are certainly not going to go away.[46]

Efforts to combat Internet gambling face significant jurisdictional issues. For example, in those states that do not allow casino gambling or off-track betting, what can a state government do if residents of the state place bets online? After all, states have no constitutional authority to regulate activities that occur in other states. Complicating the problem is the fact that many Internet sites are located outside the United States in countries where Internet gambling is legal, and no state government has jurisdiction over activities that take place in other countries.

Another problem is determining where the physical act of placing a bet on the Internet occurs. Is it where the gambler is located or where the gambling site is based? For example, suppose that a resident of New York places bets via the Internet at a gambling site located in Antigua, an island in the West Indies. Is the actual act of "gambling" taking place in New York or in Antigua? According to a New York trial court, the act of entering a bet and transmitting information

Officials at World Wide Web Casinos headquarters in Antigua demonstrate some of their activities. Technology allows Internet users from all over the world to gamble online through companies like World Wide Web Casinos outside of the United States. World Wide Web Casinos has claimed that using its service "cannot be illegal because, despite their origination, bets will technically be placed on the computer at our off-shore land-based casino site that is legally licensed and taxed by the host government." Is this statement correct? (AP Photo/ Jack Dempsey)

from New York to Antigua via the Internet was adequate to constitute gambling activity in New York.[47] How the majority of courts will decide this question, however, is not yet clear.

FIGHTING CYBER CRIME

Why not just pass a law that makes gambling in cyberspace illegal? In fact, four states—Illinois, Louisiana, Nevada, and Texas—have specifically banned Internet gambling, and Congress is considering a similar step. Simply passing a law, however, does not guarantee that the law will be effectively enforced. With 600 million users reaching every corner of the globe, transferring unimaginable amounts of information almost instantaneously, the Internet has proved resistant to regulation.[48] In the past, the U.S. government has generally adopted a "hands-off" attitude toward the Internet in order to promote the free flow of ideas and encourage the growth of electronic commerce. The terrorist attacks of September 11, 2001, seem to have changed this attitude. President Bush's efforts to increase homeland security included $722 million in funds to strengthen the nation's information security systems, a task in which law enforcement will play a crucial role.[49]

Jurisdictional Challenges

Regardless of what type of cyber crime is being investigated, law enforcement agencies are often frustrated by problems of jurisdiction (noted briefly in the section on cyber gambling and explained more fully in Chapter 8). Jurisdiction is primarily based on physical geography—each country, state, and nation has jurisdiction, or authority, over crimes that occur within its boundaries. The Internet, however, destroys these traditional notions because geographic boundaries simply do not exist in cyberspace.[50]

To see how this can affect law enforcement efforts, let's consider a hypothetical cyber stalking case. Phil, who lives in State A, has been sending e-mails containing graphic sexual threats to Stephanie, who lives in State B. Where has the crime taken place? Which police department has authority to arrest Phil, and which court system has authority to try him? To further complicate matters, what if State A has not yet added cyber stalking to its criminal code, while State B has? Does that mean that Phil has not committed a crime in his home state, but has committed one in Stephanie's?

"*One of the problems we face . . . is getting law enforcement to recognize the seriousness of the crime and then prosecute it. Internet fraud is probably the easiest thing in the world to prosecute because we have got all the information.*"

—Brad Handler, *associate general counsel and director of law and public policy for eBay* (2000)

On the Web

The National Infrastructure Protection Center (NIPC) brings together representatives from U.S. government agencies, state and local governments, and the private sector in a partnership to gather information about computer crimes. For a link to its Web site, go to the Hypercontents page for this chapter at http://cj.wadsworth.com/ gainescore2e.

Federal Law Enforcement and Cyber Crime

Of course, federal law enforcement agencies have jurisdiction over all federal crimes, no matter in which state they may take place. Because of this freedom from jurisdictional restraints, the federal government has traditionally taken the lead in law enforcement efforts against cyber crime. This is not to say that little cyber crime prevention occurs on the local level. Most major metropolitan police departments have created special units to fight cyber crime. In general, however, only a handful of local police and sheriffs' departments have the resources to support a squad of cyber investigators.[51]

The Federal Bureau of Investigation. As the primary crime fighting unit of the federal government, the FBI has taken the lead in law enforcement efforts against cyber crime. The FBI has the primary responsibility for enforcing all federal criminal statutes involving computer crimes. (See Figure 15.3 for a rundown of these laws.) In 1998, the Bureau oversaw the creation of the National Infrastructure Protection Center (NIPC), a Washington, D.C.–based agency charged with detecting and investigating cyber threats concerning the country's "critical infrastructures," such as transportation, energy, telecommunications, and financial networks.[52] Three years later, the FBI and the NIPC cosponsored Infragard, an organization that hopes to increase information sharing between law enforcement and private companies in order to combat cyber crime.

In 2000, responding to local police departments' inability to attend to problems of fraud, the FBI, along with the National White Collar Crime Center, launched the Internet Fraud Complaint Center (IFCC), discussed earlier in the chapter. The IFCC acts as a clearinghouse for reports of Internet fraud reported by businesses and individuals at the agency's Web site (**http://www.IFCCFBI.gov**). The FBI also offers instruction in cyber crime prevention for local and state police officers at its training center in Quantico, Virginia.

On the Web

The U.S. Department of Justice maintains a Web site devoted to the issue of cyber crime. For a link to its Web site, go to the Hypercontents page for this chapter at **http://cj.wadsworth.com/gainescore2e**.

INFOTRAC®
COLLEGE EDITION

Keywords:
FBI and cyber crime

FIGURE 15.3 **Federal Laws and Computer Crime**

18 U.S.C. Section 1030—It is a crime to do any of the following to and/or by means of a computer used by a financial institution, used by the federal government, or used in interstate or foreign commerce or communication:

1. gain unauthorized entry into a government computer and thereby discover information which is intended to remain confidential, information which the perpetrator either unlawfully discloses to someone not authorized to receive it or retains in violation of the law;

2. gain unauthorized entry to a computer and thereby gain access to information to which the perpetrator is not entitled to have access;

3. gain unauthorized access to a computer and thereby further the perpetration of a fraud;

4. cause damage to a computer as the result either of gaining unauthorized access to it or of inserting a program, code or information into the computer;

5. transmit, in interstate or foreign commerce, a threat to cause damage to a computer in order to extort money or property from a person or other legal entity;

6. traffic, with intent to defraud, in passwords which either permit unauthorized access to a government computer or affect interstate or foreign commerce; or

7. transmit in interstate or foreign commerce any threat to cause damage to a protected computer with intent to extort something of value.

18 U.S.C. Section 1462—It is a crime to use a computer to import obscene material into the United States.

18 U.S.C. Section 1463—It is a crime to transport obscene material in interstate or foreign commerce.

18 U.S.C. Section 2251—It is a crime to employ a minor or induce a minor to participate in making a visual depiction of a sexually explicit act if the depiction was created using materials that had been transported (including the transportation by computer) in interstate or foreign commerce.

18 U.S.C. Section 2252—It is a crime to transport child pornography in interstate or foreign commerce.

18 U.S.C. Section 1028—It is a crime to produce, transfer, or possess a device, including a computer, that is intended to be used to falsify identification documents.

Many traditional crimes encompass the use of a computer as well; for example, threatening the president's life or infringing a copyright.

Source: Susan W. Brenner, "State Cybercrime Legislation in the United States of America: A Survey," *Richmond Journal of Law and Technology* 7 (Winter 2001), 1–5; and Heather Jacobson and Rebecca Green, "Computer Crimes," *American Criminal Law Review* (Spring 2002), 280–284.

As several U.S. senators look on, President George W. Bush signs the Patriot Act in 2001. The bill allows law enforcement and intelligence agencies to "wiretap" telephone conversations and Internet usage by those suspected of terrorist activities. This form of surveillance does not require a warrant, which has led many observers to worry that it gives law enforcement officials too much power to peer into the private lives of Americans without first getting permission from a judge. Do increased concerns about terrorist activity following the September 11, 2001, attacks justify these measures? (AP Photo/Doug Mills)

"**Computer criminals may think that they operate in a new frontier without boundaries, where they won't be caught. Obviously, that's not true. We've responded by breaking down traditional borders among federal, state, county and local law enforcement.**"

—John Farmer, Jr., *New Jersey state attorney general* (1999)

INFOTRAC®
COLLEGE EDITION

**Keywords:
computer forensics**

COMPUTER FORENSICS
The application of computer technology to finding and utilizing evidence of computer and cyber crimes.

The United States Secret Service.   The USA Patriot Act,[53] passed in late 2001, greatly increased the Secret Service's role in fighting cyber crime. In the legal arena, the legislation gave the agency jurisidiction over some of the crimes listed in 18 U.S.C. Section 1030 (see Figure 15.3).[54] The Secret Service was authorized to develop a national network of electronic crime task forces based on the New York Electronic Crime Task Force, a collaboration among federal, state, and local law enforcement officers and a wide range of corporate sponsors. To date, the agency has established these task forces in Boston, San Francisco, Los Angeles, Chicago, Miami, Las Vegas, Washington, D.C., and Charlotte, North Carolina.

On the Cyber Beat: New Challenges for Law Enforcement

In trying to describe the complexities of fighting cyber crime, Michael Vatis, former director of the NIPC, imagines a bank robbery during which the police arrive just as "the demand note and fingerprints are vanishing, the security camera is erasing its own images, and the image of the criminal is being erased from the mind of the teller."[55] Cyber criminals are often able to write code that erases any traces of their presence, making the gathering of evidence much more difficult than it is in the "real" world.

Computer Forensics.   Law enforcement officers cannot put yellow tape around a computer screen or dust a Web site for fingerprints. The best, and often the only, way to fight computer crime is with technology that gives law enforcement agencies the ability to "track" hackers and other cyber criminals through the Internet. But, Michael Vatis observed, these efforts are complicated by the fact that digital evidence can be altered or erased even as the cyber crime is being committed. In Chapter 5, we discussed *forensics,* or the application of science to find evidence of criminal activity. Within the past decade, a branch of this science known as **computer forensics** has evolved to gather evidence of cyber crimes.

The basic "tool" of computer forensics is software that allows investigators to re-create the activities of the target user. A program called Silentrunner, for example, can capture and analyze all the activity on a computer network, providing a set of "electronic fingerprints" that allow authorities to retrace the user's digital movements. "Short of taking your hard drive and having it run over by a Mack truck," said one expert, "you can't ever be sure that anything is truly deleted from your computer."[56] Other software constantly monitors "conversations" a computer system has with other computer systems, making it easier to catch an intruder "in the act" before she or he is able to erase evidence of her or his presence.

Honeypots.   "Honeypots" have also proved useful in stopping hackers. These specially designed traps rely on the fact that hackers are constantly looking for unprotected computer systems from which to launch their attacks on a third party, thereby covering their tracks. A honeypot offers hackers a very inviting site from which to operate, and records all of the criminal activity while it is taking place.[57]

Private Efforts to Combat Cyber Crime

"There is no way law enforcement officials, by themselves, can effectively monitor the Internet for high-tech crimes without additional assistance." This is the message of CyberSnitch, an online network that allows citizens to learn about and report cyber crimes. Organizations such as CyberSnitch and other similar sites represent a minuscule part of the efforts among private citizens and businesses to combat cyber crime. Indeed, private Internet security has become a billion-dollar industry, in many ways proving itself more effective than the government in policing cyberspace.

Hi–Tech PIs. The client list of private investigator Kellie Carlisle of Orlando, Florida, seems average enough. It includes a woman who suspects her husband of having an affair, a family trying to find a runaway child, and a bank that suspects an employee of white-collar crimes. The difference is that Carlisle does most of her investigating without leaving the chair in front of her computer. She is part of the growing field of private investigators who specialize in computer crime. The High Technology Crime Investigation Association, formed only a few years ago, now has almost 2,500 members.[58]

Protecting Computer Information. The fear of being "hacked" has also spurred an industry that helps clients—either individuals or businesses—protect the sanctity of their computer systems. Because every computer hooked up to the Internet is a potential security breach, these experts help devise elaborate and ever-changing password systems to ensure that only authorized users access data. They also install protective software such as firewalls and antivirus software, which can limit outside access to a computer or network. Because cyber criminals are constantly updating their technology, cyberspace security firms help their clients do the same with their defensive systems.

Perhaps the most successful and, as we shall see, controversial way to protect computer information is to encrypt it. Through **encryption,** a message (plaintext) is transformed into something (ciphertext) that only the sender and receiver can understand. Unless a third party is able to "break the code," the information will stay secure. Encryption is particularly useful in protecting e-mails. Indeed, until recently the most widely used encryption program, known as P.G.P. for Pretty Good Privacy, was considered unbreakable. In 2001, however, two cryptologists announced that the program may be flawed and would require a software fix called a "patch" to restore consumer confidence.[59]

Crime Control versus Civil Liberties on the Internet

Law enforcement authorities are afraid that the wrong persons, including international terrorists, will take advantage of encryption to engage in illegal activities. For this reason, the U.S. government has tried to restrict the export of encryption codes. These restrictions have been challenged in a few cases on the ground that an encryption code is speech and therefore would be protected by the First Amendment to the U.S. Constitution. This would mean that the regulations banning its export are unconstitutional.[60]

The Internet provides yet another forum for Americans to consider the question, How much freedom is *too much* freedom? On the one hand, many law enforcement officials believe that if they are too timid in responding to cyber crime, the Internet will become a "safe haven" for criminals and terrorists.[61] On the other hand, government attempts to monitor Internet use to detect criminal conspiracies or activities are likely be challenged as violating the constitutional rights of our citizens, particularly the rights to freedom of speech and privacy, both guaranteed by the United States Constitution. (See *CJ in Focus—The Balancing Act: Hate Speech on the Net* on the next page.)

ENCRYPTION
The process by which a message is transmitted into something that the sender and receiver intend third parties not to understand.

CyberSnitch is a voluntary online crime reporting system. For a link to its Web site, go to the Hypercontents page for this chapter at **http://cj.wadsworth.com/ gainescore2e.**

Stephanie Constantino and her son Carlos, aged nine, at the public library in Camano Island, Washington. Carlos said he spotted a teenager viewing photos of naked women at one of the library's computers. In 2001, Congress passed legislation that requires all public libraries to install filters that would block pornographic sites on their computers. Does the legislation requiring filters conflict in any way with the constitutionally protected right to free speech? Which is more important: the ability of all users to gain information or the need to protect children from pornography in public access areas? (AP Photo/*The Herald,* Michael O'Leary)

CJ in F CUS

The Balancing Act: Hate Speech on the Net

Don Black is a big fan of the Internet. An ex–Ku Klux Klan member, Black is the founder of what was perhaps the first "white pride" Web site. "[T]he Net has provided us with the opportunity to bring our point of view to hundreds of thousands of people who would never have otherwise . . . been in touch with any of our organizations," he says.

This, according to many observers, is the problem. Before the Internet, extreme racists who shared Black's views existed in relative isolation. Often, they could communicate with others with the same ideology only by making a great effort. Today, even a novice Web surfer can find postings or Web sites that advocate violence against African Americans, homosexuals, Jewish people, and almost every other minority group. Although only about three thousand of the nearly 10 million sites on the World Wide Web can be described as "hate" sites, their influence may be significant. Given that nearly half of all Americans between the ages of sixteen and twenty-two regularly surf the Web, a particular

concern is that these sites will teach intolerance to the Web generation.

Some countries restrict hate speech on the Web. In Germany, for example, where Nazi propaganda and racist speech are illegal, anyone caught disseminating either over the Internet can be arrested and imprisoned. In the United States, however, the tradition of free speech is strong, and there is little call for such laws. Gerhard Lauck, for example, spent five years in prison in Germany for operating a Nazi Web site in Europe in the mid-1990s. Today, Lauck has relocated to Nebraska, and he now runs the site without government interference.

Note that just as speech that advocates harm can be regulated in this country, so can Web sites that do so. In 1999, the American Coalition of Life Activists and Advocates for Life Ministries were required to pay $107 million in damages for inciting harm against doctors who provide abortions. The jury in the case found that a list of such doctors on the site was actually a "hit list" that turned the physicians into targets, and therefore the site represented a "true threat" rather than just "speech."

FOR CRITICAL ANALYSIS
One free speech advocate has stated that the Founding Fathers had the Internet "in mind" when they added the First Amendment to the U.S. Constitution. What do you think he means by this? Do you agree?

Free Speech on the Internet. Perhaps the most controversial free speech issue in cyberspace concerns minors and pornographic material. In 1996, Congress passed the Communications Decency Act (CDA) to protect children from harmful material on the Internet by taking a broad approach. The CDA made it a crime to make available to minors online any "obscene or indecent" message that "depicts or describes, in terms patently offensive as measured by contemporary standards, sexual or excretory activities or organs."[62]

The United States Supreme Court disapproved of this approach. In *Reno v. American Civil Liberties Union* (1997),[63] the Court ruled that portions of the act were unconstitutional. In the eyes of the Court, the terms *indecent* and *patently offensive* covered large amounts of nonpornographic material with serious educational or other value. (For a further discussion of this issue, see the feature *Criminal Justice in Action—Child Pornography and the Internet* at the end of this chapter.)

Privacy on the Internet. Privacy in cyberspace is also a source of concern. Responding to these fears, Congress has passed several laws to protect Internet users in this area. The Financial Services Modernization Act, for example, forbids online financial institutions from disclosing data about their customers unless given permission.[64] Similarly, the Children's Online Privacy Protection Act requires operators of Web sites aimed at children under the age of thirteen to clearly provide notice about the information being collected from users and how it will be used.[65]

Many Americans, however, worry that the government is not doing enough to protect their rights from law enforcement efforts. These concerns were heightened when, in 2002, officials at the FBI confirmed that the agency was working to develop special technology—code-named Magic Lantern—that will allow investigators to secretly install software that can record every keystroke on a person's computer.[66] A few years earlier, the FBI had lauched the Carnivore program in order to monitor e-mail and other online transmissions to and from particular persons. Critics claim that these unprecedented forms of surveillance are a threat to privacy rights because, in addition to targeting criminal and terrorist suspects, they would allow the government to monitor the communication of innocent citizens.[67]

FIGHTING CYBER TERRORISM

Since both the use of the Internet and criminal and terrorist activity in cyberspace are going to expand significantly in the near future, law enforcement will need to use advanced technology to carry out its duties. In 2002, for example, Detective Chris Hsiung of the Mountain Valley, California, police department noticed that a large number of anonymous browsers from the Middle East and Southeast Asia were probing sensitive sites in the Silicon Valley. Detective Hsuing alerted the FBI, and federal agents were able to determine that these "visitors" had been studying the Web sites of electrical generation and transmission facilities, water storage and distribution centers, emergency telephone systems, and nuclear power plants. Then, in 2002, programs were found on computers seized from the Al Qaeda terrorist group that could conceivably control such sites via remote control.[68]

Computers alone do not have the capacity to kill. They can be used, however, as a tool of cyber terrorists to disrupt the lives of an entire community. Cyber terrorism is the use of computer technology against a person or property with the goal of intimidating a government or a population in furtherance of social or political goals. In other words, instead of using conventional methods such as bombings or hijackings, cyber terrorists can use viruses, hacking, and other "denial of service" attacks.[69] Following September 11, 2001, the New York Stock Exchange was closed for six days, affecting billions of dollars in transactions and leaving the U.S. economy in a weakened state.

Many experts feel the best way to protect against cyber terrorism is to create more intranets—that is, internal computer networks that cannot be accessed by outside sources. Indeed, the Bush administration has proposed the creation of Govnet, a secure network linking federal agencies.[70] Even if such an intranet were to exist, however, about 85 percent of the infrastructure of the Internet is controlled by private businesses.[71] In addition, there are approximately 120 million individual Internet users in the United States. Many law enforcement experts insist that controversial technologies such as Carnivore and Magic Lantern (mentioned in the previous section) are absolutely necessary to effectively police the immensity of cyberspace. Whether or not this is true, federal and state legislatures will need to find strategies for fighting cyber terrorism—and cyber crime—that achieve the proper balance between promoting crime control and protecting the ideals of personal freedom and civil liberties that the Internet often embodies.

Norwich University President Richard Schneider announces the creation of the National Center for the Study of Counter-Terrorism and Cyber-Crime at a news conference in Northfield, Vermont, in 2002. The center will focus on everything from miniaturizing communications devices worn by soldiers in combat to defending against attacks on computer networks. (AP Photo/Toby Talbot)

Criminal Justice in Action
Child Pornography and the Internet

As we have seen in this chapter, the Internet has not—for the most part—created "new" crimes. Instead, it has made old crimes easier to commit. This is particularly true with regard to child pornography. Twenty years ago, those involved in the practice relied on mail and photography labs, providing the police with plenty of opportunities to gather and trace evidence. "Child pornography was pretty much eradicated in the 1980s," says the head of the U.S. Customs Service Cyber-Smuggling Center. "With the advent of the Internet," he adds, "it exploded."[72] In this *Criminal Justice in Action* feature, we will see how law enforcement agents have dealt with this explosion and discuss how the technology of the Internet both helps and hinders this process.

HOW BIG IS THE PROBLEM?

The problem of child pornography on the Internet takes two general forms: (1) illegal exposure of children to sexual images or invitations online and (2) trafficking of photos and videos of children engaged in sexual acts. An indication of the prevalence of the first form can be found in a survey of 1,501 ten- to seventeen-year-olds conducted by the Crimes against Children Research Center at the University of New Hampshire in 2000. The survey revealed that one in five had received at least one sexual solicitation over the Internet in the past year. One in four reported unwanted exposure to photos of naked people or images of sexual behavior.[73]

As for the second form, in the past decade, a "community" of child pornographers has evolved, protected by the anonymity that the Internet offers. In 1996, the FBI was investigating 113 cases involving child pornography. By 2001, that figure had risen to 1,559 cases.[74]

These activities are also global in scope. Whereas twenty years ago an American or European interested in child pornography might have had to travel to a country where laws against it were not enforced, today he or she need only have access to a telephone connection. In the late 1990s, law enforcement agents in thirteen countries broke up the Wonderland Club, an immense child pornography ring. Based in the United States, the Wonderland Club had more than two hundred members from forty-seven different countries.[75]

THE INNOCENT IMAGES APPROACH

Parents can take certain steps to protect their children from the worst of the Internet. A number of software programs have been designed to block out certain sites—including all chat rooms—and prevent children from keying in certain words. Given children's wide access to the Internet from a number of different computer systems (at school, at the library, at friends' homes), however, it is practically impossible to protect a child at all times. Consequently, the primary responsibility for fighting cyber porn rests with law enforcement agencies.

The FBI's Innocent Images unit has been particularly successful in apprehending online pedophiles.[76] Using the anonymity that so often protects online pornographers, agents "hang out" in chat rooms, posing as either young children or sexual predators. In one such case, FBI agent Patricia Ferrante posed as One4Fun4U, a fourteen-year-old girl, in a chat room called "X Little Girl Gift." James Childress, a thirty-one-year-old Virginia native using the screen name "Sylliboy," had several sexually graphic conversations with One4Fun4U and then arranged to meet her in a Maryland mall in order to have sex. When he appeared at the mall, Childress was arrested and eventually found guilty of traveling across state lines with the intent of engaging in sexual acts with a juvenile.[77]

NAUGHTON AND THE "FANTASY DEFENSE"

The prosecution rate for those arrested by Innocent Images agents is an impressive 95 percent.[78] Most of the defendants claim that they were entrapped by the FBI or other law enforcement agents (see Chapter 6 for a review of entrapment), but this defense has generally failed. In almost every instance, the defendant entered the chat room or made "first contact" with the victim/agent. A court will rarely find that the agent "cajoled" the defendant into action simply by pretending to be a child.[79]

At least one defendant in an online solicitation case has succeeded with the "fantasy defense," however. In that case, Patrick Naughton was arrested on the Santa Monica Pier in California as he waited to meet "KRISLA," whom he allegedly believed to be a thirteen-year-old girl, but who was in fact an FBI agent. Naughton had kept up a correspondence with KRISLA over the Internet for nine months and had told her that "he wanted to get [her] alone in his hotel room and have [her] strip naked for him."[80]

During the trial, Naughton argued that he never thought that KRISLA was actually thirteen years old, but always assumed that she was an adult woman who shared his "daughter/daddy" fantasy and was playing the role of a young girl. Therefore, he did not intend to have sex with an underage girl and had not committed a crime. Enough members of the jury believed Naughton, and he was acquitted.[81]

VIRTUALLY ILLEGAL

The key to Naughton's successful defense was that those involved in the Internet culture understand that people online often do not represent themselves truthfully. Thus, Naughton could maintain that he was just involved in a fantasy courtship and had no way of knowing KRISLA's true age. This idea of the Internet as a fantasy world plays a large part in the latest controversy to arise regarding online child pornography: the depiction of "fake" minors engaged in sexual acts.

With current software programs, extremely lifelike digital images can be produced. Indeed, most Hollywood movies today use digital images, often without the viewer knowing that the images are "fake." When this relatively new and inexpensive technology is applied to pornography, the results are amazingly real. Suppose that a computer programmer, using just a computer and no human actors, creates a lifelike set of child actors and uses commands on the computer to have them engage in sexual acts. Has the programmer violated child pornography laws?

In 1996, Congress passed the Child Pornography Prevention Act.[82] This act bans the distribution and posses-sion of computer-generated images that appear to depict minors engaging in lewd and lascivious behavior. Six years later, the United States Supreme Court struck down the provisions of the law that made it a crime to create, distribute, or possess computer-generated images that appear to depict minors engaging in lewd and lascivious behavior.[83] The Court held that these provisions violated free speech protections in the First Amendment. The decision angered many observers—one politician complained that the Court had "sided with pedophiles over children"[84]—and will certainly not silence the debate over "virtual" child pornography.

MAKING SENSE OF CHILD PORNOGRAPHY ON THE INTERNET

1 Review the discussion of the mental requirements for committing a crime on pages 67–68 in Chapter 3. Do you think that Patrick Naughton, if he was indeed telling the truth, did not have the required *mens rea* to be charged with the intent to have sex with a minor?

2 What arguments can be made that the Child Pornography Prevention Act is contrary to the guarantee of freedom of speech in the U.S. Constitution? Do you agree with these arguments? Why or why not?

3 Does the government have a compelling interest in protecting children from "fake" pornography? In other words, how might banning virtual pornography protect "real" children?

INFOTRAC®
COLLEGE EDITION

Keywords: online child pornography, Patrick Naughton

Patrick J. Naughton, left, successfully used the "fantasy defense" to avoid conviction on charges of online solicitation. (AP Photo/ Lee Celano)

KEY TERMS

computer crime 382

computer forensics 394

cyber crime 382

cyber fraud 383

cyber stalking 385

encryption 395

hacker 387

identity theft 384

intellectual property 389

CHAPTER SUMMARY

❶ Distinguish a cyber crime from a "traditional" crime. Most cyber crimes are not "new" types of crimes. Rather, they are traditional crimes committed in cyberspace. Perpetrators of cyber crimes are often aided by certain aspects of the Internet, such as its ability to cloak the user's identity and its effectiveness as a conduit for transferring—or stealing—large amounts of information very quickly.

❷ Indicate how the Internet has contributed to increased instances of identity theft. In cyberspace, thieves can steal data from anywhere in the world, as long as they have the necessary computer equipment. Thus, the Internet provides a medium through which wrongdoers can appropriate the information such as credit-card numbers and Social Security numbers that is the basis for identity theft. The Internet also provides those who steal such information with an easy medium for using it. Protected by anonymity, a person who steals a credit-card number can use it to purchase thousands of dollars' worth of merchandise before the theft is noticed.

❸ Explain the activities and purposes of most hackers. A hacker is someone who uses one computer to break into another computer. Sometimes a hacker's goal is to commit cyber theft. In most cases, however, a hacker's principal aim is to "show off" the ease with which she or he can gain access to protected computer systems and cause errors.

❹ Outline the three major reasons that the Internet is conducive to juvenile cyber crime. (a) Advanced computer equipment and software allow juveniles to commit crimes without leaving their homes; (b) the anonymity of cyberspace allows young people to commit crimes such as theft that would otherwise be almost impossible, given the limitations of size, money, and experience; and (c) hacking and other cyber crimes are often not recognized as unethical in youth culture.

❺ Explain how the Internet has contributed to piracy of intellectual property. In the past, copying intellectual property such as films and music was time consuming, and the quality of the pirated copies was inferior to that of the originals. On the Internet, however, millions of unauthorized copies of intellectual property can be reproduced at the click of a mouse, and the quality of these items is often the same as the original, or close to it.

❻ Describe the challenges to enforcing online gambling laws. Although gambling is generally illegal in this country, virtually anybody with a credit card can gamble online, regardless of his or her age or place of residence. Furthermore, many Internet gambling sites are physically based outside the United States, limiting the authority, or jurisdiction, of American law enforcement agencies and courts to combat their activities.

❼ Indicate which federal law enforcement agencies are primarily responsible for preventing and investigating cyber crimes. The Federal Bureau of Investigation, as the primary crime-fighting agency of the federal government, has the most extensive jurisdiction over cyber crimes. Legislation passed in the wake of the September 11, 2001, terrorist attacks has now given considerable responsibility to the United States Secret Service, which has developed a network of electronic crime task forces across the country.

❽ List two areas in which crime control and civil liberties have conflicted on the Internet. (a) Freedom of speech, as guaranteed by the First Amendment of the United States Constitution, is constantly being tested by Web sites whose content includes hate speech, obscenity, and child pornography; and (b) privacy on the Internet is threatened, many believe, by law enforcement efforts to monitor certain citizens through programs such as Carnivore and the as-yet-untested Magic Lantern.

QUESTIONS FOR CRITICAL ANALYSIS

1 Why does the nature of online communication make it difficult to identify and prosecute those who commit cyber crimes?

2 Why are businesses often reluctant to report a security breach of their computer systems or databases?

3 Consider the following situation: Jacqueline Sharp is the sheriff of Jackson County, Missouri, population 1,434. Sheriff Sharp has only two deputies at her disposal. Mae Brown, a resident of Jackson County, is receiving threatening e-mails from someone who has the cyberspace name of johndoe1313. Mae is certain that the sender is actually Peter Brown, her ex-husband. Peter lives in Wilson County, Louisiana. What are some

of the jurisdictional problems Sheriff Sharp may face in investigating Peter's possible involvement in cyber stalking? What are some of the practical problems Sheriff Sharp may encounter? How might she solve these problems?

4 How does encryption help protect information delivered via the Internet? Is this method foolproof?

5 Why did the United States Supreme Court rule that parts of the Communications Decency Act were unconstitutional?

6 How has the Internet contributed to the spread of child pornography?

SELECTED PRINT AND ELECTRONIC RESOURCES

SUGGESTED READINGS

Casey, Eoghan, *Digital Evidence and Computer Crime: Forensic Science, Computers, and the Internet,* San Diego, CA: Academic, 2000. This is a handbook for the digital investigator. The author provides a wide survey of cyber crime law, including specific topics such as search and seizure and jurisdiction in cyberspace. He also explains the basic concepts behind forensic science and computer crime, giving an in-depth look into the gathering of evidence as a tool against cyber criminals.

Hyatt, Michael S., *Invasion of Privacy: How to Protect Yourself in the Digital Age,* Washington, D.C.: Regnery Publishing, 2001. In this book, Hyatt explains how businesses, the government, interest groups, and individuals can access personal information of those who use the Internet. The author provides a number of security measures that Web surfers can take to protect their online privacy, as well as listing Web sites and other information sources that offer advice for those with Internet privacy concerns.

Power, Richard, *Tangled Web: Tales of Digital Crime from the Shadows of Cyberspace,* Indianapolis, IN: Que, 2000. Chapter by chapter, this book examines the various types of cyber crimes and details law enforcement efforts to combat them. The author focuses on hackers, identity theft, child pornography, cyber vandalism, and cyber terrorism, as well as almost all of the other cyber crimes discussed in this chapter.

Schwartau, Winn, *Cybershock: Surviving Hackers, Phreakers, Identity Thieves, Internet Terrorists and Weapons of Mass Destruction,* New York: Thunder's Mouth Press, 2000. The author, an expert on information security, is concerned that the general public is not aware of the dangers lurking on the Internet. In this book, he tries to remedy the situation by explaining the basics of hack-

ing techniques as well as providing various means by which the user can protect himself or herself from being a victim of cyber crime. Schwartau also interviews a number of law enforcement officials, corporate security experts, and hackers in order to present a balanced view of the various takes on the hacker "ethic."

MEDIA RESOURCES

Swordfish **(2001)** Stanley Jobson (Hugh Jackman) is one of the two best computer hackers in the world. He has just been released from a prison stint for hacking into government programs. The conditions of his parole are simple: stay away from computers. Stanley is not stuck in his run-down trailer home for long, however. Succumbing to financial (and other) temptations, he is recruited by Gabriel Shear (John Travolta) to take part in a secret project. Stanley's job is to hack into the world's banking system. This film, part of the new genre of the "cyberthriller," tries to prove that a person clicking away at a computer keyboard can be exciting as long as the clock is ticking.

Critically analyze this film:

1. Stanley was initially arrested and sent to prison for hacking into an FBI program to read people's e-mails. What real-life FBI project, discussed in this chapter, provided the model for this plot device?

2. Gabriel wants Stanley to create a "multiheaded worm to sniff out digital footprints across an encrypted network." What is a "worm"? What does "encryption" mean?

3. Would you describe Gabriel and his gang as "cyber terrorists"? Why or why not?

4. How do movies such as *Swordfish* contribute to the glamorization of hackers?

LOGGING ON

Go to http://cj.wadsworth.com/gainescore2e, and click Hypercontents. There, you will find URLs for the organizations in the following list:

- Throughout this textbook, we have discussed scenarios in which the community and law enforcement agencies cooperate to prevent and fight crime. The Internet provides a very useful forum for these activities, especially for combating cyber crime. The **International Web Police,** for example, links citizens and government agencies in sixty-one different countries in an effort to make the Internet a safer place.

- Other sites also offer guidance and information regarding specific cyber crimes. If you feel that you have been the target of a cyber stalker, you should contact **Working to Halt Online Abuse.**

- One of the primary concerns of Internet users is that their privacy be respected while they are online. The **Electronic Privacy Center** and **Privacy International** have joined together to provide Web surfers with strategies to protect their privacy.

USING THE INTERNET FOR CRIMINAL JUSTICE ANALYSIS

INFOTRAC®
COLLEGE EDITION

1. Go to InfoTrac College Edition at **http://www.infotraccollege.com/wadsworth/**. After you log in, type in **"Betting the House."** This is an article that analyzes the online betting phenomenon.

   a. Why would individuals who voluntarily lost money at online gambling sites sue credit-card companies?

   b. What legal theory do such individuals use to justify their lawsuits?

   c. How can the U.S. government enforce laws against online gambling?

   d. If land-based legal casinos, such as those in Nevada, fully enter the online gambling industry, how much success will the government have at slowing down the growth in online gambling?

2. See Internet Activities 15.1 and 15.2 on the companion Web site for *CJ in Action: The Core.* To get to the activities, go to **http://www.cj.wadsworth.com/gainescore2e**, select the appropriate chapter from the drop down list, then click Internet Activities on the left navigation bar.

NOTES

1. "E-Mail Virus Masquerades as Kournikova Photo," *Wall Street Journal* (February 13, 2001), B5.

2. National Institute of Justice, *Computer Crimes: Criminal Justice Resource Manual* (Washington, D.C.: U.S. Department of Justice, 1989), 2.

3. Office of the Attorney General, *Cyberstalking: A New Challenge for Law Enforcement and Industry: A Report to the Vice President* (Washington, D.C.: U.S. Department of Justice, August 1999).

4. Anthony Deutsch, "Kournikova' Virus Creator Surrenders," *Chicago Sun-Times* (February 15, 2001), 28.

5. "New Worm Attacks Corporations Worldwide," *Business Wire* (May 9, 2001).

6. Katie Hafner and Matthew Lyon, *Where Wizards Stay Up Late: The Origins of the Internet* (New York: Simon and Schuster, 1996), 13.

7. Bradley Graham, "Lack of Disclosure Impedes Development of Safeguard," *Washington Post* (February 28, 1998), A6.

8. Michael Janofsky, "Defense Cites an Addition to the Internet in Threat Case," *New York Times* (January 13, 2000), A18.

9. Frank B. Cross and Roger LeRoy Miller, *West's Legal Environment of Business,* 4th ed. (Cincinnati, Ohio: West Legal Studies in Business, 2001), 332–33.

10. Internet Fraud Complaint Center, *Six-Month Data Trends Report* (Washington, D.C.: Federal Bureau of Investigation and National White Collar Crime Center, 2001).

11. Internet Fraud Complaint Center, *Internet Fraud Report, January 1, 2001–December 31, 2001* (Washington, D.C.: Federal Bureau of Investigation and National White Collar Crime Center, 2002), 5.

12. Jonathan Rusch, *The Rising Tide of Internet Fraud* (Washington, D.C.: U.S. Department of Justice, 2001).

13. Karen Gullo, "Internet Schemes Net 62 Arrests," *AP Online* (May 23, 2001).

14. Sheila M. Poole, "Nigeria Seeks Scam Victims," *Atlanta Journal-Constitution* (August 29, 2002), A3.

15. Sean B. Hoar, "Identity Theft: The Crime of the New Millennium," *United States' Attorney's USA Bulletin* (March 2001).

16. *Identity Theft: Is There Another You? Joint Hearing before the House Subcommittees on Telecommunications, Trade and Consumer Protection, and on Finance and Hazardous Materials, of the Committee on Commerce,* 106th Cong. 16 (1999) (testimony of Rep. John B. Shadegg).

17. Adam Cohen, "The Identity Thieves Are Out There—And Someone Could be Spying on You," *Time* (July 2, 2001), 44.

18. *Ibid.*

19. *Ibid.*

20. Cal. Penal Code Section 646.9.

21. Office of the Attorney General.

22. *Ibid.*

23. Rusch.

24. *Ibid.*

25. John Markoff, "Thief Reveals Credit Card Data When Web Extortion Plot Fails," *New York Times* (January 10, 2000), A1.

26. Deutsch.

27. *CSI/FBI Computer Crime and Security Survey* (San Francisco, CA: Computer Security Institute, 2002), 1.

28. *CERT Coordination Center 2001 Annual Report* (Pittsburgh, PA: Carnegie Mellon University Software Engineering Institute, 2002).

29. Joy D. Russell, "Curbing Cybercrime," *VAR-BUSINESS* (May 14, 2001), 32.

30. Gwen Ackerman, "'Kournikova' Virus Sweeps Through Computers Worldwide," *Jerusalem Post* (February 14, 2001), 14.

31. Bob Keefe, "Microsoft Busy Patching Security Gaps, Credibility," *Austin American-Statesman* (April 15, 2001), D1.

32. Kevin Johnson, M. J. Zuckerman, and Deborah Solomon, "Online Boasting Leaves Trail," *USA Today* (April 20, 2000), 1A.

33. Eric Newburger, *Home Computers and Internet Use in the United States: August 2000* (Washington, D.C.: U.S. Census Bureau, September 2001), 5.

34. Joseph V. DeMarco, *It's Not Just Fun and "War Games"—Juveniles and Computer Crimes* (Washington, D.C.: U.S. Department of Justice, 2001).

35. *Ibid.*

36. Rusch.

37. Peter Carbonara, "The Kid & the Con Man," *Money Magazine* (March 1, 2001), 82.

38. International Planning and Research Corporation, *Sixth Annual BSA Global Software Piracy Study* (Washington, D.C.: Business Software Alliance, May 2001), 2.

39. *2001 IFPI Music Piracy Report* (London, UK: International Federation of the Phonographic Industry, June 2001), 2.

40. 18 U.S.C. Section 2319(c) (1998).

41. 17 U.S.C. Section 1201 *et seq.* (1998).

42. "Everything Has a Price . . . ," *Business Week* (July 10, 2000), 10.

43. Kenneth V. Lanning, "Collectors," in *Child Pornography and Sex Rings*, Ann W. Burgess, ed. (Lexington, MA: Lexington Books, 1984), 83.

44. William R. Graham, Jr., "Uncovering and Eliminating Child Pornography Rings on the Internet," *Law Review of Michigan State University Detroit College of Law* (Summer 2000), 466.

45. 47 U.S.C. Section 230 *et seq.* (1996).

46. "United States—Analog Laws in a Digital World," *Monday Business Briefing* (August 4, 2000).

47. *People v. World Interactive Gaming Corp.* (N.Y.Sup.Ct. July 29, 1999); unpublished opinion.

48. Jay Krasovec, "Cyberspace: The Final Frontier for Regulation?" *Akron Law Review* (1997), 106.

49. http://www.whitehouse.gov/homeland/21st–technology.html.

50. *American Libraries Association v. Pataki*, 969 F.Supp. 168–9 (S.D.N.Y. 1997).

51. Alison Gerber, "Police Perplexed in Dealing with Cybercrime," *USA Today* (August 29, 2000), 5A.

52. Thomas T. Kubic, "Statement for the Record on the FBI's Perspective on the Cyber Crime Problem." Delivered before the House Committee on the Judiciary Subcommittee on Crime (June 12, 2001).

53. USA Patriot Act of 2001, P.L. 1076-56, 115 Stat. 272 (2001).

54. Hether Jacobson and Rebecca Green, "Computer Crimes," *American Criminal Law Review* (Spring 2002), 283.

55. Richard Rapoport, "Cyberwars: The Feds Strike Back," *Forbes* (August 23, 1999), 126.

56. May Wong, "For High-Tech Forensic Labs, a Growing Role in Corporate Crime Fighting," *APBNEWS.COM* (April 9, 2001).

57. "Whodunnit?: Forensic Computing Studies the Anatomy of Computer Crime," *Economist* (March 31, 2001), 73.

58. Dennis Blank, "Sniffing Out Crime by Bits and Bytes," *New York Times* (August 31, 2000), D8.

59. James Glanz, "Cryptologists Discover Flaw in E-Mail Security Program," *New York Times* (March 21, 2001), A14.

60. See, for example, *Bernstein v. U.S. Department of Justice*, 176 F.3d 1132 (9th Cir. 1999).

61. Kevin Di Gregory, "Statement Concerning the 'Carnivore' Controversy before the Committee on the Judiciary, United States Senate" (September 6, 2000).

62. 47 U.S.C. Section 223(a)(1)(B)(ii).

63. 521 U.S. 844 (1997).

64. 12 U.S.C. Sections 24a, 248b, 1820a, 1828b, 1831v–1831y, 1848a, 2908, 4809.

65. 15 U.S.C. Sections 6501–6506.

66. "Who Left the Light On?" *Foreign Policy* (March 1, 2002), 97.

67. John Schwartz, "Fighting Crime Online: Who Is in Harm's Way?" *New York Times* (February 8, 2001), D1.

68. Barton Gellman, "Cyber-Attacks by Al Qaeda Feared," *Washington Post* (June 27, 2002), A1.

69. *Cyber Attacks During the War on Terrorism: A Predictive Analysis* (Hanover, NH: Institute for Security Technology Studies at Dartmouth College, September 22, 2001), 18.

70. Bernard Wysocki, Jr., "Harsh Lesson for Government-Contract 'Newbies,'" *Wall Street Journal* (April 1, 2002), A14.

71. Bob Keefe, "Strategy Offered for Net Security," *Atlanta Journal and Constitution* (September 19, 2002), A4.

72. Rod Norland and Jeffrey Bartholet, "The Web's Dark Secret," *Newsweek* (March 19, 2001), 46.

73. Kimberly J. Mitchell, David Finkelhor, and Janis Wolak, "Risk Factors for and Impact of Online Sexual Solicitation of Youth," *Journal of the American Medical Association* 285 (June 20, 2001), 3011.

74. http://www.fbi.gov/hq/cid/cac/innocent/htm.

75. Michael Grunwald, "Global Internet Child Porn Ring Uncovered," *Washington Post* (September 3, 1998), A12; and Elaine Shannon, "Main Street Monsters," *Time* (September 14, 1998), 59.

76. Louis J. Freeh, "Statement on Proliferation of Child Pornography on the Internet before a Subcommittee of the Senate Committee on Appropriations" (1998).

77. *United States v. Childress,* 104 F.3d 47 (4th Cir. 1996).

78. Peter Gulotta, "An FBI Agent's Perspective" (July 31, 2000); see http://cbsnews.cbs.com/now/story/0,1597,199217–412,00.shtml.

79. Donald S. Yamagimi, "Prosecuting Cyber-Pedophiles," *Santa Clara Law Review* 41 (2001), 557–58.

80. *Ibid.,* 547.

81. *Ibid.,* 570.

82. 18 U.S.C. Section 2256.

83. *Ashcroft v. Free Speech Coalition,* 122 S.Ct. 1389 (2002).

84. John Schwartz, "Swift, Passionate Reaction to a Pornography Ruling," *New York Times* (April 17, 2002), A16.

APPENDIX A
YOU BE THE JUDGE: THE COURTS' ACTUAL DECISIONS

3.1: The court refused to throw out the charges. Although Emil was unconscious at the time his car struck the schoolgirls, he had earlier made the decision to get behind the wheel despite the knowledge that he suffered from epileptic seizures. In other words, the *actus reus* in this crime was not Emil's driving into the girls, but his decision to drive in the first place. That decision was certainly voluntary and therefore satisfies the requirements of *actus reus*. Note that if Emil had never had an epileptic seizure before, and had no idea that he suffered from that malady, the court's decision would probably have been different. Source: *People v. Decina,* 138 N.E.2d 799 (1956). A briefed (summarized) version of this case can be found at **http://www.lectlaw.com/files/lws50.htm**. Scroll down the list to the case title to view the brief.

6.1: The Court ruled that the evidence was valid and could be presented against Harold. If the police officers had known, or should have known, that the third floor contained two apartments before they entered Harold's residence, then they would have been required to search only Larry's lodging. But, the Court said, "honest mistakes" by police officers do not equal an "unreasonable search" under the Fourth Amendment. Source: *Maryland v. Garrison,* 480 U.S. 79 (1987). The full text of this case can be found online at **http://laws.lp.findlaw.com/getcase/us/480/79.html**.

7.1: The jury acquitted the four police officers of all charges in the death of Amadou. Although the jurors later admitted being uncomfortable with the number of shots fired, they said that the law was clear: if the police officers were reasonable in feeling that their lives were endangered, they were justified in using deadly force. The jury found it reasonable that Sean, Ken, Rich, and Ed felt that Amadou was threatening them with a gun. The fact that they were mistaken in this belief is, under the law, irrelevant. Source: Jane Fritsch, "4 Officers in Diallo Shooting Are Acquitted of All Charges," *The New York Times* (February 26, 2000), A1. CourtTV's Web site offers an extensive amount of information on this case at **http://www.courttv.com/national/diallo/index.html**.

10.1: The trial judge, swayed by the arguments of the defendant's lawyer, sentenced Angela to eighty-nine days of community service and one day in jail. The Washington Supreme Court, however, overruled the sentence, saying that the trial judge's light sentence was not justified given the facts of the case. The supreme court said it was up to the state legislature, and not individual judges, to decide whether an "altruistic background" can be used as a reason for leniency. Source: "High Court Says Judge Can't Levy Light Sentence," *Seattle Times* (June 24, 1995), A10.

APPENDIX B
TABLE OF CASES

GLOSSARY

A

Acquittal A declaration following a trial that the individual accused of the crime is innocent in the eyes of the law and thus absolved from the charges.

Actus reus (pronounced ak-tus ray-uhs). A guilty (prohibited) act. The commission of a prohibited act is one of the two essential elements required for criminal liability, the other element being the intent to commit a crime.

Adjudicatory hearing The process through which a juvenile court determines whether there is sufficient evidence to support the initial petition.

Administrative law The body of law created by administrative agencies (in the form of rules, regulations, orders, and decisions) in order to carry out their duties and responsibilities.

Adversary system A legal system in which the prosecution and defense are opponents, or adversaries, and present their cases in the light most favorable to themselves. The court arrives at a just solution based on the evidence presented by the contestants and determines who wins and who loses.

Affidavit A written statement of facts, confirmed by the oath or affirmation of the party making it and made before a person having the authority to administer the oath or affirmation.

Age of onset The age at which a juvenile first exhibits delinquent behavior. The earlier the age of onset, according to some observers, the greater the chance a person will become a career offender.

Aggravating circumstances Any circumstances accompanying the commission of a crime that may justify a harsher sentence.

Aging out A term used to explain the fact that criminal activity declines with age.

Appeal The process of seeking a higher court's review of a lower court's decision for the purpose of correcting or changing the lower court's judgment or decision.

Appellate courts Courts that review decisions made by lower courts, such as trial courts. Also known as courts of appeals.

Arraignment A court proceeding in which the suspect is formally charged with the criminal offense stated in the indictment. The suspect enters a plea (guilty, not guilty, *nolo contendere*) in response.

Arrest To take into custody a person suspected of criminal activity. Police may use only reasonable levels of force in making an arrest.

Arrest warrant A written order, based on probable cause and issued by a judge or magistrate, commanding that the person named on the warrant be arrested by the police.

Attorney general The chief law officer of a state; also, the chief law officer of the nation.

Attorney-client privilege A rule of evidence requiring that communications between a client and his or her attorney be kept confidential, unless the client consents to disclosure.

Authentication Establishing the genuineness of an item that is to be introduced as evidence in a trial.

Authority The power designated to an agent of the law over a person who has broken the law.

Automatic transfer The process by which a juvenile is transferred to adult court as a matter of state law. In some states, for example, a juvenile who is suspected of murder is automatically transferred to adult court.

B

Bail The amount or conditions set by the court to ensure that an individual accused of a crime will appear for further criminal proceedings. If the accused person provides bail, whether in cash or by means of a bail bond, then she or he is released from jail.

Bail bondsperson A businessperson who agrees, for a fee, to pay the bail amount if the accused fails to appear in court as ordered.

Bench trial A trial conducted without a jury, in which a judge makes the determination of the defendant's guilt or innocence.

Beyond a reasonable doubt The standard used to determine the guilt or innocence of a person charged with a crime. To be guilty of a crime, a suspect must be proved guilty "beyond and to the exclusion of a reasonable doubt."

Bill of Rights   The first ten amendments to the U.S. Constitution.

Blue curtain   A metaphorical term used to refer to the value placed on secrecy and the general mistrust of the outside world shared by many police officers.

Booking   The process of entering a suspect's name, offense, and arrival time into the police log following her or his arrest.

Boot camp   A correctional facility based on militaristic principles of discipline and physical conditioning; reserved primarily for juvenile and first-time offenders serving terms of less than six months, with the ultimate goal of deterring further criminal behavior.

Broken windows theory   Wilson and Kelling's theory that a neighborhood in disrepair signals that criminal activity is tolerated in the area. Thus, by cracking down on quality-of-life crimes, police can reclaim the neighborhood and encourage law-abiding citizens to live and work there.

Bureaucracy   A hierarchically structured administrative organization that carries out specific functions.

C

Capital punishment   The use of the death penalty to punish wrongdoers for certain crimes.

Case attrition   The process through which prosecutors, by deciding whether or not to prosecute each person arrested, effect an overall reduction in the number of persons prosecuted. As a result, the number of persons convicted and sentenced is much smaller than the number of persons arrested.

Case law   The rules of law announced in court decisions. Case law includes the aggregate of reported cases that interpret judicial precedents, statutes, regulations, and constitutional provisions.

Challenge for cause   A *voir dire* challenge for which an attorney states the reason why a prospective juror should not be included on the jury.

Charge   The judge's instructions to the jury following the attorneys' closing arguments; the charge sets forth the rules of law that the jury must apply in reaching its decision, or verdict.

Child abuse   Mistreatment of children by causing physical, emotional, or sexual damage without any plausible explanation, such as an accident.

Child neglect   A form of child abuse in which the child is denied certain necessities such as shelter, food, care, and love. Neglect is justification for a government agency to assume responsibility for a child in place of the parents or legal guardian.

Choice theory   A school of criminology that holds that wrongdoers act as if they weigh the possible benefits of criminal or delinquent activity against the costs of being apprehended. When the benefits are greater than the costs, the offender will make a rational choice to commit a crime or delinquent act.

Chronic offender   A delinquent or criminal who commits multiple offenses and is considered part of a small group of wrongdoers who are responsible for a majority of the antisocial activity in any given community.

Circumstantial evidence   Indirect evidence that is offered to establish, by inference, the likelihood of a fact that is in question.

Citizen oversight   The process by which citizens review complaints brought against individual police officers or police departments. The citizens often do not have the power to discipline misconduct, but can recommend that action be taken by police administrators.

Civil law   The branch of law dealing with the definition and enforcement of all private or public rights, as opposed to criminal matters.

Closing arguments   Arguments made by each side's attorney after the cases for the plaintiff and defendant have been presented.

Cohort   A group of persons gathered for study because they share a certain characteristic, such as age, income, or criminal background.

Common law   The body of law developed from custom or judicial decisions in English and U.S. courts and not attributable to a legislature.

Community policing   A policing philosophy that emphasizes community support for and cooperation with the police in preventing crime. Community policing stresses a police role that is less centralized and more proactive than reform era policing strategies.

Computer crime   Any wrongful act that is directed against computers and computer parts, or wrongful use or abuse of computers or software.

Computer forensics   The application of computer technology to finding and utilizing evidence of computer and cyber crimes.

Concurring opinions   Separate opinions prepared by judges who support the decision of the majority of the court but who want to make or clarify a particular point or to voice disapproval of the grounds on which the decision was made.

Confidential informant (CI)   A human source for police who provides information concerning illegal activity in which he or she is involved.

Conflict model   A criminal justice model in which the content of criminal law is determined by the groups that hold economic, political, and social power in a community.

Congregate system   A nineteenth-century penitentiary system developed in New York in which inmates were kept in separate cells during the night but worked together in the daytime under a code of enforced silence.

Consensus model A criminal justice model in which the majority of citizens in a society share the same values and beliefs. Criminal acts are those acts that conflict with these values and beliefs and are deemed harmful to society.

Consent searches Searches by police that are made after the subject of the search has agreed to the action. In these situations, consent, if given of free will, validates a warrantless search.

Consolidation A corrections model in which the inmates who pose the highest security risk are housed in a single facility to separate them from the general prison population.

Constitutional law Law based on the U.S. Constitution and the constitutions of the various states.

Contaminated When evidence of a crime is rendered useless because of exposure to a foreign agent or improper removal from a crime scene.

Control theory A series of theories that assume that all individuals have the potential for criminal behavior, but are restrained by the damage that such actions would do to their relationships with family, friends, and members of the community. Criminality occurs when these bonds are broken or nonexistent.

Coroner The medical examiner of a county, usually elected by popular vote.

Corpus delicti The body of circumstances that must exist for a criminal act to have occurred.

Courtroom work group The social organization consisting of the judge, prosecutor, defense attorney, and other court workers. The relationships among these persons have a far-reaching impact on the day-to-day operations of any court.

Crime control model A criminal justice model that places primary emphasis on the right of society to be protected from crime and violent criminals. Crime control values emphasize speed and efficiency in the criminal justice process; the benefits of lower crime rates outweigh any possible costs to individual rights.

Crime scene The physical area that contains or is believed to contain evidence of a crime.

Criminology The scientific study of crime and the causes of criminal behavior.

Cross-examination The questioning of an opposing witness during trial.

Custodial interrogation The questioning of a suspect after that person has been taken in custody. In this situation, the suspect must be read his or her *Miranda* rights before interrogation can begin.

Custody The forceful detention of a person, or the perception that a person is not free to leave the immediate vicinity.

Cyber crime A crime that occurs online, in the virtual community of the Internet, as opposed to the physical world.

Cyber fraud Any misrepresentation knowingly made over the Internet with the intention of deceiving another and on which a reasonable person would and does rely to his or her detriment.

Cyber stalking The crime of stalking, committed in cyberspace. Generally, stalking consists of harassing a person and putting that person in reasonable fear for his or her safety or the safety of the person's immediate family.

D

Dark figure of crime A term used to describe the actual amount of crime that takes place. The "figure" is "dark," or impossible to detect, because a great number of crimes are never reported to the police.

Day reporting center A community-based corrections center to which offenders report on a daily basis for purposes of treatment, education, and incapacitation.

Deadly force Force applied by a police officer that is likely or intended to cause death.

Defense attorney The lawyer representing the defendant.

Delegation of authority The principles of command on which most police departments are based; personnel take orders from and are responsible to those in positions of power directly above them.

"Deliberate indifference" A standard that must be met by inmates trying to prove that their Eighth Amendment rights were violated by a correctional facility. It occurs when prison officials are aware of harmful conditions of confinement but fail to take steps to remedy those conditions.

Departure A stipulation in many federal and state sentencing guidelines that allows a judge to adjust his or her sentencing decision based on the special circumstances of a particular case.

Deprivation model A theory that inmate aggression is the result of the frustration inmates feel at being deprived of freedom, consumer goods, sex, and other staples of life outside the institution.

Detective The primary police investigator of crimes.

Detention The temporary custody of a juvenile in a state facility after a petition has been filed and before the adjudicatory process begins.

Detention hearing A hearing to determine whether a juvenile should be detained, or remain detained, while waiting for the adjudicatory process to begin.

Determinate sentencing A period of incarceration that is fixed by a sentencing authority and cannot be reduced by judges or other corrections officials.

Deterrence The strategy of preventing crime through the threat of punishment. Assumes that potential criminals will weigh the costs of punishments versus the benefits of the criminal act; therefore, punishments should be severe.

Differential response A strategy for answering calls for service in which response time is adapted to the seriousness of the call.

Direct evidence Evidence that establishes the existence of a fact that is in question without relying on inference.

Direct examination The examination of a witness by the attorney who calls the witness to the stand to testify.

Directed patrol Patrol strategies that are designed to respond to a specific criminal activity at a specific time.

Discovery Formal investigation prior to trial. During discovery, the defense uses various methods to obtain information from the prosecution to prepare for trial.

Discretion The ability of individuals in the criminal justice system to make operational decisions based on personal judgment instead of formal rules or official information.

Discretionary release The release of an inmate into a community supervision program at the discretion of the parole board within limits set by state or federal law.

Dispersion A corrections model in which high-risk inmates are spread throughout the general prison population, in the hopes that they will be absorbed without causing misconduct problems.

Disposition hearing Similar to the sentencing hearing for adults, a hearing in which the juvenile judge or officer decides the appropriate punishment for a youth found to be delinquent or a status offender.

Dissenting opinions Separate opinions in which judges disagree with the conclusion reached by the majority of the court and expand on their own views about the case.

Diversion In the context of corrections, a strategy to divert those offenders who qualify away from prison and jail and toward community-based and intermediate sanctions.

Diversion The removal of an alleged juvenile delinquent from the formal criminal or juvenile justice system and the referral of that person to a treatment or rehabilitation program.

Docket The list of cases entered on a court's calendar and thus scheduled to be heard by the court.

Double jeopardy To twice place at risk (jeopardize) a person's life or liberty. The Fifth Amendment to the U.S. Constitution prohibits a second prosecution for the same criminal offense.

Dual court system The separate but interrelated court system of the United States, made up of the courts on the national level and the courts on the state level.

Due process clause The provisions of the Fifth and Fourteenth Amendments to the Constitution that guarantee that no person shall be deprived of life, liberty, or property without due process of law. Similar clauses are found in most state constitutions.

Due process model A criminal justice model that places primacy on the right of the individual to be protected from the power of the government. Due process values hold that the state must prove a person's guilt within the confines of a process designed to safeguard personal liberties as enumerated in the Bill of Rights.

Duress Unlawful pressure brought to bear on a person, causing the person to perform an act that he or she would not otherwise perform.

Durham **rule** A test of criminal responsibility adopted in a 1954 case: "an accused is not criminally responsible if his unlawful act was the product of mental disease or mental defect."

Duty The moral sense of a police officer that she or he should apply authority in a certain manner.

E

Electronic monitoring A technique of probation supervision in which the offender's whereabouts, though not his or her actions, are kept under surveillance by an electronic device; often used in conjunction with home confinement.

Encryption The process by which a message is transmitted into something that the sender and receiver intend third parties not to understand.

Entrapment A defense in which the defendant claims that he or she was induced by a public official—usually an undercover agent or police officer—to commit a crime that he or she would otherwise not have committed.

Ethics The rules or standards of behavior governing a profession; aimed at ensuring the fairness and rightness of actions.

Evidence Anything that is used to prove the existence or nonexistence of a fact.

Exclusionary rule A rule under which any evidence that is obtained in violation of the accused's rights under the Fourth, Fifth, and Sixth Amendments, as well as any evidence derived from illegally obtained evidence, will not be admissible in criminal court.

Exigent circumstances Situations that require extralegal or exceptional actions by the police. In these circumstances, police officers are justified in not following procedural rules, such as those pertaining to search and arrest warrants.

Expert witness A witness with professional training or substantial experience qualifying her or him to testify on a certain subject.

Extradition The surrender of a fugitive offender by one jurisdiction to another in which the offender has been convicted or is liable for punishment.

F

Federal Bureau of Investigation (FBI) The branch of the Department of Justice responsible for investigating violations of federal law. The bureau also collects national crime statistics and provides training and other forms of aid to local law enforcement agencies.

Federalism A form of government in which a written constitution provides for a division of powers between a central government and several regional governments. In the United States, the division of powers between the federal government and the fifty states is established by the Constitution.

Felony A serious crime punishable by death or by imprisonment in a federal or state corrections facility for more than a year.

Field training The segment of a police recruit's training in which he or she is removed from the classroom and placed on the beat, under the supervision of a senior officer.

Follow-up investigation The steps taken by investigative personnel once it has been determined, based on the results of the preliminary investigation, that the crime is solvable.

Forensics The application of scientific methods to finding and utilizing criminal evidence.

Forfeiture The process by which the government seizes private property attached to criminal activity.

Frisk A pat-down or minimal search by police to discover weapons; conducted for the express purpose of protecting the officer or other citizens, and not to find evidence of illegal substances for use in a trial.

Fruit of the poisoned tree Evidence that is acquired through the use of illegally obtained evidence and is therefore inadmissible in court.

Furlough Temporary release from a prison for purposes of vocational or educational training, to ease the shock of release, or for personal reasons.

G

General patrol Patrol strategies that rely on police officers monitoring a certain area with the goal of detecting crimes in progress or preventing crime due to their presence. Also known as random or preventive patrol.

"Good time" A reduction in time served by prisoners based on good behavior, conformity to rules, and other positive actions.

Graduated sanctions The practical theory in juvenile corrections that a delinquent or status offender should receive a punishment that matches in seriousness the severity of the wrongdoing.

Grand jury The group of citizens called to decide whether probable cause exists to believe that a suspect committed the crime with which she or he has been charged.

H

Habeas corpus An order that requires correctional officials to bring an inmate before a court or a judge and explain why he or she is being held in prison.

Habitual offender laws Statutes that require lengthy prison sentences for those who are convicted of multiple felonies.

Hacker A person who uses one computer to break into another.

"Hands-off" doctrine The unwritten judicial policy that favors noninterference by the courts in the administration of prisons and jails.

Hearsay An oral or written statement made by an out-of-court declarant that is later offered in court by a witness (not the declarant) concerning a matter before the court. Hearsay usually is not admissible as evidence.

Home confinement A community-based sanction in which offenders serve their terms of incarceration in their homes.

Hot spots Concentrated areas of high criminal activity that draw a directed police response.

Hung jury A jury whose members are so irreconcilably divided in their opinions that they cannot reach a verdict. In this situation, the judge may order a new trial.

I

"Identifiable human needs" The basic human necessities that correctional facilities are required by the Constitution to provide to inmates. Beyond food, warmth, and exercise, the court system has been unable to establish exactly what these needs are.

Identity theft The theft of identity information, such as name, driver's license or Social Security number. The information is then usually used to access the victim's financial resources.

Impeached As authorized by Article I of the Constitution, impeachment is voted on by the House of Representatives and then sent to the Senate for a vote to remove the president, vice president, or civil officers (such as federal judges) of the United States.

Incapacitation A strategy for preventing crime by detaining wrongdoers in prison, thereby separating them from the community and reducing criminal opportunities.

Inchoate offenses Conduct deemed criminal without actual harm being done, provided that the harm that would have occurred is one the law tries to prevent.

Incident-driven policing A reactive approach to policing that emphasizes a speedy response to calls for service.

Indeterminate sentencing An indeterminate term of incarceration in which a judge determines the minimum and maximum terms of imprisonment. When the minimum term is reached, the prisoner becomes eligible to be paroled.

Index crimes Those crimes reported annually by the FBI in its Uniform Crime Report. Index crimes include murder, rape, robbery, aggravated assault, burglary, larceny, motor vehicle theft, and arson. Also known as Part I offenses.

Indictment A charge or written accusation, issued by a grand jury, that probable cause exists to believe that a named person has committed a crime.

Information The formal charge against the accused issued by the prosecutor after a preliminary hearing has found probable cause.

Initial appearance An accused's first appearance before a judge or magistrate following arrest; during the appearance, the defendant is informed of the charges, advised of the right to counsel, told the amount of bail, and given a date for the preliminary hearing.

Insanity A defense for criminal liability that asserts a lack of criminal responsibility. According to the law, a person cannot have the requisite state of mind to commit a crime if she or he did not know at the time of the act that it was wrong, or did not know the nature and quality of the act.

Intake Following referral of a juvenile to juvenile court by a police officer or other concerned party, the process by which an official of the court must decide whether to file a petition, release the juvenile, or place the juvenile under some other form of supervision.

Intellectual property Property resulting from intellectual, creative processes.

Intensive supervision probation (ISP) A punishment-oriented form of probation in which the offender is placed under stricter and more frequent surveillance and control than usual by probation officers with limited caseloads.

Intermediate sanctions Sanctions that are more restrictive than probation and less restrictive than imprisonment. Intended to alleviate pressure on over-crowded corrections facilities and understaffed probation departments.

Internal Affairs Unit (IAU) A division within a police department that receives and investigates complaints of wrongdoing by police officers.

Interrogation The direct questioning of a suspect to gather evidence of criminal activity and try to gain a confession.

Interview The process of questioning a suspect or witness during the preliminary and follow-up investigations.

Intoxication A defense for criminal liability in which the defendant claims that the taking of intoxicants rendered him or her unable to form the requisite intent to commit a criminal act.

Irresistible impulse test A test for the insanity defense under which a defendant who knew his or her action was wrong may still be found insane if he or she was nonetheless unable, as a result of a mental deficiency, to control the urge to complete it.

J

Jail A facility, usually operated by county government, used to hold persons awaiting trial or those who have been found guilty of misdemeanors.

Judicial misconduct A general term describing behavior that diminishes public confidence in the judiciary. This behavior includes obviously illegal acts, such as bribery, and conduct that gives the appearance of impropriety, such as consorting with known felons.

Judicial waiver The process in which the juvenile judge, based on the facts of the case at hand, decides that the alleged offender should be transferred to adult court.

Jurisdiction The authority of a court to hear and decide cases within an area of the law or a geographical territory.

Jury trial A trial before a judge and a jury.

Just deserts A sanctioning philosophy based on the assertion that criminals deserve to be punished for breaking society's rules. The severity of the punishment should be determined by no other factor than the severity of the crime.

Justice of the peace Established in fourteenth-century England, a government official who oversaw various aspects of local law enforcement. The post eventually became strictly identified with judicial matters.

Juvenile delinquency Behavior that is illegal under federal or state law that has been committed by a person who is under an age limit specified by statute.

L

Lay witness A witness who can truthfully and accurately testify on a fact in question without having specialized training or knowledge; an ordinary witness.

Learning theory The hypothesis that delinquents and criminals must be taught both the practical and emotional skills necessary to partake in illegal activity.

Legalization The elimination or modification of federal and state laws that prohibit the manufacture, use, and sale of illegal drugs.

Lockdown A disciplinary action taken by prison officials in which all inmates are ordered to their quarters and nonessential prison activities are suspended.

M

M'Naughten rule A common law test of criminal responsibility derived from *M'Naughten's* case in 1843 that relies on the defendant's inability to distinguish right from wrong.

Mala in se A descriptive term for acts that are inherently wrong, regardless of whether they are prohibited by law.

Mala prohibita A descriptive term for acts that are made illegal by criminal statute and are not necessarily wrong in and of themselves.

Mandatory release Release from prison that occurs when an offender has served the length of his or her sentence, with time taken off for good behavior.

Mandatory sentencing guidelines Statutorily determined punishments that must be applied to those who are convicted of specific crimes.

Master jury list The list of citizens in a court's district from which a jury can be selected; often compiled from voter registration lists, driver's license lists, and other sources.

Maximum-security prison A correctional institution designed and organized to control and discipline dangerous felons, as well as prevent escape, with intense supervision, cement walls, and electronic, barbed wire fences.

Medical model A model of corrections in which the psychological and biological roots of an inmate's criminal behavior are identified and treated.

Medical model of addiction An approach to drug addiction that treats drug abuse as a mental illness and focuses on treating and rehabilitating offenders rather than punishing them.

Medium-security prison A correctional institution that houses less dangerous inmates, and therefore uses less restrictive measures to avoid violence and escapes.

Mens rea (pronounced mehns ray-uh) Mental state, or intent. A wrongful mental state is as necessary as a wrongful act to establish criminal liability.

Minimum-security prison A correctional institution designed to allow inmates, most of whom pose low security risks, a great deal of freedom of movement and contact with the outside world.

Miranda **rights** The constitutional rights of accused persons taken into custody by law enforcement officials. Following the United States Supreme Court's decision in *Miranda v. Arizona,* on taking an accused person into custody, the arresting officer must inform the person of certain constitutional rights, such as the right to remain silent and the right to counsel.

Misdemeanor Any crime that is not a felony; punishable by a fine or by confinement for up to a year.

Missouri Plan A method of selecting judges that combines appointment and election. Under the plan, the state governor or another government official selects judges from a group of nominees chosen by a nonpartisan committee. After a year on the bench, the judges face a popular election to determine whether the public wishes to keep them in office.

Mitigating circumstances Any circumstances accompanying the commission of a crime that may justify a lighter sentence.

Moonlighting The practice of a police officer holding a second job in the private security field.

N

Necessity A defense against criminal liability in which the defendant asserts that circumstances required her or him to commit an illegal act.

Nolo contendere Latin for "I will not contest it." A criminal defendant's plea, in which he or she chooses not to challenge, or contest, the charges brought by the government. Although the defendant may still be sentenced or fined, the plea neither admits nor denies guilt.

Nonpartisan elections Elections in which candidates are presented on the ballot without any party affiliation.

O

Opening statements The attorneys' statements to the jury at the beginning of the trial. Each side briefly outlines the evidence that will be offered during the trial and the legal theory that will be pursued.

Opinion A statement by the court expressing the reasons for its decision in a case.

Oral arguments The verbal arguments presented in person by attorneys to an appellate court. Each attorney presents reasons why the court should rule in his or her client's favor.

Organized crime A conspiratorial relationship between any number of persons engaged in the market for illegal goods or services, such as illicit drugs or firearms.

P

Pardon An act of executive clemency that overturns a conviction and erases mention of the crime from the person's criminal record.

Parens patriae A doctrine that holds that the state has a responsibility to look after the well-being of children and to assume the role of parent if necessary.

Parole The conditional release of an inmate before his or her sentence has expired. The remainder of the sentence is served in the community under the supervision of correctional officers, and the offender can be returned to incarceration if he or she breaks the conditions of parole, as determined by a parole board.

Parole board A body of appointed civilians that decides whether a convict should be granted conditional release before the end of his or her sentence.

Parole contract An agreement between the state and the offender that establishes the conditions under which the latter will be allowed to serve the remainder of her or his prison term in the community.

Parole grant hearing A hearing in which the entire parole board or a subcommittee reviews information, meets the offender, and hears testimony from relevant witnesses to determine whether to grant parole.

Parole guidelines Employed to remove discretion from the parole process, these guidelines attempt to measure the risks of an offender recidivating, and then use these measurements to determine whether early release will be granted and under what conditions.

Parole revocation When a parolee breaks the conditions of parole, the process of withdrawing parole and returning the person to prison.

Part II offenses All crimes recorded by the FBI that do not fall into the category of Part I offenses. Include both misdemeanors and felonies.

Partisan elections Elections in which candidates are affiliated with and receive support from political parties; the candidates are listed in conjunction with their party on the ballot.

Patronage system A form of corruption in which the political party in power hires and promotes police officers, receiving job-related "favors" in return.

Penitentiary An early form of correctional facility that emphasized separating inmates from society and from each other so that they would have an environment in which to reflect on their wrongdoing and ponder their reformation.

Peremptory challenges   *Voir dire* challenges to exclude potential jurors from serving on the jury without any supporting reason or cause.

Petition   The document filed with a juvenile court alleging that the juvenile is a delinquent or a status offender, and asking the court to either hear the case or transfer it to an adult court.

Plain view doctrine   The legal principle that objects in plain view of a law enforcement agent who has the right to be in a position to have that view may be seized without a warrant and introduced as evidence.

Plea bargaining   The process by which the accused and the prosecutor work out a mutually satisfactory conclusion to the case, subject to court approval. Usually, plea bargaining involves the defendant's pleading guilty to a lesser offense in return for a lighter sentence.

Police corruption   The abuse of authority by a law enforcement officer for personal gain.

Police cynicism   The suspicion that citizens are weak, corrupt, and dangerous. This outlook is the result of a police officer being constantly exposed to civilians at their worst and can negatively affect the officer's performance.

Police subculture   The values and perceptions that are shared by members of a police department and, to a certain extent, by all law enforcement agents. These values and perceptions are shaped by the unique and isolated existence of the police officer.

Precedent   A court decision that furnishes an example of authority for deciding subsequent cases involving identical or similar facts.

Predisposition report   A report prepared during the disposition process that provides the judge with relevant background material to aid in the disposition decision.

Preliminary hearing   An initial hearing in which a magistrate decides if there is probable cause to believe that the defendant committed the crime with which he or she is charged.

Preliminary investigation   The procedure, usually conducted by a patrol officer, that must be followed immediately on initial arrival at a crime scene. Includes securing the crime scene, interviewing witnesses and suspects, and searching the scene for evidence.

Presentence investigative report   An investigative report on an offender's background that assists a judge in determining the proper sentence.

Presumptive sentencing   A sentencing strategy in which legislators set the average sentence that should be served for any particular crime, leaving judges with the ability to shorten or lengthen the sentence based on the circumstances of each case.

Pretrial detainees   Individuals who cannot post bail after arrest and are therefore forced to spend the time prior to their trial incarcerated in jail.

Pretrial diversion program   An alternative to trial offered by a judge or prosecutor, in which the offender agrees to participate in a specified counseling or treatment program in return for withdrawal of the charges.

Preventive detention   The retention of an accused person in custody due to fears that she or he will commit a crime if released before trial.

Prison code   A system of social norms and values established by inmates to regulate behavior within the correctional institution.

Prisonization   The socialization process through which a new inmate learns the accepted norms and values of the prison population.

Private prisons   Correctional facilities operated by private corporations instead of the government, and therefore reliant on profit for survival.

Private security   The practice of private corporations or individuals offering services traditionally performed by police officers.

Probable cause   Reasonable grounds to believe the existence of facts warranting certain actions, such as the search or arrest of a person.

Probation   A criminal sanction in which a convict is allowed to remain in the community rather than be imprisoned as long as she or he follows certain conditions set by the court.

Problem-solving policing   A policing philosophy that requires police to identify potential criminal activity and develop strategies to prevent or respond to that activity.

Procedural criminal law   Rules that define the manner in which the rights and duties of individuals may be enforced.

Professional model   A style of policing advocated by August Vollmer and O. W. Wilson that emphasizes centralized police organizations, increased use of technology, and a limitation of police discretion through regulations and guidelines.

Property crime   Crimes committed against property, including larceny/theft, burglary, and arson.

Prosecutorial waiver   A procedure in which juvenile court judges have the discretion to transfer a juvenile case to adult court, when certain predetermined conditions as to the seriousness of the offense and the age of the offender are met.

Public defenders   Court-appointed attorneys who are paid by the state to represent defendants who are unable to hire private counsel.

Public order crime   Behavior that has been labeled criminal because it is contrary to shared social values, customs, and norms.

Public prosecutors   Individuals, acting as trial lawyers, who initiate and conduct cases in the government's name and on behalf of the people.

R

Real evidence Evidence that is brought into court and seen by the jury, as opposed to evidence that is described for a jury.

"Real offense" The actual offense committed, as opposed to the charge levied by a prosecutor as the result of a plea bargain. Judges who make sentencing decisions based on the real offense are often seen as undermining the plea bargain process.

Reasonable force The degree of force that is appropriate to protect the police officer or other citizens and is not excessive.

Rebuttal Evidence given to counteract or disprove evidence presented by the opposing party.

Rehabilitation The philosophy that society is best served when wrongdoers are not simply punished, but provided the resources needed to eliminate criminality from their behavioral pattern.

Reintegration A goal of corrections that focuses on preparing the offender for a return to the community unmarred by further criminal behavior.

Relative deprivation The theory that inmate aggression is caused when freedoms and services that the inmate has come to accept as normal are decreased or eliminated.

Release on recognizance (ROR) A judge's order that releases an accused from jail with the understanding that he or she will return for further proceedings of his or her own will; used instead of setting a monetary bond.

Relevant evidence Evidence tending to make a fact in question more or less probable than it would be without the evidence. Only relevant evidence is admissible in court.

Residential treatment programs Government-run facilities for juveniles whose offenses are not deemed serious.

Response time A measurement of police efficiency based on the rapidity with which calls for service are answered.

Retribution The philosophy that those who commit criminal acts should be punished based on the severity of the crime and that no other factors need be considered.

Rule of four A rule of the United States Supreme Court that the Court will not issue a writ of *certiorari* unless at least four justices approve of the decision to hear the case.

S

Search The process by which police examine a person or property to find evidence that will be used to prove guilt in a criminal trial.

Search warrant A written order, based on probable cause and issued by a judge or magistrate, commanding that police officers or criminal investigators search a specific person, place, or property to obtain evidence.

Searches and seizures The legal term, as found in the Fourth Amendment of the U.S. Constitution, that generally refers to the searching for and the confiscating of evidence by law enforcement agents.

Searches incidental to arrest Searches for weapons and evidence of persons who have just been arrested. The fruit of such searches is admissible if any items found are within the immediate vicinity or control of the suspect.

Seizure The forcible taking of a person or property in response to a violation of the law.

Self-defense The legally recognized privilege to protect one's self or property from injury by another. The privilege of self-defense protects only acts that are reasonably necessary to protect one's self or property.

Self-reported surveys A method of gathering crime data that relies on participants to reveal and detail their own criminal or delinquent behavior.

Sentencing discrimination A situation in which the length of a sentence appears to be influenced by a defendant's race, gender, economic status, or other factor not directly related to the crime he or she committed.

Sentencing disparity A situation in which those convicted of similar crimes do not receive similar sentences.

Sentencing guidelines Legislatively determined guidelines that judges are required to follow when sentencing those convicted of specific crimes. These guidelines limit judicial discretion.

Separate confinement A nineteenth-century penitentiary system developed in Pennsylvania in which inmates were kept separate from each other at all times, with daily activities taking place in individual cells.

Sheriff The primary law enforcement officer in a county, usually elected to the post by a popular vote.

Shire-reeve The chief law enforcement officer in an early English shire, or county. The forerunner of the modern sheriff.

Shock incarceration A short period of incarceration that is designed to deter further criminal activity by "shocking" the offender with the hardships of imprisonment.

Social disorganization theory The theory that deviant behavior is more likely in communities where social institutions such as the family, schools, and criminal justice system fail to exert control over the population.

Social process theories A school of criminology that considers criminal behavior to be the predictable result of a person's interaction with his or her environment. According to these theories, everybody has the potential for wrongdoing. Those who act on this potential are conditioned to do so by family or peer groups, or institutions such as the media.

Socialization The process through which a police officer is taught the values and expected behavior of the police subculture.

Solvability factors Those factors that affect the probability that a case will be solved.

Specialty courts Lower courts that have jurisdiction over one specific area of criminal activity, such as illegal drugs or domestic violence.

Split sentence probation A sentence that consists of incarceration in a prison or jail, followed by a probationary period in the community.

Stare decisis (pronounced ster-ay dih-si-ses) A common law doctrine under which judges are obligated to follow the precedents established under prior decisions.

Status offender A juvenile who has been found to have engaged in behavior deemed unacceptable for those under a certain, statutorily determined age.

Statutory law The body of law enacted by legislative bodies.

Stop A brief detention of a person by law enforcement agents for questioning. The agents must have a reasonable suspicion of the person before making a stop.

Stressors The aspects of police work and life that lead to feelings of stress.

Strict liability Certain crimes, such as traffic violations, in which the defendant is guilty regardless of her or his state of mind at the time of the act.

Substantial capacity test From the Model Penal Code, a test that states that a person is not responsible for criminal behavior if when committing the act "as a result of mental disease or defect he lacks substantial capacity either to appreciate the wrongfulness of his conduct or to conform his conduct to the requirements of law."

Substantive criminal law Law that defines the rights and duties of individuals with respect to each other.

Supermax prison A correctional facility reserved for those inmates who have extensive records of misconduct in maximum-security prisons; characterized by extremely strict control and supervision over the inmates, including extensive use of solitary confinement.

Suspended sentence A judicially imposed condition in which an offender is sentenced after being convicted of a crime, but is not required to begin the sentence immediately. The judge may revoke the suspended sentence and remit the offender to prison or jail if he or she does not follow certain conditions.

T

Technical violation An action taken by a probationer that, although not criminal, breaks the terms of probation as designated by the court; can result in the revocation of probation and a return to prison or jail.

Ten percent cash bail An alternative to traditional bail in which defendants may gain pretrial release by posting 10 percent of their bond amount to the court instead of seeking a bail bondsperson.

Testimony Verbal evidence given by witnesses under oath.

Time served The period of time a person denied bail has spent in jail prior to his or her trial. If the suspect is found guilty and sentenced to a jail or prison term, the judge will often lessen the duration of the sentence based on the amount of time served as a pretrial detainee.

Tithing system In Anglo-Saxon England, a system of law enforcement in which groups of ten families, known as tithings, were collectively responsible for law and order within their group.

Total institution An institution, such as a prison, that provides all of the necessities for existence to those who live within its boundaries.

Trial courts Courts in which most cases usually begin and in which questions of fact are examined.

Truth-in-sentencing laws Legislative attempts to assure that convicts will serve approximately the terms to which they were initially sentenced.

U

Uniform crime report (UCR) An annual report compiled by the FBI to give an indication of criminal activity in the United States. The FBI collects data from local, state, and federal law enforcement agencies in preparing this report.

V

Venire The group of citizens from which the jury is selected.

Verdict A formal decision made by the jury.

Victim surveys A method of gathering crime data that directly surveys participants to determine their experiences as victims of crime.

Violent crime Crimes committed against persons, including murder, rape, assault and battery, and robbery.

Voir dire The preliminary questions that the trial attorneys ask prospective jurors to determine whether they are biased or have any connection with the defendant or a witness.

W

Warden The prison official who is ultimately responsible for the organization and performance of a correctional facility.

Warrantless arrest An arrest made without first seeking a warrant for the action; permitted under certain circumstances, such as when the arresting officer has witnessed the crime or has a reasonable belief that the suspect has committed a felony.

"Wedding cake" model A wedding cake–shaped model that explains why different cases receive varying treatment in the criminal justice system. The cases at the "top" of the cake receive the most attention and have the greatest effect on public perception of criminal justice, while those cases at the "bottom" are disposed of quickly and virtually ignored by the media.

White-collar crime Nonviolent crimes committed by corporations and individuals to gain a personal or business advantage.

Widen the net The criticism that intermediate sanctions designed to divert offenders from prison actually increase the number of citizens who are under the control and surveillance of the American corrections system.

Writ of *certiorari* A request from a higher court asking a lower court for the record of a case. In essence, the request signals the higher court's willingness to review the case.

Y

Youth gangs Self-formed groups of youths with several identifiable characteristics, including a gang name and other recognizable symbols, a geographic territory, a leadership structure, a meeting pattern, and participation in illegal activities.

INDEX

Chapter opening photo credits:

Chapter 1:   AP Photo/Stephen Chernin

Chapter 2:   AP Photo/Mark Foley

Chapter 3:   AP Photo/*Tampa Tribune,*
Stephen McKnight

Chapter 4:   AP Photo/Mike Derer

Chapter 5:   AP Photo/Kevork Djansezian

Chapter 6:   AP Photo/*The Mansfield News Journal,*
Dave Polcyn

Chapter 7:   AP Photo/Mitch Jacobson

Chapter 8:   AP Photo/Steve Ueckert, Pool

Chapter 9:   AP Photo/*The Daily Oklahoman,*
Paul B. Southerland

Chapter 10:   AP Photo/David J. Phillip

Chapter 11:   AP Photo/Phil Coale

Chapter 12:   AP Photo/Donna McWilliam

Chapter 13:   AP Photo/Staff

Chapter 14:   AP Photo/Christopher Nerkey

Chapter 15:   AP Photo/Toby Talbot

Enclosed FREE in every new copy of this book!

Careers in Criminal Justice 2.0 Interactive CD-ROM

Enrich your study of the field with this interactive look at many criminal justice careers.

One of the best ways to study criminal justice is by taking a closer look at the field's varied careers. You'll learn about these careers throughout this text and with the *Careers in Criminal Justice 2.0 Interactive* CD-ROM. This essential tool guides you in exploring many dozens of careers. You can even take a self-assessment test to see which criminal justice careers match your own interests and career goals.

These reminders in the margins throughout the book and within the book's "Careers in Criminal Justice" boxes alert you to go to the CD-ROM.

At the introductory screen, click on the option of your choice:

- *Career Rolodex* features video testimonials from practicing professionals in the field and information on hundreds of specific jobs including descriptions, employment requirements, and more.

- *Interest Assessment* gives you a direct link and FREE online access to the Holland Personalized Self-Assessment Test, designed to help you decide which careers suit your personality and interests.

- *Career Planner* features helpful tips and worksheets on resume writing, interviewing techniques, and successful job search strategies.

- *Links for Reference* offers direct links to federal, state, and local agencies where you can get contact information and learn more about current job opportunities.

GIRLS' LIFE MAGAZINE

GL

The Girls' Life Guide to
Being a Style
Superstar!

**Written by
Apryl Lundsten**

**Illustrated by
Lisa Parett**

Scholastic Inc.

New York • Toronto • London • Auckland • Sydney
Mexico City • New Delhi • Hong Kong • Buenos Aires

ISBN 0-439-44984-7

12 11 10 9 8 7 6 5 4 3 2 1   4 5 6 7 8 9/0

Printed in the U.S.A.

First Scholastic printing, June 2004

Contents